HOW
CONGRESS
works

edition 5

HOW
CONGRESS
works

edition 5

CQ PRESS

$SAGE reference | CQPRESS

Los Angeles | London | New Delhi
Singapore | Washington DC

Los Angeles | London | New Delhi
Singapore | Washington DC

FOR INFORMATION:

CQ Press

SAGE Publications, Inc.

2455 Teller Road

Thousand Oaks, California 91320

E-mail: order@sagepub.com

SAGE Publications Ltd.

1 Oliver's Yard

55 City Road

London EC1Y 1SP

United Kingdom

SAGE Publications India Pvt. Ltd.

B 1/I 1 Mohan Cooperative Industrial Area

Mathura Road, New Delhi 110 044

India

SAGE Publications Asia-Pacific Pte. Ltd.

3 Church Street

#10-04 Samsung Hub

Singapore 049483

Printed in the United States of America.

Library of Congress Cataloging-in-Publication Data

How Congress works. — Fifth edition.

pages cm

Includes bibliographical references and index.

ISBN 978-1-60871-911-2 (pbk.)

1. United States. Congress. I. Congressional Quarterly, Inc.

JK1021.H69 2013
328.73—dc23   2012039629

Acquisitions Editor: Doug Goldenberg-Hart

Production Editor: Tracy Buyan

Typesetter: C&M Digitals (P) Ltd.

Proofreader: Kristin Bergstad

Indexer: Beth Nauman-Montana

Marketing Manager: Carmel Schrire

Cover Designer: Scott Van Atta

12 13 14 15 16 10 9 8 7 6 5 4 3 2 1

★ TABLE OF CONTENTS

The U.S. Congress is the branch of the federal government to which the Founders gave the most thought, writing into the Constitution considerably more detail than was given to the presidency and the court system. Despite this detailed plan, the structure, operations, and rituals that dictate how the national legislature carries out its responsibilities remain opaque and mysterious to most Americans. Millions of voters dutifully travel to polling places every two years to elect a new House and a third of the Senate, but few of these citizens understand how their elected officials actually do their work.

How Congress Works, fifth edition, is designed to help citizens—students, political activists, and voters concerned about representative government—better understand Congress as an institution and as a living organism that tries, often with mixed success, to reconcile the vast differences in political, social, and economic interests that stretch over a diverse population.

The volume is divided into four chapters that describe congressional leadership, the legislative process, committees, and staff. These are supplemented by an array of reference material in an appendix, including recorded votes, House and Senate leaders, and members' party affiliations.

Party Leadership in Congress. Many scholars and journalists have noted the increasingly high-pitched partisanship that has dominated politics in Washington in recent decades. *How Congress Works* illustrates how, in this hostile atmosphere, congressional leaders have thrived as they have become central power brokers in the art of lawmaking. Over the course of more than two hundred years, Congress has known both strong and weak leaders. In the modern period, from about 1947 onward, leaders—especially in the House—were confined to a significant degree by the iron rigidity of the seniority system and the nearly absolute power of committee chairs. This began to change with reforms in the 1960s and 1970s. Commanding leadership returned to the House in 1994, when Republicans won control for the first time in forty years. With that victory, the GOP leadership enforced a strict party line to maintain a uniform and strong position of power; Democrats similarly gave more authority to their leaders when they regained control from 2006 to 2010. The Senate remains more a temple of individualism. As leaders in

that chamber have said, trying to run the Senate is akin to herding cats. Even there, however, in what is essentially a collection of individuals, the Senate can—and has—responded to astute and determined leadership. Two of the most often cited examples of strong leaders are Lyndon B. Johnson before he became president and George Mitchell.

The Legislative Process. Congress's legislative process is an amalgam of two centuries of precedent, custom, and formal rules mixed with the alchemy of political maneuvering and deals, strategic alignment of sometimes competing, sometimes synergistic interests, and just plain arm-twisting. Policy and process are deeply intertwined in Congress, rubbing together and interacting at many stages of legislative activity. Sometimes this activity is intended only to kill a proposal, but more often it is designed to move a program ahead—embodied in bills—to enactment and law. To the casual observer, congressional actions are fairly straightforward. Legislation usually starts in a subcommittee in one or both chambers, moves to the full committee, is debated by the full House or Senate, and passes or fails. Differences between successful House and Senate bills are reconciled in a conference committee, and the final product is sent to the president for approval or rejection (veto). Getting through this labyrinth, however, is seldom easy, as *How Congress Works* explains.

The Committee System. Sometimes compared to the skeletal structure of humans and animals, the committee system in Congress is essential to the functioning of the institution; without it, the institution could not operate. Committees are where the bulk of legislative work is done, but the system has been a target of endless criticism. It has been under assault so frequently, and for so long, that it is easy to overlook how much committees still matter. In *How Congress Works,* readers will come to understand that committees are

- along with parties, a central organizing structure for Congress;
- essential to the careers of most members of the House and Senate; and
- almost always essential for legislation to be brought up for debate and up or down votes in either chamber.

Congressional Staff. Thousands of people work for members of Congress, committees, and congressional support agencies. They are a largely faceless mass of mostly young persons who, in their anonymity, are essential to the legislative process. Staff members have no vote, but their influence is felt everywhere: on bills, in political strategy, and in the positions of members who do have a vote. Critics argue staff members are too many in number, exercise too much influence, and cost the taxpayers too much money. In its examination of this debate, *How Congress Works* notes that most members of Congress disagree. They say that staffs provide expert knowledge about complex issues that come before Congress every year and that members alone could never master.

How Congress Works enables citizens to make sense of all of these elements that feed into the legislative system, turning the opaque and mysterious into the clear and explicable.

CQ Press Editors

★ CONTRIBUTORS

These authors have updated the following chapters for this edition:

Chuck McCutcheon

   1 Party Leadership in Congress

Brian Nutting

   2 The Legislative Process

Christopher J. Deering

   3 The Committee System

Christina L. Lyons

   4 Congressional Staff

chapter 1

Party Leadership in Congress

Congressional leaders have thrived in the current era of hostile partisan division, becoming the central power brokers in the interdependent arts of lawmaking, fund-raising, and campaigning. The result is a remarkably consolidated power structure in the House in which most lawmakers owe their spot on the ballot, their campaign war chest, their favorable district lines, their committee assignments, their chairmanships, their television appearances, their foreign travel, and even their late-night dinners to elected party leaders.

The Senate, by comparison, remains a bastion of individualism. However, an influx of recent House veterans into the clubby upper chamber has contributed heavily to a similar partisan dynamic taking root. Another factor has been the growing realization—by both parties—that maintaining a united front against the other side can make it far easier to block legislation.

The structure allows party leaders to develop and implement an aggressively partisan legislative and campaign agenda, often with relatively little interference from committee chairs with different plans. Over the past half-century, the "old bull" chairs who once dominated the House landscape have been gradually put out to pasture. Frustrated at their inability to advance the party's agenda, junior lawmakers seized every opportunity to break the mortal locks a long-honored seniority system conferred upon chairs.

With increased institutional power, congressional leaders take on far greater responsibility for establishing and enacting the party agenda, for articulating the party's national message, and, ultimately, for the party's success or failure at the polls. For instance, some Democrats blamed their party's inability to retain control of the House in 2010 on Speaker Nancy Pelosi, D-Calif., who had become a widely demonized figure among Republicans in that year's elections.

If a leader fails to deliver on any of those goals, he or she may be warming a new seat on the backbench or looking for a private sector job. Speaker Thomas S. Foley, D-Wash., and Senate Democratic leader Tom Daschle of South Dakota lost reelection bids after becoming too closely identified with the national party platform back home. Republican Speakers Newt Gingrich, R-Ga., and J. Dennis Hastert, R-Ill., gave up their leadership posts after Republicans lost seats in the House in 1998 and 2006, respectively. Their stepping down is a far cry from the days of Speaker Sam Rayburn (1940–1947, 1949–1953, and 1955–1961), D-Texas, who remained the Democrats' leader despite losing control of the House twice.

The risks of running the centralized and increasingly polarized parties in Congress are proportional to the rewards. When Gingrich came to power as the spiritual leader of the so-called Republican Revolution in 1994, he was able to use his personal political power to consolidate institutional authority for the leadership. His vision of Congress as a parliamentary institution with strong partisan divisions and his influence in national redistricting after the 1990 census had helped catapult Republicans into the majority by drawing distinctions between the two parties in ideology and on electoral maps.

Once in power, the new majority handed authority to its leadership by eliminating three committees, slashing committee funding, reining in subcommittees, and putting three-term limits on committee chairs. The last move, perhaps the most significant institutional change brought about by the GOP's 1994 campaign manifesto, the Contract with America, ensured that party leaders, not chairs, would be viewed as permanent power centers. Initially, the Speaker was limited to four terms, but Republicans repealed that constraint after a decade in power.

Ultimately, Texas representative Tom DeLay, who served as majority leader or majority whip for all but about one year of the twelve-year Republican run in the 1990s and 2000s, would further consolidate institutional power in the hands of party leaders and become the dominant public figure in Congress despite never holding the top post in either chamber.

Across the Capitol, Majority Leader Bob Dole, R-Kan., a Senate traditionalist, proved far less confrontational than Gingrich and DeLay. But Dole, who had long worked across party lines—on the namesake McGovern-Dole food stamp law, for example—ran for president in 1996, leaving the majority leader job to conservative Trent Lott, R-Miss. Lott, then only half a dozen years removed from the House whip's position, had used a kitchen cabinet of conservative former House colleagues to defeat Dole deputy Alan K. Simpson, R-Wyo., for the Senate Republican whip job after the 1994 election.

In his book *Herding Cats: A Life in Politics,* Lott summed up the differences between Gingrich and Dole, between Gingrich and himself, and between the House and the Senate at the time by describing Dole's reaction to Lott's suggestion that top senators join House members and candidates in unveiling the Contract with America:

> "We should join them," I told Dole. "We should sign the Contract and join them on the Capitol steps."
>
> "Nah, we don't want to do that," Dole scoffed. I knew where he was coming from: The Senate likes to think of itself as the more mature and deliberative partner in the legislative branch, and its old bulls were bound to dismiss what the young upstarts in the House were doing as foolish grandstanding. So we sat impotently in our offices and watched this remarkable ceremony on television.[1]

Despite the fanfare, a purely and aggressively conservative agenda in the House, and high-stakes battles with President Bill Clinton, it was not until George W. Bush was sworn in as president in 2001 that the Republican Revolution reached its apex. For the first time since 1955, the GOP controlled the White House and both houses of Congress.

Partisan acrimony notwithstanding—House Republican leaders had pressed for impeachment of President Clinton, which they conceded never had a chance of resulting in Senate conviction—the two sides made landmark legislative history during the Clinton years by overhauling the welfare system in 1996 and writing a balanced budget law that helped usher in a brief period of surpluses.

When a president of their own party took power in 2001, Republican congressional leaders transitioned from the role of independent guardians of their institution into the foremen for the president's agenda. They helped him pass trillions of dollars of tax cuts, including rate reductions for personal and investment income; the authorizations and laws he sought to fight the Iraq war and combat global terrorism; the privatization of previously governmental functions; and even two landmark laws opposed by many conservatives, the No Child Left Behind Act and a Medicare prescription-drug measure, which contributed to criticism of Bush's "big-government conservatism."

All of these legislative successes were made possible by a powerful congressional leadership that demanded and received nearly lockstep support for the party's program. Bush exercised his veto power just once in his first six years in office, on a bill loosening regulations for federal funding of controversial embryonic stem cell research.

Democrats, stunned by their losses in 1994, were slow to regroup. For years, long after their forty-year reign had become a distant memory, they still talked about "taking back the House" and often seemed either unsure of goals or unwilling to allow party leaders to act on a common agenda. But by 2003, with the liberal partisan Pelosi leading them in the House—and two years later with Harry Reid, D-Nev., taking the reins in the Senate—Democrats began to exhibit the type of voting unity that had allowed Republicans to draw distinctions between the parties.

Democrats had high hopes for moving their agenda through Congress with the election in 2008 of President Barack Obama, who proposed a series of ambitious measures that vastly expanded government's role in society. Those hopes rose even higher in 2009 when the Senate Democrats ended up holding 60 seats, making them theoretically able to avoid Republican filibusters. Some of their efforts did become law after following a protracted and tortuous legislative path. But others were thwarted by a fierce and passionate Republican backlash that led to Democrats losing control of the House in the 2010 mid-term elections and ushered in a more combative crowd of freshman Republicans than the lawmakers they replaced.

Since the last half of the nineteenth century, when the two-party system became firmly established on Capitol Hill, Congress has been organized on the basis of political party, with each party's congressional leaders seeking to facilitate enactment of their legislative program and to enhance their members' national image and electoral fortunes. Congressional party leaders in the early twenty-first century, even though they seemed so different from predecessors in personality and ideology, represented a long-standing institutional imperative: Congress cannot run itself.

In this partisan struggle, the majority party has a distinct advantage, because it controls not only the top leadership posts in both the House and Senate but the legislative committees and subcommittees as well. Through its party leaders and its majorities on the various committees and subcommittees, the majority party is in a position to determine the legislation Congress will consider and when. It can secure enactment of the president's agenda or label it "dead on arrival."

The minority party is not powerless, however. Depending on its numbers and coherence, the minority can influence the shape of legislation and the operation of Congress. Because of the Senate's sixty-vote threshold for ending debate and voting on legislation and nominations (invoking cloture), the minority party in the Senate is often able to thwart the will of majorities in both chambers. In the 110th, 111th, and 112th Congresses, Senate Minority Leader Mitch McConnell, R-Ky., made unprecedented and unapologetic use of the filibuster to block or slow a wide range of Democratic initiatives.

When the majority wants to legislate, it often must seek cooperation from at least a few members of the minority party, as was the case in 2003 when Democratic senators Max Baucus of Montana and John Breaux of Louisiana were invited to negotiate the details of the Medicare drug law.

However, if the majority is satisfied to use a bill as a political bludgeon against minority party members who do not support it, the majority may present the measure without consulting any minority senators and force them to choose between blocking progress or voting for legislation they had no stake in drafting.

The extent to which party leadership can control its rank and file depends on a multitude of factors, among them the personalities and abilities of the individual leaders, the institutional authority at the leadership's disposal, party unity and strength, the willingness of the rank and file to be led, the extent of the president's involvement, and the mood in the country. In the past, particularly in the House, a few party leaders dominated the chamber.

Modern-day congressional leaders have shepherded resources outside Congress, including tax-exempt entities, political action committees (PACs), adroit use of various media, policy ideas created to generate public appeal, and overarching theories of leadership.

In the last three or four decades, they have been given the authority to pursue collective goals by caucuses that increasingly want to see rapid enactment of a conservative or liberal agenda. Particularly since the post-Watergate Democratic electoral romp in 1974 and the GOP sweep to power in the 1990s as well as in 2010, the Republican and Democratic caucuses have come to be dominated by each party's ideological base.

Under a more democratic system, party leaders have more power, but they are also under tremendous pressure to develop and implement agendas that satisfy their liberal or conservative bases inside and outside of Congress while appealing to enough of the national electorate—particularly in swing districts and states—to keep their party in power.

Senate leaders have few tools with which to enforce discipline, though both the Democratic and Republican parties have begun to hand more authority to their Senate leaders in recent years.

House leaders, no longer able to rely on the mixed power structure of the middle part of the twentieth century, which gave unelected chairs greater ability to reward and punish on behalf of the elected leadership, must often contend with various factions and individuals themselves. They are limited, in that way, to using coercion only when the methods are acceptable to a large majority of the rank and file, and even then they run the risk of permanently alienating a member who will be needed to help pass future legislation through.

"In Mr. Rayburn's day," Jim Wright, D-Texas, once commented,

> about all a majority leader or Speaker needed to do in order to get his program adopted was to deal effectively with perhaps twelve very senior committee chairmen. They, in turn, could be expected to influence their committees and their subcommittee chairmen whom they, in those days, appointed. . . . We have relatively fewer rewards that we can bestow or withhold. I think that basically about all the leadership has nowadays is a hunting license to persuade—if we can.[2]

CONGRESSIONAL LEADERSHIP STRUCTURE

Although the strategies of leadership have changed substantially over time, the basic leadership structure has remained the same. In the House the leadership consists of the Speaker, who is both the chamber's presiding officer and the majority party's overall leader; the majority and minority floor leaders, who are responsible for scheduling legislation and handling it once it reaches the floor; the assistant floor leaders or whips, who try to convince party members to follow the leadership's program; the caucus or conference chairs who serve as the communications nerve center for the parties; and several political party committees that develop strategy, assign members to legislative committees, assist the leadership in scheduling and tracking legislation, and provide campaign assistance to House and Senate candidates.

The Senate has no institutional or party official comparable in power and prestige to the Speaker. The Constitution designates the vice president of the United States as the president, or presiding officer, of the Senate and a president pro tempore to preside in his absence. Aside from the vice president's tie-breaking power, neither office has been endowed with any commanding legislative or political authority, and neither has played much of a leadership role in the Senate. (See box, The Senate's Presiding Officers, pp. 48–49.)

The remainder of the Senate leadership apparatus is similar in structure and function to that of the House.

Of all the party leadership positions in Congress, the only ones that have functioned continuously since 1789 are those of Speaker and president pro tempore of the Senate—posts that were established by the Constitution. Although various members assumed the roles of floor leader and whip from time to time, the positions were not made official in the House until 1899, during a period when parties and partisanship were strong, both in Congress and throughout the country. Formal party leadership positions began to develop in the Senate in the early 1900s. But party caucuses did not officially designate majority and minority party leaders until the 1920s.

Top leaders in both chambers are elected by their respective party caucuses, or conferences, as three of the four are

Senate Majority Leader Trent Lott, R-Miss., right, and Senate minority leader Tom Daschle, D-S.D., maintained a good working relationship as leaders of opposing parties in the Senate in the mid- to late 1990s.

SOURCE: Scott J. Ferrell, Congressional Quarterly.

South, liberals and conservatives together; to work out compromises. . . . I think it takes a centrist to do that."[3] A conservative when he entered the Senate in 1959, Byrd had moved considerably leftward by the time he was first elected majority leader after the 1976 elections. By the time U.S. forces invaded Iraq in 2003, the onetime conservative stalwart had become an icon of the antiwar left.

But ideological perceptions are often deceiving, sometimes reflect a specific period of time, and can change rapidly with the shifting political orientation of the parties. For example, Gingrich, often branded a right-wing extremist by Democrats and even by some moderate Republicans when the party was a minority in the House, was later criticized as too centrist by some of the conservatives he helped elect in 1994. In 1999 Trent Lott, the Senate majority leader, who might have been considered on the far right of his party just a few years before, made a comfortable fit with the Republican Conference that had moved toward him politically and added many like-minded legislators. And the demands of institutional leadership and majority responsibility changed these leaders as well, along with their approach to politics. By 2002 conservatives were frustrated by Lott's efforts to coordinate with Senate Democrats, a dynamic that contributed to his ouster as Republican leader after he spoke at a one-hundredth-birthday party for Sen. Strom Thurmond of South Carolina. He praised Thurmond's 1948 bid for the presidency, in which the candidate expressly supported racial segregation.

formally named. (Only House Democrats refer to their partisan gathering as a caucus.) Factors such as ideological leanings, personal style, geographical balance, and length of service traditionally played an important role in the selection of the leadership. In an age of twenty-four-hour cable television news, blogs, social media, and Internet video compendiums such as YouTube, the ability of leaders to effectively speak for their party and present a legislative program to the nation has taken on new importance. A central component of this task is a talent to use the media adroitly to put forth party messages.

Modern leaders often win election to their posts in part because they have proved the strength of their ideological convictions to the party's base. But, to varying degrees and without exception, they adapt to represent the center of the party. A good example is former Speaker Pelosi, who was a leading member of the liberal Progressive Caucus before she became a House leader but navigated a more moderate path once she became responsible for unifying her party and developing its agenda. Liberals quietly groused that she had turned her back on them.

"As a member of the leadership," said Senate majority whip Robert Byrd in 1976, "it is my duty to bring North and

Leadership Functions

The powers the leaders may exercise and the ways the leadership functions differ in the House and Senate. House rules allow a determined majority to lead, while Senate rules protect minority rights. The job of a party leader has two overlapping, sometimes competing, parts. Leaders, Roger H. Davidson and Walter J. Oleszek observe, must constantly balance the needs of Congress as a lawmaking institution against Congress as a representative assembly:

> In their "inside" role, party leaders guide institutional activities and influence policy.... Good communications skills, a talent for coalition building, tactical and strategic competence, intelligence, parliamentary expertise, and sensitivity to the mood of the membership and of the electorate are important attributes of an effective leader.... In their "outside" role, party leaders . . . help recruit candidates for Congress and assist in their campaigns. Leaders also must serve as the party's link to the president, the press, the public, and the partisan faithful.[4]

In their inside role, leaders organize each chamber and each party within the chamber, setting and reviewing committee jurisdictions and assignments and institutional and party rules. Leaders of each party also work together and with their members, usually through the party caucuses, to develop the party's stand on policy issues. Leaders assign individual bills to the appropriate committee or committees and decide how best to handle each bill as it comes to the floor. Once a bill is on the floor, the leadership is responsible for monitoring the debate and using the rules and procedures in ways that will help the party's chances of legislative success. Throughout, establishing and maintaining party unity is an important goal.

Scheduling business on the floor—deciding what will come to the floor when, under what conditions, and in what order—may be the majority leadership's most important institutional task, and it is a forceful tool in achieving the party's policy agenda. "The power of the Speaker of the House is the power of scheduling," Speaker Thomas P. "Tip" O'Neill Jr., D-Mass., declared in 1983.[5]

The leadership often schedules floor action for the convenience of members. Little business is scheduled in the House on Mondays and Fridays, for example, so that members can return to their districts for long weekends. Democrats, upon returning to power in 2007, expanded the schedule to more often include work on Mondays and Fridays, which House Republicans continued in 2011. But many lawmakers, aides, and experts predicted the legislative workweek would be condensed again in future years. The leadership may delay action on a controversial bill until it is sure that it has the winning votes, it may bring a controversial bill to the floor quickly to prevent opposition from building, or it may keep a vote going while it tries to recruit or change enough votes to gain victory.

In the Senate, where bills are open to nearly unlimited amendment and debate, the majority leader generally consults with the minority leadership, the floor managers of the bill, and other interested senators to draw up unanimous consent agreements governing floor action on major legislation. These agreements can be complicated, stipulating which amendments will be offered, how long they will be debated, when they will be voted upon, and, in some cases, how many votes will be needed to pass them. Because a single member can block a unanimous consent agreement, the leaders must take care to ensure an opportunity to speak to all senators who want to be heard on the issue. The procedure is different in the House, where all but the most routine bills typically receive a rule for floor consideration. *(See "Major Legislation and the Rules Committee," p. 93.)*

Building winning coalitions is also essential to effective leadership. The absence of such coalitions has been a central source of complaint among political observers and the public, who have accused Congress of descending into dysfunction. In the House this leadership function is aided by expanded whip organizations in both parties, which poll party members on specific issues, inform them of upcoming votes, help persuade them to support the party's cause, enlist outside interest groups in persuading lawmakers to vote with the party, and ensure that the members show up to vote. On a Medicare prescription-drug vote in 2003, Virginia representative Eric Cantor, the chief deputy to Republican whip Roy Blunt of Missouri, left the floor to go to the House office buildings to find members who had not voted for the bill. Ad hoc task forces also are used in both chambers to build support for specific issues important to the leadership. Despite the partisan rhetoric and real philosophical differences, leaders of both parties traditionally tried to win support from members of the opposing party on most major legislation and amendments. But customs have changed, and the majority party, particularly in the House, has been reluctant to rely on even a small amount of minority support to win passage of legislation. More typically, minority party votes for legislation are the result of political pressure applied from back home rather than the sweet entreaties of the majority party in the Capitol.

Speaker Hastert was credited for delaying action on a restructuring of the nation's intelligence apparatus in 2004 because he demanded a majority of the Republican Party—a "majority of the majority"—to be on board to proceed. However, few leaders in recent congressional history would ever consider advancing legislation that did not have majority support within their own caucus. What was truly remarkable about Hastert's basic approach to lawmaking, and that of other Republican leaders in the modern era, was that it sought to ensure legislation would not be considered if Democratic votes were needed to achieve a majority. That is, Republican leaders wanted to build a full House majority of 218 votes from within a set that numbered from 221 to 232 over the twelve-year period. Any Democratic votes were considered gravy.

That approach, the natural outgrowth of a deepening ideological divide in Congress, was continued during Pelosi's speakership. Most major legislation was passed with little to no Republican support. On the biggest issues, most notably the 2009–2010 health care overhaul, Pelosi had to wage a strenuous all-out effort to persuade enough members of her own party to back the legislation in the face of unanimous Republican opposition.

In their outside roles, congressional leaders have become the point men and women in the perpetual electoral battle for power. Their political action committees, known informally as leadership PACs, move millions of dollars from special interest donors to candidates favored by the leaders. Party leaders also use their own campaign accounts to dole out generous sums of cash to the party committees. In addition, they fly around the country appearing at fund-raisers for scores of their party's candidates each election cycle, helping the candidates raise their own money.

The methods have been so effective at building a political constituency from grateful recipients of the campaign cash that they are now universally used both by party leaders and lawmakers who want to run for either an elected party post or any other position over which their colleagues hold sway. In the 2010 election cycle, Minority Leader John Boehner, R-Ohio, gave more than $44 million to GOP colleagues' campaigns. At the same time, Rep. Debbie Wasserman Schultz, D-Fla., established herself as a fund-raising powerhouse immediately upon her arrival in 2005 and within just six years was named chairwoman of the Democratic National Committee.

Another outside role of party leaders is to defend the institution against encroachment from the other branches of government and, in some cases, to try actively to take turf from the president and the U.S. Supreme Court. The leaders of both parties meet periodically with the president to discuss his legislative agenda, letting him know how their respective memberships are likely to respond to his proposals. The leaders of the same party as the president also generally serve as his spokespersons in the House and Senate, although they remain independent—at least in their own telling—of the president. "I'm the president's friend," Senate majority leader Byrd said of President Jimmy Carter. "I'm not the president's man."[6]

Messages through the Media

In both inside and outside roles, skilled use of the media has become a prerequisite for success and even for selection as a leader. Despite his relatively short tenure in the Senate when he ran for majority leader in 1988, George J. Mitchell of Maine won the support of many Democrats who thought he would be a more articulate and appealing public spokesperson for Senate Democrats than his opponents. Cantor and Rep. Kevin McCarthy, R-Calif., who became House majority whip in 2011, were known for their avid use of social media networking tools such as Facebook and Twitter to get their party's ideas across to the public. Cantor in 2010 launched a website, YouCut, enabling people to vote on federal projects they think deserve elimination.

Leaders in both chambers are routinely available to the news media. The Speaker of the House for many years until 1995 held a press conference before each House session began. Traditionally, the Senate majority and minority leaders gathered with journalists on the Senate floor prior to Senate sessions, to announce the schedule and answer questions. That daily tradition has become an occasional one, though both House and Senate leaders hold regular weekly news conferences. Party leaders in both the House and Senate routinely respond to presidential addresses such as the State of the Union message or other speeches calling for legislative action.

Use of the media goes beyond simply articulating party positions. Public opinion is one of the main influences on a legislator's vote, and fights on the House and Senate floor can be won not only by appealing to members of Congress but also by appealing to their constituents. Richard A. Gephardt of Missouri, the future Democratic majority and minority leader, once said: "Being a good legislator means you have to do both. If you are going to pass important legislation, you have to both deal with members and put together coalitions in the country."[7] Tactics both parties use to influence public opinion include floor speeches meant to be picked up by the television news networks, newspaper opinion page pieces written by senior members of key committees, and carefully scheduled appearances on the Sunday morning TV talk shows. Increasingly, party leaders are using the Internet and e-mail to communicate their messages to key constituencies quickly and without interference from political opponents.

One of the most adroit congressional manipulators of the media was Gingrich, a conservative Republican who arrived in the House in 1979, the same year the national Cable-Satellite Public Affairs Network (C-SPAN) began televising House proceedings. Using that medium to attack and confront the Democratic leadership, and on occasion moderate Republicans, Gingrich soon became a visible presence in the national media and a favorite of conservatives nationwide. "Conflict equals exposure equals power," the future Speaker told a reporter.[8]

Part of the secret of Speaker Hastert's success for many years was a willingness to remain in the background, credit others for Republican victories, and prevent himself from becoming a political liability for his colleagues. A congressional page scandal at the end of his tenure, however, did lightly tarnish his image as a party caretaker. In contrast, Pelosi maintained a high profile, something that made her vulnerable to frequent attacks from Republicans who sought to caricature her as a "San Francisco liberal" out of touch with the rest of the nation. Boehner, her successor, was careful to let Cantor and others take the spotlight on some issues as a way of fostering the perception that he alone did not call the shots.

Tools of Persuasion

Although the greater independence of individual members means leaders in both chambers must rely heavily on persuasion and negotiation, they are not without inducements and a few punishments to help coax their colleagues into line. A legislator who votes with his party might be rewarded with a better committee assignment or a visit by party leaders to his district during his reelection campaign. A pet program might be handled by a sympathetic committee or attached to an important bill heading for the floor. Leaders can see that a loyal member gets benefits for his district or state—a tax break for a key industry, a new flood control project, or an exemption from clean air rules. Campaign appearances and funds are also distributed judiciously to encourage loyalty.

In addition the leadership can offer many services to individual members, what House Speaker O'Neill once called the "little odds and ends":

> You know, you ask me what are my powers and my authority around here? The power to recognize on the floor; little odds and ends—like men get pride out of the prestige of handling the Committee of the Whole, being named Speaker for the day.... [T]here is a certain aura and respect that goes with the Speaker's office. He does have the power to be able to pick up the telephone and call people. And members oftentimes like to bring their local political leaders or a couple of mayors. And oftentimes they have problems from their area and they need aid and assistance.... We're happy to try to open the door for them, having been in the town for so many years and knowing so many people. We do know where a lot of bodies are and we do know how to advise people.[9]

Committee assignments and chairmanships are now, in part, given out or withheld on the basis of a lawmaker's willingness to donate campaign money to party committees and candidates.

Punishment for disloyal behavior can be subtle or brutal. A member's bid for a local dam or scheme to revamp national education grants could languish in an unresponsive committee. A request to switch or add a committee assignment or to travel abroad in a congressional delegation could be denied. Sometimes the threat of punishment may be enough to induce a member to fall into step. In the 104th Congress, Speaker Gingrich threatened to refuse to appoint members to a conference committee and to deny permission for foreign travel as a penalty for supporting a former member who opposed abortion and was running in a primary against a Republican incumbent who favored abortion rights. In the 105th Congress he endorsed a proposal that threatened to discipline members holding chairmanships who opposed the GOP position on key procedural votes, such as ordering the previous question, or rules from the Rules Committee and sustaining rulings of the chair. In rare cases legislators are stripped of committee seniority or a committee post for repeatedly betraying the party position. After Democratic representative Phil Gramm, of Texas, masterminded enactment of budgets proposed by Republican president Ronald

Reagan, Democratic leaders in 1983 stripped him of his seat on the House Budget Committee. Gramm resigned his House seat, won reelection as a Republican, and soon rejoined the committee as a GOP member. Rep. Christopher H. Smith, R-N.J., was removed from the chairmanship of the Veterans Affairs Committee in the 109th Congress after repeatedly clashing openly with party leaders over funding for veterans' health care.

Divided government—a president of one party and a Congress of another—has been an important factor in the difficulties political leaders faced in Congress in the last several decades of the twentieth century but by no means the only one. Forces within Congress and the country that had been gathering for years exacerbated partisan differences, most especially a resurgence of Republican conservatism that captured control of the GOP starting about 1964. The direct and indirect results of the reforms that Congress had put in place in the 1970s also contributed to the challenges of leadership that congressional parties faced. After 1974, Congress was filled with politicians who had never known an era in which backbenchers took care to be seen but not heard. These newcomers owed their seats and careers not to the party apparatus but also to constituents, campaign consultants, and election campaign contributors. Gone were the days when their votes were there to be delivered.

The rise of negative campaign tactics and the thirty-second sound bite made this new generation of politicians see more and more votes as perilous. Many members also concluded that party leaders no longer offered them political cover. "There is a sense that they are out there all by themselves," said Foley, "that if they are not careful, no one will be careful for them."[10]

That undertow of political vulnerability, combined with the diffusion of power that resulted from the 1970s reforms and the leadership's lack of effective tools to keep the rank and file in line, made it difficult to impose the discipline needed to legislate effectively, and especially to tackle the huge federal budget deficits that overshadowed almost all other considerations until the mid-1990s.

Over time, however, the parties were able to reassert control over most aspects of an individual lawmaker's career through their influence in the redistricting, candidate-recruitment, and fund-raising arenas. Lawmakers must weigh whether a particular vote will help or hurt them among constituents, special interest campaign donors, and party leaders.

Leaders can also gain persuasiveness by intentional inaction. In February 2011, the newly empowered Republican majority was eager to demonstrate its willingness to cut what it saw as wasteful spending. Lawmakers decided to show that not even the military budget was sacrosanct, and they proposed rejecting funds for an alternate engine for the F-35 Joint Strike Fighter aircraft that had survived previous attempts at cancellation. Boehner had the power to nullify the vote on the project, which was an important source of jobs to his

Cincinnati-area district. But he decided not to be an impediment, and the project was killed, earning the speaker credibility in the eyes of his budget-conscious GOP colleagues.

THE HOUSE SPEAKER

Widely regarded as the most powerful figure in Congress, the Speaker is the presiding officer of the House of Representatives as well as the leader of the majority party in the House. Since 1947 the Speaker has also been second in line, after the vice president, to succeed the president. "No other member of Congress possesses the visibility and authority of the Speaker," Davidson and Oleszek have written.[11]

The speakership has not always been endowed with such prestige. For the first two decades of Congress, the Speaker was largely a figurehead. Not until Henry Clay was elected to the office in 1811 did a Speaker exercise any real leadership in the House. After Clay left the House in 1825, the authority of the Speaker ebbed and flowed, but no Speaker wielded as much influence as Clay until 1890, when Republican Thomas Brackett Reed of Maine used his personal and institutional authority to ensure that the minority could no longer frustrate the legislative actions of a unified majority. (See "Speakers of the House of Representatives, 1789–2012," p. 231, in Reference Materials.)

"Czar" Reed was soon followed by Joseph G. Cannon, R-Ill., the Speaker from 1903 to 1911, whose autocratic control over the House led to a revolt against him in 1910. Ultimately the Speaker's powers as presiding officer were limited by House rules. Changes in the caucus rules of the two political parties also served to lessen the Speaker's authority.

Cannon's tyrannical rule and the rebellion against it had a lasting effect on the office and the men who have held it. Power in the House became concentrated in the hands of the chairs of the legislative committees until the mid-1970s. The reforms of the 1970s restored many of the Speaker's powers. Yet every Speaker who has been an effective House leader has achieved at least some measure of this influence through personal prestige, persuasion, brokerage, and bargaining.

In the modern era, a Speaker must take care to ensure that his or her actions have the continued support of a majority of his or her party. Democrat Jim Wright pushed his leadership close to the limits of its powers and caused resentment by acting without first consulting other party leaders or the rank and file. That exclusion, coupled with his aggressive and sometimes abrasive style, left him politically vulnerable when a challenge to his personal ethics arose. The crisis eventually forced Wright to resign both the speakership and his House seat. Republican Newt Gingrich surmounted political difficulties and personal ethics problems because he enjoyed support from a united party and from colleagues who valued strong leadership. When Gingrich's leadership no longer produced the desired results, the party replaced him in favor of a different approach.

Pelosi, the first female Speaker, was considered the most powerful and most effective lawmaker in the job since Cannon, in part because of how she skillfully maintained support within her often fractious caucus. Even after Democrats lost control of the House in 2010, she was able to remain as minority leader after no significant opposition emerged to challenge her.

Framers' Intentions

The Framers of the Constitution were silent on the role they intended the Speaker to play in the House. The Constitution's only reference to the office is in Article I, Section 2, Clause 5, which states, "The House of Representatives shall chuse their Speaker and other Officers." There is no evidence that the Founders debated this provision.

Two respected authorities on the speakership, Mary P. Follett and Hubert Bruce Fuller, have suggested that this absence of any discussion indicated that the Framers thought the Speaker would act as both presiding officer and political leader. "Surely," wrote Follett in *The Speaker of the House of Representatives*, the Speaker could not have been thought of "as a non-political moderator, as a mere parliamentary officer whom it was necessary to dissociate from politics. What [was] intended must be inferred from that with which [the Framers] were familiar." Follett's book, published in 1896, is still widely regarded as the authoritative study of the early development of the office.[12]

What the Framers knew were the colonial Speakers. In most cases these Speakers were active politicians who not only presided over the legislatures but also used their positions to further their own or their faction's legislative aims. This concept of the office differed sharply from that of the speakership of the House of Commons. The British Speaker was, and still is, a strictly nonpartisan presiding officer. (The term "Speaker" first appeared in the Commons in 1377, when Sir Thomas Hungerford assumed the post. Until the late seventeenth century, the Speaker in England was directly responsible to the Crown. The term was derived from the fact that it was the duty of the presiding officer to interpret the will of the House of Commons to the Crown.)

In any event, because political parties had not yet been formed, the first Speaker, Frederick A. C. Muhlenberg, Pa., was nonpartisan. His duties, as spelled out by the House on April 7, 1789, were to preside at House sessions, preserve decorum and order, announce the results of standing and teller votes, appoint select committees of not more than three members, and vote in cases of a tie, a practice referred to as the Speaker's "casting" vote. By the Second Congress, clearly defined party divisions had begun to develop, and Muhlenberg's successor, Jonathan Trumbull of Connecticut, displayed definite leanings toward President George Washington's legislative program. In 1796 Speaker Jonathan Dayton, a Federalist, twice voted to produce ties that resulted in the defeat of Jeffersonian motions that would have undermined the Federalist-backed Jay Treaty with Britain.

Party affiliation, although weak and more diffuse than in modern times, also became the basis for choosing the Speaker. In 1799 the Federalists elected Theodore Sedgwick of Massachusetts over Nathaniel Macon of North Carolina to the Speaker's post by a vote of 44–38, a margin that reflected that of the Federalists over the Jeffersonians in the Sixth Congress. Sedgwick, according to Follett, "made many enemies by decided and even partisan acts," so many that the Jeffersonians in the Sixth Congress refused to join in the customary vote of thanks to the Speaker at adjournment. At the beginning of the Seventh Congress, the Jeffersonians, now in commanding control of Congress, elected Macon to the speakership by a wide margin.

But throughout the early years, and particularly during Thomas Jefferson's presidency, it was the executive, and not the Speaker, who was the real political and legislative leader in the House. As Washington's Treasury secretary, Alexander Hamilton dominated the Federalist majority even during the First Congress by operating through supporters in Congress who formed what might be considered the first party caucuses. "Instead of being a forum, where every member was a peer and no man led, where great principles of government were evolved through the give and take of unrestricted discussion, Congress as such had become in effect a mere ratifying body," wrote Ralph V. Harlow in 1917. "The real work of legislation was put in shape, not in the legislature, but in secret session of the majority party."[13]

Jefferson's secretary of the Treasury, Albert Gallatin, soon became as adept as Hamilton in guiding administration measures through the party caucus and the House. Jefferson, moreover, carried his control over the legislative branch one step farther, picking his own floor leader, who was named chair of the Ways and Means Committee at the same time. One of these congressional leaders, William B. Giles of Virginia, was referred to as the "premier" or "prime minister." There was little room under Jefferson's shadow for a Speaker to carve out an independent leadership role, notes political scientist Ronald M. Peters Jr.[14]

Clay and the Shift of Power

Executive domination of the House came to an end under Jefferson's successor, James Madison. Although nominally supported by the Democratic-Republican (Jeffersonian) majorities throughout his two terms, Madison soon lost control of the party to a band of young "war hawks," who, affronted by British interference with American trade and shipping, advocated war with England. Henry Clay of Kentucky, who had served brief stints as a senator in 1806–1807 and

Henry Clay was chosen as Speaker on the day he entered the House of Representatives in 1811. A formidable presiding officer, he exerted firm control over the House.

SOURCE: AP Photo.

1810–1811, entered the House in 1811 as spokesperson for the war hawks who had swept seventy House seats in the elections of 1810. Although only thirty-four and a newcomer, he was elected Speaker on his first day in the House. He would soon become the first Speaker of national prominence and the first to use the position to achieve his own ends.

Clay's great success as presiding officer lay in his personal magnetism. "All testify," wrote Follett, "to the marvelous charm of his voice and manner, which attracted attention, awakened sympathy, and compelled obedience. He had a bold and commanding spirit, which imposed its will upon those around him. He carried all before him with his imperious nature to give him complete ascendancy over his party, and the easy leadership of the House."[15]

Employing to the full his power as Speaker to select committee chairs and appoint members to committees, Clay immediately filled key positions on the Foreign Affairs, Military Affairs, and Naval Affairs committees with fellow war hawks. On November 29, 1811, less than four weeks after Congress had convened, the Foreign Affairs Committee issued a report recommending that the nation begin immediate preparations for war. President Madison, a leader of the Constitutional Convention and a strong secretary of state under Jefferson, proved to be a weak president. Although he sought a peaceful settlement with England, he was subjected

PARTY CONTROL OF CONGRESS AND PRESIDENCY IS NO GUARANTEE OF LEGISLATIVE SUCCESS

The stalemate and gridlock that so often characterized executive-legislative relations in the 1980s, 1990s, and 2011–2012 were blamed in large part on divided government. With the Republicans in control of the White House and the Democrats in control of one or both houses of Congress between 1981 and 1993, a Democratic president and Republican Congress from 1995 through the end of the Clinton presidency in 2001, and a Democratic president and Republican House in 2011 and 2012, conflicts between the branches were inevitable.

But control of Congress and the presidency by the same party does not always guarantee cooperation between the two branches. There have been numerous occasions in American history in which determined lawmakers resisted the proposals of their own presidents, and strong-willed presidents disregarded their party leaders in Congress.

LINCOLN, WILSON, THE ROOSEVELTS

Many of the conflicts between the White House and Congress when both were controlled by the same party have come at times of strong presidential leadership. Abraham Lincoln, Woodrow Wilson, and the two Roosevelts—Theodore and Franklin D.—all had difficulties with their party's congressional leaders, although all four men were largely successful in winning enactment of their programs.

The first important clash of this kind arose during the Civil War, when Republican extremists dominated Congress. In 1861 Congress created a Joint Committee on the Conduct of the War, which went so far as to intervene in military operations. In 1864 Congress sought to undermine Lincoln's liberal reconstruction program by transferring responsibility for reconstruction from the president to Congress. Lincoln pocket-vetoed that bill and, so far as possible, ignored the extremists. He used executive orders to maintain the upper hand, but after Lincoln's assassination Congress achieved the supremacy it was seeking and retained it for more than thirty years.

Theodore Roosevelt was the next strong president to experience difficulty with his party's congressional leadership. Roosevelt clashed sharply with Sen. Nelson W. Aldrich, R-R.I., the unofficial but acknowledged leader of the Senate's Republicans. Aldrich, for example, refused to support the president's bill to regulate railroad rates in exchange for Roosevelt's agreement to drop tariff reform. After relying primarily on Democrats to report the rate bill from the Senate committee, Roosevelt won agreement from William B. Allison of Iowa, another influential Republican in the Senate, on judicial review of rate adjustments. This maneuver split the opposition and led to passage of the bill by an overwhelming vote.

Although relations between President Wilson and the Democratic congressional leadership generally were good, party leaders sometimes deserted the president on foreign policy issues. On the eve of the opening of the Panama Canal in 1914, both Speaker Champ Clark of Missouri and House Majority Leader Oscar Underwood of Alabama opposed Wilson's request to repeal a provision of a law exempting American vessels traveling between U.S. ports from having to pay canal tolls. The exemption, which Great Britain said violated an Anglo-American treaty, was eventually eliminated despite the opposition of the House leadership.

In 1917 Rep. Claude Kitchin, D-N.C., who had replaced Underwood as majority leader, opposed Wilson when the president asked Congress to declare war on Germany. Later, Clark opposed Wilson's request for military conscription. Near the end of Wilson's second term, relations between Clark and the president were nearly nonexistent.

Although Franklin Roosevelt's overall relations with Congress were as good as or better than Wilson's, he still had problems with his own party's congressional leadership. During his third term (1941–1945) the Democratic leadership deserted Roosevelt on major domestic issues. In 1944 Alben W. Barkley of Kentucky resigned as Senate majority leader when Roosevelt vetoed a revenue bill. The Democrats promptly reelected Barkley, and the bill was passed over the president's veto.

MADISON, JOHNSON, MCKINLEY

Congressional leaders also frequently clashed with less aggressive presidents of their own party. These conflicts usually occurred when Congress attempted to dominate the president by initiating its own legislative program and directives. One of the earliest examples came during the administration of James Madison when Speaker Henry Clay forced the president into the War of 1812 against Britain. Another was Clay's successful attempt to pressure James Monroe into a series of unwanted measures, including a revision of tariffs.

After the Civil War, the Radical Republicans in Congress were able to push through their reconstruction policy over President Andrew Johnson's opposition. In the process they almost managed to remove the president through an impeachment effort that historians record as entirely politically motivated.

The next major clash came in 1898. Speaker Thomas Brackett Reed, R-Maine, a strong isolationist, sought but failed to block three controversial aspects of President William McKinley's foreign policy: war with Spain, annexation of Hawaii, and acquisition of the Philippine Islands. Reed's failure to stop McKinley, which led to his retirement from Congress, was due largely to the popularity of the president's policies, not to the successful application of pressure on congressional leaders by McKinley.

MODERN PRESIDENTS: JOHNSON, CARTER, CLINTON, BUSH

In the mid-1960s President Lyndon B. Johnson demanded congressional support of his military policies in Southeast Asia. Although the Democratic Congress generally went along with Johnson's conduct of the war, the majority leader in the Senate, Mike Mansfield, D-Mont., actively opposed the president's military venture virtually from the beginning.

Congress was overwhelmingly Democratic throughout the four years Democrat Jimmy Carter was president (1977–1981). Nevertheless, many of Carter's proposals and the way they were formulated and presented to his party received less than enthusiastic support from the leadership in Congress.

President Bill Clinton failed to receive support from both ideological wings of his party on several highly contentious issues during the 103rd Congress, which contributed to loss of Democratic control of both houses for the first time in forty years in 1994. Clinton was distrusted by liberals for his campaign as a New Democrat willing to reassess traditional party orthodoxy, while more conservative members worried about his administration's initial liberal policy proposals, such as his support for the rights of gays to remain in military service. However, it was Clinton's controversial plan for a new system of national health insurance that most deeply divided the party and angered the public. It failed to receive floor consideration in either house and undermined Democratic claims that its unified control of both major branches of government would lead to substantial achievements. George W. Bush, however, found Republican congressional leaders to be uncommonly willing to help move his legislative agenda, particularly after the September 11, 2001, terrorist assault on the United States. Bush won easy authorization to use military force against Iraq, enhanced the power of U.S. law enforcement agencies through the PATRIOT Act, and implemented massive new domestic education and prescription-drug programs. He was also spared the kind of investigative oversight that previous presidents had to contend with even when members of their own party control congressional committees.

President Barack Obama took office in 2009 as his party enjoyed considerable majorities in both the House and Senate. But near-unified Republican opposition to Obama's major proposals meant Obama had to rely on the support of conservative Democrats such as Ben Nelson of Nebraska. Nelson's demands on supporting health care overhaul legislation in 2009—including a provision that gave his state a permanent exemption from the state share of Medicaid expansion that was dubbed "the Cornhusker Kickback"—led to Republican accusations of unsavory deal-making. The GOP capitalized on voter anger over such tactics to reclaim the majority in the House in 2011.

SUCCESS THROUGH BIPARTISANSHIP

Cases in which a party's congressional leadership has cooperated in a substantial way with a president of the other party are less frequent and have dealt mainly with national security and related issues. One example is Republican president Dwight D. Eisenhower, who worked with a Democratic Congress for six of his eight years in office. Yet Democratic congressional leaders cooperated actively and willingly with the White House most of the time. Speaker Sam Rayburn of Texas, who often described himself as a Democrat "without prefix, without suffix, without apology," generally acted as the president's man in the House. During Eisenhower's second term, Rayburn's liberal critics, dismayed over his seeming inattention to traditional Democratic Party causes, began referring to him as an "Eisenhowercrat."

As Senate majority leader, Lyndon Johnson was a firm believer in the bipartisan conduct of foreign policy. In 1980 House minority leader John J. Rhodes, R-Ariz., recalled Johnson sitting in on foreign aid conference committee meetings: "He was there, not to ensure the Democratic position would win, but to ensure the administration position would win. He was acting as a broker for the Eisenhower administration.... It was often said at that time that 'the president proposes while Congress disposes.' The philosophy is not very popular today, but the people running Congress then were pretty much dedicated to that idea, no matter who the president was."[1]

Ronald Reagan's first year in office was marked by a Republican Senate and a Democratic House more conservative than it had been during Carter's presidency. Working closely with Senate and House Republicans and with conservative Democrats in the House, Reagan was able to put together a string of dramatic victories, including the deepest budget cuts and largest tax reductions ever considered by Congress and a controversial arms deal with Saudi Arabia. In 1986 the Republican president and a divided Congress produced a landmark tax reform bill, largely because both parties saw political gain in passing the bill, and neither wanted to advantage the other party by blocking the reform.

President George H. W. Bush won bipartisan support from Congress to use force in the Persian Gulf crisis, but it came over the objections of Democratic leaders in both the House and Senate. Bush worked effectively with Democratic leaders in both houses to push through long-delayed legislation in 1990 to strengthen the Clean Air Act.

Clinton won bipartisan support for a number of foreign policy initiatives, including passage of the North American Free Trade Agreement (NAFTA) in the Democratic-controlled House in the 103rd Congress but with Republicans providing the majority of votes; expansion of NATO; and ratification of a chemical weapons treaty with substantial help from Senate majority leader Trent Lott, R-Miss. Congress denied Clinton controversial fast-track trade negotiating authority in 1997, which was supported by many Republicans but did not have enough support within the president's party.

Republican congressional leaders repeatedly refused to defer to the tradition that politics stops at the water's edge. Clinton's personal difficulties with a variety of scandals intruded on his foreign policy efforts, as when House majority whip Tom DeLay, R-Texas, denounced Clinton's alleged behavior as the president was touring African countries in 1998. Later that year, Speaker Newt Gingrich, R-Ga., visiting Israel, made provocative remarks that Clinton officials said harmed Middle East peace efforts. In 1999 the House, in a rare tie vote, defeated a resolution that endorsed the president's policy of bombing Yugoslavia as part of the North Atlantic Treaty Organization (NATO) campaign against that nation's attacks on ethnic Albanians in the province of Kosovo. House Speaker J. Dennis Hastert of Illinois voted to support Clinton while his deputies pressured other Republicans to oppose the president.

On domestic issues, Clinton vetoed much of the Republicans' ambitious domestic policy agenda in the 104th Congress and resuscitated himself politically by taking advantage of the missteps of the inexperienced new House majority. But he also embraced and reshaped a number of major Republican initiatives, resulting in enactment of a 1996 law repealing the long-standing federal welfare program and a 1997 law that balanced the federal budget the following year for the first time since 1969. Republicans took the lead in enacting a 1996 law making Clinton the first president to exercise a line-item veto over certain new spending and tax provisions. However, the U.S. Supreme Court declared the law unconstitutional in 1998. *(See box, Line-Item Veto Experiment Ended by Supreme Court, p. 130.)*

George W. Bush was forced to contend with Democratic control of both houses of Congress for the first time in the second half of his second term. Shortly after the 2006 election, Bush and Democratic leaders professed their desire to work across the aisle. But there was little evidence of cooperation in the first six months of the 110th Congress as the president and the Democratic Congress feuded over the future of the Iraq War. They did come to an agreement that promised to allow a series of trade pacts to move forward. Bush and congressional Democrats also found common ground on a three-part immigration overhaul aimed at improving border security, creating a new guest-worker program, and allowing illegal immigrants already in the country to become citizens. But many Republicans and some Democrats balked at the compromise, and neither chamber took up immigration for years afterward.

Barack Obama reached out to moderate Republicans during his early months in office, and some of them did back him on an expansion of the State Children's Health Insurance Program that had stalled under George W. Bush. But House Republicans stuck together on rejecting Obama's subsequent $787 billion American Recovery and Reinvestment Act stimulus law as well as health care reform, and later attempts at bipartisan cooperation proved largely fruitless.

1   "A Conservative Majority," *CQ Weekly*, 1980, 2700.

to continuous pressure for war from Clay and the war hawks. Finally, on June 1, 1812, Madison sent Congress a war message. The House voted 79–49 for war three days later.

As congressional historian George Rothwell Brown wrote, on this episode, "Clay had lifted the Speakership of the House to a point of new power and responsibility, the Speaker to a place in the state where, backed by party organization . . . he could present to the President a program determining national policy and involving a declaration of war . . . against the pacifist sentiment of the President and most of the Cabinet."[16]

According to Peters, Clay was not a particularly good parliamentarian. Another Speaker, Robert Winthrop, said of him that "he was no painstaking student of parliamentary law, but more frequently found the rules of his governance in his own instinctive sense of what was practicable and proper than in Hatsell's Precedents or Jefferson's Manual."[17] Yet Clay was widely respected for his ability to maintain order on the House floor and to bring into line some of the chamber's more unruly members.

In addition to establishing new standards of order for the conduct of business on the House floor, Clay helped to establish the committee system. There were ten standing committees in the House in 1810, the year before Clay entered the chamber. When he left the House in 1825 there were twenty-eight.[18] Historians and political scientists disagree about whether Clay fostered the committee system primarily to solidify and advance his own position or to improve the efficiency of the House.

Unlike previous Speakers, Clay remained a vigorous spokesperson for the interests of his congressional district. He was the first Speaker—and one of the few in history—to vote in instances when his vote could make no difference in the result, a practice that was revived under Speakers in the 1990s and 2000s. Clay's voting practices and his participation in debate set the precedent that Speakers forfeit none of their normal privileges as members.

Clay remained Speaker as long as he was in the House. Although he left his seat twice—in 1814, to help negotiate an end to the War of 1812, and in 1820—he was reelected Speaker as soon as he returned to the House in 1815 and again in 1823. He is the only early Speaker members elected repeatedly "irrespective of their partisan or factional allegiances, their geographic loyalties, or their views."[19]

From Clay to Colfax

For the next four decades, as the issue of slavery grew to dominate the national agenda, factional allegiances and geographic loyalties would divide both the country and Congress. In the House the speakership rarely stayed in one man's possession for more than a single term. Of the fourteen Speakers who presided between 1825, when Clay left the House, and 1861, only three—Andrew Stevenson of Virginia,

James K. Polk, the future president from Tennessee, and Linn Boyd of Kentucky—served for more than one Congress. Many election contests for the speakership were marked by multiple ballots. It took sixty-three ballots, for example, before Howell Cobb, a proslavery Democrat from Georgia, was elected Speaker in 1849 by a two-vote margin. (See box, Heated Contests for Speakership, p. 14.)

Given the brief periods that most of these Speakers served, it is little wonder that none of them achieved the stature and influence of Clay. Stevenson, who served between 1827 and 1834, may have come the closest. Although he lacked Clay's magnetism, he was an able politician, actively promoting Andrew Jackson's program in the House. "No Speaker," wrote Follett, "except perhaps Macon, has been so distinctly the president's man."[20]

Two men, both Republicans, presided over the House during the Civil War, Galusha Grow of Pennsylvania (1861–1863) and Schuyler Colfax of Indiana (1863–1869). But the real leader of the House during this period was Thaddeus Stevens, the leader of the Radical Republicans, who engineered the impeachment of President Andrew Johnson.

Grow was clearly controlled by Stevens, and Colfax, while personally popular, was not a forceful Speaker and was, like Grow, regarded by many as Stevens's man. "Colfax possessed neither will nor mind of his own," said historian Fuller. "Thaddeus Stevens furnished him with these mental attributes."[21]

Rise of Minority Obstructionism

While the speakership may have been a position of little real authority by the time the Civil War began, the emergence of the modern two-party system and a new partisanship in the House was soon to produce two of the most powerful Speakers in history. The first Speaker after the Civil War to add any new authorities to the post was James G. Blaine, R-Maine, one of the founders of the Republican Party and Colfax's successor. As Speaker from 1869 to 1875, Blaine was the first leader since Clay to organize the House in a way that favored his party's program. Blaine successfully manipulated committee assignments to produce majorities favorable to legislation he desired.

As partisan as he was, Blaine nonetheless refused to use the powers of the speakership to stop the variety of obstructionist tactics that the Democrats used to block action on legislation they did not support but could not defeat through the regular procedures. Chief among these tactics were constant demands for roll-call votes and use of the "disappearing" or "silent" quorum, in which members of the minority party refused to answer to their names even though they were present on the floor. Blaine's reluctance to restrict the rights of the minority party may have stemmed in part from his realization that the Republican Party would someday find itself in the minority and wish to avail itself of the same tactics.

When the Democrats won control of the House with the elections of 1874, they elected as their Speaker Michael C. Kerr of Indiana, who died in 1876. They then chose Samuel J. Randall of Pennsylvania, who served as Speaker until 1881 when the Republicans regained control of the House. Randall, too, refused to curb minority (this time Republican) obstructionism, but he did initiate a thorough revision of the House rules designed "to secure accuracy in business, economy in time, order, uniformity and impartiality."[22] The next such revision did not occur until 1999. The perhaps most significant of these revisions, which were adopted in 1880, made the Rules Committee a standing, instead of a select, committee. The Speaker retained chairmanship of the committee, a privilege he had enjoyed since 1858.

Republicans controlled Congress for one term (1881–1883), and when Democrats

CLEARING THE ROAD—A STRONG MAN IN THE RIGHT PLACE.

Rep. Thomas Brackett Reed, R-Maine, was one of the most powerful Speakers in House history. Known as "Czar" Reed, he established the "Reed Rules" to curb Democratic obstructionism in the 1890s. He is shown in this 1890 cartoon breaking up the roadblocks of the disappearing quorum and dilatory motion.

SOURCE: Library of Congress.

regained control of the House in 1883, they passed over Randall (who opposed the party's low-tariff policy) and elected instead John G. Carlisle of Kentucky, who served as Speaker until 1889. Carlisle was a strong Speaker, deriving much of his authority from his willingness to use his power of recognition to forestall motions he opposed. By asking "For what purpose does the gentleman rise?" Carlisle could withhold recognition from any member whose purpose opposed his own.

But like Blaine and Randall before him, Carlisle was reluctant to do anything about minority obstructionism, making him what one commentator called "the slave of filibusters." By the end of his speakership, the minority's use of delaying tactics, coupled with a disappointing legislative record, opened the House to public criticism and demands that the rules be modified "to permit the majority to control the business for which it is responsible," to quote one editorial in the *New York Tribune*.[23]

Reed Rules

Reform was to come in the person of Thomas Brackett Reed, R-Maine. Reed—a physically imposing man at six feet, three inches and nearly three hundred pounds, dressed always in

black—was Speaker from 1889 to 1891 and again from 1895 to 1899. In his rulings from the chair in his first months in office, later formally incorporated into the rules and procedures of the House, Reed expanded the powers of the office more than any other Speaker except Clay, in essence establishing the absolute right of the majority to control the legislative process.

Even as minority leader, Reed had deplored minority obstructionism. "The rules of this House are not for the purpose of protecting the rights of the minority," he had said, "but to promote the orderly conduct of the business of the House."[24] The minority's rights were preserved in their right to debate and to vote, Reed argued. The dilatory tactics the minority used controverted the essential function of the House, which was to legislate. Once elected Speaker, he determined to do something about the situation.

The Speaker's decision was risky—his Republicans commanded only a seven-vote majority in the House, 166 to the Democrats' 159—not only to his role as Speaker but also to his future political ambitions. Like Clay and Blaine before him, Reed aspired to the presidency. According to historian Barbara Tuchman, Reed confided his decision to attack the silent quorum to no one, not even to Cannon, his closest

HEATED CONTESTS FOR SPEAKERSHIP: LIVELY BUT RARE IN HOUSE HISTORY

At the beginning of every two-year term, each party caucus nominates a candidate to be Speaker of the House and the candidate of the majority party wins the office, normally on a straight party-line vote on the House floor. The Clerk of the House from the previous Congress presides until a Speaker is chosen. The Speaker is elected by a majority of members-elect voting verbally by candidate's surname, a quorum being present. Traditionally, the members nominated for Speaker vote "present," instead of for themselves. The U.S. Constitution does not require that the Speaker be a member of the House, but he or she always has been. Any member may run for Speaker.

But pro forma elections of the Speaker have not always been the case. Before the two-party system became entrenched on Capitol Hill, factions sometimes so splintered the majority party that the election of a Speaker turned into a battle royal. On two occasions, the House departed from precedent and, using special rules, chose Speakers by a plurality vote. In each case, the House by majority vote subsequently passed a resolution declaring the result.

Regional disputes, mainly over slavery, produced at least eleven hotly contested races for the speakership before the Civil War. The first was in 1809, when none of the Democratic-Republican candidates was able to achieve a majority on the first ballot. The election finally went to Joseph B. Varnum of Massachusetts after the South's candidate, Nathaniel Macon of North Carolina, withdrew because of poor health.

Other battles occurred in 1820, when an antislavery candidate, John W. Taylor, D-N.Y., won on the twenty-second ballot; in 1821, when Philip P. Barbour, D-Va., won on the twelfth; in 1825, when Taylor recaptured the post on the second ballot; in 1834, when John Bell, Whig-Tenn., won on the tenth vote; in 1847, when Robert C. Winthrop, Whig-Mass., won on the third; and in 1861, when Galusha A. Grow, R-Pa., won on the second.

In four other pre–Civil War instances the House became deadlocked for weeks or months over the election of the Speaker.

1839: NEW JERSEY CONTROVERSY

The first of these prolonged battles began on December 2, 1839, when election of the Speaker hinged on the outcome of five contested House seats in New Jersey. Excluding the five New Jersey members, the party lineup in the House was 119 Democrats and 118 Whigs. Democrats sought to organize the House (and elect the new Speaker) before the contested elections were decided. The Whigs wanted to wait until the elections were resolved.

After much debate the House on December 14 agreed with the Democratic proposal to vote for Speaker before the contested seats were decided. But Democratic leaders were then unable to hold a sufficient number of members in line to name a Speaker. On December 16, Robert M.T. Hunter, D-Va., who had declared himself an independent, was elected Speaker on the eleventh ballot.

1849: FREE-SOIL DISPUTE

The next major contest for the speakership developed in 1849, when neither the Whigs nor the Democrats could achieve a majority because the so-called Free-Soil factions in both parties decided to act independently. The resulting deadlock lasted for three weeks and sixty-three ballots.

The Free-Soilers, who opposed expansion of slavery into the territories, wanted to ensure that certain House committees were controlled by antislavery legislators.

They thus opposed the election of the leading candidates for Speaker in both parties: Robert C. Winthrop, Whig-Mass., who they felt had been lukewarm on the issue as Speaker from 1847 to 1849, and Howell Cobb, D-Ga., a strong proponent of slavery. Each faction put up its own candidate—at one time there were eleven—preventing either Winthrop or Cobb from winning a majority.

At various points compromise solutions were considered and rejected, including proposals that the Speaker be chosen by lottery and that members receive no salary or mileage reimbursement until a Speaker was elected. Finally, after the fifty-ninth vote, the House agreed to elect the Speaker by a plurality, provided that it be a majority of a quorum. On the sixtieth vote, Cobb led; on the sixty-first, Winthrop; and on the sixty-second, the vote was tied. The issue was decided on the sixty-third vote, when Cobb won a plurality of two votes. "The choice of a very pronounced pro-slavery and southern man at this crisis undoubtedly aggravated the struggles of the following decade," Mary P. Follett noted in her authoritative 1896 book on the speakership.

1855: KANSAS AND SLAVERY

Six years later another multifaction battle stemming from the slavery issue delayed election of a Speaker. The specific concern was who would be appointed to the committee investigating the admission of Kansas into the Union. Would the Speaker choose committee members who favored its entry as a free state or as a slave state?

Although antislavery forces held a majority of House seats, their ranks were so split by factions—mostly the new Republican Party and various Free-Soil groups—that they could not unite behind a single candidate. After 129 ballots, the House decided that the candidate receiving the largest number of votes on the 133rd ballot would be declared the winner. On February 2, 1856, Nathaniel P. Banks, American-Mass., was elected with 103 out of the 214 votes cast.

Banks met the expectations of the antislavery forces by giving them a majority on the Kansas investigating committee. The practical effect of that action, Follett observed, "delayed the settlement of the Kansas episode until after 1857, and this gave time for the anti-slavery forces to organize."

1859: IMPENDING CRISIS

The last of the great pre–Civil War contests over the speakership occurred in 1859. The tone was set on the first day of the session, December 5, when slavery advocates proposed a resolution that anyone who endorsed the sentiments of *The Impending Crisis of the South: How to Meet It*, a book hostile to slavery, was not fit to be Speaker.

The resolution and another introduced the next day were directed at John Sherman, R-Ohio, who had endorsed the book. "The ball thus set rolling," Follett wrote, "the discussion of slavery began, bitter and passionate on one side, eager and vehement on the other. The state of the country was reflected in the struggle for Speaker. The House was the scene of a confusion and uproar which the clerk could not control. . . . Bitter personal invectives nearly led to personal encounters. . . . It seemed as though the Civil War was to begin in the House of Representatives."

Sherman led in the early voting, falling only six votes short of a majority on the third ballot. By the end of January, however, Republicans saw that Sherman could not be elected and shifted their support to William Pennington, Whig-N.J., a new and unknown member. On February 1, 1860, after forty-four votes and two months into the session, Pennington was elected with 117 votes, the minimum needed to win. Pennington was the only Speaker other than Henry Clay ever elected to the speakership during his first term. But he did not share Clay's skill. Pennington was defeated for reelection to the House in 1860.

1923: PROGRESSIVE INSURGENCY

The only deadlock over the speakership since the Civil War occurred in 1923, when twenty Progressive Republicans held the balance of power in the House. They put up their candidate, Henry A. Cooper, R-Wis., as a protest against House procedures. After eight inconclusive votes, Nicholas Longworth of Ohio, the GOP majority leader, made an agreement with the progressives to liberalize the rules. The next day they threw their support to the Republican candidate, Frederick H. Gillett of Massachusetts.

OTHER LEADERSHIP FIGHTS

Since 1923 there have been no floor battles for the speakership. One party has always held a clear majority and has been able to elect its choice on the first ballot. But there have been fights in the party caucuses. In 1933, Democratic majority leader Henry T. Rainey of Illinois faced four candidates in his bid to win the nomination in the caucus, which was tantamount to election because the Democrats controlled the House. A northerner and a liberal, Rainey was opposed by the southern establishment that controlled the Democratic Party at the time. But with three of the other four candidates from southern states, Rainey had room to maneuver. He was nominated Speaker in a deal that ensured the southern establishment would continue to be the effective ruling power in the House.

No significant battles for the speakership have developed on the Democratic side since 1933. Each time a Democratic Speaker has left office and the party controlled the chamber, the Democratic majority leader has been elevated to the speakership without much ado. In several cases the Democratic Caucus has then elected the party whip to be majority leader. The pattern appeared to be ending in the 1970s, as Democratic whips failed to sustain long-term careers in the House, but it reemerged in the early part of the twenty-first century. John McFall, D-Calif., lost a race for majority leader in 1976. His successor as whip, John Brademas, D-Ind., was defeated in the 1980 Republican landslide. Thomas S. Foley, the last member to be chosen as whip by appointment, then got back on the ladder, rising to become majority leader and Speaker. However, the next two Democratic whips, Tony Coelho of California and William Gray III of Pennsylvania, resigned from the House before any opportunity of advancement opened up.

The Democratic pattern of leadership succession fell apart most visibly in 1976 when deputy whip Jim Wright of Texas offered himself as an alternative to the bitterly antagonistic front-runners, caucus chair Phillip Burton of California and Richard Bolling of Missouri. Whip John McFall was popular with his fellow Democrats but tainted by his association with the "Koreagate" influence-peddling scandal. He was eliminated from the race on the first ballot. Wright had seemed an unlikely winner when he announced he would enter the contest, but he eliminated Bolling by two votes on the second ballot and Burton by a single vote on the third ballot.

Speaker Nancy Pelosi, D-Calif., moved up easily from minority whip to minority leader in 2003, when Richard A. Gephardt of Missouri retired. And her successor as minority whip, Steny H. Hoyer of Maryland, handily fended off a challenge for the majority leader post from Rep. John P. Murtha of Pennsylvania, who was supported by Pelosi, after Democrats won control of the House in the 2006 election.

House Republicans have had more contests for party leader in recent decades. In 1959 Charles A. Halleck of Indiana, a conservative, deposed the more moderate Joseph W. Martin Jr., of Massachusetts, as minority leader. Martin had served as Speaker of the House in 1947–1949 and 1953–1955. Republicans had suffered massive losses in the 1958 elections.

Similarly, Gerald R. Ford of Michigan ousted Halleck as minority leader in 1965 following landslide Democratic election victories. After the 1980 elections Bob Michel of Illinois, the minority whip since 1974, was elected minority leader over Guy Vander Jagt of Michigan.

Minority whip Newt Gingrich, R-Ga., became Speaker by unanimous vote of the House Republican Conference in 1995 and was elected by a party-line vote in the House as the first Republican Speaker since Joseph Martin left office in 1955. Gingrich's political stature dropped dramatically during his first term as Speaker, and he endured a scare in 1997 as he sought reelection in the face of an ongoing ethics investigation. Despite his party's 227 members in the chamber, Gingrich received only 216 votes for Speaker, three more than the absolute majority. Four Republicans voted for other persons, either sitting Republican House members or former Republican members. Five other Republicans voted present, but their actions did not affect the race.

In November 1998, after House Republicans lost seats in the fall election that reduced their majority to a razor-thin margin, Robert L. Livingston of Louisiana challenged Gingrich for the speakership. Gingrich, sensing probable defeat, announced he would resign from Congress. (However, J. Dennis Hastert of Illinois would succeed Gingrich, not Livingston, who resigned his seat.) Other top GOP House leaders survived, although Majority Leader Dick Armey of Texas had to fight off tough challenges from other Republican colleagues. Armey finally prevailed on the third ballot—an indication of considerable unhappiness in the ranks over his leadership.

One of the most hotly contested Republican leadership races in recent memory was held in the midst of the 109th Congress, after Tom DeLay, who had been indicted on state campaign finance charges in Texas, announced he would permanently step down from the majority leader's job. Missourian Roy Blunt, the Republican whip, was the immediate front-runner and assembled a long list of public supporters quickly. But he was opposed by Reps. John A. Boehner of Ohio and John Shadegg of Arizona. Boehner, the former conference chair, was a longtime critic of DeLay's aggressive operating style, and Blunt was DeLay's hand-picked lieutenant. Shadegg argued that neither Blunt nor Boehner was the man to save Republicans from charges they were responsible for a "culture of corruption" in the Capitol.

Blunt was denied victory on the first ballot, when he garnered 109 votes, to 79 for Boehner and 40 for Shadegg. The opposition to Blunt galvanized on the second ballot and Boehner became majority leader on a 122–109 vote.

SOURCES: George B. Galloway, *History of the House of Representatives* (New York: Crowell, 1961), 43; and Mary P. Follett, *The Speaker of the House of Representatives* (New York: Longmans, Green, 1896; reprint, New York: Burt Franklin Reprints, 1974), 56, 59, 61–62, 95.

lieutenant, in part because no one else would have thought he had any chance of success, in part because he was not sure his own party, including Cannon, would support him.

On January 21, 1890, Reed took his first major step against obstructionism by refusing to consider a member's demand for a teller vote on a motion to adjourn. A few days later he announced his intention to disregard all motions and appeals, even if procedurally correct, if their purpose was simply to delay House business.

Then, on January 29, Reed made his assault on the silent quorum. When the Republicans called up the first of several contested election cases, Charles F. Crisp of Georgia, the Democratic leader who would succeed Reed as Speaker in the next two Congresses, objected to considering the Republican motion. The yeas and nays were ordered, and the vote came to 161 for, 2 against, and 165 not voting—mainly Democrats who while not voting were nonetheless present. When the vote was announced, the Democrats immediately claimed that it was invalid because a quorum (165) had not voted, whereupon Reed ordered the clerk to enter the names of those present who had refused to vote. He then ruled that a quorum was present and that consideration of the question was in order.

The House erupted into pandemonium when the quorum count began. Republicans applauded the Speaker. Democrats, wrote historian Tuchman, "foamed with rage. A hundred of them 'were on their feet howling for recognition,' wrote a reporter. 'Fighting Joe' Wheeler, the diminutive former Confederate cavalry general, unable to reach the front because of the crowded aisles, came down from the rear 'leaping from desk to desk as an ibex leaps from crag to crag.'"[25]

An appeal from the ruling was tabled by a majority of those voting (again with a quorum present but not voting). The following day, the Speaker declined to reconsider the ruling and declared that he would refuse to recognize any member rising to make a dilatory motion. The debate, angry and strident, continued for several more days. At one point, it appeared that a group of irate Democrats was preparing to pull the Speaker out of the chair. At another point, Democrats decided to leave the chamber, in an effort to deny the Republicans a quorum, but Reed ordered the doors locked, forcing Democrats to hide under their desks and behind screens. Reed was called tyrant, despot, dictator—the epithet that stuck was czar. Throughout it all he remained calm and implacable, and on the fifth day the Democrats conceded, unable to muster a majority to overturn the Speaker's decision.

On February 14, 1890, the House formally adopted new rules incorporating Reed's rulings and other new procedures. The new code, reported by the Rules Committee chaired by Reed, provided that all members must vote unless they had a pecuniary interest in the issue at hand, motions to recess or to fix a date of adjournment would not be entertained when a question was under debate, one hundred members would constitute a quorum in the Committee of the Whole, and the Speaker would entertain no dilatory motions. The House adopted the "Reed Rules" after bitter debate. The most controversial of them—counting present but nonvoting members to make a quorum—was upheld by the U.S. Supreme Court in an 1891 test case (*U.S. v. Ballin*).

The Democrats regained control of the House in 1890 with such a convincing majority that they were able to reject the Reed Rules. But Reed had not had his final word on the subject. Though the Democrats after the 1892 elections reverted to the Reed rule that set a quorum in the Committee of the Whole at one hundred members, Speaker Crisp refused to count those present but not voting. In his capacity as minority leader, Reed in 1893 and early 1894 organized several Republican filibusters in an effort to force Crisp to count the quorum. These efforts were to no avail until February 1894, when Reed attacked a Democratic-supported measure by calling for one roll call after another and then using the silent quorum tactic to delay action. Despite their majorities the Democrats were unable to muster a quorum on their own, and after two months Crisp was forced to concede. The House adopted a rule allowing the Speaker to declare a quorum when a majority of members were present, regardless of whether they answered to their names.

Crisp's tenure is notable in the evolution of the speakership for strengthening the Rules Committee as a tool of the Speaker. Historian Fuller noted that this expanded role for the Rules Committee was a "radical departure from the long-established rules and principles of parliamentary law and practice." He added that the "tyranny of Reed seemed beneficence when Crisp ruled that not even 'the question of consideration could be raised against a report from the Committee on Rules.'"[26]

"Cannonism"

During their reigns as Speaker, Reed and Crisp centralized power in the House. The Speaker was now able to take effective command of the House, and his authority to name the members and chairs of all committees gave him the power to punish or reward his colleagues. As chair of the Rules Committee, which had the right to immediate access to the floor, he could control the timing and content of bills to be brought before the House. And with unlimited power of recognition, he could determine in large measure what business would be taken up on the floor of the House. Though these authorities ensured that the House would run efficiently, if abused they could allow a Speaker to tyrannize the House. That is what happened when "Uncle Joe" Cannon was elected Speaker in 1903.

Regaining control of Congress in 1895, the Republicans returned Reed to the speakership. Having broken with

President William McKinley over the intervention in Cuba and the annexation of Hawaii and the Philippines, Reed resigned from the House in 1899. Cannon, who had already lost races for the speakership in 1881 and 1889, hoped to succeed Reed then, but the Republicans instead chose David B. Henderson, R-Iowa, who served two ineffective terms as Speaker before retiring from the House. When he was finally elected Speaker in 1903, Cannon was the oldest representative (sixty-seven) and had served longer (twenty-eight years) than any member yet to head the House of Representatives.

Cannon's first years in office gave little indication of what would develop. The affable Speaker was one of the most popular men in Congress, and in his first term "his natural kindliness and sense of humor fostered a spirit of amicability that influenced the mood of the House."[27]

But Cannon was also a devout conservative, unsympathetic to much of the progressive legislation sought by President Theodore Roosevelt and favored by a growing number of liberal Republicans and Democrats in the House. Though he was forced to accept some of these measures—including the Hepburn Act (1906), which strengthened the power of the Interstate Commerce Commission to set railroad rates, the Pure Food and Drug Act of 1906, and the Mann Act of 1910—he also made increasingly arbitrary use of his powers as Speaker to maintain control of the House.

On days set aside for approval by unanimous consent of purely local bills of minor importance, Cannon moved to reward his friends and punish his enemies. "Often on the success of these bills would depend the reelection of many men in Congress," Fuller wrote. The Speaker's "smile and assent made and unmade members, accordingly, as he bestowed or withheld these powerful benefices."[28] Although the seniority system was still not firmly embedded, Cannon's flagrant disregard for it in assigning members to committees further contributed to the chamber's growing irritation with his rule.

But it was Cannon's use, or misuse, of the Rules Committee that most offended his colleagues. Before any committee could report legislation to the full House, the committee had to obtain clearance from Rules, and clearance usually was granted only for those measures that met with Cannon's favor. The Rules Committee's special terms and guidelines for bills to be considered by the House—those acceptable to Cannon—usually placed sharp limits on debate and foreclosed floor amendments. The latter practice enabled Cannon and his associates to attach legislative riders (nongermane amendments) in committee that might have been defeated on the floor if brought to a separate vote. But because these riders were frequently attached to annual appropriations bills, the House usually accepted them rather than kill the entire bill.

Eventually the persistent use of the Speaker's powers to obstruct the legislative will—not of the majority party itself, but of a new majority of members of both parties—sparked

Autocratic Speaker Joseph G. Cannon lost much of his power in a 1910 House revolt, but he remained Speaker until his term ended in March 1911.

SOURCE: Library of Congress.

a revolt. In March 1909 the House adopted the Calendar Wednesday rule, setting aside time each Wednesday for committee chairs to call up bills that their committees had reported but that had not been cleared for floor action by Rules. *(See box, Prying Loose Legislation Stuck in Committee, p. 88.)*

At the beginning of a special session that opened a few days later, a group of Republican insurgents joined the Democrats, led by James Beauchamp "Champ" Clark, D-Mo., in a move to curb the powers of the Rules Committee. That effort failed when several Democrats joined the Republican majority in opposition to Clark, and instead the House adopted a weak alternative that made only slight inroads into Cannon's power. Chief among these was the establishment of the Consent Calendar, which set aside two days each month on which individual members could call up minor bills of particular interest to them without prior approval from the Speaker.

In March 1910 the insurgent Republicans found another opportunity to challenge Cannon's iron rule. On March 17, George W. Norris, R-Neb., the leader of the insurgents, took advantage of a parliamentary opening to move for immediate consideration of a reform resolution that would remove the Speaker from the Rules Committee and expand the committee to fifteen members. The members would be chosen by election of the House and would then choose their own chair. Cannon stalled for two days, while he pondered a point of order that Norris's motion was out of order, until Republican stalwarts who had gone to their districts for St. Patrick's Day returned to the capital. Finally, on March 19, Cannon ruled that Norris's motion was out of order. The returning Republicans were not enough. The House overturned Cannon's decision, 164–182, and then adopted the reform resolution, which Norris had modified, 191–156. The modification set the size of the Rules Committee at ten members, six from the majority and four from the minority.

In what has been described as one of the most dramatic events in the history of the House, Cannon then announced that he would entertain a motion to declare the chair vacant so that the House could elect a new Speaker. But though they were willing to strip him of his powers, most of the Republican insurgents were not willing to unseat him—or to help put a Democrat in the speakership—and Cannon remained Speaker until the term ended in March 1911.

Decline of the Speaker's Power

When the Democrats won control of the House in 1911, they named Champ Clark their new Speaker and chose Oscar W. Underwood, D-Ala., as majority leader and chair of the Ways and Means Committee. They also agreed that the Democratic members of Ways and Means would serve as their Committee on Committees to draw up committee assignments for all Democrats, a move that further weakened the powers of the Speaker. (The Democrats retained that arrangement until 1974, when the power to make committee assignments was transferred to the Steering and Policy Committee. In 1917 Republicans set up their own Committee on Committees.) Both parties now call their committee assignment bodies the Steering Committee.

Because Clark left most of the management of party business to Underwood, the floor leader quickly became the acknowledged leader in the House. "The Speaker became a figurehead, the floor leader supreme," wrote a contemporary observer.[29] Underwood made frequent use of the party caucus to develop unity on legislative issues. Democrats in 1909 had adopted rules that bound all party members to support any party position approved by two-thirds of those Democrats present and voting at a caucus meeting, provided the vote represented a majority of the Democrats in the House. A member could vote against the caucus position only if he considered the position unconstitutional or had made "contrary pledges to his constituents prior to his election or received contrary instructions by resolutions or platform from his nominating authority."

Underwood also used the caucus to develop legislative proposals, which then would be referred to the appropriate committees for formal approval; to instruct committees as to which bills they might or might not report; and to instruct the Rules Committee on the terms to be included in its special orders governing floor consideration on major bills and proposed amendments. The power that had been concentrated in the hands of the Speaker was now transferred to "King Caucus" and the person who dominated it. "Whereas Cannon had often exercised control by keeping unwanted legislation off of the floor," observed Peters, "Underwood sought to control legislation by ensuring a majority vote on the floor. The result was despotism under two different guises."[30]

Rule by caucus worked well as long as Democrats were relatively united on the issues. During President Woodrow Wilson's first term, they were able to enact a large body of domestic legislation. But the Democrats soon began to split over foreign policy, and the effectiveness of the binding caucus had disappeared by the time the Republicans took control of the House in 1919. Once again, however, the Speaker was not the true leader of the House.

The leading contender for the speakership in 1919 was James R. Mann, R-Ill., who had been minority leader since 1911. But many Republicans feared that Mann would try to centralize power in the Speaker's office, so they turned to Frederick H. Gillett, R-Mass., who, like his Democratic predecessor, Champ Clark, declined to assert political leadership. Mann refused the position of floor leader, which was then given to Franklin W. Mondell, R-Wyo. Mann, however, retained substantial influence among House Republicans.

To further ensure decentralization, the Republicans set up a five-member Steering Committee, chaired by the majority leader. "For the most part," Randall B. Ripley reported, "the Steering Committee carried out the wishes of the Republican leaders in the House, even when these were not in accord with the Republican administration." As an example, Ripley cited Steering Committee opposition that killed a bill to raise civil service pensions despite support from the Coolidge administration, the Senate, and every member of the House Civil Service Committee. Leadership under this system was so diffuse that House Republicans accomplished little during the period. House members, Ripley wrote, "including some committee chairmen, used the loose leadership structure to pursue legislative ends other than those officially sanctioned."[31]

As Speaker from 1925 to 1931, Nicholas Longworth, R-Ohio, sought to centralize power once again in the Speaker's office. Longworth held it "to be the duty of the Speaker, standing squarely on the platform of his party, to assist in so far as he properly can the enactment of legislation in accordance with the declared principles and policies of his party and by the same token to resist the enactment of legislation in violation thereof."[32] One of his first actions was to discipline Republican Progressives. Those who had opposed his candidacy for the speakership, and who had also opposed a rules change that made it much more difficult to discharge a bill from committee, found themselves stripped of their committee seniority.

Despite these moves, Longworth as Speaker had few of the powers that enabled Cannon to centralize authority in the speakership. He nonetheless was considered an effective Speaker, able, as political scientist Peters notes, to wield power and authority not so much by manipulating the rules but "by force of his character." Longworth's style was collegial. While he made little use of the Steering Committee, he established a small group of trusted associates to help him run the House. Though it appeared contradictory given his stand on strong party leadership, Longworth also was willing to deal with the Democrats not only on policy issues but also on scheduling business. He and the Democratic leader, John Nance Garner, D-Texas, began the tradition, later made famous by Sam Rayburn, of the "Board of Education"—gatherings in a Capitol hideaway where leaders from both parties met over drinks to work out accommodations on various matters.

The Power of Persuasion: Rayburn

Democrats regained control of the House in 1931, a position they lost only twice in the next sixty-four years, in 1947–1949 and 1953–1955. During the first ten years of this cycle, four different Democrats held the speakership. Garner was elected Speaker in 1931. When he became vice president in 1933, he was replaced by Henry T. Rainey of Illinois, who died in 1934. Rainey was followed in 1935 by Joseph W. Byrns of Tennessee, who died in 1936. Byrns's successor, William B. Bankhead of Alabama, served as Speaker until his death in 1940. None of them left a lasting mark on the office. That was to change with the election in 1940 of Majority Leader Rayburn, who served as Speaker until his death in 1961, except during the two Republican Congresses, when Joseph Martin of Massachusetts held the post.

Rayburn was a strong Speaker—and his reputation reached near mythic proportions in the decades following his death. But the reasons for Rayburn's strength and the style with which he led the House were in sharp contrast to those in play during the Reed and Cannon speakerships.

Rayburn entered the House in 1913, just three years after the revolt against Cannon and at a time when the powers and the stature of the Speaker were at a low ebb. By 1940 little real change had been made in the Speaker's powers. The seniority system was well entrenched, which meant that committee chairs and ranking members could act with a great deal more independence than they could at the turn of the century. In 1940 and for the next two decades most of the chairs of the major committees were southern Democrats.

At the same time, most southern Democrats began to vote with the Republicans on New Deal, and eventually on civil rights, issues, forming a conservative coalition against liberal northern Democrats. Even when the conservative coalition did not form on a particular issue, the thin Democratic majorities could make it difficult for the Democratic leadership to achieve its program. As Rayburn himself put it

in 1950, "The old day of pounding on the desk and giving people hell is gone. . . . A man's got to lead by persuasion and kindness and the best reason—that's the only way he can lead people."[33]

A man of great integrity who venerated the House of Representatives, Rayburn dealt with the individual instead of the party. He sought to bind individual members to him through friendship and favors. He did not force Democrats to vote against their conscience or constituency. Rayburn's preferences were controlling when it came to Democratic committee assignments. In 1948 he obtained the removal from the Un-American Activities Committee of three Democrats who had supported Dixiecrat Strom Thurmond in the 1948 presidential campaign. He saw to it that Democrats named to vacancies on Ways and Means were sympathetic to reciprocal trade bills and opposed to reductions in oil depletion allowances. And he turned the Education and Labor Committee from a predominantly conservative body into a more liberal one.

Despite the active presence of the conservative coalition, Rayburn was able to win House passage of an impressive amount of legislation dealing with both foreign and domestic matters, including two far-reaching civil rights bills. He accomplished his goals by working with the other power centers in the House. Rayburn, writes Peters,

> was a man carved for the role he played, yet he was also a shrewd politician who was able to create a political labyrinth in which his own skills would prove most effective. His success lay less in his ability to swing large numbers of votes than in avoiding situations in which that would be necessary. When he wanted legislation stopped, he let others stop it; when he wanted legislation passed, he worked with the committee chair to get bills that could command a floor majority. . . . [Rayburn's] emphasis upon the virtue of honesty and his reputation for fairness in dealing with members contributed to the creation of an atmosphere of comity in the House that facilitated his leadership.[34]

Transitional Speakers: McCormack, Albert

Rayburn's speakership marked the end of an era. In his later years, younger and more liberal Democrats began to demand changes that would lead to the greatest internal reforms in the history of the House. Rayburn's last major victory, in 1961, came in a battle to make the Rules Committee, dominated by conservative southerners, more responsive to the will of the Democratic majority. *(See "Major Legislation and the Rules Committee," p. 93.)*

Rayburn's two immediate successors, John W. McCormack, D-Mass., who served as Speaker from 1962 to 1971, and Carl Albert, D-Okla., who was Speaker from 1971 to 1977, had the ill luck to lead the House during a time both of great social and political upheaval within the nation and of great institutional change that neither man was well equipped to manage. McCormack was popular with his colleagues and, like Rayburn, based his leadership on his personal ties to members. But he lacked the persuasive skills of his predecessor and placed considerable reliance on Albert, his majority leader, and on the majority whip, Hale Boggs, D-La.

McCormack's weakness as a leader, coupled with his opposition to reform proposals in the House and his support of President Johnson's escalation of the Vietnam War, frustrated many of the younger, more liberal House Democrats. In 1968 Morris K. Udall, D-Ariz., challenged him for Speaker in the party caucus. McCormack easily won reelection but soon announced his decision to retire at the end of the Congress.

Albert, too, was generally considered by his colleagues to be a weak leader. His low-key style did not seem suited to the requirements of the times, although any Speaker would have been hard put to guide the House smoothly and firmly through an unparalleled period of internal reform, against the backdrop of U.S. withdrawal from the Vietnam War and the Watergate crisis, which resulted in President Richard M. Nixon's resignation.

Relations between the Republican president and the Democratic Congress were tense throughout the Nixon presidency. Intent on expanding his power, Nixon acted with minimal consultation with and concern for Congress. His administration was committed to political and economic programs opposed by the great majority of the Democrats. Their first priority was to halt administration plans to revamp or terminate many of the Great Society programs of President Lyndon B. Johnson. The prolonged congressional-executive stalemate that resulted gave rise to frustration in Democratic ranks that found expression, especially in the House, in criticism of the leadership.

Albert also drew criticism from younger and more activist House members for not supporting internal House reforms more vigorously. By the early 1970s a sharp

SOME SPEAKERS FACED A TRIAL BY FIRE

Service as Speaker of the House would have to be considered the culmination of any politician's career, but some leaders must survive a trial by fire to hold on to the post and emerge with their political and personal reputations reasonably intact. Some have succeeded better than others.

Speaker J. Dennis Hastert, R-Ill., chose not to seek election to a leadership post after Republicans were defeated at the polls in 2006. Hastert's waning days as Speaker were filled with the fallout of a flurry of criminal and ethics investigations into Republican lawmakers and aides. In October 2006, Hastert testified before the House Committee on Standards of Official Conduct (ethics committee) in the case of former representative Mark Foley, R-Fla., who sent explicit electronic messages to former House pages. Hastert, other lawmakers, and congressional aides were taken to task by the ethics panel because they "failed to exercise appropriate diligence and oversight" of Foley's interaction with pages. However, the committee found that Hastert and others had not violated any laws or rules of the House.

Speaker Newt Gingrich, R-Ga., was embarrassed during his reelection campaign for Speaker in 1997 as several Republicans cast their votes for other persons or voted "present." He then suffered a historic formal reprimand by his colleagues for ethics violations and later repelled a group of younger conservatives who, with encouragement from other members of Gingrich's leadership team, made an effort to depose him. Gingrich survived because he was in the mainstream of his party conference and lacked popular rivals positioned to take over the post. It did not last. Following unexpected GOP election losses in 1998, calls again arose for new leadership, and Gingrich was formally opposed by Robert L. Livingston of Louisiana. Faced with almost certain defeat, Gingrich said he would not stand for Speaker again and would give up his seat in the 106th Congress that was to begin in 1999. (Hastert, not Livingston, would succeed Gingrich as Speaker.)

Jim Wright, D-Texas, the only Speaker to be forced out of office during his term, was later often compared with Gingrich, one of his successors, in his desire to be a visible national leader and to use the speakership to promote a strong party agenda. But Wright never commanded strong loyalty or personal regard from his party colleagues. The link between them probably also is inevitable given Gingrich's leading role in pummeling Wright with ethics allegations for years before Wright's resignation in 1989. Wright left to avoid formal discipline by the House. Historians will likely discuss whether the controversy that ended Wright's career was more or less serious than Gingrich admitting that he violated tax laws and misled the ethics committee and subsequently received a reprimand and a $300,000 fine. There is broad consensus that Gingrich helped to create the political climate for use of ethics charges to demonize opponents, a tactic that his Democratic rivals then turned against him.

NINETEENTH-CENTURY SPEAKERS

In the early nineteenth century, Speaker Nathaniel Macon came close to being deposed. Macon was one of Thomas Jefferson's most devoted loyalists, and he was rewarded for his fealty with Jefferson's support during his election as Speaker in 1801.

But Macon later allied himself with a bitter foe of the president, John Randolph, who broke with Jefferson over a plan to acquire Florida. Jefferson retaliated against Macon by opposing his reelection as Speaker in 1805. Jefferson's effort failed, but it was a close enough decision that Macon chose not to seek another term as Speaker.

Henry Clay went to the well of the House to defend himself against allegations of impropriety while he was Speaker in 1825. In a published letter in a newspaper, another member accused Clay of cutting a secret deal to support John Quincy Adams for president in exchange for an appointment as secretary of state. Adams had been elected by the House after the popular vote leader, Andrew Jackson, failed to receive a majority of the electoral vote. The scandal died quickly. Clay asked the House to name a special committee to look into the charges, but the member who had made the allegation refused to appear.

increase in retirements and reelection defeats of much of the Old Guard had resulted in a significant infusion of new blood in the House. The average age of House members had crept steadily downward, and most of the new generation were liberal Democrats. With the dramatic turnover in membership—particularly the election of seventy-five new Democratic members in 1974—came pressure for changes in House rules and practices. Reforms adopted by the Democratic Caucus in the early 1970s, particularly in 1971, 1973, and 1974, were to have a substantial effect on the way the House and its leaders would conduct their business.

One set of reforms broke the grip senior members held on the House by subjecting committee chairs to election by secret ballot. In 1975 the caucus deposed three chairs. Committee chairs members. Other changes limited House Democrats to one subcommittee chairmanship, gave the subcommittees their own staffs, and guaranteed each party member an assignment on a major committee.

A second set of reforms granted new powers to the Speaker, making that office potentially stronger than at any time since the reigns of Reed and Cannon. The Speaker was given the right to nominate the chair and all the Democratic members of the Rules Committee, subject to caucus approval, and that panel once again became an arm of the leadership, not the independent power center it had been in the previous three decades. The Democratic Steering and Policy Committee was set up in 1973 to give coherence and strategy to the party's legislative program and was placed firmly under the Speaker's control. At the end of 1974 the committee was given the authority, formerly held by Ways and Means Democrats, to appoint the Democratic members to House committees, subject to caucus approval. Although most of these new powers became available during Albert's tenure as Speaker, he made little use of them, leaving them to his successors to exploit.

John White, Speaker from 1841 to 1843, came under fire for one of the last speeches he gave before leaving the House in 1845 to take a judgeship in Kentucky. After it was disclosed that a particularly eloquent speech he gave had been plagiarized from former vice president Aaron Burr, White committed suicide.

While James G. Blaine, R-Maine, was Speaker, he was cleared of wrongdoing by a special committee appointed to look into the Crédit Mobilier bribery scandal, in which promoters of the Union Pacific Railroad used stock to bribe members of Congress to support federal subsidies for the railroad. But other allegations of graft surfaced in 1876, after Blaine left the Speaker's office as a result of a change of party control in the House.

Blaine took to the House floor to read from letters that supposedly exonerated him. That quelled efforts to censure him, but the scandal did not help his unsuccessful quest for his party's presidential nomination at the GOP convention just months later. Blaine was finally nominated in 1884, but he lost the election to Grover Cleveland.

CANNON: STRIPPED OF POWER

The House in 1910 nearly deposed Speaker Joseph G. Cannon, R-Ill., for his heavy-handed use of power. The revolt against Cannon exploded in response to his spectacular use of the Speaker's powers to reward friends and punish foes. Cannon freely wielded his authority to control who sat on which committee, which bills went to the floor, and who would be recognized to speak.

Democrats made common cause with insurgent Republicans on March 19, 1910, and defeated Cannon on a procedural question that was, in effect, a referendum on his leadership.

The insurgents went on to ram through rules changes that stripped the Speaker of his right to make committee assignments and of his control of the Rules Committee.

Cannon refused to resign as Speaker but invited a vote on deposing him. Pandemonium broke loose on the House floor, judging from the notation in the Congressional Record: "Great confusion in the Hall."

A resolution declaring the Speaker's office vacant was put to a vote—the only time such a vote has been taken—but Cannon survived, 155–192. It suited the political purposes of some to keep Cannon in office: that made it easier to run against "Cannonism" in the 1910 elections. This was perhaps the first time a Speaker had been a major focus in an election campaign. Cannon lost the speakership after Democrats won a majority of House seats for the first time since 1895. Cannon's resistance to political change in the country and within his party, as well as his increasingly arbitrary style of leadership, had cost his office the influence it had long held within the House.

McCORMACK, O'NEILL

Speaker John McCormack, D-Mass., retired in 1971 after top aides were accused of using the Speaker's office and name for fraudulent purposes, without McCormack's knowledge. McCormack, in his seventies and under pressure from a restive younger generation of lawmakers, had other reasons for leaving the House when he did.

When Thomas P. "Tip" O'Neill Jr., D-Mass., became Speaker in 1977, he immediately faced questions raised in connection with the "Koreagate" influence-peddling scandal. The House ethics committee in January 1977 began an investigation into allegations that as many as 115 members—Republicans and Democrats—had taken illegal gifts from South Korean agents. Some people suggested that O'Neill, during a 1974 trip to Korea, had asked Korean rice dealer Tongsun Park to make contributions to House members and their wives. But other members were the principal targets, and in July 1978 the committee issued a statement exonerating O'Neill. The panel said the only thing of "questionable propriety" the Speaker had done was to let Park pay for two parties in his honor.

The Modern Speakership: O'Neill

In many respects Thomas P. "Tip" O'Neill Jr. of Massachusetts was an unlikely candidate to modernize the speakership. A New Deal liberal, he was to the political left of most of his colleagues. Intensely partisan, he was forced to work with a popular Republican president, Ronald Reagan, and a Republican Senate during six years of his decade as Speaker from 1977 to 1987. A consummate practitioner of inside politics, O'Neill faced demands from rank-and-file Democrats for greater participation in the decision-making process. A less-than-commanding public speaker, who reserved his public appearances for his Massachusetts constituents, the new Speaker was called upon to be the national spokesperson for his party. But his reluctance to temper both his liberal beliefs and his partisanship made coalition-building, even within his party, difficult at times.

Genial and enormously popular, O'Neill based his leadership on friendships, doing favors for loyal colleagues. But O'Neill also took some innovative steps to expand participation of the party rank and file in House affairs, enlarging the whip organization and setting up special task forces to help the leadership develop support and strategy on major legislation. One of O'Neill's most successful ploys was the creation of an ad hoc committee in 1977 to draw up comprehensive energy legislation, a top priority of the Carter administration. Although the tactic worked well in that case, policy differences and objections from the standing committees prevented the Speaker from ever using it again.

O'Neill also made use of several powers the House reforms had bestowed upon the Speaker, including the authority to name the Democratic members of the House Rules Committee. Although O'Neill did not demand unstinting loyalty from the Democrats on Rules, he did expect them to support him on key issues. In response to the Republican minority's penchant for offering floor amendments designed to put Democrats on the spot, O'Neill also came to rely heavily on restrictive rules, those specifying which amendments could be offered on the floor and in what order, as a potent tool to maintain control of debate on the House floor. *(See "Shift toward Restrictive Rules," p. 94.)*

O'Neill gave the speakership unprecedented visibility. He was aided by the decision to allow House floor proceedings to be televised to the public, beginning in 1979, and later spurred on by criticisms from his colleagues that he was not effectively articulating Democratic alternatives to President Reagan's legislative agenda. Soon the Speaker's office was issuing a steady stream of press releases trying to mobilize support for Democratic Party positions. Though previous Speakers had met with reporters before every House session, they usually only answered specific questions. Now O'Neill used them to volunteer information about the goals and achievements of House Democrats and to spar with Reagan on the issues.

O'Neill's attempts at public relations won mixed reviews. His sometimes garbled syntax, his physical bulk, shaggy dog appearance, and ever present cigar were reminiscent of the stereotypical backroom pol, an image that some younger members had hoped the Democratic Party could shed. Nonetheless, O'Neill affected public attitudes on a variety of questions, some more successfully than others. Nothing the Speaker said or did could have headed off support in the nation or in the House for the 1981 Reagan economic program. But on several foreign policy issues, where there was substantial doubt about Reagan's approach, O'Neill helped solidify Democratic opposition and made it credible to the public. For example, by coming out strongly against an expensive and controversial intercontinental ballistic missile, known as the MX missile, and U.S. aid to the Nicaraguan "contras," a guerrilla force that was battling to oust the leftist government of that nation, the Speaker focused media attention on the anti-Reagan position and almost certainly locked in some Democratic votes on those closely fought issues.

Yet O'Neill's speakership was not an unqualified success. His first year in the post seemed to bear out early predictions that he could be the strongest Speaker since Rayburn. But Carter's weak presidency and new militancy on the part of House Republicans combined with O'Neill's own unyielding partisanship to his disadvantage. Unable to keep his Democrats united, he lost several key votes in his first four years.

Ronald Reagan's election in 1980 and the loss of thirty-three House seats only worsened his situation in the 97th Congress (1981–1983). Not until House Democrats won twenty-six seats in the 1982 elections was O'Neill able to unite his party in opposition to Reagan's policies. The stalemate that often resulted and the heightened partisan rhetoric that it engendered led to accusations that O'Neill was a heavy-handed partisan and that the Democratic Party had no focus and could not govern. When O'Neill did try to exercise policy leadership on an issue, he was often deserted by one wing or another of his party, as he was in 1983, when a number of Democrats—including Majority Leader Jim Wright and Whip Thomas S. Foley, Wash.—voted against O'Neill to support funding for the MX missile.

Despite these setbacks, O'Neill's speakership was never in any jeopardy. But criticisms of his leadership and the clear frustrations among many House Democrats about the image the party was projecting may have weighed in his decision to retire in January 1987, the end of the 99th Congress.

The Limits of Power: Wright

As Speaker from 1987 to June 1989, Jim Wright was determined to give House Democrats the policy leadership many of them had found lacking in O'Neill. "The Congress should not simply react, passively, to recommendations from the president but should come forward with initiatives of its own," he once said.[35]

But in pursuing his activist agenda for the House, Wright may have overstepped the limits of the speakership's powers at that time, although Speaker Newt Gingrich would later seek to expand the office far beyond anything Wright had attempted. Wright exceeded the bounds of what many Democrats were willing to accept in a leader. He certainly was not what Democrats had expected when they chose him as a balanced compromise for majority leader over the ambitious liberals Phillip Burton and Richard Bolling a decade earlier.

By his second year in the office, Republicans considered him to be a match for Cannon in his treatment of the minority. Democrats were alienated by his failure to practice the politics of inclusion that had become de rigueur. As allegations of financial misconduct lodged against the Speaker by Gingrich developed into a full-blown investigation, Wright found that Democrats who were willing to support him when they were winning were not as ready to back him on a question of personal ethics. On May 31, 1989, Wright announced that he would give up the speakership effective June 6, becoming the first Speaker to be forced from office at midterm. A month later he resigned his House seat. *(See box, Some Speakers Faced a Trial by Fire, p. 20.)*

Wright was a deputy whip when he ran for majority leader in 1976, winning by a single vote. Had he lost, he would have become chair of the Public Works Committee. Unlike his three rivals, Wright had few enemies or personal negatives. He had always compromised personal differences when possible, or disagreed gently if he had to. He also had another advantage: as a member of the Public Works Committee, he had done countless small favors, making sure a dam was put up here or a federal building there. And throughout his ten years as majority leader, Wright continued to do the little favors, devoting months of precious time to public appearances and fund-raising missions in districts throughout the country.

Favors notwithstanding, many members felt a sense of unease, even mistrust, about Wright. Private, competitive, at times aggressively partisan, Wright did not inspire the sort of personal affection that O'Neill had drawn. His reputation for oratorical skills was well deserved, but now and again his speech turned florid, his smile disingenuous. "You watch him and you know when he's going to get partisan," GOP leader Bob Michel, Ill., said in 1984. "The eyebrows start to rise. The voice begins to stretch out. And the Republicans say, 'Snake oil is at it again.'"[36] Though such descriptions might be dismissed because they came from the opposition, Democrats were nonetheless concerned about the image Wright might convey to the public.

Despite these misgivings, Wright was not challenged when he ran in 1986 to succeed O'Neill. His assertions that he would be a strong, policy-oriented Speaker appealed to his Democratic colleagues who not only wanted to demonstrate that the Democrats could govern but also wanted a record to see them through the 1988 presidential campaign. And

Wright was clearly ready. As Speaker, he seemed to suddenly unleash an agenda and a pace of activity he had kept under wraps from his colleagues, and the adjustment was sometimes difficult even for members who professed to want such activism in their leader.

In his acceptance speech Wright laid out an ambitious agenda for the 100th Congress, calling for renewal of the clean water act and a new highway bill and suggesting that the tax rate for the wealthy be frozen at 1987 levels instead of dropping as scheduled, a proposal that some said put him beyond the majority of the Democrats. By the end of the 100th Congress, not only had the clean water and highway bills become law, but Congress also had overhauled the welfare system, approved the biggest expansion of Medicare since its creation, and rewritten U.S. trade law. Most of this legislation had passed the House with bipartisan support.

Although Wright's Democratic colleagues took pride in these legislative achievements, many resented being excluded from the process of achieving them. The "Lone Ranger," as Wright was sometimes dubbed, had a record of springing major decisions without consulting key colleagues. His public involvement in trying to negotiate a peace plan between the Nicaragua government and the contra rebels not only angered the administration and Republicans in the House but also unsettled Democrats who feared that they might be held accountable at the polls if the peace process failed.

Wright was also criticized for his aggressive tactics in getting legislation passed. Rules to guide floor debate grew more restrictive. No amendments, for example, were allowed on the clean water and highway bills or on a moratorium on aid to the Nicaraguan contras. Republicans complained that, under Wright, many bills were never given hearings and came to the floor of the House without being reported by committee, that substantive legislation was being enacted through self-executing rules (which provide for the automatic adoption of an amendment or other matter upon adoption of the rule), and that the minority was more often denied its right to try to recommit bills.

Wright's support among Democrats was substantially weakened early in 1989 over a proposed pay raise that would have increased congressional salaries by 51 percent. The raise was to take effect if the House and Senate did not veto it by February 9. The initial strategy was to let the pay raise take effect and then to vote on legislation to curb honoraria. But public outrage at the size of the raise—and the fact that it might take effect without a vote in Congress—was overwhelming.

Wright buckled under the pressure, his colleagues believed, failing in his duty to take the heat and protect their interests. He circulated a questionnaire to Democratic members asking whether they wanted a vote scheduled. They viewed this tactic as a major blunder, focusing additional attention on the issue and creating a mechanism that could reveal members' views. This proved to be the case, as

Rep. Nancy Pelosi, D-Calif., right, converses with Sen. Alan Cranston, D-Calif., center, and House Speaker Jim Wright of Texas, at a press conference on June 9, 1987. Ethics charges would force Wright to resign two years later and Pelosi would go on to become the first woman Speaker of the House twenty years later.

SOURCE: AP Photo/John Duricka.

members were barraged with demands from the press about how they had filled out the questionnaire. As expected, the pressure proved too great, and the questionnaire indicated that a majority of members had asked to have a vote on the issue, whether they wanted one or not.

After the Senate yielded to the pressure and voted no on the pay raise, Wright scheduled a vote for February 7. When the raise, not surprisingly, was defeated, many Democrats angrily blamed Wright for changing the strategy at the last minute.

Barely a month later, the ethics committee announced that it "had reason to believe" that Wright had violated House rules on financial conduct. In the next few weeks, new allegations of misconduct surfaced, further damaging the Speaker, as did a *Washington Post* story revealing that a top aide to Wright had a criminal record for brutally beating a woman sixteen years earlier. After Wright's attorneys failed to persuade the House Committee on Standards of Official Conduct (ethics committee) to dismiss the charges on technical grounds, the Speaker decided to resign to spare the House the embarrassment of a public investigation of its Speaker. Only days before, Democratic whip Tony Coelho, of California, had announced he would resign his House seat in the face of allegations of irregularities in his purchase of a $100,000 junk bond.

Political scientist Ronald Peters observes that "if Wright had not been vulnerable to the ethics charges brought against him, it is unlikely that his Republican opponents could have undermined his support in the Democratic Caucus.

However, if Wright had led the House differently, neither Republicans nor Democrats would have had a sufficient motive to seek to unseat him."[37]

Whether Speakers who worked more closely with their own leadership and their rank and file and who were less openly partisan would have survived the same ethics charges Wright faced is conjecture. But the Wright episode clearly shows the potential weakness of a Speaker who fails to develop an atmosphere in which consensus-building and shared decision making can flourish in a Democratic Party that had grown used to broad dispersion of power and multiple independent power centers. Wright himself seemed to recognize this. "Have I been too partisan? Too insistent? Too abrasive? Too determined to have my way?" he asked in his resignation speech. "Perhaps. Maybe so."[38]

After Wright's resignation, Democrats wanted a respite from what they regarded as excessive activism and controversy and a return to a quieter, more consensual leadership style.

End of an Era: Foley

On June 6, 1989, the Democratic Caucus nominated Majority Leader Thomas S. Foley of Washington by acclamation to succeed Wright as Speaker. Better known for bringing together warring factions than for drawing up battle plans, Foley seemed well equipped to help the Democrats—and the House—put the Wright episode behind them. In his first speech as Speaker, he called for debate "with reason and without rancor."

Foley had the most impressive resume of any House Speaker in decades. He had served in each of the Democrats' major leadership positions in succession—caucus chairmanship (1976–1980), as the last appointed whip (1980–1986), and majority leader (1986–1989). He was also the first Speaker since Rayburn to have been a committee chair. He had led the Agriculture Committee (1975–1981).

A thoughtful and articulate man, Foley was perhaps the first Speaker his Democratic colleagues felt comfortable putting in front of a television camera. With a knack for telling stories and a near-photographic memory that helped him to master the substance of most issues that came before him, Foley was a superb negotiator who was on good terms with most Democrats and a good number of Republicans. "Foley has a talent for listening and knowing what other people want," a veteran leadership aide said.[39] He chaired the task force that drew up the Democratic alternative to the 1985 Gramm-Rudman deficit reduction act. He also chaired the

1989 budget negotiations and was the lead negotiator on a comprehensive aid package for the Nicaraguan contras.

Endowed with a sense of detachment rare among politicians, Foley was a cautious, careful political navigator. "The reality," he said a few weeks before becoming Speaker, "is that in a modern, participatory Congress . . . the responsibility of leadership and the necessity of leadership is to constantly involve members in the process of decision and consensus."[40] He did not like to commit himself early on controversial issues, and he could be as skillful at making the case for the opposing side as for his own. As a result, he was criticized for being insufficiently partisan and too indecisive. "He sees three sides of every coin," noted one observer.

Foley's honeymoon as Speaker was brief. Republicans were in no mood for an olive branch. Foley's passive leadership style—trying to avoid controversy within the caucus and allowing committee chairs to compete among themselves, and with the leadership, for influence—allowed him to be overtaken by events at critical points. And he seemed especially ill-suited to confront the accelerating guerrilla warfare against Democrats, and against the institution of Congress itself, led by Minority Whip Gingrich.

Foley was surprised by the scandal that surrounded the House bank throughout 1992, when it was revealed that hundreds of sitting and former House members had routinely overdrawn their accounts without penalty. Foley had argued for limited disclosure, as recommended by the Committee on Standards of Official Conduct, but could not resist overwhelming public pressure as the Republicans forced the names of members of both parties to be made public. Of the 269 sitting members with overdrafts, 77 retired or were defeated in primary or general election bids for the House or other offices. The House Post Office also fell victim to allegations of embezzlement and drug dealing by postal clerks as well as revelations that some members had received special favors, including the ability to convert stamps received by their offices into cash. (Ways and Means Committee chair Dan Rostenkowski, D-Ill., later went to prison as a result.)

Foley said that he was not responsible for supervising these House offices, which had long operated as quasi-independent patronage operations under the nominal control of the Democratic Caucus. Both the sergeant at arms, whom many members blamed for the bank scandal, and the postmaster ultimately went to prison. The Post Office was eliminated as a separate entity, and Foley finally acceded to a caucus rules change giving him the responsibility for nominating the officers of the House, which he had previously resisted.

Many Democrats considered Foley too accommodating to the administration of President George H. W. Bush. When Democrats won the 1992 presidential election and obtained unified control of the executive and legislative branches for the first time in twelve years, the party nonetheless lost seats in the House. Foley was put in the position of having to pass an ambitious presidential program with a caucus membership that was not united either on policy or in loyalty to the new chief executive.

In pre-inauguration meetings with President-elect Bill Clinton, Foley and other congressional leaders urged him to retreat from some of his commitments as a New Democrat candidate, including a promise to press campaign reform legislation on Congress. The new administration also began inauspiciously with highly visible political missteps on numerous issues, most notably Clinton's proposed health care reform plan, which never achieved enough support even to reach the floor in the Democratic-controlled Congress. Internal divisions within the party, as well as effective opposition from a highly unified Republican minority in both chambers, limited the ability of Congress to develop a politically popular legislative record. The widely touted benefits of unified government appeared hollow to much of the public. Clinton's unpopularity also created a backlash against Congress.

Foley himself showed serious weakness in his Washington congressional district for the first time in more than a decade, falling below 40 percent of the vote in the state's all-candidate primary in September 1994. He was opposed by an attractive Republican, George Nethercutt, who was not the sort of fringe candidate who sometimes had won GOP nominations to oppose Foley. In addition to vulnerability based on his leadership post, Foley was attacked for supporting a legal challenge to Washington's newly enacted law, passed by referendum, to impose term limits on the state's congressional delegation. (The U.S. Supreme Court later threw out the law.)

Amid the national Democratic rout in 1994, Foley lost in the general election, only the third such defeat for a sitting Speaker. The last had been Galusha A. Grow, a Pennsylvania Republican, who lost in 1862; his predecessor, William Pennington of New Jersey, had lost in 1860.

The Democratic Party surrendered fifty-two seats, and control of the House shifted to the GOP after forty years of Democratic rule. Gracious in defeat, Foley offered cooperation in the transition, but Republicans responded harshly, with warnings to Democratic leaders and outgoing committee chairs not to shred documents.

After his departure from Congress, Foley joined a law firm and, following the career path of former Senate majority leader Mike Mansfield and former vice president Walter F. Mondale, was nominated to be ambassador to Japan, a post he assumed in 1997 and held for four years.

Transforming the House and Beyond: Gingrich

Even after Newt Gingrich's departure from Congress following the 1998 election setback for the GOP, evaluating his place in history would have to await future developments in the speakership and the politics of the House. But his mere presence as a Republican Speaker, after forty years of Democratic rule, guaranteed historical recognition. Gingrich's move from

House Speaker Newt Gingrich, R-Ga., won narrow reelection in 1996 after an ethics investigation, but never regained the power he had wielded prior to that inquiry.

SOURCE: Scott J. Ferrell, Congressional Quarterly.

freshman to Speaker in only sixteen years, never having chaired a committee or subcommittee, was also unprecedented in the modern era.

Gingrich was clearly a new breed of legislative leader, although his role combined recognizable elements from predecessors of both parties. Among modern Speakers, Gingrich most resembled Wright in his desire to use power. But his control of his party gave him a power unrivaled since the days of Joseph Cannon.

Gingrich was elected to the House from an Atlanta, Georgia, district in 1978 after consecutive defeats in 1974 and 1976. In the earlier races, he had campaigned as a more liberal alternative to traditional Georgia Republicans, stressing the importance of civil rights and environmental protection. But in his winning campaign he ran as a conservative promising tax cuts. For the majority of his service prior to becoming Speaker, Gingrich was the only Republican in his state's House delegation. The sea change in southern politics that helped make Republican control of the House possible was illustrated by Georgia's representation in the 104th and 105th Congresses—an eight-to-three GOP advantage.

Unlike other recent leaders of both parties, Gingrich was in no sense a "man of the House," a phrase denoting a quintessential congressional insider that Speaker O'Neill had used to characterize his own service and as the title of his autobiography. It suggested someone who allowed himself to be shaped by the institution around him, by the need to

establish relationships with the Senate and the executive branch, by shared personal and political accommodation with colleagues, and by the desire to pass legislation. A substantial part of Gingrich's apprenticeship for the speakership consisted of demonizing Congress, its leaders, the rival political party, and almost every aspect of its manner of doing business as well as creating issues to use in the future. The 1994 election platform he helped create, the "Contract with America," reflected those beliefs.

Gingrich as Speaker conceived of himself as a visionary who could make the House a vehicle for passage of legislation and a forum for ideas, principles, and values. Gingrich had these goals early. "The Congress in the long run can change the country more dramatically than the president," he said in a 1979 interview with *Congressional Quarterly*. "One of my goals is to make the House the co-equal of the White House."[41]

For years as a backbencher Gingrich had developed a political philosophy that he felt could lead eventually to Republican control of the House, a conservative but futuristic creed that called for replacing the welfare state with an "opportunity society" in which the rising technological tide of the Information Age would lift the poor to prosperity. Gingrich formed a group of members called the Conservative Opportunity Society in 1983 to foster these beliefs and mastered the use of special order speeches and other mechanisms in the House to gain public attention. He also used ethics as an issue to dramatize disagreements with his colleagues over ideas and to condemn personally opponents who fought him, most notably Speaker Wright. In 1986 he inherited the chairmanship of GOPAC, a political action committee, and turned it into an instrument to inspire Republican candidates with ideas and strategies for seeking office.

Gingrich was hardly a loyal follower of the House Republican leadership, which he viewed as too passive, too prone to negotiate with Democrats for scraps of influence, and too easily co-opted by the collegialism of the House. Many of his colleagues, including some moderates, came to share these concerns, creating an unlikely coalition that elected Gingrich as minority whip in 1989 over the opposition of Minority Leader Bob Michel of Illinois. Gingrich also opposed policies of Republican presidents that he felt compromised the party's long-term goals, such as the bipartisan 1990 budget agreement between President Bush and the Democratic congressional leadership, which repudiated Bush's "no new taxes" pledge. As political scientist Barbara Sinclair has noted, "[Gingrich] was willing to pay the policy cost in order to preserve the message."[42]

Gingrich's Republican colleagues in the 104th Congress were interested not in forming consensus or in shaping his style of leadership, which had helped elect many of them and gave them a program to run on and a list of bills to enact, but in aggressive followership. It was Gingrich's ability to inspire followership in the early days of his speakership that perhaps

CONTRACT WITH AMERICA

On September 27, 1994, six weeks before the November 8 election, approximately 350 House Republican members and candidates unveiled a ten-point campaign manifesto. They called it their Contract with America. The event, staged on the Capitol lawn and spearheaded by Minority Whip Newt Gingrich, R-Ga., was aimed at creating a high-profile national platform from which Republicans could attack the Democratic Congress and present their priorities. When the GOP won a major victory in 1994, the contract became the agenda for House Republicans' first one hundred days in office in the 104th Congress. GOP leaders promised only that the House would vote on the proposals, not that all would pass or be enacted. They vowed that on the first day they would adopt a litany of House rules changes, including the appointment of an auditing firm to look into waste, fraud, and abuse by Congress, the implementation of term limits on the Speaker (a rule that was later dropped) and committee chairs, and the prohibition of proxy voting in committee. Over the next 99 days, they would consider the portions of the Contract that would require bicameral legislative action. Here are the subject areas:

1. *Balanced Budget Amendment, Line-Item Veto.* Send to the states a constitutional amendment requiring a balanced budget and give the president the power to cancel (line-item veto) any appropriation or targeted tax break.

2. *Crime.* Require restitution to victims; modify the exclusionary rule; increase grants for prison construction; speed deportation of criminal immigrants; create block grants to give communities flexibility in using anticrime funds; and limit death row appeals.

3. *Welfare.* Cap spending on cash welfare; impose a lifetime five-year limit on welfare benefits; deny benefits to unwed mothers under age eighteen; and give states new flexibility, including the option to receive federal welfare payments as a block grant.

4. *Families and Children.* Require parental consent for children participating in surveys; provide tax benefits for adoptions and home care for the elderly; increase penalties for sex crimes against children; and strengthen enforcement of child support orders.

5. *Middle-Class Tax Cut.* Add a $500-per-child tax credit; ease the "marriage penalty" for filers of joint tax returns; and expand individual retirement account savings plans.

6. *National Security.* Prohibit use of U.S. troops in United Nations missions under foreign command; prohibit defense cuts to finance social programs; develop a missile defense system for U.S. territory; and cut funding for United Nations peacekeeping missions.

7. *Social Security.* Repeal the 1993 increase in Social Security benefits subject to income tax; permit senior citizens to earn up to $30,000 a year without losing benefits; and give tax incentives for buying long-term care insurance.

8. *Capital Gains and Regulations.* Cut capital gains taxes; allow for accelerated depreciation of business assets; increase first-year deductions for small businesses; reduce unfunded mandates; reduce federal paperwork; and require federal agencies to assess risks, use cost-benefit analysis, reduce paperwork, and reimburse property owners for reductions in value as a result of regulations.

9. *Civil Law and Product Liability.* Establish national product liability law with limits on punitive damages; make it harder for investors to sue companies; and apply a "loser pays" rule to certain federal cases.

10. *Term Limits.* Limit the number of terms that senators and House members may serve.

---

distinguished his role as a party leader most clearly from the Democrats, whose many factions had developed a distracting sense of self-importance that often made party unity and coherent leadership difficult. And it was the weakening of this loyalty, as Gingrich struggled with the transition from the rhetoric of revolution to the responsibility of governing, that threatened his hold on the speakership in the 105th Congress and ultimately forced him out after four years.

Gingrich united the Republican Conference around the plan of voting on all ten planks of the contract in the first one hundred days of the session. The strategy focused the conference and invited a high level of party loyalty, even from less enthusiastic moderates who nonetheless welcomed the title of "chair" preceding their names and gave Gingrich the benefit of the doubt. The contract was drafted to avoid divisive social issues such as abortion and school prayer and to focus on unifying conservative themes geared toward economic policy and a reduced role for government, such as balancing the budget, reforming welfare, and curbing unfunded mandates directed at the states. *(See box, Contract with America.)*

As Speaker, Gingrich enjoyed remarkable success, at least in his first year, in passing legislation through the House and in shaping a national debate over issues based on the Republicans' message of less government, more tax cuts, and a return of power to the states. He was far less successful in reaping proportionate political credit for himself or for the Republican Party in part because the speakership contained innate limitations as a bully pulpit that no amount of revolutionary zeal could overcome and that Gingrich's often bombastic personality aggravated. It was axiomatic in American politics in the twentieth century that the nation looked to the president as the nation's chief policy spokesperson and representative of the national values. Gingrich became, as polls showed, perhaps the most disliked political figure in the nation and gave President Clinton a target that helped reinvigorate a presidency some had given up for dead after the 1994 elections. Gingrich's assertiveness was often perceived by the public as arrogance, with a tendency to lecture and to appear overbearing, uncaring, and threatening. By the end of 1995, some polls gave him an approval rating hovering around 30 percent.

Congress shut down much of the government at the end of 1995, refusing to pass new versions of appropriations bills, after Clinton had vetoed the GOP leadership's ambitious domestic policy changes and tax cuts contained in a budget reconciliation bill and various spending measures. Republicans tried to blame Clinton for the ensuing disruption of vital services, but it was the president who convinced the country that he was right, and the Republicans had to retreat, pass new appropriations bills, and allow government agencies to reopen. Senate majority leader Bob Dole, who was running for president, also appeared eager to repudiate House Republicans and present a more traditional image of responsible governance. The House revolutionaries were placed on the defensive, and the defeat forced Gingrich to reevaluate GOP tactics.

In 1996 Gingrich tried a less confrontational approach, allowing appropriations to pass with fewer controversial riders and obtaining enactment of welfare reform, a major Republican policy goal for decades that Clinton was also eager to use as a centerpiece for his reelection. The public seemed to like the more cooperative style and emphasis on bipartisan legislative achievements, retaining the status quo in the 105th Congress with a slightly reduced GOP House majority.

Gingrich's leadership style could hardly be called consistent, as he switched from one manner of doing business to another during his first three years in power. He experimented with different techniques, sometimes engaging in what his critics called micromanagement, at other times withdrawing from a direct role in the House to focus on the future and long-term political themes. He could be consultative and autocratic in rapid succession.

Part of Gingrich's need for experimentation stemmed from the Republicans' long years in the minority. They had no experience in running the House, and many of their members had no significant legislative or political experience to deploy in their new roles. Many senior conservative veterans were regarded with suspicion by the freshmen as insufficiently zealous or too frequently collaborationist in earlier years with the defeated Democrats. Gingrich formed numerous task forces to develop ideas and sometimes let them draft legislation, although in the 105th Congress he deferred more frequently to the committee system.

Democrats, eager for payback against Gingrich for his attacks on Wright, filed dozens of ethics complaints against him. On December 21, 1996, the Speaker admitted, after two years of repeated denials, that he had failed to properly manage the financing of his political activities through charitable foundations. He also conceded giving the ethics committee misleading information in the course of the investigation. The admission spared the Speaker the spectacle of a trial-like proceeding to defend himself before the committee.

In 1997 the election for Speaker was held before the ethics committee submitted its final report and recommendation for punishment. Gingrich barely survived. As the election was being conducted, he was still negotiating for votes with disgruntled Republicans, four of whom defied the Republican Conference to vote for other Republicans while five others voted present. Gingrich received 216 votes, only three more than the majority required from among members who had voted for candidates for Speaker.

On January 21, 1997, the House for the first time formally reprimanded a Speaker, by a vote of 395 to 28. It adopted the report of the ethics committee that found that Gingrich had brought discredit on the House by failing to seek legal advice regarding the use of tax-exempt foundations for political purposes and for providing inaccurate information to the ethics subcommittee investigating the case. The House also fined Gingrich $300,000 to cover some of the costs of the investigation.

In the fall of 1998, Gingrich decided on a political strategy for the Republicans, criticizing misconduct by President Clinton and attempting to tar the Democrats. A major element of this strategy was Gingrich's action arranging for the immediate release of the report by special prosecutor Kenneth Starr describing sexual misconduct, perjury, and other offenses Starr considered impeachable. However, the public strategy backfired as the party of the incumbent president gained seats in the House for the first time since 1934 in a midterm election.

The election shattered Gingrich's credibility with his colleagues. One of Gingrich's close colleagues, Appropriations Committee chair Bob Livingston of Louisiana, had already been soliciting support for a future speakership campaign. When the election results placed Gingrich's future in immediate jeopardy, Livingston moved at once to challenge the Speaker, and he demonstrated such broad support that Gingrich within a few days announced he would relinquish his seat in Congress, making way for Livingston.

That, however, lasted only a little over a month before Livingston himself announced his retirement from Congress in the wake of revelations about sexual misconduct in the past.

As a result, the GOP was faced with selecting a new Speaker for the next Congress. It turned, in 1999, to a low-ranking member of the leadership, Rep. J. Dennis Hastert of Illinois, who—it was believed—could best heal the wounds left by Gingrich's contentious tenure.

Absolute Power: Hastert (and DeLay)

When Hastert was elevated from the appointive post of chief deputy whip to the speakership in 1999, no one would have guessed that the little-known lawmaker and former high school teacher from Illinois would become the longest-serving Republican Speaker in the history of the House. Elected to stabilize a party adrift after electoral losses, Gingrich's departure, and Livingston's dramatic admission of infidelity, Hastert initially was viewed as a caretaker, and he

House Speaker J. Dennis Hastert, R-Ill., left, House majority whip Roy Blunt, R-Mo., and House majority leader Tom DeLay, R-Texas, far right, attend a 2004 rally of House Republicans to celebrate ten years of majority rule.

SOURCE: Scott J. Ferrell, Congressional Quarterly.

promised a return to the "regular order" of congressional deliberation that Gingrich had sometimes abandoned in his zeal to act quickly.

Hastert had been the top lieutenant in Rep. Tom DeLay's revolutionary whip operation, a shop that mastered and institutionalized the vote-gathering process. It was DeLay who suggested that Republicans make his deputy the Speaker, and their unusually close partnership often made it difficult for outsiders to divine who held power. Hastert was well respected by his colleagues as a quiet but proficient conciliator. They often drew parallels between his leadership style in Congress and his career as a high school wrestling coach. "Coach" Hastert was good at getting the team to work together and fostered support by humbly crediting others for GOP successes.

Initially, Hastert's election was seen as creating breathing space, for the Republicans as well as the House, while both parties sought to calm the rancorous atmosphere in the chamber and to establish better and—in the words of many members—more civil relations. Hastert maneuvered carefully through the final impeachment proceedings against

President Clinton in early 1999, a volatile situation that he inherited, without inflaming the issue more than had already occurred.

The 1998 election had nearly destroyed the Republican majority in the House. The GOP held just 223 of the 435 seats, the slimmest advantage for the majority party since the 83rd Congress. It was up to Hastert to shepherd his flock through the ensuing two years. He owed his election in no small degree to the perception that higher-ranking members of the Republican leadership possessed the hard-edged contentious approach and public image of Gingrich, a perception the party was desperate to shed.

In the first months of the 106th Congress, Hastert returned to more traditional House prerogatives, particularly by allowing committees and their chairs more autonomy in developing legislation. His early leadership success was mixed. In April 1999 the House, in a rare tie vote, defeated a resolution that endorsed the president's policy of bombing Yugoslavia as part of the North Atlantic Treaty Organization (NATO) campaign against that nation's attacks on ethnic Albanians in the province of Kosovo. Hastert voted to support Clinton while his deputies pressured other Republicans to oppose the president. Later the GOP was embarrassed over gun control legislation following a deadly and much publicized shooting at a Colorado high school where fifteen youngsters died.

But by summer, Hastert had better footing as he pushed through the House a major Republican plan for huge tax cuts, which—even though the legislation faced certain death by veto of President Clinton—was designed to position the Republican Party for the 2000 election contests. In doing this, he leaned hard on many colleagues to support him, including Republicans at both ends of the spectrum who wanted much deeper cuts or who argued that reductions should be limited or delayed until other issues such as federal debt reduction and Social Security and Medicare stability were resolved.

Republicans held onto the majority, but their numbers thinned to 221 after the 2000 election, putting tremendous pressure on Hastert to find a way to deliver for the newly elected president, Republican George W. Bush, and prove the Republican Party could govern effectively. Ultimately, his colleagues would credit him for salvaging their majority.

With DeLay whipping votes by his side, Hastert sent Bush a $1.35 trillion package of tax cuts, fast-track trade negotiating authority, and the landmark education law known as the No Child Left Behind Act in 2001. On the fast-track authority vote, Hastert first exhibited his willingness to bend the norms of the House to ensure GOP victory. The vote was held open while DeLay publicly badgered recalcitrant Republicans to support the measure. That scene would be repeated time and again over the next few years, demonstrating just how far Hastert would go to win—even if it meant embarrassing colleagues. But it would not be until two years later that Hastert's tactics would draw public scorn.

After the September 11, 2001, terrorist assault on the United States, the Republican House moved legislation authorizing the president to launch wars in Afghanistan and Iraq, creating the Department of Homeland Security, and expanding the powers of law enforcement agencies. The 2002 election was a watershed for the GOP, which capitalized on voter support for the party's national security platform and a favorable round of national reapportionment and state-by-state congressional redistricting.

Hastert was revered by his Republican colleagues for his steady, determined hand in Congress and his efforts to help the party on the fund-raising circuit. He delivered, in some measure, on his promise for a return to regular order, but he made clear that the leadership would step in to resolve differences or make policy decisions at the latest stages of the legislative process. Paradoxically, he was able to consolidate even more institutional power in the hands of party leaders while still allowing standing committees and rank-and-file lawmakers to participate in the process to a greater degree than they had under Gingrich. The approach mixed a laissez-faire attitude toward the early stages of legislative development with a heavy hand in the latter stages.

Aided in large measure by DeLay, who was promoted to majority leader in 2003, Hastert gradually made changes to party and House rules that favored the leadership at the expense of committees. In 2003 a House rules change eliminated a four-term limit on the Speaker. And, for the first time, the selection of subcommittee chairs on the Appropriations Committee was subjected to the approval of the leadership.

Republican leaders moved even farther away from the seniority system that had long determined committee chairmanships. The relatively junior but fiercely loyal representative Richard W. Pombo of California was handed the gavel of the Resources Committee and Rep. Thomas M. Davis III of Virginia became Government Reform Committee chair over Rep. Christopher Shays of Connecticut. In addition to seniority, party loyalty and fund-raising prowess became important factors in a member's bid for a chairmanship. The control Hastert's leadership team exerted over members' career paths contributed heavily to voting unity. Even powerful senior lawmakers could have years of work nullified by a handful of missteps.

Part of Hastert's success in consolidating power derived from the unity of his leadership team. By 2003 all of the high-ranking elected leaders, including Hastert, had been DeLay protégés. Hastert's successor as DeLay's chief deputy whip, Roy Blunt of Missouri, had been elected whip when DeLay became majority leader. And Conference chair Deborah Pryce of Ohio had won her post with DeLay's quiet backing. In less than a decade, the party's tacticians had fully replaced the visionaries of the Republican Revolution of 1994.

Hastert capitalized on the confluence of his rising political capital, his consolidation of institutional power, and an expanded majority to enact several significant laws in the 108th Congress, most notably the Medicare prescription-drug law and a restructuring of the nation's intelligence agencies. The drug law was Hastert's crowning legislative achievement, but critics blasted the means he used to pass it as a stunning abuse of power. The bill, which expanded the government health care system for the elderly to cover prescription drugs, was sponsored by Hastert and bore the telltale number HR 1. It was the Speaker's bill. Democrats argued that the law would result in a taxpayer giveaway to the pharmaceutical and insurance industries, and they certainly did not want Republicans to win a legislative victory on an issue that they typically dominate. About two dozen conservative Republicans balked at the price tag, which came in at a reported $400 billion over ten years at the time of the final vote.

Republican leaders had held open an earlier vote on the bill for fifty-one minutes as they twisted arms, a tactic they denounced mightily when they were in the minority. Finally, they persuaded Reps. Jo Ann Emerson, R-Mo., and C.L. "Butch" Otter, R-Idaho, to support it and send it to conference.

When it came back to the House in its final form in November, the bill was clearly headed for another close floor vote. The vote began about 3 a.m. on a Saturday, and opponents quickly outnumbered supporters. At one point, the "nays" reached 219, a majority of the House with one vote to spare. But Republican leaders refused to close the vote and accept a loss. Instead, they scoured the aisles of the chamber for potential vote-switchers. Hastert and Tommy Thompson, the secretary of Health and Human Services, surrounded Rep. Nick Smith, R-Mich., hoping to elicit a change of heart. Smith would later accuse lawmakers of tying support for his son's congressional campaign to his vote. Smith did not change his vote, and his son lost his primary. (Smith later recanted, saying no arrangement had been explicitly proposed.)

For hours, GOP leaders worked anyone who might listen. Democrats, Republicans, and a handful of reporters in the press gallery watched in amazement as the clock ticked away. As dawn approached, President Bush placed calls to lawmakers. Otter and Rep. Trent Franks, R-Ariz., switched from "nay" to "yea" and the bill passed. The nearly three-hour marathon was the longest vote anyone could remember and probably the longest since an electronic clock was installed in the House in the early 1970s.

Despite the scene on the floor, Hastert expressed relief and satisfaction in the minutes after it passed. However, the willingness of Hastert's leadership team to break House norms brought criticism not only from Democrats but also from independent congressional experts. "[T]heir impressive successes have come at a steep price: in the suspect content of the legislative product, the diminished institutional standing of the Congress, and the rancorous tone of public life in Washington and the country," Thomas E. Mann and Norman J. Ornstein wrote in their book *The Broken Branch*.[43]

The House: A Woman's Place

In 2007 Nancy Pelosi became the highest-ranking woman ever in American government, second in line to the presidency, when her Democratic colleagues elected her Speaker of the House. She had led them to historically high levels of unity as minority whip and minority leader, isolating Republicans and laying the groundwork for the party's electoral victory in 2006.

Politics were in Pelosi's blood. She was the daughter of former Baltimore mayor and U.S. representative Thomas J. D'Alessandro. As a child, she helped keep track of the favors her father did, and she never forgot to reward a friend or punish an enemy. Even political allies have been known to encounter a frosty shoulder when they step out of line.

As Speaker, she wasted little time in demonstrating that she planned to use the personal political power she had accumulated as the leader of the new majority and the institutional power Republicans had consolidated in the Speaker's office to her advantage. She kept the GOP's six-year term limits for committee chairs—ensuring that she could be a

Rep. Nancy Pelosi, D-Calif., became the highest-ranking woman in U.S. government history when she was sworn in as the first female Speaker of the House in January 2007.

SOURCE: Scott J. Ferrell, Congressional Quarterly.

permanent power broker while their influence was temporary—established a select committee on global warming to circumvent senior chairs who were recalcitrant to the issue, and filled appointive spots with close allies. But she also quickly learned the limitations of her power when she tried to oust rival Steny H. Hoyer, D-Md., from the leadership by strong-arming rank-and-file Democrats to support John P. Murtha, D-Pa., for majority leader. Hoyer, then the party's whip, won handily. Pelosi's bold political maneuvers typically paid off, but many Democrats were wary of allowing her to stack the leadership deck.

Her emphasis on favor-trading and loyalty could sometimes be an Achilles' heel. She irritated Democratic colleagues with her push for Murtha, and others took umbrage at what they perceived to be threats when they did not want to vote for legislation funding the Iraq War in 2007.

Her focus in the early part of 2007 was on Democratic efforts to end the war. Pelosi forced House votes on a resolution opposing President Bush's troop surge and on a supplemental appropriations bill that established a timeline for the withdrawal of most U.S. combat forces from Iraq. But she angered liberals by promoting a more measured approach than the immediate withdrawal some of them favored.

On the domestic side of the ledger, Pelosi was able to run the Democrats' 2006 campaign agenda—dubbed "six for '06"—through the House in her first week as Speaker. She drafted the bills without putting them through the committee process and wrote rules that protected them from amendment on the floor, adopting procedures Democrats had denounced when they were in the minority. "We no longer search for the best ideas or the best policies," complained Rep. Jim Cooper, D-Tenn., an outspoken critic of Pelosi's. "There was only one health care bill offered. One Dodd-Frank [Wall Street reform bill]. Now you are either an ally or a traitor."[44] A gifted political insider, Pelosi struggled with the media demands of the modern speakership. However, she was much more visible than Hastert. She had a strong appetite for aggressive politics and was an adept motivator of her troops. She relied on a handful of trusted advisers, many of them fellow Californians such as George Miller and Henry Waxman—something that occasionally provoked grumbling from non–Golden State members. She did not let the top Democrats on committees pursue issues on a freelance basis, preferring to build consensus among a broader group.

At the same time, Pelosi made little effort to work with Republicans, complaining in April 2009 about the "radical right-wing element" that she accused of exerting power within the GOP. Angry Republicans fired back, making abundantly clear their desire to have her become the poster child for what they said was wrong with Washington. She appeared in 63 percent of the National Republican Congressional Committee's 226 advertisements during the 2010 election cycle—more than twice the number in which Obama was mentioned.

During her initial years as Speaker, Pelosi's job was made easier by her Democratic colleagues' largely single-minded opposition to Bush, whose support was fading in the polls because of the Iraq War and the perceived lax federal response to Hurricane Katrina in 2005. House Democrats set a record for party unity—92 percent—in Bush's final two years in office, according to *Congressional Quarterly*. With the election of Obama in 2008, Pelosi shifted gears and developed a close working relationship with the White House—a situation that was bolstered by Rep. Rahm Emanuel, D-Ill., one of her chief lieutenants, going to work for Obama as his chief of staff.

With a commanding majority and a like-minded White House, Pelosi's Democrats passed a stunning series of major bills in the 111th Congress. They included the $787 billion American Recovery and Reinvestment Act economic stimulus law, a reauthorization of the State Children's Health Insurance Program that had been delayed under Bush, a financial services industry overhaul in response to the abuses on Wall Street that had precipitated a financial crisis, and a revamping of food safety laws and the American Clean Energy and Security Act to regulate greenhouse gas emissions blamed for global warming. All had little to no Republican support, and all but the latter became law.

But her signature achievement was the 2010 health care overhaul, an issue in which she took an intense personal interest. As her biographer Vince Bzdek noted, "Pelosi's animating ambition has been to put so-called women's and family issues such as health care, education and the welfare of children on the same level as homeland security, foreign relations and defense."[45] At the outset, she dissuaded Obama and other Democrats from compromising with Republicans on a less sweeping measure, which she reportedly criticized as "kiddie-care." She guided the bill to passage in the House in November 2009, then successfully revived a Senate-passed version that many House Democrats disliked because it contained no government-run "public option" that could compete with private insurance companies. At the very end, she also stood firm against a last-minute effort from anti-abortion Democrats that almost derailed the legislation.

In assessing Pelosi's overall tenure as speaker, congressional scholars put her in the same lofty pantheon as Cannon and Rayburn. "We're looking at an extraordinary set of accomplishments over a brief period of time," said the American Enterprise Institute's Ornstein. "She ranks with the most consequential speakers, certainly in the last 75 years."[46] But the Republicans' relentless attacks on her leadership took their toll. By October 2010, just 29 percent of those surveyed in a *USA Today*/Gallup poll approved of her performance, with 56 percent disapproving.[47] A month later, Republicans recaptured control of the House after promising an end to the type of big-government legislation that she had so enthusiastically championed.

Despite her party's drubbing at the polls, however, Pelosi's colleagues continued to have confidence in her. She was subsequently reelected with ease as House minority leader, defeating North Carolina's Heath Shuler by a vote of 150–43. She emphasized her long experience in successfully resuscitating the party. When asked why she should remain at the helm of the Democratic Caucus, Pelosi responded, "Because I'm an effective leader. . . . Because they know that I'm the person that can attract the resources, both intellectual and otherwise, to take us to victory—because I've done it before."[48]

Boehner: A Careful Balancing Act

As Pelosi's successor under the new Republican majority, John Boehner was a more cautious figure. He had ample reason to be. When the 61-year-old Ohioan took the gavel from Pelosi in January 2011, he was far older than his young, ambitious lieutenants and was more of a creature of the Capitol than the tea party–backed Republicans elected in

2010. Though dependably conservative, he had never been considered a visionary thinker like Gingrich or a strong-willed disciplinarian like DeLay.

Nevertheless, Boehner had earned credibility among junior Republicans in part because he himself was once a young rebel. Upon coming to the House in 1991, he complained about the excesses of the incumbent Democrats who had long been in power. He fell in with the similarly reform-minded Gingrich and became Republican Conference chair after the 1994 elections gave their party control of the House. After losing the Republican Conference chairmanship in 1999, he spent five years as chair of the Committee on Education and the Workforce (now the Committee on Education and Labor), helping pass the 2001 No Child Left Behind education reform law and other measures. As minority leader, he rallied Republicans to pass the Troubled Asset Relief Program for the ailing financial industry in 2008 after an initial vote failed, even though he famously derided the $700 billion rescue plan as a "crap sandwich."

In his initial months as speaker, Boehner employed a hybrid strategy of leadership. On day-to-day matters, he granted committee chairs more latitude than any speaker since Foley, an action that stemmed from his own experience chairing the Committee on Education and the Workforce. He let the new Budget Committee chair, Wisconsin's Paul Ryan, craft a controversial budget blueprint that immediately came under attack from Democrats for reshaping Medicare. He also lived up, at least initially, to his earlier promises to open up the legislative process. In the first five months of the 112th Congress, the House considered and voted on more than 430 amendments and took up six bills with modified open rules allowing for wide-ranging debate. During the entire 111th Congress, Democrats permitted one bill under a modified open rule and considered 810 amendments. Part of the reason for Boehner's approach came from his inability to rely on one of the chief tools of his predecessors: House Republicans took umbrage at and banned special-interest appropriations "earmarks."

But on the significant issues that divided the two parties, Boehner used a centralized, top-down style similar to that of Pelosi. He assumed the lead role on negotiating a fiscal year 2011 budget deal with Obama that avoided a government shutdown—something many tea party–backed Republicans said they were willing to let occur. During an even more polarizing subsequent debate on raising the federal debt ceiling—another idea that tea party members vehemently opposed—Boehner sternly called for party unity. "Get your ass in line," he bluntly told House Republicans at a closed-door meeting at which the debt ceiling legislation was discussed. His admonishment led several Republicans to drop their opposition.[49]

Boehner used a different tactic several months later, when he sought to bring his caucus on board to support a

House Minority Leader John A. Boehner, R-Ohio, attends a news conference for Democratic leaders' plans to set an ultimate deadline of August 2008 for U.S. combat troop removal from Iraq. Boehner became his party's House minority leader in November 2006.

SOURCE: Scott J. Ferrell, Congressional Quarterly.

short-term spending bill known as a continuing resolution, or CR, to fund the federal government. Forty-eight Republicans joined Democrats in opposing the measure; Republican leadership aides said Boehner was aware the stopgap bill would fail and wanted to send a message to the defecting Republicans how their actions would subsequently force party leaders to negotiate with Democrats to win passage of a much less desirable bill.

HOUSE LEADERSHIP: A HIERARCHY OF SUPPORT

The party leadership structure is particularly important in the House because of its size and consequent potential for unwieldiness. In his 1963 study of the House, *Forge of Democracy,* Neil MacNeil described the chamber's leadership organizations as its "priesthood." Though the younger, media-savvy, sound-bite quoting, expert fund-raisers who rose to the leadership late in the twentieth century might laugh at such a description, the leadership remains a structure separate from other members.

> Indeed, over the years, a hierarchy of leaders has been constructed in the House to support the Speaker, and opposing this hierarchy has been another, created by the minority party and led by the "shadow" Speaker, the leader of the opposition party. With the hierarchy also has been built a vast array of political and party organizations to assist the Speaker and his lieutenants in the complicated task of making the House a viable, responsible legislative body.[50]

The Majority Leader

In the modern House, the second in command is the majority leader, whose primary responsibility is to manage the legislative affairs of the chamber. To that end, he or she helps formulate, promote, negotiate, and defend the party's program, particularly on the House floor. A majority leader was not officially designated in the House until 1899, when Sereno E. Payne, R-N.Y., was named to the post. But from the earliest days, Speakers have appointed someone to help them guide their party's legislative program through the House. Occasionally this person was a trusted lieutenant. More often the chair of the Ways and Means Committee also served as the floor leader, largely because until 1865 the committee handled both revenues and appropriations and thus the bulk of the legislation that came before the House. Payne, for example, was also chair of Ways and Means. *(See "House Floor Leaders, 1899–2012," p. 231, in Reference Materials.)*

After the Appropriations Committee was established, its chair sometimes served as majority leader. At other times, the Speaker chose a leading rival within the party, presumably either to promote party harmony or to neutralize an opponent. Thus in 1859 William Pennington, R-N.J., the only House member besides Clay to be elected Speaker in his first term, chose as his majority leader his chief rival for the speakership, John Sherman, R-Ohio. And in 1889 Reed named as his majority leader William McKinley Jr., R-Ohio, who had challenged Reed for the speakership and who, like Reed, had presidential ambitions.

The revolt against Cannon in 1910, which stripped the speakership of many of its powers, also stripped the Speaker of the right to name the majority leader. Since 1911 Democratic majority leaders have been elected by secret ballot in the party caucus. The first two, Oscar W. Underwood and Claude Kitchin of North Carolina, also chaired the Ways and Means Committee. When the GOP returned to power in 1919, their Committee on Committees named the majority leader. However, since 1923 the Republican Conference has selected the majority leader.

Franklin Mondell of Wyoming, the Republican floor leader chosen in 1919, had been chair of the Ways and Means Committee, but he gave up his committee assignments to help the Speaker manage the House. The first Democratic majority leader to give up his committee assignments was Henry T. Rainey, who resigned his seat on the Ways and Means Committee upon his election as majority leader in 1931. Beginning in the 1970s, Democratic majority leaders held leadership-designated slots on both the House Budget Committee and, later, on the Permanent Select Intelligence Committee, to be able to intervene when needed in difficult budget negotiations and maintain access to sensitive national security information. However, after the Republican takeover in 1995, the practice was not continued by the new majority. Majority Leader Dick Armey, R-Texas, held no committee assignment. His successor, fellow Texan Tom DeLay, followed suit, as did the next two men to hold the job, Republican John A. Boehner of Ohio and Democratic majority leader Steny H. Hoyer of Maryland. After stepping down as majority leader amid legal troubles in the 109th Congress, DeLay was allowed to return to his seat on the Appropriations Committee.

Underwood, the first elected majority leader, was one of the strongest majority leaders in the history of the House. Champ Clark, the Democrat who succeeded Cannon as Speaker, gave Underwood a free hand to manage both legislation and the party. "Although I am going to be Speaker . . . I am going to sacrifice the Speaker's power to change the rules," he declared.[51] As a result of Clark's attitude and the limitations placed upon the Speaker's office, Underwood was able to dominate the House through the Democratic Caucus and his chairmanship of Ways and Means, which assigned members to the standing committees. "Oscar Underwood became the real leader of the House," wrote historian George B. Galloway.[52]

But changing circumstances in the years following World War I made it more difficult for Underwood's successors to wield such power. Internal party divisions made the caucus ineffective, while strong Speakers such as Longworth and Rayburn elevated the prestige and thus the power of the Speaker. The majority leaders eventually came to give up their committee chairmanships and assignments, and between 1937 and 1975 the Rules Committee ceased to be an arm of the leadership. The majority leader under the Democrats was seen as the chief lieutenant to the Speaker, not his rival. The majority leader, Wright wrote in 1976, "must work with the Speaker, in a supportive role, and never against him."[53]

The unusual events surrounding Hastert's ascension to the Speaker's office helped DeLay become the most powerful majority leader in the modern era. When Gingrich was pushed from the leadership and Speaker-designate Livingston resigned, DeLay, then the whip, promoted Hastert, his top lieutenant, to the Speaker's office. Majority Leader Dick Armey, R-Texas, who had been sparring with DeLay since an aborted coup against Gingrich, announced in the 107th Congress that he would retire. By 2003 all of the top House

House Majority Whip Kevin McCarthy, R-Calif. (left), and Majority Leader Eric Cantor, R-Va. (right), applaud as President Barack Obama delivers an address on jobs and the economy to a Joint Session of Congress at the Capitol in Washington, D.C., on Thursday, September 8, 2011.

SOURCE: Ed Reinke/AP/Corbis.

leaders, including new whip Roy Blunt and Conference chair Deborah Pryce, were DeLay acolytes. The complex nature of the Hastert-DeLay relationship is hard to untangle, but DeLay was given a long leash to execute party goals. DeLay was often seen as the "bad cop" to Hastert's "good cop." In addition to having tremendous influence with the Speaker, DeLay proved an expert floor manager and kept close tabs on the vote-counting operation he had built and bequeathed to Blunt.

Hastert's election to Speaker from the post of chief deputy whip broke a nearly century-long string of Speakers advancing from the next-highest rung of their party's leadership ladder. Every Speaker between 1900 and 1989, when Foley took office, advanced to that position from either the majority or minority leadership position. Gingrich effectively continued the tradition because he had been the highest-ranking sitting leader of his party—minority whip—as the Republican-controlled 104th Congress organized itself.

(Minority Leader Bob Michel had retired in 1995 at the end of the 103rd Congress.)

Three of the six Democratic Speakers elected between 1945 and 1989 also served as whip. The exceptions were Rayburn, who was chair of the Interstate and Foreign Commerce Committee when he was chosen majority leader in 1937; McCormack, who was chair of the House Democratic Caucus; and Wright, who was a deputy whip and next in line to chair the Public Works Committee when he bid for, and won by a single vote, the floor leader position in 1976.

The duties of the majority and minority leaders are not spelled out in the standing rules of the House, and no official provision is made for them, except through periodic appropriations specifically made for their offices. House rules do provide preference in recognition for the party leaders to offer certain specified procedural motions on the House floor. Both leadership positions are also enumerated in their respective party rules.

In practice, the majority leader's job has been to formulate the party's legislative program in cooperation with the Speaker and other party leaders, to steer the program through the House, to persuade committee chairs to report bills deemed of importance to the party, and to arrange the House legislative schedule. The majority leader is also the party's field general on the floor, coordinating with the bill's manager and others to anticipate problems before they develop.

Like the Speaker, the majority leader is in a position to do many favors for colleagues—scheduling floor action at a convenient time, speaking on behalf of a member's bill (or refraining from opposing it), meeting with a member's important constituents, holding fund-raising events and donating money to a member, or campaigning for a member in his or her home district. The modern-day majority leader, like other party leaders, is a tremendous source of campaign cash for party incumbents and challengers alike. Such favors clearly help the leadership build coalitions and maintain party unity. The opportunity to campaign for colleagues has been, in recent years, eagerly sought after by party leaders of both parties.

After Republicans regained control of the House in 2011, Majority Leader Eric Cantor, R-Va., became a national figure in part because of the widespread perception that he was closer to the conservative rank and file than Speaker Boehner. The Cantor-Boehner relationship became a frequently watched barometer of how successfully the GOP could govern with a restive majority. The two men insisted there was no friction between them, and Boehner gave Cantor a number of important duties, such as assigning him to take part in bipartisan negotiations with Vice President Joe Biden over reducing the deficit. Those negotiations reportedly had been making progress before Cantor quit in June 2011, citing his unwillingness to allow tax increases to be part of a final budget deal.

The Minority Leader

Although individual members occasionally stepped forward to lead the loyal opposition against the majority position on specific bills or issues, the position of House minority leader first became identifiable in the 1880s. Since then the post has always been assumed by the minority party's candidate for the speakership. The titular head of the minority party, or shadow Speaker as he or she has sometimes been called in the past, is chosen by the party caucus.

The basic duties of the minority leader were described by Bertrand Snell, R-N.Y., who held the post from 1931 to 1939: "He is spokesman for his party and enunciates its policies. He is required to be alert and vigilant in defense of the minority's rights. It is his function and duty to criticize constructively the policies and program of the majority, and to this end employ parliamentary tactics and give close attention to all proposed legislation."[54] Snell might also have added that if the minority leader's party occupies the White House,

he is likely to become the president's chief spokesperson in the House. And if Snell were alive today, he might amend his statement to reflect that a woman can be minority leader, too. Before she was Speaker, Pelosi served as minority leader for four years, and she returned to the post when Republicans regained the majority in 2011.

Because the minority's role is to counter the legislative program of the majority or advance the president's legislative agenda if he or she is of the same party, it rarely offers its own comprehensive legislative program. However, given the success of the minority House Republicans' Contract with America proposals in unifying the party prior to the 1994 election, this pattern is changing to some degree—particularly as the House increasingly resembles a parliament.

Bob Michel, the Illinois Republican who became the GOP minority leader in 1981, described his job as twofold: "To keep our people together, and to look for votes on the other side."[55] Michel's greatest success in this regard came in 1981, when Congress, aided by a Republican Senate and a popular president of the same party, passed the Reagan administration's unprecedented budget and tax-cut package. Large-scale defections by conservative Democrats in the House made the Republican successes possible.

But such victories are rare for the minority. "One of the minority leader's greatest problems," wrote Randall Ripley, "is the generally demoralizing condition of minority party status."[56] Minority members want the same things majority members do—information, legislative success, patronage, and the like. When they do not get them, the minority leader is often the target of their frustrations. Throughout his term as minority leader Michel was pushed by younger and more conservative and aggressive colleagues who urged him to turn the House floor into a theater for all-out partisan warfare. But Michel was just the last in a long line of Republican minority leaders who were put on the hot seat by aggressive junior members. Gerald Ford, R-Mich., helped Charles Halleck of Indiana oust Minority Leader John McCormack in 1959 and then knocked Halleck out of the job in 1965. Ford's successor, John Rhodes of Arizona, was succeeded by Michel after he was criticized by Gingrich and others for being too comfortable with minority status and chose to step down to avoid facing removal. The election of Gingrich as minority whip in 1989 accelerated this trend and further eroded remaining patterns of bipartisan cooperation. *(See box, Partisan Tensions in the House, p. 37.)*

Michel did grow increasingly confrontational during Wright's tenure as Speaker, when he, along with most other House Republicans, believed the Democrats were becoming more brazen in using the rules to deny them their rights. Republicans' intense personal dislike of Wright made this easy. And Michel made a Republican takeover of the House in the 1992 elections—the first to be held after the decennial redistricting—a top priority, working with various Republican groups in the House to develop GOP alternatives on

PARTISAN TENSIONS IN THE HOUSE: STRIDENCY INCREASED AROUND THE TURN OF THE TWENTY-FIRST CENTURY

Political and personal disagreements reached a level of vituperation and nastiness beginning in the 1980s not previously seen in the modern Congress. The proverbial gloves came off. The weakening of personal relationships among members and traditions of comity on the House floor accelerated the process. And new members entering the House were less willing to recognize the legitimacy of opposing viewpoints or to allow their respective party leaderships to negotiate as readily with "the enemy."

Some referred to it as "the politics of personal destruction" as opponents were no longer satisfied simply to win an argument and move on, perhaps working together on the next issue. Instead, some sought to destroy a rival both personally and politically, using investigations, demands for special prosecutors, ethics charges, or seemingly any other technique that would garner advantage. Rep. Newt Gingrich, R-Ga., was credited or blamed for pioneering this technique and using it successfully to publicize and escalate partisan tensions in the ethics investigation of Speaker Jim Wright, which led to Wright's resignation.

PARTISAN WARFARE

One other factor that accounted for the increased stridency was divided government—a Congress controlled by one party and a president of the other (1987–1993; 1995–2001), or a Congress split between the parties, as was the case in 1981–1987, for most of the 107th Congress (2001–2003) and the 112th Congress (2011–2012). Democrats lost control of the White House for twelve years during the Ronald Reagan and George H.W. Bush administrations, and House Republicans had been in the minority from 1955 to 1995. This led to frequent clashes over policy that often left both parties frustrated by the inevitable "half-a-loaf" results. Members of the Republican minority concluded that they could benefit if they sharpened the conflict and demonstrated strong disagreements between the parties, ultimately forcing the public to make a choice between them, instead of engaging in compromise and bipartisanship that tended to cloud distinctions between the parties.

Partisan tensions escalated rapidly during the first term of Gingrich's speakership (1995–1997) as Democrats reeled from their sudden loss of power and Republicans, including many newcomers unschooled in the mechanics of legislating, exulted in their ability to pass quickly most elements of their Contract with America legislative agenda that was used effectively in the 1994 election campaign. In doing so, they sometimes ran roughshod over the minority rights that they had long complained Democrats had ignored during that party's long era of House control. When Democrats took control of the chamber in 2007, they initially bypassed committees and ran their "six for '06" agenda through the House without regard to the rights they had clamored for when in the minority. Even after the first week, Democrats continued to circumvent the "regular order" of the committee process to speed legislation to the floor when it suited them. Such was the case in July when they decided at the last minute to consider a bill calling for a sharp reduction of U.S. forces in Iraq by April 2008. Rather than going through the Armed Services Committee, Speaker Nancy Pelosi, D-Calif., chose to put the measure on the floor without committee consideration. Several Democratic members of the Armed Services Committee voted against the measure when it came to the floor.

In the aftermath of Gingrich's narrow reelection as Speaker in 1997 and subsequent formal reprimand by the House, both parties made some effort to cool tensions, with mixed results. But numerous investigations of President Bill Clinton and of allegations of campaign finance abuses in the 1996 presidential campaign further exacerbated partisan warfare. The GOP was accused of conducting a vendetta against the president and first lady Hillary Rodham Clinton and abusing its subpoena powers to investigate alleged campaign violations by Democrats while ignoring Republicans. Majority Leader Dick Armey and Whip Tom DeLay, both of Texas, broke precedent by criticizing Clinton in highly personal terms, but Dan Burton of Indiana outdid both by calling the president a "scumbag." The battle culminated in impeachment of the president by a near party-line vote by a lame-duck Republican House following an election in which the party unexpectedly lost seats, sparking bitter attacks on the floor.

Gingrich's later action relinquishing the speakership and voluntarily resigning from Congress following surprising GOP losses in the fall 1998 elections removed a flashpoint from House partisan warfare. Eventually Republicans settled on J. Dennis Hastert of Illinois as the new Speaker. Hastert and his party allies, as well as Democrats, promised new efforts at bipartisanship and cooperation.

After the Gingrich episode, Democrats and Republicans engaged in an informal ethics truce in which members did not file complaints against each other. But that was broken in 2004, when one-term representative Chris Bell, D-Texas, filed a complaint against Majority Leader Tom DeLay. Bell accused DeLay of illegally financing state legislative races with corporate donations, promising legislative favors in exchange for campaign contributions, and improperly involving the Federal Aviation Administration in an effort to locate state lawmakers who fled Texas to avoid being forced to make a quorum so the legislature could approve a DeLay-driven redistricting map.

DeLay and Bell were both admonished by the ethics committee—Bell for improperly preparing his complaint—and DeLay was later indicted in Texas on charges of funneling corporate contributions into state legislative races through the Republican National Committee. A jury convicted him in November 2010 of committing a felony. DeLay was later sentenced to three years in prison but was allowed to remain free while he appealed his conviction.

The long-dormant ethics committee became more active under Chair Joel Hefley, R-Colo., and DeLay was ultimately removed from the post under term-limit rules.

In earlier years, House Speakers Thomas P. "Tip" O'Neill Jr. of Massachusetts, who retired from the House in 1987, and Jim Wright of Texas, who resigned in June 1989, were both highly partisan Democrats who were not comfortable regularly working with Republicans. Republicans were outraged in the early 1980s when the Democrats under O'Neill stacked key committees to deny Republicans representation proportional to their numbers in the House. (Republicans adopted a similar practice when they assumed control with a substantially smaller majority.) Democrats eventually agreed to increase the number of seats on most major committees. In 1985 a drawn-out fight over a contested election in Indiana's Eighth District further embittered Republicans, who walked out of the House chamber en masse after the Democratic candidate, Rep. Frank McCloskey, was declared reelected by a four-vote margin. Although O'Neill maintained cordial relations with many Republicans,

(Continued)

(Continued)

including Minority Leader Bob Michel of Illinois, which helped to cool passions, his successor, Wright, was unable to do so.

Republicans were even more incensed at what they considered to be Speaker Wright's heavy-handed partisanship. One of the most divisive incidents occurred October 29, 1987, when Wright forced passage of a major deficit-cutting budget reconciliation bill that called for taxes Republicans opposed. The Speaker, who has sole authority under House rules to determine when to announce the result of a vote after the normal time allotment has expired, held the vote open so a Texas ally, Rep. Jim Chapman, could be persuaded to change his vote, making the result 206–205. Angry GOP House members booed Wright after the vote and accused him of stealing their victory. After assuming the speakership in 1995, Gingrich used this authority to extend voting time for much longer periods to persuade members to change their positions. He said he was following the "regular order" of House practice in doing so. During one such interlude, a Democrat asked Gingrich from the floor whether he was planning to apologize to Wright for the earlier criticism.

THE GINGRICH FACTOR

Much of the partisan tension was deliberately fomented over a long period of time by a group of Republicans led by Gingrich. Younger Republican conservatives effectively demonized the Democrats not only as political and policy adversaries but also personally as "corrupt" and "evil" in their ultimately successful campaign to seize power in the chamber. Such feelings, and such language, made it virtually impossible for the parties to communicate and hamstrung those who still were willing to attempt bipartisan cooperation. Democrats used their own rhetoric to help regain control of the House in the 2006 election. They charged that Republicans had presided over a "culture of corruption" and used as examples the ethics of the chamber and of individual lawmakers to sway public support and win Republican-held open seats.

The use of dilatory tactics on the House floor increased. The use of motions to adjourn, demands for roll-call votes on routine matters, and other techniques to disrupt the schedule of the House proliferated. These tactics had been used in the past, usually in response to some specific event that angered the minority or to try to run out the clock for action on legislative business at the end of a session. But more aggressive conservatives such as Gingrich had little concern with the majority's reaction to the frequency of these techniques. They did not care that they could not win these votes or have significant impact on the end product of legislation. Delaying tactics helped mobilize and unite the minority, created

Speaker Thomas P. "Tip" O'Neill Jr.'s partisan quarrel with Newt Gingrich led to the Speaker's words being stricken from the record.

SOURCE: Library of Congress.

uncertainty in the majority's otherwise firm control of the chamber, attracted the media's notice, and made bipartisan collaboration more difficult.

In 1984 Gingrich endeared himself to Republican conservatives when he humiliated Speaker O'Neill on the House floor. Addressing a nearly empty chamber during the special order period after the close of regular business one night in May, Gingrich denounced Majority Leader Wright and nine other Democrats for writing a

issues such as child care, education, and health policy. Although some judged Michel to be one of the most effective House leaders on either side of the aisle since Rayburn, many Republicans felt a need for the strident partisanship offered by Gingrich and other members of his Conservative Opportunity Society. In 1989 Gingrich defeated Michel's friend and candidate Edward R. Madigan of Illinois, 87–85, to succeed Dick Cheney of Wyoming as minority whip.

"What that says to me," Michel told reporters immediately after Gingrich's election, "is that they want us to be more activated and more visible and more aggressive, and that we can't be content with business as usual."[57] As minority whip,

Gingrich often eclipsed Michel as the Republicans aggressively attacked the majority and planned the strategy that led to the Republican takeover of the House in the 1994 elections.

When Democrats lost control of the House beginning in the 104th Congress in 1995, the new minority leader was Missouri's Richard A. Gephardt, who had earlier been caucus chair (1984–1988) and majority leader (1989–1995) and had run unsuccessfully for the party's presidential nomination in 1988. In contrast to his earlier roles in developing policy and serving as a national party spokesperson, Gephardt had to devote substantial energy just to the mechanics of obtaining committee assignments for members displaced

conciliatory letter to Nicaraguan leader Daniel Ortega, addressing him as "Dear Commandante" and calling for a settlement between political factions in that country. Gingrich said the letter was undermining U.S. foreign policy. O'Neill retaliated by ordering the television cameras to pan the chamber during special order speeches so that viewers would see that Gingrich and his supporters were addressing an empty chamber.

A few days later, when Gingrich repeated his charges during regular debate, O'Neill took the floor himself to denounce the Georgian's tactics as "the lowest thing that I have ever seen in my 32 years in Congress."[1] That remark, an obvious violation of House rules of decorum, brought a demand from GOP whip Trent Lott of Mississippi that O'Neill's words be "taken down," that is, be reread to the House and examined by the Speaker, who determines whether they should be stricken from the record. Speaker pro tempore Joe Moakley, a Massachusetts Democrat with close ties to O'Neill who was presiding at the time, had no choice but to agree with Lott—the first time the words of a Speaker had been taken down since February 12, 1797, when Speaker Jonathan Dayton of New Jersey was called to order for using "improper language" during debate on the House floor. O'Neill's comment never became part of the official record.

DEMOCRATS GROW COMBATIVE

The partisan tensions in the House grew during the late 1990s and early 2000s, but it was not until Nancy Pelosi, D-Calif., became minority leader in 2003 that Democrats effectively used Gingrich's tools to challenge Republican control of the House. In 2003 Pelosi led Democrats to their highest level of party unity since *Congressional Quarterly* began tracking the statistic in 1956, using procedural warfare and partisan rhetoric to draw sharp divisions between Democrats and Republicans and build unity within her own caucus.

Democrats' unity forced Republicans to win legislative victories on their own. The results were sometimes embarrassing for the majority party. Votes were held open far longer than the typical fifteen minutes so leaders could twist arms among the rank and file and pass bills. The final vote on prescription-drug legislation in November 2003 was held open for three hours. Democrats charged that Republicans were routinely bending the rules to win and would, a few years later, tie that argument into their larger, successful electoral theme that the GOP had established a "culture of corruption" in the nation's capital. DeLay was admonished by the ethics committee for offering to endorse a lawmaker's son in exchange for the member changing his vote on the drug bill, though the member refused to do so.

Partisan unity increasingly helped Democrats draw distinctions between themselves and Republicans, especially as a slew of scandals began to threaten the Republican majority in the 109th Congress (2005–2007). Former representative Randy "Duke" Cunningham, D-Calif., was sent to prison for arranging defense contracts in exchange for cash and gifts from contractors. Former representative Bob Ney would admit to making false statements and conspiracy to commit fraud as part of the Jack Abramoff lobbying scandal. Ney sought to give favorable legislative treatment to Abramoff's clients in return for cash, lavish trips, and gifts.

Exit polling from the 2006 election showed that three-quarters of voters said corruption was an issue important to their vote and most of them voted Democratic, according to the Associated Press.

PARTISANSHIP TARNISHES CONGRESS'S IMAGE

With Republicans' return to the minority, partisan tensions again became inflamed. The GOP focused much of its criticism on Pelosi, branding her a "San Francisco liberal" who was out of step with much of the rest of the country. When Pelosi contended in 2009 that the Central Intelligence Agency had misled her seven years earlier about its controversial use of "waterboarding" terrorism suspects, angry Republicans accused her of being irresponsible and unpatriotic. That summer, Democrats were met with a firestorm of criticism at their August recess town-hall meetings, much of it from participants in the limited-government "tea party" movement.

When Republicans regained control of the House in 2011, they promised to take steps to open up debate and enable Democrats to have a greater say in the legislative process. But the hostility between the two parties only deepened. Obama was subjected to prolonged and punishing attacks from conservatives who castigated him as a "socialist" and with other epithets, while Democrats branded the new crop of tea party–influenced House Republicans as unreasonable extremists for their unwillingness to raise the federal debt ceiling in 2011.

All of the infighting did serious damage to Congress's image. In September 2011 its public approval rating in several polls had sunk to 12 percent, matching the all-time low recorded in 2008 during the Wall Street economic crisis. Respondents in a *New York Times*/CBS News poll were just slightly more disapproving of the Republicans in Congress than of the Democrats, with 19 percent approving of Republicans, compared with 28 percent for the Democrats.

1 "Televised Partisan Skirmishes Erupt in House." In *CQ Almanac 1984*, 40th ed., 208. Washington, D.C.: Congressional Quarterly, 1985. library.cqpress.com/cqalmanac/cqal84-1152500.

by the election results and calming various party factions that wanted to assess blame for the election defeat. The press reported that he and Gingrich almost never spoke, inhibiting the development of a sustainable relationship between the majority and minority leaderships under the new regime. Gephardt's inability to lead Democrats back into the majority and accusations that his own presidential ambitions were of paramount importance to him hurt his stature as minority leader.

When he gave up the post at the end of the 107th Congress—after voting to authorize the president to invade Iraq and not asking Democrats to take a unified position on the

question—he was succeeded by the hard-charging Pelosi. Pelosi rallied her troops in opposition to the Republican agenda in a manner reminiscent of Gingrich and developed a 2006 campaign agenda called "six for '06" that gave Democrats a set of alternative priorities to point to on the campaign trail.

As minority leader in the 111th Congress, Boehner took a similarly hard-line stance against the Pelosi-led Democratic majority seeking to implement new president Barack Obama's agenda. In addition to aggressive rhetoric—"All the talk of a post-partisan atmosphere was a ruse," he complained in April 2009—Boehner demonstrated a willingness to engage in political theater.[58] He angrily tossed a copy of the 1,100-page American Recovery and Reinvestment Act stimulus bill onto the House floor during a debate and later deployed his rarely used privilege as minority leader to speak for more than an hour in opposition to the 2009 American Clean Energy and Security Act imposing a "cap-and-trade" program aimed at reducing greenhouse gas emissions. His maneuver delayed the vote until after that evening's network news broadcasts.

Party Whips

The term "whip" comes from British fox-hunting lore; the "whipper-in" was responsible for keeping the foxhounds from leaving the pack. It was first used in the British Parliament in 1769 by Edmund Burke. Though neither party in the House of Representatives designated an official whip until 1897—Rep. James A. Tawney, Republican of Minnesota, was the first—influential members played that role from the outset, working to forge consensus on important issues and for particular floor fights.

Unlike the British system, where political parties are well disciplined and a whip's major concern is good party attendance, whips in the U.S. House cajole votes as well as count noses, gather information as well as impart it. "We try to keep our people . . . informed of the leadership's position on things—what they'd like, what we're seeking, what we're trying to do," a member of the Democratic whip organization said. "Not only on policy, but also on scheduling and programming. . . . We pick up static from our people and relay it to the leadership, so that they know what's going on, but we also pick up information from the leadership and convey it back. It's a two-way conduit."[59]

Specifically, whips of both parties help their floor leaders keep track of the whereabouts of party members and lobby them for their votes. Whips also serve as the party's acting floor leaders in the absence of the regular leaders. They handle the mechanics of polling members both on their views on issues and on the stands on specific floor votes, information that the majority leader uses to determine whether and when to bring legislation to the floor. Through weekly whip notices, whips inform members about upcoming floor action, including key amendments. Increasingly, whips gather support for party initiatives from inside Congress as well as from outside interest groups. They marshal coalitions of business lobbyists or other interested groups to help put pressure on wavering members and to raise money for party candidates.

The whips are also responsible for ensuring that members are present for tight votes. Sometimes, whips and their assistants stand at the door of the House chamber, signaling the leadership's position on a vote by holding their thumbs up or down. They also put out information sheets to members describing the vote. During recorded votes, a computer on the floor prints out how members have voted. If the vote is close, the whips can use that list as a guide to seek possible vote switches before the result of the vote is announced. Occasionally the whip organization goes to extremes. In 1984, for example, deputy whip Marty Russo, D-Ill., carried Daniel K. Akaka, D-Hawaii, onto the House floor in an effort to persuade him to change his vote.

House Republicans have always elected their whip. The Democratic whip was appointed by the Speaker and majority leader until 1986, when the Democratic Caucus elected Tony Coelho of California. In recent decades the Democratic whip position has frequently been a first step toward the speakership. The change to elective status had been demanded and passed years earlier by caucus members who did not want an appointed member to gain the advantage of such an important post, with its potential for advancement on the leadership ladder. But implementation of the new rule was delayed until a vacancy developed in the whip post, which it did when Thomas S. Foley moved up to become majority leader. Members also wanted the whip to act as a liaison between the leadership and the rank and file, and not simply as an enforcer and intelligence gatherer. Coelho shocked his colleagues by resigning suddenly in 1989 in the midst of an ethics controversy that developed simultaneously with, but unrelated to, Speaker Wright's troubles. He was succeeded by the first African American to win a major leadership position, Rep. William H. Gray III of Pennsylvania, who had previously been Budget Committee chair (1985–1989) and moved up to whip from the chairmanship of the Democratic Caucus.

In the last years of Democratic rule in the House, the whip system was expanded into a continuous information-gathering and strategizing mechanism. Congressional scholar Sinclair notes that in the 103rd Congress, with more than ninety-five members involved, the whip system had evolved "from a sporadically active body more inclined to count than persuade . . . into a continuously active organization that perceived persuasion as its central mission."[60]

Coelho and Gingrich were very influential, Coelho for his fund-raising skills and Gingrich as a political strategist, which gave them both power beyond the technical rank of their leadership positions. DeLay, who became majority whip in 1995, was an aggressive conservative activist who enjoyed considerable success in the 104th Congress in helping pass most elements of the Contract with America and other items on the new majority's legislative agenda. Called "The Hammer," he was often credited—or blamed—for revolutionizing the whip operation by demanding fealty from lobbyists who wanted access to the Republican leadership and input in the congressional agenda and from members who wanted party support in their campaigns. He was admonished by the ethics committee for creating the impression that special access would be given in exchange for political donations and that the personal interests of a member would be served by voting with the party. DeLay's legendary effectiveness as a vote-getter perhaps was cemented by the public arm-twisting sessions Republican leaders engaged in during the 108th Congress after he had moved on to the majority leader's job. Though DeLay remained a part of the leadership team—and helped whip votes—he was no longer primarily responsible for having the votes in hand.

In recent years the politics of inclusion and the need to build coalitions have induced both parties to expand and enhance their whip organizations. By the late 1980s virtually every bill of significance was given a task force by the Democrats, made up of committee members and noncommittee members with an interest in the issue. The task force's job was to round up support for the bill. Task force members discussed which arguments would work best with which members of Congress and who was best suited to push those points with individual members. Sometimes task forces reached out to unions, trade associations, and others who were lobbying on the issue. If the votes were not there, the task force and key committee members, under the aegis of the leadership, might even tinker with the substance of the legislation to try to reach a compromise acceptable to a majority.

The tactic proved successful in getting legislation through the House and in involving more members, especially junior members, in the process. "It's helped the leadership to get to know the new members and the new members to get to know the leadership," one member told Barbara Sinclair. "And it's certainly helped the new members . . . understand the need for leadership and followership. I think the guys who have served on task forces know a lot more about the need for a party structure with some loyalty than those who haven't."[61]

Republicans used, and built on, many of the same tactics in the majority. DeLay was heavily criticized for involving outside interest groups more visibly in the process of garnering support for legislation, but Republicans countered that Democrats had always consulted labor and liberal groups.

The whip system of both parties has expanded over time to involve more members in the process and to gather greater amounts of political intelligence. For example, in mid-1999 DeLay had one chief deputy whip, Roy Blunt of Missouri, eight deputy whips, and thirty-one assistant whips. The whip's responsibilities as formally defined by the Republican leadership included floor strategy, counting votes, identifying member concerns, providing information on floor activities, an automatic call system for Republican members, a Republican job bank, and a member ombudsman program.

The majority whip in the 110th and 111th Congresses was South Carolina's James Clyburn, who relied more on persuasion than pressure to assemble votes, in contrast to Pelosi's more aggressive approach to leadership. After Republicans regained the majority in 2011, Pelosi created a new position for Clyburn, "assistant minority leader," rather than have him undergo a head-to-head challenge with Maryland's Steny Hoyer, who reclaimed the whip's post after serving as majority leader.

The majority whip for House Republicans in the 112th Congress became California's Kevin McCarthy, a former congressional aide known for his political strategizing and close relationship with new Majority Leader Cantor. McCarthy took on the challenge of acknowledging the independence of the dozens of tea party–inspired conservatives elected in 2010 while also stressing to them the importance of hewing to the GOP agenda. "Kevin probably has a better handle on the freshmen than anybody else here," Boehner said in July 2011.[62]

The Party Caucuses

The use of party caucuses—the organization of all members in each party in the House—has waxed and waned since the First Congress. In the Jeffersonian period, the Democratic-Republicans, in conjunction with the president, used the caucus to formulate their party's legislative strategy. During Henry Clay's terms as Speaker, most important legislative decisions were still made in the Democratic-Republican caucus. Less than two weeks after being seated in 1813, Federalist Daniel Webster concluded that "the time for us to be put on the stage and moved by the wires has not yet come," because "before anything is attempted to be done here, it must be arranged elsewhere."[63]

The nominees for president and vice president were chosen by congressional caucuses from 1800 to 1824. By the 1830s the importance of the caucuses had diminished, and except to nominate the party's candidate for Speaker at the beginning of each Congress, they met rarely during the next sixty years.

In the 1890s the caucus was revived as a forum for discussing legislative strategy. Speaker Reed used the Republican Caucus to a limited extent to discuss policy questions. For the most part, though, the caucus under Reed functioned only to give the party's stamp of approval to decisions Reed had already made. In the early 1900s Speaker Cannon called caucus meetings occasionally but manipulated them much as Reed had. It was not until the revolt against Cannon and the return of control of the House to the Democrats that the caucus was restored to its earlier legislative significance.

The Democratic Caucus

In 1909 the Democrats adopted a party rule that the caucus, by a two-thirds majority, could bind its members on a specific vote. Throughout President Woodrow Wilson's first term, the Democratic leadership used this rule and the caucus effectively, achieving remarkable party unity on a wide range of domestic legislation. But the party began to split over foreign policy issues, and the caucus fell into disuse in Wilson's second term. The binding caucus rule was used during Franklin D. Roosevelt's first term as well, but subsequently it was invoked only on procedural or party issues, such as voting for Speaker, and the rule was finally abolished in 1975.

In recent decades the Democratic Caucus has been revived. In the late 1960s younger House Democrats with relatively little seniority sought to revitalize the caucus as a means of countering the arbitrary authority exercised by committee chairs and other senior members. The campaign, led by the House Democratic Study Group, began when Speaker McCormack established regular monthly caucus meetings in 1969, and it gained momentum in the early 1970s. The result was a basic transfer of power among House Democrats and eventually throughout the House.

The most important change modified the seniority system by making committee chairs subject to secret-ballot election by the caucus. This modification was achieved in steps and took its final form—automatic secret votes on all chairmen—in December 1974. Early in 1975 the caucus rejected three chairs, a clear signal that all chairs in the future would be held accountable to their colleagues and could not expect to exercise the absolute powers they had held when the seniority system all but guaranteed them tenure as chairs. Other chairs were unseated in 1984 and 1990. However, seniority was observed strictly when Democrats won a majority in the 110th Congress, although Speaker Pelosi confronted John D. Dingell, D-Mich., chair of the House Energy and Commerce Committee, over the global-warming issue by proposing a select committee on that subject. Pelosi also chose Silvestre Reyes, D-Texas, over two more senior members to chair the House Permanent Select Committee on Intelligence, but she was considered to have more leeway in this decision because that panel is not a permanent standing committee. The Democratic Caucus instituted other changes that helped transform the House into a more open and accountable institution. It opened many of its own meetings to the public and the media between 1975 and 1980. It limited House Democrats to one subcommittee chairmanship and guaranteed each party member a seat on a major committee. It also created a "bill of rights" for subcommittees that gave them considerable independence from committee chairs. On purely party matters it transferred the authority to make committee assignments from the Democratic members of the Ways and Means Committee to a revamped Steering and Policy Committee and placed that committee firmly under the control of the leadership.

Although the Democratic Caucus focused primarily on procedural reforms during this period, it also gave some attention to substantive issues. In 1972, for example, it forced a House vote on a nonbinding, end-the-Vietnam-War resolution. In 1975 it went on record as opposing more military aid to Indochina, and it voted to order the Rules Committee to allow a floor vote on an amendment to end the oil depletion allowance.

These forays into substantive legislation plunged the caucus into new controversy, partly because it was seen as usurping the powers of the standing committees and undermining the committee system. At least that was the argument expressed by conservative Democratic opponents of the resolutions, which were drafted and backed mainly by the party's liberal bloc. The conservatives insisted that caucus meetings, which had been closed, be opened to the public. That killed the role the caucus played as a "family council" and greatly diminished its usefulness.

Under the chairmanship of Gillis W. Long, D-La. (1980–1984), the Democratic Caucus once again closed its meetings following substantial losses in the 1980 election. This made it easier to keep party disputes within the family. Long also set up a Committee on Party Effectiveness early in 1981 to reassess the party's direction after its election losses in 1980. Members of the committee covered a spectrum of political opinion, including several rising stars such as Richard Gephardt, who succeeded Long as caucus chair. Gephardt ran for president in 1988 while holding the post. Gray, the outgoing Budget Committee chair, succeeded him at the caucus. (Rep. Shirley Chisholm of New York had been caucus secretary, a post at that time traditionally reserved for a woman, in the 1970s. The title was later changed to the more prestigious "vice chair," which, ironically, had the effect of eliminating the automatic claim to it by women members.) When Gray became whip in 1989 after Coelho resigned, the vice chair, Steny Hoyer of Maryland, was elected to fill the vacancy and was then reelected twice for full terms, ultimately holding the post for five and one-half years. When Democrats lost control of the House in 1994, the party did not hold it against Vic Fazio of California, who was both vice chair of the caucus and chair of the Democratic Congressional Campaign Committee. It elevated him to caucus chair until his retirement from the House at the beginning of 1999.

The caucus elects a variety of party leaders, including the nominee for Speaker when Democrats hold a majority. Other elected posts in the 110th Congress were the majority leader, whip, caucus chair and vice chair, and chair of the Democratic Congressional Campaign Committee, though in practice that position was filled by nomination of the Speaker. In 1999 the new position of assistant to the leader was created, to be nominated by the leader and then elected by the caucus. Its purpose was to place a woman in a visible spot, though it was held in the 110th Congress by Rep. Xavier Becerra, D-Calif., and in the 109th Congress by Rep. John Spratt, D-S.C. Those selections allowed Pelosi to give visibility to a member of the Congressional Hispanic Caucus and a conservative Democrat, respectively. The chair and vice chair of the caucus serve two full consecutive terms, the only major positions in the Democratic leadership required under the rules to rotate.

After Democrats lost their House majority in 2010, some disgruntled conservative Democrats took aim at Pelosi's practice of appointing the cochairs of the Steering and Policy Committee as well as the chair of the Democratic Congressional Campaign Committee and the top Democrat on the Rules Committee. But their efforts to hold a caucus vote on those jobs went nowhere, as did their attempt to unseat Pelosi as minority leader.

The Republican Conference

The counterpart of the Democratic Caucus, the Republican Conference, is the umbrella organization for House Republicans. The conference sets party rules and elects the leadership. In the majority, it chooses its nominee for Speaker and also elects a majority leader, whip, conference chair, vice chair, secretary, policy committee chair, and chair of the National Republican Congressional Committee. The positions are not term limited.

The conference builds party unity through retreats and other meetings of the rank and file, and it helps to identify campaign issues. The conference also produces legislative status reports and research information on issues pending before the House, coordinates use of talk radio, and provides training sessions for members and staff on efficient use of House resources.

The Republican Conference rarely served as a policy-setting body, although in the 1965–1969 period it was used occasionally to develop policy positions for consideration by the party's leadership. The conference occasionally passed resolutions stating House Republican views on particular issues. In what was widely seen as a slap at Republican president George H. W. Bush, the conference in 1990 approved a resolution opposing any new taxes. Bush had recently renounced his "no new taxes" campaign pledge in an effort to reach agreement with the Democrats on a budget deficit reduction measure.

The Republican Conference was revitalized by Gingrich and often served as the vehicle pressing the GOP leadership to implement the Contract with America and other items on its legislative agenda. There were frequent policy discussions, including votes on strategy, such as a conference majority urging continuation of the controversial government shutdown at the end of the 1995 session.

Gingrich also summoned members to conference meetings to explain votes at variance with party policy, such as what occurred when defections derailed the 1997 committee funding resolution. The most dramatic conference event of Gingrich's tenure as Speaker was a session in the summer of 1997 at which various party leaders were asked to explain their roles in an aborted coup aimed at toppling the Speaker.

Gingrich set up task forces to develop legislation, and he allowed the conference chair, John Boehner of Ohio, a major strategic role. Boehner was later accused of participating in the coup discussions, but his position in the leadership was not challenged at the time. However, he lost his job to J. C. Watts of Oklahoma, 121–93, when Republicans organized for the 106th Congress. Boehner would return to be elected majority leader in a three-way race after DeLay stepped down from the job amid legal troubles in the 109th Congress. One problem with the new Republican leadership structure after the party achieved its majority was the absence of clear lines of authority on some matters, as Gingrich experimented with different strategies and combinations of party personnel. For example, to reward Rep. Bill Paxon, R-N.Y., who had led the campaign committee successfully to achieve the majority, Gingrich in 1997 created the title of "chair of the Republican leadership" to give Paxon continuing status among the top leadership. However, several months later Paxon was forced to resign, and the new post was abolished, when his loyalty to the Speaker was questioned in the aftermath of the coup discussions. The job was revived by Hastert for Rep. Rob Portman, R-Ohio, a close ally who had not built a strong enough constituency among his colleagues to win a leadership job outright but whose relationships throughout the Republican establishment, including with President George W. Bush, made him an important strategic asset.

As both minority leader and House Speaker, Boehner gave broad latitude to the Republican Conference chairs. In both cases, those individuals had previously served as chairs of the Republican Study Committee, the caucus of the House's most conservative members, and had occasionally been in conflict with Boehner. The first was Mike Pence of Indiana, who had challenged Boehner for minority leader in 2006 and lost overwhelmingly. The second was Texas's Jeb Hensarling, a close ally of Boehner's rival Eric Cantor. Hensarling wielded extraordinary power apart from chairing the conference—in 2011 he also cochaired the Joint Select Committee on Deficit Reduction, the bipartisan twelve-member "super committee" created by the protracted impasse over raising the federal debt ceiling.

Making Committee Assignments

After the House revolt against Joseph Cannon in 1910, the power to appoint members of standing committees was taken from the Speaker and vested in the party caucuses. In 1911 the Democratic Caucus delegated the authority to choose the party's committee members to a special Committee on Committees, which was composed of all Democrats on the Ways and Means Committee.

The reforms of the 1970s also affected the committee assignment process. In 1973 the Democratic Caucus expanded the Committee on Committees to include the Speaker, who served as chair, the majority leader, and the caucus chair. In December 1974 the caucus transferred the assignment power to the Steering and Policy Committee, which is composed of the Democratic leaders and their appointees and regionally elected members. The Steering and Policy Committee's recommendations were subject to ratification by the caucus, as were those of Ways and Means, but ratification, particularly of committee chairs, was no longer perfunctory. The policy functions were later split off into another body, and the committee assignment function is now performed by the Steering Committee.

In 1917 the Republican Conference also established a Committee on Committees, which traditionally is chaired by the GOP House leader. Committee chairmanships when in the majority, or ranking minority positions otherwise, as well as committee assignments, are subject to approval by the conference. In 1989 Republicans gave their minority leader the same authority to appoint the GOP members of the Rules Committee that Democratic Speakers had obtained for their Rules members in 1974. When Republicans took control of the House in 1995, the Committee on Committees was called the Steering Committee and was chaired by Speaker Gingrich.

Speakers often have exercised great influence on committee assignments, even when they were not on the panel making the choices. In the late 1920s, for example, Speaker Longworth had four uncooperative members of the Rules Committee replaced with his own choices. In the 1940s and 1950s Speaker Rayburn intervened frequently to influence the makeup of the Ways and Means Committee, which he insisted be stacked with members opposed to reductions in the oil and gas depletion allowance. Speaker Gingrich made sure that members of the aggressive and conservative 1995 freshman class received assignments to the most important committees, both to cement their loyalty and spread their activism.

Policy and Strategy Committees

During the twentieth century both parties established groups called steering committees to assist the leadership with legislative scheduling and party strategy (not to be confused with the entities with similar names in the 1990s that now handle only committee assignments). The Republican Steering Committee, established in 1919, dominated the business of the House until 1925, when power again shifted to the Speaker. Speaker Longworth largely ignored the Steering Committee. In 1949 the committee was expanded and renamed the Policy Committee. The Policy Committee was considered the chief advisory board for the minority leader from 1959 to 1965, when it was replaced in the role by the Republican Conference. In its role after the Republicans assumed majority status in 1995, the Policy Committee issues and disseminates policy statements on matters of concern to the conference, considers policy resolutions, writes reports, and conducts policy forums. It helps develop the legislative agenda for House Republicans.

Democrats established a Steering Committee in 1933, abandoned it in 1956, and reconstituted it in 1962. Its duties and role in the party structure were vague. In 1973 the Democratic Caucus voted to create a new Steering and Policy Committee to give coherence and direction to the party's legislative strategy. In 1974 the caucus gave the new Steering and Policy Committee the authority to make Democratic committee assignments, removing that power from the Democratic members of the Ways and Means Committee.

However, this and other periodic efforts by Democrats in later years to create a separate leadership entity to deal with policy floundered on opposition from both party leaders, who thought a new structure hampered their flexibility, and committee chairs, who did not want a potential rival intruding on their turf.

The size of the Steering and Policy Committee expanded over time as members of the leadership were added to the panel. The Speaker was also given the right to make additional appointments of members of his choice, the number of which also increased. The caucus membership at large could seek elective seats from geographic regions.

In 1992 the caucus created a Speaker's Working Group on Policy Development to satisfy demands for a separate, smaller entity to deal with policy matters, because the Steering and Policy Committee focused on little besides committee assignments and that was the reason members sought to be on it. Speaker Foley promptly expanded the size of the working group, which made the new entity unwieldy, and it exercised little influence. After becoming the minority in 1995, Democrats created a new, separate Policy Committee.

The Democratic Study Group (DSG), created in 1959, functioned as the primary source of research on legislative issues for the Democrats and exercised considerable influence, particularly during the height of the reform period. It was one of many legislative service organizations (LSOs) that hired staff and used office space in the House funded by members from their office allowances. DSG's legislative reports, which explained the content of bills, and its more political special reports that often had a partisan slant were widely read even by Republicans. But the DSG and similar entities were effectively abolished in 1995 when the new Republican majority eliminated LSOs and the ability of members to pool resources. This action damaged the Democrats' ability to gather and coordinate legislative information and weakened the party's ability to compete effectively with the Republican Conference, which published similar legislative materials for its own party members. DSG's staffers were subsequently hired by *Congressional Quarterly* to put out nonpartisan legislative analyses called *House Action Reports,* and the publication is still in circulation today.

LEADERSHIP IN THE SENATE: "WE KNOW NO MASTERS"

Sen. Daniel Webster in 1830 described the upper chamber as a "Senate of equals, of men of individual honor and personal character, and of absolute independence. We know no masters, we acknowledge no dictators."[64] At the time and for several decades thereafter, the Senate had no structured leadership apparatus. Not until the early twentieth century did either party formally designate a leader to oversee and guide its interests in the Senate. Now both parties name a leader, an assistant leader, and others who head party committees that help them formulate policy and strategy and win reelection. The degree to which senators follow or stray from the party line depends on a variety of factors, including shift in institutional power, the personal political power of the party leader, and the tools the caucus gives the leader to bind senators to the party.

But Webster's words still hold true. The Senate is essentially a collection of individuals, each of whom is a leader in his or her own sphere. The independence of each senator is further ensured by Senate rules, which protect the rights of the minority against the will of the majority. As Ripley has observed, Senate floor leaders are not "automatically invested with a specific quota of power; they still must create much of their own."[65] Effective leadership in the Senate, even more than in the House, thus depends on the leaders' personal and negotiating skills.

Evolution of Senate Leadership

As with the House, the Constitution did not offer much direction about Senate leadership. Its two references to leadership posts and responsibilities in the Senate (Article I, Section 3) stipulate that the vice president shall be president of the Senate and that the Senate shall choose a president pro tempore to preside in the vice president's absence. Neither of these offices has ever been an effective leadership position.

Thus legislative leadership was left to individual senators. Here, as in the House, Alexander Hamilton acted much like a stage manager, controlling floor action through his many friends in the chamber. Jefferson and his Treasury secretary, Albert Gallatin, exercised as much control over the Senate as they did over the House. Jefferson, wrote Thomas Pickering of Massachusetts, tries "to screen himself from all responsibility by calling upon Congress for advice and direction. . . . Yet with affected modesty and deference he secretly dictates every measure which is seriously proposed."[66]

The first significant move toward party organization did not occur until 1846, when the parties began to nominate members of the standing committees. Until 1823 the Senate had chosen committee members by ballot. That year the Senate turned over the appointment process to the presiding officer. Initially this officer was the president pro tempore, but in 1825–1827 Vice President John C. Calhoun assumed the power. Hostile to the administration of John Quincy Adams, he used the power to place supporters of Andrew Jackson in key positions. In 1828 the Senate amended its rules to return the appointment power to the president pro tem, who was selected by the Senate itself. In 1833 the Senate reverted to selection by ballot.

By this time the seniority system had begun to develop, and chairmanships of Senate committees rotated less than they had in the past. Parties began to control assignments, committees began to divide along ideological lines, and minority reports began to appear. By 1846 the routine was formalized. When the second session of the 29th Congress met in December, the Senate began balloting for committee chairs. Midway through the process the balloting rule was suspended, and on a single ballot the Senate accepted the list of committee assignments that had already been agreed upon by the majority and minority. For the most part, that routine has been followed since.

Immediately before and during the Civil War, party authority extended to substantive as well as organizational matters. In 1858, for example, the Democratic Caucus removed Stephen A. Douglas as chair of the Committee on Territories, despite his seniority, because he had refused to go along with President James Buchanan and the southern wing of the party on the question of allowing slavery in the territories.

With the end of the Civil War, however, party influence on substantive matters declined. By the time Ulysses S. Grant entered the White House in 1869, political parties required unity only on organizational matters. Disputes over committee assignments were settled in the party caucuses, and pressing issues were discussed there, but senators could not be bound by a vote of the majority of their caucus. "I am a senator of the United States," Charles Sumner, R-Mass., once declared. "My obligations as a senator were above any vote in a caucus."[67]

Beginning in the 1870s, Republicans sought to strengthen party control of the Senate by appointing a caucus chair, who was considered to be the party's floor leader, and setting up a Committee on Committees to recommend committee assignments to the caucus and then to the full Senate. But the power of the caucus chair, then Henry Anthony, R-R.I., was overshadowed by a Republican faction led by Roscoe Conkling of New York that held sway for roughly ten years. Though the faction generally controlled the Committee on Committees, it never controlled the Senate's proceedings. Eventually in the early 1880s, it dissolved as a consequence of a series of unsuccessful feuds with Republican presidents over patronage in New York state.

Emergence of Republican Leaders

The emergence of another Republican faction in the 1890s led to establishment of a permanent leadership organization in the Senate. The leader of this faction was Nelson W. Aldrich of Rhode Island, who worked in close alliance with William B. Allison of Iowa, Orville H. Platt of Connecticut, and John C. Spooner of Wisconsin. Aldrich had, in the words of one historian, "made himself indispensable to the party organization [in the Senate], rising step by step as the elders passed out, until in the end he made himself the dictator of the cabal which for a time was the master of the government."[68] Already an influence in the Senate, this group took complete control after Allison, as the member with the longest period of Senate service, was elected chair of the Republican Caucus in March 1897.

Previous caucus chairs had not seen the office as a vehicle for consolidating party authority, an oversight that Allison and Aldrich were quick to correct. Since the mid-1870s the Republicans had appointed a Steering Committee to help schedule legislative business. Unlike previous caucus chairs, Allison assumed the chair of this committee and filled it with his allies. For the first time a party organization arranged the order of business in minute detail and managed proceedings on the Senate floor.

Allison also controlled the Committee on Committees. By this time committee chairmanships were filled through seniority, and Allison and Aldrich made no attempt to overturn this practice (to which they owed their committee chairmanships—Allison of Appropriations, Aldrich of Finance). But seniority did not apply to filling committee vacancies, and here the two found an opportunity to reward their supporters and punish their opponents. "Realizing the potentialities for control in the chamber," wrote historian David J. Rothman, Allison and Aldrich "entrenched and tightened personal leadership and party discipline. Their example would not always be emulated. . . . Nevertheless, they institutionalized, once and for all, the prerogatives of power. Would-be successors or Senate rivals would now be forced to capture and effectively utilize the party post."[69]

Like Speaker Joseph Cannon, who dominated the House for much of the same period, Allison and Aldrich were largely successful in imposing their conservative political views upon the chamber. Defeats were rare until President Theodore Roosevelt was able to push a part of his legislative program through Congress. The group retained much of its power even after Allison's death in 1908. Though Allison had held the formal positions of power, Aldrich exercised power through the sheer force of his personality. He was considered by many to be the most powerful man in the Senate. But as the number of Republican insurgents in the Senate increased, the once all-powerful group began to weaken, and it quickly disintegrated after Aldrich retired in 1911.

Emergence of Democratic Leaders

A centralized Democratic organization in the Senate developed in the same period. Under the leadership of Arthur P. Gorman of Maryland, who served as chair of the Democratic Caucus from 1889 to 1899, the Democratic power structure was similar to that put together by Allison and Aldrich. Gorman consolidated his power by assuming all of the party's top leadership posts himself, including floor leader and the chairmanship of both the Steering Committee and the Committee on Committees. He further solidified his control by appointing his political allies to positions of influence.

Historian Rothman has concluded that the Democratic Party structure under Gorman may have been more conducive than the Republican structure to the emergence of an effective and energetic leadership. Rothman notes that Gorman was elected chair of the caucus not on the basis of seniority, but because of his standing among his colleagues. And Gorman eventually came to appoint the same group of men to the Steering Committee and the Committee on Committees, concentrating power over the party organization in a relatively small number of Democrats. For all but two of his ten years as caucus chair, however, Senate Democrats were in the minority, and they were often badly divided on substantive issues. As a result Gorman never attained the same degree of power and authority as the Allison-Aldrich team.

Early Effective Leaders

Few of the Senate leaders in the twentieth century were particularly effective. One of the stronger leaders was Democrat John W. Kern of Indiana, whose election as caucus chair in 1913, after only two years in the Senate, was engineered by progressive Democrats after they first deposed conservative Thomas S. Martin of Virginia. The Democratic Steering Committee, appointed by Kern and dominated by the progressives, assigned members sympathetic to President Woodrow Wilson's programs to key committees. (See "Senate Floor Leaders, 1911–2012," p. 233.)

Kern worked hard to push Wilson's progressive program through the Senate, achieving passage of a steep reduction in import duties and imposition of the first income tax under the Sixteenth Amendment, establishment of the Federal Reserve and the Federal Trade Commission, and enactment of antitrust laws, among others. Kern served as leader for only four years (he was defeated for reelection to the Senate in 1916). Yet until the 1950s few other floor leaders of either party attained the effectiveness he had achieved.

President Franklin D. Roosevelt was fortunate in having Joseph T. Robinson of Arkansas as the Senate majority leader from 1933 to 1937. Robinson revived the Democratic Caucus and won agreement from Senate Democrats to make caucus decisions on administration bills binding by majority vote. There is no evidence that Robinson ever made use of the binding rule, but nonbinding caucuses were frequently held to mobilize support. In his four years as majority leader, Robinson pushed through the Senate most of the president's controversial New Deal legislative program, including measures he personally opposed.

Alben W. Barkley of Kentucky, who was elected majority leader after Robinson died of a heart attack in 1937, was also influential with his colleagues, but, like a growing number of Senate Democrats, he did not always support Roosevelt on domestic issues. In 1944 Barkley resigned his leadership post when Roosevelt vetoed a revenue bill. He was promptly reelected by the Democrats, and the bill was passed over the president's veto.

The Johnson Years

In the decades immediately after World War II two Republicans were widely acclaimed as effective Senate leaders.

In this 1968 photo, Senate Majority Leader Mike Mansfield, D-Mt. (left), speaks with President Lyndon B. Johnson at the White House. Johnson himself was considered the most effective Senate majority leader ever. The Texas Democrat was famous for his ability to persuade and sometimes traded favors in an effort to achieve his goals.

SOURCE: LBJ Library photo by Frank Wolfe.

"Mr. Republican," Robert A. Taft of Ohio, was the majority leader for only a few months before he died in 1953, but he had been the de facto Republican power in the Senate since the early 1940s, just as Richard B. Russell of Georgia was the real leader of the Senate Democrats. Everett McKinley Dirksen of Illinois, known as the "wizard of ooze" for his florid style, was one of the more colorful personalities to grace the modern Senate. A conservative, he served as minority leader from 1959 until his death in 1969.

Taft and Dirksen employed two different styles—Taft won unity through his intellectual command of the issues; Dirksen won it through negotiation and compromise. Both men centralized the Republican leadership apparatus, controlling the formulation of Republican policy in the Senate and taking an active part in scheduling and setting floor strategy.

Taft and Dirksen may have had great influence among their Republican colleagues, but their leadership talents were eclipsed by those of Lyndon B. Johnson. Johnson, wrote political scientist John G. Stewart, "set for himself no less an objective than *running* the Senate, in fact as well as in

theory."[70] Elected minority leader by the Democrats in 1953 after only four years in the Senate, Johnson became majority leader when the Democrats regained control of the Senate after the 1954 elections and served in that position until his resignation to become John F. Kennedy's vice president in 1961.

As a leader Johnson quickly became famous—some would say notorious—for his power of persuasion and his manipulative skills. Johnson was adroit at doing favors for and extending courtesies to his colleagues, their families, and staffs, at maneuvering his supporters onto desired committees and keeping his opponents off. He revitalized the Senate Democratic Policy Committee and modified the seniority system to ensure freshman Democrats at least one major committee assignment, a practice the Republicans also eventually adopted. On the floor he exploited to the fullest the majority leader's right of first recognition by the chair to control what was debated and under what terms. He was the first majority leader to make extensive use of unanimous consent agreements to control debate on legislation. He also used night sessions to wear down senators who might, if

THE SENATE'S PRESIDING OFFICERS

The only two Senate leaders mentioned in the U.S. Constitution have little effective leadership power. Article I, Section 3 provides that the vice president "shall be President of the Senate, but shall have no vote, unless they be equally divided." It also provides that the "Senate shall choose … a President pro tempore, in the absence of the Vice President, or when he shall exercise the office of President of the United States." The Constitution also provides that the chief justice of the United States will preside during an impeachment trial of a president. This has occurred only twice, in 1868 in proceedings against President Andrew Johnson and in 1999 in the impeachment trial of President Bill Clinton.

DUTIES OF THE PRESIDING OFFICER

As presiding officer, the principal function of the vice president and the president pro tem is to recognize senators, but this is rarely significant because Senate rules usually require the presiding officer to recognize the senator who first seeks recognition. The presiding officer also decides points of order, subject to appeal to the full Senate; appoints senators to House-Senate conference committees (although it is customary for the presiding officer to take the recommendations of the floor manager of the bill in question); enforces decorum; administers oaths; and appoints members to special committees. The president pro tem may appoint a substitute to replace him in the chair; the vice president may not.

As a senator, the president pro tem may vote on all matters. The vice president may vote only if the Senate is evenly divided on a question, as stipulated by the Constitution, and then only if he is available and chooses to participate.

Such votes may be widely separated in time. Between 1945 and March 2008, when thirteen different vice presidents served, only forty-three such votes were cast. Of these, Vice President Richard B. Cheney, R-Wyo., cast eight votes. Four other modern vice presidents, Lyndon B. Johnson, D-Texas (1961–1963), Gerald R. Ford, R-Mich. (1973–1974), Nelson A. Rockefeller, R-N.Y. (1974–1977), and Dan Quayle, R-Ind. (1989–1993), did not cast any. As of September 2011, Vice President Joe Biden, D-Del., had not cast any tie-breaking votes.

THE VICE PRESIDENT AS PRESIDING OFFICER

It is little wonder that the Senate has not placed any real power with the vice president, who is not chosen by the Senate, may not be a member of the majority party in the chamber, and may not be sympathetic with the aims of its majority. Precedent was established by John Adams, who, although in agreement with the majority of the Senate during his terms as vice president (1789–1797), perceived his role simply as that of presiding officer and made little effort to guide Senate action. His successor, Thomas Jefferson (1797–1801), could not have steered the Federalist-controlled Senate even if he had wanted to.

A few vice presidents have attempted to use their position as presiding officer to achieve a partisan purpose, with varying degrees of success. John C. Calhoun, vice president to John Quincy Adams, was hostile to the Adams administration. Taking advantage of an 1823 rule change giving the presiding officer the right to appoint committee members, Calhoun placed supporters of Andrew Jackson on key committees. But he refused to use the authority exercised by earlier vice presidents to call senators to order for words used in debate.

Nelson A. Rockefeller, vice president to Gerald R. Ford, once used his authority to refuse to recognize a senator who wanted to filibuster a Ford administration bill. Senators from both parties were incensed at Rockefeller's action and made it clear that the president's program would suffer if Rockefeller did not desist.

Most vice presidents preside only upon ceremonial occasions or when a close vote on a bill or amendment of interest to the administration is likely to occur. But as president of the Senate, the vice president is well positioned to lobby on behalf of the president's program. Walter F. Mondale, D-Minn., who left his Senate seat to become Jimmy Carter's vice president, proved to be an effective spokesperson for the White House on numerous occasions and tried to fill part of the gap caused by Carter's lack of experience in Washington, D.C., and the absence of any long-standing political or personal relationships with congressional leaders. Vice President Al Gore wielded even more influence during the Clinton administration, exercising significant power over federal appointments and several key areas of

---

fresher, choose to engage in extensive floor debate. Perhaps most important, Johnson kept himself informed about the views and positions of his Senate colleagues through an active intelligence operation headed by Robert G. "Bobby" Baker, secretary to the Senate Democrats.

Johnson, whose entire tenure as both minority and majority leader was spent with Republican president Dwight D. Eisenhower in the White House, was also a master of compromise. He made sure to have allies among conservative southern Democrats and Republicans as well as among northern liberals. Like his mentor, House Speaker Sam Rayburn, Johnson worked to pass those elements of Eisenhower's legislative program that did not challenge basic tenets of Roosevelt's New Deal or Harry S. Truman's Fair Deal. As a result Johnson presided over some of the most productive years in Senate history.

The future president was renowned for what came to be known as the "Johnson Treatment," a tactic he carried with him into the White House. Rowland Evans and Robert Novak gave a vivid description in their book, *Lyndon B. Johnson: The Exercise of Power:*

> The Treatment could last ten minutes or four hours. It came, enveloping its target, at the LBJ Ranch swimming pool, in one of LBJ's offices, in the Senate cloakroom, on the floor of the Senate itself—wherever Johnson might find a fellow senator within his reach. Its tone could be supplication, accusation, cajolery, exuberance, scorn, tears, complaint, the hint of threat. It was all of these together. It ran the gamut of human emotions. Its velocity was breathtaking, and it was all in one direction.[71]

Johnson's effectiveness lost some of its edge after the 1958 elections added substantially to the Democrats' majority in the Senate. Members began to lose patience with Johnson's intensity. As one observer said, "After eight years of Lyndon Johnson, a lot of senators were just worn out."[72] An influx of liberal Democrats rejected the long-standing notion that junior senators were to be seen and not heard, and they

government policy, most notably on government reorganization, technology, and the environment. Richard B. Cheney, under George W. Bush, expanded the vice presidency's powers even further, particularly on national security matters after the September 11, 2011, terrorist attacks.

THE PRESIDENT PRO TEMPORE

The first president pro tempore, John Langdon of New Hampshire, was elected on April 6, 1789, before John Adams appeared in the Senate to assume his duties as presiding officer. When the first vice president took his seat on April 21, Langdon's service as president pro tem ended. For the next one hundred years, the Senate acted on the theory that a president pro tempore could be elected only in the vice president's absence and that his term expired when the vice president returned. (Unlike modern practice, the vice president frequently presided over the Senate in the nineteenth century.) By 1890 the Senate had elected presidents pro tempore on 153 occasions. In the 42nd Congress alone (1871–1873), ten such elections, all of the same senator, were held.

In 1890 the Senate gave the president pro tem tenure of a sort by adopting a resolution stating that "it is competent for the Senate to elect a president pro tempore, who shall hold the office during the pleasure of the Senate and until another is elected, and shall execute the duties thereof during all future absences of the vice president" until the Senate otherwise orders. That practice was still in use in 2011.

By law, the president pro tem is third in line, behind the vice president and the Speaker of the House of Representatives, to succeed to the presidency. Like the Speaker, he is a member of the majority party, and his election, if contested, is usually by a straight party-line vote. By custom the most senior member of the majority party in terms of Senate service is elected president pro tem. Only one of those elected since 1945 did not follow this pattern: Arthur H. Vandenberg, R-Mich., was the second-ranking Republican when elected in 1947.

Before 1945 there were some notable exceptions to the custom. George H. Moses, R-N.H., ranked only fifteenth in party seniority when he was elected president pro tem in 1925, and Willard Saulsbury, D-Del., was still in his first term when elected to the post in 1916.

Strom Thurmond, of South Carolina, who switched to the GOP in 1964, was considered the most senior Republican when he was elected president pro tem in 1981 even though John Tower of Texas had served longer as a Republican. Thurmond, a former Democratic governor, began his Senate service in 1955 after winning election as a write-in candidate, the only senator ever to do so. He resigned the following year and was absent from the Senate for most of 1956 to run again, and win, as a Democrat. When Thurmond became a Republican in 1964, the Republican Conference agreed to base his seniority on the date he entered the Senate, not the date he switched parties. Thurmond resumed the president pro tempore post when Republicans regained Senate control in 1995.

Few presidents pro tem in the twentieth century had much influence on the Senate. One who did was Vandenberg, who was also chair of the Foreign Relations Committee. Vandenberg "no doubt exerted as much influence in what was done and not done as the Speaker of the House," Floyd M. Riddick, who would later become Senate parliamentarian, wrote in 1949.[1] When Robert C. Byrd of West Virginia became president pro tempore (1989–1995, 2001–2003, 2007–2010), he liked to preside over complicated procedural situations. As chair of the Appropriations Committee and a former majority and minority leader, Byrd brought far more stature to the position than could accrue simply through seniority. Succeeding Byrd in the job in the 111th and 112th Congresses was Hawaii Democrat Daniel K. Inouye, who continued the low-key presence he had established as a veteran member of the Appropriations Committee.

1   Floyd M. Riddick, *The United States Congress: Organization and Procedure* (Washington, D.C.: National Capitol Publishing, 1949), 67.

began to chafe under Johnson's centralized leadership. In response Johnson added more caucus meetings and named some freshmen Democrats to the Policy Committee. But calls from younger liberal members for greater inclusion in party matters continued to build.

By all accounts, Johnson was the most effective leader the Senate had ever seen, if not always the most liked. ("I know he comes off with high marks for getting things done, but he was repugnant to me," one senator recalled.[73]) Like the strong leaders before him, he derived his power primarily from his own force of personality, aided by his skill at finding out what his colleagues needed. As one observer put it, Johnson "worked at being better informed than anyone else, and that information then made him better equipped than anyone else to broker many agreements."[74]

The Age of Collegiality

Meanwhile, other factors were changing the Senate substantially. Between the 1950s and the mid-1970s, southern domination and the seniority system gave way to a more decentralized, more democratic institution, in which junior members played a greater role. Party leaders on both sides of the aisle eschewed the arm-twisting tactics that Johnson used so effectively and engaged in a more collegial style of leadership, dependent for its success not on the leader's ability to bend the Senate to his will but on his ability to meet the expectations of his colleagues and to facilitate the conduct of Senate business.

Johnson's successor, Mike Mansfield, D-Mont., could not have provided a greater contrast in leadership styles. Known as the "gentle persuader," Mansfield, who served longer than any other majority leader in Senate history (1961–1977), was a permissive, at times even passive, leader. "I rarely asked for votes on specific legislation," Mansfield told political scientist Robert L. Peabody in 1972. "I assumed that these people are mature, that they have been sent back here by their constituents to exercise their own judgment."[75]

LEADERSHIP FIRSTS

From the very first, when Oliver Ellsworth of Connecticut exercised "more practical leadership in the day-to-day activities" of the Senate, the upper chamber has had unofficial leaders. But congressional scholars disagree as to who were the first official Senate floor leaders.

Some scholars, among them Randall B. Ripley, hold that the position of floor leader emerged around 1911. The chairs of the Democratic Caucus—Thomas S. Martin of Virginia from 1911 to 1913 and John W. Kern of Indiana from 1913 to 1917—were clearly the party's leaders in the Senate, although it is unclear that the term "floor leader" was formally applied to either man.

In a 1988 pamphlet on the origins of Senate leadership, Senate parliamentarian emeritus Floyd M. Riddick wrote that neither party's caucus minutes used the term "leader" until 1920, when the Democratic minutes referred to Oscar W. Underwood, D-Ala., as "minority leader." (Underwood had also served two terms as majority leader in the House before being elected to the Senate.) According to Republican Caucus minutes, the first GOP Senate floor leader was Charles Curtis of Kansas (1924).

SOURCE: Walter J. Oleszek, "John Worth Kern," in *First among Equals*, eds. Richard A. Baker and Roger H. Davidson (Washington, D.C.: CQ Press, 1991), 9–10.

Though Mansfield was criticized for not being sufficiently partisan and for sometimes failing to provide direction, he was working with a larger, more liberal, and less cohesive group of Senate Democrats than Johnson had led. As congressional scholar Roger H. Davidson noted, "Most senators flourished under Mansfield's regime, for its very looseness gave them the leeway they needed to pursue their increasingly diverse legislative and career goals."[76]

When Mansfield retired from the Senate at the end of 1976, Democrats chose Robert Byrd of West Virginia as his successor for the first of two cycles as majority leader (1977–1981; 1987–1989). Byrd had been whip from 1971 to 1977, taking the post on a dramatic secret ballot away from Edward M. Kennedy, D-Mass., who had been distracted by the consequences of a 1969 accident at Chappaquiddick in Massachusetts, which resulted in the death of a passenger in a car driven by the senator. Byrd was in many ways an old-style Senate personality, but he had to contend with a rapidly changing body that was more partisan, less patient, and with younger and more independent colleagues even more willing to employ the Senate's rules to press their interests and less susceptible than ever to party discipline. More significant, Byrd had to survive and adapt a leadership style to a Senate no longer with a firm Democratic majority, as the Republican Party took control from 1981 to 1987 and relegated him to minority leader.

While other senators built their careers on national issues and oratorical flair, Byrd was the quintessential insider, working quietly and diligently to build support through a combination of service to his colleagues and knowledge of Senate rules and procedures, skills he honed to near perfection during his six years as Democratic whip. As majority leader he so disadvantaged his opponents through the artful use of his parliamentary talents that the Republicans later hired the parliamentarian Byrd had fired, Robert B. Dove, to improve their procedural strategies. (Dove became Senate parliamentarian again in 1995.)

A more activist leader than Mansfield, Byrd emphasized the need for strong party loyalty and said he wanted to bring about a resurgence of party spirit. He did not see his role as forcing an unpopular measure on his colleagues, who probably would not have accepted such a role in any event, but as trying to find consensus. Byrd tended to go to his colleagues with only the hint of an objective. If a consensus could be found that would attract the necessary number of votes, he would take the bill under his wing. "I talk to senators, I have meetings with senators, I try to stimulate a consensus for a party position on issues where one is necessary," he explained.[77] Byrd had an uneasy relationship with President Carter, who came to the White House in 1977, the year Byrd became majority leader. Byrd seemed to regard Carter as an amateur with little aptitude for the exercise of power. Nonetheless, he repeatedly saved the Democratic administration in difficult legislative situations. Byrd played an indispensable role in the passage of Carter's energy policy package and in the extension of the deadline for ratification of the Equal Rights Amendment, among other matters. Perhaps his most dramatic rescue operation came in 1978, when he amassed enough votes to ratify the Panama Canal treaties—giving canal ownership to Panama—through nonstop negotiation with wavering senators, personal diplomacy with Panamanian officials, and last-minute language changes.

Despite his obvious love and respect for the Senate, Byrd was a private man, withdrawn from his colleagues. A former aide once noted that "Byrd was most comfortable in a room by himself."[78] His inability to develop a personal rapport with fellow senators, combined with his emphasis on Senate procedures and prerogatives, meant that, though he was respected, Byrd was regarded by some as more of a technician than a leader. Dissatisfaction grew louder after the 1980 elections, when Republicans took control of the Senate and Byrd was relegated to what for him was the uncomfortable role of minority leader.

Byrd worked hard to reunite the party, scheduling weekly luncheon meetings of the Democratic Caucus, which had rarely met during the Carter years, and holding a series of weekend retreats in West Virginia where Democratic senators could work through many of their disagreements. He also set up several task forces to propose Democratic alternatives to President Reagan's legislative proposals.

But perceptions lingered that Byrd was too stilted and old-fashioned to be the Senate Democrats' national spokesperson in the age of television. After the 1984 elections Lawton Chiles of Florida challenged Byrd for the leadership post but lost, 36–11. Never before had anyone challenged an incumbent Democratic leader in the Senate, and it was a sign of simmering discontent that Chiles, a cautious, moderate-to-conservative figure, had chosen to undertake it. J. Bennett Johnston of Louisiana spent much of 1986 preparing to challenge Byrd, but when the Democrats regained control of the Senate, and by a much wider margin than had been expected, he quietly dropped his plans.

In his second tour as majority leader Byrd played the partisan spokesperson that his party seemed to want, rallying the Democrats behind an ambitious legislative agenda meant to show that the Democrats could govern. But criticisms of his leadership style and his media image continued, and in the spring of 1988 Byrd announced that he would retire from the leadership post at the end of the year to take up the chairmanship of the Senate Appropriations Committee and to become president pro tempore, where he was more active than previous occupants, sometimes choosing to preside over complex parliamentary situations in which his knowledge of Senate rules was especially valuable. And on the Appropriations Committee, Byrd was in an even better position to direct billions of dollars to his home state. Even in the minority after 1994, Byrd remained an aggressive institutionalist, leading opposition to the enactment of the line-item veto in 1996 and challenging it in the U.S. Supreme Court. He was ultimately vindicated in 1998 when the Court, in a case brought by other persons, declared the law unconstitutional. In the twenty-first century, the one-time proponent of escalation during the Vietnam War became an unlikely hero to liberal antiwar activists with powerful denunciations of President George W. Bush's decision to go to war in Iraq. *(See box, Line-Item Veto Experiment Ended by Supreme Court, p. 130.)*

The Modern Leadership: Mitchell

The winner in a three-way race to succeed Byrd as majority leader was George J. Mitchell of Maine, unsuccessful Democratic nominee for Maine governor in 1974 and former federal judge. Mitchell was appointed to the Senate to fill the vacancy caused in 1980 by President Carter's appointment of Sen. Edmund Muskie as secretary of state and did not have to run for election in that year. He quickly caught the notice of his colleagues with his keen memory for detail and his command of facts, particularly on environmental issues. Mitchell further impressed his fellow senators with his political skills when he came from thirty-six points behind to win election to a full term in 1982 with 61 percent of the vote.

Chosen to chair the Democratic Senatorial Campaign Committee for the critical 1986 elections, Mitchell was instrumental in helping the party regain control of the Senate with a wider-than-expected margin. As a reward he was made deputy president pro tempore, a post created for Hubert H. Humphrey, D-Minn., in 1977 and not occupied since. Appointed in 1986 to the joint committee investigating the Iran-contra scandal, the secret sale of U.S. arms to Iran and diversion of some of the profits to "contra" rebel forces in Nicaragua, Mitchell proved himself to be an able performer before national television cameras, a factor considered crucial to his election as majority leader over Bennett Johnston of Louisiana and Daniel K. Inouye of Hawaii.

Mitchell's background left him flexible enough for a variety of tasks awaiting the leader of a rapidly changing body that had just endured two shifts of partisan control. "The role of party leaders has changed so that . . . they have become conciliators who must set broad goals and then prepare themselves for incremental progress that may yield both policy change and eventual political support," *National Journal* reporter Richard E. Cohen has written.[79]

In his first year in the position, Mitchell won high marks for his legislative savvy and administration of the Senate. Early in 1990 he demonstrated the effectiveness of negotiation and persistence, working out a comprehensive compromise with the White House on a clean air bill when it became clear that the committee version could not overcome a filibuster and then fighting to protect the compromise from major amendment. The bill was assembled over a month of extraordinary closed-door meetings just off the Senate floor run by Mitchell, who assembled key senators and administration representatives to thrash out details for a package that could be protected by a bipartisan majority coalition. Mitchell attributed his victory on the floor to direct, personal, face-to-face talks with his colleagues, urging them to stick with the compromise or see the entire bill collapse under the weight of controversial amendments. Mitchell also cemented his leadership by successfully staring down his predecessor, Byrd, whose efforts to protect coal miners threatened to unravel the bill. Byrd's key floor amendment was defeated by a single vote.

Republicans considered Mitchell partisan, but his judicial demeanor often served to mask that aspect of his leadership. His more matter-of-fact debate style was a far cry from the sometimes emotional, florid performances of Johnson, Dirksen, and Byrd. Nonetheless, Mitchell often found the Senate as frustrating as they had. His announcement that he would not seek reelection in 1994 shocked colleagues. He quickly became the front-runner for a vacancy on the Supreme Court in that year, but Mitchell issued a statement asking that he not be considered and noting the importance of his presence as majority leader in trying (ultimately unsuccessfully) to push health care legislation through the Senate.

The contest to succeed Mitchell as Democratic leader began as a contest between younger senators close to

Sen. Tom Daschle, D-S.D., served as the Senate's Democratic leader from 1995 until his reelection defeat in 2004. He was later Obama's first nomination for Secretary of Health and Human Services, but withdrew due to ethical concerns including tax delinquencies. He speaks before the Senate Democratic Caucus luncheon in October 2002.

SOURCE: Scott J. Ferrell, Congressional Quarterly.

Mitchell and more senior traditionalists, although like any struggle by secret ballot in a highly personalized body the alliances did not always follow obvious or expected patterns. Mitchell's mantle fell on Sen. Tom Daschle of South Dakota, elected in 1986, who had been made cochair of the Policy Committee. Because the original senior contender for majority leader, Budget Committee Chair Jim Sasser of Tennessee, appeared a likely loser in his reelection race, his supporters switched quickly to Christopher Dodd of Connecticut. When the Democrats lost control of the Senate in the 1994 elections, the battle became one over who would become minority leader. Dodd, elected in 1980, had substantial seniority over Daschle. But he lost to Daschle by one vote, 24–23, indicating, as did Mitchell's election, that senators had different criteria than seniority in mind in choosing leaders.

Daschle had served in the House and was attuned to the needs of a media-conscious Senate to develop a united party message. From 1995 to 1999, Daschle enjoyed considerable success as Senate minority leader. Although his Democratic colleagues in the Senate were further reduced to forty-five for

the 105th and 106th Congresses—which was also the party's low point in strength during the 1980s—Daschle was able to keep the Democrats together during many cloture votes. But Daschle's adroit command of Democrats in Washington made him vulnerable back home in South Dakota, where he was accused of having abandoned his constituents' values in favor of the national Democratic Party's. He lost his 2004 reelection race, suffering the first election defeat for a Senate party leader in fifty-two years, losing to former representative John Thune. He was replaced as minority leader by then Democratic whip Harry Reid of Nevada.

Reid: The Return of the Insider

Reid became leader as the quintessential Senate insider. A moderate Democrat from a swing state, he built his constituency within the chamber as a backroom deal-cutter on the Appropriations Committee and spent long hours on the floor developing a keen sense of parliamentary procedure. He lacked the charisma of some party leaders but was trusted as an institutionalist by both Democrats and Republicans. As minority leader, and as Democratic whip before that, Reid proved himself capable of building consensus among his colleagues and counting votes. He used Senate rules and a largely unified caucus to thwart much of the GOP's legislative agenda in the 109th Congress.

But some Democrats cringed a little bit when Reid, who is prone to outbursts, became the public face of the majority party. He called the president a "loser" in May 2005 when Bush was overseas, abrogating a long-standing tradition that lawmakers do not speak ill of the president when he is abroad. In 2007 he declared that the Iraq War "is lost," going farther than many Democrats preferred. He was also dogged by ethical questions. He was forced to amend Senate financial disclosure forms to report a previously undisclosed $700,000 profit on a land deal with a friend in 1998.

A former amateur boxer, Reid seldom backs down from a fight. Eric Herzik, a University of Nevada political scientist and longtime Reid watcher, said, "He likes to say he'd rather dance than fight, but a lot of people have gotten bruised dancing with him."[80] Though he initially had a solid working relationship with Minority Leader Mitch McConnell, R-Ky., a fellow appropriator, the two men often scrapped over what Reid saw as the GOP's reflexive obstructionism. The two men did manage to work out an agreement on rules changes at the outset of the 112th Congress as a response to several Democratic proposals to dramatically curtail the use of filibusters. Their changes included an end to secret legislative "holds," a reduction in the number of presidential nominations subject to the lengthy Senate confirmation process, an end to mandatory readings for amendments if they have been publicly available for at least three days, an agreement by Republicans to limit filibusters of motions to begin debate, and an agreement by Democrats to limit instances in which they limit the number of amendments Republicans can put to a given piece of legislation, a procedural practice known as "filling the tree."

Reid showed himself to have an understanding of the psychology of his colleagues. He paved the way for Pennsylvania Republican Sen. Arlen Specter's switch to the Democratic Party in 2009, and his persistence helped guide several of President Barack Obama's major initiatives to passage in the Senate that year, such as health care reform and the $787 billion American Recovery and Reinvestment Act economic stimulus law. But his accommodating approach toward Democratic colleagues limited his abilities. As the *New Yorker*'s George Packer observed, Reid

Minority Leader Mitch McConnell, R-Ky., and Majority Leader Harry Reid, D-Nev., pose for photographs in Reid's office in November 2006, shortly after each was elected by colleagues to lead his party in the Senate. Although miles apart ideologically, McConnell and Reid work to keep a professional relationship for times of needed compromise.

SOURCE: Scott J. Ferrell, Congressional Quarterly.

has achieved his position, in spite of his public shortcomings, by being the senator who helped other Democrats, always answered their calls, and got them what they wanted through masterly maneuvering. This has made him enormously popular within the Democratic caucus, but it doesn't give him the leverage of McConnell, let alone of Lyndon Johnson.[81]

The year 2010 was an especially difficult one for Reid. McConnell proved to be a determined adversary, regularly employing the filibuster. The lack of legislative progress led many observers to regard the Senate as incapable of doing its job. Reid also found himself in the nation's most closely watched reelection race. His Republican opponent, tea party favorite Sharron Angle, won a national following by relentlessly criticizing both Nevada's dismal economic picture and Reid's insider status.

But Reid avoided Daschle's earlier fate and pulled out a narrow victory, keeping pace with Angle by raising almost $25 million to her $28 million. Upon returning to Congress in the post-election lame-duck session that year, he notched several significant achievements, including an economic stimulus bill that renewed expiring tax cuts; a repeal of the military's "don't ask, don't tell" policy forbidding openly gay service members; and the New START nuclear arms treaty with Russia. He saw the results as a vindication of his backroom style. "I don't have people saying, 'He's the greatest speaker, he's handsome, he's a man about town,' Reid said at the end of the session. "But I don't really care. I feel very comfortable with my place in history."[82]

The Republican takeover of the House in 2010 forced Reid into more of a defensive role and set up further clashes with the unabashedly partisan McConnell, who openly boasted that his central goal was to make Obama a one-term president. Action in the Senate ground to a near-standstill; by June 2011 only 86 roll-call votes had been held, compared with 206 at the same stage in the 111th Congress and 207 in the 110th.

Modern Republican Leadership

Republican leadership styles in the age of collegiality paralleled those of the Democrats. Hugh Scott of Pennsylvania, who was narrowly elected to succeed Dirksen in 1969, was less assertive but perhaps even more flexible than Dirksen. His leadership style of compromise and accommodation was much like Mansfield's, but Scott was considered an ineffective leader. His moderate-to-liberal politics sometimes made it difficult for him to serve as a spokesperson for the Nixon and Ford administrations, and his support, first of U.S. action in Vietnam long after many of his colleagues and constituents had turned against it and then of Nixon well into the Watergate crisis, further undermined his standing.

Scott, who retired at the end of 1976, was succeeded by Dirksen's son-in-law, Howard H. Baker Jr. of Tennessee. Baker had sought the post twice before, running unsuccessfully against Scott in 1969 and 1971. Baker was best known for adopting an aura of bipartisanship during the televised

1973 hearings of the Senate Watergate Committee, where he served as the ranking Republican to folksy Chair Sam Ervin, D-N.C., and for asking the famous question "What did the President know and when did he know it?" In 1977 his colleagues, apparently convinced that he would be a more articulate spokesperson for the party, elected Baker minority leader over minority whip Robert P. Griffin of Michigan by a single vote. When the Republicans took over the Senate in 1981, Baker was made majority leader with no opposition.

A relaxed manner and close friendships with many of his Republican colleagues were Baker's principal assets. He was open and accessible to GOP senators of every ideology and was committed to protecting their rights. As majority leader, Baker was able to hold the disparate group of Republicans together on most issues during Reagan's first year in office. But when the economy faltered in late 1981, old divisions between moderate and conservative Republicans reopened, and unity became more difficult to achieve.

Baker's job was increasingly frustrated by the procedural chaos that gripped the Senate. His penchant for accommodation created a situation in which nearly every senator expected the schedule to conform to his or her personal needs. Floor action was delayed by senators who asked for holds on legislation—guarantees that a particular matter would not be taken up until the senator was present to protect his or her interests. Baker eventually announced that he would no longer consider holds sacrosanct, and he would not stack votes for the convenience of members who wanted more time to return to their home states. But there was little Baker could do to prevent individual members from tying up the Senate with filibusters and other delaying tactics.

In January 1983 Baker announced that he would retire from the Senate after the 1984 elections. To succeed him as majority leader, Republicans elected Bob Dole of Kansas over four other candidates.

Dole: Sharp Tactics, Hard Edges

After four years of Baker's easy-going stewardship, Republican senators opted for a leader whom they thought would restore some discipline and sense of purpose to a chamber increasingly bogged down in procedural chaos.

Five candidates entered the lists: Dole; Ted Stevens of Alaska, the majority whip; Richard G. Lugar of Indiana; Pete V. Domenici of New Mexico; and James McClure of Idaho. It was the first time since 1937 that the selection of a Senate majority leader came down to a vote in a party body. On the first ballot, McClure fell out of the race, followed on subsequent ones by Domenici and then Lugar. On the fourth ballot, Dole won, 28–25.

Dole was chair of the Republican National Committee at the time of the Watergate burglary in 1972 but was forced out of the post at the beginning of 1973 and was never associated with the scandal. Dole, as the nominee for vice president on the Republicans' unsuccessful 1976 national ticket, had

suffered a memorable embarrassing moment in debate with the Democratic nominee, Sen. Walter F. Mondale, D-Minn., by referring to World Wars I and II as "Democrat Wars." It cemented the public image of Dole as a harsh and humorless partisan, which he tried with only mixed success to mellow in later years. He also ran briefly for president in 1980 but dropped out without mounting a serious effort.

However, despite his often-glowering persona on national television, in the Senate Dole moved steadily into the position of insider who was willing to negotiate and valued legislative achievement. Dole had a hand in much of the important legislation of a generation, from taxes to Social Security to civil rights to protections for the disabled. He ably chaired the Finance Committee for four years (1981–1985) before ascending to the leadership, and ultimately Dole was to become the longest serving Republican Senate leader in history (1985–1996).

In addition to his image as a decisive leader, Dole was known as a superb negotiator with an ability to find compromises where others had failed. "You don't try to cram things down people's throats," he once said. "You try to work it out." Many of his colleagues, especially those up for reelection in 1986, thought he would also be willing to stand up to the Reagan White House when needed to protect their political interests. Of the candidates for majority leader, Dole was considered the least likely to toe the White House line on legislation. He had disagreed with President Reagan on issues as diverse as food stamps, civil rights, and tax policy.

That did not mean that Dole was anything less than an aggressive advocate for the administration on a broad range of issues. With a thin 53–47 Republican majority in his first term as majority leader, Dole produced significant victories, helping to pass tax revision, a new immigration law, a new farm bill, and aid to the Nicaraguan contras. Although Dole restored a modicum of discipline to the Senate, some of his methods—lengthy sessions and complicated parliamentary tactics intended to disarm obstructionists—were not popular with his colleagues and in some instances had only minimal effect. Democrats often gleefully used Dole's past image as a tough political hatchet man against him. They successfully ran against the Republicans' conservative budget priorities as well as the weaknesses of many members of the Republican class of 1980, who proved too weak to withstand a campaign without an accompanying presidential landslide.

Dole was relegated to minority leader from 1987 to 1995. He ran again for the Republican presidential nomination in 1988, winning the Iowa caucuses before losing the New Hampshire primary to Vice President George H. W. Bush's better focused effort. As minority leader, Dole was considered a tough partisan who was particularly effective in mobilizing Republicans against President Clinton's 1993 economic stimulus package, which was killed by a filibuster signaling that Republicans would give Clinton no honeymoon.

In his second incarnation as majority leader in 1995 and part of 1996, Dole became the front-runner for the Republican presidential nomination, but as a congressional leader he played second fiddle to Speaker Gingrich during the first session of the 104th Congress. Known to be skeptical of elements of the Contract with America, Dole was uncomfortable with the House's breakneck pace and what he regarded as careless legislating. However, Dole pushed aggressively for elements of the GOP plan, particularly the constitutional amendment requiring a balanced federal budget that had passed the House for the first time in 1995. Dole's aggressive tactics angered Democrats, who accused him of breaking an agreement by delaying a final vote that would have defeated the proposal, as he tried to secure one additional vote. However, the defection of Sen. Mark Hatfield, chair of the Appropriations Committee and the only Republican to oppose the amendment, killed any chance of it passing and deeply embarrassed Senate Republicans.

After Speaker Gingrich was badly weakened following the fiasco of the two government shutdowns during the winter of 1995–1996, Dole took the initiative to force an end to the controversy and to repudiate conservative House members who wanted to continue the shutdown.

Democrats in 1996 successfully tied down Dole in the Senate, blocking legislation and making him appear frustrated and ineffective. Realizing that trying to run the Senate was incompatible with his ambitions for the White House, Dole surprised his colleagues by resigning not only from the leadership but also the Senate itself in the spring of 1996. After losing the presidential election to Clinton overwhelmingly, Dole joined a law firm. He also became an occasional television pitchman, appearing in commercials for products as diverse as Viagra, Visa, and Pepsi-Cola.

Lott: Pragmatic Ideologue

Sen. Trent Lott, R-Miss., had crashed his way into the GOP leadership in 1994 by defeating the combative but less conservative incumbent Alan Simpson of Wyoming for majority whip by a single vote. Speculation arose that Lott, in his new role, would push Dole to the right, but the two leaders moved to put aside their initially uneasy relationship. The challenge of mustering votes from the minority side in the House gave Lott formidable training for his whip role in the Senate. And it gave him valuable ties to colleagues of both parties, many of whom had since been elected to the Senate.

Lott became majority leader in mid-1996 after squashing a campaign by his senior Mississippi colleague and longtime rival, Thad Cochran, 44–8. Lott seemed well suited to lead the most conservative Senate since the 1920s, with a 55–45 Republican majority in the 105th and 106th Congresses. He came into office with high expectations. Once considered a sharp-edged ideologue from his days in the House as minority whip from 1981 to 1989, Lott did not use the Senate's top post, as some thought he would, to transform the chamber into an engine of conservative activism similar to the House. That perception may have been buttressed by an increasing number of conservative Republican senators who had served in the House and agreed with many of the views of Gingrich and the 1994 GOP freshman class.

However, Lott had broad legislative experience that characterized House leadership. He also had an accommodating personal style, unlike the often harsh tones Gingrich took in the House. The nature of the Senate itself made such a strategy impractical. Like many Senate leaders, Lott found that a more successful approach was to accommodate a leadership style to the institution of the Senate rather than to change that body to suit outside constituencies.

Lott did not often employ the all-or-nothing tactics employed by House Republicans in 1995. Faced with an opportunity for legislative achievement at the expense of ideological purity, Lott grabbed it eagerly, overseeing the passage of major legislation to raise the minimum wage, improve the safety of drinking water, guarantee health insurance coverage for displaced workers, and overhaul the nation's welfare system. The fact that some of these initiatives were favored by Democrats and passed over the opposition of conservatives did not prevent Lott from claiming credit for substantial legislative accomplishments and increasing the GOP majority by one in the 1996 election even as President Clinton was trouncing his predecessor, Dole, in the presidential election. Lott's impeccable conservative credentials enabled him to strike deals with Democrats without arousing the mistrust of Republicans.

As the 105th Congress neared its end, Lott had not yet become a high-profile national figure, as had Gingrich. With the Speaker weakened politically, it had been anticipated that Lott, with a larger GOP majority in his chamber—at least in percentage terms—would assume a more prominent role as party spokesperson. However, Lott demonstrated no rush to fill such a role. And when he did step forward as a party spokesperson, Lott sometimes was too open for his troops' tastes, as when early in 1998 he called on special prosecutor Kenneth Starr to wrap up his investigation of the Clinton presidency, when many Republicans considered the variety of alleged presidential scandals ripe for lengthy political exploitation. And in the 106th Congress Lott worked with Daschle to ensure that the Senate's prerogatives were protected in the impeachment trial.

Lott's willingness to reach across the aisle, and to exercise independence from the White House, eventually angered many Republicans, particularly when he worked closely with Daschle during a 107th Congress that saw a year and a half of Democratic control and six months of a 50–50 split between the parties. That mistrust contributed to his downfall as leader in late 2002. Lott stepped down after praising the 1948 presidential campaign of Sen. Strom Thurmond, R-S.C., who ran as a segregationist, during a one-hundredth birthday party for Thurmond. His comments were played over and over again by the national media. As he tried to hold on to his job, Lott ran into opposition from some Republican senators and White House aides. Republican whip Don Nickles, R-Okla., called for his resignation. White House ally Bill Frist, R-Tenn., announced he would challenge Lott and got a quick endorsement from veteran Sen. John W. Warner, R-Va. Lott bowed out within twenty-four hours of Frist's announcement. Lott would not be out of the leadership for long, however. He spent the next four years rebuilding his political base among colleagues and won the job of Republican whip for the 110th Congress by one vote. However, he abruptly left the Senate in December 2007 to become a lobbyist. In 2011, he was named one of the ten highest-earning lobbyists who previously served in Congress.

Frist: The Outsider Within

Lott's Senate critics and President George W. Bush got precisely what they sought in Frist: a White House loyalist who pressured the Senate from within to act on the president's priorities.

Because his primary constituency was at the other end of Pennsylvania Avenue, Frist had to manage the Senate for four years without having built up the political capital with colleagues that usually leads a senator to be promoted into the party leadership. The combination of having little institutional power as majority leader and little personal power as a relatively junior senator left Frist with few tools to enforce discipline.

A heart-transplant surgeon who entered politics in 1994, Frist portrayed himself as a citizen legislator, an outsider in the tradition-bound Senate. He did little to hide his presidential ambitions, and critics saw calculations for a White House bid in his every move. They contended that he gave too little deference to the traditions of the institution. He led the Senate to the precipice of a rules showdown known as the "nuclear option" that would have used a majority of senators, not the sixty needed for cloture, to get Bush's judicial nominees through the Senate. Not only was the threat unpopular with Democratic senators, but many Republicans, especially those who remembered life in the minority, also were uncomfortable with the prospects of majority rule.

During Frist's tenure, he often angered House Republicans and some of his Senate colleagues with an unpredictable management style in which he was perceived to alternately bend too easily to the will of the White House or the most boisterous moderate GOP senators. In a body of political insiders, Frist stood out for his lack of political ability. His 2006 suggestion that the government combat rising gas prices by providing $100 rebates to consumers was laughed at on both sides of the aisle. His 2005 Senate floor diagnosis of the recovery prospects of Terry Schiavo, a brain-dead Florida woman whom conservatives hoped to keep on life support,

was delivered after he watched video of Schiavo—an episode that led some to call into question both his medical judgment and his political skills. Frist also did himself no favors as a party leader by honoring a self-imposed two-term limit, which allowed his foes to wait him out.

His limitations as a leader were perhaps most evident in his handling of the most basic tasks of Congress. Only three of the annual appropriations bills won Senate floor approval in 2006, and less than half did in 2003 and in 2004.

Frist was nevertheless able to shepherd some of the president's top priorities through a bitterly divided Senate, including the confirmations of Supreme Court Justices John G. Roberts Jr. and Samuel A. Alito Jr., tax cuts, and the 2003 law that added prescription-drug coverage to the Medicare program. But he was hamstrung by an essential lack of regard for and understanding of Senate norms. His decision to campaign against Minority Leader Daschle in 2004 permanently frayed his relationships with Democrats. Daschle's successor, Harry Reid, D-Nev., made little effort to hide his own dissatisfaction with Frist. In November 2005 Democrats shut down the Senate by invoking a little-known rule to force a closed session. Frist called it a "slap in the face" and said "it means, from now on, for the next year and a half, I cannot trust Sen. Reid."[83]

It was in such an environment of partisan and intrapartisan hostility that Frist tried to operate. The labeling of the 109th Congress as a "do nothing" Congress stemmed in no small measure from intransigence in the Senate, and the moniker contributed heavily to Republicans' loss of the Senate in the 2006 election.

McConnell was elected minority leader in November 2006 as Frist's replacement. He faced no opposition, having established himself as a powerful figure among Senate Republicans. He had twice chaired the National Republican Senatorial Committee and served as majority whip under Frist. He also had chaired the Rules Committee, which handles internal Senate housekeeping matters, and was the leader of the Republicans' opposition to overhauling campaign finance legislation, which he regarded as an infringement on the First Amendment. Liberals often derided McConnell for his owlish, tight-lipped demeanor, and he was not known as a great orator. But in stark contrast to Reid, he took great care in his precise and disciplined delivery of his party's message. "The idea of an off-the-cuff comment is anathema to him," observed his biographer, John David Dyche. As Reid's frequent foil, McConnell acted more like the opposition leader in a parliamentary system than someone in partnership with the majority. He preached unity among his GOP colleagues, discouraged bipartisan deal-making, and routinely held up nominations to executive branch posts. "The only tool we have against the most stridently left-wing administration we've seen in this country . . . is the confirmation process. And we intend to use it," he said.[84]

The Republican leadership—Senate Majority Whip Mitch McConnell, R-Ky., Vice President Dick Cheney, and House Speaker J. Dennis Hast-ert, R-Ill.—accompany Senate Majority Leader Bill Frist, R-Tenn., to the Senate chamber for Frist's farewell address in December 2006.

SOURCE: Scott J. Ferrell, Congressional Quarterly.

PARTY SUPPORT STRUCTURE IN THE SENATE

The leadership hierarchy in the Senate is not as strong as that in the House, but the apparatus follows many of the same patterns. The party support structure is composed of party whips, leaders of the party conference, and leaders of other party committees.

Party Whips

The first whips appeared in the Senate about the same time the floor leader positions were being institutionalized. The Democrats designated J. Hamilton Lewis of Illinois their first whip in 1913; the Republicans named James W. Wadsworth Jr. of New York their first GOP whip in 1915.

Although the duties of Senate whips are essentially the same as those of their House counterparts, the whip organizations are much less prominent in the Senate than in the House. For one thing, their functions and duties are less institutionalized, and their organizations much less elaborate. The majority and minority leaders in the Senate also generally assume some of what the whip's responsibilities would be in the House.

Senate whips at times have openly defied their own party leaders. Both parties elect their whips in the Senate, and the political maneuvering entailed in running for the office has sometimes led members to back certain senators for reasons that may have little to do with leadership effectiveness.

A serious breach occurred between Majority Leader Mansfield and Russell B. Long of Louisiana, the Democratic whip from 1965 to 1969. The two first clashed in 1966 over Long's proposal for federal subsidies for presidential election campaigns. Long exacerbated the dispute in 1967 by sending a newsletter to constituents in which he listed his disagreements with President Johnson (and Mansfield) on the issue. Mansfield sought to circumvent Long's influence by appointing four assistant whips. Long was defeated for whip by Edward Kennedy in 1969 (although Long eventually won the policy battle in 1971, when Congress finally approved public financing legislation).

Long lost his bid for reelection perhaps as much because he had been insufficiently attentive to the day-to-day details of the whip's job as because of any lingering ill-feeling between him and Mansfield. His successor, Kennedy, was neither a particularly active nor an effective whip and was crippled early in his tenure by the auto accident at Chappaquiddick. In 1971 he lost his bid for reelection to West Virginia's Byrd, then secretary of the Democratic Conference.

Alan Cranston, of California, who was elected Democratic whip when Byrd became majority leader, was particularly effective in that post. A liberal able to build bridges to Senate moderates and conservatives, he demonstrated a remarkable ability to sense shifts in sentiments as legislation moved toward the Senate floor and through the years put together numerous winning coalitions.

Traditionally, Senate whips do not move up the leadership ladder as regularly as House whips do. Although Johnson, Mansfield, Byrd, and Reid all did so, Cranston did not even seek the leadership spot when Byrd announced he would vacate it in 1989. When Cranston left the Senate in 1993, the more conservative and low-key Wendell H. Ford of Kentucky, who did not run in the 1994 race to replace Mitchell, succeeded him. Daschle never served as whip. On the Republican side the whips who moved up to floor leader in recent times have been Dirksen, Scott, Lott, and McConnell, with Robert Griffin and Ted Stevens trying and losing.

When Democrats regained control of the Senate in 2006, Illinois Democrat Richard Durbin became the majority whip. Like Reid, he was a savvy insider who was well liked within his party; he was voted the most admired senator in a *National Journal* poll of Democratic congressional insiders in 2009. He had a particularly warm relationship with Barack Obama when Obama served as his Senate colleague, and he continued to enjoy close ties to Obama's White House.

But there were indications of potential friction between Durbin and Sen. Charles Schumer, D-N.Y., a hard-charging lawmaker who had helped propel the Democrats to the majority in 2006 as chair of the Democratic Senatorial Campaign Committee. Schumer was given the number-three leadership position as a reward for his efforts and made no secret of his ambition to eventually ascend even higher. Both men—who roomed together in a Capitol Hill townhouse—endured repeated speculation that they would be forced to challenge each other for Democratic leader if Reid lost his reelection bid. With his fund-raising acumen, Schumer had closer ties to the lobbying world than Durbin, and after the 2010 election Reid put the New Yorker in charge of the Senate Democratic policy and messaging effort—a move widely interpreted within Washington as a slap at Durbin.

Party Conferences

The development of party caucuses (now called conferences) in the Senate paralleled that of the House. In 1846 the party caucus increased in importance by acquiring the authority to make committee assignments. During the Civil War and Reconstruction era, Republicans used the caucus frequently to discuss and adopt party positions on legislation.

In the 1890s Republican leaders Allison and Aldrich used the caucus extensively and effectively. As Rothman observed, "The Republican caucus was not binding, and yet its decisions commanded obedience for party leadership was capable of enforcing discipline. Senators could no longer act with impunity unless they were willing to forgo favorable committee posts and control of the chamber proceedings."[85]

It is unlikely that any Senate Democrats ever were penalized for not abiding by a binding caucus rule adopted in 1903. But they used the rule to achieve remarkable unity in 1913–1914 in support of President Wilson's legislative objectives. Twenty years later, charged with enacting Franklin Roosevelt's New Deal, Democrats readopted the rule. It was not employed, but frequent nonbinding caucuses were held to mobilize support. Since that time neither party has seriously considered using caucus votes to enforce party loyalty on legislative issues.

Both party conferences elect the various party leaders and ratify committee chairmanship and ranking minority member posts and other committee assignments. After resuming control of the Senate in the 104th Congress, Republicans amended their conference rules to limit service in elected party leadership posts, except floor leader and president pro tempore, to no more than three Congresses. The affected positions would be majority whip, conference chair and conference secretary, chair of the policy committee, and chair of the National Republican Senatorial Committee, though that post has traditionally rotated. In recent years both parties have used the conference to collect and distribute information to members, to perform legislative research, and to ratify decisions made by the policy committees. Each conference meets weekly for luncheons to discuss scheduling and strategy. Administration officials sometimes attend their party's sessions. In September 2011, the Republican Conference chair, Lamar Alexander of Tennessee, took the highly unusual step of announcing he would depart from the post the following January to work more frequently across the aisle with Democrats. "Any time you take a leadership role, you give up some of your independence. I'm giving that up and getting my independence back," he said.[86]

Other Party Committees

The two Senate parties each have a policy committee, a Committee on Committees (called the Steering Committee by the Democrats), and a campaign committee. Traditionally the Democratic leader chaired the party conference as well as the Policy and Steering committees, giving him or her significant potential power to control the party apparatus. Breaking with that custom, George Mitchell gave responsibility for the Steering Committee to Inouye and made Daschle cochair, with Mitchell, of the Policy Committee. Daschle continued the practice. The Republican Conference and party committees traditionally are chaired by different senators, thus diffusing power among Senate Republicans.

The first of the party committees to be created was the Committee on Committees, which originated during the Civil War era, when Republicans, then in the majority, used a

CAMPAIGN AID: PRIORITY ROLE FOR PARTY LEADERS

Helping their members win reelection and wresting seats away from the other party are top-priority jobs for party leaders in Congress. Given the ever mounting cost of House and Senate election campaigns, fund-raising is probably the most valuable service the leadership can provide. In addition to attending fund-raising dinners and receptions in members' home districts or states, every party leader, and many rank-and-file lawmakers who have leadership or chairmanship aspirations, operate their own political action committees (PACs) that solicit money from unions, corporations, and other contributors, which the leaders then channel to candidates. Commonly referred to as leadership PACs, these fund-raising tools are formed by ambitious members to help party candidates win seats, expand party representation, and establish a sense of gratitude among beneficiaries when leadership positions are decided. They have become increasingly important since the 2002 enactment of a campaign finance law that banned unlimited soft money contributions to party committees.

Still, the major campaign efforts are handled by special party committees set up expressly for the purpose of electing Republicans or Democrats: the Democratic Congressional Campaign Committee and the National Republican Congressional Committee (NRCC) in the House; and the Democratic Senatorial Campaign Committee and the National Republican Senatorial Committee in the Senate. Chaired by members of Congress, these committees help identify candidates to challenge incumbents of the other party or to run for open seats. They brief candidates on the issues and help them with all phases of campaigning, advising—even supplying—campaign managers, finance directors, and press secretaries. They also play an increasingly important role in recruiting candidates.

These committees also raise and disburse millions of dollars. For the 2010 elections, the Democratic congressional committees raised more than $290 million on behalf of their candidates; the Republican congressional committees, nearly $230 million, according to the Center for Responsive Politics. However, Republicans were by far the greater beneficiary of spending by outside groups that poured money into campaigns as a result of the Supreme Court's 2010 *Citizens United v. Federal Election Commission* decision. Conservative interest groups gave more than $190 million, while liberal groups gave nearly $99 million, according to the CRP. The party campaign committees are important to candidates because they spend large sums of money on independent advertisements that serve to help the candidate, devote resources to voter-turnout efforts, and attract funding from other contributors. Given the high cost of campaigns and the limits on campaign contributions, a commitment from a congressional party entity can help a candidate cross an important threshold of credibility with other potential sources of funding. The party committees almost invariably support incumbents of their party if there is a challenge in the primary, except in unusual circumstances. For example, in 1998 the NRCC worked aggressively to shore up William Goodling, R-Pa., chair of the House Committee on Education and the Workforce, in a primary against an opponent who had won 45 percent of the vote against him two years earlier. Goodling won the rematch easily. But at the same time it refused to support Jay Kim, R-Calif., for renomination in 1998 after he had pleaded guilty to campaign finance law violations in earlier campaigns, was sentenced to house arrest, and was forced to campaign from Washington, D.C., where he had been required to wear an electronic monitoring device. Kim lost in the primary.

Incumbents are routinely asked to contribute to the party committee in their chamber and also for special purposes, such as hotly contested special elections that may arise in the House.

The party committees often decline to openly support candidates for an open seat that is being contested in a primary. But if one candidate is believed to be visibly stronger for the general election, early intervention can help that candidate win the primary and begin an earlier focus on the general election. With party control of Congress closely divided, especially in the House, such intervention has become much more common. Recruitment activities by the party committees have also intensified.

Because the parties play such a dominant role in fund-raising, they have tremendous influence in deciding which candidates make it to the general election ballot. Elected officials up to and including the president often try to get desired candidates to run and then work to clear the primary field for them. In 2010, President Obama and New York Democrats discouraged several House members from challenging new Sen. Kirsten Gillibrand, D-N.Y., after Gillibrand was the surprise choice to fill Hillary Rodham Clinton's seat when Clinton became secretary of state. Gillibrand went on to win reelection easily.

To help attract additional funding, the party committees work on selling their candidates to PACs through meetings with the candidates, briefings, even newsletters. The ability of congressional leaders to raise money for leadership PACs from their donors and then give it away to colleagues makes them an increasingly valuable source of funds. Lawmakers may give unlimited amounts of money from their individual reelection accounts to the party committees, and leaders will often give as much as $500,000 in excess campaign funds to the party. They may also appear at fund-raisers for their colleagues to help encourage donors to give to lesser-known lawmakers.

Raising campaign funds for one's colleagues is not new. In his book *The Path to Power*, Robert A. Caro wrote that in 1940 Lyndon B. Johnson, then in his third year in the House, tapped into Texas oil money, directing it to Democratic colleagues. His endeavors were credited with saving thirty to forty Democratic seats, which kept the House from going Republican. Campaign finance laws, and the amounts of money potentially available, have changed dramatically since then, but the leadership's interest has not.

In more recent times, House majority whip Tony Coelho, D-Calif., and Senate majority leader George J. Mitchell, D-Maine, won their leadership positions in part because of their success in directing their respective campaign committees. Mitchell ran the committee for the 1986 election cycle, when Democrats regained control of the Senate. Similarly, Rep. Bill Paxon, R-N.Y., used his success running the NRCC before the 1994 election, when the Republicans gained control of the House, to position himself for a run for higher office in the GOP leadership before suddenly announcing his retirement in 1998 to spend more time with his family. Fund-raising for colleagues seems to have become a prerequisite for anyone who wants to join the party leadership. Mitchell's two challengers for the post of majority leader in 1988 both set up PACs to direct campaign funds to colleagues. Mitchell did not set up a PAC but indirectly channeled money to colleagues when asked for advice from other PACs and contributors.

Today, campaign aid is one of the services that leaders are expected to provide their rank and file. It is a service that can also benefit the leadership when the time comes to ask for support for the parties' legislative programs in Congress. The money chase has filtered down to other levels of leadership activities, such as the assignment of members to committees and the awarding of chairmanships. It is not uncommon for members on the leadership panels making such assignments to examine how financially supportive an applicant for an important legislative committee has been to other, more vulnerable, colleagues.

special panel appointed by their party caucus to make both Republican and Democratic committee assignments. Senate Democrats set up a Committee on Committees in 1879. Committee assignments made by each of these committees are subject to ratification by the respective party conference and the full chamber.

What was, in effect, the first Senate Steering Committee was established in 1874, when the GOP Conference appointed a Committee on the Order of Business to prepare a schedule for Senate floor action. That committee was replaced in the mid-1880s by a Steering Committee appointed by the caucus chair. Democrats established a Steering Committee in 1879 but abandoned it when the Republicans regained control of the Senate and the legislative agenda. They did not set up another Steering Committee until 1893 when the Democrats once again controlled the Senate.

In 1947 both parties created policy committees that were assigned the scheduling functions of the old Steering committees. At the same time the Democratic Steering Committee, while retaining its name, was reconstituted as the party's Committee on Committees. The Policy committees—which prepare material on issues and legislation and discuss broad questions of party policy—have been more or less active, depending on the needs of the party leadership and whether the party was in or out of the majority.

Under Daschle's leadership, for example, the Democratic Policy Committee stepped up its analysis of the issues and put together an ambitious policy agenda for Senate Democrats. Sen. Byron L. Dorgan, D-N.D., used his chairmanship of the Democratic Policy Committee in the 109th Congress to conduct investigations into mismanagement of Iraq war contracts and Gulf Coast hurricane recovery efforts. When Dorgan retired in 2011, Charles Schumer was given the helm of the committee at the start of the 112th Congress as part of his added messaging and policy responsibilities.

★

NOTES

1 Trent Lott, *Herding Cats: A Life in Politics* (New York: Regan Books, 2005), 127–128.

2 Christopher J. Deering and Steven S. Smith, "Majority Party Leadership and the New House Subcommittee System," in *Understanding Congressional Leadership,* ed. Frank B. Mackaman (Washington, D.C.: CQ Press, 1981), 288–289.

3 Roger H. Davidson and Walter J. Oleszek, *Congress and Its Members,* 7th ed. (Washington, D.C.: CQ Press, 2000), 184.

4 Ibid., 164.

5 Ibid., 185.

6 Richard E. Cohen, "Byrd of West Virginia: A New Job, a New Image," *National Journal,* August 20, 1977, 1295.

7 Richard E. Cohen, "Taking Advantage of Tax Reform Means Different Strokes for Different Folks," *National Journal,* June 22, 1985, 1459.

8 Howard Fineman, "For the Son of C-SPAN, Exposure Equals Power," *Newsweek,* April 3, 1989, 23.

9 Michael J. Malbin, "House Democrats Are Playing with a Strong Leadership Lineup," *National Journal,* June 18, 1977, 942.

10 Janet Hook, "Budget Ordeal Poses Question: Why Can't Congress Be Led?" *CQ Weekly,* October 20, 1990, 3472. library.cqpress.com/cqweekly/WR101401737.

11 Davidson and Oleszek, *Congress and Its Members,* 165.

12 Mary P. Follett, *The Speaker of the House of Representatives* (New York: Longman, Green, 1896. Reprint. New York: Burt Franklin Reprints, 1974), 25–26.

13 George B. Galloway, *History of the House of Representatives* (New York: Crowell, 1961), 20.

14 Ronald M. Peters Jr., *The American Speakership: The Office in Historical Perspective* (Baltimore: Johns Hopkins University Press, 1990), 31.

15 Follett, *The Speaker of the House of Representatives,* 82.

16 George Rothwell Brown, *The Leadership of Congress* (New York: Arno Press, 1974. Reprint. Indianapolis: Bobbs-Merrill, 1922), 37–38.

17 Peters, *The American Speakership,* 35–36.

18 Steven S. Smith and Christopher J. Deering, *Committees in Congress,* 2nd ed. (Washington, D.C.: CQ Press, 1990), 28.

19 Peters, *The American Speakership,* 36.

20 Follett, *The Speaker of the House of Representatives,* 84.

21 Hubert B. Fuller, *The Speaker of the House* (Boston: Little, Brown, 1909), 26.

22 Galloway, *History of the House of Representatives,* 51.

23 Ibid., 132.

24 Ibid., 133.

25 Barbara W. Tuchman, *The Proud Tower: A Portrait of the World before the War: 1890–1914* (New York: Macmillan, 1966), 127.

26 Fuller, *The Speaker of the House,* 244.

27 Peters, *The American Speakership,* 77.

28 Fuller, *The Speaker of the House,* 257.

29 Robert Luce, *Congress: An Explanation* (Cambridge, Mass.: Harvard University Press, 1926), 117.

30 Peters, *The American Speakership,* 94.

31 Randall B. Ripley, *Party Leaders in the House of Representatives* (Washington, D.C.: Brookings Institution, 1967), 101.

32 Galloway, *History of the House of Representatives,* 144.

33 *U.S. News and World Report,* October 13, 1950, 30.

34 Peters, *The American Speakership,* 140–141.

35 John M. Barry, *The Ambition and the Power* (New York: Viking Penguin, 1989), 4.

36 Alan Ehrenhalt, ed., *Politics in America: Members of Congress in Washington and at Home, 1986* (Washington, D.C.: CQ Press, 1985), 1507.

37 Peters, *The American Speakership,* 280.

38 Phil Duncan, ed., *Politics in America, 1990* (Washington, D.C.: CQ Press, 1989), 2.

39 Christopher Madison, "The Heir Presumptive," *National Journal,* April 29, 1989, 1036.

40 Ibid., 1035.

41 *1995 Congressional Quarterly Almanac* (Washington, D.C.: Congressional Quarterly, 1996), I-21.

42 Barbara Sinclair, "Transformational Leader or Faithful Agent? Innovation and Continuity in House Majority Party Leadership: The

104th and 105th Congresses," paper presented at 1997 meeting of the American Political Science Association, Washington, D.C., 9.

43 Thomas E. Mann and Norman J. Ornstein, *The Broken Branch: How Congress Is Failing America and How to Get It Back on Track* (Oxford, U.K.: Oxford University Press, 2006), 175.

44 Joe Nocera, "The Last Moderate," *New York Times*, September 6, 2011.

45 Vince Bzdek, "Why Did Health-Care Reform Pass? Nancy Pelosi Was in Charge," *Washington Post*, March 28, 2010.

46 Linda Burstyn, "Watch Out John, Nancy's Still on the Job," Ms.Magazine.com, January 5, 2011.

47 *USA Today*/Gallup poll, August 28, 2011. www.pollingreport.com/p.htm.

48 Jonathan Allen and John Bresnahan, "Pelosi Survives Democratic Revolt," *Politico*, November 17, 2010.

49 Jake Sherman and John Bresnahan, "Boehner Tries to Tame GOP on Debt Ceiling Plan," *Politico*, July 27, 2011.

50 Neil MacNeil, *Forge of Democracy: The House of Representatives* (New York: McKay, 1963), 87.

51 Peters, *The American Speakership*, 92.

52 Galloway, *History of the House of Representatives*, 108.

53 Barbara Sinclair, *Majority Leadership in the U.S. House* (Baltimore: Johns Hopkins University Press, 1983), 46.

54 Floyd M. Riddick, *Congressional Procedure* (Boston: Chapman and Grimes, 1941), 345–346.

55 Irwin B. Arieff, "Inside Congress," *Congressional Quarterly Weekly Report*, February 28, 1981, 379.

56 Ripley, *Party Leaders in the House of Representatives*, 29.

57 Duncan, *Politics in America, 1990*, 470.

58 Chuck McCutcheon and Christina L. Lyons, eds., *CQ's Politics in America 2010* (Washington, D.C.: CQ Press, 2009), 794.

59 Sinclair, *Majority Leadership in the U.S. House*, 57.

60 Sinclair, "Transformational Leader," 20.

61 Barbara Sinclair, "Majority Party Leadership Strategies for Coping with the New U.S. House," in *Understanding Congressional Leadership*, ed. Frank H. Mackaman (Washington, D.C.: CQ Press, 1981), 202.

62 Robert Draper, "How Kevin McCarthy Wrangles the Tea Party in Washington," *New York Times Magazine*, July 13, 2011, 38.

63 Galloway, *History of the House of Representatives*, 130.

64 Sinclair, *Majority Leadership in the U.S. House*, 96–97; and George H. Haynes, *The Senate of the United States: Its History and Practices* (Boston: Houghton Mifflin, 1938), Vol. 2, 1003.

65 Randall B. Ripley, *Power in the Senate* (New York: St. Martin's Press, 1969), 24.

66 W. E. Binkley, *The Powers of the President* (New York: Russell and Russell, 1973), 52.

67 David J. Rothman, *Politics and Power: The United States Senate 1869–1901* (Cambridge, Mass.: Harvard University Press, 1966), 19.

68 Charles O. Jones, *The Minority Party in Congress* (Boston: Little, Brown, 1970), 48.

69 Rothman, *Politics and Power*, 44.

70 John G. Stewart, "Two Strategies of Leadership: Johnson and Mansfield," in *Congressional Behavior*, ed. Nelson W. Polsby (New York: Random House, 1971), 61–92.

71 Rowland Evans and Robert Novak, *Lyndon B. Johnson: The Exercise of Power* (New York: New American Library, 1966), 104.

72 Roger H. Davidson, "The Senate: If Everyone Leads, Who Follows?" in *Congress Reconsidered*, 4th ed., eds. Lawrence C. Dodd and Bruce I. Oppenheimer (Washington, D.C.: CQ Press, 1989), 280.

73 Ross K. Baker, *Friend and Foe in the U.S. Senate* (New York: Free Press, 1980), 203.

74 Barbara Sinclair, "Congressional Leadership: A Review Essay," in *Leading Congress: New Styles, New Strategies*, ed. John J. Kornacki (Washington, D.C.: CQ Press, 1990), 141.

75 Robert L. Peabody, "Senate Party Leadership: From the 1950s to the 1980s," in *Understanding Congressional Leadership*, ed. Frank B. Mackaman (Washington, D.C.: CQ Press, 1981), 59.

76 Davidson, "The Senate," 281.

77 Congressional Quarterly, *Congress and the Nation, Vol. IV: 1973–1976* (Washington, D.C.: Congressional Quarterly Service), 875.

78 Janet Hook, "Mitchell Learns Inside Game; Is Cautious as Party Voice," *Congressional Quarterly Weekly Report*, September 9, 1989, 2294.

79 Richard E. Cohen, *Washington at Work: Back Rooms and Clean Air* (Needham Heights, Mass.: Allyn and Bacon, 1995), 96.

80 Jackie Koszczuk and Martha Angle, eds., *Politics in America* (Washington, D.C.: CQ Press, 2007), 616.

81 George Packer, "The Empty Chamber," *The New Yorker*, August 9, 2010, 44.

82 John Harwood, "With Major Bills Passed, Reid Takes a Victory Lap," *New York Times*, December 19, 2010.

83 Daphne Retter, "Senate Lights Go Down, Tempers Go Up," *CQ Weekly*, November 7, 2005, 2991. library.cqpress.com/cqweekly/weeklyreport109-000001950592.

84 Major Garrett, "Leading from Behind," *National Journal*, June 9, 2011, 26.

85 Rothman, *Politics and Power*, 60.

86 Tim Mak, "Lamar Alexander: Getting My Independence Back," *Politico*, September 21, 2011.

SELECTED BIBLIOGRAPHY

Ahuja, Sunil, and Robert E. Dewhirst. *Congress Responds to the Twentieth Century.* Columbus: Ohio State University Press, 2003.

Aldrich, John H. *Why Parties? The Origin and Transformation of Political Parties in America.* Chicago: University of Chicago Press, 1995.

Alexander, De Alva S. *History and Procedure of the House of Representatives.* Boston: Houghton Mifflin, 1916.

Ardis, Lawrence P. *Party Leaders in Congress, 1789–2002: Vital Statistics and Biographical Sketches.* New York: Nova Science, 2002.

Baker, Richard A., and Roger H. Davidson, eds. *First among Equals: Outstanding Senate Leaders of the Twentieth Century.* Washington, D.C.: Congressional Quarterly, 1991.

Baker, Ross K. *Friend and Foe in the U.S. Senate.* New York: Free Press, 1980.

———. *House and Senate.* 4th ed. New York: Norton, 2008.

Baldwin, Louis. *Hon. Politician: Mike Mansfield of Montana.* Missoula, Mont.: Mountain Press Publishing, 1979.

Barry, John M. *The Ambition and the Power.* New York: Viking Penguin, 1989.

Bianco, William T. *Congress on Display, Congress at Work.* Ann Arbor: University of Michigan Press, 2000.

Bolles, Blair. *Tyrant from Illinois: Uncle Joe Cannon's Experiment with Personal Power.* New York: Norton, 1951.

Bond, Jon R., and Richard Fleisher, eds. *Polarized Politics: Congress and the President in a Partisan Era.* Washington, D.C.: CQ Press, 2000.

Brady, David W., and Mathew D. McCubbins, eds. *Party, Process, and Political Change in Congress: Further New Perspectives on the History of Congress.* Stanford, Calif.: Stanford University Press, 2007.

———. *Party, Process, and Political Change in Congress: New Perspectives on the History of Congress.* Stanford, Calif.: Stanford University Press.

Brown, George Rothwell. *The Leadership of Congress.* Indianapolis: Bobbs-Merrill, 1922. Reprint. New York: Arno Press, 1974.

Burns, James MacGregor. *Leadership.* New York: Harper and Row, 1978.

Busbey, L. White. *Uncle Joe Cannon.* New York: Henry Holt, 1927.

Byrd, Robert C. *The Senate, 1789–1989: Addresses on the History of the United States Senate.* 2 vols. Washington, D.C.: Government Printing Office, 1988.

Campbell, Colton C., and Nicol C. Rae. *The Contentious Senate: Partisanship, Ideology, and the Myth of Cool Judgment.* Lanham, Md.: Rowman and Littlefield, 2001.

Cheney, Richard B., and Lynne V. Cheney. *Kings of the Hill: Power and Personality in the House of Representatives.* Rev. ed. New York: Simon and Schuster, 1996.

Clancy, Paul, and Shirley Elder. *Tip: A Biography of Thomas P. O'Neill, Speaker of the House.* New York: Macmillan, 1980.

Clark, Joseph S. *The Senate Establishment.* New York: Hill and Wang, 1963.

Cohen, Richard E. *Washington at Work: Back Rooms and Clean Air.* Needham Heights, Mass.: Allyn and Bacon, 1995.

Cox, Gary W., and Mathew D. McCubbins. *Legislative Leviathan: Party Government in the House.* Berkeley: University of California Press, 1993.

———. *Setting the Agenda: Responsible Party Government in the U.S. House of Representatives.* New York: Cambridge University Press, 2005.

Davidson, Roger H., Susan W. Hammond, and Raymond W. Smock. *Masters of the House: Congressional Leadership over Two Centuries.* Boulder, Colo.: Westview Press, 1998.

Davidson, Roger H., and Walter J. Oleszek. *Congress and Its Members.* 13th ed. Washington, D.C.: CQ Press, 2012.

Davis, Christopher M. *The President Pro Tempore of the Senate: History and Authority of the Office.* Washington, D.C.: Congressional Research Service, 2010.

DeGregorio, Christine A. *Networks of Champions: Leadership, Access, and Advocacy in the U.S. House of Representatives.* Ann Arbor: University of Michigan Press, 1997.

Dodd, Lawrence C., and Bruce I. Oppenheimer, eds. *Congress Reconsidered.* 9th ed. Washington, D.C.: CQ Press, 2009.

Dyche, John David. *Republican Leader: A Political Biography of Senator Mitch McConnell.* Wilmington, Del.: ISI Books, 2009.

Eilperin, Juliet. *Fight Club Politics: How Partisanship Is Poisoning the House of Representatives.* Lanham, Md.: Rowman and Littlefield, 2006.

Evans, C. Lawrence, and Walter J. Oleszek. *Congress under Fire: Reform Politics and the Republican Majority.* Boston: Houghton Mifflin, 1997.

Evans, Rowland, and Robert Novak. *Lyndon B. Johnson: The Exercise of Power.* New York: New American Library, 1966.

Fiorina, Morris P., and David W. Rohde, eds. *Home Style and Washington at Work: Studies of Congressional Politics.* Ann Arbor: University of Michigan Press, 1989.

Follett, Mary P. *The Speaker of the House of Representatives.* New York: Longmans, Green, 1896. Reprint. New York: Burt Franklin Reprints, 1974.

Fuller, Hubert Bruce. *The Speakers of the House.* Boston: Little, Brown, 1909.

Galloway, George B. *History of the House of Representatives.* 2nd ed. New York: Crowell, 1976.

Geraghty, Jim. *Voting to Kill: How 9/11 Launched the Era of Republican Leadership.* New York: Simon and Schuster, 2006.

Gillespie, Ed, and Bob Schellhas, eds. *Contract with America.* New York: Times Books, 1994.

Green, Matthew N. *The Speaker of the House: A Study in Leadership.* New Haven, Conn.: Yale University Press, 2010.

Grossman, Mark. *Speakers of the House of Representatives.* Amenia, N.Y.: Grey House Publishing, 2009.

Hardeman, D. B., and Donald C. Bacon. *Rayburn: A Biography.* Austin: Texas Monthly Press, 1987.

Haynes, George H. *The Senate of the United States: Its History and Practice.* 2 vols. Boston: Houghton Mifflin, 1938.

Hertzke, Allen D., and Ronald M. Peters Jr. *The Atomistic Congress: An Interpretation of Congressional Change.* New York: Sharpe, 1992.

Hinckley, Barbara. *Stability and Change in Congress.* 4th ed. New York: Harper and Row, 1988.

Jacobs, John. *A Rage for Justice: The Passion and Politics of Phillip Burton.* Berkeley: University of California Press, 1997.

Jones, Charles O. *The Minority Party in Congress.* Boston: Little, Brown, 1970.

Kiewiet, D. Roderick, and Mathew D. McCubbins. *The Logic of Delegation: Congressional Parties and the Appropriations Process.* Chicago: University of Chicago Press, 1991.

Koopman, Douglas L. *Hostile Takeover: The House Republican Party, 1980–1995.* Lanham, Md.: Rowman and Littlefield, 1996.

Kornacki, John J., ed. *Leading Congress: New Styles, New Strategies.* Washington, D.C.: CQ Press, 1990.

Krehbiel, Keith. *Pivotal Politics: A Theory of U.S. Lawmaking.* Chicago: University of Chicago Press, 1998.

Kura, N.O. *Congressional Leadership.* New York: Nova Science Publishers, 2004.

Lee, Frances E. *Beyond Ideology: Politics, Principles, and Partisanship in the U.S. Senate.* Chicago: University of Chicago Press, 2009.

Loomis, Burdett A. *The Contemporary Congress.* 5th ed. Belmont, CA: Thomson/Wadsworth, 2006.

———. *The New American Politician.* New York: Basic Books, 1988.

———. *The U.S. Senate: From Deliberation to Dysfunction.* Washington, D.C.: CQ Press, 2012.

Mackaman, Frank H., ed. *Understanding Congressional Leadership.* Washington, D.C.: CQ Press, 1981.

MacNeil, Neil. *Dirksen: Portrait of a Public Man.* New York: World Publishing, 1970.

———. *Forge of Democracy: The House of Representatives.* New York: McKay, 1963.

Maltzman, Forrest. *Competing Principals: Committees, Parties, and the Organization of Congress.* Ann Arbor: University of Michigan Press, 1997.

Mann, Thomas E., and Norman J. Ornstein, eds. *The Broken Branch: How Congress Is Failing America and How to Get It Back on Track.* New York: Oxford University Press, 2008.

———. *The New Congress.* Washington, D.C.: American Enterprise Institute, 1981.

Marshall, Bryan W. *Rules for War: Procedural Choice in the U.S. House of Representatives.* Burlington, Vt.: Ashgate, 2005.

Mayhew, David R. *America's Congress: Actions in the Public Sphere, James Madison through Newt Gingrich.* New Haven, Conn.: Yale University Press, 2000.

———. *Divided We Govern: Party Control, Lawmaking, and Investigations, 1946–2002.* 2nd ed. New Haven, Conn.: Yale University Press, 2005.

O'Neill, Thomas P., Jr., with William Novak. *Man of the House: The Life and Political Memoirs of Speaker Tip O'Neill.* New York: Random House, 1987.

Palazzolo, Daniel J. *The Speaker and the Budget: Leadership in the Post-Reform House of Representatives.* Pittsburgh: University of Pittsburgh Press, 1992.

Peters, Ronald M., Jr. *The American Speakership: The Office in Historical Perspective.* 2nd ed. Baltimore: Johns Hopkins University Press, 1997.

————, ed. *The Speaker: Leadership in the U.S. House of Representatives.* Washington, D.C.: CQ Press, 1995.

Peters, Ronald M., and Cindy Simon Rosenthal. *Speaker Nancy Pelosi and the New American Politics.* New York: Oxford University Press, 2010.

Ranney, Austin. *Channels of Power.* New York: Basic Books, 1983.

Reedy, George E. *The U.S. Senate: Paralysis or a Search for Consensus?* New York: Crown, 1986.

Riddick, Floyd M. *Majority and Minority Leaders of the Senate: History and Development of the Offices of the Floor Leaders.* Washington, D.C.: Government Printing Office, 1988.

————. *Riddick's Senate Procedure: Precedents and Practices.* Rev. ed. Edited by Alan S. Frumin. Washington, D.C.: Government Printing Office, 1992.

Ripley, Randall B., and Grace A. Franklin. *Congress, the Bureaucracy, and Public Policy.* 5th ed. Pacific Grove, Calif.: Brooks/Cole, 1991.

Robinson, William A. *Thomas B. Reed: Parliamentarian.* New York: Dodd, Mead, 1930.

Rohde, David W. *Parties and Leaders in the Post-Reform House.* Chicago: University of Chicago Press, 1991.

Rothman, David J. *Politics and Power: The United States Senate, 1869–1901.* Cambridge, Mass.: Harvard University Press, 1966.

Saturno, James, Richard S. Beth, and Alfred T. Zubrov, eds. *Speakers of the House 1789–2002.* Hauppauge, N.Y.: Novinka Books, 2002.

Sinclair, Barbara. *Legislators, Leaders, and Lawmaking: The U.S. House of Representatives in the Post-Reform Era.* Baltimore: Johns Hopkins University Press, 1995.

————. *Majority Leadership in the U.S. House.* Baltimore: Johns Hopkins University Press, 1983.

————. *Party Wars: Polarization and the Politics of National Policy Making.* Norman: University of Oklahoma Press, 2006.

————. *The Transformation of the U.S. Senate.* Baltimore: Johns Hopkins University Press, 1989.

Smith, Steven S. *Party Influence in Congress.* Cambridge, U.K.: Cambridge University Press, 2007.

Steinberg, Alfred. *Sam Rayburn.* New York: Hawthorne Books, 1975.

Stonecash, Jeffrey M., Mark D. Brewer, and Mack D. Mariani. *Diverging Parties: Social Change, Realignment, and Party Polarization.* Boulder, Colo.: Westview Press, 2003.

Sulkin, Tracy. *Issue Politics in Congress.* New York: Cambridge University Press, 2005.

Sundquist, James L., ed. *Back to Gridlock? Governance in the Clinton Years.* Washington, D.C.: Brookings Institution, Committee on the Constitutional System, 1995.

Theriault, Sean M. *Party Polarization in Congress.* Cambridge, U.K.: Cambridge University Press, 2008.

Valeo, Frank. *Mike Mansfield, Majority Leader: A Different Kind of Senate, 1961–1976.* Armonk, N.Y.: Sharpe, 1999.

chapter 2

The Legislative Process

Nowhere are policy and process more intertwined than in the Congress of the United States. They interact at many stages of the legislative drama as skillful senators and representatives use the rules of procedure—largely fashioned with the aim of producing an orderly consideration of legislative proposals—to advance their policy goals or kill those they oppose.

Bill sponsors tinker with wording to ensure the proposal goes to a sympathetic, not a hostile, committee. The Senate may attach major tax legislation to a minor House revenue bill, adhering to the letter of a constitutional requirement that all revenue bills must originate in the House while circumventing its spirit. Wording of a House rule for consideration of a bill on the floor may rewrite the underlying measure or greatly constrict the ability of opponents to alter it. Senators may seek to end or continue debate on a proposal to position themselves to force action on an entirely unrelated matter. All of these maneuvers, and many more, routinely go on in a session of Congress.

Although the Constitution and the rules of the House and Senate set forth the manner in which laws are made, legislating is often much more of an art than a science. As a practical matter, the rules and procedures for moving a bill along its legislative journey—from an idea, to a bill, to a law—are often altered, ignored, or bypassed. To do otherwise would slow down even further a legislative process that can be maddeningly inefficient.

On the surface, the actions of Congress appear fairly straightforward. To become law proposed legislation must be approved in identical form in both the House and the Senate.

Most legislative proposals are first considered in subcommittee and committee. After reaching the floor, legislation is debated, possibly amended further, and passed by the full House or Senate. After both chambers have acted, any differences in the two versions of the legislation must be resolved, either by passing the bill back and forth between the houses or through an ad hoc conference committee. The final version is sent to the White House for the president's signature, which completes the process. If the president vetoes the legislation, Congress may enact the measure into law by overriding the veto with a two-thirds supermajority vote in each chamber.

Both the House and Senate use procedures to expedite minor and noncontroversial legislation, but negotiating this lawmaking course for controversial measures is complicated and time-consuming. Throughout the process Congress must consider the opinion of the executive branch, constituents, and special interest groups. At any point the bill is subject to delay, defeat, or substantial modification. At each step of the way the bill's proponents must assemble a majority coalition through continual bargaining and compromise. "It is very easy to defeat a bill in Congress," President John F. Kennedy, a former representative and senator, once observed. "It is much more difficult to pass one."[1]

The success rate is low. In the 110th Congress (2007–2008) only 3.6 percent of the bills and joint resolutions introduced became law. In the 111th Congress (2009–2010), the enactment rate was only slightly higher—4.1 percent.

RULES GUIDE THE PROCESS

Reinforced by more than two centuries of precedent and custom, congressional rules and procedures can speed a bill to final passage or kill it, expand the policy alternatives or narrow them, disadvantage the minority or thwart the will of the majority. (See box, House and Senate Rules, p. 72.)

Legislators who know the rules and procedures are better able to influence the legislative process than those who do not. "If you let me write the procedure," Rep. John D. Dingell, D-Mich., once said, "and I let you write the substance, I'll [beat] you every time."[2]

The rules and procedures of the House of Representatives are designed to allow a majority to prevail consistently. But, in both houses, skillful use of the rules can permit a majority to achieve its objectives more quickly, bargain with the other chamber and with the president from strength, and reap maximum political advantage. Ineffective use of the rules can splinter a potential majority, require unwelcome concessions to opponents, create a potentially damaging

TERMS AND SESSIONS

The two-year period for which members of the House of Representatives are elected constitutes a Congress. Under the Twentieth Amendment to the U.S. Constitution, ratified in 1933, this period begins at noon on January 3 of an odd-numbered year, following the election of representatives the previous November, and ends at noon on January 3 of the next odd-numbered year. Congresses are numbered consecutively. The Congress that convened in January 2011 was the 112th in a series that began in 1789.

Prior to 1935, the term of a Congress began on March 4 of the odd-numbered year following the election and coincided with the inauguration of the president (also changed by the Twentieth Amendment to January 20 beginning in 1937). Under the Constitution, Congress is required to "assemble" at least once each year. The Twentieth Amendment provides that these annual meetings shall begin on January 3 unless Congress "shall by law appoint a different day," which it frequently does. For example, before the second session of the 111th Congress adjourned it passed a law, later signed by the president, to convene the first session of the 112th Congress on January 5, 2011. Each Congress, therefore, has two regular sessions beginning in January of successive years.

The Legislative Reorganization Act of 1970 stipulates that unless Congress provides otherwise the Senate and House "shall adjourn sine die not later than July 31 of each year" or, in nonelection years, take at least a thirty-day recess in August. The provision is not applicable if "a state of war exists pursuant to a declaration of war by the Congress." Congress routinely dispenses with this restriction by passing a concurrent resolution. In practice the annual sessions may run the entire year. In recent years, Congress has had to return after the congressional elections in early November to complete its work. These "lame duck" sessions were held in every even-numbered year from 1998 through 2010.

Adjournment *sine die* (literally, without a day) ends a session of Congress. Adjournment of the second session is the final action of a Congress and all legislation not passed by both houses expires. However, following adjournment there may still be some delay before legislation that has passed near the end of the session is enrolled and formally presented to the president for action. Members frequently include in the adjournment resolution language to authorize their leaders to call them back into session if circumstances require it. This occurred in 1998 when the House returned to consider impeachment charges against President Bill Clinton.

The president may "on extraordinary occasions" convene one or both houses in special session or threaten to do so to achieve a political or legislative objective. For example, in 1997 President Clinton threatened to delay the adjournment of the first session of the 105th Congress by calling a special session to consider campaign finance reform legislation. The Senate quickly took up the major legislation, but the proposal succumbed to a filibuster.

Within a session either house of Congress may adjourn for holiday observances or other brief periods of three days or less. In a typical week, for example, the Senate or House may meet through Thursday and then, by unanimous consent or by motion, convene on the following Monday. By constitutional directive neither house may adjourn for more than three days without the consent of the other, which they give through passage of a concurrent resolution.

The second session of the 110th Congress and the third session of the 76th Congress were the longest sessions in history, each lasting 366 days.

---

record of controversial and divisive votes, and portray a chamber or an entire Congress in disarray.

House and Senate rules and procedures differ significantly. Because House actions are intended to mirror the will of a national majority, its procedures are intended to ensure that the majority of the nation's representatives prevail. Because the Senate was designed to check what Thomas Jefferson called the "irregularities and abuses which often attend large and successful legislative majorities," its procedures are intended to ensure that the voice of the individual will be heard. This tradition survived the Senate's radical transformation from a body whose members were originally selected by state legislatures to one elected directly by popular vote, as stipulated by the Seventeenth Amendment, ratified in 1913. "Senate rules are tilted toward not doing things," House Speaker Jim Wright, a Texas Democrat, said in 1987. "House rules, if you know how to use them, are tilted toward allowing the majority to get its will done."[3]

Without tight procedural constraints to promote order, the House—with a membership more than four times that of the Senate—would be nearly impossible to operate. Thus the House is organized hierarchically and relies on tighter structure. Because debate is restricted and the amending process frequently limited, the House is able to dispose of legislation more quickly than the Senate.

By comparison, the Senate's smaller size allows it to be more personal and informal in its operations. Although the Senate has an elaborate network of rules and procedures, it may ignore or override them to suit the political needs of the moment, often increasing the difficulty of predicting how the Senate may operate at any particular time. However, it most often conducts business (such as deciding what legislation to consider, the length of time for debate, the number of amendments, and even when to pass bills large and small) by unanimous consent. Each member, even the most junior, is accorded a deference not seen in the House, and failure to recognize this could result in paralysis of the chamber's business. The privileges of engaging in unlimited debate—the filibuster—and offering nongermane amendments are cherished traditions in the Senate that are not permitted under House rules. Thus it is not surprising that the Senate may spend days or weeks considering a measure that the House debates and passes in a single afternoon. While the Senate is renowned for its slower pace, the tradition of using unanimous consent requests to conduct business, rather than making debatable motions, can facilitate the chamber moving expeditiously on matters that are either noncontroversial or on which members want to move quickly.

Evolution of Rules

Congressional rules and procedures are not static but evolve in response to changes within Congress. In the modern era several external developments and internal reforms have led to significant changes in the ways the two chambers conduct their business.

As in military doctrine, or even football strategy, in Congress there is a constant battle between offense and defense; the minority party devises ingenious ways, within the rules, to frustrate the majority—to slow or thwart the majority's efforts to enact legislation reflecting its policy priorities. Then, the majority party must find a way to overcome the newly implemented tactic, and that leads the minority to develop another strategy.

A major change in the 1970s was a new openness in congressional proceedings. For the first time many committees, including Senate-House conference committees, were required to open their meetings to the public. In practice, the conference only needs to have one open meeting, however, and the negotiations may occur outside the public eye. Outsiders could sit in as committee members bargained over provisions and language to be included or deleted from bills and resolutions.

Magnified further by the antipolitical atmosphere fostered by the Watergate scandal, which led to the resignation of President Richard M. Nixon, the emphasis on openness even extended to the traditionally secret meetings of the House Democratic Caucus, the organization of House Democrats. The caucus, which met in the House chamber, opened the public galleries to visitors and to the press from 1975 to 1980 for certain types of business.

A rules change in the House in 1971 made it possible to record how each individual voted on floor amendments considered in the Committee of the Whole, one of the procedures used to consider legislation. Formerly, the House recorded only the total number voting for or against such an amendment. The rules change meant that members could not vote one way while telling their constituents they voted another.

Many of these changes were favored by more liberal members of both parties, who correctly believed that a more open process would weaken long-established power centers in congressional committees, where conservative committee chairs wielding immense power often frustrated their legislative goals. (*See box, Methods of Voting in the House and Senate, p. 96.*)

Another major development in the 1960s and 1970s was an increase in the number of amendments offered on the floor of each chamber. Several factors contributed to this development. Constituents and special interest groups pressured individual members to take specific stands on issues of concern to them. Members, with one eye always on reelection, responded in ways to gain them wide recognition with their constituents and in later years with organizations that donated money to their reelection campaigns. Increased opportunities to obtain recorded votes in the House made it much easier to be visibly on the public record. In addition, increasing partisanship in Congress since the 1960s has broken down political norms of earlier eras—exemplified by the admonition of Speaker Sam Rayburn, D-Texas, to "get along, you have to go along"—which had tended to discourage members who wanted to be considered serious legislators from presenting issues and seeking confrontation solely to score political points.

This trend magnified in the late 1990s and into the twenty-first century, as lawmakers, political scientists, and other observers have all bemoaned the increasingly strident tones of congressional debates and the hyperpartisan refusal of many lawmakers to consider compromise. Lee Hamilton, D-Ind., who served in the House from 1965 to 1999, noted in an opinion piece in 2011, "There is room in politics for elected leaders who won't back down on their principles. But if they dominate the political sphere, representative government becomes impossible, as making progress on the many ills that beset us takes a back seat to declarations of principles."[4]

Congressional Quarterly, which began studying congressional voting behavior in 1945, reported that in 2010 almost 80 percent of all the votes taken in the Senate pitted one party against the other—the highest percentage *CQ* had ever noted. And, early in 2011, *CQ* reported that in the first four months of the year, the House had split into party-line positions almost 80 percent of the time, also an all-time high.

That growing partisanship has resulted in an ebb and flow in the number of amendments offered, as the majority party uses the power of the Rules Committee to structure floor proceedings to its advantage. Often that has meant restricting the number of amendments that can be offered. At other times, particularly when control of the House changes hands, the newly in-charge majority makes a point of trumpeting how much more open and fair it is than the previous majority, and permits more amendments to be offered.

Other factors have also influenced the rules governing amendments over time. Not only do amendments allow their authors to appeal to constituents, party leaders, and special interest supporters, but they also are often designed to make members of the other party cast votes that could be politically perilous back home. In response, leaders in each chamber began to develop ways to limit amendments. The number of amendments brought to the House and Senate floors decreased somewhat in the 1980s, partly because each house developed strategies to reduce amendments to avoid and partly because massive federal budget deficits meant that fewer new programs—and therefore fewer amendments to them—were being initiated.

From the mid-1980s onward the nation's budget deficit—and the special process Congress had devised for dealing with it—has been by far the single most time-consuming issue before Congress. It had also led to the increased use of omnibus bills: the packaging of many, often unrelated, proposals in a single, massive piece of legislation. Budget reconciliation measures, for example, revised existing laws touching every aspect of government to bring federal programs into conformity with the overall budget plan for the year. In addition, it became common practice to package all or most of the year's appropriations bills in a single piece of legislation. The opportunities to debate and amend these bills were often severely limited.

Rank-and-file House members were particularly affected by this narrowing of their opportunities to influence legislation. "What we have now is a technique for returning to a closed system where a few people make all the decisions," said Indiana Democrat Philip R. Sharp.[5]

In the 1980s and 1990s the tough choices posed by the need to reduce the deficit, frustration over the drop in opportunities to enact new programs, the new assertiveness of individual lawmakers, and increased partisanship posed procedural challenges in both chambers.

When they were in the minority, House Republicans complained, sometimes bitterly, that the Democratic leadership restricted floor debate and amendments in ways that trampled minority rights. In the minority themselves in both houses starting in 1995 in the 104th Congress, Democrats made the same claims against Republicans, who became increasingly adept at using the rules to their advantage in the early part of the twenty-first century. But when Democrats recaptured control of the House in the 110th Congress, they employed many of the same tactics. In each instance, the aggrieved minority members complained, without acknowledging the irony, about the same tactics that they themselves had used when they were in control. In the modern era, the majority-dominated House Rules Committee is essentially an arm of the Speaker's office that is detailed to engineer the outcomes desired by majority party leaders.

Members in both houses complained that it was politically difficult to make tough decisions in open committee meetings, and majority members were reluctant to allow the minority too many opportunities for procedural and political counterattack. An uneasy balance began to evolve between the ideals of process and the realities of politics. Many members of Congress who were reformers of the 1960s and 1970s had risen to power as committee barons in the 1980s and 1990s. They began to squirm in the limelight under multiple pressures from the public, the press, interest groups, and the

opposition party. These committee chairs were ready to make some compromises.

A few committees began to close their doors occasionally to the public, although the vast majority of meetings remained open. Conference committees, required by rule to operate in the open unless the full House of Representatives closed them by recorded vote, often finessed the rules by holding one or two open meetings and then having closed subconferences, caucuses of conferees and staff negotiations to make the real decisions. In 2003 House Democrats cried foul when a small set of Republican party leaders and senior committee members locked them out of discussions on the Medicare prescription-drug law, allowing only a pair of friendly Democratic senators to sit at the negotiating table.

These kinds of mechanisms proved essential to enact complex legislation such as omnibus budget reconciliation bills potentially involving two dozen committees and hundreds of conferees. In these cases, it was often physically impossible to squeeze all of the conferees into the same room at the same time, and any meeting could merely be ceremonial or procedural, not substantive. The large, deliberative conference meetings of the 1980s—one budget reconciliation measure involved nearly half of Congress in the conference negotiations—had been entirely abandoned by the late 1990s and early 2000s.

The conference almost became a thing of the past. According to *Congressional Quarterly*, during the 110th Congress, only nine bills were cleared via a conference process—an all-time low. In the 111th Congress, there was only one truly open conference—on a measure to overhaul financial regulations.

The procedural problems have been most acute in the Senate, where individual members can, and often do, bring the chamber to a standstill. Many senators have been vocal about their dissatisfaction with Senate procedures that let individual members pursue their own and their party's legislative interests at the expense of the Senate's interests. Two-term Indiana Democratic Sen. Evan Bayh, who grew up in Washington, D.C., while his father, Birch, was serving eighteen years in the Senate, expressed his displeasure in a surprise announcement in early 2010 that he would not seek reelection that year. Bayh cited the lack of bipartisan comity as one of the main reasons for the decision. "There is too much partisanship and not enough progress—too much narrow ideology and not enough practical problem-solving," he said.[6]

Even as rules have converged to tie more and more lawmaking to the budget, attempts to reduce the federal deficit and balance the federal budget have generated rules of their own. Throughout the 1970s and 1980s, the development of new procedures to enhance the ability to set priorities made little progress toward these goals. In the 1990s, Congress adopted a new budget ethos based on "pay as you go"

(PAYGO), which required new mandatory spending and tax cuts to be offset by spending cuts or tax increases elsewhere. The success in balancing the budget at the end of the 1990s was ultimately made possible by a booming economy that increased tax revenues and by mechanisms and events essentially outside of process—budget summit deals negotiated between key executive branch and congressional leaders and then sold to a majority of both chambers as a package. But after the September 11, 2001, terrorist attacks, and the expensive U.S. military involvement in Iraq and Afghanistan, budget deficits returned in explosive fashion. Even so, over time, Congress routinely waived PAYGO rules to ensure that President George W. Bush's tax cuts and spending on popular programs did not require concomitant cuts in entitlements. Statutory PAYGO spending caps were allowed to expire in 2002, and battles over whether the rules should be applied to tax cuts played a significant role in the failure of Congress to complete budget resolutions several times in the early 2000s.

When Democrats were returned to the majority in the House and Senate in 2007, they vowed to adhere to PAYGO rules for both new mandatory spending and tax cuts, adding provisions to House and Senate rules—and enacting statutory PAYGO provisions in 2010. In 2009, Democrats changed the PAYGO rules, permitting the majority to attach an "emergency" designation to entitlement spending bills to exempt those measures from the pay-as-you-go mandates. The legislation could receive an emergency designation "if such provisions are necessary to respond to an act of war, an act of terrorism, a natural disaster, or a period of sustained low economic growth," according to a Rules Committee summary of the package. In addition, the rules allowed a bill that did not meet PAYGO requirements to be linked procedurally with another piece of legislation that does have offsets.[7]

In 2011, when Republicans took control of the House, they replaced the PAYGO rules with a "cut-as-you-go" rule that requires new mandatory spending to be offset with cuts to existing programs. The rule did not require offsets for tax cuts and barred the use of tax increases to offset mandatory spending. The GOP rules also required that each appropriations bill contain a "spending reduction" account. The account would contain the total amount of spending removed from the bill through the amendment process. Amendments to cut certain accounts or lower funding levels in appropriations bills would be counted toward spending reduction, and the removed funds could not be spent on other programs.

Change in Party Control

For all its powers, rules, and traditions, Congress is dominated by forces beyond its control, such as the shifting will of the electorate. Just when consistent trends and historical patterns observed over several decades in Congress seem ripe for analysis and placement in historical perspective, the political environment can change rapidly.

Two-term Sen. Evan Bayh, D-Ind., is pictured with President Barack Obama on Air Force One. After just two terms, Bayh announced he would not seek reelection, citing partisanship as the reason for his departure. This partisanship has greatly impacted the rules that govern the lawmaking process.

SOURCE: MAI/Landov.

The evolution of congressional procedures and practices over the thirty years from the end of the 1960s reflected the emergence of younger, more liberal Democratic congressional members, especially in the House, who began as insurgents in the 1950s and 1960s, assumed control of both chambers in the 1970s, and became the power brokers and senior committee members of the 1980s and early 1990s. There was a period of brief conservative resurgence in the House following the landslide election of Ronald Reagan in the 1980s, which was complemented by Republican control of the Senate from 1981 to 1987. By the early 1990s, with the Democrats back in control of both houses of Congress, however, these GOP inroads on Democratic power seemed transitory and did not leave any fundamental changes in either body.

The Democratic dominance ended abruptly in 1995, as a new Republican majority containing large numbers of young, militant conservatives joined frustrated and angry senior GOP members who had long felt victimized and impotent in their legislative careers. Suddenly Republicans found themselves the guardians of congressional practices that many either knew little about or had railed against for years.

The most significant evolution during the years of Republican control of the House from 1995 to 2007, and the Senate for all but a year and a half of that time, was the further consolidation of power in the hands of party leaders at the expense of once-powerful committee and subcommittee chairs. In the House, Republican leaders instituted term limits for chairs that did not apply to party leaders, making clear that the positions held by chairs were temporary and that the elected party leaders would wield power indefinitely. They also chipped away at a nearly sacrosanct seniority system that had long determined who would become a chair, often dipping far down into the seniority ranks of a committee to choose its leader, frequently awarding chairmanships to committee members who had shown more fealty to them and raised more money for the party than their more senior colleagues.

Though the rules of the Senate were not changed to give more power to the institutionally weak party leaders, an influx of highly partisan House veterans in the 1990s and early 2000s empowered both Republican and Democratic leaders to impose party discipline and challenge the institutional norms that favor individualism. In a highly partisan era, these trends continued when Democrats reclaimed control of the House and the Senate in 2007. Speaker Nancy Pelosi, D-Calif., and Senate Majority Leader Harry Reid, D-Nev., demonstrated early on that they intended to consolidate power to an even greater degree than their Republican predecessors. For example, Pelosi, backed by her caucus, maintained the Republican-written term limits on Democratic committee chairs for the first time and created a new select committee on environmental issues to try to circumvent Energy and Commerce chair John D. Dingell, D-Mich., who disagreed with her over policy on vehicle emissions and fuel-efficiency standards. Reid routinely sought cloture on bills as soon as they were brought to the floor as a means of getting the Senate to decide quickly whether legislation had a chance.

At the beginning of the 112th Congress, with Democrats holding a narrow advantage in the Senate, Reid and Republican leader Mitch McConnell of Kentucky came to a "gentleman's agreement" about floor procedures. The majority Democrats would allow Republicans to offer more amendments to legislation, and in return, Republicans vowed not to block legislation from coming to the Senate floor. In the House early in the 112th Congress, the majority GOP Rules Committee produced rules that permitted significantly more amendments than were offered in the Democratic-controlled 111th Congress.

Pitfalls to Passage

As President Kennedy said, it is easier to defeat legislation than to pass it. And the route a bill must travel before it wins final approval allows many opportunities for its opponents to defeat or delay it. "Legislation is like a chess game more than anything else," Representative Dingell has said. "It is a seemingly endless series of moves, until ultimately somebody prevails through exhaustion, or brilliance, or because of overwhelming public sentiment for their side."[8]

Even if the majority party favors a bill, it still must be navigated through the legislative labyrinth before it is enacted. The first place a bill might run into trouble is in subcommittee or committee. Most bills, lacking the interest or support

of party leaders or the relevant committee chair, simply die without any consideration after they are referred to the committee of jurisdiction.

If a bill is marked up—that is, considered—by a subcommittee or a full committee, it likely receives close scrutiny by members and aides who, in part through their work on the committee, have developed expertise in the subject matter at hand. An open committee amendment process allows members to significantly modify the legislation in committee. Some amendments may make the legislation unpalatable to lawmakers who originally supported it, hurting its chances for full committee approval or for passage by the full chamber later in the process. Often, a committee chair will agree to modify a bill—or to work for later modifications—to secure its approval by the full committee.

The second place a bill may be delayed is in scheduling for floor action. When, and sometimes whether, a bill is brought to the floor of either the House or Senate depends on many factors, including what other legislation is awaiting action, how controversial the measure is, whether the leadership judges its chances for passage to be improved by immediate action, and whether its consideration or delay can be used as leverage by party leaders to win support for other priorities. Near the end of the 108th Congress, for example, House Majority Leader Tom DeLay, R-Texas, was accused by colleagues of bottling up noncontroversial bills favored by certain senators who had voted against cloture on an energy bill that carried a provision shielding producers of the gasoline additive MTBE from lawsuits. When asked, DeLay grinned and said, "I wouldn't know anything about that."

More typically, the leadership might decide to delay taking up a controversial bill until its proponents can gather sufficient support to guarantee its passage.

In the Senate, bills often cannot be scheduled much in advance until all of the interested senators have given clearance and holds by individual senators or groups of senators have been removed. (A hold is a request by a senator to delay action on a matter. The intent may be to delay indefinitely or postpone action until some concern is addressed. A hold carries an implicit threat that a filibuster would begin if the hold is not honored.) Even then, absent a unanimous consent agreement, filibusters are possible unless a supermajority of sixty senators (or three-fifths of the entire membership) intervenes to move the process forward. In the Senate, even if a bill itself is delayed or blocked, that does not prevent controversial issues from reaching the floor unexpectedly because they can be offered as nongermane amendments to other legislation at almost any time.

The next hurdle a bill must surmount is amendment and passage on the chamber floor. The amending process is at the heart of floor consideration in both chambers. Amendments have many objectives. Members may offer amendments to dramatize their stands on issues, even if their proposals are not likely to win adoption. Some amendments are offered at the request of the executive branch, a member's constituents, or special interests. Some become tactical tools for gauging sentiment for or against a bill. Others are used to stall action on a bill. In the Senate, the majority leader, who has the choice of always being the first to be called upon to speak or make a motion when multiple senators seek to control the floor, may offer amendments to prevent other senators from offering amendments, which is called "filling the amendment tree." (There are limits on the number of amendments that can be pending, and the majority leader uses this process to take up the available slots.) In the House, where debate is more strictly limited, a member may offer a pro forma amendment solely to gain a few additional minutes to speak on an issue. That amendment, often introduced in the form of a motion to "strike the last word," is deemed withdrawn when the "sponsor" finishes his or her remarks.

Still other amendments may be designed to defeat the legislation. One common strategy is to try to load a bill with so many amendments that it will eventually collapse under its own weight. Another strategy is to offer a killer or poison pill amendment, which, if adopted, would cause members who initially supported the bill to vote against it on final passage. Conversely, amendments known as sweeteners may be offered to attract broader support for the underlying measure. And finally, in the House, a motion to recommit the bill back to committee, either to kill it outright or send it back to the floor forthwith with additional amendments, gives opponents a final chance to persuade their colleagues to back away from the proposal or change it significantly.

The tactical use of such procedural tools as the motion to recommit can cause fits for party leaders, particularly those who are new to their jobs. Republicans took advantage of their own procedural expertise and Democrats' inexperience running the floor repeatedly in the years after Democrats assumed control of the House for the first time in a dozen years in 2007. Republicans were able to amend several bills through motions to recommit with instructions. Then, when Democrats tried to pass legislation that would expand the membership of the chamber from 435 to 437 by giving the District of Columbia's representative full voting rights in the House and by adding a seat in Utah, Republicans employed a rarely used (and now banned) wrinkle to frustrate the Democratic majority. They offered a motion to recommit with instructions that the bill be reported back promptly with an amendment nullifying gun control laws in the nation's capital. Republicans thus would put Democrats on record on gun owners' rights, while the use of the word "promptly" instead of "forthwith" meant that the committee would not have to report back at all if the motion was agreed to. Also, unlike a "forthwith" motion, in which the bill remains the pending business on the House floor, the committee would have needed to act again.

Democratic leaders pulled the bill off the floor and vowed to bring it back with a new rule for debate that would prohibit a similar motion from being considered. To illustrate the complexity of House rules, the motion to recommit on the gun language was germane only because of a seemingly unrelated effort by Democrats to offset the bill's costs with a revenue enhancement necessary to keep the bill in compliance with Democrats' own pay-as-you-go budget rules.

A bill that fails to clear any hurdle along the legislative process in either the House or the Senate is likely to be abandoned for the remainder of the Congress. Those measures that survive passage by both houses must still be reconciled through processes that hold a host of additional dangers and delays. The House and Senate may trade the bills back and forth like Ping-Pong balls, adding, subtracting, and modifying provisions. Or the legislation may face a conference committee, a temporary panel of House and Senate members established solely to work out the differences between the measures passed by the two chambers. The conference committee is sometimes known as the third house of Congress. Conferees bargain and compromise until they reach a version of the legislation acceptable to both chambers. Sometimes the legislation is substantially rewritten in conference, although rules changes in 2007 made it harder to add completely new items. Occasionally conferees cannot strike a compromise, and the legislation dies. The challenge of a conference lies in writing compromise legislation that can win the support not only of a majority of conferees from each chamber but also from party leaders in both chambers and the rank-and-file members in each chamber who must vote to adopt it.[9]

For a small number of measures the final hurdle is approval by the president. All modern presidents have used the veto threat to persuade Congress to pay attention to the executive viewpoint as it considers specific measures. Because presidents most of the time can muster the necessary support to defeat override attempts in Congress, lawmakers usually try to compromise with the chief executive. Sometimes, however, such efforts fail, and the bill is vetoed. In his first six years in office, President George W. Bush vetoed just one bill, but he found the threat of a veto to be an effective manner of pressuring Congress, particularly during Republican control, to alter legislation before it came to his desk. In his last two years, with Congress under Democratic control, Bush issued eleven vetoes, four of which were overridden.

All of these steps, repeated in endless variation for dozens of major bills, must be completed within the two-year cycle of a single Congress. Any bill that has not received final approval when a Congress adjourns automatically dies and must be reintroduced in the next Congress to begin the entire procedure over again. When a Congress is drawing to a close, the pressure to act can be intense. Lawmakers, who have put off making difficult choices, often find themselves rushing to keep their bills from dying. In a sentiment as apt in the twenty-first century as it was in the 1820s, Davy Crockett, a legendary frontiersman who served four House terms, once

HOUSE AND SENATE RULES

Article I, Section 5, of the U.S. Constitution stipulates that "Each House may determine the Rules of its Proceedings." In addition to the standing rules adopted under this authority, the House and Senate each have a separate set of precedents, practices, and customs that guide their conduct of business.

The standing rules of the House are set forth in the *Constitution, Jefferson's Manual, and Rules of the House of Representatives*, or the House Manual as it is commonly called, which is published with revisions during the first session of each Congress. The content is also available on the Government Printing Office's website. *(See "Congressional Information on the Internet," p. 237, in Reference Materials.)*

This is the most important single source of authority on the rules and contains voluminous annotations. In addition to the written chamber rules, the document contains the text of the Constitution, portions of the manual on parliamentary procedure that Thomas Jefferson wrote when he was vice president, budget rules, and the principal rulings and precedents of the House. The formal rules of the Senate are found in the *Senate Manual Containing the Standing Rules, Orders, Laws, and Resolutions Affecting the Business of the United States Senate*.

In the House, on the day when a new Congress convenes, the chamber has no formal rules and no committees, which are created in the rules. It operates under what is called general parliamentary law, which relies on *Jefferson's Manual* and many House precedents. Prior to opening day, the rules have been drafted by the majority party's conference or caucus. Amendments suggested by individual majority members are considered at such party meetings.

Following the election of the Speaker and the administration of the oath of office to members, the proposed rules of the House are offered directly from the floor as a resolution, usually by the majority leader or the person who will become the Rules Committee chair. The minority may be given the opportunity to offer a substitute. However, in the 110th, 111th, and 112th Congresses, the minority was not permitted to offer amendments. The only way amendments would have been permitted was for opponents to defeat the previous question. Then, they could seek to recommit the rules package to change it. The previous question has not been defeated on a rules package since 1971, when a conservative coalition of Republicans and southern Democrats defeated the previous question and forced the Democratic leadership to drop a provision for a "twenty-one-day rule," a procedure that would have allowed legislation to reach the floor without action by the Rules Committee.

The majority's rules package is often formally adopted on a party-line vote and becomes effective immediately. Once adopted, House rules continue in force through the Congress, unless further amended, and expire at its end.

In the 106th Congress, for the first time since 1880, the House recodified its rules, reducing them in number, reorganizing provisions without making substantive changes, and eliminating archaic language.

The Senate does not readopt its rules at the beginning of a Congress. Because only one-third of the chamber turns over every two years, the Senate considers itself a continuing body. Any proposed changes in existing rules are adopted subject to provisions already in the rules, such as Rule XXII, the cloture rule requiring a supermajority to cut off debate. This interpretation of the Senate's continuing nature was challenged by liberals for years as conflicting with Article I, Section 5, of the Constitution, but their contention that the Senate could cut off debate on proposed rules changes by majority vote at the beginning of a Congress was unsuccessful. The issue was raised again when Republicans wanted to circumvent the filibuster to confirm President George W. Bush's judicial picks in the 109th Congress, but Majority Leader Bill Frist, R-Tenn., did not attempt to execute a rules change.

In the controversy leading to the most recent important change in the cloture rule, the Senate did cast a series of votes in 1975 that appeared to support the right of a simple majority to avoid a filibuster and change Senate rules. But agreement

said: "We generally lounge or squabble the greater part of the session, and crowd into a few days of the last term three or four times the business done during as many preceding months."[10] As adjournment draws near, lawmakers, realizing that their last chance for passage of their own high-priority bill is at hand, often are able to gain the acquiescence of their largely indifferent colleagues and obtain passage of dozens of noncontroversial measures that are collectively referred to as "dogs and cats."

Controversial and far-reaching proposals are seldom enacted in a single Congress. More often they are introduced and reintroduced, incubating in a legislative cauldron as national sentiment on the issue coalesces and the necessary compromises are struck. The comprehensive revision of the Clean Air Act finally approved in 1990 had been stalled in Congress since 1977—over such controversial issues as acid rain—before the right combination of supporters and political circumstances emerged simultaneously to free it finally.

The addition of prescription-drug coverage to Medicare in 2003 concluded a debate that had been raging in health care circles for at least two decades. A 1988 catastrophic care law had expanded Medicare coverage to include prescription drugs, but that provision and others were repealed almost as soon as they had been enacted.

Congress enacted welfare reform in 1996, ending a sixty-one-year federal guarantee and representing the first time a major entitlement program for individuals was transformed into a block grant to states. Republicans had advocated radical changes in welfare for decades, and they revived these ideas as part of the Contract with America, a grouping of legislative and philosophical proposals the GOP used in the 1994 elections in its campaign to win control of the House. *(See box, Contract with America, p. 27.)*

Bill Clinton in his 1992 campaign for the presidency had promised to "end welfare as we know it." But it was only after initial presidential vetoes of Republican bills in 1995 and 1996, the intervention of the nation's governors who were greatly burdened by welfare costs, GOP fears of political reprisals from a partial shutdown of the federal government in late 1995 after a deadlock with Clinton, and Clinton's desire in his 1996 reelection bid to claim a major promise had

was subsequently reached to change Rule XXII by invoking cloture first by a two-thirds vote. Before doing so the Senate cast procedural votes that, it was argued, reversed this majority precedent.

House precedents, based on past rulings of the chair, are contained in three multivolume series: Hinds's *Precedents of the House of Representatives* covers the years 1789 through 1907; Cannon's *Precedents of the House of Representatives* covers from 1908 through 1935; and Deschler's *Precedents of the United States House of Representatives,* volumes one to nine, and Deschler-Brown *Precedents of the United States House of Representatives,* volumes ten to sixteen, cover 1936 through 1999. In addition, *Procedure in the U.S. House of Representatives* is a summary of all the important rulings of the chair through 1984. *House Practice: A Guide to the Rules, Precedents and Procedures of the House,* published in 1996 and updated in 2003, is a single volume by retired House parliamentarian William Holmes Brown that discusses selected precedents and the operation of current House rules in a less intimidating format and includes material on rules changes following the shift in party control in the 104th Congress.

Riddick's Senate Procedure: Precedents and Practices, by retired parliamentarian Floyd M. Riddick and Alan S. Frumin, who was parliamentarian when the book was last revised in 1992, contains precedents and related standing rules and statutory provisions through the end of the 101st Congress.

In addition to precedents, each chamber has particular traditions and customs that it follows—recognition of the Senate majority leader ahead of other senators seeking recognition from the chair is an example of such a practice. Moreover, each party in each chamber has its own set of party rules that can affect the chamber's proceedings.

Many public laws also contain provisions that affect House and Senate procedures. Prominent examples are the Congressional Budget and Impoundment Control Act of 1974, the Base Realignment and Closing laws of 1988 and 1990, and so-called fast-track or trade promotion legislation. The latter two laws basically force each chamber to deal with proposals presented to it on a short timetable with only up-or-down votes permitted. The fast-track law expired in 2007, but treaties negotiated under its provisions could still be brought to Congress after that. Other examples would be numerous statutory provisions, rendered moot by the U.S. Supreme Court's 1983 *Immigration and Naturalization Service v. Chadha* decision, which provided for various schemes of approval or disapproval of actions by the executive branch or independent agencies by either one or both houses.

Such rulemaking statutes obviate the need for each chamber to create special procedures on an ad hoc basis whenever it takes some action on the subject matter dealt with in these laws. Without fast-track authority, for example, the president would find it difficult to negotiate credibly with foreign nations without the advance assurance that each chamber would not amend the agreements in potentially unpredictable ways, ultimately rendering them unacceptable to these nations. The existence of procedures set out by law is particularly significant in the Senate, where they serve to limit debate and prevent filibusters. However, such statutes, even though they are laws passed by both chambers and signed by the president, still remain subservient to each chamber's constitutional power to amend its rules at any time. (For example, the House could always adopt a special rule allowing amendments to a fast-track trade agreement. And in 2008 the House Democratic majority, declaring that under the fast-track law, the procedures and timetable for congressional action were rules of the House and Senate that could be changed by either chamber, refused to consider a trade agreement with Colombia submitted by President George W. Bush. In the Senate, which has no equivalent of the House's Rules Committee, any alterations in process would be far more difficult.)

been kept that the necessary compromises were reached to ensure enactment of welfare reform.

More recently, the sweeping health care overhaul law enacted in 2010 was the result of decades of legislative efforts. Rep. Dingell, for instance, who came to Congress in 1955, had introduced a national health care bill in every Congress since then. And the major legislative battle of 1993 was the unsuccessful effort by President Clinton (publicly joined by his wife, Hillary Rodham Clinton) to enact a national health care system.

Of course, even enactment of a law does not always signal the end of the battle—as proven by the repeal of the 1988 prescription drug law and the effort by House Republicans in 2011 to repeal the 2010 health care law.

The legislative process and its various stages seem clear enough. Those interested in either passing or defeating legislation will ultimately win, lose, or accept some compromise. However, sometimes long-standing patterns of congressional behavior, the seemingly fixed interrelationships with other branches of government, and the comfortable access to the legislative process enjoyed by a mix of influential special interest groups can shift abruptly with the public mood.

An extraordinary, modern example of the effects of a sudden radical change in the traditional approach to legislating occurred during the first few months of the 104th Congress in 1995, after the Republican Party had assumed control of both houses for the first time in four decades. The House Republican majority, apparently sensing a popular mandate after its landslide 1994 victory and gain of fifty-two seats, briefly appeared to be ushering in a new era of congressional government. The Senate was relegated to playing second fiddle. The president was purportedly seen as almost irrelevant. The House worked feverishly to rush the legislative components of its Contract with America proposals to the floor, sometimes without even holding hearings or allowing amendments. When Democrats took control of the House following the 2006 election, Speaker Pelosi, the highest-ranking woman ever in American government, followed a similar model by pushing Democratic-written bills through the House without so much as a committee hearing. But in both cases, the new House majorities were most effective at implementing new rules to govern the chamber, action that could be taken without the consent of the Senate and the president. The most significant feat of the Contract with America was a restructuring of the institution to centralize power in the hands of the Speaker by reining in subcommittee chairs and committee chairs.

In the 104th Congress, the controversies associated with the ambitious new agenda led to gridlock between the GOP-led Congress and a Democratic president, vetoes of tax and appropriations bills, two shutdowns of some government departments and agencies in the period from December 1995 to January 1996, a near collapse of Republican control of the chamber in the 1996 election, and the easy reelection of the once seemingly crippled President Clinton.

Congress found itself in similar circumstances in 2011, with the Republican takeover of the House, abetted by the arrival of 87 GOP freshmen, most of whom campaigned on a platform of reducing the size and role of the federal government. Much like the Capitol Hill–White House gridlock that had led to government shutdowns in 1995 and 1996, the crisis in 2011 was over whether, and under what terms, Congress would pass legislation to increase the national debt limit.

DEVELOPING LEGISLATION

Procedures for introducing legislation and seeing it through committee are similar in the House and Senate.

Legislative proposals originate in different ways. Members of Congress develop ideas for legislation. Assistance in drafting legislative language is available from each chamber's Office of Legislative Counsel. Special interest groups—business, labor, farm, civil rights, consumer, trade associations, and the like—are another fertile source of legislation. Many of these organizations and their lobbyists in Washington, D.C., provide detailed technical knowledge in specialized fields and employ experts in the art of drafting bills and amendments. Constituents, either as individuals or groups, also may suggest legislation. A member of Congress may introduce a bill for the administration or a private organization, such as a trade association, and the bill will have "by request" printed on it.

Much of the legislation considered by Congress originates in the executive branch (although key members of Congress may participate in the formulation of administration programs). This is especially true if Congress and the president are of the same political party. However, the periodic emergence of an entirely separate congressional agenda, such as the GOP's 1994 contract or the Democratic "six for '06" agenda, illustrates the ability of Congress to confront the president aggressively and push ahead independently on a vast range of issues. For example, as one of its first acts in 2007, the Democratic House passed an embryonic stem cell research measure that President George W. Bush had vetoed in the 109th Congress. Although Congress may not be dependent on the

executive if it wants to pass legislation, the presidential veto usually remains the ultimate arbiter of whatever is enacted into law. This proved true again, as Bush vetoed the stem cell bill in June 2007 and Congress did not attempt an override. (Bush's ban on federal funding for stem cell research was lifted in 2009 by President Barack Obama by presidential directive.)

Each year after the president outlines his legislative program, executive departments and agencies transmit to the House and Senate drafts of proposed legislation to carry out the president's program or ideas. Because only members can introduce bills, these presidential initiatives may be introduced "by request" by the chair of the committee or subcommittee having jurisdiction over the subject involved, or by the ranking minority member if the chair is not of the president's party. The congressional leadership may designate a group of bills as key legislative initiatives and give them low bill numbers (such as HR 1 or HR 2) to emphasize their importance. Bill numbers HR 1–10 and S 1–10 are typically reserved for party leaders to use for the designation of important legislation. Recent bills tagged with HR 1 include a funding bill in the 112th Congress that would have cut $100 billion from fiscal 2011 appropriations, the implementation of National Commission on Terrorist Attacks Upon the United States (known as the 9/11 commission) security recommendations in the 110th Congress, the Medicare drug legislation in the 108th Congress, the No Child Left Behind measure in the 107th Congress, and the Family and Medical Leave Act in the 103rd Congress.

Committees may also consider proposals that have not been formally introduced. The committee may work from its own preliminary text, called the chair's mark, and a bill is introduced at a later stage. When legislation is heavily amended in committee, all the changes, deletions, and additions, together with whatever is left of the original bill, may be organized into a new bill.

In an ideal world, cooperation between the two branches throughout the legislative process would smooth out the rough edges in legislation and help ensure that no one is surprised either in committee or on the floor. This assumes that there is a desire for cooperation. It may appear to be to the political advantage of one branch or the other, or both, to engage in a confrontation. Enactment of legislation may not be the primary goal in such circumstances, or even be desired. Someone wants to create an issue, so he or she picks a fight. Fights involve risks, so one side must perceive some political reward for taking them. The president often gains the advantage in such situations because of the White House's ability to present a case more clearly and consistently to the public, while Congress has many potential spokespeople of lesser stature who may not all be of the same opinion or able to command attention.

Introduction of Legislation

No matter where a legislative proposal originates, it can be introduced only by a member of Congress. In the House, a member may introduce any of several types of bills and resolutions by handing them to the clerk of the House or by placing them in a mahogany box near the clerk's desk called the hopper. The member need not seek recognition for the purpose. The resident commissioner of Puerto Rico and the delegates of the District of Columbia, Guam, American Samoa, the Virgin Islands, and the Northern Mariana Islands also have this right.

Senators introduce legislation from the floor during the morning hour or other period of the day set aside for doing so, but increasingly they have gone to the House practice of leaving them at the desk.

There is no limit to the number of bills and resolutions members may introduce and no restrictions on the time during a Congress when they may do so. It is rare to find a day when Congress is in session when someone does not introduce something. House and Senate bills may have joint sponsorship and carry several members' names. The Constitution stipulates that "all bills for raising revenue shall originate in the House of Representatives," and the House has successfully insisted that it reserves the power to originate appropriation bills as well. All other bills may originate in either chamber.

Major legislation often is introduced in both houses in the form of companion (identical) bills, primarily to speed up the legislative process by encouraging both chambers to consider the measure simultaneously. Sponsors of companion bills also may hope to dramatize the importance or urgency of the issue and show broad support for the legislation. At the beginning of a Congress, members vie to be the sponsors of the first bills introduced and to retain the same bill number in consecutive Congresses on legislation that has not been enacted. The House and Senate majority leadership typically reserve low bill numbers for measures that are key elements of their legislative program. In 1995 Speaker Gingrich gave many Contract with America items the first bill numbers assigned, including designating as HR 1 the Congressional Accountability Act, which applied workplace laws in the private sector to Congress (this was S 2 in the Senate), and as House Joint Resolution 1 a proposed constitutional amendment to require a balanced federal budget.

WHEN A SUPERMAJORITY VOTE IS REQUIRED BY CONGRESS

The U.S. Constitution created two houses of Congress, each of which could act, with a quorum present, by simple majority vote except with respect to certain extraordinary matters that required support from a supermajority. *Jefferson's Manual* states: "The voice of the majority decides . . . where not otherwise expressly provided." These principles have also applied to actions taken in congressional committees, unless otherwise provided by rule or statute.

The Constitution requires a two-thirds majority vote of both the House and Senate to

- Override a presidential veto
- Pass a constitutional amendment
- Remove political disabilities (Fourteenth Amendment)
- Overrule a disabled president's declaration that he is capable of resuming duties (Twenty-fifth Amendment)

The Constitution requires a two-thirds majority in the Senate to

- Convict in an impeachment trial
- Ratify a treaty

The Constitution requires a two-thirds majority of either the House or the Senate to expel a member.

The House and Senate also have adopted supermajority requirements for various procedural actions. In the House, a two-thirds majority is required to

- Suspend the rules and pass a measure
- Consider a report from the Rules Committee relating to a rule or special order of business on the same legislative day it is reported to the House (a legislative day starts when the Senate meets after an adjournment, and it ends when the Senate adjourns next)
- Dispense with Calendar Wednesday
- Dispense with the call of the Private Calendar

In the Senate, a two-thirds vote is required to suspend a rule of the Senate (a rarely used procedure) and to invoke cloture and end debate under Rule XXII on any measure to change the rules of the Senate. (Senate rules themselves may be amended by a simple majority.)

The Senate rules otherwise require sixty votes ("three fifths of the senators duly chosen and sworn," assuming no vacancies in the Senate) to invoke cloture under Rule XXII on debate on all other debatable matters including bills, nominations, and motions.

A supermajority of sixty members is also required in the Senate to override various points of order under the 1974 Congressional Budget and Impoundment Control Act and to appeal rulings of the presiding officer related to those provisions.

In the 110th Congress, the Senate adopted two rules involving earmarks and conference reports that require sixty votes to overcome. One rule bars consideration of any bill or conference report unless all earmarks had been identified on the Internet at least 48 hours before the Senate voted on the measure. Also, if a conference report contains an item or earmark that was added in conference—a so-called air-dropped provision—that provision can be stricken. A sixty-vote majority would be required to waive the point of order.

Speaker Pelosi and Majority Leader Reid followed suit in 2007. Pelosi numbered bills addressing Democrats' six campaign promises—implementing recommendations of the 9/11 commission, raising the minimum wage, allowing the government to negotiate lower prescription-drug prices under Medicare, expanding embryonic stem cell research, lowering student loan rates, and promoting alternative energy—HR 1 through HR 6. Reid made the same bills S 2 through S 7, leaving the first slot for a lobbying reform bill.

Thousands of bills are introduced in every Congress, but most never receive any consideration, and consideration is not expected. Lawmakers introduce measures for a variety of reasons—to stake out a stand on an issue, as a favor to a constituent or a special interest group, to get publicity, or to ward off political attack. As congressional expert Walter J. Oleszek writes, once such a bill has been introduced, the legislator can claim that he or she has taken action "and can blame the committee to which the bill has been referred for its failure to win enactment."[11]

However, in the House, a number of factors have operated to reduce the number of bills introduced substantially since the 1980s and 1990s. The most significant was a rules change in 1979 that allowed an unlimited number of members to cosponsor any legislation introduced, obviating the need for members to introduce duplicate bills to get their names onto them. (Before 1967, House rules barred representatives from cosponsoring legislation. From 1967 to 1979, the rules limited the number of cosponsors to twenty-five). The effect was immediate, reducing the number of bills introduced from 14,414 in the 95th Congress to 8,456 in the 96th. Since then, the number continued to decline, averaging fewer than 6,000 over the next five congresses. In the 111th Congress, 6,562 bills were introduced in the House.

Nonetheless, the modern Congress considers and enacts fewer measures than its predecessors. But it is impossible to measure congressional workload by the number of measures passed. After enactment of the Congressional Budget and Impoundment Control Act of 1974, Congress tended to package many, often unrelated, proposals in lengthy pieces of legislation known as omnibus bills.

During the 1980s, the number of commemorative bills—those designating commemorative days, weeks, or months, for example—increased. Commemoratives were often introduced as joint resolutions, which required a presidential signature to become law and carried the possibility of a signing ceremony and media coverage. However, their sheer volume was often used by critics and by the media to ridicule the work product of a Congress whose principal achievements might be contained in a massive omnibus budget reconciliation bill and a continuing resolution.

When the Republicans took control of the House in 1995, they prohibited by rule the introduction of commemorative legislation or its consideration in that chamber, which

also had the effect of shutting off similar Senate action. The impact of the new rule can easily be seen in the drop in the number of joint resolutions introduced in the House, from 429 in the 103rd Congress to 140 in the 105th, and in the Senate from 232 in the 103rd to 60 in the 105th. In the 109th Congress, those numbers dropped to 102 in the House and 41 in the Senate. However, lawmakers still name post offices and other federal facilities after people ranging from musician Ray Charles (the postal facility on West Washington Boulevard in Los Angeles, California) to President Ronald Reagan (the postal facility on Minton Road in West Melbourne, Florida).

Bills not enacted die with the Congress in which they were introduced and must be reintroduced in a new Congress if they are to be eligible for further consideration. Resolutions adopted by the House affecting its operations during a Congress also expire automatically. However, similar Senate resolutions may remain in effect, as the Senate considers itself a continuing body. Nominations pending in the Senate expire at the end of each session of Congress but are usually carried over into the next session of the same Congress by unanimous consent. Treaties pending in the Senate, once submitted by the president, remain pending from one Congress to another. Nominations, however, lapse under those conditions and must be resubmitted in the next Congress.

Major legislation goes through changes in nomenclature as it works its way through the legislative process. When a measure is introduced and first printed, it is officially referred to and labeled as a bill. When it has been passed by one house and sent to the other body it is reprinted and officially labeled an act. When cleared by Congress and signed by the president, it becomes a law (and also may still be referred to as an act).

Types of Legislation

The types of measures that Congress may consider and act on (in addition to treaties and nominations submitted by the president to the Senate) are bills and three kinds of resolutions (joint, concurrent, and simple). The first to be introduced is designated as number 1 of its type, and numbers increase with the chronological introduction of additional measures.

Bills are prefixed with HR when introduced in the House and with S when introduced in the Senate, followed by a number assigned to the measure. The vast majority of legislative proposals dealing with either domestic or foreign issues and programs affecting the U.S. government or the population generally are drafted in the form of bills. These include both authorizations, which provide the legal authority and spending limits for federal programs and agencies, and appropriations, which provide the money for those programs and agencies. When passed by both chambers in identical form and signed by the president (or if Congress overrides a presidential veto), they become laws. Under specific circumstances the president also may allow a bill to become law without his signature.

Joint resolutions are designated H J Res or S J Res. A joint resolution, like a bill, requires the approval of both houses and (usually) the signature of the president. Proposed amendments to the Constitution, which begin as joint resolutions, are not sent to the president. If they win two-thirds majorities in both chambers, they require ratification of three-fourths of the states—but not the approval of the president—to be adopted. Some proposed amendments to the Constitution require ratification within a certain time period and some do not. The joint resolution that became the Twenty-seventh Amendment was introduced in 1789 and was not ratified by three-fourths of the states until 1992. Joint resolutions have the force of law if approved. There is no real difference between a bill and a joint resolution. The latter generally is used when dealing with a single item or issue, such as a continuing or emergency appropriations bill.

Concurrent resolutions are designated as H Con Res or S Con Res. Used for matters affecting the operations of both houses, concurrent resolutions must be passed in the same form by both houses, but they are not presented to the president for his signature, and they do not have the force of law. Concurrent resolutions are used to fix the time of adjournment of a Congress or to express the "sense of Congress" on an issue. Some concurrent resolutions, such as the annual congressional budget resolutions setting Congress's revenue and spending goals for the upcoming fiscal year, set rules or other procedures for one or both houses and, as such, can have a substantial impact on all other legislation that Congress considers.

Resolutions, also referred to as simple resolutions, are designated as H Res or S Res. A simple resolution deals with matters entirely within the prerogative of one house of Congress, such as setting the spending levels for its committees, revising the chamber's standing rules, or expressing the opinion of that house on a current issue, and is acted on only by that chamber. A simple resolution is not considered by the other chamber and does not require action by the president. Like a concurrent resolution, it does not have the force of law. However, adoption of resolutions can have effects outside the chamber. For example, the Senate adopts resolutions of ratification for treaties. At the end of the 100th Congress (1987–1989) adoption of a Senate resolution had the effect of carrying over into the next Congress impeachment proceedings against a federal judge. In the House, simple resolutions embody the special orders of business, or rules, reported by the Rules Committee that set guidelines for floor consideration of legislation.

Bill Referral

Once a measure has been introduced and given a number, it is almost always referred to committee. (Rarely a member might ask unanimous consent that a bill be taken up for consideration on the House or Senate floor immediately.

Such bills are usually either noncontroversial or of great urgency.) The Speaker of the House and the presiding officer in the Senate are responsible for referring bills introduced in their respective chambers to the appropriate committees, but the job is usually left to the House and Senate parliamentarians, respectively.

House and Senate rules require that all bills be read three times before passage, in accordance with traditional parliamentary rules. In the House, the first reading occurs when the bill is introduced and printed by number and title in the *Congressional Record*. The second reading occurs when floor consideration begins. Often the bill is read section by section for amendment. The third reading comes just before the vote on final passage. Senate rules require bills and resolutions to be read twice, on different legislative days (a legislative day starts when the Senate meets after an adjournment, and it ends when the Senate adjourns next), before they are referred to committee. The third reading follows floor debate and voting on amendments.

The jurisdictions of the standing committees are spelled out in House Rule X and Senate Rule XXV, and referrals are generally routine—tax bills go to House Ways and Means and Senate Finance, for example. However, bills can cover a multitude of subjects that need not have any relationship to each other, which can lead to complications in the referral process.

Many issues that come before Congress cut across the jurisdictions of several committees. Three House committees—Foreign Affairs, Energy and Commerce, and Ways and Means—might all lay claim to jurisdiction over a trade measure, for example, and the Speaker might refer it to all of them for consideration.

The authors of a bill often try to manipulate or anticipate the referral process to ensure it goes to a sympathetic committee or avoids a hostile one, a consideration that often figures into the manner in which legislation is drafted initially. The mechanics of this strategy have changed over the years, especially in the House, where the rules on committee referral have been modified on several occasions. Prior to 1975, measures introduced in the House could be referred to only a single committee, no matter how many subjects they might encompass. Any bill containing a tax provision, for instance, was always referred to the Ways and Means Committee.

During the reform period of the mid-1970s, in an attempt to prevent some committees from monopolizing legislation, to provide additional opportunities for a larger number of members to participate in the legislative process, and to strengthen the role of the Speaker, House rules were changed to allow the Speaker to refer legislation to more than one committee and to impose time limits on referrals. The Speaker was given several options. The Speaker could refer a bill to several committees at once, which was called a concurrent or joint referral; refer a bill first to one committee and then later to others, called a sequential referral; and send portions of bills to different committees, called a split referral.

As a result, some bills could be referred to numerous committees simultaneously, making it difficult to plot a path for them to the floor. Open warfare often developed among committees that sought opportunities to expand their power by claiming jurisdiction, with the Speaker placed in the middle. The Energy and Commerce Committee under the Democrats, with a mammoth portfolio and chaired by the aggressive John D. Dingell, D-Mich., from 1981 to 1995, was especially noted for its expansive, repeated, and contentious jurisdictional claims.

If necessary, legislation could be referred from one committee to another by unanimous consent to correct any errors that arose.

In referring bills, the House Speaker may set deadlines for committee action. At the beginning of the 1983 session, Speaker Thomas P. "Tip" O'Neill Jr., D-Mass., announced that in some multiple referrals he would designate one committee the primary committee and might "impose time limits on committees having a secondary interest following the report of the primary committee." The use of multiple referrals gave House leaders greater opportunities to bargain with and bring together key legislative players and opened the process to a broader range of views. But multiple referrals also created potential additional obstacles for a bill to surmount before it reached the floor. While the referral reforms of the 1970s in the House democratized the process and prevented one committee from monopolizing a particular subject matter, there were distinct negative trade-offs in terms of increased complexity, confusion, and lack of ultimate accountability for legislation. The House-Senate conference process also was affected, as conferences grew in size to accommodate all the new participants. But in recent years, party leaders have tried to limit the number of members who participate in conference committees.

Sometimes the subject matter of a bill, or the political situation surrounding it, proved to be so complex that the normal rules could not work. House rules were amended to provide that, in addition to referring bills to more than one committee, the Speaker, with the approval of the House, may set up an ad hoc committee to consider a bill. Speaker O'Neill did that in 1977 when he created a temporary committee to consider President Jimmy Carter's energy package.

When the Republicans took over the House in 1995, they had little stake in the existing system or in the various formal and informal jurisdictional accommodations that had been reached over the years to satisfy key Democrats. They reacted to complaints that the referral process was too confusing by changing the rules again and further enhancing the role of the leadership. The earlier version of the joint referral was abolished. Instead the Speaker was required to designate a primary committee to manage the major workload related to a bill. Other committees would participate through an additional initial referral or through later sequential referrals at the Speaker's discretion and under possible time limitations. Speaker Newt Gingrich used ad hoc committees to craft legislation. His successor, J. Dennis Hastert, R-Ill., sought a return to employing the traditional committee process or regular order, instead of ad hoc or select committees, to write legislation. But during Hastert's reign, from 1999 to 2007, party leaders maintained a strong hand not only in rewriting bills but also in selecting the subcommittee and committee chairs charged with writing them. In one of her first acts as Speaker in 2007, Pelosi established a select committee to consider climate change issues. In doing so, she created a temporary panel, which existed from 2007 to 2011, outside the jurisdictions of a pair of powerful chairs, Dingell at Energy and Commerce and Henry A. Waxman, D-Calif., at Oversight and Government Reform, as well as other chairs at other committees with jurisdiction over such issues. (Waxman replaced Dingell as chair of Energy and Commerce in the 111th Congress.) The climate change committee had no legislative jurisdiction—that is, it could not act on legislation. Its authority was solely "to investigate, study, make findings, and develop recommendations. . . ."

The Senate usually refers bills to more than one committee by unanimous consent. Bills may be referred to two or more committees concurrently or sequentially, or a bill may be split so that part of it is referred to one committee, part to another. Also, the majority and minority leaders or their designees, acting jointly, may offer a motion providing for a joint or sequential referral. In the Senate multiple referrals may contain a deadline for action by one or more of the committees. However, bills are almost always referred to just one committee for consideration. The Senate is also more likely to discharge a committee from consideration of a measure so that it can be brought to the floor without that committee having taken action.

Often, different committees of the House and Senate can claim jurisdiction of the same subject matter, because the committee systems of the two bodies do not coincide. The result can be a dramatically different reception for a measure, depending on the composition of the panel. A classic example of this strategy was the 1963 civil rights bill. The House version was referred to the Judiciary Committee, whose chair supported the measure. The chair of the Senate Judiciary Committee, however, opposed it. Thus the Senate version was drafted in such a way that it would be referred to the more sympathetic Senate Commerce Committee. (The measure guaranteed minorities access to public accommodations, which fell within the Commerce Clause of the Constitution.)

In Committee

Although the House and Senate handle bills in different ways when they reach the floor, the committee system in both chambers is similar. The standing committees of Congress determine the fate of most proposals. A bill comes under the sharpest scrutiny at the committee stage, in part because committee members and staff frequently are experts in the subjects under their jurisdiction. If a measure is going to be substantially revised, that revision usually occurs at the committee or subcommittee level instead of during floor consideration, though leaders of the Congresses around the turn of the twenty-first century often made significant changes to legislation on the floor through manager's amendments or self-executing rules that altered the measure. Committees usually use hearings as the first step of their process, to receive testimony and information. But if legislation moves forward, further revision occurs at meetings where a bill is marked up when amendments are offered, debated, and voted on.

Legislation may be disposed of by a committee in several ways.

- It may be ignored if the chair never puts it on the agenda at a committee meeting, which is by far the most frequent disposition of most legislation.

- It may be approved, or reported favorably with or without amendments, which is the normal result for most legislation that is allowed to reach the stage of a committee markup.

- It may be reported negatively or without recommendation, which might still allow full House or Senate consideration. For example, in a highly unusual action the House Rules Committee in 1996 reported a rule providing procedures for consideration of a controversial campaign reform bill without recommendation, an indication of distaste for the House GOP leadership's decision to schedule floor action on this controversial proposal. (Thirty years earlier, when the committee was still an autonomous power center instead of an arm of the House leadership that it later became, the panel would probably have simply refused to grant a rule.) In 2005 the Senate Foreign Relations Committee reported the nomination of John R. Bolton to become ambassador to the United Nations without recommendation, presaging two filibusters on the floor that blocked his confirmation by the Senate and ultimately led to a recess appointment by President George W. Bush.

- It might be taken up and killed outright through a tabling motion, a rare event but one that occurred in 1997 in the House Judiciary Committee, which used this means to give sponsors of legislation abolishing affirmative action programs a vote while demonstrating that the proposal was not yet ripe for action.

Hearings

The full committee may decide to consider a bill in the first instance, but, particularly in the House, more often the committee chair assigns it to a subcommittee for study and hearings. The rules of many committees in the House were amended starting in the 1970s to require the referral of bills to subcommittees, and the House Democratic Caucus

Stephen Colbert, host of the mock news program The Colbert Report *on Comedy Central, testifies before a House Judiciary Committee Immigration, Citizenship, Refugees, Border Security, and International Law Subcommittee hearing regarding migrant farm workers and the agricultural industry on Capitol Hill in Washington, September 24, 2010. Publicity for important issues is one intended consequence of Congressional hearings. However, some argued that by appearing in character, Colbert made a mockery of the proceedings.*

SOURCE: UPI/Roger L. Wollenberg/Landov.

adopted a rule urging a greater role on the floor for subcommittees that had initiated major legislation. The Republican-controlled House of the late 1990s, while continuing to use subcommittees, subjected them to greater discipline and control by the leadership in pursuing a party agenda than was true when Democrats were in the majority.

Assigning bills to a sympathetic or unsympathetic subcommittee is one of the ways a committee chair can influence the legislative outcome. No longer able to dictate committee activities the way they could prior to 1970s procedural reforms, committee chairs now negotiate with committee members to work out arrangements that will accommodate as many members as possible. But the chair still controls the committee's funds and can hire and fire committee staffers. Chairs therefore are in a position either to promote expeditious action on legislation they favor or to encourage delay and inaction on measures they oppose.

Few bills reach the House or Senate floor without first being the subject of hearings. Hearings are used to receive testimony from members of Congress, executive branch officials, policy experts, interest groups, and the general public, and they are usually held at the subcommittee level. Testimony may be delivered by witnesses either in person or through written submissions that may later be published as part of the hearing transcript. Most persons who come before committees offer prepared statements, after which they may be questioned by subcommittee members.

Hearings are used for a variety of purposes—to gather information, to attract media attention, to test initial reaction to a legislative idea. Hearings may be held by either a subcommittee or a full committee—sometimes both. Full committees will sometimes hold hearings as well on subjects of major public controversy, or when witnesses from the top levels of government are called to testify. Senate hearings in 1997 on alleged campaign finance scandals were held by the full Committee on Governmental Affairs, instead of its investigations subcommittee, and a companion House inquiry was run by the full Committee on Government Reform and Oversight. Major League Baseball stars appeared before that same House committee in 2005 to testify about steroid use in their sport.

Hearings are intended as fact-finding forums to educate both members of Congress and the public about specific problems. They may also be used to assess the degree of support or opposition to a particular bill or to promote support or opposition to a bill in Congress and among the public. Some hearings are held primarily to score political points and buttress the views of the majority party. Many hearings are brief and perfunctory. Because demands on legislators' time are so great, only a few members with a special interest in a subject are likely to participate.

The presence of television, along with controversial subject matter, can attract substantial interest from members even on subjects on which they might not otherwise actively participate. The creation of the Cable-Satellite Public Affairs Network (C-SPAN), which usually televises some hearings on any day that Congress is in session, has forced Congress to accommodate the new medium. Television's powerful intrusiveness is coupled with the medium's need for interesting or dramatic events that readily provide heroes and villains and promote controversy. Members with the skill to accommodate these channels of communication to the public have a powerful force to influence the outcome of policy debates. Increasingly, committees are making their proceedings available through webcasts that can be viewed live or later on. *(See box, Televised Floor Debates Here to Stay, p. 82.)*

Some hearings do not directly involve legislation. The Army-McCarthy hearings in the early 1950s turned public opinion against Sen. Joseph R. McCarthy, R-Wis., who had made a career of accusations of communist penetration of the government. Senate Foreign Relations Committee hearings in the mid-1960s, under Sen. J. William Fulbright, D-Ark., mobilized opposition to the Vietnam War. Senate committee hearings in 1973 into a variety of illegal activities in the White House that came to be known collectively as the Watergate scandal, and the ensuing 1974 House Judiciary Committee impeachment proceedings against President Nixon, destroyed the remnants of popular support for Nixon and, in the process, made folk heroes of the committees' chairs, Sen. Sam Ervin, D-N.C., and Rep. Peter W. Rodino Jr., D-N.J. Televised Senate Judiciary Committee hearings in 1987 helped fuel the controversy over the nomination of Robert H. Bork to a seat on the Supreme Court, moving public opinion decisively against him and ensuring his defeat. Explosive 1991 hearings by the all-male Senate Judiciary Committee on sexual harassment accusations against Supreme Court nominee Clarence Thomas charged a national debate that continued years later. While public opinion about Thomas was sharply divided and he was ultimately confirmed by a 52–48 vote, the most immediate impact of the hearings was to focus more attention on issues of sexual harassment and gender politics in the 1992 political campaigns, contributing to the election of four additional women to the Senate in a period that their supporters called the Year of the Woman. Such oversight or confirmation hearings may air issues that lend themselves to legislation later on.

In less historic or controversial circumstances, a reasonable amount of national press coverage will result from testimony by popular actors and other celebrities who are active in a particular cause, such as Bono, the lead singer of U2, on debt relief and AIDS (acquired immune deficiency syndrome) in Africa and actor Michael J. Fox on Parkinson's disease. Ordinary citizens with good stories to tell can also hit a nerve, especially on subjects of broad public interest.

In the last three decades, most hearings and meetings of congressional committees occurred in open session, although committees dealing with national security and other sensitive or classified information often close their meetings. The congressional Intelligence committees nearly always meet in closed session. The Senate Armed Services and House Armed Services committees use a combination of open and closed (executive) hearings. Until 1971 the House Appropriations Committee held all its hearings in closed session.

House rules by 1995 made it extremely difficult for most committees and subcommittees to close meetings or hearings except for a few specified reasons relating to national security, use of law enforcement information, or protection of the rights of witnesses testifying. A rules amendment in 1995 liberalized media access to open sessions and made coverage by radio, television, and photographers a right to be exercised by the press, not a privilege to be granted or withheld by committees.

Markup

Once the hearings are concluded, the next step in the House is usually a subcommittee markup. In the Senate, most committees skip the subcommittee markup phase and begin the process at the full committee level. Exceptions to this practice in the Senate in recent years have been the Appropriations and Armed Services Committees and the Judiciary Committee when a proposed constitutional amendment is the subject.

The subcommittee may take no action, in effect killing a bill. Or it may mark up the bill, considering the contents of each provision and section of the measure, amending some provisions, discarding others, and perhaps rewriting the measure altogether. When the markup is finished, the subcommittee sends its version of the legislation, presuming it has not rejected the measure, to the full committee. In some instances, the full committee may exercise its authority to take up the bill directly, bypassing a separate subcommittee markup stage.

The full committee may repeat the subcommittee procedures, sometimes even including additional hearings. It may conduct an amending process, especially if the stage of subcommittee action has been bypassed, or it may simply ratify the action of the subcommittee. Frequently the full committee will propose additional amendments to alter the proposal. If the amendments are not extensive, the original bill is reported with amendments.

If a bill is to be rewritten extensively after it is referred to committee, as is often the case with major pieces of legislation, the chair may offer a full substitute amendment that replaces the original language with a new version incorporating all of the changes agreed upon behind closed doors. Legislation may also be marked up as a draft bill—one that has not been formally introduced in the House—and later introduced with all of the changes incorporated. This method, traditionally used by the Appropriations Committee and its subcommittees, has been employed on occasion in recent years by authorizing committees.

Committee chairs may also choose to introduce a new version of the bill—called a clean bill—after it has been marked up, particularly if major changes have been made. The original bill is then set aside, and the clean bill, with a new number, is the version voted out of committee and reported. This practice has become less common in recent years as the use of substitute amendments and draft bills has come more into favor.

Incorporating all of the widely supported changes to a bill before it hits the floor reduces the amount of time spent on floor amendments and makes moot the issue of whether the provisions are germane. If a provision is in a bill when it comes to the floor, it cannot be ruled to be nongermane, but if a lawmaker attempts to attach it to a bill through a floor amendment, it can be ruled out of order.

So any amendments made part of a clean committee bill, a draft measure that serves as the text for a bill, or a bill that has been altered with a full committee substitute, are usually protected from points of order on the floor. (There are exceptions that can be used to delete provisions from bills that include tax or tariff matters not reported by the Ways and Means Committee and provisions in appropriations bills that violate the jurisdictions of authorizing committees.)

In 1973 both chambers adopted new rules to encourage more committees to open their markup meetings to the public, and most committee meetings were opened. Some markups, for example many subcommittee markups of appropriations or defense authorization bills, were closed, however. Advocates of closed sessions believed that members would make politically difficult decisions more easily in the absence of lobbyists and interested constituents. The minority, which often objected to the decisions made, pressed for greater openness and attacked closed sessions as a symbol of majority arrogance.

When the Republicans assumed control of the House in 1995, they amended rules for the conduct of meetings and hearings to make closed sessions more difficult. For example, the new rules allowed a committee majority, by a roll-call vote, to close all or part of a meeting to consider legislation only by determining that an open meeting would endanger national security; compromise sensitive law enforcement information; tend to defame, degrade, or incriminate any person; or violate a law or rule of the House. Arguments to close as a matter of convenience or to satisfy members' desire for privacy no longer carried weight. All meetings and hearings open to the public were also open automatically to broadcast and photographic media, without the need for advance permission.

When a committee votes to approve a measure, it is said to order the bill reported. Occasionally, a committee may order a bill reported unfavorably or without recommendation. The House Judiciary Committee, for example, voted 19–17 in June 1990 to report without recommendation a proposed constitutional amendment barring desecration of the American flag. In such cases, the committee may be acting only because of overwhelming political pressure to deal with legislation a majority of its members disapprove of but feel that they cannot avoid. This situation occurred after the Supreme Court threw out a statute barring the practice on constitutional grounds. The constitutional amendment later passed in the House but failed in the Senate.

But because a committee can effectively kill a measure by not acting on it, a committee generally schedules a markup only when its intention is to move the legislation along the process, and committee reports almost invariably recommend passage. Those bills reported favorably have usually been amended to satisfy a majority of the committee's members.

Committee Reports

House rules and Senate custom require that a written report accompany each bill reported from a committee to the floor. The report, written by the committee staff, typically describes the purpose and scope of the bill in plain English, explains committee amendments, indicates proposed changes in existing law, estimates additional costs to the government of the recommended program changes, and often includes the texts of communications from department and agency officials whose views on the legislation have been solicited. Committee members opposed to the bill or specific sections of it often submit minority views in a separate section of the report. Bills discharged from a committee prior to formal committee

TELEVISED FLOOR DEBATES HERE TO STAY

At noon on March 19, 1979, the U.S. House of Representatives made its live television debut. That appearance was the culmination of years of hard work by proponents of the idea. First proposed in 1944 by then-Senator Claude Pepper, D-Fla., the movement to open the chambers to television cameras took hold only slowly in a body often resistant to change. Senate floor action has been televised only since June 1986.

Al Gore, a Tennessee Democrat who became vice president under Bill Clinton, led the fight for television in the House, where he served from 1977 to 1985, and in the Senate, where he served from 1985 to 1993. "The marriage of this medium and of our open debate have the potential . . . to revitalize representative democracy," Gore said in the first televised speech in 1979, a one-minute address to the House before the regular legislative day began.

Because members can use television to keep up with the action, said political scientist Steven S. Smith in 1989, "[they] are not quite as reliant on a colleague at the door telling them whether to vote up or down."

DAWN OF A NEW AGE

Until the early 1970s, televised congressional proceedings were just a dream to proponents. But the arrival in Congress of reform-minded members in the wake of political scandals in the 1970s, particularly the Watergate affair that led to President Richard M. Nixon's resignation, contributed to an atmosphere more amenable to transparency.

In 1977 the Democratic leadership directed the House Select Committee on Congressional Operations to conduct a ninety-day experiment using closed-circuit telecasts of House floor proceedings to members' offices. The experiment was labeled a success, and on October 27, 1977, the House tentatively agreed to go ahead, although it took some time to iron out the details.

In June 1978 news organizations began broadcasting House proceedings over radio, and by March 1979 television had arrived. The Cable-Satellite Public Affairs Network (C-SPAN), the private, nonprofit cooperative of the cable television industry, was launched in 1979 with the express purpose of televising Congress. House employees remain in control of the cameras.

The Senate proceeded more slowly in bringing in the cameras. Majority Leader Howard H. Baker Jr., R-Tenn., began the effort in earnest in 1981. In February 1986 the Senate passed a resolution to allow television broadcasting.

For a month the Senate permitted closed-circuit transmissions into members' offices, followed by six weeks of public broadcasts. At the conclusion of the six-week test period, the Senate voted to keep the cameras permanently. And on June 2, 1986, the Senate premiered on a second C-SPAN channel.

Senate rules are fairly strict. Cameras are operated by congressional staff and usually remain fixed on a single speaker. Initially the House rules were similar. Since May 1984, however, House cameras began to slowly pan the room during votes and special orders, a period at the end of a daily session when members may speak on various topics, usually to a mostly empty chamber.

Speaker Thomas P. "Tip" O'Neill, D-Mass., ordered that the cameras show the viewing audience that future Speaker Newt Gingrich, R-Ga., and his conservative allies were fulminating to an empty chamber when they began gaining attention as partisan bomb-throwers in the 1980s.

When Gingrich and Republicans took control of the House in 1995, procedures for panning the chamber changed. The camera would focus on individual members talking on benches in the chamber or reading the newspaper, practices that appeared to give some degree of editorial control to the camera operators and raised concerns about possible partisan abuse of the television coverage. After protests at the new intrusiveness, Speaker Gingrich ordered that such close-ups of members who are not directly participating in the business on the floor be stopped.

THE VIEWING AUDIENCE

The public does watch Congress on television, though not as much as it once did. In January 1998, C-SPAN had 72.5 million subscribing households who received its cable channel showing House proceedings (C-SPAN1), and 49.5 million for its Senate channel (C-SPAN2). Based on Pew Research Center for the People and the Press research, C-SPAN estimated that in 2006 it had 52 million adult viewers. In 2010, the *New York Times* cited a recent poll by Fairleigh Dickinson University that found that 52 percent of voters said they watched C-SPAN at least once in a while.

Time is a precious commodity for members of Congress. Televised proceedings and committee hearings often allow them to gauge their time better during votes and other floor activities. Members follow the proceedings and committee hearings to keep abreast of the latest developments.

---

action and brought up on the floor are not accompanied by a written report.

Often there is a considerable delay between the day that a committee orders a bill reported and when the bill is actually reported to the floor.

After enactment of the Legislative Reorganization Act of 1970, committees were required to publish in their reports all votes taken on amendments disposed of during markup as well as the vote to report the bill. Only vote totals were required, not the position of individual members on roll calls. Following rules changes in 1995, House committees were required to publish in the report how members voted individually both on the bill and on any amendments considered and disposed of by roll-call vote, whether successful or not.

House committees are required to keep a record of all roll calls and make it available to the public on request, which provides another source of information if a bill has never been reported. The Senate has similar, if somewhat looser, procedural requirements. It requires that the results of all votes, including the votes of individual senators, be included in the committee report unless previously announced by the committee.

Reports are numbered, by Congress and chamber, in the order in which they are filed (for example, S Rept 110-1, S Rept 110-2, H Rept 110-1, H Rept 110-2, and onward, with the first number referring to the Congress in which the bill is reported) and immediately printed. The report number and the date the bill was reported formally are also shown on the bill. The reported bill is also printed with any committee

MIXED VERDICTS ON MEDIA IMPACT

Members of Congress and political scientists agree that the cameras are a fixture in the chambers and the public would not allow their removal. "The horror stories that were supposed to happen didn't happen," political scientist Larry Sabato said in 1989.

While passage of rules changes allowing television coverage of floor proceedings was probably inevitable, the ultimate effect on the legislative process at the heart of Congress remains difficult to evaluate. Around the turn of the twenty-first century, widespread complaints were aired by members about the increasing partisanship and meanness in debate, and some observers—both in and out of Congress— blamed the live coverage for encouraging use of floor speeches to produce sound bites for the evening news. A substantive and spontaneous legislative process, it is argued, has too often been sidelined by staged events. Not only television, but also the advent of talk radio shows that specialized in inciting listeners, contributed to a debasement of political dialogue. In recent years, that phenomenon has extended to the twenty-four-hour cable news television networks and websites that capture footage or transcripts of floor proceedings.

In the House, use of one-minute speeches for this purpose has become widespread, with outside political committees and interest groups sending suggested remarks for members to recite. Both parties often carefully organize their presentations in this daily forum. The use of charts and exhibits likely to be visible on a television screen has proliferated. Even opposing political candidates have gotten into the act, using excerpts of speeches by House members in campaign commercials and then attacking them. A House rule prohibits use of the televised proceedings for political purposes, but it is enforceable only against sitting members. Democrats had been considering a proposal to modify this rule, effective with the 104th Congress, to allow members to better defend themselves against opponents who might use excerpts of floor proceedings in potentially misleading ways, but the idea died with the 1994 election that turned over House control to Republicans.

In *Civility in the House of Representatives*, political scientist Kathleen Hall Jamieson argued that traditional methods for striking inappropriate language from the *Congressional Record* and letting tempers cool had been rendered obsolete by television. "Not only is it impossible to strike words taken down from the C-SPAN record but the process, designed to enhance civility, may instead diminish it, as the offending Member plays to the cameras. C-SPAN footage also increases the likelihood that moments of incivility will be replayed on the news."

Potentially embarrassing clips of members are e-mailed around Washington, D.C., and posted on websites quickly, some just for humor and others to do political damage.

Some of these concerns reflect twenty-first-century sensibilities about the way a political process should be conducted. In earlier times, members of Congress sometimes fought each other in physical brawls on the floor and had duels with political opponents. So recent instances of incivility, while disturbing, pale in historical comparison.

Most observers of Congress agree that despite all the attention generated by televised debate, Congress survived the television revolution. It was a change the public would have forced eventually if the two houses had not acted. Television made the work of members of Congress more real and immediate to constituents, giving a sense of elected officials that voters often saw only in campaign commercials. In that sense, television strengthened Congress as an institution.

In recent years, televised coverage of Congress has expanded into committee meetings. Under House rules, committee proceedings must be open to television and radio coverage unless the panel votes by majority at a public meeting to go into executive session. Committees have taken advantage of new technology and often make their proceedings available through webcasts, which allow viewers to watch live transmissions without having to get to Capitol Hill.

SOURCES: John Schachter, "Congress Begins Second Decade under TV's Watchful Glare," *Congressional Quarterly Weekly Report,* March 11, 1989, 507–509; "New Survey: 22 Million Watch C-SPAN Weekly," C-SPAN news release, January 6, 1997; Brian Stelter, "C-Span Puts Full Archives on the Web," *New York Times,* March 16, 2010, C-1; and Kathleen Hall Jamieson, *Civility in the House of Representatives,* Report Series No. 10 (Philadelphia: University of Pennsylvania, Annenberg Public Policy Center, 1997).

amendments indicated by insertions in italics and deletions in stricken-through type.

Sometimes, a House committee will rework legislation well after the time it is reported using the Rules Committee as a means to make final changes to its liking, to accommodate other committees' interests, or to deal with concerns raised by the leadership. In these cases, the Rules Committee may make a new bill, often referred to as an amendment in the nature of a substitute, the vehicle for formal debate and amendment on the floor, while retaining the shell of the bill's HR number. Adoption of the rule could substitute this new text for the original language, which would never be formally acted on and would disappear entirely once the bill is passed. Or the Rules Committee may allow consideration of a new bill with an entirely new number, making the legislative history of an issue into a tricky maze in which the original bill, along with its committee report, appears to die through lack of House consideration while forming the basis of eventual chamber action.

Legislative Intent

In some situations, the language of the report is as important as the bill itself. It has been common practice for committees, including House-Senate conference committees, to write in their reports instructions directing government agencies on interpretation and enforcement of the law. Moreover, courts have relied on these guidelines in establishing what is known as legislative intent.

Some legal scholars, judges, and members of the Supreme Court have expressed skepticism about relying on these reports because they are not written into law, or relying on floor debate, complaining that Congress is often sloppy in its preparation for floor action. The most prominent and outspoken critic of legislative intent has been Supreme Court Justice Antonin Scalia. Critics say they prefer to rely on the text of the measure as the basis for statutory interpretations. Others counter that divorcing a bill from the circumstances surrounding its passage can lead to misinterpretations.

Legal scholar Robert A. Katzmann, a judge for the U.S. Court of Appeals for the Second Circuit, notes: "The more authoritative Congress is as to the appropriate use of such material, the more likely that legislative history will have the intended weight. Thus it is imperative that Congress develop means to clarify the use of such materials if courts are to better interpret legislative meaning." Katzmann suggests that Congress take care to use "more precise drafting, more authoritative legislative histories, and refinement of the process of revising statutes."[12]

Lobbyists are also vitally interested in the report language as one way to promote or protect their clients' interests. Many appropriations bills, for example, set out only the amount of money an agency or department might spend. But the accompanying committee report often contains directives on how Congress expects the money to be spent or warnings to bureaucrats not to take certain actions.

The use of report language, instead of bill text, to earmark federal funds for specific recipients became the subject of serious debate in the early 2000s, particularly in the 109th Congress when Republican spending hawks sought to crack down on earmarks only to be frustrated by their inability to amend report language. The divide between Republicans who enjoyed earmarking funds for their home districts or states and those who publicly excoriated their colleagues for doing so—sets that sometimes overlapped—proved one of the trickiest fractures for party leaders to bridge in the 109th Congress.

In 2007 the White House directed federal agencies to ignore earmarks written into congressional reports and instead award grants and other federal funds based on their own priorities. However, agencies have long understood that they risk displeasing their congressional overseers if they ignore directives issued through reports. The reports protect the earmarks from removal and also give the administration flexibility to redirect the funds if a particular project no longer needs the money. If the earmarks were written into law, agencies could face legal hurdles to redirecting the funds.

HOUSE FLOOR ACTION: STRUCTURED EFFICIENCY

Because of the sheer number of representatives in the House—435—the chamber can appear disorderly, especially at the end of a session, with members milling about in small groups and streaming in and out of the chamber to answer to roll calls. But underlying this general hubbub is a structure for considering legislation that allows the House to act relatively efficiently and expeditiously. There is only one important rule in the House: the majority rules. *(See box, Dilatory Tactics Are Limited in the House, p. 92.)*

Scheduling Floor Action

Bills can reach the House floor in a number of ways. Most are reported first by a committee. However, no requirement exists in the rules that a bill be reported by or even considered by a committee, or that any report be available for members prior to floor action unless the bill was in fact reported. By unanimous consent, noncontroversial bills and resolutions can even be offered from the floor, considered, and passed without being formally introduced and given a number first. (They may be given a number when called up.) Some bills receive committee consideration but may be called up for a vote without any final committee action or a report being filed. Major legislation, however, nearly always must survive the full stages of committee action culminating in a committee vote and report, and it also receives a rule from the Rules Committee before being brought up for action. In practice, even a noncontroversial bill brought up under an expedited procedure called suspension of the rules is often accompanied by a committee report, or has received some committee action, to reassure members that the bill's presence on the floor has legitimacy and that interested members have been given sufficient opportunity to participate in the process.

After a bill is reported from a House committee and before it is scheduled for floor action, it is placed on one of three legislative calendars: Union, House, or Private. Another calendar, Discharge, is used only for motions to discharge committees from consideration of a measure when such motions have received the signatures of a majority of members on a discharge petition. Each day the House is in session it publishes a Calendar of the House as a formal document that includes all matters on each of the calendars, and it also provides a history of action on them by committees, the House and Senate, conferences, and the president.

All bills, including authorization bills, having any effect on the Treasury go on the Union Calendar, which is by far the most important. Technically it is the Calendar of the Committee of the Whole House on the State of the Union, so called because bills listed on it are first considered in the Committee of the Whole and reported back to the House for a final vote on passage. Other types of matters, such as investigative reports approved by committees, may also appear on the Union Calendar even though they will not be considered by the House. Legislation on the Union Calendar may be considered on the floor, debated, and amended in a wide variety of different ways under the rules of the House. *(See "Action in the Committee of the Whole," p. 100.)*

Matters that have no direct effect on the Treasury are placed on the House Calendar. These bills or, far more commonly, resolutions, generally deal with administrative and procedural matters and are usually not considered by the Committee of the Whole but taken up directly by the House. However, some legislation of great significance, such as constitutional amendments and approval of compacts among states, appear on the House Calendar. Simple and concurrent resolutions also go on the House Calendar, including the concurrent resolution that starts off yearly action on the budget process and special rules reported from the Rules Committee allowing consideration of other legislation. On the floor, matters from this calendar may also be considered in several different ways.

Two calendars, the Consent Calendar and the Corrections Calendar, have been eliminated.

The Corrections Calendar was established in 1995 when Republicans took control of the House. It was created by the new Republican majority as a vehicle to consider bills that would correct mistakes in previously enacted legislation or in government actions or regulations. The Republican Conference considered these types of measures to be a class of legislation that deserved special recognition and easy access to the floor. After an initial flurry of partisan strife in 1995, the Corrections Calendar quickly fell into disuse. Still, the House continued to provide nearly $1 million in funding annually for a Corrections Calendar Office that did not occupy any space and paid staffers who worked for members of the congressional leadership in both parties. After *Congressional Quarterly* exposed the bloated payroll and lack of work—only one of twelve staffers interviewed said they worked on the Corrections Calendar—lawmakers closed the account and the 109th Congress eliminated the Corrections Calendar when it approved its rules in January 2005.

The Consent Calendar, eliminated in 1995 in favor of the Corrections Calendar, was a device used to group bills that could be approved by unanimous consent. But such measures are now considered under suspension of the rules.

Private immigration bills and bills for the relief of individuals with claims against the United States are placed on the Private Calendar. This calendar must be called on the first Tuesday of each month, unless dispensed with by a two-thirds vote or by unanimous consent, which is what usually occurs unless there are a number of bills on the calendar ready for passage. The Private Calendar may also be called on the third Tuesday of each month at the Speaker's discretion. If two or more members object to the consideration of a bill it will be recommitted to the committee that reported it, but if there is some concern or uncertainty about a bill it may be passed over without prejudice by unanimous consent and still remain eligible for action on a future call of the Private Calendar. Both major political parties appoint several members as official objectors to monitor such bills and ensure that

only those that have overwhelming support pass using the Private Calendar. Most private bills are called up from the calendar and simply passed by unanimous consent without debate and without a recorded vote, but debate may occur under a procedure that allows any member to speak for five minutes. Amendments may be offered and debated for a maximum of five minutes in support and five minutes opposed.

The Judiciary Committee handles most private relief bills, which typically deal with various claims against the government, and immigration status. Once enacted, private laws receive separate private law numbers, as opposed to the numeration given to public laws that Congress enacts. The quantity of private bills enacted into law, however, has dropped precipitously since the 96th Congress (1979–1981), when 123 private laws were enacted. In the 109th Congress, just 1 private bill became law. In the 110th Congress, there were none, and in the 111th Congress, just 2. Congressional scholar Walter Oleszek has suggested that the transfer of jurisdiction over some of these issues to federal agencies, fears of scandals over favoritism to individuals, and reluctance to disburse federal funds for private concerns in an era of deficit spending led to a decline in popularity of the private law mechanism. As a result, the House now seldom calls the Private Calendar.

The House also has a Discharge Calendar. It is used to list motions to discharge committees from further consideration of bills or resolutions, when a majority of the total membership of the House—218—signs a discharge petition at the desk in the House chamber. Discharge motions are taken up on the second and fourth Mondays of each month. The procedure exists to allow a majority of members to bring up favored legislation if it has been bottled up by a powerful committee chair or the leaders of the majority party.

Members can try to discharge a legislative committee from consideration of an unreported bill after it has been referred for thirty legislative days or discharge the Rules Committee from consideration of a reported bill or an unreported rule. Efforts to discharge legislative committees, however, are difficult, as House rules provide means for the committees to circumvent, and effectively kill, them just before or just after the necessary signatures are collected.

The most useful practice is for members to draft a special rule for debate of the measure that is to be discharged. If the petitioners have 218 signatures, the committee of jurisdiction has reported the bill or held it for thirty days, and the rule has not been acted upon by the Rules Committee, a motion to discharge the Rules Committee from consideration of the rule making the bill in order may be offered.

If the motion is adopted, the measure discharged will then be considered in a number of possible ways. Because the discharge procedure is rarely attempted, and few discharge

A TYPICAL SCHEDULE IN THE HOUSE

The House conducts different types of business on different days, so its daily routine varies. However, from week to week, a pattern is usually followed.

- The House convenes early for morning hour debate for five-minute speeches on Mondays and Tuesdays sixty to ninety minutes prior to the formal opening of the day's session, even if that is in the afternoon. No votes or legislative business can occur. The House then recesses until the formal convening of the day's session.

- The chaplain, or sometimes a guest chaplain invited for the day, delivers the opening prayer, and a House member leads the chamber in the Pledge of Allegiance.

- The Speaker approves the Journal, the record of the previous day's proceedings. Sometimes a member demands a roll-call vote on the approval of the Journal, which can be used to determine who is present and to allow the leadership to "whip" them on other matters. The minority may call for a roll-call vote on the Journal as a form of protest against some action taken by the majority. There were thirteen such votes in the 111th Congress, and in the first session of the 112th Congress, there were eighteen votes on approval of the Journal. The Journal vote can also be postponed by the Speaker until later in the day and clustered with other votes that may be occurring.

- After the House receives messages from the Senate and the president and privileged reports from committees, and conducts other similar procedural activities, members are recognized by unanimous consent for one-minute speeches on any topic. The Speaker can limit the number of these speeches.

- The House then turns to its legislative business. On Mondays, Tuesdays, and Wednesdays, the House usually considers less controversial bills, sometimes dozens in a day, under the suspension of the rules process requiring a two-thirds majority for passage, and recorded votes are postponed until late in the day, or until the next day. Measures that are even less controversial may be passed by unanimous consent. Though only so-called suspension bills are generally considered on the first three days of the week, more controversial legislation may also be considered on those days. Typically, debate and votes on major bills are held Wednesday, Thursday, or Friday.

- Virtually every bill of any significance is considered under a special rule, reported from the Rules Committee, that sets guidelines for floor action. The rule may be approved with little opposition, but the vote can also be a first test of a bill's popularity. If the rule restricts the amendments that may be offered, those members barred from offering amendments may work with opponents of the bill itself to defeat the rule or to defeat the previous question so that amendments to the rule can be offered. However, party leaders have become adept in recent years at enforcing discipline even on the procedural votes.

- After the rule is adopted, the House resolves into the Committee of the Whole to consider the bill. The Speaker relinquishes the gavel to another member, who serves as chair of this committee and presides over the activities.

Debate time is controlled by the managers of the bill, usually the chair and ranking minority member of the standing committee with jurisdiction over the measure. *(See "Action in the Committee of the Whole," p. 100.)*

After time for general debate has expired, amendments that are permitted under the rule may be offered and debated. Debate on an amendment may be for a fixed time. If none is specified in the rule, it is conducted under the "five-minute rule," which limits each side to five minutes. However, members may obtain additional speaking time by offering amendments to strike the last word, a pro forma action that allows additional time for discussion and debate.

Voting may be conducted in three different ways plus variations depending on whether the House or the Committee of the Whole is sitting: by voice, the usual procedure; by division, a seldom-used method in which members stand to be counted but no record of names is kept; or by electronic device, referred to as "the yeas and nays" or a "recorded vote" depending on the parliamentary circumstances. Certain matters in the House require a roll-call vote under the U.S. Constitution (for example, to reconsider a vetoed bill) or the rules of the House (for example, passing a general appropriations bill or closing a conference committee meeting to the public). The first vote in a series of electronic votes lasts at least fifteen minutes, as do most votes on major legislation that party leaders expect to be close. Technically, the rules set a minimum time frame, not a maximum. Members of Republican and Democratic minorities cried foul when party leaders left votes open to lobby recalcitrant lawmakers. When they came to power in 2007, Democrats changed House rules to prohibit keeping a vote open beyond the allotted time to change the outcome, but that rule was rescinded two years later. If several votes in sequence are conducted, the second and any subsequent votes are usually reduced to a minimum of five minutes. *(See box, Methods of Voting in the House and Senate, p. 96.)*

- After the amending process is complete, the Committee of the Whole rises, and the chair reports to the Speaker on the actions taken. The House votes on whether to accept the amendments adopted in the Committee, usually a pro forma action. The House then votes on final passage of the bill, sometimes after voting on a motion by opponents to recommit the bill to its committee of origin, which would kill it, or to recommit the bill with instructions to report it back forthwith with additional amendments that would be adopted prior to final passage. After final passage, a motion to reconsider is in order but is usually announced as "laid on the table" by the Speaker to save time.

- After the House completes its legislative business, members may speak for longer periods of time, called special orders. Members must reserve the time in advance but can speak on any topic—often to an almost deserted chamber. Members seeking recognition for short periods of time, such as five or ten minutes, are recognized first, alternating between the parties. These speeches are not referred to in the House rules, but rather in a policy statement made at the beginning of each Congress by the Speaker. In 2011, new Speaker John A. Boehner announced that special order speeches could last for as many as four hours, as long as they did not extend beyond 10 p.m. The time allotted is to be divided equally between the parties.

petitions obtain the 218 signatures, the Discharge Calendar usually consists of a restatement of the discharge rule followed by a blank page.

Of 563 discharge petitions filed from 1931 through 2002, forty-seven obtained the requisite number of signatures. The House discharged committees only twenty-six times. Only nineteen times did the measure pass the House once it was considered, and only four ultimately changed House rules or became law. But a successful discharge petition may prompt party leaders to advance the measure on their own, thereby allowing them to keep nominal control of the process. In such cases, the discharge motion will not carry, but the sponsors will get what they are after. The most recent example was the 2002 Shays-Meehan overhaul of campaign finance laws.[13]

In the four years from 2007 through 2010, thirty-one discharge petitions were filed; none received the necessary number of signatures. Discharge motions that have been filed but have not obtained the requisite signatures can be found listed in the *Congressional Record* and the House of Representatives' website, along with their signers. *(See box, Prying Loose Legislation Stuck in Committee: Use of Discharge and Calendar Wednesday, p. 88.)*

The four calendars (Union, House, Private, and Discharge) are printed in one document titled *Calendars of the United States House of Representatives and History of Legislation.* This calendar is printed daily when the House is in session. The first issue of the week lists in numerical order all House and most Senate measures that have been reported by committees, with a capsule history of congressional action on each. It also includes a general index and other valuable reference material.

Bills are placed on the calendars in the order in which they are reported. But they do not come to the floor in chronological order. In fact, some never come to the floor at all. The Speaker of the House, working with the majority leader, committee chairs, and the Rules Committee, determines which bills will come to the floor and when. How the bill will be handled on the floor depends on whether it is noncontroversial, privileged, or major legislation that requires a special rule from the Rules Committee.

Unanimous Consent

The House may accomplish almost any action by unanimous consent, but the procedure is most commonly used to act quickly. Sometimes the actions desired can be accomplished only by unanimous consent because no readily available motion can be used to force the matter before the House for debate and vote. In other instances, available motions might waste the time of the House with debate or votes because the matter is noncontroversial.

If the Speaker recognizes a member to make a unanimous consent request it will be granted unless another member objects. The Speaker can prevent a unanimous consent request from being placed before the House simply by withholding recognition, after inquiring "for what purpose does the gentleman [gentlelady] rise?"—in effect signifying his or her own opposition to the request. Unanimous consent requests relating to action on legislation normally must be cleared in advance by the majority and minority or the Speaker will not entertain them. No debate is in order and no vote is held on unanimous consent requests, saving substantial time for the House. However, for the House to understand the purpose of a unanimous consent request, in many cases, when the Speaker asks "is there objection?" another member who supports the request will often "reserve the right to object" and yield to the maker of the request for an explanation. Several members may participate in an informal discussion in this manner until a legislative record has been made.

Unanimous consent requests are used dozens of times each day, most commonly to insert material into the *Congressional Record;* to address the House when no legislation is pending, such as during one-minute speeches at the beginning of the day and special order speeches at the end; to extend the time a member may speak on an amendment; to obtain a leave of absence from a House session; to discharge committees from consideration of noncontroversial matters and bring them directly to the floor; and to dispose of various motions that could normally be voted on if demanded by any member.

Suspension of the Rules

Under House Rule XV, bills considered to be noncontroversial may be brought to the floor under a motion to suspend the rules, a procedure that dispenses with parliamentary objections, limits debate to twenty minutes per side, and requires two-thirds of those present and voting for passage. Such suspensions may be considered only on the first three days of each week or at any time during the last six days of a session of Congress. Often, suspension bills can be passed by unanimous consent, without a recorded vote. There is no "suspension calendar," though a slate of bills scheduled for consideration under suspension of the rules is often mistakenly referred to that way.

Amendments to a suspension measure are generally prohibited. However, a member may include an amendment as part of a motion to suspend the rules and pass the bill as amended.

The suspension procedure is most often used to bring to the floor noncontroversial measures on the Union or House Calendars that have been reported from committee. In addition, measures never considered by a committee or even those just introduced also may be taken up. The Speaker has total control over bringing legislation to the floor under this procedure, and he or she invariably recognizes only members of the majority party to offer motions to suspend the rules. However, bipartisan cooperation is required for passage of suspension motions because a two-thirds majority is needed.

PRYING LOOSE LEGISLATION STUCK IN COMMITTEE: USE OF DISCHARGE AND CALENDAR WEDNESDAY

The House has two special procedures—the discharge petition and Calendar Wednesday—designed to bring to a vote legislation that has been blocked from floor consideration. Both devices were instituted during the speakership of Joseph G. Cannon, R-Ill. (1903–1911), in an effort to circumvent the near-complete control the strong-arm Speaker held over the legislative agenda. These procedures have been used rarely and are even more rarely successful. However, the threat of using a discharge petition has sometimes been successful in prompting action through the normal legislative process. *(See "Cannonism," p. 16.)*

DISCHARGE PETITION

The House's modern discharge motion was first adopted in 1910, reached approximately its present form in 1931, and was then further modified in the 1990s as public attention to the procedure increased. The discharge petition enables a majority of the membership to bring before the House any public bill blocked in a standing committee. With respect to the Rules Committee, it allows discharge of resolutions proposing changes in House rules and of resolutions providing special rules for consideration of any bill that has been before a standing committee.

While the discharge rule is specifically directed against committees, its use also serves as a check on the majority leadership. This is true because, in cases in which discharge is attempted, a committee is usually working in concert with or at the direction of the leadership. (If the leadership wanted a vote on a measure, it could simply use the Rules Committee to bring it out to the floor.)

The discharge procedure may be used if a bill has been referred to a standing committee for at least thirty legislative days without having been reported. Members also have the option, in such cases, of introducing a special rule providing for consideration of the bill that, if not reported in seven legislative days, becomes subject to discharge. Any member may then file a motion to discharge a committee from further consideration, popularly known as a discharge petition, which members may sign at the clerk's desk in the chamber whenever the House is in session. Members may withdraw their names until 218—a majority—have signed, at which point the motion to discharge is placed on the Discharge Calendar and the complete list of the names of the signers and the order of their signatures are published in the Calendar and in the *Congressional Record*. Once 218 have signed, no more may do so.

The identity of the members signing a discharge petition was kept secret until 1993. Up until then, the petition had been considered an internal matter in the House. Secrecy was intended to ensure that the process was considered a last resort and to permit quiet efforts to persuade members to withdraw their names and to preserve opportunities to reach a compromise on an issue through the normal legislative process. From time to time, some members would threaten to reveal the names of their colleagues who had or had not signed a petition, to subject them to

pressure from outside interest groups. There had been stories of members asking to view a petition, with each memorizing several names and then leaving to write them down until a comprehensive list was obtained.

The sponsors of the 1993 rules change, principally from the Republican minority, intended that it would pressure more members to sign such petitions. They viewed a discharge petition as a legislative mechanism that should be subjected to public scrutiny, much like a member's cosponsorship of a bill. The handful of members publicly opposed to opening the process worried that it might result in the more frequent consideration of irresponsible legislation and undermine the committee system.

Ironically, the resolution to open up the process to public view was passed only after itself being discharged from the Rules Committee. However, no significant changes in the normal legislative process were immediately evident. The names of members signing a discharge petition are published in the *Congressional Record* on a weekly basis and made public on the Clerk of the House's website.

A motion to discharge must remain on the Discharge Calendar for seven legislative days before it can be called up for floor action. On the second and fourth Mondays of each month, except during the last six days of the session, any member who has signed the discharge petition may be recognized to move that the committee be discharged. Debate on the motion is limited to twenty minutes, divided equally between proponents and opponents. If the motion carries, any member who signed the petition can move for immediate consideration of the discharged measure, which then becomes the business of the House until it is resolved. Depending on the nature of the measure discharged, it may be considered either in the House or in the Committee of the Whole. If the House postpones action on the discharged measure, it is placed on the appropriate calendar, to be available for potential floor action just as other measures are.

Partly because the process is so cumbersome and time-consuming, and partly because members are usually reluctant to challenge committees so directly, the discharge petition has seldom been successful. Of 563 discharge petitions filed from 1931 through 2002, just 47 obtained the requisite number of signatures. The House discharged committees only 26 times. Just 19 times did the measure pass the House once it was considered, and only 4 ultimately changed House rules or became law. When the requisite signatures are obtained, party leaders may concede and bring the measure forward under their own power to maintain control of the process. The most recent example was the 2002 Shays-Meehan overhaul of campaign finance laws. The numbers, therefore, are somewhat misleading, because a handful of laws have been enacted as the result of discharge petitions that were rendered moot once the leadership allowed the bill to be considered under normal procedures.[1]

Discharge petitions nonetheless can serve a purpose by focusing attention on a particular issue and sometimes forcing the recalcitrant committee to take action. In 1985, after two hundred members signed a petition filed by Harold L. Volkmer,

Any member may move to suspend the rules and pass a measure, although it is generally a committee or subcommittee chair, with the concurrence of the ranking minority member, who is recognized for the purpose. The motion suspends all rules of the House that normally affect consideration of the measure, including referral to a committee and

requirements for committee action such as preparation of a committee report. This precludes points of order against the legislation.

If a suspension motion is not approved, the measure may be considered later under regular House procedures. In 1979 the House amended its rules to give the Speaker

D-Mo., to discharge from the Judiciary Committee a Senate-passed bill weakening federal gun controls, that committee hastily reported out gun control legislation. Ultimately Volkmer's version of the measure passed the House, in part because his discharge petition, which was eventually signed by 218 members, forced the Rules Committee to make his version in order on the floor.

In modern practice, instead of discharging legislation, discharge supporters usually target the Rules Committee, especially if they intend to make a serious effort to obtain 218 signatures. They introduce and attempt to discharge a special rule that brings up the legislation and does so employing procedures of the sponsors' choosing that provide maximum prospects for passage. (Discharging legislation directly to the floor without a rule can subject it to potentially cumbersome floor procedures that might inhibit passage.)

Constitutional amendments are frequently the subjects of discharge petitions. For example, in 1990, 1992, and 1994 special rules were discharged from the Rules Committee providing for consideration of constitutional amendments requiring a balanced budget. The Judiciary Committee, which had jurisdiction over the amendments, along with the Rules Committee and the majority leadership, opposed floor action through normal procedures. In each case, the House ultimately fell short of the two-thirds majority required for passage. In 1995 the constitutional amendment was part of the Republicans' Contract with America and was reported out of committee and passed by the House using the normal legislative process. It failed by one vote in the Senate, however. The same thing happened again in 1997.

Longtime advocates of discharge understandably lost interest in it following the shift in party control, and no measures were discharged during the first four years of Republican majorities starting in 1995. But, in another example of partisan turnabout, minority Democrats attempted to discharge campaign finance reform legislation in 1997 over the opposition of the Republican leadership. The effort stalled when Speaker Newt Gingrich, R-Ga., promised a vote on the issue in the spring of 1998.

However, Republican supporters of campaign finance reform who had shunned the discharge strategy later cried betrayal when Gingrich allowed the issue on the floor using the two-thirds majority suspension process, which prevented passage of any major legislation. Gingrich also barred action on the most important bipartisan proposal. Denouncing the Speaker for a cynical ploy, they quickly got behind the discharge petition sponsored by Rep. Scotty Baesler, D-Ky., which would have discharged an essentially open rule allowing consideration of the bill with substitute amendments made in order that embodied several major proposals. The rule used a "queen-of-the-hill" process in which, if any substitutes passed, the one receiving the most votes would become the basis for further action. As the petition moved above two hundred signatures in April 1998, Gingrich capitulated and promised consideration under an open rule reported by the Rules Committee using a normal legislative process. It would be several years before a successful discharge petition would bring about a change in campaign finance laws.

CALENDAR WEDNESDAY

Calendar Wednesday is a little-used method for bringing to the House floor a bill that has been blocked by the Rules Committee. Under the procedure, each Wednesday standing committees may be called in alphabetical order for the purpose of bringing up any of their bills that have been reported, except those that are privileged, on the House or Union Calendar. General debate is limited to two hours, and action must be completed in the same legislative day. Bills called up from the Union Calendar are debated in the Committee of the Whole with amendments considered under the five-minute rule.

Until the 112th Congress, the call of the Calendar was routinely dispensed with by unanimous consent. In the 112th, the House changed its rules so that the Calendar is not called unless the chair of a committee requests is.

Several limitations made the process cumbersome to use. Because committees are called alphabetically, those near the end of the list may have to wait several weeks before they are reached, and once a committee has brought up one bill under the procedure it may not bring up another until all other committees have been called. Because the bill must be disposed of in a single day, opponents need only delay to kill the bill.

During the 98th Congress (1983–1985) Republicans regularly objected to dispensing with Calendar Wednesday and forced a call of the Calendar to protest the Democratic leadership's failure to schedule action on legislation they supported, such as school prayer measures and a constitutional amendment calling for a balanced budget. The protests were purely symbolic because the committees to which these measures had been referred had never reported them, and the reading clerk simply read the name of each committee in alphabetical order before the House moved on to other business. On January 25, 1984, the Democratic leadership allowed a minor agricultural bill to be considered under the Calendar Wednesday procedure—the first such passage since May 1960. Finding the process as cumbersome and ineffective as its earlier users had, the Republicans eventually stopped objecting to dispensing with Calendar Wednesday.

On March 29, 2007, minority Republicans objected to a routine unanimous consent request to dispense with Calendar Wednesday. But they, too, found that a roll call of committees has little practical effect.

1   Richard S. Beth, *The Discharge Rule in the House: Recent Use in Historical Context* (Washington, D.C.: Library of Congress, Congressional Research Service, April 17, 2003); Richard S. Beth, *The Discharge Rule in the House of Representatives: Procedure, History, and Statistics* (Washington, D.C.: Library of Congress, Congressional Research Service, March 2, 1990); Richard S. Beth, *The Discharge Rule in the House: Recent Use in Historical Context* (Washington, D.C.: Library of Congress, Congressional Research Service, September 15, 1997); and Richard S. Beth, *The Discharge Rule in the House: Principal Uses and Features* (Washington, D.C.: Library of Congress, Congressional Research Service, February 18, 1999).

discretion to delay final votes until all the suspension bills scheduled for the day have been debated. The measure then may be called up at some time within the next two days and voted on, in succession, along with other suspension bills previously debated. The Speaker also was given discretion to shorten the time for each of those serial recorded votes to five minutes from fifteen minutes after the first vote in a sequence. These procedures have since become the normal means of considering suspensions.

The availability of the suspension motion has changed repeatedly over time. Originally in order on any day, in 1847 it was restricted to Mondays only, and in 1880 to the first and third Mondays of each month; in the 93rd Congress (1973–1975) it was made available also on the Tuesdays following those Mondays, and in the 95th Congress (1977–1979) the House rule was amended to allow for consideration of suspension bills on Mondays and Tuesdays of every week. From time to time, especially toward the end of a session, or if Congress is returning to work at midweek, the Rules Committee reports and the House passes resolutions making the motion available at other times as well. In the 112th Congress, bills could be considered under suspension of the rules on Monday, Tuesday, or Wednesday.

However, Republican leaders in 2011 announced that they intended to cut back on the number of bills considered under suspension of the rules. Majority Leader Eric Cantor, R-Va., told his colleagues, "The goal for this Congress is to stress quality over quantity." Noting that 70 percent of the bills dealt with on the House floor in the 110th Congress were considered under suspension, including congratulating individuals, institutions, or sports teams and supporting the designation of a particular day, week, or month, Cantor said, "Gone are congratulatory resolutions. Post office naming will be handled on a less frequent basis." The House did not pass any congratulatory resolutions or measures designating days, weeks, or months for the observance of a particular worthy cause in the first session of the 112th Congress. The House continued to name post offices and courthouses, however.[14]

As adjournment nears there usually is a considerable backlog of legislation awaiting action. Members who might have voted against a measure under the suspension procedure earlier in the session because of the bar to floor amendments might in the final days support a suspension motion on the grounds that the unamended measure is better than no measure at all. Conversely, members opposed to a bill under suspension have maximum leverage to force the bill's manager to incorporate amendments in the motion or risk losing it altogether.

In some cases, the rules are suspended simply to expedite important legislation, even it if it is controversial.

The House declared war on the Axis powers in World War II through passage of joint resolutions under suspension of the rules. Ironically, when the House convened on Monday, December 8, 1941, following the attack on Pearl Harbor the day before, it was neither the first nor the third Monday, and the House needed unanimous consent to use the procedure to consider a declaration of war on Japan. Later in the week, the House followed a similar procedure to deal with Germany and Italy.

The Twenty-Fourth Amendment to the Constitution, abolishing the poll tax, was passed by the House using the suspension procedure on August 27, 1962, by a vote of 295–86. On November 15, 1983, an attempt to again pass the so-called Equal Rights Amendment, which had expired without being ratified by a sufficient number of states, failed to receive the requisite supermajority under suspension of the rules by a vote of 278–147.

In the late 1970s, the Republicans accused the Democrats of using the shortcut procedure to push through some complex or controversial legislation without adequate debate or the opportunity to offer amendments. By 1978 the procedure had become as much of an issue as the bills themselves. The Democrats were embarrassed that year when a controversial education aid bill supported by President Carter failed under suspension on a vote of 156–218, in part because members were angry about the large numbers of suspension bills.

In 1979 the Democratic Caucus formalized guidelines that prohibited any bill with an estimated cost of more than $100 million in a single year from being taken up under suspension unless the Democratic Steering and Policy Committee granted a waiver to the Speaker. When the Republicans assumed control of the House in 1995, they continued to use the suspension procedure much as the Democrats had done. The Republican Conference rules largely mimicked the Democratic rules. Major legislation, however, is still sometimes passed under suspension, either because there is substantial bipartisan support for it or because an emergency situation warrants it.

The Republican leadership in 1995 used the Rules Committee on several occasions to bring noncontroversial bills to the floor under open rules—bills that might ordinarily have been considered under suspension. An open rule allows any germane amendment to be offered. The Democrats complained that the new majority was avoiding the suspension process to inflate artificially the Rules Committee's claims that it was reporting a greater percentage of open rules than had been the case previously. The majority used these statistics to bolster its claims to have brought greater openness and fairness to House procedures.

Sometimes the suspension process has been used as a safe way to test sentiment on an issue or to allow members to go on the record while avoiding passing legislation. For example, in February 1998, following more than a year of bitter partisan strife, the House dismissed an election challenge against Rep. Loretta Sanchez, D-Calif., after failing to find proof of sufficient voting irregularities to question the result. The Republican majority, however, still wanted to make a statement expressing concern about allegations that noncitizens had voted in the election. Their method of doing so was to immediately call up for consideration under suspension controversial legislation that would have required proof of U.S. citizenship for voting. The unsuccessful 210–200 vote for passage demonstrated some House interest in the concept, but the close margin also served as a warning that a full-fledged airing of the issues in the normal legislative process was called for before the bill made a reappearance on the floor.

Formal Order of Business and Privileged Legislation

House Rule XIV provides a detailed order of business for the House each day, which has changed little since 1890. The rule (in slightly shortened form) reads as follows.

First. Prayer by the chaplain.

Second. Reading and approval of the Journal.

Third. The Pledge of Allegiance to the Flag.

Fourth. Correction of reference of public bills.

Fifth. Disposal of business on the Speaker's table.

Sixth. Unfinished business.

Seventh. The morning hour for the consideration of bills called up by committees.

Eighth. Motions to go into Committee of the Whole House on the State of the Union.

Ninth. Orders of the day.

The House routinely ignores this order of business because many of its elements have become obsolete or different practices more efficiently accomplish the objectives. For example, the morning hour has not been used for decades, and the House, while it often resolves into the Committee of the Whole to debate and amend legislation, arrives there in a manner different from that contemplated by the rule.

The only elements of the order of business that always occur in the House are the first, second, and third. After that, other rules procedures, such as motions to suspend the rules or special orders of business from the Rules Committee, are used to determine the House's agenda. In addition, other informal practices, such as the period at the beginning of the day when the Speaker, at his or her discretion, recognizes members to speak for one minute, occur routinely but are not mentioned in Rule XIV.

The House operates by putting aside that formal order in which to proceed and making in order other matters in their place. Some observers have described this as the use of privileged interruptions in the order of business. This new business derives from the use of other rules of the House, or through the use of resolutions from the Rules Committee, to make legislation privileged for consideration, which means it cannot be stopped simply by the objection of a single member. The House must then decide whether it wants to conduct this privileged business. But assuming it does, legislation comes up for debate and votes.

In the House, the term "privilege" may have several meanings. The House's standing rules create privilege for certain measures or motions to come up on the floor, which might depend on the subject matter of the legislation, the committee reporting the measure, or both. For example, general appropriations bills that are reported from the Appropriations Committee may simply be placed before the House,

requiring some action be taken as a result. The class of such privileged matters is relatively small compared with the total number of measures that the House considers each year. A bill revising criminal laws, however, is not privileged because neither the subject matter itself nor the committee that reported it—in this case, Judiciary—have been given any special recognition in the rules for such a purpose. Such a bill may not be brought up unless the rules are suspended to allow it to interrupt the order of business or unless the House adopts a resolution reported from the Rules Committee to make it privileged. Such a resolution is called a special rule, a "rule providing a special order of business." More often, it is simply called the rule.

In some cases, not only can committees call up bills they have reported without going first to the Rules Committee, but they also can create and report out a measure without even introducing it first. Under House rules, these committees have leave to report at any time.

Among the most significant types of legislation in this category are:

- General appropriations bills, as well as continuing appropriations resolutions reported after September 15.

- Concurrent budget resolutions reported by the Budget Committee in accordance with the Congressional Budget and Impoundment Control Act of 1974.

- Resolutions providing biennial committee funding and disposing of House election contests reported by the House Administration Committee.

- Measures amending the rules of the House, or providing a special order for future consideration of a bill on the floor, reported by the Rules Committee.

- Resolutions dealing with ethics complaints against members reported by the Committee on Standards of Official Conduct.

- Resolutions of inquiry. Such resolutions are addressed to the president or the head of an executive branch department requesting the official to provide information to the House specified in the resolution. Such resolutions are deemed essential for the House to perform its oversight and legislative responsibilities. For many years, lawmakers rarely availed themselves of this tactic. But in the early 2000s, with Republican George W. Bush in the White House, and with Republicans controlling the House, Democrats filed dozens of resolutions of inquiry, generally seeking information that would embarrass the Bush administration, such as information about how the decision to go to war with Iraq was made, or whether top administration officials knew of and condoned waterboarding and other interrogation practices. House Republicans also have made use of the resolution of inquiry.

DILATORY TACTICS ARE LIMITED IN THE HOUSE

The House does not permit the range of delaying tactics common in the Senate. This is because of its much larger size, which does not allow for the same degree of recognition for the interests of individuals; its rules, which limit the ability of members to obtain the floor except for specified purposes and which provide several mechanisms for cutting off debate; and its traditions of bringing business to some conclusion.

The House has a number of rules and practices not used in the Senate that operate to restrict debate.

- The motion for ordering the previous question in the House, which, if adopted on a simple majority vote, ends all debate and forces an immediate vote.

- The "one-hour rule," which prevents any member from being recognized for more than one hour at a time for debate or to call up legislation. Business directly before the House, such as a conference report or a special rule from the Rules Committee, can be considered for no more than one hour unless additional time is granted by unanimous consent, the previous question motion ending debate is defeated, or a special rule is passed extending debate time.

- The Rules Committee, which can bring before the House a resolution providing a special rule for a debate and amending process that limits opportunities for delay and can force the House to consider such a resolution. Most special rules in the modern Congress are written to curtail unwanted amendments and points of order against the bill and amendments to be considered.

- An 1890 rule that "no dilatory motion shall be entertained by the Speaker."[1] On January 31, 1890, Speaker Thomas B. Reed ruled: "The object of a parliamentary body is action, and not stoppage of action," in refusing to allow the House to consider a motion to adjourn, one of the few procedural matters directly mentioned in the U.S. Constitution. The prohibition also may be applied to other motions, including appeals from the ruling of the chair as well as to amendments. Its application is extremely rare.

Despite its rules, the House does not always operate like clockwork. Proceedings can be delayed by forcing electronic votes on matters that might not otherwise merit one, such as on the Speaker's approval of the Journal, or by offering and then forcing electronic votes on motions to adjourn, motions to table, ordering the previous question, moving to rise (end proceedings) in the Committee of the Whole, reconsidering actions taken by the House, and offering resolutions raising questions of the privileges of the House. Sometimes motions long forgotten or almost never seen on the floor, such as Texas representative Lloyd Doggett's 1997 motion to reconsider the vote by which the yeas and nays were ordered on a pending motion to adjourn, are resurrected to provide additional delaying tactics. Eventually, all of these options will be exhausted after some hours have elapsed and the House can conclude its legislative business.

On October 8, 1968, in an extraordinary example of just how far a leader may go to ensure the House can conduct its business, the Speaker used his authority in the standing rules to order the doors of the chamber locked so that members could not leave while a quorum call was in progress. The House was attempting to complete the reading of the Journal, which had been demanded, so that it could move on to other business. During these proceedings, which lasted into the next day, thirty-three quorum calls delayed action. The House ultimately adopted a motion providing that the doors would be locked until the conclusion of the reading. Once a quorum had been established and with members locked in the chamber, the Journal was disposed of and the House got down to business.

Underlying the obscure parliamentary pyrotechnics were questions of the rawest politics. First, the minority Republicans wished to preserve their lead in the 1968 presidential election. Richard M. Nixon, the GOP nominee, was refusing televised debates with the Democratic candidate, Vice President Hubert H. Humphrey, and Democrats sought to embarrass Nixon.

The unsuccessful delaying tactics were intended to prevent consideration of a special rule and, following that, a bill suspending the equal time requirements of the Communications Act of 1934, the enactment of which would have allowed Nixon and Humphrey to debate in the absence of other candidates. While the House went on to pass the bill, it did not clear the Senate and was not enacted.

Second, the minority wanted to make a major issue of the Democrats' refusal to consider reform proposals recommended by a 1965–1966 joint committee on the reorganization of Congress prior to final adjournment. Their delaying tactics were a means to draw attention to that issue. (The legislation was not considered until the next Congress when the Legislative Reorganization Act of 1970 was passed.)

The potential for seemingly endless delay through repeated quorum calls was later eliminated by House rules changes in the 1970s.

When unanticipated delays arise, the majority can always employ the Rules Committee to remedy the situation. In 1997 the Democratic minority used delaying tactics on several occasions to signal its displeasure over what it considered the majority's failure to resolve the election challenge filed by former representative Robert K. Dornan, R-Calif., against Democrat Loretta Sanchez, who had defeated him in a close race in 1996. In November 1997, Democratic members announced their intention to present nearly two dozen consecutive privileged resolutions—each offered by a different member—in an effort to pressure the majority to dismiss the challenge. Pushing all of these resolutions out of the way, by moving to table each after it had been read but before any debate, would have disrupted the schedule of the House for a considerable period of time.

In a preemptive strike, the majority adopted a resolution from the Rules Committee barring such resolutions for the rest of the session unless offered by either the majority or minority leader. As expected, after its adoption the minority leader chose not to offer all of these resolutions himself. (The Democrats ultimately achieved their objective the following February when the election challenge was dismissed.)

In 2009, Republicans employed a range of delaying tactics to express their displeasure over a rule that limited amendments to an appropriations bill—a measure that traditionally had been considered under an open rule. Republicans demanded roll-call votes on amendments—both in the Committee of the Whole and again in the House, motions to reconsider votes and motions to recommit the bill. And the GOP appealed numerous rulings of the presiding officer. Action on the bill took most of three days and culminated in an all-time record of 53 roll-call votes on June 18. For the rest of the year, Democrats brought up other appropriations bills under structured rules that limited amendments.

1   Asher C. Hinds, ed., *Hinds' Precedents of the House of Representatives.* Vol. 5 (Washington, D.C.: Government Printing Office, 1907), sec. 5713, 358.

Most privileged measures must lie over (await action) for some short period of time after they have been reported. This includes, for example, one day in the case of special rules from the Rules Committee and committee funding resolutions (with some exceptions), and three days for general appropriations bills and the concurrent budget resolution, to give members time to read the legislation.

While privilege may convey status to a committee, it does not necessarily automatically convey additional power or political advantage on the floor. The Ways and Means Committee lost its power to report legislation as privileged in 1975, but the committee has not suffered a loss in power as a result.

Certain other legislative matters in the House also are considered privileged and may be called up quickly. In this category, for example, are conference reports (after a three-day layover) and any bill vetoed by the president and returned to the House, which may be called up immediately for disposition.

Although a rule is not required to bring privileged legislation to the floor, the managers will often seek a rule anyway to waive the time layover requirements, eliminate points of order that might be lodged against the bill, and restrict or prevent the offering of floor amendments. Appropriations bills, for example, frequently contain authorizing language or provide funds for programs whose authorizations have expired, which violates House rules. A waiver protects such language from a point of order, which, if upheld, would have allowed any single member to strike the provision.

To prevent floor amendments from unraveling compromises on complex legislation, committees routinely seek rules that permit only specified amendments to be offered on the floor. The Budget Committee, for example, effectively abandoned use of its power to call up budget resolutions as privileged in 1980 because the resolutions would be subjected to perfecting amendments in the Committee of the Whole on virtually any subject large or small without effective restrictions and could remain on the floor for weeks at a time. Instead, using the Rules Committee, the leadership can usually pass the measure in a day. Invariably it obtains a rule barring all amendments except a handful of complete substitute budgets offered by the minority party and various factions such as the Congressional Black Caucus, the Republican Study Committee, conservative Democrats known as the Blue Dog Coalition, and the liberal Progressive Caucus. The increasing use of the Rules Committee to protect even privileged legislation from points of order and a potentially lengthy amendment process is one of the most significant developments of the last several decades. It represents an increase in the ability of House leaders to exert control over virtually every committee and a corresponding loss of power by the House membership at large to alter legislation once it reaches the floor.

Gone are the days when the chairs of the Appropriations subcommittees, the so-called College of Cardinals, would pride themselves on drafting their own bills, bringing them to the floor without a rule or consultation with the Speaker, and managing them as they saw fit. Floor time is too limited, and the potential for embarrassing surprises too great, for the kind of uncertainty this style of committee independence might generate, and the majority party has increasingly sought to structure floor action around its agenda instead of the long-standing traditions of committees or the egos of chairs.

In 1997, at a leadership meeting, Speaker Gingrich was reported to have upbraided Appropriations Committee chair Bob Livingston, R-La., for allowing a subcommittee chair, Rep. Sonny Callahan, R-Ala., to make policy decisions on the bill he managed without approval of the leadership. Just a few years earlier, such criticism by a Speaker, along with the concept that the full committee chair should control a subcommittee chair, would have been considered an unprecedented assault on the integrity of the Appropriations Committee.

Major Legislation and the Rules Committee

Virtually all major legislation, including privileged bills and any measure considered controversial, is routed through the Rules Committee before going to the floor. The purpose is twofold. First, a special rule makes a bill in order for floor consideration even though it is not at the top of whichever calendar it is on. It might not ordinarily be considered at all without a rule. If bills were called in the order in which they appeared on the House calendars, much significant legislation would never reach the House floor. Second, the special rule sets out the guidelines for floor debate and amendment on the legislation.

Because it controls the flow of legislation from the committees to the full House, the Rules Committee has considerable power and its role in the legislative process is crucial. In the modern era, the majority-dominated House Rules Committee is essentially an arm of the Speaker's office that is detailed to engineer the outcomes desired by majority party leaders. The majority party has nine seats on the committee, while the minority has only four. In addition, the party leaders, who appoint the members of the committee, take care to name only lawmakers who will accede to the leaders' wishes—no mavericks are found on the Rules panel. Because the committee comprises party loyalists, and because the majority always enjoys a supermajority, the Rules Committee produces the kind of rules that the ruling party's leaders desire.

The Rules Committee chair, who is the Speaker's personal choice for the post, has wide discretion in arranging the panel's agenda. The chair may call an emergency meeting of the committee whenever he or she wishes. Many Rules Committee meetings are held late at night, after majority party leaders have agreed upon a strategy, so that a rule could be drafted enabling floor action the next day. Scheduling—or not scheduling—a Rules hearing on a bill usually determines whether it ever comes before the House for debate.

For many years in the middle part of the twentieth century, the committee used that power to kill bills it opposed even though they were supported by the majority leadership and a majority of the House. However, since a showdown between Speaker Sam Rayburn, D-Texas, and Rules Committee chair Howard W. Smith, D-Va., in 1961—and to a far greater degree after the House reforms of the 1970s—the Rules Committee has become an arm of the majority leadership and usually works with the Speaker and majority leader to expedite their priorities and block items they oppose. The committee and the leadership also consult often on the terms of debate and amendment that will be allowed for each bill.

Rules Committee Hearings

Usually the chair of the committee that reported a bill requests a rule. At Rules Committee hearings the chair of the legislative committee, supported by the bill's sponsors and other committee members, proposes a rule to the Rules Committee. Members who oppose the bill or who want to offer floor amendments to it also may testify.

Rules Committee hearings serve as a dry run for the bill's floor managers. As political scientist Bruce I. Oppenheimer has pointed out, "The Rules Committee dress rehearsal gives them a chance to make errors and recover before going to the floor."[15]

Drafting the Rule. All rules limit the time for general debate on the House floor. The time permitted varies (it is often one hour equally divided between the two parties), depending largely on the extent of controversy surrounding a bill. Many rules also waive points of order against certain provisions of the bill or against specified amendments that are expected to be offered on the floor. This waiver permits the House to violate its own rules by barring any objections to such matters.

Since the 1980s the committee has granted an increasing number of blanket waivers, barring all points of order that might be raised against a particular bill. Blanket waivers are most often granted for conference reports and omnibus bills. The committee justified the increase by pointing to the growing number and complexity of procedural requirements, such as those added by the Gramm-Rudman-Hollings deficit reduction law, which made it difficult to specify exactly which rules needed to be waived. Failure to waive a specific rule would give opponents of the bill an opening to challenge it.

The minority party often has expressed displeasure with the trend toward blanket waivers. They "are indicative of the [majority] leadership's willingness to permit committees to circumvent and violate House rules in order to advance their legislative agenda," Rep. Trent Lott, R-Miss., himself a member of the Rules Committee, said in December 1977.[16]

Rules also govern amending activity on the floor. The committee traditionally grants three kinds of rules affecting amendments: open, closed, or modified, the last of which is sometimes referred to as a structured rule. These terms are not defined in the rules of the House or of the committee, are often used colloquially, and can have different meanings depending on the circumstances and the opinion of the person using the term. An open rule usually permits any germane amendment to be offered on the floor at the appropriate time. A rule that bars all amendments, or all but committee amendments, is referred to as closed. A modified rule generally permits amendments only to certain provisions or sections of the bill, or to specific subjects dealt with in the bill, or only allows certain specific amendments. Sometimes the terms "modified open" and "modified closed" are used as well, and the difference is usually in the eye of the beholder.

In some cases, the Rules Committee writes structured rules that provide procedural protections for desired amendments that would otherwise be vulnerable to points of order on the floor. In such an instance, the amendment stands a better chance of adoption than it would under an open rule.

Shift toward Restrictive Rules

Until the 1980s the vast majority of rules were open. Closed rules were generally reserved for tax bills and other measures too complicated or technical to be tampered with on the House floor. But in the 1970s a number of developments led the Rules Committee to begin to draft more modified rules that specified which amendments could be offered and often stipulated in what order they would be considered.

For one thing, the decision to allow recorded votes on floor amendments significantly increased the number of amendments offered. Before 1971 only vote totals, not individual votes by members, were recorded on floor amendments in the Committee of the Whole, which made members much more accountable to their colleagues than to their constituents. Once their votes were routinely made public, however, members found it to their advantage to offer and vote for amendments their constituents supported even if those amendments were opposed by the reporting committee. Activist junior Republicans also took advantage of recorded votes to force the Democrats to vote repeatedly on politically sensitive issues such as abortion.

The erosion of seniority and the rise of subcommittees also had its effects. When most bills were managed by the chair of the committee reporting the bill, or his or her designee, rank-and-file members tended to accept committee bills on the floor, in part because the chair, and often others on the committee, had developed expertise in the subject area and because members might need cooperation from the chair in the future. With the increase in the importance of subcommittees in the late 1970s, many bills came to be managed on the House floor by junior members often inexperienced in House procedure and without acknowledged expertise in the subject matter. In these situations, rank-and-file members were less inclined to defer to the subcommittee's judgment and more likely to offer amendments of their own on the House floor.

Consequently, the number of amendments offered on the floor increased substantially. According to political scientists Stanley Bach and Steven S. Smith, the number of floor amendments more than doubled, from 792 in the 92nd Congress (1971–1973) to 1,695 in the 95th Congress (1977–1979) before beginning to decline again.[17] And with this explosion of amendments the Democratic leadership and bill managers found it more and more difficult to know what was likely to be offered on the floor, whether it would win, and how long the whole process might take.

This pressure to regain control over the amending process was reinforced by several other developments.

First, the decision to allow a bill to be referred to more than one committee created a need for mechanisms by which conflicting recommendations could be resolved on the House floor in an orderly fashion. Bills that have been referred to more than one legislative committee can present special problems to the Rules Committee, particularly if the legislative committees report conflicting provisions. To prevent divisiveness, embarrassment, and perhaps defeat on the House floor, the Rules panel will often ask the committees to try to negotiate their differences before a rule is granted. The resulting compromise, not the original reported legislation, is then made the basic legislation to be debated and amended on the House floor. This is called an amendment in the nature of a substitute considered as original text. If negotiations are unsuccessful, the Rules Committee may write a rule that allows members to vote on the alternatives.

Second, many members were eager to open Ways and Means Committee bills, which had traditionally been considered under closed rules, to at least some adjustment on the floor. In 1973 the Democratic Caucus began to require committee chairs to give advance notice in the *Congressional Record* whenever they intended to seek a closed rule. The caucus also adopted a rule allowing it to instruct Democrats on Rules to vote to make certain specific amendments in order during floor consideration. But after a brief flurry of activity in the 1970s, the power fell into disuse as the Rules Committee became a reliable arm of the party leadership and, as such, more representative of the views of the majority of the caucus.

Third, the increased partisanship in the House beginning in the 1970s erased earlier norms that had inhibited members of the minority from offering controversial proposals purely to embarrass the opposition. These votes created a record that could be attacked by interest groups in their voting scorecards and related materials disseminated to their membership. The majority, while it could not prevent all such votes, sometimes moved to restrict amendments to limit the damage.

Fourth, the increased political independence of members from their political parties, and the need to maintain a fundraising apparatus, encouraged more members to freelance on the floor by offering amendments that might give them greater visibility. In many cases, while such amendments might have accomplished the objectives these members desired, they also might not contribute much of substance to the bill and could delay and distract the House, and the Rules Committee moved to limit them.

The Rules Committee began to draft more rules controlling the amendment process. In the 95th Congress (1977–1979) only 15 percent of the rules reported to the House were closed or restrictive; by the end of the 101st Congress (1989–1991), that number had risen to 55 percent. Another way of looking at the change is through statistics kept by the minority parties, both Republican and Democratic, on open rules from the 95th Congress through the 107th Congress (2001–2003). The percentage of open rules under the Democrats declined from 85 percent in 1977–1979 to 30 percent in 1993–1995, the last years they controlled the House before 2007. Under the GOP, open rules rose to 44 percent in the 104th Congress (1995–1997) but had dropped to 28 percent in the 107th Congress. As part of their broader critique of Democratic dominance of the chamber, Republicans attacked the majority constantly for using restrictive rules to stifle debate and block amendments. Democrats would later voice the same outrage when they were cast into the minority in the 104th Congress and the roles would reverse again in the 110th Congress.

In the 104th Congress, with a Republican-controlled Rules Committee, the new majority trumpeted important victories for openness in House procedures during consideration of its critical Contract with America bills, claiming to have issued open rules 72 percent of the time. The Democratic minority, however, responded that the correct figure was 26 percent. Predictably, each side differed on the definition of "openness" and which legislation should be included in the statistics.

In 2009, minority House Republicans ratcheted up parliamentary warfare in their fight to reduce federal spending, and Democrats retaliated by severely limiting the opportunity to offer floor amendments. Appropriations bills had traditionally been considered under an open rule—as long as the amendments did not increase total spending in the bill beyond limits set forth in the annual budget resolution and allocated among the spending bills by the Appropriations Committee. But when the first fiscal 2010 spending bill reached the House floor, Republicans proposed more than one hundred amendments to the Commerce-Justice-Science bill. Democrats reacted with a floor rule that allowed no more than thirty-three amendments. Republicans retaliated with a barrage of parliamentary delaying tactics that brought action to a crawl. On June 18, the House took fifty-three votes on the bill, a modern record for a single day.

From then on that year, House Democrats brought all the other appropriations bills to the floor under restrictive rules, to the great outrage of Republicans.

METHODS OF VOTING IN THE HOUSE AND SENATE: PUTTING MEMBERS' POSITIONS ON THE RECORD

The House and Senate have each developed their own procedures for voting. Guiding them are voting rules spelled out in the U.S. Constitution. Most specific are requirements for roll-call votes, which are set forth in Article I, Section 5, Clause 3: "The yeas and nays of the members of either house on any question shall, at the desire of one fifth of those present, be entered on the Journal." The provision is aimed at preventing secret ballots.

HOUSE

The House has also developed a complex set of rules governing how members make demands on the House floor to have their votes recorded. The House uses three types of votes: voice, division, and votes recorded by the name of the member ("yeas and nays" or "recorded votes"). The House may take several votes on the same proposition, using the most simple method first and then increasingly more complex voting methods, before a decision is reached. *(See "Action in the Committee of the Whole," p. 100.)*

A voice vote is the quickest method of voting and the type nearly always used first when a proposition is first put to the membership. The presiding officer calls for the "ayes" and then the "nays," members shout in chorus on one side or the other, and the chair decides the result.

If the result of a voice vote is in doubt or a single member requests a further test, a division, or standing, vote may be demanded. In this case those in favor of the proposal and then those against it stand up while the chair takes a head count. Only vote totals are announced; there is no record of how individual members vote. Few issues are decided by division vote. After a voice vote, members usually skip the division vote and ask for a vote in which members are recorded by name. This kind of vote, which is nearly always taken using the electronic voting system, draws most members to the chamber. It is called the yeas and nays or a "recorded vote" depending on the circumstances under which it is taken, but the result is identical.

Since 1973 the House has used an electronic voting system for recording members' votes. Members insert identification cards into one of forty-four voting stations mounted on the backs of chairs along the aisles of the House chamber. When a member punches a button to indicate his position, a giant board on the wall of the press gallery above the Speaker's desk immediately flashes green for "yes" and red for "no" next to the legislator's name. Members may also vote "present," which shows up as a yellow light on the board. Members may change their votes at any time until the result is announced. The Speaker may vote on any matter but, by tradition, rarely does.

The yeas and nays, provided for by the Constitution, is used only when the House itself is sitting and never in the Committee of the Whole. This method of voting may be ordered by one-fifth of those present regardless of how few members are on the floor. House rules also provide that it may occur automatically whenever a quorum is not present on the floor when the question is put and any member objects to the vote on those grounds. The resulting vote both establishes a quorum and settles the question at issue.

A recorded vote, provided for by House rules, may be demanded both in the House and in the Committee of the Whole, but it works differently in each case. In the House, it may be ordered upon demand of one-fifth of a quorum of 218, which is 44. For example, as a matter of strategy, a member would demand a recorded vote, not the yeas and nays, whenever a majority of the members were present on the floor because the requisite number (44) would always be less than one-fifth of those present. In the Committee of the Whole a recorded vote is always ordered by 25 members. However, in practice, a request for a recorded vote may not need the visible support of 25 members to be ordered.

Once the first vote in a series of votes by electronic device begins, members have a minimum of fifteen minutes to record their votes. The voting time is often shortened to five minutes, if a number of votes have been clustered, for each vote beyond the first one; again, an additional two minutes may be allowed. Regardless of the time limit, which is technically a minimum and not a maximum, any member who is in the chamber at the time the result is to be announced has the right to record a vote or to change one already cast. The time period was extended regularly in the early years of the twenty-first century so that party leaders could have extra minutes—or in one case extra hours—to try to change the outcome of a vote. Once the result has been announced, however, the vote is closed and members may not subsequently vote or change their votes, even by unanimous consent. Often members who miss a vote will insert statements in the *Congressional Record* immediately following the missed vote indicating what their position would have been, though there is no requirement that they do so.

Until 1971 the yeas and nays were the only votes on which House members were individually recorded. Votes in the Committee of the Whole were taken by methods that did not record the stands of individual members. Many questions were decided by "teller votes" under which the chair appointed tellers representing opposite sides on a vote and directed members to pass between them up the center aisle to be counted—first the ayes and then the nays. Only vote totals were announced on teller votes.

In the 1960s members and outside interest groups began to object to unrecorded votes in the Committee of the Whole. They believed that members could not be held accountable for saying one thing to their constituents but voting the opposite way by tellers. Members could effectively hide their votes on key amendments, which were sometimes closely contested and usually determined the final form of the bill, while going on the record on the less controversial matter of final passage in the House. Liberals also believed that their views might have a better chance to prevail against established institutional power centers, which were more conservative, if members were forced to go on record.

A provision of the Legislative Reorganization Act of 1970 opened the way for "tellers with clerks," more commonly called "recorded teller votes." This procedure,

---

In the 112th Congress, with the House again under GOP control, Republican freshmen clamoring to transform the federal government persuaded new Speaker John Boehner, R-Ohio, to open bills to more amendments. In 2011, the House cast 516 roll-call votes on amendments, compared with only 21 in all of 2010, when the Democrats were in charge.

"To find the last time the House worked in this way, with really open access to the floor, you need to reach back to the 1970s," says Sarah A. Binder, a political scientist at George

used in 1971 and 1972, made it possible to record the votes of individual members in the Committee of the Whole. When the change first went into effect, members were required to write their names on red or green cards, which they handed to tellers. The consequence of the rules change was swift. Many more members appeared for these votes because absentees could now be noted by name in the *Congressional Record*. After the electronic voting system was installed in 1973, the recorded teller vote process became known simply as a recorded vote. The advent of recorded teller votes, and then the electronic voting system, rendered the old unrecorded teller votes essentially obsolete. However, unrecorded teller voting still remained as a potential fallback option in the rules until its formal abolition in 1993.

When members' votes first began to be recorded in the Committee of the Whole on amendments and other motions, only twenty members were required to stand and demand a recorded vote. This number was later raised to twenty-five in 1979 after some members complained that it was too easy to force votes. But there has been no evidence that the change to twenty-five made any significant difference. The requirement has essentially become a formality, and recorded votes are often requested and granted with fewer than twenty-five members in the chamber.

In the Committee of the Whole, unlike the House, there is no means to force a vote automatically by claiming that a quorum (one hundred) is not present. In such cases, a member usually demands a recorded vote and, pending that, makes the point of order that a quorum is not present. By doing so the member gains time to ensure the presence of at least twenty-five supporters when the chair announces whether sufficient support exists for a recorded vote. If a quorum is not present, the chair orders a quorum call to establish one before determining whether twenty-five members support the demand for a recorded vote. The chair has two choices: to order a regular quorum call, which summons all 435 members, whose names are recorded in the *Congressional Record* after the vote; or a "notice quorum call," in which the chair simply stops the proceedings after one hundred members have responded and no permanent record of those responding is kept.

In many cases, to save time, enough members rise informally to indicate their support for a recorded vote while the chair is still counting for a quorum. The point of no quorum then is withdrawn and a recorded vote occurs. If both the quorum call and then the recorded vote are used, the quorum call is fifteen minutes long, followed, if ordered, by a recorded vote, which the chair may reduce to five minutes.

Before the electronic voting system was installed, yeas and nays were taken by calling the roll, a time-consuming process in the 435-member House. Each roll call took about half an hour. The Speaker still retains the right to call the roll instead of using the electronic voting system. The old-fashioned method may be used when the electronic system breaks down, as it has from time to time. An archaic provision still exists in the rules that allows the Speaker to direct the clerk to "tell" the members by name in the House. In practice, the only time each member's name is called is on the opening day of each Congress when the clerk calls each name to elect a Speaker. Members shout out the name of the person they support. Usually there are only two candidates, one Republican and one Democrat, but the 1997 election was unusual as four Republican members voted for persons other than Speaker Newt Gingrich, R-Ga., for reelection because of ethics controversies surrounding him at the time. They voted either for another sitting Republican member or for former House members. In 2011, most Democrats voted for Nancy Pelosi, D-Calif., but seven other Democrats received votes. On several occasions members have voted present.

Use of the electronic voting system opened the possibility of ghost voting in which an absent member would give his voting card to a colleague. Such instances are rare, but the House has banned the practice by rule and has disciplined members suspected of violations. Occasionally, a member might be seen handing a voting card to his or her child to cast the vote, which is also against the rules.

No member may be deprived of his or her right to vote. House rules direct members to refrain from voting on an issue on the House floor if they have a conflict of interest. The rules also admonish members in a Code of Official Conduct (Rule XXIII in the 110th Congress) not to vote on the floor or in committees if they have been convicted of crimes for which a sentence of two or more years imprisonment may be imposed. Compliance with these rules is strictly at the discretion of the member affected. However, convicted members who have continued to vote in such circumstances have been threatened with expulsion.

SENATE

Only two types of votes are in everyday use in the Senate—voice votes and roll-call votes (yeas and nays). Standing votes are seldom employed. The Senate does not use the teller vote and has no electronic voting system.

As in the House, the most common method of deciding issues is by voice vote. The presiding officer determines the outcome. Under the Constitution, one-fifth of the senators present must support a demand for a roll call. (Unlike the House, the Senate assumes that an actual quorum—fifty-one—is present when this demand is being made, so a minimum of eleven senators must rise in support. When a request for a roll call occurs immediately after a roll call or a live quorum call has occurred, the number needed is one-fifth of the senators who responded, to a maximum of twenty. Informal practices have evolved in which a vote may be ordered by the chair if only a few senators are present and the two parties' floor managers agree.)

Unlike the House, where a demand for a roll-call vote comes only when debate has been concluded and the chair has put the question, senators may demand the yeas and nays on pending business at a time long in advance of the vote. The Senate usually allows fifteen minutes for a roll-call vote, although unanimous consent requests may shorten the voting time in specific situations. The fifteen-minute period also may be extended to accommodate late-arriving senators. Senators who miss a vote cannot be recorded after the result has been announced. However, unlike the House, a senator who voted but was not recorded or was incorrectly recorded may, by unanimous consent, have the proper vote recorded if it would not change the result.

Washington University.[18] The Republican-led Rules Committee offered another measure of what it termed the new "spirit of openness and accountability." According to the panel, 810 amendments were considered during the entire 111th Congress. In just the first seven months of the 112th Congress, according to the Rules Committee, 437 amendments had been considered.

The kinds of restrictive rules vary considerably. The Rules Committee may simply require that amendments will be in order only if they have been printed in the *Congressional*

Record in advance of the debate. This practice may increase the number of amendments, not reduce them. "When you see you are fixin' to be cut off and not be able to have an opportunity to offer an amendment you start conjuring up all possible amendments and you put them in the *Record*," Lott said.[19] But advance notice does help the leadership anticipate floor action and develop strategy to deal with it.

Structured Rules

A structured rule is a rule that can have many different forms. It usually can be anything other than a simple open rule but its principal purpose is to supply a sense of order on the floor as amendments are offered and debated in the Committee of the Whole. Such rules may specify the amendments that can be offered, by whom, and, sometimes, in what order they will be considered. Structured rules may also set time limits on debate for the amendments. Most such rules are restrictive in that they prevent members from offering some amendments. However, structured rules may also be expansive, by making it in order for the House to consider amendments that are not germane to the bill. They may attempt to focus debate around entire substitutes for a bill, instead of numerous minor perfecting amendments. This invariably happens during consideration of the congressional budget resolution, because debate there deals with broad issues of policy and philosophy, not the nuts and bolts of programs.

In the 1980s and 1990s, as party leaders tried to engineer policy outcomes on the floor without denying rank-and-file members the ability to offer and vote on alternatives, they began to use highly stylized rules that ensured their bills would pass intact.

"King-of-the-Hill Rules"

The granddaddy of those highly stylized structured rules is known as the "king-of-the-hill rule." First used in 1981, it made in order a series of alternatives to the bill under consideration and provided that even if a majority votes for two or more of the alternatives, only the last one voted on wins.

This procedure circumvented House rules that prohibit amending any portion of a bill that has already been amended. Under the normal rules, if a substitute for a bill is offered and adopted as an amendment, further substitutes or other amendments are precluded and the House moves to final passage. But king-of-the-hill rules allow amendments to continue to be offered.

In cases in which the alternative favored by the majority leadership was sure of winning, this procedure provided a means to satisfy various factions within the House by letting them present, and the members vote on, their alternatives. In cases in which the outcome was uncertain, positioning the preferred alternative last could give it an edge over its competitors.

Minority Republicans bristled when Democrats employed the tool, arguing that it allowed lawmakers to vote for, and campaign on their support of, amendments that would ultimately die at the hands of a complex rule they supported.

"It is a complex machination that in this case, as in every case, stacks the deck against the adoption of any of the amendments offered," Rep. Porter Goss, R-Fla., explained during debate of a king-of-the-hill rule in 1994. "We are giving cover to members to say they voted for something that they thought their people wanted back in their district. But when it came really to the end, the last vote they had to vote for is the one that the majority party wanted in the first place, the party position, and that is the one they vote for to be members of the party and adhere to the discipline in their party position." According to a Congressional Research Service (CRS) report in 2008, king-of-the-hill procedures were authorized in sixty-three rules between 1981 and 1994.

"Queen-of-the-Hill Rules"

A variation that replaced king-of-the-hill in the 104th Congress is sometimes referred to as the "queen-of-the-hill rule." As in king-of-the-hill rules, several substitutes for a bill can be voted on in succession, and a majority vote for any one of them does not result in the termination of the amending process. However, instead of endorsing the last such amendment considered that received a majority, under queen-of-the-hill rules, the amendment that passed with the largest number of affirmative votes, after voting on all substitutes, prevails. If two amendments received an equal number of affirmative votes, the last one voted on wins.

Rules Committee chair Gerald Solomon, R-N.Y., argued that king-of-the-hill rules were flawed because they "allowed lawmakers to be on both sides of an issue and violated the democratic principle that the position with the strongest support should prevail."[20] Queen-of-the-hill rules, similar to king-of-the-hill rules, allow the leadership to appease various factions and allow members to vote on various sides of a question. For example, during consideration in 1997 of a constitutional amendment limiting the number of years a member could serve in Congress, eleven substitute amendments were made in order under the queen-of-the-hill process so that members from particular states could vote for the congressional term limit scheme adopted by those states. (Attempts by states to limit the terms of members of Congress by statute were later thrown out by the U.S. Supreme Court, thus necessitating a change in the U.S. Constitution to accomplish the purpose.) All of the substitutes were rejected, as was the constitutional amendment itself. The queen-of-the-hill process was utilized six times in the 104th, 105th, and 107th Congresses, according to the CRS report. It has not been used since.

Self-Executing Rules

Another innovative mechanism that Rules began to use in the 1980s was the self-executing rule, under which adoption of the rule also resulted in adoption of an amendment or amendments. Self-executing rules were devised originally to expedite consideration of Senate-passed amendments to House bills and to make technical corrections, but they have also been used to enact more substantive and controversial measures.

In 1987, for example, a vote for a rule on a continuing appropriations resolution also had the effect of excluding members of Congress from a controversial pay raise. A vote for a rule on another continuing resolution earlier in the year was also a vote to provide $3.5 billion in humanitarian assistance to Nicaraguan contras fighting the Sandinista government there. The move, which was supported by the leadership of both parties, avoided a direct vote on the controversial issue of continued aid to the contras. The rule was adopted by voice vote.

In 1990, passage of a conference report on a major immigration bill was unexpectedly threatened when opposition developed to one of its provisions, leading to defeat of the rule. A second rule was then prepared and passed that self-executed adoption of a concurrent resolution changing the offending section of the conference report. Once the Senate sent a message that it had adopted the concurrent resolution, the conference report, as newly modified, was immediately available under the terms of the rule for consideration in the House. It then passed.

In February 2010, faced with an unpopular vote to raise the debt ceiling, House leaders packaged the debt ceiling increase with legislation to impose pay-as-you-go budget rules that would require Congress to offset new entitlement spending or tax cuts to avoid increasing the deficit. Then, the Rules Committee drafted a self-executing rule that included language automatically approving the debt limit increase. Adoption of the rule also served to approve the debt limit increase.

Republicans blasted the maneuver as a scheme to shield Democrats from accountability. "This is a legislative sleight of hand to protect members," Minority Leader Boehner said. "It is the kind of backroom deal the American people don't like."[21]

Just a month later, House Democratic leaders seriously considered using a self-executing rule to pass the final version of the health care overhaul bill, but scrapped that idea in the face of withering condemnation from conservatives—both in Congress and elsewhere. They complained that the so-called Slaughter rule—named after Rules Committee chair Louise M. Slaughter, D-N.Y.—which would deem the Senate version of the bill to be passed by the House upon its adoption of the rule, would be an affront to the Constitutional requirement that both chambers pass the same version of the bill.

House Floor Procedures

Procedural differences between the House and Senate are most visible on the chamber floors. Because of its size, the House adheres strictly to detailed procedures for considering legislation. These procedures, which limit debate on bills and amendments, are designed to ensure majority rule and to expedite action. Although the opposition can slow legislation from time to time in the House, it usually cannot impede it altogether. It is often said that the House minority can delay, but not deny. In contrast, the much smaller Senate emphasizes minority rights and virtually unlimited debate.

Historically, the House has operated on a Monday- or Tuesday-to-Thursday schedule, with the first day of the legislative week reserved primarily for noncontroversial legislation considered under shortcut procedures such as suspension of the rules. Sessions occasionally are scheduled for Friday, and more rarely on Saturday or Sunday, but that day is often left free so that legislators can return to their districts for the weekend. In the 112th Congress, GOP leaders announced a schedule that called for more Monday-through-Friday work-weeks, combined with more complete weeks out of session to be devoted to work in members' home districts.

Meeting times now vary. Daily sessions may begin at any hour, although earlier daily meetings are common as a session progresses. After some preliminary activities (*see box, A Typical Schedule in the House, p. 86*), the House turns to the legislative business of the day. If the House is to take up legislation under its shortcut procedures, it remains sitting as the House, with the Speaker presiding. The rules for considering and passing legislation under these expediting procedures have been described above. Most major legislation, however, comes to the House floor under a special rule and is subject to a much more elaborate procedure. The process involves four steps: adoption of the rule governing debate on the bill, general debate on the bill itself, consideration of any amendments in the Committee of the Whole, and final passage of the bill by the full House.

Adoption of the Rule

Floor action on a major House bill ordinarily begins when the Speaker recognizes the member of the Rules Committee who has been designated to call up the rule for the bill. The rule may be debated for up to one hour, with, by custom, half the time allotted to the minority party. A simple majority is sufficient to adopt a rule.

Rules are seldom rejected. In 1987 the House voted 203–217 to reject the rule for consideration of budget reconciliation legislation because it included the text of a major welfare reform bill. The Democratic leadership realized that it had made a political error by overloading the process with too many divisive issues at once. The Rules Committee revised the rule by dropping the welfare provisions.

Democrats' inability to pass a rule on the 1994 crime bill became a metaphor for their disintegrating majority. And Republicans, known for their strict discipline on parliamentary votes under Speaker Hastert, nonetheless lost a vote on the rule for a bill that would have made it more difficult for consumers to avoid paying debts by filing for bankruptcy. Republican abortion foes sided with Democrats to sink the rule, 172–243, because the bill contained language aimed at blocking abortion protesters to skirt court-ordered fines by filing for bankruptcy.

Opponents may also seek to amend a rule by defeating the previous question. The previous question, a parliamentary device used only in the full House, is a motion that, if adopted, cuts off all further debate and amendments and requires an immediate vote on the matter at hand. Routinely, the Rules Committee member handling the rule will move the previous question to bring the rule to a vote. If that motion is defeated, the rule is then open to amendment. However, the tactic is rarely successful, because defeat of the previous question has the effect of turning control of the floor over to opponents of the rule, who are likely to be members from the minority. Even majority members opposed to a rule are loath to do that, preferring instead to vote against the rule itself and have the Rules Committee report out another, while retaining control of the process.

One of the most controversial and dramatic instances of defeat of the previous question on a rule occurred in 1981, when a coalition of Republicans and conservative Democrats blocked a deficit reduction package pushed by the Democratic leadership and substituted instead an alternative containing many elements of President Reagan's legislative program, embodied in the so-called Gramm-Latta bill. This conservative coalition defeated the previous question, adopted an amendment to the rule, adopted the revised rule, and went on to successful passage of their version of the legislation. In some instances the leadership may not realize that a rule faces defeat until it is being debated on the floor. In 1999, for example, a rule for consideration of the Department of Defense authorization bill was withdrawn during debate when it became clear that defeat was possible.

Action in the Committee of the Whole

Once the rule has been adopted, the House resolves itself into the Committee of the Whole House on the State of the Union to debate and amend the legislation. Not a committee as the word is usually understood, the Committee of the Whole is a parliamentary framework to expedite House action. Although all 435 House members, as well as the nonvoting delegates, are members of the Committee of the Whole, business may be conducted with a quorum of 100 members instead of the 218 members required in the full House.

The Committee of the Whole has no counterpart in the Senate, although for many years the Senate had a Committee of the Whole to deal with treaties. The concept developed in the British House of Commons when the Speaker was once considered to be an agent of the king. During periods of strained relations between the king and the lower house of Parliament, the procedure allowed members of Commons to elect a chair of their own and to discuss matters, particularly matters pertaining to the king's household expenses, without observing the normal restrictions that applied to a formal session of the House of Commons.

The Speaker does not preside over the Committee of the Whole but selects another member of the majority party to take the chair. The Mace is lowered from its position behind the Speaker's chair when the Committee of the Whole sits.

Amendments are debated in the Committee of the Whole under the five-minute rule, which in theory but not always in practice limits debate to five minutes for and against the amendment. They may then be voted on by voice vote or by division (standing) vote. There is only one way to obtain a recorded vote on an amendment or any other matter in the Committee of the Whole, unlike the situation in the House, where there are several possibilities. Twenty-five members must stand in support of a demand for a recorded vote in the Committee of the Whole. If a quorum is not present, a quorum call may be demanded to bring additional members to the floor. To avoid using this time, members will often routinely grant a colleague a recorded vote even on matters that have little substantive support. (*See box, Methods of Voting in the House and Senate, p. 96.*)

The Committee of the Whole cannot pass a bill. Instead it reports the measure back to the full House with whatever changes it has made. The House then may adopt or reject the Committee of the Whole's proposed amendments, amend a bill further through a motion to recommit with instructions, recommit it to the legislative committee where it originated, and finally, if the bill is still on the floor, pass or reject it.

Amendments adopted in the Committee of the Whole are always put to a second vote in the full House, which is usually a pro forma voice vote with all amendments considered en bloc. However, if the initial vote on an amendment in the Committee of the Whole was close, the second vote in the House might also be a recorded vote as the losing side seeks to change the outcome.

Republican leaders postponed final action on a spending bill for the District of Columbia in 2003 when Democrats sought a second vote on an amendment authorizing a private school voucher program in the nation's capital. Republicans had prevailed on the first vote, in the Committee of the Whole, 205–203, but they were not sure they could hold a majority. When a second vote was held four days later, they reprised their success on a 209–208 vote, with District Del. Eleanor Holmes Norton, a foe of the plan, unable to cast a vote against it because of her status as a delegate and not a full voting member of the House.

Sometimes proponents of an adopted amendment will attempt to discourage such reconsideration in the House, or express their displeasure, by threatening to demand recorded votes on all amendments reported back to the House, even of the most minor nature.

In 1993 Republicans led by Rules Committee ranking member Gerald Solomon of New York instituted a practice of demanding a separate recorded vote in the House on every amendment adopted by a recorded vote in the Committee of the Whole. They objected to a new House rule adopted at the beginning of that Congress granting the four delegates and the resident commissioner from Puerto Rico, all of whom sat with the Democratic Caucus, the right to vote in the Committee of the Whole even though the rule prevented their votes from affecting the outcome. However, these five could not vote in the full House. The minority demanded that more than sixty such votes be rerun without the delegates' participation after the Committee of the Whole rose to report its actions to the House. The delegates and resident commissioner lost their right to vote in the Committee of the Whole when Republicans took control in 1995. When delegates regained the ability to vote on amendments in 2007, Republicans again protested by calling for several re-votes on bills that had been amended by the Committee of the Whole. The voting rights of the delegates and resident commissioner were once again taken away when Republicans regained control of the House in 2011.

The Committee of the Whole itself may not recommit a bill, although it may recommend to the full House that the enacting clause be stricken—a parliamentary motion that, if adopted, kills the measure. However, the motion to strike the enacting clause is almost never successful, because members desiring to kill the underlying legislation can express themselves more clearly by defeating the rule prior to its consideration, or the bill itself on final passage. The motion to strike the enacting clause is sometimes made anyway because it guarantees five minutes of debate to the maker even under circumstances when debate may not be in order. After the member finishes, he or she withdraws the motion by unanimous consent without a vote. Recommittal must be voted on in the House, not in the Committee of the Whole.

General Debate

After resolving into the Committee of the Whole, the first order of business is general debate on the bill. General debate, as Oleszek noted, serves both practical and symbolic purposes: complicated or controversial provisions of the legislation may be explained, a legislative record may be developed for the administrative agencies responsible for implementing the bill and the courts that interpret it, and a public record may be built on which legislators later campaign. In the process, Oleszek wrote, general debate "assures both legislators and the public that the House makes its decisions in a democratic fashion with due respect for majority and minority opinion."[22]

But he and other congressional observers have questioned whether general debate influences members' views and policy outcomes in an era when there is little time to sit on the House floor or watch the proceedings on television.

A 1992 examination of floor procedures by a group of scholars led by Thomas E. Mann and Norman J. Ornstein concluded that "[g]eneral debate . . . has become a time of reading prepared statements by the floor managers and is widely considered a filler time between adoption of the rule and voting on amendments, during which members can leave the floor for other activities."[23]

Most debate occurs with only a handful of members on the floor, leaving first-time visitors to the public and press galleries above the chamber to wonder where everyone is.

The rules on most bills allot an hour for general debate, although more time may be granted for particularly controversial measures. The allotted time is divided equally between and controlled by the floor managers for the bill. Ordinarily the chair of the committee or subcommittee that reported the measure acts as the floor manager for the bill's supporters, while the ranking minority member or his or her designee leads the opposition. If both support the legislation, which often happens on noncontroversial bills, they may allot some of their time to members of their party opposing the bill. A bill that has been referred to more than one committee might have multiple floor managers, each of whom is responsible for the part of the bill that was before his or her committee and each controlling a small chunk of time. The importance of the managers is evident in their physical location on the House floor. They occupy designated seats at tables on either side of the center aisle, and they are permitted to bring several committee staff members onto the floor to assist them.

Floor managers marshal speakers and support for the majority or minority position. Regardless of his or her personal view on the measure or amendments, the majority floor manager is responsible for presenting the committee's bill in the most favorable light and for fending off undesirable amendments. Traditionally, the mark of a successful majority floor manager is the ability to get a bill passed without substantial change. The minority manager, if opposed to the bill, is expected to line up convincing arguments against the legislation and for amendments, if the rule permits, that would make the measure more acceptable to the opposition.

However, the role of the floor manager has been diminished in the era of highly restrictive rules that limit amendments.

The Amending Process

In recent years, the number and type of amendments allowed on the floor have been sharply limited by the restrictive rules for floor debate favored by both Democratic and Republican majorities. As a result, many of the procedures described here, including second-degree amendments, are not as commonly employed as they once were.

Amendments, which provide a way to shape bills into a form acceptable to a majority, may change the intent, conditions, or requirements of a bill; modify, delete, or introduce

PRIVATE BILLS SERVE AS COURT OF LAST RESORT

A private bill in Congress is legislation intended for the benefit of a specific individual or entity, not the general public. At one time, hundreds, even thousands, of these would be enacted into law during a Congress, but in recent decades the number has dropped dramatically. In the 109th, 110th, and 111th Congresses combined, just three private laws were enacted.

Private legislation is used essentially as a court of last resort because those seeking relief must have exhausted all reasonable administrative and judicial procedures before asking Congress to intercede on their behalf. Courts and federal administrative agencies can make decisions based only on interpretations of public laws. Congress reserves to itself the privilege of aiding some parties who, for various reasons, are seen as deserving of special treatment. Most private bills deal with claims against the federal government and immigration and naturalization matters. Their titles usually begin with the words "For the relief of...."

A 2005 law enacted to try to spare the life of Terry Schiavo, a brain-dead Florida woman whose feeding tube was due to be disconnected, began with those words but was actually a public law. The process for enacting a private law has become so cumbersome that the mechanism was not viable for those who wanted to prevent the removal of her feeding tube.

A fine line sometimes separates public and private bills. House parliamentarian Asher C. Hinds offered the following explanation in his 1907 *Precedents of the House of Representatives:* "A private bill is a bill for the relief of one or several specified persons, corporations, institutions, etc., and is distinguished from a public bill, which relates to public matters and deals with individuals only by classes." As an example, Hinds cited bills benefiting soldiers' widows: a bill that granted pensions to soldiers' widows as a class would be a public bill, but a bill that granted a pension to a particular soldier's widow would be a private bill.

The history of private bills dates at least from Roman times when they were called *constitutionis privilegia,* privileges accorded to specified individuals. They came to Congress by way of the English Parliament. The first private bill was passed by Congress September 24, 1789, and signed by President George Washington five days later. The bill gave seventeen months' back pay at the rank of captain to the Baron de Glaubeck, a foreign officer in the service of the United States.

FLUCTUATING USAGE

Private bill usage has fluctuated over the years, largely because changes in federal law have made exceptions for individuals more necessary sometimes and less necessary other times. For example, when Congress passed legislation giving people other avenues to pursue their claims against the government the numbers would decline, or if Congress enacted a stricter immigration law the numbers would jump.

Ten private bills were enacted into law in the First Congress (1789–1791), which was the same number enacted in the 105th Congress (1997–1999). But over

those more than two hundred years the numbers varied substantially. For example, there were 6,248 private laws enacted in the 59th Congress (1905–1907) but only 234 enacted in the next Congress. There were 457 enacted in the 80th Congress (1947–1948) and 1,103 in the 81st Congress.

In modern times there has been a sharp decline in the use of private bills. Since the early 1980s the totals have dropped to double—sometimes single—digits.

REASONS FOR DECLINE

There have been several reasons for the decline in the use of private bills. The most important of these is that Congress has taken steps over the years to limit the need for private bills. These steps have included the establishment of the U.S. Court of Claims (now the U.S. Court of Federal Claims) with the authority to decide certain claims cases and to issue advisory reports on private bills when requested by the House or Senate. Congress also has approved a series of public laws authorizing executive agencies to act on other cases previously handled by Congress. Title IV of the 1946 Legislative Reorganization Act, known as the Federal Tort Claims Act, provided for settlement of certain claims by executive agencies and U.S. district courts. Another title of the 1946 act provided for the correction of military records by civilian review boards. When passage of the Immigration and Nationality Act of 1952 resulted in a marked increase in requests for relief from immigration restrictions, Congress adopted amendments easing some of the restrictions or authorizing the attorney general to do so.

Congressional scholar Walter J. Oleszek noted in *Congressional Procedures and the Policy Process* additional reasons for the decline in private bills. Scandals involving private bills have resulted in tighter procedures for their consideration and have contributed to the drop-off. Members are reluctant to assign staff to handle private bills because they can be so time-consuming and the claims can sometimes be incorrect or fraudulent. Budget deficits in the 1980s and much of the 1990s also made it more difficult for members to focus on the needs of just one individual or entity while they were cutting back on programs for the general public.

TYPES OF BILLS

The two kinds of private legislation that Congress deals with most often are claims and immigration cases. Before 1950 private bills dealing with land claims, military justice, and pensions were more common.

In the 111th Congress, of a total of 116 private bills, 105 were referred to either the House or Senate Judiciary Committees, which handle immigration matters. It has been the practice of immigration officials to stay the removal or deportation of a person if they receive an official request for information about that person from either of the Judiciary panels.

The Constitution provides in Article I, Section 8, Clause 1 that "the Congress shall have Power . . . to pay the Debts . . . of the United States." This provision has been

provisions; or replace a section or the entire text of a bill with a different version. Amendments that seek to revise or modify parts of bills or of other amendments are called perfecting amendments.

Amendments that would add extraneous matter to the bill under debate are sometimes referred to as riders. They are

far more common in the Senate than in the House, where a rule of germaneness limits unexpected proposals. Riders often appear on appropriations bills where they may restrict the use of funds for a controversial program. For example, a 1976 rider to the annual spending bill for labor, health, and education programs banned the use of federal funds to pay

construed broadly to include not only legal but also moral obligations. Bills introduced in Congress for payment of private claims against the government include refund cases that aim to wipe out individuals' obligations to give back money the government paid them in error; waiver cases that allow the government to honor a claim after the government's obligation has expired; and tort (wrongful act, injury, or damage) claims not covered by the Federal Tort Claims Act of 1946.

Private laws are also used to provide relief to aliens because public immigration and naturalization laws do not cover all hardship cases. Private laws permit them to come to the United States, to remain here, or to become citizens, even though they technically may not be eligible.

ENACTMENT PROCESS

The general course of a private bill, from introduction to presidential approval, is much the same as that of a public bill. But there are some important differences.

A private bill generally is initiated at the request of the individual, company, group, or locality that stands to benefit from its enactment. By contrast, public laws usually originate in the executive branch or in Congress itself. The intended beneficiary of a private bill may get in touch with a member directly or use an intermediary, such as a lawyer or lobbyist, to present the facts and considerations believed to justify the introduction of a bill.

Virtually all private bills are referred to the House or Senate Judiciary committees. Once a private bill is reported out of committee, it is placed on the Private Calendar in the House and on the Calendar of Business in the Senate.

In the House, the Private Calendar, also known as the Calendar of the Committee of the Whole House, must be called on the first Tuesday of the month (unless dispensed with by a two-thirds vote or moved to another day by unanimous consent) and may be called on the third Tuesday at the Speaker's discretion. In the Senate, private bills may be taken up on any day after the conclusion of the morning hour.

The House uses a formal system of objectors to monitor private bills. The majority and minority leaders each select three party members to serve as objectors who screen the bills for controversial provisions. They also answer questions that arise during floor consideration.

A bill must be on the Private Calendar for at least seven days before it can be called up for floor consideration. If one House member objects to a bill's consideration, the bill is passed over for later consideration. If two or more object, the bill is recommitted, a procedure that usually kills the bill.

For all of these reasons, the measure enacted to keep Terry Schiavo alive would not have been able to move quickly as a private bill and was thus considered as a public matter.

Bills passed over for later consideration may be pulled together into an omnibus bill, which is given preference over other bills when the Private Calendar is called on the third Tuesday. When such an omnibus bill is passed, the bills within it are considered to have been passed separately. This type of omnibus bill, however, has rarely been used in recent decades.

When a private bill is taken up on the floor, it is considered in "the House as in Committee of the Whole," which means the House is operating under a combination of procedures from the general rules of the House and rules of the Committee of the Whole. No time is allotted for general debate, and amendments are considered under expedited procedures.

As with public bills, once a private bill has been passed in identical form by both chambers, it is sent to the president. If the president signs it into law, the measure is given a private law number. Vetoes of private bills are handled in the same manner as vetoes of public bills. There may be an immediate vote to override or sustain the veto, the vote may be postponed to a fixed date, or the veto message may be referred to a committee. Committee referral in effect kills the bill in most cases.

ABUSES OF THE SYSTEM

Private bills occasionally have given rise to impropriety, or at least the appearance of it.

A newspaper investigation in 1969, for example, produced accusations of wrongdoing in the introduction of hundreds of private immigration bills to help Chinese seamen stay in the United States. Knight Newspapers reported evidence that New York lawyers and Washington, D.C., lobbyists had been getting $500 to $2,500 for each Chinese immigration bill involved. The disclosures resulted in a preliminary investigation by the Senate ethics panel into allegations that some senators or their aides received gifts and campaign contributions for introducing bills to help Chinese ship-jumpers escape deportation. Senate leaders moved to put an end to the practice of allowing staff aides to introduce private bills.

Rep. Henry Helstoski, D-N.J., was indicted by a federal grand jury in 1976 on charges that he solicited and accepted bribes in return for introducing bills to delay deportation of Chilean and Argentinian immigrants living illegally in the United States. The indictment alleged that Helstoski received "at least" $8,735 for his sponsorship of the immigration bills. But the charges were thrown out after the U.S. Supreme Court ruled in *United States v. Helstoski* that because of the Constitution's grant of immunity to members of Congress under the Speech and Debate Clause, federal prosecutors could not use any evidence relating to Helstoski's legislative acts against him.

The power to introduce private immigration legislation proved ruinous to the members of Congress caught in the Federal Bureau of Investigation (FBI) Abscam operation in 1980. Agents of the FBI, posing as Arab sheiks or their representatives, asked the members to introduce private bills to permit wealthy "Arabs" to enter the United States in exchange for money. Although the investigation turned up no evidence of bills introduced on behalf of the fictitious Arabs, the videotapes and recorded conversations of the members and the government agents were enough to end seven congressional careers.

for abortions. The rider's sponsor, Henry J. Hyde, R-Ill., ultimately settled for a House-Senate compromise that created an exception for cases in which a woman's life would be endangered by carrying the pregnancy to term.

Riders can be local in nature, too. One has prevented the District of Columbia from using federal money for a needle-exchange program for drug users. Once the House has added a rider to an annual appropriations bill, the committee will often incorporate the language into the base text of the bill in subsequent years.

In the case of the Hyde amendment, further revisions to the language were made over the ensuing thirty years, including exceptions for pregnancies resulting from rape or incest, but the rider and subsequent add-ons became part of the base text of the annual Labor-Health and Human Services-Education appropriations bill.

House rules require amendments to be germane, or relevant, to the bill itself. Any member may raise a point of order on the floor that an amendment is not germane, but if there is general agreement on the need or desirability of a nongermane amendment it may be protected from a point of order by the Rules Committee.

Riders are often controversial for two reasons: the substantive provisions they contain and the potential that disagreements about them between the House and Senate, or between Congress and the president, will cause a deadlock delaying or preventing enactment of the main bill. It is precisely because the underlying bills, particularly must-pass appropriations bills, are headed toward passage that controversial riders, unlikely to be enacted as stand-alone measures, are added to them. In 1997 a supplemental appropriations bill providing disaster relief to several states after heavy flooding was delayed because several controversial riders opposed by President Clinton were attached. One of these sought to alter the manner in which the 2000 census was scheduled to be conducted. The president vetoed the bill, and Congress succumbed to public pressure and passed it without the extraneous matters.

Debate on Amendments. Once general debate is completed the measure is read for amendment, which constitutes the second reading of the bill. The special rule may specify that each part of a bill must be considered in sequential order. The bill may be read paragraph by paragraph, section by section, or title by title, and amendments are offered to the appropriate part as it is read. Once the reading of that part is completed, amendments to it are no longer in order except by unanimous consent. On occasion, the Rules Committee may allow the bill to be considered as read and open to amendment at any point. Alternatively, the floor manager may make a unanimous consent request that the bill be open to amendment. Committee amendments are always considered before amendments offered from the floor.

Debate on any amendment is theoretically limited to five minutes for supporters and five minutes for opponents. Members regularly obtain more time, however, by offering pro forma amendments to "strike the last word" or "strike the requisite number of words." Under the Legislative Reorganization Act of 1970, ten minutes of debate, five minutes on each side, are guaranteed on any amendment that has been published in the *Congressional Record* at least one day before it is offered on the floor (assuming that the amendment is otherwise in order) even if debate has been closed on the portion of the bill to which the amendment is proposed. The change thus ensured that opponents could not block even an explanation of an important pending amendment, but it has

also been used on a few occasions as a delaying device by members who have had dozens of amendments to a bill printed in the *Record,* all of which may be called up and debated for up to ten minutes. Committee floor managers encourage members to print their amendments in the *Record,* to obtain as complete a picture as possible of the political problems a bill may face. When the Republicans took power in the House in 1995, they often reported rules that allowed the chair of the Committee of the Whole to give preference in recognition to members who had preprinted their amendments.

Degrees of Amendments. Provided the special rule on the bill has not imposed specific restrictions, four types of amendments may be pending at any one time: a perfecting amendment to the text of the bill, also called a first-degree amendment; an amendment to that amendment, which is called a second-degree or perfecting amendment; a substitute amendment for the original amendment; and a perfecting amendment to the substitute. An amendment to an amendment to an amendment, known as an amendment in the third degree, is barred under House rules.

Amendments to the original amendment are voted on first. Only one first-degree amendment is in order at a time, but once it has been disposed of another may be offered immediately. When all amendments to the original amendment have been disposed of, perfecting amendments to the substitute amendment are voted on one at a time. The amended substitute is voted on next, followed by a vote on the original amendment as amended. If the substitute has been adopted, this last vote will be on the perfected original amendment as amended by the substitute. Once an amendment has been offered in the Committee of the Whole, its author may modify it or withdraw it only by unanimous consent and if no action has occurred but may not offer an amendment to it directly. A diagram of a so-called amendment tree and the order in which amendments must be voted on are shown on the next page.

This description may seem complex, but it gives only a hint of the total universe of amending possibilities. It can be mind-boggling when a substitute for the entire bill may be pending along with the base legislation, and such substitute may attract yet another substitute to itself as well as a panoply of perfecting amendments.

More than one vote may be taken on any given amendment. The Committee of the Whole may first take a voice vote and then, if members request, move on to a recorded vote before finally deciding the question. First-degree amendments (original amendments as amended) and amendments in the nature of substitutes, as amended, adopted in the Committee of the Whole are subject to roll-call votes after the committee rises and the chamber resumes sitting as the full House. Few roll-call votes are taken, and the full House rarely

TEXT OF BILL

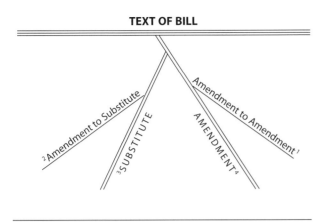

SOURCE: CQ Press.

rejects amendments adopted in the Committee of the Whole. Amendments defeated in the Committee of the Whole cannot be offered again at this stage because the previous question has usually been ordered on the bill when the House adopted the rule for its consideration, barring additional amendments or debate once the Committee of the Whole has risen back to the House with its recommendation that the bill as amended be passed.

Action by the Full House

When the Committee of the Whole has completed its work on the bill, it rises, according to the House's parliamentary terminology. The Speaker or the Speaker's designee returns to the chair, and the chair of the Committee of the Whole formally reports the bill to the House, with any amendments that have been adopted and a recommendation that the bill pass.

If the previous question has been ordered by the special rule governing the bill—the usual procedure—the full House then votes immediately on amendments approved by the Committee of the Whole. Members may demand a roll call on any amendment adopted in the Committee of the Whole. Such roll calls are called separate votes.

Amendments not considered separately are approved en bloc by a pro forma voice vote.

Once the amendments have been disposed of the question is on engrossment (the preparation of an accurate version of the bill including all amendments) and third reading, by title only, of the bill. This, too, is nearly always pro forma. Prior to 1965, any House member could demand that the bill be engrossed, that is, printed on special paper, prior to further proceedings. This was sometimes used as a dilatory tactic.

After engrossment and third reading, a member opposed to the bill may offer a motion to recommit the measure to the committee that reported it. The Speaker will inquire of a member attempting to make the motion whether he or she so qualifies. The Speaker typically asks "Is the (member) opposed to the bill?" and if the response is yes then that member is recognized. In practice, the motion to recommit belongs to the minority party, and the Speaker looks first to the floor manager of the minority, then to other minority members of the committee, and then to any other minority member.

There are two kinds of recommittal motions: a nondebatable simple motion to recommit, sometimes called a straight motion, which kills the bill if it is adopted by sending it back to committee; and a motion to recommit with instructions, which, if approved, may have the effect of removing the bill from the floor or amending it before final passage. The minority often moves to recommit with instructions directing the committee to report the bill back with amendments forthwith. This tactic offers the minority members one last chance to amend the bill to their satisfaction. The minority may offer any germane amendment as part of its instructions, even one that had previously been offered and rejected in the Committee of the Whole. If the motion to recommit is adopted, the floor manager announces that the committee has reported the bill back to the House with the amendments contained in the instructions. Republicans used the motion to recommit with instructions to great effect in the early days of the 110th Congress. The bill in this case is not recommitted to the committee that reported it. The amendment is then voted on again directly. This is usually a pro forma voice vote.

In March 2007 the Republicans added a wrinkle by offering a motion to recommit with instructions that the committee report back promptly. The gambit, which forced Democratic leaders to postpone consideration of the bill, would have given GOP leaders a vote on a firearms amendment that would have been politically difficult for Democrats. In addition, if the motion had been agreed to, the underlying bill, which they opposed, would have been sent back to committee indefinitely.

The motion to recommit is privileged and the right to offer it is guaranteed by House rules, but its use has been regulated by the Rules Committee. From 1934 to 1995 the majority reserved the right to restrict the motion in certain circumstances. The Rules Committee is forbidden by a House rule to report a rule for consideration of a bill or joint resolution that denies the right to offer a motion to recommit. However, a series of precedents was established that construed the rule so that members were guaranteed the right to offer only the straight motion to recommit without instructions.

A motion to recommit with instructions was, on occasion, barred by a special rule governing consideration of a bill. This might occur if the majority feared that last-minute amendments could pull apart the support built up for the pending legislation during the original amendment process or if a minority proposal was considered potentially popular enough to pass. The House Republicans, while in the minority for four decades prior to 1995, often used a recommittal motion with instructions to present their alternative to the Democratic-crafted legislation being considered. They roundly criticized the constraints under rules governing recommittals that they considered a denial of basic rights and frequently appealed rulings of the Speaker on this issue but always lost.

When Republicans gained control of the House in 1995, the new majority effectively wiped out the earlier precedents that had allowed the Rules Committee to prevent a motion to recommit with instructions from being offered to bills and joint resolutions, and it amended House rules to guarantee that right to the minority leader or the minority leader's designee. In this respect, the Republicans increased the rights of the Democratic minority beyond what they themselves had enjoyed. However, other parliamentary restrictions may still apply to such a motion, such as the requirement that amendatory instructions be germane to the underlying bill.

Democrats appeared to acknowledge, at their own peril, the importance of giving the minority an opportunity to recommit bills when they won control of the House. At the start of the 110th Congress, motions to recommit were allowed, and Republicans used them repeatedly to put Democrats on record on issues and amend legislation.

A rules change in the 111th Congress allowed for debate on a straight motion to recommit, which had not been debatable. A motion to recommit a bill or joint resolution with instructions may be debated for ten minutes, evenly divided, although, since 1985, the majority floor manager—but not the minority floor manager—may ask for up to an hour of debate, which is then divided evenly between the two sides. That change was a direct result of a motion by Rep. Dan Lungren, R-Calif., in September 1984 to recommit the fiscal 1985 continuing appropriations resolution with instructions to add to it a Senate-passed crime bill. The House version of the crime bill had been bottled up in the Judiciary Committee. The motion was debated for ten minutes, and the House, to the majority leadership's embarrassment, adopted it on a vote of 243–166. The continuing resolution was then passed, and the crime package was eventually enacted.

Another example of amending strategy and clever use of the motion to recommit occurred in 1995 when Massachusetts Democrat Edward J. Markey offered a motion to recommit a telecommunications bill, with instructions to include a provision mandating use of V-chip circuitry in televisions to allow parents to control more effectively their children's viewing habits. Markey had earlier offered a perfecting amendment to the bill in the Committee of the Whole to accomplish this, but he had been prevented from getting a direct vote when his proposal was altered by adoption of a second-degree Republican-sponsored amendment. The Republican proposal encouraged, but did not require, the new technology.

However, use of the motion to recommit in the House offered Markey, in effect, a "second bite of the apple" under parliamentary circumstances when a counterproposal could not be offered. Now forced to go on the record in an up-or-down vote on Markey's popular plan, the House effectively reversed its earlier vote and adopted the mandatory requirement.

These victories were once unusual because few controversial recommittal motions are ever adopted. A competent majority can usually anticipate and head off such dangers before a bill is reported or through the amendment process on the floor as they attempted to do, ultimately unsuccessfully, in the Markey case.

But in the 110th Congress, minority Republicans used the motion to offer targeted and politically popular changes to legislation that Democrats were forced to accept or twist arms to defeat.

In 2007 alone, the GOP was successful on twenty-one motions to recommit. In contrast, during the preceding dozen years, the Democratic minority had won fourteen out of 349 attempts.

Beyond that, Republicans made clever use of the effective difference between a motion to recommit "promptly" and a motion to recommit "forthwith." A motion to recommit a bill to committee with instructions to "promptly" report back the changes specified in the motion effectively meant that the committee would have to hold a business meeting to approve the changes. In practice, that meant that the bill was seriously delayed, or killed entirely. On the other hand, a motion to recommit a bill to committee with instructions to "forthwith" report back the changes specified in the motion meant that the new language would be automatically added to the bill and it would immediately come up for another floor vote.

The majority Democrats closed that option in the 111th Congress, adopting a new rule that requires that motions to recommit must include instructions that the measure be returned to the floor "forthwith," meaning the House must vote on the amended bill within minutes.

If the motion to recommit is rejected, the next step is the vote on final passage. If the bill is passed, a pro forma motion to reconsider the final vote is usually offered. A supporter of the bill then offers a countermotion to lay the motion on the table, or kill reconsideration, thus safeguarding final passage. More often, the Speaker will simply say, "Without objection the motion to reconsider is laid upon the table." With that, the bill is considered to be formally passed by the House. At this point, the bill officially becomes an act, although it generally still is referred to as a bill.

An engrossed copy of the bill, including changes made during floor action, is certified in its final form by the clerk of the House and transmitted to the Senate for its consideration.

(An engrossed bill in the Senate must be certified by the secretary of the Senate.)

If a similar Senate bill has already reached the House, the rule providing for floor action on the House version might also have included a provision permitting the House to take it up, strike out the text, insert the text of the House-passed legislation, pass the "S" numbered bill, and send it back to the Senate to await further amendments or a Senate request for a conference. Or the House itself could ask for the conference first. In these legislative scenarios, the House bill passed earlier would be laid on the table (killed) because it is no longer needed as a vehicle for further proceedings.

SENATE FLOOR ACTION: FLEXIBILITY, INFORMALITY

House members elected to the Senate are inevitably struck by the difference in the way the two chambers operate. Although the Senate has an elaborate framework of parliamentary machinery to guide its deliberations, in practice its procedures are far more flexible than those of the House. Almost anything can be done by unanimous consent. That very flexibility also means that a single member can delay or threaten to delay action on a bill until his or her wishes are accommodated or a compromise is struck. The Senate also effects changes in its procedures from time to time, without formally changing its rules, by overruling decisions made by the presiding officer. The result of such a vote can establish a new precedent that would govern future proceedings.

From time to time the Senate reviews its procedures in an attempt to pick up the pace and predictability of action in the chamber. But the Senate is rarely receptive to the proposals for change that come forth from these reviews, largely because they almost always entail curbs on the rights of the individual member.

In 1982 Howard H. Baker Jr., R-Tenn., then the majority leader, expressed the prevailing attitude: "The Senate is a great institution. It is the balance wheel which keeps democracy on track. It is the framework on which the Republic is constructed. It is the essence of compromise. It is the only place where there is unfettered expression of individual views. It is the last fortress that can be used to defend against the tyranny of a temporary majority. I would not change a thing about that."[24]

Scheduling in the Senate

In a chamber devoted to preserving individual rights, the challenge of scheduling floor action can sometimes be formidable. Senators can—and do—insist that the legislation in which they are interested be scheduled for floor action at a time convenient to them. At the same time senators faced with ever increasing political, constituent, and legislative demands on their time have sought greater predictability in the Senate schedule.

In the months preceding a presidential election, scheduling votes around the campaign appearances of party hopefuls for the White House is an added challenge for Senate leaders.

Scheduling in the Senate is primarily the responsibility of the majority leader, who works closely with the majority party's policy committee, committee chairs, and other partisan colleagues to develop a legislative program acceptable to a majority of the party. Because of the need to secure unanimous consent to bring up a bill, the majority leader also works closely with the minority leader and his or her staff in working out the schedule. This bipartisan cooperation is in sharp contrast to the House, where scheduling is solely a responsibility of a majority party that has the ability to enforce its decisions by majority vote.

A system based largely on unanimous consent also necessitates that the membership be kept informed about the status of pending legislation. The majority leader regularly begins each session with an announcement of the day's anticipated schedule and concludes it with the likely program for the next session. Whip notices, televised floor proceedings, and an automatic telephone connection to each member's office help the leadership keep the membership informed.

To the extent possible the modern leadership tries to accommodate the schedules of individual senators. Most leaders have acknowledged the frustration inherent in the job. "It is extremely difficult to deal with the wishes of 99 other senators, attempting to schedule legislation," Majority Leader Robert C. Byrd, D-W.Va., said in 1987, "because in almost every case, at any time it is scheduled, it inconveniences some senator."[25]

All legislation reported from Senate committees is placed on the Calendar of General Orders, while all treaties and nominations that require the Senate's advice and consent are placed on the Executive Calendar. To consider treaties or nominations, the Senate resolves into executive session either by motion or unanimous consent. There are no restrictions on when the Senate may enter executive session. Despite its connotations, the term "executive session" is an open session of the Senate just like any other.

Senate rules require bills and reports on nonprivileged matters to lie over on the calendar for one legislative day before they are brought to the floor. This rule is usually waived by unanimous consent, and the Senate often stays in the same legislative day for a considerable period of time. Another rule requires that printed committee reports be available to members for two calendar days before a measure is debated. It, too, may be waived by unanimous consent.

The leadership evolved several ways to handle the various scheduling problems it regularly confronts. Different majority leaders have had their own ideas of how best to conduct business while giving their colleagues adequate down time. In 1988, for example, the Senate worked for three weeks and then took a week off, giving members a set time to return to their states without running the risk of missing votes in the Senate or other legislative work of importance to them. However, this practice did not become institutionalized.

In the early 1970s Majority Leader Mike Mansfield, D-Mont., devised a system that allowed several pieces of legislation to be considered simultaneously by designating specific periods each day when the measures would be considered. The track system, still in use today, affects all aspects of Senate procedure. When a filibuster is under way, the filibustered bill occupies one track while the Senate proceeds by unanimous consent to other legislation on the second track. But the ability of the Senate to continue its more routine work also encourages senators to threaten to filibuster more frequently, because it is not as important to leaders and colleagues to stop a filibuster.

The Senate normally recesses from day to day, instead of adjourning. The effect is the same—an end to the day's session—but a recess avoids creating a new legislative day that can, in some circumstances, create unwanted procedural complications when the Senate next convenes.

Unanimous Consent Agreements

The leadership has been innovative with its use of unanimous consent requests, traditionally the mechanism the Senate uses to expedite business by circumventing its rules. As its name implies, a unanimous consent request may be blocked by a single objection. Once the request is agreed to, however, its terms are binding and can be changed only by another unanimous consent request.

There are two kinds of unanimous consent requests. Simple requests, which can be made by any senator, usually deal with routine business—asking that staff members be allowed on the floor, that committees be allowed to meet while the Senate is in session, that material be inserted in the *Congressional Record,* and the like. Noncontroversial matters, including minor legislation, private bills, and presidential nominations may be considered by unanimous consent. Generally these matters are cleared with the leadership beforehand. At times unanimous consent requests can be made to pass major legislation.

Complex unanimous consent requests set out the guidelines under which a piece of major legislation will be considered on the floor. In some respects like a special rule for guiding debate in the House, these unanimous consent requests usually state when the bill will come to the floor and set time limits on debate, including debate on motions, amendments, and final passage. For that reason they are often referred to as time agreements. Frequently the agreements stipulate that any amendments offered must be germane but, unlike House rules, they cannot prevent a senator from offering a particular amendment because the senator would have to be accommodated somehow to ensure there would be no objection to the request.

Lyndon B. Johnson, D-Texas, widely acknowledged to have been the most powerful majority leader in history, began to develop complex unanimous consent agreements during his tenure as majority leader from 1955 to 1960. Such agreements steadily grew more complex and were applied to more legislation. Negotiating a complex unanimous consent agreement can be complicated and time-consuming, involving the majority and minority leaders, the chair and ranking minority member of the committee or subcommittee with jurisdiction for the bill, and any senator who has placed a hold on or otherwise expressed strong interest in the measure. The leadership tries to negotiate a unanimous consent agreement before the measure comes to the floor, but additional agreements—to limit time spent on a specific amendment, for example—may be fashioned on the floor.

The fundamental objective of a unanimous consent agreement, as Oleszek has observed, "is to limit the time it takes to dispose of controversial issues in an institution noted for unlimited debate."[26] The agreements are also valuable because they bring some predictability to Senate business.

In mid-March 2007, Majority Leader Reid and Minority Leader McConnell worked out an unusual unanimous consent agreement for debate on a series of Iraq War–related proposals after weeks of being deadlocked over which plans would be allowed on the floor, whether they could be amended, and even how many votes it would take to pass each one. Ultimately, they agreed to consider three proposals: a Democratic leadership plan calling for a timetable for withdrawal of U.S. forces; a counterproposal by Sen. Judd Gregg, R-N.H., stipulating that Congress should not cut funds for troops in harm's way; and a counter-counterproposal by Sen. Patty Murray, D-Wash., affirming America's commitment to its soldiers and returning veterans. The agreement stipulated that only those garnering sixty votes or more would pass. The Gregg and Murray initiatives cleared that hurdle, but the Democratic leadership resolution did not.

Still, unanimous consent agreements "must not be viewed as rigid restrictions comparable to those found in House special rules," Steven S. Smith cautions. The need to obtain unanimous consent to ward off a potential filibuster "forces leaders to make concessions before and during floor debate on a scale that would seem quite foreign in the House. As a result, the new use of complex agreements on the floor does not alter the basic principles of Senate floor politics, which remain rampant individualism and the protection of minority rights."[27]

Holds

One scheduling complication the leadership has been unable to do away with is the practice of placing holds on bills or nominees. A hold is a request by a senator to the party leadership asking that a certain measure not be taken up. The

THE PRESIDING OFFICER

Members of the House and Senate take turns presiding over floor debate, a job some view as drudgery and others see as an honor requiring finesse and skill. The Speaker of the House typically puts a trusted ally in the chair to preside over particularly acrimonious debates. Members may speak on the floor and offer legislation, amendments, or motions for consideration only if the presiding officer permits, or recognizes, them.

The presiding officer also rules on points of order and delivers other pronouncements that regulate floor debate. Members may appeal, or challenge, the presiding officer's decisions, and in the House these rulings can always be overturned by majority vote. Some rulings by the chair in the Senate, related to the budget process, require sixty votes to overturn. In the House, while rulings are occasionally appealed, none has been overturned since February 1, 1938. In the Senate, where procedure is more fluid and often yields to the political needs of senators, rulings of the chair have been appealed and overturned on various occasions in recent decades.

SPEAKER OF THE HOUSE

The presiding officer in the House is called the Speaker, a position designated by the U.S. Constitution. When the House convenes to begin a new Congress, it is first presided over by the clerk from the previous Congress. After a quorum is established, the first order of business is to elect the Speaker. The election is nearly always pro forma because the decision had been made earlier by the majority party's caucus or conference.

The Speaker need not be a member of the House but always has been. In the speakership election in January 1997 in the 105th Congress, two Republican members cast votes for former members of the House to protest the candidacy of Rep. Newt Gingrich, R-Ga., who was seeking reelection as Speaker but was also about to be disciplined for ethics violations. In 2003, three Democrats voted present and one voted for Rep. John P. Murtha, D-Pa., instead of their party's candidate, Nancy Pelosi, D-Calif. In 2011, after Democrats had lost control of the House, most observers expected Pelosi to step down as her party's leader. But she ran again and was nominated for Speaker. Eleven Democrats instead voted for Heath Shuler, D-N.C. Seven votes were cast for other members, and one Democrat voted present.

The Speaker effectively serves as political leader of the majority party and also has rights as an elected representative to participate fully in all activities of the chamber. The Speaker may vote at any time but does so only on occasion.

By statute, the Speaker is second in line, behind the vice president, to become president of the United States in the event of a vacancy, although this has occurred only on television and in the movies. The president pro tempore of the Senate follows the Speaker in order of succession.

The Speaker cannot preside over the House all of the time. When the Speaker is not present, a member of the majority party is designated as Speaker pro tempore, although any member may preside if called to the chair. The Speaker's office has a small list of lawmakers who are used in rotation as Speakers pro tempore.

Unlike in the Senate, in the House the presiding officer has broad authority to choose which member to recognize and inquires "for what purpose does the gentleman [gentlelady] rise" to ascertain whether he or she wishes to recognize the member. Members seeking to conduct business made privileged under House rules have priority in recognition.

When the House is considering bills for amendment in the Committee of the Whole, the Speaker steps down and appoints another member, who is called the chair, to preside. When sensitive bills are under consideration, the Speaker's choice for the chair usually turns to senior members who are skilled parliamentarians or who are close to the leadership. Sometimes a tradition develops that the same member always presides over a certain bill whenever it comes to the floor. For example, Rep. Dan Rostenkowski, D-Ill., best known as the longtime chair of the powerful Ways and Means Committee, was usually named to preside over consideration of the annual defense authorization bill. Speaker J. Dennis Hastert, R-Ill., often turned to home-state colleague Ray LaHood, a longtime aide to Minority Leader Robert H. Michel, R-Ill., to preside over contentious debates.

VICE PRESIDENT AND PRESIDENT PRO TEMPORE

The Speaker is far more powerful than his counterpart in the Senate, the vice president, who is not a member of the Senate and cannot speak except to recognize senators or make parliamentary rulings.

In the Senate, the presiding officer is always referred to as "Mr. (or Madam) President." The vice president of the United States serves formally as president of the Senate under the Constitution. It once was common for the vice president to preside over floor debates. In the modern Senate, the vice president seldom is called in unless his or her vote might be needed, if the Senate is evenly divided, to vote to break a tie. In this case, only an "aye" vote can affect the result because a tie is considered defeat of a pending proposition. The vice president may not vote to create a tie. In theory, the vice president can vote when the Senate is evenly divided on matters requiring a supermajority vote for approval, but because the proposition would thereby have been defeated anyway, the vice president could not affect the result. The vice president is rarely called on to vote. The Senate Historical Office identified only 244 tie-breaking votes by a vice president through the end of the first session of the 112 Congress. Only 26 had been cast since 1965.

The president pro tempore is a position created by the Constitution and is usually held by the senior member of the majority party in the Senate. In the 112th Congress, for example, it was Daniel K. Inouye, D-Hawaii. This senator has the right to preside in the absence of the vice president, but generally the Senate puts a freshman member in the chair. That relieves more senior members of a time-consuming task and gives newcomers firsthand lessons in Senate rules and procedures. Not surprisingly, new senators are heavily dependent on the parliamentarian for advice. In the Senate, the rules require the presiding officer to recognize "the Senator who shall first address him [her]" if several senators are seeking to speak. However, by custom, the majority and minority leaders are always recognized first if they seek recognition when no one else holds the floor.

Many senators tend to view presiding as drudge work to be avoided, because the job frequently involves presiding over quorum calls that interrupt business while agreements are being worked out privately or senators are coming to the floor. However, some have embraced it, and a custom has developed of giving a Golden Gavel to those who have presided for one hundred hours.

Some House members also actively seek to preside. In an institution as large as the House, it is one way for members to increase their visibility. The House puts no premium on giving new members experience in the chair. However, during routine business, it is not uncommon to see them there, visible to their constituents on the Cable-Satellite Public Affairs Network (C-SPAN).

In both the House and Senate, only members of the majority party preside. Until 1977 members of each party took turns presiding in the Senate. The bipartisan practice was ended abruptly following an incident the previous year. The presiding officer, Sen. Jesse Helms, R-N.C., a member of the minority, broke with Senate custom by denying recognition to the majority leader, Sen. Mike Mansfield, D-Mont., in favor of conservative senator James B. Allen, D-Ala. The Democratic leadership then decided that the majority should retain control of the chair at all times, unless the vice president, who might be a member of the opposite party, decided to occupy it. Republicans continued this practice when they controlled the Senate.

leadership usually respects holds. To do otherwise would likely be self-defeating because the senator could easily block any unanimous consent request to consider the measure.

Traditionally, most holds were kept confidential and were requested simply so that the senator would be told when the bill is likely to come up. But some senators have used them extensively as bargaining tools, to ensure that they will be able to offer their amendments or to force the leadership to call up some unrelated piece of legislation that otherwise might not have been scheduled for the floor. There have been instances of rolling holds, in which one senator withdraws a hold when it is discovered but another then steps in to retain the block in place, and even cases in which a Senate staffer has applied a hold in a senator's name.

In most cases, the holds were done anonymously—only the party leader knew the senator's identity—making it difficult for the backers of the legislation to negotiate to assuage the concerns. And many times, the reason for the hold had nothing to do with the substance of the bill held hostage. Some senators, notably Ron Wyden, D-Ore., and Charles E. Grassley, R-Iowa, had worked for years to eliminate the secret holds. Finally, at the beginning of the 112th Congress, Wyden and Grassley, joined by Sen. Claire McCaskill, D-Mo., were able to win approval of a Senate rule to do away with secret holds. The rule requires disclosure of the identity of a senator within two days of the time the senator notifies his or her party leader of an intent to place a hold. If the senator does not step forward publicly, the hold would be attributed to that member's party leader. "What's different here is every hold will have a public owner and there will be consequences," said Wyden.[28]

Identification of the senator placing a hold makes it easier for opponents to apply pressure to allow consideration of a measure or a nomination.

A TYPICAL DAY IN THE SENATE

A typical day in the Senate might go like this.

- The Senate is called to order by the presiding officer. The constitutional presiding officer, the vice president, is seldom in attendance. Sometimes the president pro tempore presides over the opening minutes of the Senate session. During the course of the day, other members of the majority party take turns presiding.

- The Senate chaplain delivers the opening prayer.

- The Pledge of Allegiance is recited.

- The majority and minority leaders are recognized for opening remarks. The majority leader usually announces plans for the day's business, which are developed in consultation with the minority leadership.

- The Senate usually conducts morning business (which need not be in the morning and should not be confused with the morning hour, so if morning business is put off other business necessarily precedes it). During morning business senators may introduce bills and the Senate receives reports from committees and messages from the president and conducts other routine chores. Senators who have requested time in advance are recognized for speeches on any subject.

- The Senate may turn to consider legislative or executive matters. To begin work on a piece of legislation the majority leader normally asks for unanimous consent to call up the measure. If any member objects, the leader may make a debatable motion that the Senate take up the bill. The motion gives opponents the opportunity to launch a filibuster, or extended debate, even before the Senate officially begins to consider the bill. Certain types of measures, such as budget resolutions, omnibus budget reconciliation bills, and reports from House-Senate conference committees, are privileged, and a motion to consider them is not debatable.

Floor debate on a bill is generally handled by managers, usually the chair and ranking minority member of the committee with jurisdiction over the measure. Most measures are considered under a unanimous consent, or time, agreement in which the Senate unanimously agrees to limit debate and to divide the time in some prearranged fashion. In the absence of a time agreement any senator may seek recognition from the chair and, once recognized, may talk for as long as he or she wishes. Unless the Senate has unanimously agreed to limit amendments, senators may offer as many as they wish. In most cases, amendments need not be germane, or directly related, to the bill.

Many noncontroversial bills are passed by voice vote with only a handful of senators present. And, at times, senators agree in advance to automatically pass certain legislation if it passes the House so that they can go home for an upcoming recess or adjournment. Any member can request a roll-call vote on an amendment or motion or on final passage of a measure. Senate roll calls are casual affairs. Senators stroll in from the cloakrooms or their offices and congregate in the well (the area at the front of the chamber). When they are ready to vote, senators catch the eye of the clerk and vote, sometimes by indicating thumbs up or thumbs down. Roll-call votes are supposed to last fifteen minutes, but some have dragged on for more than an hour.

- Often, near the end of the day, the majority leader and the minority leader quickly move through a wrap-up period, during which minor bills and confirmations that have been cleared by all members are passed by unanimous consent.

- Just before the Senate finishes its work for the day, the majority leader seeks unanimous consent for the agenda for the next session—when the Senate will convene, which senators will be recognized for early speeches, and specific time agreements for consideration of legislation.

In the Clinton administration, the president and even the chief justice of the United States objected to the practice by conservative senators of placing holds on large numbers of judicial nominations. The practice was not new, just more visible and seemingly more organized. Senators have also placed holds on legislation on behalf of the administration or an interest group. Sen. Jesse Helms, R-N.C., frequently placed holds on ambassadorial nominations to pressure the State Department into adopting policies more to his liking. Sen. Howard Metzenbaum, D-Ohio, placed holds on all types of legislation, especially during the end of each session as the Senate rushed toward adjournment, to ensure that he was not unpleasantly surprised by unexpected developments.

Other Scheduling Methods

Because the Senate allows non-germane amendments on most legislation, it has little need for procedures to wrest bills out of reluctant committees. A member may simply offer the legislation bottled up in committee as an amendment to another measure being considered on the floor. However, a senator may bring a bill to the floor in three other ways, although none of them is used with any frequency.

First, all measures introduced in the Senate, including House-passed bills, must be read twice on successive legislative days before they are referred to committee. If any senator objects to the second reading of a bill, it is placed immediately on the calendar. This tactic was used to avoid sending the House version of the 1964 civil rights legislation to the Senate Judiciary Committee, which opposed it.

The Senate may also vote to suspend the rules by a two-thirds vote, but the procedure bears little relation to the similarly named House practice and has little practical use. While approval of the motion requires a two-thirds vote, it only suspends a rule but does not simultaneously pass a measure. The motion and the measure also remain subject to potential filibusters.

Finally, the Senate may discharge a bill from committee. The motion to discharge, which is debatable, must be made during morning hour. However, morning hour is rarely used in the Senate, and even if it were, opponents would have ample opportunities to delay and render the discharge procedure inoperative. If debate is not completed by the time morning hour ends, the motion is placed on the calendar, where it can be subjected to another series of delays.

Senate Floor Procedures

While the Senate's rules establish elaborate procedures to conduct certain types of business, in practice many of these rules are either ignored or altered by unanimous consent. This is because efforts to invoke the formal rules may prove too cumbersome, provoking retaliation from opponents. The purported cure for a parliamentary stalemate or obstacle may be worse than the disease. And some of the rules simply do not work.

Senate Majority Leader Bill Frist, R-Tenn., welcomes Rear Admiral Barry C. Black, left, in June 2003. Black is the first African American and first military chaplain to hold the job of Senate chaplain. The Senate's business day begins with the chaplain delivering an opening prayer and with the reciting of the Pledge of Allegiance.

SOURCE: AP Photo/Stephen J. Boitano.

The Senate may set a standard daily meeting time for noon, but it frequently alters its meeting times by unanimous consent each day to accommodate the demands of the daily workload and the scheduling needs of individual senators who wish to be present for particular items of business. As in the House, the chaplain gives an opening prayer, the Pledge of Allegiance is recited, and the previous day's Journal is approved. A rules change in 1986 made approval nondebatable, although amendments to correct the Journal may still be offered and filibustered. The majority leader and then the minority leader are recognized for brief periods. Usually they discuss the Senate's schedule for the day.

What happens next depends on whether the Senate is beginning a new legislative day. If the Senate recessed at the end of its previous session, it may proceed immediately to any unfinished business. If it adjourned, it must begin a new legislative day, which, after the opening preliminaries, requires the Senate to enter a two-hour period called morning hour (though this is almost always waived by unanimous consent). During that period members conduct what is known as morning business—introducing bills, filing committee reports, and receiving messages from the House and the president.

In the second hour, or at the conclusion of morning business, members may move to consider any measure on the calendar. This motion is not debatable, in theory, but in practice efforts to employ it to avoid a filibuster have been thwarted by the use of other provisions of the rules, making this shortcut effectively obsolete. After morning hour, because a motion to consider a nonprivileged measure is debatable, opponents of a measure have found ways to tie up the morning hour with other business and votes to prevent the leadership from forcing it up.

In an attempt to avoid a certain filibuster on the fiscal 1988 defense authorization bill, on May 13, 1987, Majority Leader Byrd sought to call up the bill during morning hour. But before he could do that, the Journal of the previous day's proceedings had to be approved. Republicans requested a roll call on approval of the Journal and then used more arcane procedural tactics, demanding time to explain their individual votes and calling for votes on excusing them from voting, to further slow the proceedings. By the time the ensuing wrangle over the rules between Byrd and the Republicans had been untangled, seven roll-call votes had occurred, the period for morning hour had long since expired, and the motion to call up the defense bill was once again debatable. Future majority leaders were thus put on notice that a similar parliamentary maelstrom could erupt if the use of the morning hour to circumvent a filibuster were ever attempted again.

Morning Business

The Senate rarely conducts morning business and the morning hour as stated in its rules because the formal procedures are too cumbersome and do not work to help the leadership avoid filibusters. However, it can conduct morning business at any time by unanimous consent.

The decision to adjourn or to recess at the end of the day is made by unanimous consent or by motion, usually by the majority leader. The leadership generally prefers to recess from day to day because it can maintain greater control over the daily schedule. Senators seeking to delay action on a measure, however, may push for adjournment because the convening of a new legislative day offers them more opportunities to slow Senate deliberations.

If the Senate has recessed and there is no morning hour when it next reconvenes, it may still conduct morning business by unanimous consent. Within morning hour, morning business may be followed by the call of the Calendar of General Orders. During this procedure, which is almost always set aside by unanimous consent, the chair calls each bill in the order in which it appears on the calendar. If objection is raised to considering the bill, the chair moves on to the next measure. No senator may speak for more than five minutes on any one bill during the call of the calendar.

Morning hour may be followed by a period when members are given permission to speak for brief periods on virtually any topic. The Senate next turns to any unfinished business. If there is none, or if it is set aside by unanimous consent, the Senate may then take up new business.

Most major bills are brought up under unanimous consent agreements worked out in advance by the leadership. If a member objects to a unanimous consent request, the leadership may decide to renegotiate the consent agreement, or it may move that the Senate take up the bill. Because most such motions are debatable, a filibuster could be launched against the bill before it is even technically on the floor. Motions to proceed to consider some measures, such as House-Senate conference reports, are not debatable, though the conference reports themselves may be filibustered once they become the pending business.

Floor Debate

Once a bill is brought to the floor for consideration, floor managers take over the task of guiding the legislation through the amendment process and final passage. As in the House, the chair and ranking minority member of the committee or subcommittee with jurisdiction for the bill act as the majority and minority floor managers. Floor managers play much the same role in the Senate as they do in the House, mapping strategy for passing the bill, deflecting debilitating or undesirable amendments, offering amendments to attract additional support, and seeing that members in favor of the bill turn out to vote for it.

On measures brought to the floor under a unanimous consent agreement, the time allotted for debate is usually divided evenly between the two opposing sides. The chair gives preferential recognition first to the majority manager and then to the minority manager, who, if they control time, yield it to other senators. If there is no time agreement, any senator may seek recognition from the chair. Once recognized, in the absence of a time agreement, a senator may speak as long as he or she likes and on any subject, unless he or she violates the rules of the Senate. A senator may yield temporarily for the consideration of other business, after asking unanimous consent to do so without losing the floor, or to another senator who wants to ask a question, but he or she may not parcel out time to other members as floor managers in the House typically do and as Senate managers may when time is controlled. Typically, senators yielded to find ways to make broader statements within the guise of asking their questions.

The Senate does not consider bills in a Committee of the Whole or set aside a period for general debate before the amending process begins. Amendments are in order as soon as the bill is made the pending order of business.

Debate in the modern Senate is a far cry from debate during the Senate's Golden Age, when great orators such as Daniel Webster, John C. Calhoun, and Henry Clay fought an eloquent war of words over slavery and states' rights. While a few issues still engender lively debate on the floor, Senate speeches are seldom spontaneous. Most are prepared by staff and read to a nearly empty chamber or inserted, unread, in

SENATE PROCEDURES USED TO THWART SUBSTANTIVE ACTIONS

In a notable example in 1997 of the impact of Senate rules on debate and amendment strategy on controversial legislation, Senate majority leader Trent Lott, R-Miss., agreed to call up major campaign finance reform legislation, the so-called McCain-Feingold bill, named for sponsors John McCain, R-Ariz., and Russ Feingold, D-Wis. As the most heavily promoted campaign reform vehicle in the Senate, that bill would have banned soft money contributions to political campaigns, a method of support for candidates that fell outside the legal restrictions on contributions. It also would have curbed issue ads, often presented on television and radio by special interest advocacy groups that in many election contests were aimed more at electing or defeating candidates than at promoting debate on issues.

The legislation was certain to be filibustered, with Lott and Sen. Mitch McConnell, R-Ky., among its principal opponents. But supporters, consisting of the Democratic minority and a handful of Republicans, hoped that by getting the bill to the floor they could attract enough media attention and popular support, and work out compromises through the amendment process, to gain legislative momentum and overcome this obstacle.

Action stalled when the Republican leadership insisted on offering an amendment that would have required labor organizations, banks, and corporations to secure voluntary authorization from their members before using any membership dues, initiation fees, or other payments to fund political activities. They called the proposal the "paycheck protection act." Democrats, allied with labor and the primary beneficiaries of financial support from union leaders, filibustered against the amendment, knowing its adoption would prevent them from supporting the bill on final passage. That was exactly the outcome Republicans were seeking as each side tried to blame the other for the failure to reform the nation's widely criticized and ineffective campaign finance laws. In the meantime most Republicans continued to filibuster the bill itself.

These stark partisan and ideological cleavages, exacerbated by the Senate's loose amendment rules and reliance on a sixty-vote supermajority needed to stop a filibuster, prevented compromise and smothered direct consideration of the legislation even as campaign finance scandals implicating both parties were being played out daily in highly publicized committee hearings in both chambers and on the front pages of major newspapers.

However, the amending process of the Senate, which allows unrelated amendments to be offered to virtually any piece of legislation, often prevents the permanent demise of an issue. McCain-Feingold was resuscitated when its proponents threatened to attach it to other legislation as an amendment and to

filibuster if the majority leadership used its prerogatives to prevent this course of action. They blocked a major transportation reauthorization bill, which contained billions of dollars for highway construction and mass transit operations throughout the country, until an agreement was reached to allow a direct vote on campaign finance reform in 1998.

But when the issue returned to the floor for a week in February 1998, the political and procedural dynamics remained essentially unchanged. In this case, Lott presented paycheck protection as the base bill; McCain-Feingold was a substitute.

While supporters of McCain-Feingold demonstrated a majority for their proposal and in opposition to paycheck protection, they got nowhere near the sixty votes required to end debate. No votes were taken on adoption of the various proposals. Instead, as is often the case in the Senate, procedural votes were employed as a safe test of strength. Each side retained its full rights to filibuster if it did not get its way.

McConnell failed to table McCain-Feingold, 48–51. Sen. Olympia J. Snowe, R-Maine, proposed an amendment to the McCain-Feingold substitute to prohibit use of labor and corporate money to broadcast campaign ads shortly before a primary or general election. This was intended to weaken the appeal of paycheck protection and win over additional moderate Republicans to support cloture. It failed to do that, but a tabling motion to kill it was defeated 47–50. Snowe's amendment was then adopted by voice vote. Another effort to table McCain-Feingold, as amended, was rejected 48–50. A cloture vote on the McCain-Feingold substitute failed, 51–48. Lott could not obtain cloture on his paycheck protection base bill. The 45–54 vote meant that his motion did not even secure a simple majority.

All of the key votes, except for Snowe's amendment, were on either tabling motions or cloture. No direct votes were permitted on McCain-Feingold or the Lott bill. Lott then used his leadership prerogative to be recognized to offer multiple amendments and motions to recommit—to fill the amendment tree—with his proposals, which effectively precluded other senators from offering anything else and prevented further action on the bill.

One lesson that can be drawn from the McCain-Feingold battle is that even though an energized minority can use Senate rules to block action, public attention can either force that minority to back down or prompt voters to change the constitution of the Senate. McCain and Feingold won enactment of their law in 2002. By then, several Senate seats had changed hands, and it passed with exactly sixty votes.

---

the *Congressional Record*. "Floor debate has deteriorated into a never-ending series of points of order, procedural motions, appeals and waiver votes, punctuated by endless hours of time-killing quorum calls," Sen. Nancy Landon Kassebaum, R-Kan., wrote in the *Washington Post* in 1988. "Serious policy deliberations are a rarity. 'Great debate' is only a memory, replaced by a preoccupation with procedure that makes it exceedingly difficult to transact even routine business."[29]

"There is dialogue and debate, but most of it does not take place on the floor under public scrutiny," Sen. Paul Simon, D-Ill., said in 1985.[30]

Comparatively few limits are placed on the debate that does occur on the Senate floor. Most unanimous consent agreements limit the time to be spent debating amendments and on debatable motions, points of order, and appeals of rulings. Some agreements also limit the overall time that the entire bill, including amendments, may be debated. A few statutes, such as the 1974 Congressional Budget and Impoundment Control Act, also effectively prohibit unlimited debate on such matters as budget resolutions and budget reconciliation bills. A motion to table, if adopted, also serves to cut off debate on an amendment or motion, but it does not affect the right to offer additional amendments. And under Rule XXII, the filibuster rule, sixty senators may vote to invoke cloture, which limits debate to a potential maximum of thirty hours and requires amendments to be germane. The previous question motion, which brings debate to a close in the House, is not used in the Senate.

Senate rules bar members from speaking more than twice on the same subject in the same legislative day. This has not been an effective limit on debate, however, because each amendment is considered a different subject, and the "two-speech rule" was effectively gutted by a Senate vote in 1986 overturning a ruling of the presiding officer after the issue of enforcing the rule was raised.

As in the House, the Senate presumes that a quorum is present until a member suggests otherwise. During floor debate a senator will often suggest the absence of a quorum. This is a tactical maneuver designed to occupy time while the leadership negotiates a procedural agreement or to give a senator time to reach the floor to speak or to offer an amendment. Except in limited circumstances, the presiding officer is not permitted to count the senators on the floor to see whether a quorum exists, as the House does, but must proceed to a call of the roll. When the reason for requesting the quorum call is resolved—that is, when the negotiation is completed or the senator is in the chamber and ready to proceed—the call may be suspended by unanimous consent.

This sort of quorum call differs from a live quorum, when a member insists upon a majority of the members appearing on the Senate floor. By refusing to answer the roll call, opponents of a bill or an amendment can delay action or even try to deny the Senate a quorum. In the absence of a quorum, no business or debate may take place, and the Senate must wait for one to appear, direct the sergeant at arms to obtain the presence of absentees, or adjourn.

A dramatic example of an attempt to force a quorum to appear occurred in 1988 during debate on a controversial campaign finance bill. To break a Republican filibuster, Majority Leader Byrd sought to keep the Senate in session all night. Republicans countered by calling for repeated live quorums and then refusing to come to the floor. That forced Democrats to keep enough members present to maintain the quorum needed for the Senate to remain in session. When the Democrats came up short around midnight, Byrd resorted to a motion directing the sergeant at arms to arrest absent senators and bring them to the floor. The sergeant at arms arrested Sen. Bob Packwood, R-Ore., after forcing his way into the senator's office, and escorted him to the entrance of the Senate chamber. When Packwood refused to go in under his own steam, two Capitol police officers lifted the senator and carried him feet first into the Senate chamber. Byrd had established his quorum, but he was ultimately unable to break the filibuster and the bill died.

The Amending Process

The flexibility that marks the Senate's rules of procedure also characterizes its amending process. When a bill is taken up for consideration on the Senate floor, it is not read for amendment by section, or title, as in the House, where amendments to the beginning of the bill are offered first, and so on. Any part of the measure is open immediately to amendment in the Senate, so the subject matter of debate may shift repeatedly while the bill is on the floor. Unlike the House, the Senate is not bound by a five-minute rule governing debate on amendments. Unless limited by a unanimous consent agreement or a cloture, debate on amendments may continue until no senator seeks recognition to offer further amendments. The majority leader can obtain recognition at any time no other senator has the floor, to try to advantage his party's positions on a pending bill.

Tax legislation is particularly susceptible to nongermane amendments for a special reason. The Constitution requires revenue measures to originate in the House, a stipulation that restricts the Senate to amending House-passed bills that contain tax provisions. The Senate cannot simply add a tax provision to a House-originated measure that does not contain any. If the Senate attempts to circumvent the constitutional restriction and send a tax provision to the House on its own, the House will blue slip the legislation—adopt a resolution as a question of the privileges of the House, sending the offending matter back to the Senate without action. Opponents were able to use the threat of a blue slip to snarl a Senate-passed immigration bill in 2006 because it contained provisions affecting the tax code. Despite this constitutional stricture, the Senate, nonetheless, takes the initiative on tax issues from time to time under its constitutional power to amend all tax bills as it may all other House-passed measures. It even may act first on its own tax bill and add the provisions later as an amendment to a House-passed tax bill.

A noteworthy example occurred in 1982, when Congress approved a $98 billion tax increase that the House considered for the first time when it took up the conference report on the bill. The tax increase was required by the fiscal 1983 budget resolution. The House Ways and Means Committee took no action, in part because its members were unable to agree on what should go into a revenue-raising package and in part because Democrats wanted to force Republican President Ronald Reagan to share some of the blame for raising taxes in an election year. The Republican-led Senate Finance Committee wrote a bill raising revenue and then attached it to a minor tax bill the House had passed in 1981. After the Senate passed its version, the full House agreed with the Ways and Means Committee's recommendation to go straight to conference on the House-passed bill as amended by the Senate.

Moreover, amendments need not be germane, except in the case of general appropriations bills (this restriction was gutted by Senate votes in 1995 but restored in 1999), bills on which cloture has been invoked, concurrent budget resolutions, budget reconciliation bills, and measures regulated by unanimous consent agreement. Increasingly, Senate leaders have used complex unanimous consent agreements to limit amendments, either by disallowing nongermane amendments or specifying which amendments may be offered to legislation. Majority leaders have also employed a tactic known as filling the amendment tree to prevent other senators from offering amendments. The majority leader is able to employ that parliamentary tool effectively because the Senate affords him or her the right to be recognized first when more than one senator seeks to control the floor.

Once cloture is invoked, the Senate may consider only germane amendments. When a cloture petition is filed, senators anticipating that cloture may be invoked on a measure and wishing to protect their rights must submit first-degree amendments by one o'clock in the afternoon on the day following the submission of the petition and second-degree amendments by one hour prior to the beginning of the cloture vote.

The right of senators to offer nongermane amendments is a primary means of ensuring that legislation does not get bottled up in an unsympathetic committee. In 1983, for example, Senate Finance Committee chair Bob Dole, R-Kan., vehemently opposed a proposal to repeal a provision of the 1982 tax bill that required tax withholding on interest and dividends. But when proponents of repeal threatened to attach it to important jobs and Social Security legislation, the Senate leadership agreed to allow it to be offered as an amendment to an unrelated trade bill.

However, on the occasions in which the Senate requires that amendments be germane, the test is stricter than that in the House. An amendment in the Senate is considered germane only if it deletes something from the bill, adjusts a figure up or down, or restricts the scope of the bill. An amendment is considered nongermane if it in some way expands the scope of the bill, no matter how relevant the subject matter of the amendment may be to the underlying legislation. An amendment adding a fourth country to a bill granting normal trade relations status to three countries would be just as nongermane as an amendment revising the criminal code.

A sponsor may modify or withdraw an amendment at any time before a roll-call vote is ordered on it or it becomes the subject of a unanimous consent agreement. The amendment may then be modified or withdrawn only by unanimous consent. A sponsor may agree to modify an amendment to make it more acceptable to a greater number of senators. If a senator has offered an amendment simply to make a point, he or she may choose to withdraw it before it comes to a vote. Amended language cannot be changed again unless the change is part of an amendment that also changes other unamended parts of the legislation.

Amendments offered by the reporting committee are taken up before other amendments. Sometimes, the Senate agrees to the committee amendments en bloc, particularly if the amendments are extensive, and then provides that the bill as amended is to be considered as an original text for the purpose of further amendment. Or the Senate might agree en bloc to all but one or two of the committee amendments, which are then considered separately. Such amendments are themselves open to amendment and must be disposed of before other unrelated amendments are proposed.

The principles governing consideration of amendments in the Senate are similar to those in the House. Legislation may be amended in the first and second degree, which means that a proposed amendment to a bill may itself be amended. And, again, substitutes may be proposed for pending amendments as well as for the bill itself.

The Senate process, however, is more complex in its treatment of the precedence of different types of first- and second-degree perfecting amendments and substitutes. It differs somewhat from the House process in that there is an order in which they may be offered. Another difference is the ability of senators to modify their amendments virtually at will and, in some cases, to offer second-degree amendments to their own amendments.

In voting on amendments, the Senate makes frequent use of a procedural device known as tabling to block or kill amendments. When approved, a motion to lay on the table is considered the final disposition of that issue. The motion is not debatable, and adoption requires a simple majority vote. In the Senate, a motion to table is usually offered after an amendment has been debated, rather than as a means to prevent debate. By voting to table, a senator can appear to avoid being recorded directly on a controversial amendment to a politically sensitive issue, though the substantive result is the same. In a major floor showdown in 2006, Appropriations chair Thad Cochran, R-Miss., successfully tabled an amendment by Sen. Tom Coburn, R-Okla., that would have cut $700 million from an emergency war-spending bill for the relocation of a rail line important to Cochran's hurricane-ravaged home state. The rail spending became a cause célèbre for fiscal conservatives and a hot political button for senators from around the country. Cochran's motion for a procedural vote instead of a roll call on the amendment itself certainly made it easier for colleagues to support his position.

Like the House, the Senate has available motions to recommit a bill under consideration on the floor to a

DILATORY TACTICS: AS OLD AS THE SENATE

The most defining and controversial characteristic of the Senate is the ability of a determined minority to block the majority by refusing to curtail debate and move to a vote. In the modern Senate, debate on a matter can be ended only when sixty senators vote for cloture. An effort to prolong debate and avert a vote is called a filibuster.

In every Congress, the majority party accuses the minority party of obstructionism and of thwarting the will of the electorate. The level of rancor over filibusters rises and falls over time based on a number of factors, including the state of the relationship between the majority and minority leaders, pressure from interest groups that are pushing a particular bill or nomination, and the proximity of the next election.

The Senate was just six months old in 1789 when delaying tactics were first used by opponents of a bill to locate the nation's capital on the Susquehanna River. The first full-fledged filibusters occurred in 1841, when Democrats and Whigs squared off first over the appointment of official Senate printers and then over the establishment of a national bank. Slavery, the Civil War, Reconstruction, and ex-slaves' voting rights in turn sparked the increasingly frequent and contentious filibusters of the nineteenth century. Because the Senate repeatedly rejected efforts to restrict debate, the majority's only recourse was to win unanimous consent for a time limit on considering a bill, on a case-by-case basis.

Minor curbs on debate were adopted early in the twentieth century. But they did not hinder Republican filibusterers from killing two of President Woodrow Wilson's proposals to put the nation on a war footing—bills in 1915 concerning ship purchases and in 1917 to arm merchant ships.

As a political scientist in 1882, Wilson had celebrated "the Senate's opportunities for open and unrestricted discussion." After the 1917 defeat, he railed, "The Senate of the United States is the only legislative body in the world which cannot act when the majority is ready for action. A little group of willful men . . . have rendered the great government of the United States helpless and contemptible."[1]

On March 8, 1917, the Senate yielded to public outcry and adopted a cloture rule (Rule XXII), which required a vote of two-thirds of those present to end debate. The rule's framers predicted it would be little used, and for years that was the case.

The first successful cloture motion came in 1919, ending debate on the Treaty of Versailles, which nonetheless failed to be ratified. Nine more motions were voted on through 1927, of which three succeeded. Over the next thirty-five years, until 1962, only sixteen were voted on and not one was adopted.

In large part that reflected the politics of civil rights. Southern Democrats successfully filibustered legislation against the poll tax, literacy tests, lynching, and employment discrimination by building an anticloture coalition that included Westerners and some Republicans. In 1949 proponents of the right to filibuster gained a further advantage when they were able to amend Rule XXII to require a two-thirds vote of the total Senate membership to invoke cloture. That change occurred after a coalition of Northern Democrats and moderate Republicans sought to make it easier for the majority to invoke cloture.

Undaunted by its failure, a liberal-moderate coalition sought to ease Rule XXII nearly every time a new Congress convened. A key strategy was to assert the right of a majority to amend Senate rules at the beginning of a Congress. They received support from sympathetic vice presidents Richard M. Nixon, Hubert H. Humphrey, and Nelson A. Rockefeller. Filibuster supporters maintained that the Senate was a continuing body not subject to wholesale revision with each new class of senators who, after all, constituted only one-third of the chamber.

In 1959 Rule XXII was amended to provide for limitation of debate by a vote of two-thirds of the senators present and voting, with the vote to occur two days after a cloture petition was submitted by sixteen senators. If cloture was adopted, further debate was limited to one hour for each senator on the bill itself and on all amendments affecting it. Amendments that were not germane to the pending business and dilatory motions were out of order. The rule applied both to regular legislation and to motions to change the Standing Rules of the Senate.

Slowly, the anticloture coalition began to dissolve. In 1964 the Senate for the first time invoked cloture on a civil rights bill, cutting off one of the longest filibusters in Senate history, a fourteen-hour, thirteen-minute talkfest by Robert C. Byrd of West Virginia. A year later cloture was approved for another civil rights measure, the Voting Rights Act, and in 1968 a filibuster on an open housing bill was cut off. Sen. Strom Thurmond of South Carolina staged a twenty-four-hour, eighteen-minute filibuster against the Civil Rights Act of 1957, but cloture was not needed to end debate when he was finished because his Southern allies had already agreed not to prevent consideration of the measure. "None of his fellow Southerners would join him, and they were furious at him because they felt he was showing

committee, which would terminate action on it. The Senate may also choose to recommit a bill to a committee with instructions to take certain actions, such as to report back forthwith with amendments, and such a motion if agreed to would immediately bring the bill back to the floor in an altered form. The Senate motion to recommit is more flexible than its House equivalent, because it can be offered at any time during consideration of a measure, not just at the end of the amendment process; may be offered more than once; may be amended by proposing instructions or by offering amendments to instructions offered in the initial motion; and may be proposed by any senator without preference to those in the minority. The motion also has precedence over the offering of amendments.

Filibusters and Cloture

In its most extreme form, the Senate's tradition of unlimited debate can turn into a filibuster—the deliberate use of extended debate or procedural delays to block action on a measure supported by a majority of members. Filibusters once provided the Senate's best theater. Practitioners had to be ready for days or weeks of freewheeling debate, and all other business was blocked until one side conceded. In the modern era, drama is rare. Disappointment awaits visitors

them up for not filibustering themselves," Robert A. Caro wrote in the third volume of his biography of Lyndon B. Johnson.[2]

As it did in the 109th Congress, the Senate came close to eviscerating the cloture rule in 1969, when Vice President Humphrey ruled that the Senate could end debate on a rules change by a majority vote at the beginning of a new Congress. However, the Senate promptly overruled Humphrey.

By the early 1970s the liberals' victories on civil rights had cooled their ardor for cloture reform. Moreover, they had become the ones doing much of the filibustering—against President Nixon's Vietnam policies, weapons systems, and antibusing proposals.

In 1973, for the first time in years, the new Senate did not fight over the cloture rule. But in 1975 the liberals tried again—and won. After the Senate seemed ready on a series of procedural votes to adopt the principle that a simple majority could change the rules at the beginning of a Congress without having to invoke cloture, senators opposed to cloture reform agreed to relax the supermajority requirements if this precedent were overturned. Under Rule XXII as amended, three-fifths of the total membership of the Senate, or sixty votes if there were no vacancies, could shut off a filibuster—seven votes less than was needed under the old rule if every senator voted. (A two-thirds vote of those present and voting was still required to cut off debate on proposed rules changes.)

The 1975 revision made it easier for a majority to invoke cloture. But much of the revision's success relied on the willingness of the senators to abide by the spirit as well as the letter of the chamber's rules. When cloture was invoked on a particular measure, senators had generally conceded defeat and proceeded to a vote without further delay.

In 1976 conservative James B. Allen, D-Ala., began violating this unwritten rule of conduct and finding ways around the existing restrictions. By capitalizing on a loophole that permitted unlimited postcloture quorum calls, parliamentary motions, and roll-call votes on amendments introduced before cloture was invoked, Allen was able to delay a vote on the issue itself for far longer than the hour allotted to him under the 1959 rules revision. In 1977, with Vice President Walter F. Mondale presiding, Majority Leader Byrd took the floor to have ruled out of order dozens of amendments filed by liberal senators Howard Metzenbaum, D-Ohio, and James Abourezk, D-S.D., who were staging a postcloture filibuster on energy legislation, a major legislative priority of the Carter administration. The vice president refused to entertain appeals of his rulings or to recognize anyone other than the majority leader. Mondale and Byrd were subsequently criticized for heavy-handed and arbitrary tactics, but their actions stood amid indications that the Senate's tolerance for delaying tactics pushed to a potentially infinite degree was waning.

The Senate closed the postcloture loophole in 1979, when it agreed to an absolute limit on such delaying tactics. The rule provided that once cloture was invoked, a final vote had to be taken after no more than one hundred hours of debate. All time spent on quorum calls, roll calls, and other parliamentary procedures was counted against the one-hundred–hour limit. In 1986 the Senate reduced that limitation to thirty hours. The change, enacted as part of the Senate's decision to allow live television coverage of its floor action, was intended to quicken the pace of the proceedings.

Republican control of the Senate in 1981–1987, and for most of the years from 1995 to 2007, largely eliminated interest by liberals in further changes in the cloture rule. The filibuster became an important tool used by Democrats to restrain Republican presidents and, later, to block key parts of the political agenda of House Republicans.

In 2011, disgusted with the explosive increase in the number of cloture votes in the previous two Congresses, a small band of senators tried to change the rules—with a predictable lack of success. Three resolutions were offered:

- A measure to reduce the number of votes needed to invoke cloture if multiple votes were held: 60 on the first, 57 on the second, 54 on the third, and 51 on the fourth. It was defeated, 12–84. A similar proposal in 1995 had been tabled, 76–19.

- A resolution that, among other things, would have eliminated the possibility of filibustering the motion to proceed to a bill. It was rejected 44–51.

- A resolution to require that after an unsuccessful cloture vote, debate on the measure shall be brought to a conclusion if no senator is seeking recognition. That would have required senators to engage in an old-time filibuster. It was defeated 46–49.

1 Robert C. Byrd, *The Senate, 1789–1989*. Vol. 2 (Washington, D.C.: Government Printing Office, 1991), 122.
2 Robert A. Caro, *The Years of Lyndon Johnson: Master of the Senate* (New York: Alfred A. Knopf, 2002), 998.

to the Senate gallery who expect a real-life version of Jimmy Stewart's climactic oration in the 1939 movie *Mr. Smith Goes to Washington*. They are likely to look down on an empty floor and hear only the drone of a clerk reading absent senators' names in a mind-numbing succession of quorum calls. Often today's filibusterers do not even have to be on the floor, nor do the bills they are opposing. In the modern Senate, a filibuster typically continues until the majority party can obtain sixty votes to cut off debate and move to a vote. To ensure that all business is not stopped by a filibuster, the Senate has developed a means of considering other bills as part of a "dual track" system in which the measure being filibustered is temporarily set aside. *(See box, Dilatory Tactics: As Old as the Senate, p. 116.)*

Despite the lack of drama, filibusters—and even just the threat of a filibuster—are still effective weapons. Any controversial legislation that comes to the floor without a prearranged time agreement is vulnerable to filibuster. Success is most likely near the end of the session, when a filibuster on one bill may imperil action on other, more urgent legislation. Filibusters may be intended to kill a measure outright by forcing the leadership to pull the measure off the floor so that it can move on to other business, or they can be mounted to force a compromise on the measure. Time is such a precious commodity in today's Senate that individual members who even threaten to hold a bill hostage to lengthy debate can usually force compromises on the measure, either in committee or on the floor. Filibusters always have generated intense controversy. Supporters view filibusters as a defense against hasty or ill-advised legislation and as a guarantee that minority views will be heard. Detractors contend that filibusters allow a minority to thwart the will of a majority and impede orderly consideration of issues before the Senate.

Silencing a Filibuster. A filibuster can be ended by negotiating a compromise on the disputed matter or by mustering a determined supermajority of senators to shut it off. Since 1917 the Senate has also been able to vote to invoke cloture to cut off a filibuster, though the supermajority required to do so has changed over the years.

The procedure to end a filibuster is contained in Senate Rule XXII. This cumbersome procedure requires sixteen senators to sign a cloture petition and file it with the presiding officer of the Senate. Two days later, and one hour after the Senate convenes, the presiding officer establishes the presence of a quorum and then poses the question: "Is it the sense of the Senate that the debate shall be brought to a close?" If three-fifths of the Senate (sixty senators) votes in favor of the motion, cloture is invoked. (A two-thirds majority of those present and voting, which would be sixty-seven senators if all were present, is needed to invoke cloture on proposals to amend the Senate's standing rules, including Rule XXII. This means that an even larger majority would be needed to change the rule. In practice, it puts an almost impossible task in front of advocates of ending the cloture rule entirely and creating a situation of simple majority rule in the Senate.)

There is no limit on how long a filibuster must go on before a cloture petition can be filed. "Years ago, even Lyndon Johnson wouldn't try to get cloture until after a week," Sen. Strom Thurmond, R-S.C., said in 1987. "But now, after one day, if the leaders see you are really going to fight, they'll apply cloture immediately."[31] Thurmond's record for the longest filibuster by a single individual—twenty-four hours and eighteen minutes on a 1957 civil rights bill (which became law despite his efforts)—is likely to stand in the modern era.

No limitations are set on the number of times the Senate can try to invoke cloture on the same filibuster. "There used to be an unwritten rule that three [cloture votes] was enough," said Robert B. Dove, who was Senate parliamentarian during periods of Republican control in the 1980s and 1990s.[32] But in 1975 the Senate took six cloture votes in a futile effort to cut off debate on a dispute over a contested Senate seat in New Hampshire. And in 1987–1988, the Senate took eight cloture votes to shut off a Republican filibuster of a campaign spending bill before conceding defeat and shelving the measure.

Increased Use of Filibusters. For most of the Senate's history, the filibuster was used sparingly and for the most part only on legislative battles of historical importance, such as peace treaties and civil rights matters. Since the mid-1970s the Senate has seen a significant increase in its use. Members, Sen. Thomas F. Eagleton, D-Mo., said in 1985, "are prepared to practice the art of gridlock at the drop of a speech or the drop of an amendment."[33] In some cases the majority leader, aware of potential controversy surrounding a bill, may offer a motion to proceed to its consideration and then immediately file for cloture on that motion to get a more accurate sense of the intensity of the opposition. If sixty votes are not available, he or she may not attempt to advance the legislation further.

Ironically, a change in Senate rules that made it easier to invoke cloture to cut off a filibuster coincided with their increased use. In 1975, after years of trying, Senate liberals succeeded in pushing through a change in the Senate's cloture rule. Instead of two-thirds of those voting (sixty-seven if all senators are present), three-fifths of the membership, or sixty senators, could invoke cloture on a filibuster.

Several factors account for the increased number of cloture votes. More issues come before the Senate, making time an even scarcer commodity than in the past. More issues are controversial and, in a period of divided party rule between Congress and the White House, which has prevailed much of the time since the 1970s, more partisan. In addition, constituents and special interest groups put more pressure on members, and members are more apt to pursue their political goals even if it means inconveniencing their colleagues. In recent years, filibusters and threats of filibuster have been common weapons of senators hoping merely to spotlight or change as well as delay or kill legislation. The track system, which allows the Senate to set aside a filibustered measure temporarily while it considers other legislation, also may have contributed to the heightened use of filibusters. "For senators peripheral to the fight on a filibustered measure, separate tracking made filibusters more tolerable, made them less resentful of the filibustering senators, and even may have reduced the incentive to vote for cloture," Steven Smith wrote. "And for the filibustering senators, tracking may have improved the chances of success and reduced the costs of filibustering."[34]

Increasingly, majority leaders of both parties have filed cloture motions upon bringing a bill to the floor, or shortly thereafter, instead of waiting for a lengthy floor debate to tie up legislation. In the four-year period of 2007 through 2010, the Senate held 203 votes on cloture—22 percent of all the cloture votes it had held in the ninety-four-year history of cloture. Cloture was invoked 124 times in those four years—30 percent of all successful cloture votes in the ninety-four-year history of cloture.

From left, Sens. John Warner, R-Va., John McCain, R-Ariz., Mike DeWine, R-Ohio, and Susan Collins, R-Maine, attend a 2005 news conference after a meeting of the bipartisan "Gang of 14" senators to strike a deal that averted a showdown on the "nuclear option"—a parliamentary maneuver that, if successful, could have spelled the end of the filibuster over President Bush's judicial nominations.

SOURCE: Scott J. Ferrell, Congressional Quarterly.

However, Majority Leader Reid and Republican leader McConnell reached a two-part gentlemen's agreement: majority Democrats would allow Republicans to offer more amendments to legislation, and in return, Republicans vowed not to block legislation from coming to the Senate floor. That agreement between the two leaders, however, did not prevent several other members of the Senate from using the filibuster, or the threat of one, to delay the Senate from beginning work on a bill. However, the Reid-McConnell agreement, combined with the Senate's much slower pace of work in 2011, served to diminish the number of cloture votes somewhat. In 2011, the Senate conducted 34 cloture votes and cloture was invoked 20 times.

The Nuclear Option. In 2005 the bruising battle over Democratic filibusters of President George W. Bush's most controversial judicial nominees brought Senate Republicans to the brink of initiating a parliamentary maneuver dubbed the "nuclear option" that, if successful, could have spelled the end of the filibuster.

Under the plan, Majority Leader Bill Frist, R-Tenn., would make a point of order that a filibuster against a judicial nominee was out of order. The Senate president, Vice President Dick Cheney, would rule in favor of Frist's point of order. Democrats would likely appeal the ruling of the chair, only to have it upheld by a majority of senators. In that manner, the supermajority of sixty votes needed to thwart a filibuster would be reduced to a simple majority.

Democrats, some conservative Republicans outside the Senate, and independent analysts warned that the nuclear option could destroy Senate comity and rob the chamber of one of the few practices that distinguishes it from the majority-rules House.

"The Senate would by fiat overrule an established procedural principle to serve the immediate interests of the president and respond to the demands of a vocal constituency. And in doing so, it would establish a precedent that would threaten to change the essential character of the institution, making the Senate much more like the House," congressional scholars Thomas E. Mann and Norman J. Ornstein wrote in their book *The Broken Branch*.[35]

It was clear from the outset that even some of the senators who said they would vote for the nuclear or constitutional option did not want to see it exercised. Sen. Trent Lott,

R-Miss., despite his role in formulating the nuclear option, was always eager to make a deal. He and Sen. Ben Nelson, D-Neb., began negotiating a compromise that could have led to the confirmation of more of Bush's nominees, while preserving the filibuster. Ultimately, Lott walked away from the discussions, saying he was convinced that Frist, then considering a presidential bid, wanted to pull the trigger on the nuclear option and that he did not want to be seen as undermining the leader.

But the initial talks gave rise to the "Gang of 14," a set of seven senators from each side of the aisle who signed an agreement to not help sustain filibusters against judicial nominees except under loosely defined "exceptional" circumstances and to not vote in favor of the nuclear option.

The immediate result was the approval of several of Bush's nominees to the federal bench and temporary détente. The deal also paved the way for easy confirmation of two of Bush's Supreme Court nominees, Chief Justice John G. Roberts Jr. and Associate Justice Samuel A. Alito Jr.

Early in 2011 Reid and McConnell said that in the 112th and 113th Congresses, neither would use parliamentary force to change Senate rules through a simple majority vote, a promise that would require all significant rules changes to garner the support of two-thirds of senators voting and present. The agreement means that as long as either Reid or McConnell is majority leader, the chamber will not resort to the "constitutional" or "nuclear option," invoking a procedural maneuver using a simple majority to approve a change in certain procedures and rules. "The Senate is governed by a delicate mix of rules, rights and responsibilities," Reid said. "To that mix, we must add respect." [36]

The Rise and Fall of the Postcloture Filibuster. Traditionally, filibusterers bowed to the inevitable in the face of a successful motion to invoke cloture, abandoning any further attempts to delay action on the disputed measure. After the Senate made it easier to invoke cloture in 1975, however, a postcloture filibuster quickly appeared. The tactic took advantage of the fact that the hour allotted each senator did not count time spent on procedural motions and that all germane amendments filed before cloture was invoked were in order. By filing dozens of amendments, demanding roll calls and quorum calls, and engaging in other parliamentary procedures, senators could delay final action for days or weeks.

The postcloture filibuster was developed largely by James B. Allen, a conservative Democrat from Alabama. But two Northern liberals, James G. Abourezk, D-S.D., and Howard M. Metzenbaum, D-Ohio, exploited the tactic fully in 1977, tying up the Senate for two weeks after cloture had been invoked on a bill to deregulate natural gas. The postcloture debate was ended only after the presiding officer, Vice President Walter F. Mondale, in close consultation with Majority Leader Byrd, took the then-extraordinary step of recognizing only Byrd, ruling amendments offered by the two senators out

of order, and refusing recognition to appeal his rulings. While these actions stood, effectively killed the filibuster, and ensured passage of the president's energy legislation, their arbitrary nature disturbed some senators because they placed ends (passage of a bill) ahead of means (each senator's right to use the rules). Byrd's use of the rules to crush the postcloture filibuster was cited as a precedent by Republicans who wanted to use the nuclear option to kill filibusters of judicial nominees.

In 1979 the Senate moved formally to eviscerate the postcloture filibuster by including all time spent on procedural activities as well as on substantive debate against each senator's allotted hour. That put a one hundred-hour cap on postcloture debate. Senators were also barred from calling up more than two amendments until every other senator had an opportunity to call up two amendments. And the presiding officer was authorized to rule clearly dilatory motions out of order. In 1986 the Senate agreed to cap postcloture debate at thirty hours. Senators could still be recognized for an hour, but the time was allocated on a first-come, first-served basis. Any senators who had not yet been recognized at the end of thirty hours were each entitled to receive ten minutes.

Final Senate Action

Once debate and voting on all amendments has ended and no senator wishes to speak, a final vote on the pending legislation is taken. Senate observers are often surprised to discover that some bills pass by voice vote with only a handful of senators present. Any member, however, can request a roll call on final passage, and the Senate nearly always grants such a request. Under the Constitution, at least eleven senators (one-fifth of a quorum) must request a roll-call vote, but that requirement is often ignored in practice.

After the final vote is announced, the Senate must dispose of the usually routine motion to reconsider before a bill is considered finally passed. A senator who voted for the bill (or who did not vote) moves to reconsider the vote. A second senator who voted for the bill moves to table the motion to reconsider, and the tabling motion is almost always agreed to, usually by voice vote. Occasionally, the Senate does reconsider its action. It happens most often when supporters of a measure that is narrowly defeated have hopes of changing a few senators' minds and gaining passage. As a roll-call vote comes to an end and it appears headed for defeat, one backer of the bill will change his or her "yea" vote to a "nay"—in order to be on the prevailing side. That senator, most often the majority leader, then moves to reconsider the vote. Backers of the measure then endeavor to change a few minds. If they can do so, then the Senate will vote on whether to reconsider the previous vote.

FINAL ACTION: RESOLVING DIFFERENCES

Before a bill can be sent to the White House for the president's signature, it must be approved in identical form by both chambers of Congress. However, in 2006, after a clerical error resulted in the House and Senate passing different versions of a budget reconciliation bill, Hastert and Senate president pro tempore Ted Stevens, R-Alaska, certified in writing that the same version had passed both chambers.

There are three ways of resolving differences between the two houses: one chamber may yield to the other and simply accept its amendments; amendments move back and forth between the two houses until both agree; or a conference committee may be convened. The strategy that is used can be determined by many factors—the nature of the legislation, the time of year it is being considered, and the desire to avoid procedural entanglements.

On many noncontroversial measures the second chamber may simply agree to the version approved by the first chamber. When that occurs, no further legislative action is required, and the bill can be submitted to the president.

On virtually all major legislation, however, the second chamber approves a version that differs, sometimes radically, from the measure adopted by the first chamber. (Often the second chamber already has a similar measure under consideration.) When that happens, the second chamber has two options. It may return the bill to the chamber of origin, which then has the choice of accepting the second chamber's amendments, accepting them with further amendments, or disagreeing to the other version and requesting a House-Senate conference. Or, the second house itself may request a conference. On occasion, one chamber may accept major amendments made by the other to avoid further floor action that might jeopardize the bill. Congressional staff often work behind the scenes to hammer out agreements before formal conferences are convened to expedite the process or, in some cases, eliminate the need for a conference.

CQ Weekly in 2010 took note that formal conferences had become a rarity in recent years:

> Such temporary panels, which since the 18th century have been used to resolve differences between the House and Senate on the most complex and contentious legislative details, have all but disappeared from Congress over the past few decades. . . .
>
> Since the time of Republican rule in the mid-1990s and persisting under the Democrats, precedent and civics textbooks have largely been tossed aside. Conference committees, which have played such an important role historically as to be dubbed the "third house of Congress," have taken a back seat to out-of-view dealmaking by a handful of leaders or the volleying of competing versions of a bill across the Rotunda.

The reason for that, according to *CQ Weekly*, is that "[i]t is easier for lawmakers to cut a deal in private than to negotiate a position in the open." According to former House Ways and Means Committee chair Charles B. Rangel, D-N.Y., "historians will say it was a much more open and knowledgeable Congress when we had open conferences. . . . Politically,

it's easier to make a deal behind closed doors, but it certainly is not the best way to legislate."[37]

In recent years, many of the formal conferences that were held were called only after agreements had been reached in informal negotiations. In those cases, the appointment of conferees did not signal that negotiations were about to start, but rather that a deal had been struck behind the scenes.

Much negotiating over the final details of legislation—whether a conference committee has been appointed or the behind-the-scenes negotiations are informal—is done by staff. The procedures described in the following pages are still common elements of the conference process, but House and Senate staffers have a strong hand in putting together the final product.

Just as neither chamber may offer amendments beyond the second degree, neither chamber may amend the other's amendments more than twice. Like other rules, however, this one can be waived and sometimes is. The budget reconciliation act of 1985 was shuffled between the two chambers nine times before agreement was finally reached the following year.

Conference Action

Sen. Joel Bennett Clark, D-Mo., once introduced a resolution providing that "all bills and resolutions shall be read twice and, without debate, referred to conference." He was joking, but his proposal highlights the historical role of conference committees in drafting the final form of complex and controversial legislation. Everything the bill's sponsors worked for and all the efforts exerted by the executive branch and private interests to help pass or defeat it can be won or lost during these negotiations. Some of the hardest bargaining in the entire legislative process takes place in conference committees, and frequently the conference goes on for days, weeks, and even months before the two sides reconcile their differences.

During floor consideration of a bill, members may adopt certain tactics solely to better position themselves for the bargaining and compromise that is the hallmark of all conference negotiations. A senator, for example, may demand a roll call on a particular amendment to demonstrate to the House the Senate's solid support for the amendment—or its solid opposition. A committee may add some provisions to its version that can be traded away in conference. Or it may deliberately keep out a provision it knows the other chamber favors, again to have something to trade in conference. A floor manager may agree to an amendment, especially if he or she can persuade the sponsor not to ask for a recorded vote, knowing that it can be dumped in the conference.

Once in conference, conferees generally try to grant concessions only insofar as they remain confident the chamber they represent will accept the compromises. That is not always possible, however. The threat of a Senate filibuster on a conference report, for example, may influence

CONGRESSIONAL RECORD

The *Congressional Record* is the primary source of information about what happens on the floors of the Senate and House of Representatives. Published daily when Congress is in session, the *Record* provides an officially sanctioned account of each chamber's debate and shows how individual members voted on all recorded votes.

The *Record* is not the official account of congressional proceedings. That is provided in each chamber's Journal, which reports actions taken but not the accompanying debate. But the *Record* is often used by the courts to determine legislative history—what Congress intended when it passed a law.

By law the *Record* is supposed to provide "substantially a verbatim report of the proceedings." Exchanges among legislators can be lively and revealing, though watching Congress on television conveys far more of the flavor of the debate than reading the *Record.* Until recent years, there was broad discretion for members to edit their remarks for the *Record,* fixing grammatical errors or even deleting words spoken in the heat of floor debate. Speeches not given on the floor were often included, although both the House and Senate have tightened rules about inserting remarks, as the process is known. There have been complaints from time to time that this practice had been abused. The full texts of bills, conference reports, and other documents, rarely read in full on the floor, are often printed in the *Record.*

When Republicans took control of the House in 1995, the rules were changed to limit alterations that members might make "only to technical, grammatical and typographical corrections," which prohibited removal of remarks made. Written statements can still be inserted in the *Record,* even within the text of remarks made by a member on the floor, as long as they appear in a distinctive typeface. The new stringency was ruled to apply even to the Speaker, who had customarily refined rulings made from the chair after the fact to ensure clarity. Now the Speaker's comments appear verbatim.

The Speaker often inserts written material into the *Record,* especially at the beginning of a Congress, to elaborate certain practices that he or she will follow in recognizing members, referring bills, and addressing other subjects.

HISTORY

Before 1825 reports of congressional debates were sporadic. In 1789–1790 Thomas Lloyd of New York took down congressional debates in shorthand. Four volumes exist of his *Congressional Register.* Between 1790 and 1825 debate in the House was reported haphazardly by some of the better newspapers. Senate debates scarcely were reported at all. In 1834 Gales and Seaton published the first of forty-two volumes of *Annals of Congress,* which brought together material from newspapers, magazines, and other sources on congressional proceedings from the 1st Congress through the first session of the 18th Congress (March 3, 1789, to May 27, 1824).

From 1824 through 1837 Gales and Seaton published a *Register of Debate,* which directly reported congressional proceedings. In 1833 Blair and Rives began to publish the *Congressional Globe,* but debates were still not reported systematically until 1865, when the *Globe* took on a form and style that later became standard. When the government contract for publication of the *Globe* expired in 1873, Congress provided that the *Congressional Record* would be produced by the Government Printing Office.

PROCEEDINGS

The *Record* contains four sections. Two of them, the proceedings of the Senate and of the House, are edited accounts of floor debate and other action taken in each chamber. A member may request "unanimous consent to extend my remarks at this point in the *Record,*" or to include extraneous matter, at any time he or she is able to gain recognition on the floor. When the request is granted, and it almost always is, a member may include a statement, newspaper article, or speech, which will appear in the body of the *Record* where the member requested.

Until March 1978 there was no way to tell whether a lawmaker had delivered his or her remarks or had them inserted. Since then, inserted remarks are indicated in the House proceedings by a different typeface. In the Senate, they are denoted by black dots, or bullets. If a member read only a few words from a speech or article, it would appear in the *Record* as if the member had delivered it in its entirety. The House in 1995 restricted this practice to require all undelivered remarks to appear in a separate typeface.

Since 1979 time cues have marked House floor debate to show roughly when a particular discussion occurred. Senate proceedings have no indication of time.

EXTENSIONS OF REMARKS

In addition to inserting material, senators and representatives are given further space to extend their remarks in a third section of the *Record* labeled "Extensions of Remarks." By unanimous consent, they may add such extraneous material as speeches given outside Congress, selected editorials, or letters. Such material may also be included in the body of the *Record* by unanimous consent if a representative or senator prefers.

DAILY DIGEST

The fourth section of the *Record* is the Daily Digest, which summarizes House and Senate floor action for the day as well as Senate and House committee meetings and conferences. It also notes committee reports filed and the time and date of the next House and Senate sessions and all committee meetings. The last issue of the Digest in the week lists the program for the coming week, including legislation scheduled for floor action if it has been announced, and all committee meetings. At the beginning of each month the Digest publishes a statistical summation of congressional activity in the previous month. An index to the *Record* is published semimonthly.

COSTS

According to Senators Herb Kohl, D-Wis., and Tom Coburn, R-Okla., about 4,551 copies of the *Record* were printed at the start of the 112th Congress, at a cost of about $8 million annually ($240 per page). In 2011, they introduced a bill to reduce the number of copies printed to only archival copies and those explicitly requested by the vice president or a member of Congress. Rules require that any insert of more than two pages include an estimate of printing costs by the Government Printing Office. One of the most expensive inserts appeared in the issue of June 15, 1987, when Rep. Bill Alexander, D-Ark., inserted 403 pages covering three and a half years of congressional debate on an amendment barring military aid to the antigovernment contra guerrillas in Nicaragua. Estimated cost of the insertion was $197,000.

WEB ACCESS

The public has free access to the daily *Congressional Record* through websites run by the U.S. Government Printing Office (www.fdsys.gov) and the Thomas service provided by the Library of Congress (http://thomas.loc.gov). Copies of the *Record,* dating back to 1989, are online in searchable format. The rise of the Internet is one reason that fewer copies of the *Record* are now printed than in past years. *(See "Congressional Information on the Internet," p. 237, in Reference Materials.)*

House conferees to drop a provision that they believe too many senators might find distasteful. Time also may be a factor, especially at the end of a Congress when delay might cause a bill to die in conference.

Calling a Conference

Either chamber can request a conference once both have considered the same legislation. Generally, the chamber that approved the legislation first will disagree to the amendments made by the second body and request that a conference be convened. Sometimes, however, the second body will ask for a conference immediately after it has passed the legislation, assuming that the other chamber will not accept its amendments. The distinction can be important, because the chamber that requests the conference nearly always, by custom, acts last on the conference report. Depending on the political situation, this may have strategic importance affecting the legislation's chances for final passage.

Both chambers technically must go to conference on a single bill. Thus one chamber often takes up the other's version of the measure, strikes everything after the enacting clause, and substitutes its version for everything but the other chamber's bill number. Both versions can then be considered by the conference committee. Tax bills that are sent to conference always have an "HR" designation because of the constitutional requirement that revenue bills originate in the House. A conference cannot change the number of the bill committed to it or create a different-numbered bill.

A conference cannot take place until both chambers formally agree that it be held. The Senate usually requests or agrees to a conference by unanimous consent. However, a motion to do so is debatable and may be filibustered. In the House this action generally is taken by unanimous consent, by special rule, or, since 1965, by motion, if authorized by the committee managing the legislation and if the floor manager is recognized at the discretion of the Speaker for that purpose. Before 1965, if there was objection to unanimous consent, the House could go to conference only if it suspended the rules with a two-thirds majority or if the Rules Committee granted a rule that the House could adopt by majority vote. On some occasions, the Rules Committee refused to report a rule allowing a conference, which gave the conservative coalition that often controlled that committee prior to its expansion in 1961 another means of blocking legislative action.

Selection of Conferees

The two chambers have different rules for selecting conferees, or managers, as they are formally called, but in practice both follow similar procedures. House rules grant the Speaker of the House the right to appoint conferees, but the Speaker usually does so only after consultation with the minority leader and the chair and ranking minority member of the committee or subcommittee having jurisdiction over the legislation. As in the selection of members of standing committees, the minority makes its choices for conferees, which, by custom, are appointed by the Speaker without change.

In 1993 the House amended its rules to give the Speaker formal authority to replace any conferee whenever he or she wished. A Speaker might be more inclined to overcome a recalcitrant conferee by appointing two new loyal conferees instead of removing the troublesome lawmaker. While the new power has rarely been used for any substantive purpose, it does give the leadership substantial power over conference negotiation and restrains conferees from bringing back a conference report that includes provisions opposed by party leaders or omits those they favor.

Senate rules allow the chamber as a whole to elect conferees, but that rarely happens. The common practice is for the presiding officer, by unanimous consent, to appoint conferees on the recommendation of the appropriate committee chair and ranking minority member. The process of going to conference and appointing conferees is debatable, however, and provides another potential choke point for opponents of a measure.

Those members who are usually selected as conferees are the chairs of the committee(s) that handled the legislation, the ranking minority member(s), and other members of the committee(s) most actively involved. If a subcommittee has exercised major responsibility for a bill, some of its members may be chosen. Seniority once governed the selection of conferees, but it is common today for junior members in each chamber to be chosen, especially if they are particularly knowledgeable about the bill or have earned the trust of party leaders. Occasionally a member from another committee with expertise in the subject matter of the bill may be named to the conference or one who sponsored a major amendment adopted on the floor.

Even on major legislation, once unwieldy conference committees made up of dozens or scores of legislators from various committees have been replaced by small clutches of legislators, sometimes including party leaders. On the 2003 Medicare prescription-drug law, for example, Speaker Hastert appointed eight conferees, including the chairs and relevant subcommittee chairs from the tax and commerce panels and Majority Leader Tom DeLay, R-Texas. The nine-member Senate contingent included Majority Leader Frist. Democrats complained angrily that all but two of their conferees, Max Baucus of Montana and John Breaux of Louisiana, were locked out of the negotiations.

The increase in the size of conference committees in the 1970s and 1980s led to limitations on the role of some conferees, particularly those who are not members of the principal committee of jurisdiction. General conferees have overall responsibility for the whole bill. Additional conferees consider and vote only on specific subjects or sections of the legislation. Exclusive conferees are the sole negotiators for their chambers on specified subjects or sections. Members

Speaker of the House Nancy Pelosi, D-Calif., Senate Majority Leader Harry Reid, D-Nev., Senate Banking Committee Chair Christopher Dodd, D-Conn., and House Financial Services Committee Chair Barney Frank, D-Mass., attend the signing ceremony for the Dodd-Frank Wall Street Reform and Consumer Protection Act at the Ronald Reagan Building and International Trade Center on July 21, 2010, in Washington, D.C.

SOURCE: UPI/Chip Somodevilla/Pool/Landov.

who are general conferees may vote on the same issues as additional conferees but may not participate in the areas reserved for exclusive conferees unless they are also so named.

The number of conferees each chamber selects does not have to be the same. A majority in each delegation will be from the majority party in the chamber, however. Bills that have been referred to more than one committee once entailed large conferences because multiple conferees were selected from each of the committees of jurisdiction.

Twenty-three committees, for example, sent conferees to the conference committee on the omnibus trade bill enacted in 1988. Budget reconciliation bills generally engender some of the largest conferences because they may affect the jurisdictions of almost every House and Senate committee. More than 250 conferees from both houses were appointed as conferees on the 1981 budget reconciliation bill, for example. Such large conferences usually divide up into smaller working groups, or subconferences, that deal only with specific parts of the bill. In more recent years, Congress has moved in the opposite direction, sometimes limiting

conferences to as few as three members from a chamber—the chair, another majority member, and the ranking minority member—to expedite the process and ensure leadership control.

The diminishing size of conference committees can be seen in the appointment of sixty conferees to the budget reconciliation measure enacted in early 2006. The figure is staggeringly large by today's standards but dwarfed by the 1981 reconciliation measure.

Conferees in both the House and Senate generally are expected to support the legislative positions of the chamber they represent. In an effort to ensure that its conferees would uphold its position, the House in 1974 modified its rules on conferees selection. The revised rule said that "the Speaker shall appoint [as conferees] no less than a majority of members who generally supported the House position as determined by the Speaker." A further revision, in 1977, said that "the Speaker shall name members who are primarily responsible for the legislation and shall, to the fullest extent feasible, include the principal proponents of the major provisions of the bill as it passed the House." Some of these changes were intended to further strengthen the Speaker and to give him or her authority to resist demands by committee chairs that might not be in the majority's interest. The Speaker's conference appointments may not be challenged in the House. The 1993 rules change giving the Speaker power to name and replace conferees at will has effectively limited the independent power of conferees, individually or collectively, to actively defy the majority party's agenda.

Sometimes questions have arisen about whether conferees are likely to uphold the chamber's position on key points in conference deliberations, particularly when party goals are at stake. If the party leadership prefers provisions passed by the other body, conferees may be inclined to depart from their own chamber's position in conference. Each chamber has remedies in such situations that restrain conferees—motions to instruct conferees, motions to recommit a conference report, the filibuster in the Senate, and the Speaker's power to change conferees in the House. The ultimate power is to defeat a conference report or prevent its consideration by demonstrating that opponents could sink it on the floor.

But most lawmakers are reluctant to vote against major legislation, often bills that address pressing national issues and include money for local projects, because they find some provisions offensive. That has led to frustration among members of the rank and file over their inability to access conference negotiations and their inability under the rules to amend conference reports once they are presented for a vote.

In an effort to address the concerns of junior colleagues and give the Senate more leverage in its negotiations with the House, the Senate passed legislation in the 109th Congress that would have given the Senate the ability to strike individual provisions from a conference report without killing it and send it back to the House.

The provision was modeled after the "Byrd Rule" for budget reconciliation measures, which has given the Senate considerable leverage over the House since the 1990s. But the provision was included in a bill, not presented as a simple rules change, and the bill was not enacted.

In 1995 Speaker Gingrich used his appointment power in a new way to highlight divisions in the minority over legislation headed to conference. For example, on one occasion he appointed a conservative Democrat, Rep. Gary A. Condit of California, to a conference on legislation relating to curbing unfunded federal mandates to the states and localities. In another, conservative representative Mike Parker, D-Miss., was appointed a conferee on the concurrent budget resolution. (Parker later switched parties.) These members had been passed over by Minority Leader Richard A. Gephardt, D-Mo., when the Democrats announced their choices from among more senior members. But Gingrich did not violate the custom of allowing the minority exclusive power over its

choices. The slots he gave to these Democrats were taken from the Republicans' own allotment.

Political scientist Barbara Sinclair described the process in choosing conferees for the 1995 budget reconciliation bill, which was later vetoed by President Clinton. The Republican Party leadership in both houses sought to ensure close control over the bill, both to achieve a satisfactory result and to conclude negotiations quickly. The conference consisted of forty-three senators in twelve subgroups and seventy-one House members in fourteen subgroups.

> Had Gingrich not assertively exercised the Speaker's discretion . . . the House delegation could easily have been much larger. . . . Gingrich chose whenever possible members who could do double duty because they served on the Budget Committee and another concerned committee. A subgroup of eight House members had authority over the entire bill and included . . . a number of party leaders—Majority Leader Dick Armey of Texas, Majority Whip Tom DeLay of Texas, and Conference Chair John A. Boehner of Ohio on the Republican side and Minority Whip David Bonior on the Democratic side. In the Senate, the group of three that had authority over the entire bill was confined to the Budget Committee leaders. The other subgroups consisted of members from committees with provisions in the bill and had authority over those provisions only.[38]

Instructing Conferees

Either chamber may try to enforce its will by instructing its conferees how to vote in conference, but the rules do not obligate the conferees to follow the instructions. The Senate rarely instructs its conferees, but the practice may be becoming more common. In both chambers, conferees may be instructed just prior to their appointment by the chair. In the House, they may be instructed again, day after day, if they have failed to report after twenty calendar days have elapsed. (One day's advance warning must be given in the House of the intention to offer such motions, along with the exact wording.)

Efforts to instruct conferees may reflect the degree of support in the chamber for certain provisions in either the House or Senate versions of a bill. Depending on the circumstances, votes to instruct may serve as warnings that conferees had better not stray too far from the language the chamber originally approved or they may have just the opposite intent and signal receptivity to a provision originated in the other chamber. In the House motions to instruct can be used to react to Senate provisions that the House, under its germaneness rules, would never have had the opportunity to consider.

The potential political advantages of forcing a vote on a motion to instruct have led to its frequent use in the House. The minority has used the right to offer motions to instruct to embarrass the majority or to force repeated votes on controversial issues. For example, during the 103rd Congress, the Republican minority offered numerous motions to instruct

LEGISLATIVE ANOMALIES

Peculiar situations have arisen occasionally as Congress searches for an appropriate manner to achieve a new or unique result. And even if Congress cannot find one, it may do what it wants to anyway. Here are several examples.

A not-so-insignificant problem was created during consideration of a five-year, $40 billion spending-cut package the House passed and cleared for the president's signature on February 1, 2006. The text was different, albeit only slightly, from the version passed by the Senate. The version sent from the Senate to the House indicated the Senate had approved it in the agreed-upon form, which it had not. A clerk, realizing that the Senate had passed the wrong version, attempted to correct the situation by changing the number of months affecting a particular provision in the copy sent to the House. In order to become a law, a bill has to pass both chambers in identical form.

House leaders, though aware of the discrepancy, chose to pass the version the Senate said it had passed, not what the Senate had, in fact, passed. The House could have amended it with the correct language and sent it back to the Senate, but the bill had already survived dozens of obstacles, including the vitiation of a conference report by the Senate on a technicality a little more than a month earlier. So the House, on a tight, nearly party-line vote, cleared the spending cuts. Despite the glitch, Speaker J. Dennis Hastert, R-Ill., and Senate president pro tempore Ted Stevens, R-Alaska, both signed the measure, as is required before presentation to the president. The law was subject to a number of court challenges, all unsuccessful.

In 1978 Congress attempted a new form of legislative enactment to extend the time permitted for ratification of a proposed constitutional amendment. The so-called Equal Rights Amendment (ERA), passed by Congress in 1972 and intended to enhance women's rights, carried within it a seven-year time limit for ratification by the requisite three-fourths of the states. It would die on March 22, 1979, unless ratified by thirty-eight states. Congress had first set time limits on amendment ratifications beginning in 1917 to ensure that the initial proposal of an amendment and its ultimate ratification were roughly contemporaneous.

With the deadline nearing Congress wanted to keep the amendment alive to see if several additional states might ratify the amendment. A joint resolution was passed extending the life of the amendment by thirty-nine additional months, until June 30, 1982. Congress first had determined, by simple majority, that a two-thirds vote was not required for passage of the time extension. (It also would have been more difficult to obtain a two-thirds vote in 1978 than in 1972 because the amendment had become far more controversial after its passage.)

Once passed by both houses, the joint resolution was sent to President Jimmy Carter, who proceeded to sign it even while raising doubt that he had any role in the process and questioning whether the joint resolution was a law. The archivist of the United States, who received the joint resolution next, did not give it a public law number but instead notified the states of its existence. A federal judge ruled in 1981 that Congress had acted improperly, but the question became moot when additional states failed to ratify the amendment even under the extended timetable. The U.S. Supreme Court dismissed the case in 1982 and vacated the lower court's decision, leaving the ultimate validity of the congressional action in constitutional limbo.

Other examples of unusual legislative actions have involved constitutional amendments. Congress does not need to take any formal action once an amendment has been ratified. In 1868, however, Congress passed a concurrent resolution to declare that the Fourteenth Amendment to the U.S. Constitution had been ratified by the requisite number of states. Several states had ratified the amendment and later rescinded their endorsements, and others ratified it after first having rejected it. A number of other states signed on years after the adoption. Maryland ratified it in 1959, and Kentucky waited more than one hundred years, until 1976, to do so.

In 1992, reeling from scandals and low public approval ratings, members rushed to identify themselves with the so-called Madison Amendment, which would require that an election intervene before any congressional pay raise could take effect. The amendment, originally proposed by Congress in 1789, suddenly

as a conference on major crime legislation dragged on for months. The tactic was so effective, and annoying, that the Democratic majority considered changing House rules for the next Congress to restrict such motions, but the subsequent shift in party control prevented any action.

To protect rank-and-file lawmakers from having to cast politically tricky votes, Speaker Hastert would often wait until an informal conference had come to agreement before formally appointing conferees and starting the twenty-day clock for motions to instruct them.

Authority of Conferees

Theoretically House and Senate conferees are limited to resolving matters in disagreement between the two chambers. They are not authorized to delete provisions or language that both chambers have agreed to or to draft entirely new provisions. This is called staying within the scope of disagreements between the two chambers. When the disagreement involves numbers, such as the

level of funding in appropriations bills, conferees are supposed to stay within the amounts proposed by the two houses.

But in practice the conferees have wide latitude, except where the matters in disagreement are specific. If one chamber has substituted an entirely new version of the bill for that approved by the other chamber—which is nearly always the case on major bills, except for appropriations—the entire subject is technically in disagreement, and the conferees may draft an entirely new bill if they so choose. In such a case, the Legislative Reorganization Act of 1946 stipulates that they may not include in the conference version of the bill "matter not committed to them by either house." But they may include "matter which is a germane modification of subjects in disagreement." The tight reins party leaders use to control conference committees put them in a unique position to insert provisions into law at the last minute—in some cases after all of the conference's work has been completed— prompting their colleagues to cry foul.

reemerged in 1978 after more than a century in limbo since the last time a state legislature had approved it, and began a flurry of new ratifications. Previous historical concerns by Congress about contemporaneous enactment of constitutional amendments were thrown to the winds as members rushed to embrace what was still one of the most popular forms of Congress-bashing—denying themselves pay raises.

Each house passed a concurrent resolution stating that the new Twenty-seventh Amendment was properly ratified, but neither house passed the concurrent resolution adopted by the other. Not satisfied with that, the Senate also adopted a simple resolution declaring ratification of the amendment. Adding to the confusion, the archivist of the United States had already declared the amendment ratified on May 18, 1992, before Congress acted.

The Republican-led House late in 1998, following midterm elections in which the GOP lost seats, approved articles of impeachment against President Bill Clinton, forcing the issue to the Senate. Under the Constitution, the House by majority vote can initiate articles of impeachment that could result in a trial by the Senate, where a two-thirds majority is required for conviction and removal from office. The Senate in 1999 took up the articles but voted not to convict the president.

In the course of this, members in both chambers—but particularly the Senate—looked for ways to express strong disapproval of Clinton's actions involving a female White House intern and his response to legal proceedings that grew out of the matter. Senate majority leader Trent Lott, R-Miss., suggested a censure of the president by Congress if the charges against Clinton were insufficient for impeachment conviction. The Senate had done this before, to President Andrew Jackson in 1834, in a political dispute over the Bank of the United States (whose reauthorization Jackson had vetoed), but the action carried no legal weight and was never repeated by any future Congress. The Constitution does not recognize any punishment other than impeachment and removal from office. Jackson's allies later expunged the censure from the Senate Journal. In 1999, once conviction of Clinton

was defeated, the idea of censure was not raised again. Presumably, if Lott's suggestion were to be followed, either chamber could initiate a concurrent resolution to censure the president or act separately by simple resolution, but such measures would not be privileged for consideration in either chamber and would be subject to a filibuster in the Senate.

The Senate reached back to rewrite history in 1997. In 1996 the House had passed a conference report containing continuing appropriations funding government agencies. However, to deal with possible Senate opposition the House also passed the funding as a separate bill that the Senate might amend if it chose to do so. Ultimately, the Senate passed both bills. The conference report was sent to the president and signed into law. However, instead of simply killing the unnecessary separate bill, it was passed without amendment by a roll-call vote and the Daily Digest of the *Congressional Record* noted that it was cleared for the president. However, this did not happen. The Senate never sent a message to the House formally notifying it of the bill's passage, which prevented the House from enrolling it for presentation to the president, as required. Presumably, had this been done, the president could simply have disposed of the bill with a quiet pocket veto. With the bill in limbo, the 104th Congress expired, preventing any enrollment.

Nevertheless, Rep. David Skaggs, D-Colo., concerned with setting a precedent that a bill passed in identical form by both houses of Congress could be kept from the president by direction of the majority leadership of one chamber, called Majority Leader Lott and demanded an explanation. He also inserted a letter to Lott and a history of the incident into the *Record*.[1] In response, in February 1997 Senate majority whip Don Nickles, R-Okla., rose on the floor to ask unanimous consent to amend the Senate Journal of the preceding Congress to state that the bill had been indefinitely postponed.

1 "Concerning a Congressional Failure to Comply with the Constitution During the 104th Congress," *Congressional Record*, daily ed., 105th Cong.,1st sess., January 7, 1997, E2.

"After the conference was finished at 6 p.m., Senator Frist marched over to the House side of the Capitol about 4 hours later and insisted that over 40 pages of legislation, which I have in my hand, 40 pages of legislation that had never been seen by conferees, be attached to the bill," Rep. David Obey, D-Wis., said of a provision added to the fiscal 2006 defense appropriations law. "The Speaker joined him in that assistance so that, without a vote of the conferees, that legislation was unilaterally and arrogantly inserted into the bill after the conference was over in a blatantly abusive power play by two of the most powerful men in Congress."[39]

Both houses have scope requirements, but these are often ignored or difficult to enforce. In practice, House and Senate conferees can agree to virtually anything, so long as the overall package wins support in the respective chambers.

The House has long objected to the inclusion in conference reports of Senate-passed amendments that are not germane. Because conference agreements may not be amended

on the floor of either chamber, the House was often put in a take-it-or-leave-it situation, forced either to accept a nongermane amendment it may never have debated or to recommit or vote down the entire conference report, including provisions it favored. A series of rules changes in the 1970s, including one in 1972 that allows the House to take separate votes on nongermane amendments in conference reports, has given the House some leverage both in conference and on the Senate floor. Senate floor managers sometimes tried to turn away nongermane floor amendments by arguing that they might prevent the entire bill from winning approval in the House.

However, in more recent practice, the trend has been toward allowing conferees, with the concurrence of the leadership, greater flexibility to negotiate and present conference reports that produce the desired policy results, irrespective of procedural inadequacies. The House leadership has worked with the committees to protect conference reports from points of order and possible dismemberment on the floor by having the Rules Committee waive points of order, including the scope-of-the-conference matter about which Obey complained, the germaneness of Senate provisions, or the inclusion of legislation on appropriations bills. Today it is common practice for the House to waive all points of order against a conference report.

Appropriations bills used to return from conference with hundreds of amendments in disagreement at the insistence of the House. Disposition of compromise language on these amendments was considered separately after the House had adopted the conference report. Most of these amendments were reported in technical disagreement, which meant there were technical violations of House rules involved, and an agreement was not placed in the body of the conference report to avoid potential points of order against the entire report. The conferees had reached agreement on these issues, but each such item was theoretically subject to separate debate and votes to ratify the decisions and even potentially to additional amendment. Sometimes there were substantial issues in true disagreement that the two chambers sent back and forth until an agreement was reached. Both houses had to attain final agreement on all of these amendments to conclude action on a bill and send it to the president.

After the Republicans took control of Congress in 1995 they stopped this practice, insisting that conferees reach agreement on all issues whenever possible before returning to the floor. Every provision was placed within the body of the conference report and, in the House, was protected by a rule waiving points of order. The result was a considerable simplification of the conference procedure that reduced the ability of individual members to challenge the contents of conference reports.

After the mid-1970s, the growing power of the House leadership of both parties at the expense of committees, as well as the creation of committee memberships more representative of their respective parties, decreased the importance of procedural protections for the membership as a whole because the ability of committees and conferees to defy the majority was drastically curtailed.

Since the Senate's adoption in 1985 of the Byrd Rule barring extraneous matters in budget reconciliation bills, the Senate has had a distinct advantage in negotiating budget laws. The Byrd Rule allows points of order against any matter in a reconciliation bill that violates the rule, including major provisions in a conference report that might have survived from the House version, unless sixty votes waive the point of order.

The House has complained bitterly that its ability to legislate on reconciliation bills and to negotiate in conference has been restricted because conferees on the bill risk rejection of their entire product if it includes a provision that violates the Senate rule and cannot command sixty votes. The Senate argues that the Byrd Rule is vital to protect the Senate tradition of unlimited debate because reconciliation bills, by statute, are immune to filibusters. In the absence of the Byrd Rule, the House could use conference reports on such bills to force the Senate to act on matters that might be filibustered if considered separately outside the budget process.

In 2007, in the aftermath of a series of scandals, Congress enacted a lobbying and ethics measure that included new Senate rules for conference reports. The new law included provisions that changed Senate rules to bar consideration of any bill or conference report unless all earmarks had been identified on a publicly accessible congressional website at least forty-eight hours before the vote. If they were not, consideration of the bill would be subject to a point of order. Also, provisions added during a conference—so-called air-dropped provisions—could be challenged in the Senate through points of order that required sixty votes to waive. Such challenges do not endanger the rest of the conference report. In November 2007, conferees on the fiscal 2008 Labor-HHS-Education appropriations bill added provisions to fund military construction projects and the Veterans Affairs Department. The House adopted the conference agreement. When the Senate considered it, a point of order was raised against the added portions, which was sustained. The Senate then voted to send an amended bill back to the House, minus the military construction-VA language, and the House agreed to the slimmed-down bill.

If conferees find they are unable to reach agreement, they may report their failure to reach agreement to the parent chamber and allow the full House or Senate to act as it wishes. If neither chamber is willing to yield, the legislation will die.

House rules allow conferees to be discharged and replaced by new conferees if they fail to reach agreement within twenty calendar days (or within thirty-six hours of their appointment during the last six days of a session), but this authority is rarely invoked.

Adoption of the Conference Report

When a majority of the conferees from each chamber have reached agreement on a bill, conference committee staff—generally the staff of the committees with jurisdiction over the measure—writes a conference report indicating changes made in the bill and explaining each side's action. If the two sides have been unable to reach a compromise on particular House or Senate amendments, those amendments are reported in disagreement and are acted on separately after the conference report itself has been adopted.

The conference report must be signed by a majority of conferees from each chamber and submitted in document form to each house for approval. Minority reports or statements of minority views are not permitted, though sometimes a member will note next to his signature "except section ____" or a similar notation indicating partial disapproval. Until the 1970 Legislative Reorganization Act required House and Senate managers to prepare a joint explanatory statement discussing the specific changes made by the conferees, the conference report was printed only in the House, together with an explanation by the House conferees. The joint statement ensures that both houses have the same interpretation of the actions taken by the conferees, in addition to having an identical bill text. Although the conference report is supposed to be printed in the Senate, that requirement is frequently waived by unanimous consent. The report is always published in the *Congressional Record.* House rules require that conference reports lie over three days before the House takes them up, but that rule was routinely waived in the 1990s and early 2000s. The Senate requires only that copies be available on each senator's desk.

Each chamber must vote on a conference report as a whole. No new amendments may be considered. The Senate can still filibuster a conference report. Lawmakers are often forced to consider huge bills with little notice or even without access to the written text of the legislation. In 1997, for example, members complained that copies of huge budget reconciliation and tax reduction legislation, which was supposed to lead to a balanced federal budget, were not available except for a few copies in the hands of the floor managers.

For complex legislation, the House Rules Committee is usually asked to report a rule waiving points of order. Protection from points of order may be critical because a point of order against the conference report—for example, that it contains matter beyond the scope of the disagreements committed to conference—would, if sustained, kill the conference report immediately without any vote and return the bill to its parliamentary status prior to the conference. There may be no time for a new conference, and the result would be the death of the legislation.

The house that agreed to the other chamber's request to go to conference on a bill acts first on the conference version. This procedure, followed by custom instead of by rule, is sometimes ignored. The Senate, for example, asked for the conference on the 1981 tax cut, and it acted first on the conference report.

Which chamber acts first or last can occasionally influence the outcome. The chamber to act first has three options: it can agree to the conference report, reject it, or recommit it to the conference committee for further deliberation. Once the first chamber has acted, however, the conference committee is dissolved, and recommittal is no longer an option. The second chamber must vote the conference report up or down.

The pressure on reluctant members to support a report that the other chamber has already approved can be intense. Rep. Jack Brooks, D-Texas, counted on that intense lobbying when he maneuvered in 1979 to have the House take up the conference report creating the Department of Education after the Senate had already adopted it. Brooks's strategy worked. The House, which had originally approved creation

of the department by a four-vote margin, adopted the conference report with fourteen votes to spare.

While the conference version of the bill must be approved or rejected in its entirety by both bodies, in the House exceptions may be made for nongermane Senate amendments. Unless a special rule has waived all points of order, any member of the House may make the point of order that a particular section of a conference report contains nongermane material and move to reject the offending language. Forty minutes of debate, equally divided between opposing sides, is allotted for such motions. If the motion carries, the nongermane material is deleted, the conference report is considered rejected, and the House may go on to approve the remaining text of the conference report, minus the deletion, as a further amendment to the bill. The bill as amended must then go back to the Senate, which can either accept the amendment by the House, reject it, amend it further, or ask for a new conference.

If conferees have been unable to agree on any of the amendments in disagreement, separate votes are taken in both houses to resolve the differences. One chamber may insist on its amendment, or it may move to recede and concur in the other chamber's position. Occasionally the amendment in disagreement will be returned to conference for further compromise efforts.

Conference reports are seldom rejected, in part because legislators have little desire to begin the entire legislative process all over again and in part because members tend to defer to the expertise of the conferees, just as they tend to defer to the recommendations of the legislative committees. If a bill dies once it has reached conference, it is more likely that conferees have been unable to reach a compromise before the end of the Congress. That is what happened to the 1990 campaign finance bill.

Sometimes the House Rules Committee has been asked to make changes in a pending conference report through the device of allowing passage of a concurrent resolution changing the enrollment of a conference report. These changes, for example, might be altering the text to enhance chances for adoption or to correct errors discovered after passage. If the Senate also adopts such a concurrent resolution, the conference report is modified by the enrolling clerk and ultimately sent to the president in its new, improved form.

Final Legislative Action

After both houses have given final approval to a bill, a final copy of the measure, known as the enrolled bill, is prepared by the enrolling clerk of the chamber in which the legislation originated, printed on parchment-type paper, and certified as correct by the secretary of the Senate or the clerk of the House, depending on which chamber originated the measure. No matter where the bill originated, it is signed first by the Speaker of the House and then by the vice president or president pro tempore of the Senate and sent to the White House.

LINE-ITEM VETO EXPERIMENT ENDED BY SUPREME COURT

Congress's historic enactment in 1996 of a law giving the president a line-item veto began a short-lived experiment with a power that Republicans had long sought for the executive branch. The line-item veto lasted only until June 1998, when the U.S. Supreme Court declared it unconstitutional. There have been efforts since then to revive it in a form more likely to survive the high court, but none has been enacted.

The Line-Item Veto Act, which took effect on January 1, 1997, gave the president the power to strike out, or cancel, dollar amounts of discretionary spending, new direct spending, and certain forms of new tax benefits in bills signed into law. Congress could vote to pass the item(s) again, but the president could then use his constitutional veto power to kill this legislation, forcing Congress to find a two-thirds majority to override the veto in the normal manner.

Proponents of the line-item veto, generally political conservatives opposed to government spending and programs, argued that the overwhelming majority of state governors possessed the line-item veto in some form and that it had proved to be a useful tool in controlling expenditures. They responded to constitutional concerns by arguing that there was a long history of presidential action declining to carry out spending passed by Congress and that Congress could properly delegate authority to the president to declare cancellations of spending authority.

Opponents argued that the U.S. Constitution clearly required that bills be approved or rejected by the president in their entirety, not in pieces. They said that the new procedure gave the president the power to change laws after their enactment—in effect, to make laws, a power reserved exclusively to Congress—and to leave on the statute books truncated laws in a form that Congress might never have chosen to enact. The most fundamental argument, however, went to the balance of power between Congress and the executive branch. Opponents warned that a line-item veto would upset this balance among the branches of government by ceding too much political power to the president while Congress considered legislation. Beyond the basic principle, they feared the executive branch would have enormous leverage to offer to withhold cancellations if members backed unrelated presidential priorities.

A version passed by the House in 2006 at the urging of President George W. Bush would have guaranteed expedited congressional consideration for packages of cuts identified by the president. Proponents argued the approach would give the president a stronger hand in the spending process without running afoul of the Constitution.

OPERATION OF THE LINE-ITEM VETO

The 1996 law allowed the president not only to look at the specific language of new spending and tax laws but also to examine other elements of the legislative package that described these laws, including tables, charts, or explanatory text included in the statement of the managers accompanying a conference report. In other words, the president was allowed to locate spending wherever it tried to hide,

subject to limitations of the act. If an item of spending could be clearly identified, the president could cancel only the entire amount (not simply reduce it in part).

It was anticipated that the president's use of the line-item veto would focus on appropriations bills, because there were thirteen of them (now twelve) that contain discretionary spending. But when President Bill Clinton first employed his new power in 1997, appropriations bills had not yet reached his desk. Consequently, he targeted other forms of spending defined by the law—new direct spending and limited tax benefits contained in the Balanced Budget Act and the Taxpayer Relief Act of 1997.

The president was allowed to use the line-item veto to cancel items of new direct spending, which encompassed any new entitlement programs Congress passed. (He could not attack existing entitlements.) The president was also allowed to block limited tax benefits, a provision that was put into the law to satisfy members who believed that tax benefits were just as much a form of spending as appropriations and deserved the same treatment.

The law allowed the president to target federal tax benefits that went to one hundred or fewer beneficiaries and in certain other limited situations. The Joint Committee on Taxation also could include a statement in legislation specifying which provisions qualified as limited tax benefits, and if it did so the president would be able to examine only those provisions. If it did not, he could examine the whole bill to make a determination based on definitions in the act.

The president had to use the line-item veto within five days (excluding Sundays) of his signature on a bill or forfeit the power. He could not use it on bills he allowed to become law without his signature. If he used it, he had to send a message to Congress enumerating the items he had chosen and including other information, such as the impact on the federal budget and the specific states and congressional districts affected. The effect of sending the message was to immediately cancel the item in question.

THE PRESIDENT AS FISCAL GUARDIAN

Presidents dating back to Ulysses S. Grant (1869–1877) have advocated a line-item veto for themselves or their successors. President Clinton had long supported a line-item veto, a version of which he employed at the state level as Arkansas governor. It finally sprang to life as part of the House Republicans' Contract with America in the 104th Congress.

The intellectual concept behind the law was that Congress had demonstrated many times it could not restrain its urge to spend. In an era of huge and seemingly ever expanding and intractable deficits, Congress needed to be held in check by the president, who was—in this concept—defined as an opponent of waste and pork barrel politics. The idea of the president as a fiscal disciplinarian and opponent of increased spending was without historical foundation, but it fit especially well into the political rhetoric of the 1980s and early 1990s, when a Congress usually

The president has ten days (not counting Sundays) from the day he receives the bill to act on it. Often, Congress quickly performs the final required paperwork and ships the bill down Pennsylvania Avenue. But it is not uncommon that the bill does not make its way to the White House for approval for quite some time. For example, Congress cleared a National Institutes of Health reauthorization bill on December 9, 2006, but did not present it to the president until January 3, 2007.

In modern practice, an enrolled bill may be sent to the president even after the Congress that passed it has expired, and the president still may act on it even though a new Congress has convened. If he approves the measure he signs it, dates it, and usually writes "approved" on the document. The Constitution requires only the president's signature.

A bill may become law without the president's signature in one of two ways. If the president does not sign a bill within

controlled by liberal Democrats faced conservative Republican presidents Ronald Reagan and George H.W. Bush. Historically, many presidents of both parties—including such unquestioned conservatives as Dwight D. Eisenhower and Richard M. Nixon—backed huge spending programs.

Once the new law was passed, however, times had changed. The Republican Congress postponed the effective date until after the 1996 election to prevent President Clinton from using it during his first term. Clinton was reelected, and when the historic moment for the unveiling of the first line-item veto finally came in 1997, it was a Democratic president facing off with a Republican Congress that controlled the purse strings and had its own spending and tax reduction priorities. Instead of huge deficits, federal red ink was decreasing each year and a large and growing budget surplus was anticipated as early as fiscal 1998.

CLINTON V. CONGRESS

When President Clinton employed the new tool to cut spending he opposed, he was accused of playing politics by Republicans in Congress. Some said that the administration was using veto threats to bargain with members on unrelated issues, such as the renewal of fast-track authority for trade agreements. In other words, the dreaded fears of line-item veto opponents that the law would give a president unprecedented political leverage might prove to be true. Some earlier veto proponents switched sides and suggested repeal of the law.

In reality, the line-item veto was used sparingly in its debut. Clinton employed it eighty-two times in 1997, for an estimated savings of $1.9 billion over five years. But this was only about two-tenths of a percent of the $9 trillion the federal government was estimated to spend during that time.

In addition to the entitlement and tax provisions that Clinton had initially targeted to unveil his new power, and which became the basis for Supreme Court review in 1998, he canceled items on nine of the appropriations bills enacted in 1997. The cancellations represented a tiny amount of total spending in each bill.

In another court case, Judge Thomas F. Hogan, who was to later declare the line-item veto unconstitutional, blocked on statutory grounds Clinton's use of a line-item veto to kill a provision allowing federal employees to change pension plans. The administration agreed that the veto had been improperly cast, because the provision did not fit the definition of spending items the president could cancel, and the provision was restored as law.

In 1997, following procedures in the act, Congress passed a bill to reinstate all of the president's cancellations of $238 million for items in a military construction appropriations bill. This had been Clinton's most controversial use of the new power and was the only time he was seriously challenged within Congress. The president admitted that some cancellations he made in the bill had been in error, but he vetoed the restoration bill that would have undone all of them. Both houses easily overrode him, the Senate in 1997 and the House following the convening of the second session of the 105th Congress in 1998.

VETO DECLARED UNCONSTITUTIONAL BY COURT

Two federal district judges agreed that the law was unconstitutional in decisions in 1997 and 1998. The Supreme Court turned back the first challenge to the law, in *Byrd v. Raines*, in 1997. The Court did not rule on the line-item veto's constitutionality because it said that the members of Congress who brought the lawsuit lacked legal standing to do so. The president had not used the line-item veto yet at that point.

The second case combined *City of New York v. Clinton* and *Snake River Potato Growers Inc. v. Rubin*, which were responding to the president's use of the line-item veto, enabling the new plaintiffs to argue directly that they had been injured by its use.

On February 12, 1998, Federal District judge Hogan ruled that the line-item veto was unconstitutional. The Clinton administration immediately appealed his decision to the Supreme Court. On June 25, 1998, in a 6–3 decision, the Court upheld the lower court ruling, affirming the unconstitutionality of the veto.

The majority of the Court ruled that Congress had gone beyond the Constitution in allowing the president the power to cut out individual elements within a single spending bill. In a sense, this veto gave the president an unconstitutional role in altering legislation. Justice John Paul Stevens wrote for the majority:

> There is no provision in the Constitution that authorizes the President to enact, to amend, or to repeal statutes....
>
> If the Line-Item Veto Act were valid, it would authorize the President to create a different law—one whose text was not voted on by either House of Congress or presented to the President for signature....
>
> If there is to be a new procedure in which the president will play a different role in determining the final text of what may "become a law," such change must not come by legislation but through [constitutional] amendment.

After the decision was announced, congressional supporters of the line-item veto immediately vowed to press the search for a constitutional means of giving such power to the president. With the end of the federal deficit, the main impetus for the line-item veto, and the unhappiness of many members of Congress over President Clinton's use of the veto, most analysts felt that Congress's experiment with sharing its legislative power would not be repeated any time soon.

But the return of annual deficits during George W. Bush's presidency—and Congress's growing appetite for earmarking federal dollars—revived fervor for line-item authority. The 2006 version fell short in the Senate, where it lacked the sixty votes necessary to overcome a filibuster, and the fervor subsided again when Democrats took control of Congress the following year. The debate is sure to continue, at various levels of intensity, in the coming decades.

---

ten days (Sundays excepted) from the time he receives it, the bill becomes law provided the Congress that passed it is in session. A bill may also become law without the president's signature if Congress overrides a veto.

When the president signs some bills, especially major legislation, he may stage a signing ceremony at the White House or some other appropriate location to draw attention to the new law and to honor its congressional sponsors and other supporters. The president, in such circumstances, uses numerous pens to affix his signature to the document and passes them out to his audience.

Another variation of the method of presidential signing might be called the "yes, but . . ." approach. During the 1980s, Presidents Ronald Reagan and George H. W. Bush occasionally issued signing statements when they approved some bills, objecting to certain provisions as unconstitutional and stating that they would ignore them. President George W. Bush made more regular and expansive use of such signing statements. Pennsylvania Republican Arlen Specter, then the Senate Judiciary Committee chair, introduced a bill in 2006 that would allow the Senate or House to request that a court determine the legality of any signing statement and that would instruct courts not to consider a presidential signing statement as a source of authority. Democrats also held hearings during the 110th Congress on the use of presidential signing statements.

The idea was not new and had appeared occasionally in more radical forms. In 1842 President John Tyler sent Congress a message noting that he had signed a bill and that it had been filed with the secretary of state with "an exposition of my reasons for giving it my sanction." Tyler was promptly criticized for this action by Rep. John Quincy Adams of Massachusetts, a former president (1825–1829), who successfully moved to have a select committee examine the matter. Adams later filed a critical report from the select committee, which also submitted a resolution warning "of evil example for the future." The resolution was not, however, adopted by the House. The select committee noted in its report that it

> can find . . . no authority given to the President for depositing in the Department of State an exposition of his reason for signing an act . . . and most especially none for making the deposit in company with the law . . . unless disavowed and discountenanced. . . . [I]ts consequences may contribute to prostrate in the dust the authority of the very law which the President has approved with the accompaniment of this most extraordinary appendage, and to introduce a practice which would transfer the legislative power of Congress itself to the arbitrary will of the executive.[40]

A House committee also criticized President Andrew Jackson for an 1830 action when he had signed a bill and then written on the bill itself his views as to its meaning, views not shared by many in Congress.

The Veto Power

If the president does not want a bill to become law, he may veto it by returning it to the chamber in which it originated without his signature and with a message stating his objections. If no further action is taken, the bill dies.

The Constitution provides that Congress may attempt to enact the bill into law "the objections of the president to the contrary notwithstanding." A two-thirds vote of those present and voting in both chambers is required to override a veto. There must be a quorum present for the vote, which must be by roll call, and whether the two-thirds majority is achieved is determined only from the number of "yea" and "nay" votes. Those who vote "present" are not considered.

Despite the Constitution's provision that Congress "shall proceed to reconsider" veto messages, the language has been interpreted to give each chamber various procedural

options under its rules that do not require an immediate vote to override or sustain the veto. In the House, a vetoed bill is usually handled in one of four ways.

1. It may be called up and debated for one hour, after which a vote on an override is held.

2. It may be immediately referred back to its committee of origin by motion, with the expectation that it will remain there and no veto override vote will ever be held.

3. It may be referred back to committee to be parked for a while, awaiting a decision on scheduling a future override vote. The committee may not amend the bill but could theoretically hold further hearings on it to generate or increase public support for an override. (A motion on the floor to discharge a vetoed bill from a committee is privileged and may be made by any member each day.)

4. It may remain at the Speaker's table but with further action postponed to a later date, either by motion or unanimous consent.

The last two options may be employed either to gain additional time to assemble the needed two-thirds majority or to schedule a vote closer to the next election for maximum political visibility. A vetoed bill may not be amended in any manner, only repassed or rejected.

In the Senate, if a vetoed bill is not considered immediately on receipt, the majority leader is normally permitted to bring it up at any time. A vetoed bill may be subject to a filibuster, but this rarely occurs because if there is any realistic chance of overriding the veto the bill's supporters would almost certainly have at least the sixty votes needed to end the filibuster. If they did not, there would be little point in taking up the bill at all. Vetoed bills are normally considered subject to a time agreement arrived at by unanimous consent.

The Senate has used another procedural mechanism, the motion to reconsider (the meaning of which differs from the Constitution's use of the same word), to give itself two chances to override a veto. In 1987, following President Reagan's veto of a major highway and mass transit funding bill, the House overrode but the Senate appeared about to sustain the veto by a single vote, with all senators voting, as a previously undecided Sen. Terry Sanford, D-N.C., voted "nay." Majority Leader Robert C. Byrd changed his vote to "nay" before the result was announced—making the final vote 65–35—to vote on the prevailing side and be eligible under Senate rules to make a motion to reconsider the vote. His action kept the vetoed bill on parliamentary life support until the following day, when Sanford changed his mind, the Senate adopted Byrd's motion to reconsider the earlier vote, and then the Senate finally overrode the veto by a 67–33 vote.

This is an excellent example of occasional disparity in the practices of the two houses even on such a supposedly fixed constitutional procedure as a veto override. House precedents would have barred a motion to reconsider the result of a veto override vote. Under Senate precedents, had the veto initially been overridden, no motion to reconsider would have been permitted as the bill would have effectively left the chamber and become law.

If the first house to act fails to override the veto, the bill is dead and the matter ends there. If the vote to override succeeds, the measure is sent to the second house. If the veto is overridden there, the bill becomes law without the president's signature; otherwise, the veto stands and the bill is dead. The attempt to override can occur at any time during the Congress that passed the legislation. For example, a vote in the House on overriding President Reagan's veto of a textile bill was delayed from December 1985 to August 1986, when the veto was finally sustained.

The Pocket Veto

The Constitution also provides that a bill shall not become law if "Congress by their adjournment prevent its return." The president can then pocket veto the bill because he does not have an opportunity to return it to Congress for further consideration. Unlike the veto specifically provided for in the Constitution, which is sometimes called a return veto because it is returned to Congress without the president's signature and with a statement of his objections, a pocket veto is accomplished wholly by inaction. However, it has become a common practice in recent years for the president, at his discretion, to issue a statement called a memorandum of disapproval with such pocket vetoes explaining the reason for his refusal to sign, and Congress has published these in the *Congressional Record.*

The president clearly may pocket veto any bills that are still awaiting his approval when Congress adjourns *sine die.* The Supreme Court ruled in the 1929 *Pocket Veto* case that the president may pocket veto a bill when Congress has adjourned its first session *sine die* fewer than ten days after

presenting it to him or her for its approval. But whether it is proper for the president to pocket veto bills during congressional recesses of more than three days or between sessions of the same Congress when the two houses have made arrangements to receive presidential messages is still unsettled in the law.

Federal courts have ruled such pocket vetoes to be unconstitutional, but the Supreme Court has not made a definitive ruling on the issue. President Gerald Ford, after losing a case in a federal appeals court, entered into a consent decree agreeing to use the return veto during intersession and intrasession adjournments when each house had provided for the receipt of such messages. The Supreme Court in 1987 threw out a federal appellate court ruling against an intersession Reagan pocket veto as moot (*Burke v. Barnes*), without reaching the merits of the issue. President George H. W. Bush raised these issues again in two of his fifteen pocket vetoes during his term. Sometimes Congress has refused to recognize a purported pocket veto and has treated it as a return veto and conducted a vote to override it, leading to further confusion. In the second session of the 93rd Congress (1974), for example, President Ford returned a bill to Congress without his signature while asserting that he had pocket vetoed it during an adjournment of the House to a day certain. However, each house treated it as a return veto and then proceeded to override. The bill was sent to the National Archives to receive a public law number. The administrator of general services, on advice from the Justice Department, refused to promulgate the bill as law. Without acquiescing in this interpretation, both houses then passed an identical bill that the president signed.

The House has authorized its clerk, and the Senate its secretary, to receive veto messages when either body is in recess when a veto message arrives. Both houses have asserted that this procedure allows them to properly receive the vetoes while awaiting the reconvening of the receiving chamber for formal action. But presidents have not accepted this mechanism as a means of restricting their broad claims of authority to issue pocket vetoes.

★

NOTES

1 Walter J. Oleszek, *Congressional Procedures and the Policy Process,* 7th ed. (Washington, D.C.: CQ Press, 2007), 19.

2 *National Review,* February 27, 1987, 24.

3 Janet Hook, "Speaker Jim Wright Takes Charge in the House," *Congressional Quarterly Weekly Report,* July 11, 1987, 1486.

4 Lee Hamilton, "We Need to Embrace Compromise, Not Insult It," The Center on Congress at Indiana University, May 10, 2011. congress.indiana.edu/we-need-embrace-compromise-not-insult-it.

5 *Congressional Quarterly Almanac, 1986,* vol. 42 (Washington, D.C.: Congressional Quarterly, 1987), 33.

6 Chris Cillizza, "Evan Bayh Won't Seek Re-election, Senate Majority in Play?" *Washington Post,* February 15, 2010, voices.washingtonpost.com/thefix/senate/evan-bayh-to-retire.html.

7 Bennett Roth, "House Adopts Package of Rule Changes," *CQ Weekly,* January 12, 2009, 75–76. library.cqpress.com/cqweekly/weeklyreport111-000003006904.

8 *Washington Post,* June 26, 1983, A14.

9 Walter J. Oleszek, *Congressional Procedures and the Policy Process,* 6th ed. (Washington, D.C.: CQ Press, 2004).

10 Quoted in *Congress A to Z,* 4th ed. (Washington, D.C.: CQ Press, 2003), 215.

11 Oleszek, *Congressional Procedures,* 7th ed., 80.

12 Robert A. Katzmann, *Congress and Courts* (Washington, D.C.: Brookings Institution, 1997), 64–65.

13 Richard S. Beth, *The Discharge Rule in the House: Recent Use in Historical Context* (Washington, D.C.: Library of Congress, Congressional Research Service, 2003); Richard S. Beth, *The Discharge Rule in the House of Representatives: Procedure, History, and Statistics* (Washington, D.C.: Library of Congress, Congressional Research Service, 1990); Richard S. Beth, *The Discharge Rule in the House: Recent Use in Historical Context* (Washington, D.C.: Library of Congress, Congressional Research Service, 1997); and Richard S. Beth, *The Discharge Rule in the House: Principal Uses and Features* (Washington, D.C.: Library of Congress, Congressional Research Service, 1999).

14 House Minority Leader Eric Cantor, R-Va., in a letter to colleagues. December 8, 2010. majorityleader.gov/Calendar/EC_LETTER.pdf.

15 Bruce I. Oppenheimer, "The Changing Relationship between House Leadership and the Committee on Rules." In *Understanding Congressional Leadership,* ed. Frank H. Mackaman (Washington, D.C.: CQ Press, 1981), 217.

16 Walter J. Oleszek, *Congressional Procedures and the Policy Process,* 3rd ed. (Washington, D.C.: CQ Press, 1987), 127.

17 Stanley Bach and Steven S. Smith, *Managing Uncertainty in the House of Representatives: Adaptation and Innovation in Special Rules* (Washington, D.C.: Brookings Institution, 1988), 28.

18 Stephen Gettinger, "Return of the Floor Vote," *CQ Weekly,* May 2, 2011, 961–962. library.cqpress.com/cqweekly/weeklyreport112-000003860135.

19 Janet Hook, "GOP Chafes under Restrictive House Rules," *Congressional Quarterly Weekly Report,* October 10, 1987, 2452.

20 Walter J. Oleszek, *Congressional Procedures and the Policy Process,* 4th ed. (Washington, D.C.: CQ Press, 1996), 149.

21 Greg Vadala and David Clarke, "Record Increase in Debt Limit Clears," *CQ Weekly,* February 8, 2010, 334. library.cqpress.com/cqweekly/weeklyreport111-000003291636.

22 Ibid., 169.

23 Thomas E. Mann and Norman J. Ornstein, *Renewing Congress: A First Report* (Washington, D.C.: Brookings Institution and American Enterprise Institute, 1992), 49.

24 Steven S. Smith, *Call to Order: Floor Politics in the House and Senate* (Washington, D.C.: Brookings Institution, 1989), 243.

25 Jacqueline Calmes, "Byrd Struggles to Lead Deeply Divided Senate," *Congressional Quarterly Weekly Report,* July 4, 1987, 1422.

26 Oleszek, *Congressional Procedures,* 7th ed., 207.

27 Smith, *Call to Order,* 128.

28 Brian Friel and Niels Lesniewski, "Senate Limits 'Holds,' Keeps Filibuster," *CQ Weekly,* January 31, 2011, 260. library.cqpress.com/cqweekly/weeklyreport112-000003802944.

29 Nancy Landon Kassebaum, "The Senate Is Not in Order," *Washington Post,* January 27, 1988, A19.

30 Oleszek, *Congressional Procedures,* 4th ed., 231.

31 Jacqueline Calmes, "'Trivialized' Filibuster Is Still a Potent Tool," *Congressional Quarterly Weekly Report,* September 5, 1987, 2120.

32 Ibid.

33 Smith, *Call to Order,* 97.

34 Ibid., 96.

35 Thomas E. Mann and Norman J. Ornstein, *The Broken Branch: How Congress Is Failing America and How to Get It Back on Track* (New York: Oxford University Press, 2006), 166.

36 Friel and Lesniewski, "Senate Limits 'Holds,'" 260.

37 Edward Epstein, "Dusting Off Deliberation," *CQ Weekly,* June 14, 2010, 1436–1442. library.cqpress.com/cqweekly/weeklyreport111-000003681823.

38 Barbara Sinclair, *Unorthodox Lawmaking: New Legislative Processes in the U.S. Congress* (Washington, D.C.: CQ Press, 1997), 202.

39 U.S. Congress. *Congressional Record,* 109th Cong., 1st sess., Vol. 151, December 22, 2005, H13181.

40 Asher C. Hinds, ed., *Hinds' Precedents of the House of Representatives.* Vol. 4 (Washington, D.C.: Government Printing Office, 1907), sec. 3492, 336–338. The Tyler quote appears on p. 336, the Adams quote on p. 338, and the select committee's quote on p. 337.

SELECTED BIBLIOGRAPHY

Adler, E. Scott, and John S. Lapinski, eds. *The Macropolitics of Congress.* Princeton, N.J.: Princeton University Press, 2006.

Bach, Stanley. *The Amending Process in Congress.* New York: Novinka Books, 2003.

Bach, Stanley, and Steven S. Smith. *Managing Uncertainty in the House of Representatives: Adaptation and Innovation in Special Rules.* Washington, D.C.: Brookings Institution, 1988.

Becker, Lawrence. *Doing the Right Thing: Collective Action and Procedural Choice in the New Legislative Process.* Columbus: Ohio State University Press, 2005.

Berman, Daniel M. *A Bill Becomes a Law: Congress Enacts Civil Rights Legislation.* 2nd ed. New York: Macmillan, 1966.

Bessette, Joseph M. *The Mild Voice of Reason: Deliberative Democracy and American National Government.* 2nd ed. Chicago: University of Chicago Press, 1997.

Bianco, William T., ed. *Congress on Display, Congress at Work.* Ann Arbor: University of Michigan Press, 2000.

Binder, Sarah A. *Stalemate: Causes and Consequences of Legislative Gridlock.* Washington, D.C.: Brookings Institution, 2003.

Birnbaum, Jeffrey H., and Alan S. Murray. *Showdown at Gucci Gulch: Lawmakers, Lobbyists, and the Unlikely Triumph of Tax Reform.* New York: Random House, 1987.

Black, Amy E. *From Inspiration to Legislation: How an Idea Becomes a Bill.* Upper Saddle River, N.J.: Pearson Prentice Hall, 2007.

Brady, David W. *Critical Elections and Congressional Policy-Making.* Stanford, Calif.: Stanford University Press, 1988.

Brady, David W., and Mathew D. McCubbins, eds. *Party, Process, and Political Change in Congress: New Perspectives on the History of Congress.* Stanford, Calif.: Stanford University Press, 2002.

———. *Party, Process, and Political Change in Congress. Further New Perspectives on the History of Congress.* Vol. 2. Stanford, Calif.: Stanford University Press, 2007.

Brown, William H., and Michael E. O'Hanlon. *House Practice: A Guide to the Rules, Precedents, and Procedures of the House.* Washington, D.C.: Government Printing Office, 2003.

Byrd, Robert C. *The Senate, 1789–1989.* Vol. 2. Washington, D.C.: Government Printing Office, 1991.

Cannon, Clarence, ed. *Cannon's Precedents of the House of Representatives.* 6 vols. Washington, D.C.: Government Printing Office, 1936.

Connelly, William F., Jr., and John J. Pitney Jr. *Congress' Permanent Minority.* Lanham, Md.: Rowman and Littlefield, 1994.

Cooper, Joseph, and G. Calvin Mackenzie. *The House at Work.* Austin: University of Texas Press, 1981.

Cox, Gary W., and Mathew D. McCubbins. *Setting the Agenda: Responsible Party Government in the U.S. House of Representatives.* Cambridge, U.K.: Cambridge University Press, 2005.

Davidson, Roger H., and Walter J. Oleszek. *Congress and Its Members.* 13th ed. Washington, D.C.: CQ Press, 2012.

Davies, Jack. *Legislative Law and Process in a Nutshell.* 3rd ed. St. Paul, Minn.: Thomson/West, 2007.

Deering, Christopher J., and Steven S. Smith. *Committees in Congress.* 3rd ed. Washington, D.C.: CQ Press, 1997.

Deschler, Lewis. *Precedents of the House of Representatives.* Washington, D.C.: Government Printing Office, 1977.

Deschler, Lewis, and William H. Brown. *Procedure in the House of Representatives.* Washington, D.C.: Government Printing Office, 1982; 1987 supplement.

Dodd, Lawrence C., and Bruce I. Oppenheimer, eds. *Congress Reconsidered.* 9th ed. Washington, D.C.: CQ Press, 2009.

Eidenberg, Eugene, and Roy D. Morey. *An Act of Congress: The Legislative Process and the Making of Education Policy.* New York: Norton, 1969.

Evans, C. Lawrence, and Walter J. Oleszek. *Congress under Fire: Reform Politics and the Republican Majority.* Boston: Houghton Mifflin, 1997.

Evans, Diana. *Greasing the Wheels: Using Pork Barrel Projects to Build Majority Coalitions in Congress.* Cambridge, U.K.: Cambridge University Press, 2004.

Fenno, Richard. *Congressmen in Committees.* Boston: Little, Brown, 1973.

Finocchiaro, Charles J. *Procedural Efficiency, Leadership Centralization, or Both? Unconventional Patterns of Bill Referral in the Republican Congress.* East Lansing: Michigan State University, 2000.

Fiorina, Morris P. *Divided Government.* 2nd ed. New York: Allyn and Bacon, 1996.

Fox, Harrison W., Jr., and Susan W. Hammond. *Congressional Staffs: The Invisible Force in American Lawmaking.* New York: Free Press, 1977.

Froman, Lewis A., Jr. *The Congressional Process: Strategies, Rules, and Procedures.* Boston: Little, Brown, 1967.

Galloway, George B. *The Legislative Process in Congress.* New York: Crowell, 1953.

Gold, Martin. *Senate Procedure and Practice.* 2nd ed. Lanham, Md.: Rowman and Littlefield, 2008.

Harrison, Robert. *Congress, Progressive Reform, and the New American State.* New York: Cambridge University Press, 2004.

Hinckley, Barbara. *Less Than Meets the Eye: Foreign Policymaking and the Myth of the Assertive Congress.* Chicago: University of Chicago Press, 1994.

Hinds, Asher C., ed. *Hinds' Precedents of the House of Representatives.* 11 vols. Washington, D.C.: Government Printing Office, 1907–1941.

Irwin, Lewis G. *A Chill in the House: Actor Perspectives on Change and Continuity in the Pursuit of Legislative Success.* Albany: State University of New York Press, 2002.

Jewell, Malcolm E., and Samuel C. Patterson. *The Legislative Process in the United States.* 4th ed. New York: McGraw-Hill, 1986.

Johnson, Charles W. *Constitution, Jefferson's Manual, and Rules of the House of Representatives of the United States, One Hundred Eighth Congress.* Washington, D.C.: Government Printing Office, 2003.

———. *How Our Laws Are Made.* Rev. ed. Washington, D.C.: Government Printing Office, 2003.

Katzmann, Robert A. *Courts and Congress.* Washington, D.C.: Brookings Institution, 1997.

Keefe, William J., and Morris S. Ogul. *The American Legislative Process: Congress and the States.* 10th ed. Upper Saddle River, N.J.: Prentice Hall, 2001.

King, David C. *Turf Wars: How Congressional Committees Claim Jurisdiction.* Chicago: University of Chicago Press, 1997.

Kingdon, John W. *Congressmen's Voting Decisions.* 3rd ed. Ann Arbor: University of Michigan Press, 1989.

Kornacki, John J., ed. *Leading Congress: New Styles, New Strategies.* Washington, D.C.: CQ Press, 1990.

Krehbiel, Keith. *Information and Legislative Organization.* Ann Arbor: University of Michigan Press, 1991.

———. *Pivotal Politics: A Theory of U.S. Lawmaking.* Chicago: University of Chicago Press, 1998.

Krutz, Glen S. *Hitching a Ride: Omnibus Legislating in the U.S. Congress.* Columbus: Ohio State University Press, 2001.

Luce, Robert. *Legislative Procedure: Parliamentary Practices and the Course of Business in the Framing of Statutes.* Boston: Houghton Mifflin, 1922. Reprint. New York: Da Capo Press, 1972.

Lynch, Megan Suzanne. *Queen-of-the-Hill Rules in the House of Representatives.* Report No. RS20313. Washington, D.C.: Library of Congress, Congressional Research Service, 2008.

Maass, Arthur. *Congress and the Common Good.* New York: Basic Books, 1983.

Malbin, Michael J. *Unelected Representatives: Congressional Staff and the Future of Representative Government.* New York: Basic Books, 1980.

Mann, Thomas E., and Norman J. Ornstein, eds. *The New Congress.* Washington, D.C.: American Enterprise Institute, 1981.

———. *Renewing Congress: A First Report.* Washington, D.C.: Brookings Institution and American Enterprise Institute, 1992.

———. *Renewing Congress: A Second Report.* Washington, D.C.: Brookings Institution and American Enterprise Institute, 1993.

Mucciaroni, Gary, and Paul J. Quirk. *Deliberative Choices: Debating Public Policy in Congress.* Chicago: University of Chicago Press, 2006.

Nickels, Ilona B., and Thomas P. Carr. *Congressional Parliamentary Reference Sources: An Introductory Guide.* New York: Nova Science, 2004.

Oleszek, Walter J. *Congressional Procedures and the Policy Process.* 8th ed. Washington, D.C.: CQ Press, 2011.

Ornstein, Norman J., ed. *Congress in Change: Evolution and Reform.* New York: Praeger, 1975.

Panagopoulos, Costas, and Joshua Schank. *All Roads Lead to Congress: The $300 Billion Fight over Highway Funding.* Washington, D.C.: CQ Press, 2008.

Parker, Glenn R., ed. *Studies of Congress.* Washington, D.C.: CQ Press, 1985.

Parker, Glenn R., and Suzanne L. Parker. *Factions in House Committees.* Knoxville: University of Tennessee Press, 1985.

Peabody, Robert L., et al. *To Enact a Law: Congress and Campaign Financing.* New York: Praeger, 1972.

Pickerill, J. Mitchell. *Constitutional Deliberation in Congress: The Impact of Judicial Review in a Separated System.* Durham, N.C.: Duke University Press, 2004.

Price, David. *Who Makes the Laws?* Cambridge, Mass.: Schenkman, 1972.

Redman, Eric. *The Dance of Legislation.* New York: Simon and Schuster, 1973. Reprint. Seattle: University of Washington Press, 2001.

Reid, T. R. *Congressional Odyssey: The Saga of a Senate Bill.* New York: Freeman, 1980.

Riddick, Floyd M. *Riddick's Senate Procedure: Precedents and Practices.* Rev. ed. Edited by Alan S. Frumin. Washington, D.C.: Government Printing Office, 1992.

Rieselbach, Leroy N. *Congressional Reform.* Washington, D.C.: CQ Press, 1986.

Ripley, Randall B. *Congress: Process and Policy.* 4th ed. New York: Norton, 1988.

Setting Course: A Congressional Management Guide. 11th ed. Washington, D.C.: Congressional Management Foundation, 2008.

Sheppard, Burton D. *Rethinking Congressional Reform: The Reform Roots of the Special Interest Congress.* Cambridge, Mass.: Schenkman, 1985.

Siff, Ted, and Alan Weil. *Ruling Congress: How House and Senate Rules Govern the Legislative Process.* New York: Grossman, 1975.

Sinclair, Barbara. *Unorthodox Lawmaking: New Legislative Processes in the U.S. Congress.* 4th ed. Washington, D.C.: CQ Press, 2012.

Smith, Steven S. *Call to Order: Floor Politics in the House and Senate.* Washington, D.C.: Brookings Institution, 1989.

Smith, Steven S., Jason M. Roberts, and Ryan J. Vander Wielen. *The American Congress.* 7th ed. New York: Cambridge University Press, 2011.

Stein, Robert M., and Kenneth N. Bickers. *Perpetuating the Pork Barrel: Policy Subsystems and American Democracy.* New York: Cambridge University Press, 1995.

Strom, Gerald S. *The Logic of Lawmaking: A Spatial Theory Approach.* Baltimore: Johns Hopkins University Press, 1990.

Sulkin, Tracy. *Issue Politics in Congress.* Cambridge, U.K.: Cambridge University Press, 2005.

———. *The Legislative Legacy of Congressional Campaigns.* Cambridge, U.K.: Cambridge University Press, 2011.

Sullivan, Terry O. *Procedural Structure: A Success and Influence in Congress.* New York: Praeger, 1984.

Thurber, James A., and Colton C. Campbell, eds. *Congress and the Internet.* Upper Saddle River, N.J.: Prentice Hall, 2003.

Tiefer, Charles. *Congressional Practice and Procedure: A Reference, Research, and Legislative Guide.* Westport, Conn.: Greenwood Press, 1989.

Uslaner, Eric M. *The Movers and the Shirkers: Representatives and Ideologues in the Senate.* Ann Arbor: University of Michigan Press, 1999.

Vital Statistics on Congress. Washington, D.C.: American Enterprise Institute for Public Policy Research/Brookings Institution Press, 1980.

Vogler, David J. *The Third House: Conference Committees in the United States Congress.* Evanston, Ill.: Northwestern University Press, 1971.

Wawro, Gregory J., and Eric Schickler. *Filibuster: Obstruction and Lawmaking in the U.S. Senate.* Princeton, N.J.: Princeton University Press, 2006.

Whalen, Charles, and Barbara Whalen. *The Longest Debate: A Legislative History of the 1964 Civil Rights Act.* Washington, D.C.: Seven Locks Press, 1985.

Wise, Charles R. *The Dynamics of Legislation: Leadership and Policy Change in the Congressional Process.* San Francisco: Jossey-Bass, 1991.

chapter 3

The Committee System

"Congress in session is Congress on public exhibition, whilst Congress in its committee-rooms is Congress at work," then-Professor Woodrow Wilson famously wrote in 1885.[1] Since then, the committee system in Congress has been under assault so frequently, and for so long, that it is important to remember that committees still matter.

- Along with parties and leaders, committees are a central structural feature of Congress.

- The vast majority of members find committees essential to their House and Senate careers.

- Both tradition and rule make it difficult to consider legislation that has not been vetted in committee.

Thus committees endure despite efforts to weaken their chairs, rotate chairs out of office, and transfer committee powers to political party bodies or ad hoc entities. And as we head toward the 2020s, the committee system looks remarkably like that of the early 1920s. Although scholars and participants alike still see many deficiencies in the system, members clearly believe that it works and that experimentation with other means of processing legislation should be attempted only incrementally and with careful monitoring.

Committees are the infrastructure of Congress. The bulk of legislative work is done there—they are the institutional location where expertise resides, where policies incubate, where most legislative proposals are written or refined, where many necessary compromises are made, where the public can make its views known, and where members of Congress build influence and reputations.

Committees have enormous power, especially in the House of Representatives. They hold hearings, conduct investigations, and oversee government programs. They initiate bills, approve and report legislation to the floor, control most of the time for debate on the floor, have preference in offering amendments, and take the lead in representing their chamber in conferences with the other house. Committee inaction on a bill generally spells defeat. In the Senate, where individual senators' prerogatives may hold sway over collective interests and where the ability to offer amendments is practically unlimited, committees can be bypassed more easily and do not perform the same gatekeeper role in determining access to the floor. Still, the ability of committees to influence the ultimate disposition of an issue remains substantial.

It is difficult—at times virtually impossible—to circumvent a committee determined not to act. A bill that is approved by a committee may be amended when it reaches the House or Senate floor, but extensive revisions generally are more difficult to achieve at that stage. The actions of the committees, or their failure to act, more often than not give Congress its record of legislative achievement or failure. As congressional expert Walter J. Oleszek has observed, the rules and precedents of both chambers reinforce committee prerogative: "[C]ommittee members and their staffs have more expertise on matters within their jurisdiction than members of Congress as a whole, the fundamental outlines of committee decisions generally will be accepted."[2]

COMMITTEES IN TRANSITION

As the twenty-first century begins to unfold, it is readily apparent that committees lack the clout they once had. They are no longer the "little legislatures" of political science literature that once dominated the presentation of legislation to Congress and set the agenda, from floor action through presidential action. Committees are affected by the same factors that transformed the broader operations of Congress and the relationships between politicians and the American public. Changes in membership, shifts in power in relation to the leadership, the evolution of new rules and procedures, demands of partisan political agendas, extensive media coverage, legions of lobbyists, and the availability of new sources of information and technology all have served to alter the balance of power within Congress. Sometimes these changes have pulled the institution in opposite directions over relatively short periods of time.

HOUSE GOP CONFERENCE, DEMOCRATIC CAUCUS CONTROL POWER STRUCTURE

The organizations of the House's two political parties—the Republican Conference and Democratic Caucus—exercise complete control of committee assignments, committee chairs, and ranking minority member positions. Committee assignments and seniority rankings are ratified by the House through the adoption of privileged resolutions offered by direction of the parties and may be altered at any time.

The longtime Democratic majority from 1955 to 1995 created an increasingly complex system to resolve competing claims for committee chairs and assignments while giving members hope that they would be considered fairly for important posts at some time in their careers. Party leadership exercised considerable influence over the process but sometimes could be effectively pushed or challenged by the general membership, depending on the salience of the issue involved. Many of the major committee-related reforms of the 1970s, for example, along with the principal efforts to unseat conservative committee chairs, were driven by less senior, more liberal members, usually over leadership opposition or passive acquiescence.

The Republican minority, without real power, quarreled with the Democrats over committee ratios, sued them unsuccessfully in court, offered reform proposals on the House floor at the organization of each new Congress, and developed a critique of Democratic control that gradually became the "forty years of corruption" theme used successfully in the 1994 elections.

During the reform period of the 1970s, the Democratic Caucus had threatened to intrude on committee independence and to direct action on legislative matters by instructing committee members, but this quickly sparked a counterreaction and these caucus initiatives did not last long. Changes in committee chairs and memberships accomplished the objective of ensuring greater responsiveness to the caucus using more traditional means.

The activist tradition reemerged briefly in 1993 with a demand by junior members to discipline subcommittee chairs who had voted against President Bill Clinton's budget reconciliation legislation, which had passed by only two votes over unified Republican opposition. But the effort faded rapidly after liberals had vented their anger.

The Republican Conference, once in the majority in 1995, immediately assumed an aggressive posture. The conference, new to power, had little tradition of deferring to committees that it had not controlled for forty years. The GOP conference had an activist agenda coming out of the 1994 election campaign and wanted action as quickly as possible.

Far more than the Democrat leadership, the Republican leadership, led by Speaker Newt Gingrich, R-Ga., who was credited with masterminding the campaign for majority status, was deferred to by rank-and-file party members with little political experience. The Speaker intervened freely in the legislative process, sometimes reaching down to the level of dictating subcommittee chairs and subcommittee agendas. He exercised far greater influence over the committee system than Democratic leaders could have ever dreamed of doing. Demands were even made for individual dissenters to explain to the conference their votes against the party's positions on the floor. For example, a handful of rebellious members who voted against, and helped defeat, the rule for consideration of the 105th Congress's committee funding resolution in 1997 were called upon to explain themselves. Later in the year senior members of the GOP leadership were forced to explain their knowledge of and roles in a celebrated and unsuccessful effort to replace Gingrich as Speaker.

As the House majority changed hands following the 2006 and 2010 elections, party leaders have retained greater control over committee assignments than they had during the earlier long Democratic majorities.

COMMITTEE ASSIGNMENTS

The two parties developed rules dividing the various committees into different classifications, to ensure a fair distribution of desirable committee assignments and mechanisms to distribute committee and subcommittee chair and ranking minority member posts. Both parties consider the Appropriations, Energy and Commerce, Financial Services, Rules, and Ways and Means committees as exclusive, meaning that no member of one of them may serve on any other committee. There also are various grandfather clauses and waivers allowing certain members to escape these restrictions. In addition, members of exclusive committees are allowed to serve on committees on House Administration, Standards of Official Conduct, and the Budget, which is required by House rules to have some members from Appropriations and Ways and Means.

Members who are not awarded exclusive posts—just over half the House given current committee sizes (214 total slots)—usually serve on two standing legislative committees. Exceptions are sometimes made when the majority party needs members on less desirable panels to ensure its numerical control. The Democrats grappled for years with the problem of temporary members serving on committees, principally to fill vacancies that other members did not want and to provide proxy votes to the committee chair. Temporary assignments were often denounced by reformers, but in the absence of any rules governing committee sizes, the caucus realized it could not dispense with the practice entirely. The Democratic leadership sometimes encouraged it by promising politically vulnerable members additional assignments.

The Republicans in 1995 passed new rules in the House itself purporting to regulate and rationalize the number of committee and subcommittee assignments, restricting members to two standing committees and four subcommittees. But they

During the 1970s, reforms initiated by a new generation of younger, activist Democrats came to fruition with the election of the large 1974 class of "Watergate babies," as they were known after their election in the wake of the political scandal that drove President Richard M. Nixon from office. Their numbers, seventy-five newly elected Democrats, provided the votes to complete an institutional revolution that overthrew several committee chairs and weakened others, dispersed power to subcommittees, strengthened the leadership, increased accountability to the House Democratic Caucus, and fostered the growth of staff on both sides of the Capitol. Power was diffused and rival power centers emerged. Many lawmakers no longer deferred to committees on the details of legislation. Floor challenges to committees became more

soon found themselves in the same bind as the Democrats, further complicated by the fact that the new majority had deprived itself of the convenience of proxy voting. (*See box, Proxy Voting, p. 152.*) Exceptions to the rules again quickly followed. This problem was exacerbated in the 110th and 111th Congresses as Democrats expanded committee sizes somewhat. But the new Republican majority pared them back a bit in the 112th.

ROLE OF MAJORITY AND MINORITY RULES

The voluminous House Democratic Caucus rules illustrated the importance of process for regulating the many ways in which power was dispersed. Because committee and subcommittee chairs, assignments, and seniority represented raw power and could make or break members' careers, the application of the rules assumed tremendous importance. The existence of increasingly complex rules became essential to maintain a balance between different factions, to let members feel they were being treated fairly, and to settle contests for important posts with highly structured competition. They provided checks and balances among the leadership, the committees, and the general caucus membership.

Committee chairs held great power, but mechanisms existed that could remove them and allow others to run against them directly in the caucus. The Steering Committee dominated by the Democratic leadership could almost always get its way in selecting members of the most important committees, but other candidates could run from the floor. Members could bid by order of seniority for subcommittee chairs on their committees, but challengers could announce opposition, run elaborate campaigns to reject the senior members on secret ballots, and then, if successful, claim the posts themselves.

The caucus rules reflected decades of adjustments and accommodations made for different reasons at different times. Eventually, they became so filled with multiple classifications of committees and with service and chair limitations, all further layered with exceptions geared to specific individuals, that the system became increasingly difficult to comprehend and administer. Issues such as the proper size of committees and their jurisdictional workloads, which might have been used to distinguish between major as opposed to non-major committees, were often ignored and took a back seat to the political needs of members or the leadership's desire to grant special favors.

After Democrats became a minority in 1995 and lost their power to control committee ratios and a legislative agenda, the need for such a complex rules structure diminished. Members had less interest in their share of a minority with little power, which opened the way for a further enhanced leadership role in the committee assignment process and even returned some power to the former

committee chairs, now the ranking minority members. The new decisions that had to be made reflected ways to limit the pain of minority status, instead of to distribute additional rewards, so members were more willing to leave such decisions to the leadership's discretion.

The most important rules change by the new Democratic minority weakened the "subcommittee bill of rights" created during the reform period of the mid-1970s that had allowed each subcommittee chair the right to hire one staffer. The Republican majority in 1995 dramatically cut back the number of committee staff, claiming that it was making a one-third cut. That change, along with minority status, so decimated available Democratic staff positions that it made less sense to guarantee staff to ranking subcommittee members and created an argument for recentralization so that the core committee staff had enough resources to function. A new rule allowed each committee's Democratic caucus to decide the staff allocations, and some chose to return control over them all to the ranking minority member.

The Republican Conference rules remained far simpler because in the minority complex rules had not been needed. When majority status did come, the leadership found itself with fewer constraints. Republicans had never undergone the relentless push for democratization reflected in Democratic rules fights over more than two decades. Republican Conference rules gave the Steering Committee the right to nominate candidates for committee chairs, without regard to seniority, until a nominee was approved. They also gave committee chairs the right to take the initiative in selecting subcommittee chairs and members, subject to modification by the full committee caucus, which allowed the chairs greater influence over assignments.

The first years of the House Republican majority starting in 1995 emphasized party discipline and the need to enact the party's political and legislative agenda. Strict adherence to party rules, seniority, and accommodations with individuals were of secondary importance and were dispensed with when they interfered with the primary objectives. With Gingrich's departure and the ascendance of J. Dennis Hastert, R-Ill., as Speaker, the reins were loosened somewhat. But continued party polarization meant that both leadership teams would retain power even after the Democrats returned to majority status in 2007.

Two additional rounds of party change have resulted in relatively minor changes. Upon regaining power in 2007, Democrats elevated their most senior committee members to chair House committees—though new Speaker Nancy Pelosi of California did choose a less senior colleague, Silvestre Reyes, D-Texas, to chair the Intelligence Committee. Two years later the Democrats repealed the House rule limiting chairs to six years of service. But the Republicans promptly restored the rule in 2011.

common once members had gained the expertise and staff needed to make independent judgments.

Unchallenged in previous Congresses, committee leaders became accountable for their actions and could be ousted by a secret-ballot vote of their party. This happened to Democratic committee chairs six times in the House between 1975 and 1990, though never in the Senate. (Nearly two

decades later, in 2008, Rep. Henry Waxman, D-Calif., bested Rep. John Dingell, D-Mich., in a contest to lead the Energy and Commerce Committee.) House reformers struggled repeatedly over a period of more than twenty years to find better ways to control, restrict, discipline, or challenge chairs and to remind them that they were always under scrutiny. No ideal formula ever emerged, and committees and their leaders remained imperfect vehicles for fulfilling the aspirations of their fellow politicians. Some prominent leaders, such as former Ways and Means Committee chair Dan Rostenkowski, D-Ill., maintained an often tense relationship with substantial segments of their party membership.

Committees routinely shared their once exclusive domains with other committees, particularly in the House, through the use of bill referrals to more than one committee. Committees had to comply with timetables for action set by the House Speaker. The traditional authorizing committees found their power diluted, if not eclipsed, by the Appropriations and Budget committees as Congress had less time for floor action on committee initiatives. Summits, task forces, and other ad hoc groups were convened on occasion to handle controversial issues as traditional channels worked less well. Massive pieces of omnibus legislation often were used to conduct the most important business and on occasion were the only way to get work done. Congressional leaders frequently failed to orchestrate a changing legislative process that sometimes seemed out of control.

As the decade of the 1970s closed, the committee structure was still firmly entrenched in Congress, but much of the power and prestige that had been held by the full committees had devolved to the subcommittees and to a new, larger corps of chairs, especially in the House. Subcommittees took on the institutional characteristics and vested interests of their parent committees. People began to talk about "subcommittee government" instead of "committee government" on Capitol Hill.

This empowerment of subcommittees furthered the decentralization of power and heavier legislative workloads for members of both houses. Critics noted a slowing down of the legislative process. "On balance, Congress has become more decentralized, more responsive to a multitude of forces inside and outside its halls, and, as a result, more hard pressed to formulate and enact coherent, responsible public policies," wrote Leroy N. Rieselbach.[3] So great was the proliferation of subcommittees that limits on their number were set in both chambers. Other changes and accommodations were made as well.

By the early 1990s, before a recentralization of power in the House undermined their autonomy, subcommittees were widely blamed for the inability of Congress to act coherently on major issues. Other factors—the increasing political independence of members from their parties, weak congressional leadership, multiple jurisdictional requirements, and increased partisanship in both houses—also created unpredictable obstacles in the traditional paths to legislative achievement.

The mix of historic precedents and contemporary reforms placed committees in a state of flux. "[L]ike other institutional features, congressional committees are dynamic rather than static. Indeed, in a variety of small ways committees change almost constantly," political scientists Christopher J. Deering and Steven S. Smith observed.[4] On the one hand, committees were still the central players in the legislative process. On the other hand, committees were much less autonomous than they were just a few decades earlier.

When Republicans gained control of both chambers of Congress after the 1994 elections, for the first time in four decades, many of the common patterns of congressional organization were disrupted. The new majority had a well-defined political and legislative agenda but inherited traditional legislative institutions to enact it. Speaker Newt Gingrich, R-Ga., made and unmade committee leaders at will, even influencing subcommittee chair selections. The role of committees and subcommittees, relationships between committees and the leadership, and seniority all became subordinate to the need to build a record that would allow continued GOP control of Congress. Committees and their procedures had little claim to legitimacy based merely on past history. New rules placed six-year term limits on chairs, returned the hiring of subcommittee staff to the full committee, limited each committee (save Appropriations) to five subcommittees, eliminated proxy voting, and enhanced the influence of party leaders in the chair selection process.

After the Republican takeover, House committees initially were eclipsed by the leadership using the Republican Conference, the organization of all House GOP members, and ad hoc task forces as vehicles to adopt within one hundred days a conservative policy agenda known as the Contract with America that Republican candidates had touted during the 1994 elections. Given this aggressive schedule, when committees did consider contract legislation early in 1995, their actions were often pro forma, while the Democratic minority's ability to offer amendments and debate the proposals in committee were sometimes curtailed to an unusual degree. "I am a transmission belt for the leadership," said Judiciary Committee chair Henry J. Hyde, R-Ill. "Either I don't live up to the Contract, or I move faster than both I and the Democrats want."[5] There also was no doubt that the party leadership would go around committees to attain important political goals. Thus the extremes of subcommittee government and party government have emerged in the recent past. Most recently, however, they have been closer to the latter but at neither extreme.

In the 105th Congress, starting in 1997—following a series of legislative defeats at the hands of President Bill Clinton and his allies and the GOP's near loss of their House majority in the 1996 election—the value of the committee process became more apparent to Republican leaders and attempts to bypass it were less blatant. A less impatient GOP took more time to learn how to use the traditional tools of committee leadership. By this route, committees came to serve many political masters who were no longer reluctant to crack the whip to obtain the legislative performance desired. Twice during this period of Republican majorities incumbent chairs (Christopher H. Smith of New Jersey on House Veterans' Affairs and Joel Hefley of Colorado on Standards of Official Conduct) were denied reappointment to their positions. And fully half of the chairs elected by the Republican Steering Committee for the 107th Congress (2001–2003), the first big round of chair replacements mandated by term limits, were not the most senior members of their respective panels. Instead, party loyalty, measured by voting records and contributions to party election efforts, figured prominently in the decisions reached by Steering.

THE HISTORY OF COMMITTEE EVOLUTION

Congressional committees became a major factor in the legislative process by evolution, not by constitutional design. Committees are not mentioned in the U.S. Constitution. The committee concept was borrowed from the British Parliament and transmitted to the New World by way of the colonial legislatures, most notably those of Pennsylvania and Virginia. But the committee system as it developed in Congress was modified and influenced by characteristics peculiar to American life.

In the early days of the Republic, when the nation's population was small and the duties of the central government carefully circumscribed, Congress had little need for the division of labor that the modern committee system provides. Just as the American people viewed the delegation of authority to elected representatives with grave suspicion, so too, were they served by a Congress that only grudgingly delegated any of its own powers to committees.

In the earliest Congresses, members were few in number and their legislative workload was light. Temporary committees served their needs. But as the nation grew and took on more complex responsibilities and problems, Congress had to develop expertise and the mechanisms to deal with the changing world. And so, from a somewhat haphazard arrangement of ad hoc committees evolved a highly specialized system of permanent committees—so-called because they are written into the standing rules of the two chambers.

Standing (or permanent) committees were institutionalized and multiplied in the nineteenth century. Efforts in the twentieth century to consolidate the burgeoning committee system—especially through the 1946 Legislative Reorganization Act—served to strengthen the streamlined committee system and its leaders. So overriding did the influence of committees in the legislative process become that scholars over the years called them "little legislatures."[6] And their chairs were dubbed "petty barons."[7]

None of this could have been foreseen during the First Congress, when many of the Founders served and took major roles in every issue that came along. In the early Congresses, legislative proposals were considered first in the Senate or House chamber, after which a special or select committee was appointed to work out the details of the legislation. Once the committee submitted its report on the bill, it was dissolved. Approximately 350 such committees were created during the Third Congress alone.[8]

The House led the way in the creation of standing committees. The Committee on Elections, created in 1789, was followed by the Claims Committee in 1794 and by Commerce and Manufactures and Revision of the Laws committees in 1795. The number had risen to ten by 1810. The next substantial expansion of committees did not occur until the administration of President James Monroe (1817–1825). Between the War of 1812 and the Civil War the standing committee system became the standard vehicle for consideration of legislative business by the House, but it was not yet fully exploited as a source of independent power. The dramatic growth of the House and its workload contributed to the institutionalization of committees. House Speaker Henry Clay of Kentucky also found a responsive committee system helpful to his policy goals and thus encouraged the creation of committees.[9]

The Senate was somewhat slower in establishing standing committees. In the first twenty-five years of its existence only four, largely administrative, standing committees were created. Most of the committee work fell to select committees, usually of three members, appointed as the occasion demanded and disbanded when their task was completed. These occasions were so frequent that during the session of 1815–1816 between ninety and one hundred select committees were appointed. Frequently, however, related legislation would be referred to special committees already in existence, and the same senators often were appointed to committees dealing with similar subjects.

In 1816 the Senate, finding inconvenient the appointment of so many ad hoc committees during each session, added a core group of eleven standing committees, most of which continue to the present day. By 1863 the number had grown to nineteen and continued to climb into the twentieth century.[10] But prior to the Civil War committees still played a relatively small role in the Senate.

Expansion of the Standing Committee Systems

The standing committee system, firmly established in the first half of the nineteenth century, expanded rapidly in the second half. Several factors influenced the role of committees, Smith and Deering wrote.

> First, dramatic economic, geographic, and population growth placed new and greater demands on Congress, which responded with more legislation and new committees. Second, further development of American political parties and the increasing strength of congressional party leaders, especially in the late nineteenth century, led to an

even greater integration of congressional parties and committee systems. Third, members of Congress, first in the Senate and then in the House, came to view service in Congress as a desirable long-term career, which in turn gave more personal significance to congressional organization, particularly the committee systems.[11]

The number of standing committees reached a peak in 1913, when there were sixty-one in the House and seventy-four in the Senate. The House Appropriations, Rules, and Ways and Means and the Senate Finance committees, in particular, exercised great influence. Meanwhile, others were created and perpetuated chiefly to provide members with offices and clerical staff they could otherwise not attain.

Initial efforts to consolidate the House committee system occurred in 1909, when six minor committees were dropped. Two years later, when Democrats took control, six more superfluous committees were abolished. In 1921 the Senate dramatically reduced the number of its committees from seventy-four to thirty-four. In many respects this rationalization of the committee structure was simply the formal abandonment of long-defunct bodies such as the Committee on Revolutionary Claims. The House in 1927 reduced the number of its committees by merging eleven expenditures committees, those dealing primarily with oversight, into a single Committee on Expenditures in the Executive Departments.

DATES COMMITTEES WERE ESTABLISHED

Only permanent committees in existence at the outset of the 112th Congress (2011–2013) are listed. Where major committees have been consolidated, the date cited is when the component committee was established first. Names in parentheses are those of current committees when they differ from the committees' original names.

HOUSE

1789—Rules (originally as select committee; became permanent in 1880)
1789—Enrolled Bills (House Administration)
1795—Commerce and Manufactures (Energy and Commerce)
1802—Ways and Means
1805—Public Lands (Natural Resources)
1808—Post Office and Post Roads (Oversight and Government Reform)
1808—District of Columbia (Oversight and Government Reform)
1813—Judiciary
1813—Pensions and Revolutionary Claims (Veterans' Affairs)
1816—Expenditures in Executive Departments (Oversight and Government Reform)
1820—Agriculture
1822—Foreign Affairs
1822—Military Affairs (Armed Services)
1822—Naval Affairs (Armed Services)
1837—Public Buildings and Grounds (Transportation and Infrastructure)
1865—Appropriations
1865—Banking and Currency (Financial Services)
1867—Education and Labor
1941—Select Small Business (Small Business)
1958—Science and Astronautics (Science and Technology)
1967—Standards of Official Conduct
1974—Budget
1977—Permanent Select Intelligence
2005—Homeland Security

SENATE

1789—Enrolled Bills (Rules and Administration)
1816—Commerce and Manufactures (Commerce, Science, and Transportation)
1816—District of Columbia (Homeland Security and Governmental Affairs)
1816—Finance
1816—Foreign Relations
1816—Judiciary
1816—Military Affairs (Armed Services)
1816—Naval Affairs (Armed Services)
1816—Post Office and Post Roads (Homeland Security and Governmental Affairs)
1816—Public Lands (Energy and Natural Resources)
1825—Agriculture (Agriculture, Nutrition, and Forestry)
1837—Public Buildings and Grounds (Environment and Public Works)
1842—Expenditures in Executive Departments (Homeland Security and Governmental Affairs)
1867—Appropriations
1869—Education and Labor (Health, Education, Labor, and Pensions)
1913—Banking and Currency (Banking, Housing, and Urban Affairs)
1950—Select Small Business (Small Business and Entrepreneurship)
1958—Aeronautical and Space Sciences (Commerce, Science, and Transportation)
1961—Special Aging
1964—Select Standards and Conduct (Select Ethics)
1970—Veterans' Affairs
1975—Budget
1976—Select Intelligence
1977—Indian Affairs

NOTE: Both the House and Senate Select Intelligence committees are permanent committees, but for reasons relating to congressional rules on committee organization they are called select committees.

SOURCES: *Constitution, Jefferson's Manual and Rules of the House of Representatives* (110th Congress); *House Practice;* and George Goodwin Jr., *The Little Legislatures: Committees of Congress* (Amherst: University of Massachusetts Press, 1970).

The next major overhaul of the committee structure took place in 1946 with enactment of the Legislative Reorganization Act. By dropping minor committees and merging those with related functions, the act achieved a net reduction of eighteen Senate committees (from thirty-three to fifteen) and of twenty-nine in the number of House committees (from forty-eight to nineteen). The act also codified the jurisdictions of each committee and attempted to set ground rules for their operations.

For the next three decades, until a partial reorganization of Senate committees in 1977, only minor changes were made in the committee structure in Congress. During that period many of the achievements of the 1946 act were weakened by the creation of additional committees as well as the proliferation of subcommittees.

In 1993 the House began a modest cycle of reexamination of its committee system. It abolished four constituent-dominated select committees, temporary entities that had acquired seemingly permanent status. And in 1995, following a shift in party control from Democrats to Republicans, the House abolished three minor standing committees: District of Columbia, Post Office and Civil Service, and Merchant Marine and Fisheries.

The Legislative Reorganization Act of 1946 had led to the rapid increase of subcommittees, reaching more than one hundred in the House and more than eighty in the Senate by 1964. Smith and Deering found that

> [t]he growth in the number of subcommittees had roots in the practical problems involved in managing larger and more complex workloads, in the desire of larger numbers of senior members for a "piece of the action," and in isolated efforts on individual committees to loosen the grip of chairs on committee activity.[12]

But the larger network of subcommittees did not mean that power automatically gravitated there. Until the early 1970s, most House committees were run by chairs who were able to retain much of the authority for themselves and a few trusted senior members, while giving little power to junior members or subcommittees. This all changed with the 1970s reforms that simultaneously empowered party leaders and subcommittees at the expense of full committee chairs. In the House this meant another surge in the creation of subcommittees. By the end of the 1970s, however, constraints adopted in both chambers led to sharp declines in these panels.

In 1995, House Republicans adopted a rule limiting committees (other than Appropriations) to no more than five subcommittees. But exceptions to that rule and the addition of the Homeland Security Committee allowed the number to creep upward slightly. At the outset of the 112th Congress in 2011, the House had twenty standing committees, one permanent select committee, and ninety-seven subcommittees.[13] The Senate had sixteen standing committees, two permanent select committees, one special committee, the Indian Affairs

committee, and seventy-three subcommittees.[14] There also were four joint committees as well as the Joint Select Committee on Deficit Reduction that made its report on November 21, 2011, and formally expired in January 2012.

Committee Membership

Each chamber has developed its own method of making appointments to committees. A rule established by the House in 1789 reserved to the whole House the power to choose the membership of all committees composed of more than three members. That rule quickly gave way in 1790 to another delegating this power to the Speaker, with the reservation that the House might direct otherwise in special cases. Eventually, however, the Speaker was given the right to appoint the members as well as the chairs of all standing committees, a power retained until 1911. The principle that committees were to be bipartisan, but weighted in favor of the majority party and its policies, was established early.

In making committee appointments and promotions, certain principles governed the Speaker's choices. The wishes of the minority leaders in filling vacancies going to members of their party usually were respected. Generally, seniority—length of service on the committee—and factors such as geographical distribution and party loyalty were considered. But the Speaker was not bound by such criteria, and there were cases in which none of those factors outweighed the Speaker's wishes. Despite complaints and various attempts to change the rule, the system remained in force until 1911, when the House again exercised the right to select the members of standing committees. In practice, this means House confirmation of committee lists drawn up by the Republican Committee on Committees and the Democratic Steering Committee. (See "Committee Assignments," p. 169.)

In the Senate, assignment to a committee was made by vote of the entire membership until 1823. Members wishing to serve on a particular committee were placed on a ballot, with the choicest committee assignments going to those receiving the most votes. The senator with the largest number of votes served as chair.

By the 1820s a number of difficulties with the ballot system had become evident—not least that it proved tedious and time-consuming. But also it provided no guarantee that the party in control of the chamber would hold a majority of seats on the committee or retain control of the committee chairs in the event of a vacancy. Several times in the ensuing years the Senate amended its rules to provide for appointment to committees by a designated official, usually the vice president or president pro tempore. But abuse of the appointment power and a transfer of power between parties compelled the Senate to return to use of the ballot.

In 1823 senators rejected a proposal that the chairs of the five most important committees be chosen by the full Senate and that the chairs then have the power to make all other committee assignments. The Senate instead amended the standing rules to give the presiding officer authority to make committee assignments, unless otherwise ordered by the Senate. Because Daniel D. Tompkins, vice president during the administration of James Monroe, scarcely ever entered the chamber, committee selection was left to the president pro tempore, who in effect had been chosen by and was responsible to the Senate majority leadership. But when the next vice president, John C. Calhoun, used the assignment power with obvious bias, the Senate quickly and with little dissent returned to the election method to fill committee vacancies.

This time the chairs were picked by majority vote of the entire Senate, and then ballots were taken to select the other members of each committee, with members' rank on the committee determined by the size of their plurality. In 1828 the Senate changed its rules to provide for appointment to committees by the president pro tempore, but in 1833 it reverted to selection by ballot when control of the Senate changed hands. Since 1833 the Senate technically has made its committee assignments by ballot, although the last time a formal ballot appears to have been taken—on assigning new committees to Sen. Wayne Morse of Oregon, a Republican-turned-independent—was in 1953.

To avoid the inconveniences inherent in the ballot system, it became customary between 1833 and 1846 to suspend the rule by unanimous consent and designate an officer (the vice president, the president pro tempore, or the presiding officer) to assign members to committees.

The method of selecting committee members in use today was, with some modification, developed in 1846. In that year a motion to entrust the vice president with the task was defeated, and the Senate proceeded under the regular rules to make committee assignments by ballot. But after six chairs had been selected, a debate began on the method of choosing the other members of the committees. At first, several committees were filled by lists—arranged in order of a member's seniority—submitted by the majority leader. After a number of committees had been filled in this manner, the ballot rule was suspended and the Senate approved a list for the remaining vacancies that had been agreed upon by both the majority and minority leadership.[15]

Since 1846 the choice of committees usually has amounted to routine acceptance by the Senate of lists drawn up by special committees of the two major parties (as of 2012, the Committee on Committees for the Republicans and the Steering Committee for the Democrats).

The Seniority System

As the committee system grew, so, too, did a system that awarded power on committees to the longest serving member. Seniority—status based on length of continuous service, to which are attached certain rights and privileges—pervades

Many southern Democrats who opposed the national party programs held committee chairmanships in the decades following World War II, thanks to seniority. Sen. James O. Eastland, D-Miss., who chaired the Senate Judiciary Committee from 1956 to 1978, was notorious for bottling up civil rights bills sought by party leaders.

SOURCE: Time & Life Pictures/Getty Images.

nearly all social institutions. And it has been particularly strong in the U.S. Congress.

Despite frequent references to a seniority rule and a seniority system, observance of seniority in Congress has never been dictated by law or formal rule. It developed as a practice and later became a dominant institutional norm. Formal rules simply stated that the House or Senate should determine committee memberships and chairs. *(See box, Seniority under Fire, p. 156.)*

Seniority on Capitol Hill is based on the length of service in Congress, referred to as congressional seniority, or on the length of consecutive service on a committee, called committee seniority. As the system developed in both houses, it affected the assignment of office space, Senate seating arrangements, access to congressional patronage, and deference shown members on the floor. But seniority was most apparent—and important—in the selection of committee chairs and in filling vacancies on committees, although state and regional considerations, party loyalty, legislative experience, and a member's influence with his or her colleagues always were important factors in making committee assignments.

Seniority had been relatively unimportant in the early years of Congress, when political parties were weak, turnover of congressional membership was frequent, and congressional careers were brief. By 1846, however, party control had become so firm that committee assignment lists supplied by the parties were approved routinely. With party domination of assignments, the principle of seniority also appeared. Seniority came to be applied both to committee assignments and to advancement within a committee.

The seniority norm caught hold earlier in the Senate than in the House. As the Civil War neared, southern Democrats, who dominated Senate committee chairs, "supported the hardening of seniority to protect their position so that they could defend slavery," Randall B. Ripley wrote.[16] During the Civil War and Reconstruction period, between 1861 and 1875, Southern Democrats virtually disappeared from Congress, and Republican senators disregarded seniority in committee assignments. But when larger numbers of Democrats began to reappear in the Senate, the Republican majority returned to the seniority system to keep peace among party members. Republican leaders found they had to rely on the support of all their party colleagues, Ripley wrote. And one way to gain this support was to agree to an "automatic and impartial rule for committee advancement. The leaders of the party thus helped institute this limit on their own power."[17]

As committees developed into powerful, autonomous institutions, committee chairs assumed ever greater powers over legislation. So great was their influence that in 1885 Woodrow Wilson wrote: "I know not how better to describe our form of government in a single phrase than by calling it a government by the chairmen of the standing committees of Congress."[18]

In the House, committee chairs and the evolving seniority system suffered a temporary setback during the speakership of Joseph G. Cannon, R-Ill., in the early 1900s. The period from the Civil War to 1910 had seen the gradual development of an all-powerful Speaker. Through the power to name committee members and chairs, the Speaker was able to control legislation, grant favors or impose political punishments, and ride roughshod over the minority party. So much so, in fact, that the press frequently referred to the Speaker as "Czar" Cannon.

Finally, in 1910, insurgent Republicans in the House, led by Nebraska's George Norris, combined with Democrats to strip Speaker Cannon of much of his power. The Speaker could no longer name committee members, chair or even serve on the Rules Committee, or hold unchallenged control over recognizing representatives who wished to bring legislation to the floor. (See "Cannonism," p. 16.) With the revolt against Cannon, the right to appoint committee members and chairs returned to the political party structures.

After World War II, lengthening congressional careers, committee consolidation produced by the Legislative Reorganization Act of 1946, and the Democrats' largely unbroken dominance in Congress meant relatively little turnover in their membership and long tenure for chairs elected from the Democrats' safest seats—those in the South and in urban areas dominated by party machines. Chairs thus grew increasingly unrepresentative of the party as younger members were elected in the political landslides of 1958 and 1964. Many of these younger members came to be identified with advocacy of new social programs, civil rights, and, later, opposition to the Vietnam War.

Members who were out of step with their party's program or with the mood of the country, because of advanced age or ideology, or both, chaired important committees thanks to seniority. James O. Eastland, D-Miss., chair of the Judiciary Committee from 1956 to 1978, routinely tried to bottle up civil rights bills and initially opposed the appointment of Thurgood Marshall to the federal judiciary. A party loyalist, Sen. Carl Hayden, D-Ariz., became chair of the Appropriations Committee at age seventy-eight and served until he was ninety-one, setting a (then) record for longest service in Congress, nearly fifty-seven years (counting both House and Senate service). Emanuel Celler, D-N.Y., longtime House Judiciary Committee chair and liberal stalwart, ended his career as an opponent of the proposed constitutional amendment providing equal rights for women and lost a primary to a liberal feminist in 1972. F. Edward Hébert, D-La., a stalwart supporter of military programs and the Vietnam War who chaired the Armed Services Committee, opposed the appointment of African Americans and women to his committee. When antiwar liberals Ronald V. Dellums, D-Calif., an African American, and Patricia Schroeder, D-Colo., were added to the committee in 1973, Hébert provided only one chair for them in the committee hearing room, until the leadership intervened. He saw his career ended by the 1974 Democratic newcomers after he referred to them condescendingly as boys and girls.

On June 12, 2006, West Virginia Democrat Robert C. Byrd became the longest serving senator in American history. On November 18, 2009, he became the longest serving member of Congress. During his career Byrd served as majority whip, majority leader, minority leader, president pro tempore, ranking minority member, and chair of the Appropriations Committee. Sen. Strom Thurmond, R-S.C., the oldest person ever to serve in Congress, held the previous record for Senate service (1955–1956, 1956–2003). During his career Thurmond chaired both the Judiciary and Armed Services committees at different times and served as president pro tempore (1981–1987; 1995–2003), which made him third in line for the presidency. John D. Dingell,

HOUSE RULES COMMITTEE FUNCTIONS AS ARM OF MAJORITY LEADERSHIP

The Rules Committee is among the most powerful committees in the House. Often described as the gatekeeper to the floor, the committee works with the majority leadership to control the flow of legislation and set the terms of floor debate. The Speaker and minority leader nominate all of its members. Because the majority party in recent decades has always insisted on holding a two-to-one-plus-one ratio in the committee's membership (a 9:4 ratio in the 112th Congress, for example), even if it controls only a small majority in the House, an occasional defection on a vote does not affect its control.

GRANTING A RULE

Controversies have occurred frequently throughout the House's history over the function of the Rules Committee in the legislative process: whether it should be a clearinghouse (or traffic cop) for legislative business, the agent of the majority leadership, or a superlegislative committee editing the work of the other committees.

For major bills, the committee writes a resolution or special rule that, subject to the approval of the House, alters the calendar position of the bill, sets a time limit on general debate, and regulates whether and how the bill may be amended.

Before granting a rule, the committee usually holds a hearing at which only members of the House are able to testify. The chair of the committee reporting the bill usually requests the kind of rule desired. Members testify for and against the bill and ask that their amendments be made eligible for consideration. The hearing procedure is usually informal, with members being added to or dropped off the witness list on a continuing basis. The committee usually will listen to any member who wishes to be heard. It then may grant a rule immediately or meet again later after controversies and strategies have been considered privately.

When the committee orders a rule reported, the chair and ranking minority member decide who will manage the one hour of House floor debate on it. Once the rule is filed on the House floor, it may be considered on the next legislative day, on the same day if a two-thirds majority of the House votes to do so, or at any time if a special rule is adopted to waive the two-thirds vote (House Rule XIII 6(a)).

In many cases, the committee will restrict amendments. It may forbid all amendments, allow only amendments proposed by the legislative committee that handled the bill, allow only certain specified amendments, allow only amendments that are printed in the *Congressional Record* prior to their consideration on the floor, or allow only amendments that can be called up within a fixed time limit.

On complex bills, the committee may create its own original text, called an amendment in the nature of a substitute, that incorporates provisions desired by the various committees to which a bill might have been referred or represents a compromise. The committee also may propose perfecting amendments to a bill, which it self-executes within the proposed rule—that is, adoption of the rule automatically adopts the amendments, even before the bill is formally considered on the floor.

CHANGING ROLE OF THE COMMITTEE

Established in 1789, Rules originally was a select committee authorized at the beginning of each Congress. Because the rules of one Congress usually were readopted by the next, this function was not initially of great importance, and for many years the committee never issued a report.

In 1858 the Speaker was made a member of the committee, and in subsequent years Rules gradually increased its influence over legislation. The panel became a standing committee in 1880, and in 1883 it began the practice of issuing rules— special orders of business—for floor debate on legislation. (The Senate Committee on Rules and Administration has never developed a similar function, marking a key House-Senate distinction.) Other powers acquired by the committee over the years included the right to sit while the House was in session, to have its resolutions considered immediately, and to initiate legislation on its own.

Before 1910 the Rules Committee worked closely with the leadership in deciding which legislation to allow on the floor and often was chaired by the Speaker himself. But in the Progressive revolt of 1910 against the arbitrary reign of Speaker Joseph G. Cannon, R-Ill., a coalition of Democrats and insurgent Republicans succeeded in enlarging the committee and excluding the Speaker from it. Alternative methods of bringing legislation to the floor while avoiding the committee—the Discharge Calendar, Calendar Wednesday, and the Consent Calendar (repealed in 1995)—were created and added to standing rules.

By the late 1930s the committee had come under the domination of a coalition of conservative Democrats and Republicans. From then until the 1970s it repeatedly blocked or delayed liberal legislation. Opposition to the obstructive tactics led, in 1949, to adoption of the "twenty-one-day rule." It allowed a committee chair whose panel approved a bill to call it up on the House floor if the Rules Committee failed to act within twenty-one days of receiving a request to grant a rule. The Speaker was required to recognize the chair for this purpose. Two years later, after the Democrats had lost twenty-nine seats in the midterm elections, the House repealed this procedure. Although used only eight times, the threat of its use was credited with prying other bills out of the Rules Committee.

HOUSE REVOLT

After the Rules Committee in the 86th Congress (1959–1961) blocked or delayed measures that later were to become key elements in the new Kennedy administration's legislative program, Democratic reformers pressured Speaker Sam Rayburn, D-Texas, to act against it. In 1961 the House by a 217–212 margin agreed to enlarge the committee from twelve to fifteen members. That gave Rayburn and the incoming administration a delicate eight-to-seven majority on most issues coming before the committee.

Nevertheless, dissatisfaction continued, and following a 1964 Democratic election sweep the twenty-one-day rule was revived. The new version adopted by the House in 1965 gave the Speaker discretion whether to recognize a committee chair to call up legislation. The new rule, employed successfully only eight times, was abandoned in 1967 following Republican gains in the 1966 midterm elections.

The House adopted a rule in 1965 that curbed the committee's power to block conferences on legislation. Before 1965 most bills could be sent to a conference committee only through unanimous consent, suspension of the rules, or adoption of a special rule from the Rules Committee. The change made it possible to send any bill to conference by majority vote of the House if the committee that reported the bill authorized such a motion and the Speaker recognized a member to make it.

Despite repeal of the twenty-one-day rule in 1967, the committee generally continued to pursue a stance more accommodating to the leadership. Contributing to this was the loss of its chair of twelve years, Rep. Howard W. Smith, D-Va., who was defeated in a 1966 primary election. Smith was a skilled parliamentarian and the acknowledged leader of the House's conservative coalition, a voting alliance of

House Rules chair David Dreier, R-Calif., right, leaves a meeting of the Republican caucus in May 2006. The Rules Committee is one of the most influential in the House. After an interlude of Democratic control, Dreier once again became chair of the committee in 2011.

SOURCE: Scott J. Ferrell, Congressional Quarterly.

Republicans and southern Democrats. He was replaced by Rep. William M. Colmer, D-Miss., who was unable to exert the high degree of control over legislation that Smith had exercised. In addition, new rules governing committee procedures reduced the power of the chair. The rules took from the chair the right to set meeting dates, a power Smith frequently had used to postpone or thwart action on bills he opposed.

Another effort to revive a twenty-one-day rule in 1971 failed when a conservative coalition blocked the Democrats' rules package on the House floor at the opening of Congress and passed an amendment excising the provision.

Effective leadership control over the Rules Committee finally came when the Democratic Caucus voted in December 1974 to give the Speaker the power to nominate all of its Democratic members, subject to caucus approval. Using this power, Speaker Carl Albert of Oklahoma nominated liberals to fill two vacant positions. The Republican leader later acquired the same power over GOP members.

Although the committee's power remains immense, the loss of influence by its members as individuals has reduced the panel's attractiveness as an assignment. Ambitious members seeking power in the institution, or a base to aid their constituencies, look to committees such as Appropriations, Energy and Commerce,

and Ways and Means. The era of recent Rules Committee members considered powerful in their own right, such as chairs Howard Smith, D-Va., and Richard Bolling, D-Mo., is probably over.

RESTRICTIVE RULES

No matter who was Speaker, the panel was used increasingly to limit amendments and debate on the House floor, provoking an outcry from Republican members usually in the minority. Democratic leaders argued that the Rules panel was an essential tool of a well-managed House. Such limits, they argued, helped focus debate on central issues, weed out dilatory amendments, and still ensure that major alternatives were considered. The Republicans themselves, despite decades of complaints about the committee, adopted and even expanded some of these restrictive practices when they took control in 1995.

Use of more complex rules also reflected institutional changes that had little to do with a deliberate strategy of closing off amendments. After 1974, when House rules were changed to allow more than one committee to handle a bill, the Rules

(Continued)

(Continued)

Committee had to set guidelines for resolving conflicts and eliminating overlap when several committees marked up a single bill. Moreover, faced with huge budget deficits and waning public enthusiasm for government programs in the 1980s, the House considered fewer authorizing bills, the sort of legislation that had usually received an open rule. Increasingly, authorizing legislation was folded into omnibus measures, which usually were not entirely open to amendment.

ERA OF RAPID CHANGE

The chair of the Rules Committee turned over several times in the 1970s and 1980s, accommodating a variety of diverse personalities in an era of rapidly increasing partisanship in the House. Leadership influence, cemented by the Speaker's power to select all Democratic members, ensured that the committee would operate as a loyal instrument of the Democratic Caucus. When party control shifted in 1995, ranking Republican member Gerald B.H. Solomon of New York, an aggressive partisan, assumed the chair. Former Democratic chair Joe Moakley of Massachusetts stayed on as the leader of a four-member Democratic minority. *(See box, Rules Committee Seniority, p. 150.)*

The Republican-controlled Rules Committee became a more visible forum for advocates of changes in House rules, though the majority had already implemented its most controversial proposals directly on the floor during the first two days of the 104th Congress. The committee held hearings on issues such as how changing technologies would affect the operations of the House in the twenty-first century. Under the Democrats, the committee had largely shunned institutional oversight. It left nearly all such activities to be handled privately in the Democratic Caucus, out of concern by the leadership that hearings or other formal action on controversial matters in a public setting might prove divisive or provide Republicans with a forum to launch attacks. This posture effectively marginalized the Rules Committee as a vehicle for dealing with institutional problems in the years preceding the loss of Democratic control of the House.

Solomon acted quickly in response to leadership directives to modify, or repeal, long-standing institutional practices when they inhibited achieving the majority's political agenda. In 1995 and 1997 it gave the staff of the Government Reform and Oversight Committee, which was investigating scandals in the Clinton administration, the power to take depositions from witnesses under oath. In 1997 it overrode GOP rules changes passed just two years earlier limiting the number of subcommittees to give Government Reform an extra one to deal with controversy surrounding conduct of the year 2000 census. And in 1997 it repealed a long-standing rule, inspired by the excesses of the McCarthy era, that had given witnesses appearing at House committee hearings under subpoena the right to bar photographs and television and radio broadcasts of the proceedings.

Solomon was succeeded by David Dreier, R-Calif., in 1999. Dreier, a rule maven, had been the primary author of the Republican rules package adopted in 1995, having cut his teeth on reform as ranking House minority member to the Joint Committee on the Organization of Congress (1993). And his chair, which ended with the Democratic victory in the 2006 elections, continued the period of highly aggressive majority leadership in the House.

In 2004 this led then-minority leader Nancy Pelosi, D-Calif., to call for a "minority bill of rights"—which would have allowed debate on more amendments authored by minority Democrats. Pelosi even pledged to allow greater minority rights upon a Democratic takeover of the House—which occurred in 2007. At that point ranking minority member Louise Slaughter, D-N.Y., acceded to the Rules Committee chair but Democrats, to hear minority Republicans tell the story, failed to make good on their pledge. During the two-congress Democratic rule, minority Republicans took to offering numerous motions (over 120 by one count) to recommit bills with instructions (amendments) that are routinely permitted by the Rules Committee. Thus the tit-for-tat exploitation of Rules continued in the 112th Congress—with Dreier regaining the chair and Slaughter reverting to ranking member.

D-Mich., holds the record for House service. Dingell served as chair or ranking member of the Energy and Commerce Committee from 1981 to 2009 (when he was unseated by Rep. Henry Waxman, D-Calif.). Rep. Jamie Whitten, D-Miss. (1941–1995), held the previous record for service in the House.

The lengthy terms served by these men testify to the growing careerism in Congress that gradually also spread to members who could rely on mastery of the media, campaign skills, and a strong fund-raising base to compensate for an unsafe seat. But tenure and age made it increasingly difficult for elderly members to adjust to changing political climates and younger, more demanding, and less deferential colleagues.

With the long tenure of senior members, a generation gap developed. Roger H. Davidson observed:

> In 1973 the average House committee chair was 66 years old and had almost 30 years of congressional service behind him; the average Senate chair was 64 years old and had 21

years' experience. Not only did such a situation squander talent in the mid-seniority ranks, but it eventually generated frustration and resentment.[19]

The gap between leaders and backbenchers, covering not only age but also region, type of district, and ideology, "lay at the heart of the Democrats' seniority struggles in the 1970s," Davidson wrote.

The regional imbalance in top committee posts was especially irksome to Democratic liberals. In 1973 the six chairs of the most powerful committees in Congress—those dealing with taxes, appropriations, and the armed services—came from just four states in the south central part of the country: Arkansas, Louisiana, Mississippi, and Texas. Congress was ready for change.

Harbingers of Reform

Though it preceded the period of sustained reform by more than a decade, the fight for expansion of the size of the Rules Committee in 1961 represented a sign of things to come.

Speaker Sam Rayburn, D-Texas, allied himself with the incoming Kennedy administration to break the conservative coalition that frequently stymied the majority's ability to bring legislation to the floor or to go to conference with the Senate. By a vote of 217 to 212, with many conservative Democrats opposing Rayburn, the House increased the size of the committee from twelve (an eight-to-four party ratio) to fifteen (a ten-to-five party ratio). Chair Howard W. Smith, D-Va., and William M. Colmer, D-Miss., had often joined the Republicans to create a tie, paralyzing legislative action. The new configuration, with two additional Democrats handpicked by Rayburn, prevented that and gave the Speaker greater assurance that Rules would not routinely stymie the party's more activist legislative agenda. But the leadership's control of the committee was still far from ensured.

In 1965, a push for further reforms led to the creation of the Joint Committee on the Organization of Congress, headed by Sen. A.S. Mike Monroney, D-Okla., and Rep. Ray J. Madden, D-Ind. The following year the panel recommended a wide-ranging set of reforms, including proposals to curtail the powers of committee chairs, limit committee assignments, and increase committee staff resources. But no consensus immediately emerged, and the proposals were not enacted.

Some of the joint committee's procedural recommendations were enacted into law in the Legislative Reorganization Act of 1970. The recommendations opened Congress to greater public view and fostered participation by more members but did not directly attack the power bases of senior members. The law encouraged open committee proceedings, required that committees have written rules, required that all committee roll-call votes be made public, allowed radio and television coverage of committee hearings, and safeguarded the rights of minority party members on a committee. The law made only minor revisions in the committee structure and it left the seniority system intact. The most significant change for the House required recorded teller votes in the Committee of the Whole. This forced members to vote publicly on key amendments and undermined the control by senior committee members who had once stage-managed legislation with sparse attendance.

Although the 1970 law had limited effects, it marked a turning point in the reform movement, signaling an end to an era when committee chairs and senior members could block reforms and the beginning of nearly a decade of change. Loosening the grip of seniority was seen as a crucial step toward changing committee operations. The issue of committee seniority was treated as strictly a party matter. Democratic leaders feared that if seniority changes were proposed through legislation instead of through party rules, a coalition of members of both parties could upset the majority party's control of the legislative program. When changes

in seniority were offered as amendments on the floor of the House and Senate, they consistently had been defeated.

Because the reform goals of the two chambers were different and the pressure for change was greatest in the House, subsequent attempts at change took the form of intrachamber reform efforts, not bicameral action. And with one exception—the failed 1993 Joint Committee on the Organization of Congress—this go-it-alone strategy for congressional reform has prevailed for each chamber ever since.

Revival of the Democratic Caucus

The House Democratic Study Group (DSG), founded in 1959 to counterbalance the conservative coalition, accelerated the drive to overhaul the seniority system and open House procedures. The outlook for the DSG agenda brightened with the revival of regular meetings of the House Democratic Caucus in 1969 following a challenge to the reelection of Speaker John W. McCormack, D-Mass. The retirement of McCormack at the end of the 1970 session deprived the dominant committee chairs of a powerful ally at the top of the House leadership structure and opened the way for the liberal wing to operate more freely under his successor, Carl Albert, D-Okla.

Caucus revival meant that frustrated moderate and liberal Democrats elected to the House in the 1960s or earlier now had a vehicle to change House procedures. Their actions were directed at undercutting the power of committee chairs and strengthening the role of the subcommittees, where the opportunity lay for them to gain a greater role and make an impact on the legislative process. The drive had a sharp generational edge. Between 1958 and 1970, 293 Democrats entered the House. Between 1970 and 1974, another 150 Democrats were elected. From this group, many of whom tended to be more moderate or liberal than their predecessors, sprang pressure for reform.

1970s Reform Movements

The reformist trend in Congress on domestic policy was greatly accelerated by the election of John F. Kennedy to the presidency in 1960. Responsibility for the obstruction of liberal policy goals focused squarely on congressional impediments within the congressional majority party, where seniority reigned supreme until the early 1970s—at which point Democrats had controlled both House and Senate for all but four years since 1933. So frustration with the existing system led to a drumbeat of demands for reforms. As Deering and Smith noted:

> These demands were especially strong among junior members and some long-standing liberal Democrats, who found their efforts to shape public policy stymied by their more conservative senior colleagues.... These members, and the

outsiders whose causes they supported, were concerned about issues that were not receiving active committee consideration and did not fall easily into existing committee jurisdictions. A nascent environmental movement, opposition to the Vietnam conflict, and a continuing interest in civil rights legislation placed new challenges before congressional committees.[20]

No longer did new members, and not a few of their elders, accept the admonition credited to Speaker Sam Rayburn: "to get along, go along."

The 1970s revolt began in the House as membership turnover accelerated and the proportion of first- and second-term members increased. These lawmakers demanded fundamental changes in the way Congress—and particularly the committees—operated. Major changes in Democratic Caucus rules and, to a lesser extent, in the standing rules of the House and the Senate diluted the authority enjoyed by committee chairs and other senior members and redistributed the power among the junior members.

On the House side, newcomers breathed life into a dormant Democratic Caucus and gave would-be reformers the votes they needed to effect change. The single most important factor that undermined chairs' authority was the decision by Democrats in both chambers to allow chairs to be elected by their party's caucus. The change came gradually, beginning in 1971. But by 1975 Democrats had adopted rules providing for secret-ballot election of the top Democrats on committees. A secret vote was automatic in the House and held at the request of 20 percent of Senate Democrats. That year three House chairs were ousted in caucus elections. (Other Democratic ousters followed in 1985, 1992, and 2008, for example.)

RULES COMMITTEE SENIORITY

For decades, few committees illustrated the importance of seniority more vividly than did the House Rules Committee. Rep. Thomas P. "Tip" O'Neill Jr., D-Mass., a longtime committee member before giving up his seat in 1973 to become majority leader, joked that he had served for eighteen years on the panel (1955–1973) and had moved from eighth to fifth in seniority.

The Rules Committee had once been a strong arm of the majority party leadership, chaired by the Speaker himself, until the revolt against Speaker Joseph G. Cannon, R-Ill., resulted in his removal from the committee in 1910. *(See "Cannonism," p. 16.)*

For most of the decades after that until the early 1960s, Rules served as a power center for conservatives opposed to the Democratic congressional leadership and presidential administrations. Its independence began to be curbed beginning in 1961, when its size was expanded, and continued in the 1970s with party rules changes giving the Speaker control of Democratic appointments.

From 1949 until 1979, except for a two-year interval when Republicans ran the House, the Rules Committee was chaired by two elderly Democrats from the rural South and three others who came out of big-city machine politics. They were Reps. Adolph Sabath of Chicago (chair in 1949–1953), who died at age eighty-six while still chair; Howard W. Smith of Virginia (chair in 1955–1967), leader of the southern bloc in the House, who at age eighty-three was upset in his party's 1966 primary; William M. Colmer of Mississippi (chair in 1967–1973), who retired from Congress upon reaching age eighty-two; Ray J. Madden of Gary, Indiana (chair in 1973–1977), who became chair at age eighty and was defeated in the Democratic primary four years later; and James J. Delaney of New York City (chair in 1977–1979), who succeeded Madden for one Congress.

"Judge" Smith, as he was known, was so antagonistic to liberal Democratic programs and worked so well with Republicans that Speaker Sam Rayburn, D-Texas, reluctantly agreed in 1961 to increase the committee's size to fifteen, from twelve. The new ten-to-five party ratio (instead of eight-to-four) diminished the prospect of tie votes, when Smith and Colmer had voted with Republicans to create a deadlock. Rayburn agreed to pack the Rules Committee with two additional Democrats willing to vote for programs of the newly elected administration of John F. Kennedy. The passage in 1974 of a Democratic Caucus rule giving the Speaker the power to nominate the chair and all other Democratic members of the Rules Committee finally secured full control of the committee for the party leadership. *(See box, House Rules Committee Functions as Arm of Majority Leadership, p. 146.)*

Richard Bolling, D-Mo., chair from 1979 to 1983 and the most significant figure to head the committee since Smith, was recognized as one of the ablest legislators in the House and was one of only a handful of Rules Committee members in recent decades who had significant expertise and interest in the rules and structure of the institution. He had chaired the Select Committee on Committees in the 93rd Congress (1973–1975), which proposed a number of significant reforms but is perhaps best remembered for its radical, and unsuccessful, scheme to reorganize the House committee system and limit members' committee assignments. A power broker in his own right who had run unsuccessfully for majority leader, and the author of several books on Congress, Bolling served as a link between the committee's jurisdictional responsibilities for the structure of the House and its other role as a loyal processor of special rules to promote the majority's agenda.

After Bolling retired for health reasons, the committee entered a period of drift. With its perceived loss of influence came reduced desirability as a committee assignment. Would-be power brokers now had little room to operate. Relatively junior members were recruited to fill vacancies because there was less need for the leadership to require members to serve an apprenticeship elsewhere to see if they had the temperament for the job. Committee size varied from the fifteen established by Rayburn in 1961, to sixteen from 1975 to 1985, then back to thirteen.

There was an effort in 1983 to persuade octogenarian representative Claude Pepper, D-Fla., not to assume the chair, but Pepper quickly dismissed that suggestion. The Speaker named him, and he held the post until his death in 1989, when he was the House's oldest member. Pepper was regarded as an ineffective chair whose

The election requirement made chairs accountable to their colleagues for their conduct. Caucus election of committee chairs was only one of a number of changes that restricted the chairs' power. Under the 1970 Legislative Reorganization Act committees were required to have written rules and committee operations and votes were opened to the public eye. In 1973 House Democrats adopted a "subcommittee bill of rights" that guaranteed subcommittee autonomy. Before the decade was over, the committee system had been radically restructured. The era of the autocratic committee chair who answered to no one was over. Junior and minority party members of Congress now had positions, privileges, and resources earlier members had been denied.

In later years House Democrats gave members of each committee the power to determine the number of subcommittees their committee would have. Most committees were required to have subcommittees. Because of concerns over their proliferation, however, the number of subcommittees was subsequently further limited by caucus rule and, after the Republican takeover in 1995, by House rule—though somewhat loosened in later years.

Staffing prerogatives were extended to members other than the chair. This change made members less subservient to the chair by giving them professional staff help on legislative issues. Both chambers also tried to limit the influence of chairs and other senior members by restricting the number of chairs and committee slots that any one member could hold.

House Committee Changes

The first blow to seniority in the House came when both parties decided that the selection of committee leaders no longer

principal interest remained issues affecting elderly Americans, which he had long championed. Other Democratic members assumed more visible roles to fill the vacuum. Rep. Joe Moakley, D-Mass., an O'Neill protégé who served as chair from 1989 to 1995, restored a sense of order to the committee's role in reporting special rules and coordinating business with the leadership. But the committee largely sat on the sidelines during controversies over whether, and how, to reform the House and over how to respond to the Republicans' increasingly effective institutional attacks on Congress and the Democratic Party in the 1980s and 1990s. When Democrats lost control of the House in 1994, Moakley stayed on as ranking minority member.

Despite—or possibly because of—the 1974 Democratic Caucus rule giving the Speaker the power to nominate all Democrats on the Rules Committee, the seniority system continued to be followed rigidly. Speakers always appointed the senior Democratic member as chair and reappointed all serving members. Ironically, instead of opening the door for membership changes, the rule may have had the opposite effect. With leadership control of the committee secured, the threat of potential removal controlled committee votes without the need for violations of seniority, which might have seemed threatening to the rest of the caucus.

Also in the 1970s, the pattern of the Republican minority's assignment process on the Rules Committee began to evolve to reflect its more aggressive, partisan role and the minority's increasing willingness to use its limited resources more effectively. The minority leader, like the Speaker, exercised the power to select his or her party's membership. For years, the most visible Republican member of the committee, even though he was not the senior member, was Minority Whip Trent Lott, R-Miss., who served as the leadership spokesperson on the committee until his election to the Senate in 1988. The seniority tradition was formally breached during the 1990s, and the weakening of the practice had important consequences when the party finally took over the House.

In 1991 Republicans moved aside their longtime ranking minority member, seventy-five-year-old James H. "Jimmy" Quillen, R-Tenn., and replaced him with Gerald B. H. Solomon, R-N.Y., a younger, more aggressive partisan who had served on the committee for only two years. Solomon was made chair in 1995 by Speaker Newt Gingrich, R-Ga., and was a vigorous advocate for the Contract with America and the party's conservative agenda. Solomon retired from Congress in January 1999 and was succeeded by David Dreier, R-Calif., who at age forty-seven was the youngest member to chair the panel.

Dreier's service as chair extended for four Congresses, the 106th through the 109th, which necessitated a change of Rule X, waiving the three-term limit for chairs. Democrats retained the term limit rule at the outset of the 110th Congress, but they also retained the Rules Committee exception. And, with the elevation of their ranking minority member, Louise M. Slaughter of New York became the first woman to chair the House Rules Committee. Slaughter retained the position for the 110th and 111th Congresses but returned to the ranking member post in the 112th Congress as Republicans swept back into power. At that point Dreier, who had been serving as ranking member, returned to chair the committee—marking seven consecutive congresses as either chair or ranking member.

Close ties to the leadership and increased party polarization have had an important unintended consequence for committee seniority, however. They have diminished the attractiveness of a Rules Committee assignment—which as an "exclusive" committee carried with it the penalty of not receiving an additional committee assignment. For their part, Republican leaders did appoint a couple of newly elected members to the committee during their decade plus in the majority. But they also lost four committee members who resigned to join other House committees. In 2007, Democrats went a step farther in filling four of their newly regained slots on the committee with freshmen. To do so, however, the leadership effectively had to abandon Rules' status as an exclusive committee as all Democrats on the panel except the chair were permitted an additional committee assignment. Republicans followed suit in 2011 by naming four freshmen—all from the South—to Dreier's committee.

PROXY VOTING

Proxy voting in House committees was abolished in 1995 as part of the Republican majority's new rules package. It continues to be used on amendments in Senate committees and in House-Senate conferences by members from both chambers. Proxy voting is not permitted on the floor of the Senate or House.

Proxies permit one committee member to authorize another to cast votes for that person in the member's absence. The device is a convenience for members of Congress caught between conflicting demands of busy schedules, which often include more than one committee or subcommittee meeting at the same time. A proxy is nearly always given to a committee or subcommittee chair or, if the member differs from the chair on an issue, to another member who is on the same side of the issue as the absentee. Although proxy voting may seem an innocuous practice, it was the bane of the minority party in Congress and a target of reformers for years.

Controversy over proxy voting focused principally on the House, where one member could cast many proxies. The practice is viewed less harshly in the Senate because of the large number of committee and subcommittee assignments held by each senator and the tradition of accommodating the convenience of individuals. In addition, committees do not have the same power or importance in the Senate.

HOUSE

Proxy voting was a noteworthy tool for the majority in operating committees because it allowed members to cope with multiple simultaneous scheduling commitments while ensuring that political control could not slip away to a well-organized minority that might concentrate its strength at a single location for a sneak attack on the majority. In this respect, proxy voting was simply a means of ensuring majority control over committees as subunits of the House and preventing such control from succumbing to whims of committee scheduling or flukes of member absences.

Proxy voting was denounced by the minority members and reform advocates outside the House for encouraging absenteeism and irresponsibility. Perhaps more significant, it tended to discourage efforts to improve the coordination of the scheduling of committee and subcommittee meetings as well as to reduce the number of subcommittees and member assignments.

Before 1970 the use of proxies was regulated by custom or by guidelines established by individual committees and differed from committee to committee.

Some committees never used them. Before the power of House chairs was diminished by the Democratic Caucus in the 1970s, proxy voting reinforced their domination of committees. A chair had little trouble procuring and using proxies, while opponents had to appear, and in significant numbers, to change the outcome on a key vote unless they were capable of organizing themselves around a proxy campaign as well.

The Legislative Reorganization Act of 1970 was the first measure to alter proxy voting. That act prohibited proxy voting unless a committee's written rules specifically allowed it, in which case it was limited to a specific bill, amendment, or other matter. Proxies also had to be in writing, designating the person on the committee authorized to use them.

In October 1974, as part of the Select Committee on Committees' resolution making changes in the committee system, the House voted 196–166 to ban proxy voting entirely, effective at the beginning of the subsequent Congress. But the ban never took effect. The Democratic Caucus, voting this time without the Republicans, modified the ban before the 94th Congress convened in 1975 to adopt House rules on a party-line vote. The revision once again gave committees the authority to decide whether to permit proxy voting. If a committee allowed proxy voting, it was to be used only on a specific measure or matter and related amendments and motions. General proxies, covering all matters before a committee for either a specific time period or for an indefinite period, were prohibited, except for votes on procedural matters. As before, they had to be in writing, with a member designated to cast the proxies. The proxy vote also had to be dated and could not be used to make a quorum.

During its brief consideration of reform proposals recommended by the Joint Committee on the Organization of Congress as adjournment approached in 1994, the House Rules Committee considered amendments to the rules that would have further restricted or abolished the practice of proxy voting. With several Democrats reportedly considering support for such reforms the committee recessed and never resumed the markup, preventing any votes on the joint committee's proposals.

Ironically, following the abolition of proxy voting when House rules were adopted in January 1995, the Republicans endured immediate political pain for their decision. They were forced to conduct numerous simultaneous committee meetings and House floor votes to ensure prompt passage of the legislative agenda

had to be dictated solely by seniority. In January 1971 the House Democratic Caucus voted to adopt modest changes recommended by its Committee on Organization, Study, and Review, created in 1970 to examine the party's organization and the seniority system. The committee was headed by Julia Butler Hansen, D-Wash.

The principal changes agreed upon were as follows.

■ The Democratic Committee on Committees, composed of the Democratic members of the Ways and Means Committee, would recommend to the caucus

nominees for the chair and membership of each committee, and such recommendations did not have to follow seniority. (The committee's power was transferred in December 1974 to the Steering and Policy Committee, a leadership entity.)

■ The Committee on Committees would make recommendations to the caucus, one committee at a time. Upon the demand of ten or more caucus members, nominations could be debated and voted on. If a nomination were rejected, the Committee on Committees would submit another nomination.

promised in the election campaign, while struggling to maintain voting control with the narrowest House majority in forty years.

Although pleas by a few members for a return to proxy voting were not heeded, the Republicans eventually loosened some of the other restrictions they had passed on the number of committee and subcommittee assignments members might hold, so they would be able to place enough majority members in the right places to ensure control. Also, a rule change adopted at the outset of the 108th Congress in 2003 allowed committee chairs to postpone votes on a variety of substantive matters. The effect of this change, Democrats claimed at the time, was essentially the same as allowing proxies, because chairs could simply wait for favorable majorities to appear and thereby conclude business to their advantage. That said, the Democrats retained the rule when they took control of the House in January 2007.

SENATE

For Senate committees the 1970 act provided little restraint on the use of proxies, and they are still used on amendments offered during committee markups. The law said proxy votes could not be used to report legislation if committee rules barred their use. If proxies were not forbidden on a motion to report a bill, they nevertheless could be used only upon the formal request of a senator who planned to be absent during a session. To prevent the use of general proxies, Senate rules bar the use of a proxy if an absent member "has not been informed of the matter on which he is being recorded and has not affirmatively requested that he be so recorded." Proxies cannot be counted toward the quorum needed for reporting legislation.

In addition to proxy voting, some Senate committees permit polling—holding an informal vote of committee members instead of convening the committee. Such votes usually are taken by sending a voting sheet to committee members' offices or by taking members' votes by telephone.

Because Senate rules require a quorum to be present for a committee to report legislation, polling is supposed to be restricted to issues involving legislation that is still pending before the committee, to matters relating to investigations, and to internal committee business.

If polling is used to report a matter, any senator can challenge the action by raising a point of order. Such was the case in December 1980 when opponents of a Carter nominee for a federal judgeship charged that the nomination had not been properly reported because the Judiciary Committee had approved it by a written poll. The issue was dropped and the nominee was approved when Judiciary chair Edward M. Kennedy, D-Mass., gained Republican support by agreeing not to push other Carter lame-duck judicial nominations pending in the committee.

FROM PROXY VOTING TO A CYBER-CONGRESS?

Neither chamber of Congress has ever allowed members to vote by proxy on the floor, and the House has disciplined members who used another member's voting card. But in recent years some members raised the issue of voting from other locations, as long as it was concurrent with voting on the floor and their votes could be verified through a secure system. Improving technology could, at some point, allow members of Congress working in their states or districts to participate in real time in congressional debates.

Members broached these ideas as a way of enhancing their personal convenience and allowing them to perform more of their congressional functions, but perhaps at the expense of Congress's broader purposes. The concept of representation and the role of members of Congress changed in the latter part of the twentieth century as Congress stayed in session longer and members had less time to spend in their districts. The demands of campaign fund-raising and the need for direct constituent contact at town meetings and other events increased pressure on congressional schedules. Members also had less time to spend with their families.

Congress traditionally fears change and has resisted even modest technological intrusions. Both chambers long resisted television. The House in 1995 banned the use on the floor of any personal electronic office equipment, including cellular telephones and computers. The Senate, similarly, banned the use of laptop computers on the grounds that they would disrupt floor proceedings and distract senators.

Critics of the use of technology to allow absent members to legislate say this development would contradict the very essence of Congress, which requires an interaction of legislators face to face. In addition, the Constitution requires that Congress assemble to exercise its power. It is doubtful that video-conferencing or a "Congress Online" could qualify.

■ No Democrat could chair more than one legislative subcommittee. That change made it possible to break the hold of the more conservative senior Democrats on key subcommittees, and it gradually made middle-level and even some junior Democrats eligible for subcommittee chairs. In its first year, sixteen Democrats who came to the House after 1958 gained their first subcommittee chairs.

Also in 1971, House Republicans agreed that the ranking Republican on each committee would be selected by vote of the Republican Conference, which is made up of all House Republicans, and not automatically elevated by seniority. They also bypassed Armed Services Committee member Alvin O'Konski, R-Wis., who was next in line to be ranking member, by allowing the more senior Minority Whip Les Arends, R-Ill., to take the post even though party rules would have prevented him from holding both jobs. In 1973 the Republican Conference confirmed moderate Frank Horton of New York as ranking member of the Government Operations Committee, deflecting a challenge from the junior but more conservative John N. Erlenborn of Illinois. So long as

Republicans remained in the minority, they had little incentive to violate seniority or formally remove an incumbent committee leader. But this would change after their 1995 takeover.

House Democrats in January 1973 altered their chair selection procedures by allowing a secret-ballot vote on any committee chair when 20 percent of the caucus demanded it. The expectation was that votes would be taken on all candidates. (This cumbersome procedure was replaced in 1974 by an automatic secret vote.) In 1973 all the chairs survived, as did the seven ranking Democrats marked for elevation by the retirement of their predecessors.

Subcommittee "Bill of Rights"

The House Democratic Caucus in January 1973 adopted the so-called subcommittee bill of rights. The new caucus rules created a party caucus for Democrats on each House committee and forced chairs to start sharing authority with other Democrats. Each committee caucus was granted the authority to select subcommittee chairs (with members allowed to run for chair based on their seniority ranking on the full committee), establish subcommittee jurisdictions, set party ratios on the subcommittees to reflect the party ratio of the full committee, write the committee's rules, provide a subcommittee budget, and guarantee all members a major subcommittee slot when vacancies made that possible. Each subcommittee was authorized to meet, hold hearings, and act on matters referred to it. And under the bill of rights, committee chairs were required to refer designated types of legislation to subcommittees within two weeks. They no longer could kill measures they opposed by pocketing them, at least not at the subcommittee stage.

Compromise Hansen Plan

Further procedural changes, along with minor committee jurisdictional shifts, were approved by the House in 1974 in a new package of recommendations put forward by Hansen's study committee. The Hansen plan was a substitute for a much broader bipartisan proposal, drafted by a select committee headed by Rep. Richard Bolling, D-Mo. The Bolling committee's call for wholesale restructuring of the committee system had triggered a flood of protests from adversely affected chairs and committee members. The Hansen substitute made some jurisdictional shifts—such as giving the Public Works Committee control over more transportation matters—but mainly retained the existing committee structure dating from 1946.

Under the Hansen plan, each standing committee's permanent staff, beginning in 1975, was increased from six to eighteen professionals and from six to twelve clerks, with the minority party receiving one-third of each category. And in what would prove to be one of the most controversial provisions, the plan gave the minority party control of one-third of a committee's investigative staff funding. As the 94th Congress (1975–1977) convened to adopt its rules, the Democratic Caucus engineered repeal of the one-third provision for investigative staffing before it could take effect. Nevertheless, each side received more staffing and subcommittee chairs, and ranking members were allowed to hire one staff person each to work directly for them on their subcommittees.

In other changes, which also took effect in 1975, committees with more than fifteen members (later increased to those with more than twenty members) were required to establish at least four subcommittees. This change was directed at the Ways and Means Committee, which had operated without subcommittees during most of the sixteen-year chair of Wilbur D. Mills, D-Ark. It also created an important precedent in that it institutionalized subcommittees in House rules for the first time. The larger committees also were required to set up an oversight subcommittee or to have their legislative subcommittees carry out oversight functions. In addition, the Hansen plan gave the Speaker new powers to refer legislation to more than one committee and banned proxy voting in committee. (Proxy voting was almost immediately restored, however, in 1975 by the Democratic Caucus and remained in effect for twenty years until Republicans took control in 1995.) *(See box, Proxy Voting, p. 152.)*

More Blows to Seniority

Further changes in House committee operations unrelated to the Hansen plan were made in late 1974 and early 1975 by the Democratic Caucus after the party's overwhelming victory in post-Watergate elections resulted in a two-to-one majority. Meeting in December 1974 to organize for the next Congress (as had been required under the Hansen plan), Democrats decided to adopt a secret-ballot vote on the election of each committee chair. The new procedure allowed competitive nominations for chairs if the original Steering Committee nominee was rejected. Democrats immediately made use of their new rule by deposing three committee chairs. *(See box, Seniority under Fire, p. 156.)*

In other changes the Democratic members of the Ways and Means Committee were stripped of their power to select the party's members of House committees. This authority was transferred to a revamped Democratic Steering and Policy Committee, chaired by the Speaker. Many of the other members served in the leadership or were appointed by the Speaker, along with members elected from specific geographic regions. Over time, both the size of the Steering Committee and the number of leadership-influenced appointments increased. At the same time the caucus increased the size of the Ways and Means Committee from twenty-five to thirty-seven members, a change designed to give the committee a more liberal outlook and thus make it more likely to support party-backed proposals on tax revision, health insurance, and other issues.

In actions affecting the independence of subcommittees, the caucus directed that the entire Democratic membership of each committee, not the chair alone, was to determine the number and jurisdiction of a committee's subcommittees. The Democratic Caucus of each committee drafted and approved a committee's rules, which often incorporated the number, size, and jurisdiction of its subcommittees. And the caucus specified that no Democratic member of a committee could become a member of a second subcommittee of that committee until every member of the full committee had chosen a subcommittee slot—a process called "bidding." (A grandfather clause allowed sitting members on subcommittees to protect two subcommittee slots, but this protection for the second subcommittee slot was eliminated in 1979.)

One group of subcommittees always had been semiautonomous—the powerful units of the House Appropriations Committee. The thirteen subcommittees were organized roughly parallel to the executive departments and agencies, and most of the annual budget review was done at that level. The staggering size and complexity of the federal budget required each subcommittee to develop an expertise and an autonomy respected and rarely challenged by other subcommittees or by the full committee—leading these thirteen chairs to be referred to as the "cardinals." Because of the panels' special role, the caucus decided that, like full committee chairs, all nominees for chair of these subcommittees would have to be approved by the Democratic Caucus. (Nominees for Appropriations subcommittee chairs were selected by the membership of each subcommittee, with members bidding for a subcommittee chair in the order of their seniority on the subcommittee.)

The Speaker's powers were further buttressed by allowing him or her to nominate the Democratic members of the Rules Committee, subject to caucus approval. Moreover, in a change adopted by the Caucus in December 1976, the chairs of the Ways and Means and Appropriations committees were stripped of their power to nominate members from their committees to serve on the Budget Committee. That power was transferred to the Speaker-dominated Democratic Steering and Policy Committee.

In December 1978 the House Democratic Caucus voted to prohibit, as of the next Congress, a committee chair from serving as chair of any other standing, select, special, or joint committee. Some chairs were exempt because they were required by law to also chair joint committees.

Each House Democrat was limited to five subcommittee seats on House standing committees. In 1987 waivers to the five-subcommittee rule—which had become routine— were barred in most cases, but the change proved ineffective. To maintain effective control of a subcommittee, it was sometimes necessary to add members who might violate the assignment limit. Attempts to restrict subcommittee assignments were frequently disregarded, especially when the leadership supported exceptions. In addition, the caucus decided that the bidding for subcommittee chairs would be based on a member's seniority rank on the full committee, with the exception of Appropriations subcommittee chairs.

Decline of Reform Zeal

Toward the end of the 1970s, the broad agenda for House reform among Democrats abated. The leadership had been strengthened, chairs had been weakened, and junior members were assured of acquiring subcommittee chairs along with increased staff resources relatively early in their careers.

Not surprisingly, reform projects that did emerge received a less than hospitable reception. The House Commission on Administrative Review, headed by Rep. David Obey, D-Wis., concluded that members had too many committee assignments and that existing committee jurisdictions were too confused. But its recommendations went down to defeat in October 1977. The House also declined to consider its proposals to change the administrative operations of the House. This decision would come back to haunt Democrats in the early nineties when several embarrassing administrative scandals came to light.

The House in March 1979 once again set up a Select Committee on Committees to recommend how to improve the House's internal organization and operations. But the effort failed because substantive changes would have proven too threatening to a wide variety of entrenched interests. When the panel chaired by Jerry M. Patterson, D-Calif., closed its doors in April 1980, it left behind barely a trace of its thirteen-month-long effort. Only one recommendation— a plan to create a separate standing committee on energy— went to the House floor, where the proposal was promptly gutted. In place of the select committee's plan, the House merely decided to rename its Commerce Committee as the Energy and Commerce Committee and to designate that panel as its lead committee on energy matters. Proposals to limit subcommittee assignments as well as the number of subcommittees were dropped.

Two years later, in 1982, House Democrats did amend their caucus rules to limit the number of subcommittees and similar committee subunits. Under the new rule, the Appropriations Committee could retain all of its thirteen panels, but all other standing committees were restricted to a maximum of either eight (if the standing committee had at least thirty-five members) or six (for smaller committees). A decade later, in 1992, Democrats again amended their caucus rules to limit most committees to a maximum of five subcommittees, but, in a gesture to the importance of placating individuals and avoiding sacrifice, they also guaranteed that no subcommittee chair would lose a post.

Seniority Under Fire: House Ousts Chairs, Senate Follows Tradition

Both political parties in the House and Senate in the 1970s decided that seniority—status based on length of continuous committee service—should no longer be the sole determinant in selecting committee leaders. The House took substantive steps to implement this reform, as did Senate Republicans. But even the threatened use of this authority gave rank-and-file members a potent weapon.

The House Democratic Caucus shook the foundations of the committee structure by ousting three autocratic chairs in 1975. It was a watershed that redirected the flow of institutional power in the House. The caucus rules required an automatic up-or-down vote on a candidate for chair nominated by the Steering and Policy Committee if the nominee was either the incumbent chair or the senior Democrat seeking the post if the chair was vacant. Other candidates were only allowed to run if the chair or senior member were rejected by the Steering and Policy Committee or by the full caucus. In 1992 the rules were further liberalized to allow others to run directly if fourteen or more members opposed the nomination of the chair or senior member in the Steering and Policy Committee or if fifty members signed a petition.

The House Republican Conference took a somewhat different approach to seniority. Few direct challenges were made to ranking minority committee members because those posts had little power relative to chairs controlled by the majority. Moderate representative Frank Horton, R-N.Y., was challenged as ranking minority member of the Government Operations Committee in 1972 by conservatives supporting Rep. John N. Erlenborn, R-Ill. But Horton easily won confirmation in the up-or-down vote. In 1992 an attempt by the Steering Committee to nominate Rep. Paul Gillmor, R-Ohio, as ranking member of the House Administration Committee over incumbent representative William M. Thomas, R-Calif., whose relations with the leadership were sometimes testy, also was rejected by the conference.

Upon taking power in Congress in 1995, however, the GOP immediately demonstrated it was less concerned about seniority than the Democrats. Speaker Newt Gingrich, R-Ga., hand-picked chairs of the Appropriations, Commerce, and Judiciary committees, bypassing more senior members. Rep. Carlos Moorhead, R-Calif., senior member of both the Commerce and Judiciary committees, was denied either chair. Moorhead retired in 1997. Rep. Joseph M. McDade, R-Pa., was denied the Appropriations chair in 1995 because he was under a federal indictment for corruption. Gingrich then skipped over the next two senior members to select Rep. Robert Livingston, R-La., as chair. After McDade was acquitted, however, Livingston remained chair and McDade had to be satisfied with the title of vice chair and a subcommittee chair. He announced his retirement at the end of the 105th Congress.

HOUSE CHAIRS OUSTED

In 1971 House Democrats and Republicans decided that seniority need not be followed in the selection of committee leaders. In 1973 Democrats permitted one-fifth of their caucus to force a vote on a nominee for committee chair, and in 1974 that vote became automatic for all nominees.

Rank-and-file Democrats in January 1975 asserted their new power by unseating three incumbent chairs: Armed Services Committee chair F. Edward Hébert of Louisiana; Agriculture Committee chair W.R. Poage of Texas; and Banking, Currency, and Housing Committee chair Wright Patman of Texas. Hébert and Poage were both replaced by the next ranking Democrat on their committees, but, in yet another blow to the seniority system, the fourth-ranking Democrat on the Banking Committee, Henry S. Reuss of Wisconsin, was elected to succeed Patman. The autocratic manner in which the three chairs had run their committees was primarily responsible for their downfall, but each also refused to interview with the Democratic Class of 1974 (the "Watergate babies").

In 1984 the Democratic Caucus voted narrowly to remove elderly Melvin Price of Illinois from the chair of the Armed Services Committee and replace him with Les Aspin of Wisconsin, the panel's seventh-ranking Democrat, despite an impassioned plea on behalf of Price from Speaker Thomas P. "Tip" O'Neill Jr., D-Mass. Many Democrats had complained that Price's infirmity allowed the Republican minority to exercise effective control of the conservative panel.

Aspin nearly suffered the same fate two years later. Many liberal Democrats were distressed at what they considered his betrayals on several controversial defense issues. Aspin lost his chair in early January 1987 in a yes-or-no vote in the Democratic Caucus on his reelection, with no other name on the ballot. But two weeks later, pitted against three other committee members, Aspin won it back on the third ballot over the more conservative representative Marvin Leath of Texas.

Democrats ousted two more committee chairs in December 1990, as they organized for the 102nd Congress. Public Works Chair Glenn M. Anderson, D-Calif., and House Administration Chair Frank Annunzio, D-Ill., were regarded as weak, ineffective leaders. They were rejected and then replaced by younger Democrats: Rep. Robert A. Roe of New Jersey, the second-ranking Democrat on Public Works, defeated third-ranking representative Norman Y. Mineta of California (who would become chair in the next Congress); and Rep. Charlie Rose of North Carolina, the third-ranking Democrat on House Administration.

Use of caucus rules to challenge committee chairs usually was at the behest of the rank-and-file membership and was often unsuccessfully opposed by some in the party leadership, who feared disruptions from ongoing competition for committees and subcommittee posts. There were important exceptions, however.

Rep. David Obey, a senior member of the Appropriations Committee and one of the House's most aggressive and partisan liberals, benefited from the weakening of the seniority tradition in 1994 when Chair William H. Natcher, D-Ky., became terminally ill. Obey, the fifth-ranking member, was supported by the leadership and

Having ignored administrative reforms earlier, twin 1992 scandals regarding overdrafts on the House bank and the House post office forced reform back into the headlines. Thus in the 103rd Congress a new Joint Committee on the Organization of Congress was created and was structured similarly to the previous joint committees of 1946 and 1970. But ultimately that was all it had in common with them. The joint committee discussed many ideas for reform but accomplished nothing as there was little appetite among House Democrats for change. In the words of *CQ Weekly* reporter Janet Hook:

easily won a vote of the Steering and Policy Committee to succeed Natcher as acting chair over the third-ranking Democrat, Neal Smith of Iowa, who argued that he deserved the post as a veteran liberal who had served for thirty-five years. Obey automatically assumed the chair upon Natcher's death.

Republicans too have proven willing to depose chairs over substantive disagreements. In January 2005 the Republican Steering Committee refused to renominate Christopher H. Smith of New Jersey as chair of the Veterans' Affairs Committee. Smith had repeatedly opposed his party's position on the funding of veterans' programs and occasionally voted pro-labor. That same month, Republican leaders ousted Joel Hefley of Colorado from the chair of the House ethics committee. During the 108th Congress, Hefley presided over the committee while it admonished Majority Leader Tom DeLay, R-Texas, three times.

The most recent episode, though, occurred at the outset of the 111th Congress, when longtime second-in-waiting Democrat Henry Waxman of California decided to challenge John Dingell, D-Mich., for the Energy and Commerce chair. He had served as the No. 2 Democrat on the committee for 16 years. Although allied on many policies, Waxman and Dingell differed on some energy and clean air proposals, and Waxman longed to promote national health care legislation. In a contest that went to the Democratic Caucus, Waxman ultimately carried the day on a 137–122 vote.

Use of caucus rules to challenge committee chairs usually has been at the behest of the rank-and-file membership and often has been unsuccessfully opposed by some in the party leadership, who feared disruptions from ongoing competition for committees and subcommittee posts. There have been important exceptions, however, as Republican leaders were instrumental in the ousters of Smith and Hefley. And, although officially silent, there is no particular evidence to suggest that Pelosi was saddened by Waxman's elevation.

SENATE ADHERES TO SENIORITY

The Senate also decided in the 1970s that seniority should not dictate the choice of committee leaders. Senate Republicans adopted the policy in 1973 and the Democrats in 1975. Yet the Senate continued to adhere to the seniority tradition, and in the smaller body longtime personal relationships among senators also worked to smooth over arguments that ideology should be a more significant determinant in the acquisition of a committee chair.

In 1977, in the most visible attempt to undermine seniority, the liberal-dominated Democratic Conference took a secret-ballot vote on all nominees for chairs, with opposition centering on Finance Committee chair Russell Long of Louisiana. He won overwhelmingly, 42–6.

A battle in 1987 over the position of ranking minority member on the Foreign Relations Committee was settled primarily on the issue of seniority. The contest was between Jesse Helms, R-N.C., and the more moderate Richard G. Lugar, R-Ind. The situation was somewhat unusual because Lugar had been chair of the Foreign Relations panel for the previous two years while the Republicans controlled the Senate. Helms tended to North Carolina issues as chair of the Agriculture Committee in part due to a campaign promise he had made to lead the panel. But when the Senate reverted to the Democrats, Helms, who had joined the Foreign Relations panel the same day as Lugar, decided he wanted the position of ranking Republican on the committee and claimed seniority by virtue of his four years of longer service in the Senate.

Under the rules of the Senate Republican Conference at the time, each committee chose its top-ranking member, subject to confirmation by the entire conference. Republicans on the Foreign Relations Committee nominated Lugar as ranking member, but the full Republican Conference rejected him, 24–17. Helms—and the seniority system—won out. Lugar then became ranking minority member of the Agriculture Committee, and both he and Helms became chairs of these committees when Republican Senate control resumed in 1995.

The apparent personal animus between Helms and Lugar lingered, and the fallout from their contest had interesting repercussions for years to come. Lugar led the opposition to Helms's refusal in 1997 to hold a confirmation hearing for William Weld, a moderate Republican nominated as ambassador to Mexico. In an unprecedented action, a committee majority forced Helms to schedule a meeting at which they intended to discuss the Weld nomination, but Helms successfully used his powers to deny most other senators, including Lugar, a chance to speak. Lugar, in turn, threatened to use his powers as Agriculture chair against North Carolina tobacco interests.

Despite dramatic conservative gains in the Republican Conference, more moderate senators continued to rely on seniority to obtain and keep important positions on committees. Sen. Mark O. Hatfield, R-Ore., a veteran liberal, was not removed as Appropriations Committee chair during the 104th Congress after he cast the lone—and decisive—vote to kill a balanced budget constitutional amendment, and Sen. John H. Chafee, R-R.I., assumed the chair of the Environment and Public Works Committee. In the 105th Congress, a rumored challenge to Sen. James M. Jeffords, R-Vt., for the open chair of the Labor and Human Resources Committee by conservative senator Dan Coats, R-Ind., never developed. And even after angering some fellow Democrats by running as an independent, Joseph I. Lieberman of Connecticut was granted approval by the Democratic Conference in 2007 to switch from ranking member to chair of the Homeland Security and Governmental Affairs Committee.

The adoption of chair term limits by Senate and House Republicans, of course, now makes challenges to incumbent GOP chairs far more unlikely. But the absence of such rules for House and Senate Democrats means that challenges and seniority violations, such as the Waxman-Dingell contest, remain a distinct possibility.

[T]he obstacles to major change are monumental. Many Democratic leaders are lukewarm. Powerful committee chairs are downright hostile. Even among junior lawmakers, the interests vested in the status quo are legion. Many members wonder if it is worth the trouble to even try.[21]

So although the Democratic leadership wanted the issue to go away, they continued to make (unfulfilled) commitments to consider the committee's recommendations on the House floor. Meanwhile Republicans were anxious to take credit for the idea of reform and to use institutional corruption as a theme in the next, decisive, campaign. David Dreier, R-Calif., spearheaded the minority effort on the committee and authored an aggressive reform package to the rules that was dismissed by majority Democrats. That rules package would become a blueprint for Republicans in 1995 upon their ascendance to majority status.

In the end, the joint committee foundered over bitter partisanship in the House and poisonous bicameral relations when Senate Republicans angered Democrats by employing filibusters against Clinton administration proposals. House Democrats refused to consider enhanced minority rights for Republicans, such as a guarantee that the minority could offer amendatory instructions in the motion to recommit bills to committees, unless the Senate agreed to reforms in the filibuster, a proposal anathema to key senators from both parties. These issues were difficult enough without the addition of changes in committee structure and jurisdiction.

After the 103rd Congress expired, party control of both chambers shifted and reforms again became a unicameral, partisan initiative, this time in GOP hands. In 1995 the House abolished the District of Columbia, Merchant Marine and Fisheries, and Post Office and Civil Service committees. Although the absence of these three minor panels had little effect on the operation of the chamber, Democrats believed it was payback by the new majority, because the three had, on balance, liberal-leaning constituencies. Moreover, two other small committees—Small Business and Veterans' Affairs—were retained. And these, if anything, had Republican-leaning constituencies.

The Republican rules package went far beyond this, as the new majority sought to quickly place its imprint on the chamber. Among other things, the new rules package:

- Placed six-year term limits on committee and subcommittee chairs.

- Placed an eight-year term limit on the Speaker (later rescinded).

- Eliminated three standing committees, changed a number of committee names, and implemented some jurisdictional shifts.

- Limited nearly all committees to five subcommittees.

- Abolished joint referrals while enhancing the Speaker's authority over split and sequential referrals.

- Prohibited the use of rolling quorums in committee.

- Prohibited the use of proxy voting in committee.

- Enhanced the authority of party leaders in the committee and chair assignment process.

- Cut back member assignments to two full and four subcommittee slots.

All together, these reforms were nearly as dramatic as anything achieved by Democrats in the early 1970s. And they moved in precisely the opposite direction, by undercutting subcommittees and re-empowering the corporate Republican leadership. Once again, full committee chairs had lost.

Senate Committee Changes

While most of the attempts to reorganize the committee system in the 1970s were directed at the House, the Senate committee system was altered in 1977 by the first major committee consolidation in either house since passage of the 1946 reorganization act. Earlier in the decade the Senate had adopted important procedural changes involving committees. As previously noted, a later attempt, the Joint Committee on the Organization of Congress, ended in failure.

Committees and committee assignments in the Senate are less important in the work of the chamber and in determining the course of a member's career than in the House. Although parties influence the assignment process in the Senate, some assignment limitations are set out in the chamber rules. Consequently, proposed reforms open the door to the delicate subject of amendments to Senate rules. The Senate often adjusts committee structure and assignment issues by creating new exceptions, irrespective of the rules, that benefit individual senators. Each party also privately determines policies affecting its own members, which has the advantage of avoiding messy floor debate and keeps the parties out of each other's affairs.

Challenges to Seniority

The Senate struck the first successful blow to the seniority system in the post–World War II period. As Senate minority leader in 1953, Lyndon B. Johnson proposed that all Democratic senators be given a seat on one major committee before any Democrat was assigned to a second major committee. The proposal, which became known as the "Johnson Rule," was a stunning blow to seniority. But it had the backing of Sen. Richard Russell of Georgia—the powerful leader of the southern Democratic bloc that dominated the Senate for years—and was approved by the Democratic Steering Committee that made Democratic committee assignments in the Senate. It was fitting that Johnson had successfully staged the breakthrough because he was a junior senator, chosen as his party's leader while still in his first Senate term. He had served six terms in the House, however, and had become a protégé of House Speaker Sam Rayburn, D-Texas. Senate Republicans adopted the same party rule, first informally in 1959 and then through the Republican Conference in 1965.

In 1971, under renewed pressure to modify the seniority system, Majority Leader Mike Mansfield, D-Mont., announced that a meeting of the Democratic Conference would be held at the request of any senator and any senator could challenge any nomination by the Steering Committee. For their part, Republicans adopted a proposal that a senator could be the ranking minority member of only one standing committee.

They later applied the same rule to the selection of committee chairs upon taking control of the Senate in 1981.

A major challenge to the seniority system was blocked in 1971 when a resolution embodying it failed on a 48–26 vote. The resolution had provided that in making committee assignments "neither [party] conference shall be bound by any tradition, custom, or principle of seniority." But in 1973 Senate Republicans adopted a plan to limit the seniority system by having members of each standing committee elect the top-ranking Republican on that committee, subject to approval by a vote of all Senate Republicans. In 1975 Senate Democrats also voted to choose committee chairs without regard to seniority. A secret ballot would be taken whenever one-fifth of their conference requested it. The provision was first used in 1977 when twelve senators made a request for a secret ballot, though several of them said they still intended to support the committee chairs.

Unlike the changes under way in the House, the new rule failed to reveal any significant dissatisfaction with the traditional seniority system even on a secret ballot, as only a handful of votes were cast against any chair nominees. Sen. Russell Long, D-La., supposedly a longtime target of reformers, was easily renominated by a 42–6 vote. Appropriations Committee chair John McClellan, D-Ark., received an identical tally. Majority Leader Robert C. Byrd, D-W.Va., later forced a separate Senate vote on Long's election as chair to demonstrate what he called the democratic nature of Senate rules. Long won 60–0.

Also in 1975, junior senators obtained committee staff assistance for the first time. A new rule authorized them to hire up to three committee staffers, depending on the number and type of committee assignments they had, to work directly for them on their committees. In the past, committee staff members had been controlled by the chairs and other senior committee members. *(See Chapter 4, Congressional Staff.)*

1977 Committee Reorganization

The 1977 Senate reorganization consolidated a number of committees, revised jurisdictions of others, set a ceiling on the number of committees and subcommittees on which a senator could serve or chair, gave minority members a larger share of committee staff, and directed that schedules for committee hearings and other business be computerized to avoid conflicts. These latter changes, in particular, had already been put forward by the Commission on the Operation of the Senate (Culver Commission), which studied these matters from mid-1975 through the end of 1976. But the ultimate package of organizational and procedural changes was the product of a special panel, the Temporary Select Committee to Study the Senate Committee System chaired by Sen. Adlai E. Stevenson III, D-Ill.

One of the biggest organizational changes was the consolidation of most aspects of energy policy, except taxes, in one committee. Although the final result fell short of the Stevenson committee's goals for consolidating and merging committees, three committees were abolished: District of Columbia, Post Office, and Aeronautical and Space Sciences, as well as the joint committees on Atomic Energy, Congressional Operations, and Defense Production. (The decision to end the joint committees was a unilateral Senate action. The House continued the Congressional Operations panel as a select committee for another two years.) Special interest groups were able to preserve several other committees slated for extinction, such as Small Business.

Changes also were made in Senate committee procedures and bill referral—where a joint leadership motion could lead to multiple referrals. Senate reformers, like their House counterparts, were concerned with the proliferation of committees and subcommittees. In 1947 most senators served on two or three subcommittees. By the 94th Congress (1975–1977) they held an average of eleven assignments on subcommittees of standing committees.[22] Stevenson's Temporary Select Committee to Study the Senate Committee System stated in its report:

> Proliferation of committee panels means proliferation in assignments held by Senators. And the burdens and frustrations of too many assignments, whatever the benefits, produce inefficient division of labor, uneven distribution of responsibility, conflicts in the scheduling of meetings, waste of Senators' and staff time, unsystematic lawmaking and oversight, inadequate anticipation of major problems, and inadequate membership participation in committee decisions.[23]

As part of the 1977 reorganization, the Senate prohibited a senator from serving as chair of more than one subcommittee on any given committee. This placed an indirect cap on subcommittee expansion by limiting the number of subcommittees of any committee to the number of majority party members on the full committee.

Although initially there were many exceptions, each senator was nominally limited to membership on two major committees and one minor committee. Each senator also was limited to membership on three subcommittees on each of his or her major committees (the Appropriations Committee was exempted from this restriction) and two subcommittees on his or her minor committee.

Though it was not made a requirement, the Senate adopted language, similar to the practice in the House, stating that no member of a committee should receive a second subcommittee assignment until all members of the committee had received their first assignment. The Senate also prohibited a senator from serving as chair of more than one committee at the same time; prohibited the chair of a major committee from serving as chair of more than one subcommittee on the senator's major committees and as the chair of more than one subcommittee on his or her minor committee; prohibited the chair of a minor committee from chairing a subcommittee on that committee; and prohibited a senator

TERM LIMITS ON COMMITTEE CHAIRS AND SERVICE

Congress historically has resisted limiting the length of time members may serve on committees. To do so, it was argued, would detract from the expertise that committees possess in dealing with complex legislation. Limitations also would disrupt the concept of seniority that provides a stable mechanism for determining committee leaders over long periods of time and helps to avoid power struggles.

In 1995, however, the new Republican majorities in the House and Senate took important steps toward legitimizing term limitations for top committee posts. They amended House rules at the beginning of the 104th Congress to place a three-term service limit on all committee and subcommittee chairs and a four-term limit on the speakership, although this was later repealed. The House rule does not apply to ranking minority members of committees and subcommittees, and the Democratic Caucus in 1997 overwhelmingly rejected a proposal to implement a term limitation through the party's caucus rules. The House rule change was effective immediately.

The Senate's term limitation is a Republican Conference rule, not an amendment to the chamber's rules. It was adopted prospectively to limit full committee chairs or ranking members to six years of service, and the clock began to run only in 1997.

The three-term and six-year chairmanship limits were a significant movement away from seniority and toward a broader sharing of power in Congress.

The Contract with America, a GOP political agenda used in the 1994 elections, contained a proposal for a constitutional amendment requiring term limits on service in Congress itself. However, the amendment was easily defeated in 1995 and 1997 when brought to a vote. *(See box, Contract with America, p. 27.)*

Whether the changes would hold up was uncertain at the time. Although many Republicans had second thoughts as the deadline approached, they retained the rule and denied several requests for exemptions. As a result, at the outset of the 107th Congress (2001–2003), thirteen new chairs were anointed by the Republican Steering Committee and approved by the Conference. This was the most dramatic shift in committee leadership in modern congressional history, not counting circumstances of majority party change. Smaller shifts followed in 2003 and 2005.

On the Senate side, no similar drama accompanied chair or ranking member rotations when the rule finally kicked in. But the 1995 rule's vagueness about service as chair and ranking member did cause Republicans to revisit the language. So in June 2002 a reworded version was adopted—defeating a strict six-year limit and abandoning the rule altogether—that took something of a middle ground. Under the revised language Republicans were allowed up to twelve years combined as chair and ranking member—six years of each. But once they had served six years as chair, they would be forced to step down even if they had not yet served six years as a ranking member. In addition, the entire 107th Congress was treated as if the Republicans had been in the minority, a circumstance caused by James Jeffords's departure from the GOP conference. This effectively put off the first round of Senate musical chairs to the 109th Congress, at which point senior or retiring chairs were simply replaced by the next most senior member.

Democrats gained control of the House and Senate in 2007. Despite considerable grumbling, particularly among more senior members of the Democratic Caucus, the House term limit rule was initially retained. But after further consideration it was abandoned in the 111th Congress—only to be returned by Republicans in 2011.

Reformers in the past have argued for even broader committee service limitations for the entire House membership to break up entrenched oligarchies on committees and encourage members to explore new interests across the jurisdictional spectrum. The idea never attracted significant support because by disrupting seniority it removed the most significant source of stability and predictability for members as they planned their congressional careers. There also were legitimate questions about how any wholesale rotation would work when hundreds of members might be affected at once.

The use of term limits in limited circumstances is not new in Congress, however. Three House standing committees—Budget, Intelligence, and Ethics—currently have service limits stipulated by House and/or party rules. The Budget Committee, which is supposed to have a broad range of membership, including mandatory representation from the Appropriations and Ways and Means committees, began with a two-term limit and gradually expanded to three terms, then to four terms in the 104th Congress. Technically, the rule limits members to no more than four terms out of six successive Congresses, thus preventing them from leaving the committee and quickly being brought back. The chair can serve for an additional term, if necessary, to allow him or her a minimum of two terms in that post. But

from chairing more than one of each of his or her major committees' subcommittees.

The Senate also required the Rules and Administration Committee to establish a central computerized scheduling service to keep track of meetings of Senate committees and subcommittees and House-Senate conference committees. Finally, the Senate required the staff of each committee to reflect the relative size of the majority and minority membership on the committee. On the request of the minority party members of a committee, at least one-third of the staff of the committee was to be placed under the control of the minority party, except that staff deemed by the chair and ranking minority member to be working for the whole committee would not be subject to the rule.

1980s Reform Attempts

Frustration with Senate procedures ran high in the 1980s, but despite several serious proposals for reform no major changes were achieved by the end of the decade.

A 1983 report by former senators James B. Pearson, R-Kan., and Abraham Ribicoff, D-Conn., urged major changes in the Senate structure and procedures, including restrictions on subcommittees and a reduction in the number of committees. Under their plan, subcommittees would not have been permitted to report legislation to the full committee. And the panels would not have been staffed, a move aimed at eliminating what they saw as time-consuming specialization at the subcommittee level.

CONFERENCE COMMITTEES

The conference committee is an ad hoc joint committee appointed to reconcile differences between Senate and House versions of pending legislation. The conference device, used by Congress since 1789, had developed its modern form by the middle of the nineteenth century.

Before a bill can be sent to the president, it must be passed in identical form by both chambers. Whenever different versions of the same bill are passed, and neither chamber is willing to yield to the other or make modifications by sending a bill back and forth, a conference becomes necessary to determine the final shape of the legislation. It is unusual for the Senate or House to reject the work of a conference committee.

In the past, conference committees were composed of senior members of the committees that handled the bill. This remains generally true today, but there are opportunities for junior members to be appointed and occasionally even members who were not on a committee that originally reported the bill. Conferees are appointed by the Speaker and the presiding officer of the Senate on the recommendations of the committee chairs and ranking minority members. They are subject to influence by the respective party leaderships. Although the chairs, by tradition, have played the principal role in picking conferees, in the House the Speaker retains the substantive power to make the appointments, subject only to the restrictions in Rule I, Clause 11, that he or she "shall appoint no less than a majority of Members who generally supported the House position as determined by the Speaker" and "shall name Members who are primarily responsible for the legislation and shall, to the fullest extent feasible, include the principal proponents of the major provisions of the bill as it passed the House." The Speaker's appointments may not be challenged on a point of order for alleged violations of these criteria.

Recent Speakers have intervened more frequently to select members they want to serve as conferees and to bar those they do not. Speaker Newt Gingrich, R-Ga., even appointed members of the Democratic minority to serve in conference slots reserved for the majority to highlight differences within the minority.

In 1993 the House changed its rules to give the Speaker the power, after a conference has been appointed, to appoint additional conferees and to remove conferees as he or she wishes. Before then, any changes in the composition of a conference after its appointment had required unanimous consent. While the change by 1999 had no dramatic impact on the operation of conferences, it effectively prevented conferees from defying the will of the majority leadership. Largely because of complexities in the House created by multiple referrals of bills to different committees and the increasing use of massive omnibus bills to deal with budget and tax matters, the size of conference delegations increased during the 1980s and in subsequent years. Scholars C. Lawrence Evans and Walter J. Oleszek have noted that committee chairs in the 1980s often demanded positions on conferences from Democratic Speakers, who frequently found it politic to accommodate them. In 1981, for example, more than 250 members of Congress participated in a conference on a budget reconciliation bill, making it the largest conference in history. The conference split up into fifty-eight subgroups to consider various sections of the legislation.

The 1995 rules changes in the House requiring that a primary committee be designated for each bill, instead of the previous practice of joint referrals, could swing the trend back toward less complex conference structures. Evans and Oleszek have observed that the new rule gave Speaker Gingrich "the procedural rationale for resisting chairs' demands for conference slots."[1] Data indicate that, for legislation in conference that received multiple referrals, the average size of the House delegation dropped from 42.7 members to 29.1 between the 103rd and 104th Congresses. And conferences in general have receded in size from their peak in the 1980s.

In addition, conferences themselves are simply not used as frequently in recent congresses. Instead party leaders increasingly have cleared legislation via leadership "ping-ponging" whereby the final versions of bills are simply hashed out behind closed doors and without a formal conference being formed. By the 110th Congress (2007–2009) only 2 percent of the statutes produced by Congress had been subject to a conference—down from 13 percent in the 103rd.[2]

CONDUCTING A CONFERENCE

There need not be an equal number of conferees (or managers, as they are called) from each house. Each house's delegation has a single vote, which is determined by a majority vote of its conferees. Therefore, a majority of both the Senate and House delegations must agree before a provision emerges from conference as part of the final bill. Both chambers permit proxy voting in conferences.

Republicans weakened the chairmanship rule by allowing John R. Kasich of Ohio to hold the post continuously from 1995 to 2007.

The Democrats refused to adopt the new four-term limit, retaining the three-term limit in their caucus rules and making Budget the only committee in Congress in which each party uses a different term limit. The Democrats' decision did not represent a judgment of the appropriate length of service on the committee. Instead, they sought to use the already scheduled three-term rotation to create some vacant seats to give to members because so few committee assignments were available under the ratios created by the new Republican majority.

In the case of the Committee on Ethics, term limits have varied. Effective in 1999 a service limitation of no more than three Congresses in any period of five successive Congresses was imposed. However, there is no demand for service on the committee. The size of the committee was fixed at fourteen by the Ethics Reform Act of 1989, but the controversy associated with the committee's workload made that number unrealistic. Only ten seats were occupied in each of the 104th, 105th, and 106th Congresses. Rules changes in 1997 allowed twenty members who do not serve on the committee—ten from each party—to serve in a pool from which members could be drawn to join regular committee members in filling subcommittees to investigate ethics violations.

The lone House select committee, Permanent Intelligence, originally had a six-calendar-year service limitation, which was changed to four-terms-out-of-six successive Congresses in 1995, as had been recommended by the Joint Committee on the Organization of Congress. Proponents of term limits had argued at the committee's inception that a limitation would refresh the membership and prevent it from being co-opted by the intelligence community. The rule also was amended to allow a member selected as chair in his or her fourth Congress of service to be eligible to serve for a fifth term if reappointed as chair, to ensure greater continuity of the committee's work. Subsequently, this rule was further changed to place no limit on the committee's chair. And both the four-in-six provision and the no-limit provision were retained by Democrats in 2007. Because of defects in the operation of the original six-year rotation rule, criticism arose that the committee had been weakened because nearly all of its chairs (except the first) had been limited to only

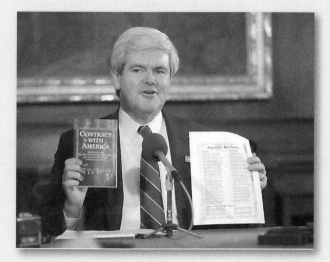

House Speaker Newt Gingrich, R-Ga., holds up his "Contract with America" and a paperback bestseller list during a January 1995 meeting with reporters. As part of the Contract with America agenda the Republican majority sought to impose term limits on committee chairs.

SOURCE: AP Photo/John Duricka.

two years in that post and could not establish strong and stable working relationships with executive branch entities. Thus, at present, there is no limit on service for the chair or ranking member of the committee (Rule XI 11(a)(4)(B)).

The Senate does not employ rotation on any of its standing committees, so the shifting members of the House Budget Committee face a Senate counterpart with long-term permanent membership. So, for example, the Senate chair in 1999, Pete V. Domenici of New Mexico, also held the post during an earlier period of Republican Senate control in the 1980s.

---

also fixes their size. Of the four permanent joint committees functioning in the 112th Congress (2011–2013), none had the authority to report legislation. The Joint Economic Committee is directed to examine national economic problems and review the execution of fiscal and budgetary programs. The Joint Committee on Taxation, made up of senior members of both parties from the House Ways and Means and Senate Finance committees, serves chiefly to provide a professional staff that long enjoyed a nonpartisan reputation on tax issues. When the Republicans assumed control of both houses in 1995, the new majority used it as a resource to develop its agenda for enacting major tax cuts. The other two joint committees deal with administrative matters: the Joint

Committee on Printing oversees the Government Printing Office, and the Joint Committee on the Library oversees the Library of Congress and works of art in the Capitol.

Chairs of permanent joint committees generally rotate from one chamber to the other at the beginning of each Congress. When a senator serves as chair, the vice chair is a representative and vice versa. The last standing joint committee to have legislative responsibilities was the Joint Committee on Atomic Energy, which was abolished in 1977.

The most recent temporary body, the Joint Committee on Deficit Reduction, was created in 2011 as part of an agreement to raise the federal debt ceiling and cut federal deficits (P.L. 112-25). The twelve-member committee, with House

The following year another Temporary Select Committee to Study the Senate Committee System, chaired by Dan Quayle, R-Ind., recommended, among other things, strictly limiting the number of committee and subcommittee assignments each senator could have. The panel urged strict enforcement of existing rules allowing senators to serve on two major committees and one minor committee.

The Senate Rules and Administration Committee in 1988 proposed changes in committee and floor procedures. To reduce the number of competing demands on senators' time, the panel proposed allowing subcommittees to hold only hearings, thus requiring all legislative drafting sessions to be held at the full committee level.

In 1993 the Joint Committee on the Organization of Congress proposed a variety of ideas to revise committee structure, assignments, and procedures, although it did not recommend abolition of any existing committee. Among its proposals were limiting senators to three committees; restricting major committees (called "super A" and "A") to three subcommittees (except Appropriations) and minor "B" committees to two subcommittees; limiting senators to service on two subcommittees per "A" committee (except Appropriations) and one per "B" committee; requiring bipartisan leadership approval and a Senate recorded vote for extra assignments; allowing majority and minority leaders to make committee assignments, subject to party rules; setting meeting days for the various classifications of committees to reduce scheduling conflicts; and barring use of proxies if they affected the result of a vote.

The joint committee's recommendations were reworked by a Republican task force appointed by incoming majority leader Bob Dole, R-Kan., in 1994, which called for Senate floor action on limiting subcommittees, enforcing committee membership rules, abolishing joint committees, phasing out several small unpopular panels, and restricting proxy voting. But again, none of these proposals was adopted.

By the 104th Congress (1995–1997), however, with Republicans back in the majority, reforms gained new life within the Republican Conference. The effort emerged after Appropriations Committee chair Mark O. Hatfield, R-Ore., voted against a balanced budget amendment to the Constitution (which failed by one vote). Angered at Hatfield's vote, a group of activist Republicans, including Sen. Connie Mack of Florida, approached Dole about seeking the chair's ouster. Dole refused to pursue the ouster but put Mack in charge of a task force to investigate possible changes to the Republican Conference rules.

The group returned to the conference in July 1995 with a package of reforms, nearly all of which were adopted and became effective at the outset of the following Congress (1997). They included:

- Six-year term limits for committee chairs.
- Six-year term limits for Republican Party leaders (except the floor leader and president pro tempore).
- A prohibition on reclaiming seniority upon returning to a committee on which a senator had previously served.
- Secret-ballot elections for committee chairs in committee and in the conference (with a provision for the party leader to nominate a successor in the event of a defeat).
- The adoption of a formal legislative agenda prior to the selection of committee chairs.

The last item, it was believed, would include support for the balanced budget amendment and defeat of Hatfield's reappointment as Appropriations chair. Republicans did include the amendment in their agenda for the next Congress, but by then Hatfield had retired. *(For more on term limits, see box, Term Limits on Committee Chairs and Service, p. 160.)*

COMMITTEE STRUCTURE

There are three principal classes of committees in Congress.

1. Standing committees, by far the most important and most numerous, that have permanently authorized staff and legislative jurisdictions fixed in each chamber's standing rules.

2. Select or special committees that have limited or no legislative jurisdiction, are frequently investigative, and are generally temporary in that they are authorized to operate for a specific period of time or until the project for which they are created has been completed.

3. Joint committees that have a membership drawn from both houses of Congress and usually are investigative or housekeeping in nature.

Conference committees, a special variety of joint committee, serve only on an ad hoc basis to resolve differences in Senate and House versions of the same legislation. *(See box, Conference Committees, p. 164.)*

Below the committee level are a plethora of subcommittees that are functional subdivisions of the committees. They are composed of members of the majority and minority parties in roughly the same proportion as the party ratios on the full committees. Beginning in the 1970s additional mechanisms, such as ad hoc committees and task forces, were developed to consider legislation apart from the traditional committee structure. Appearing principally in the House, rarely used ad hoc committees deal with complex legislation within the normal jurisdiction of several committees. This mechanism requires formal approval by the House, includes members of committees with relevant jurisdiction, and should be considered a variation of a multiple referral. By contrast, informal leadership task forces develop or refine legislation and occur outside the committee process entirely, at least until the bill is ready to be considered more formally.

Standing Committees

Standing committees, sometimes referred to as full committees to distinguish them from subcommittees, are at the center of the legislative process. Legislation usually must be considered and approved in some form at the committee level before it can be sent to the House or Senate for further action. *(See Chapter 2, The Legislative Process.)*

The 1946 reorganization act organized the Senate and House committees along roughly parallel lines, although some divergences subsequently emerged. One of the act's purposes was to eliminate confusing and overlapping jurisdictions by grouping together related areas. The authorizing committees (as distinct from the Appropriations committees) generally were regrouped to follow the major organizational divisions of the executive branch.

Subcommittees

Most standing committees have a number of subcommittees that provide the ultimate division of labor within the committee system. Although they enable members of Congress to develop expertise in specialized fields, they often are criticized on grounds that they fragment responsibility, increase

the difficulty of policy review, and slow down the authorization and appropriation process.

Subcommittees play a much larger role in the House than in the Senate. In the House, subcommittees usually are responsible for hearings and the first markup of a bill before a measure is sent on to the full committee. In the Senate, subcommittees may hold hearings, but the full committee generally does the writing of legislation. And, Deering and Smith write, "on nearly all Senate committees the work of subcommittees on important legislation is shown little deference by the full committees."[24]

Subcommittees also vary in importance from committee to committee. Some, especially the Appropriations subcommittees in both chambers, have well-defined jurisdictions and function with great autonomy. In both the House and Senate, their work is often ratified by the full committee without significant change.

A few committees such as House Ways and Means and Senate Finance long resisted the creation of subcommittees even though there were logical subdivisions into which their work could be divided. Subcommittees were established by the Finance Committee in 1970 and by Ways and Means only in 1975, after the House Democratic Caucus voted to require them. The subcommittee requirement was established in part because of dissatisfaction with the power and performance of Ways and Means chair Wilbur Mills. But these subcommittees, unlike those on the Appropriations Committee, never became autonomous legislative power centers because tax bills were put together as a unified package that required negotiations with all members of the full committee.

Ways and Means subcommittee chairs became subject to caucus election in 1990 after two chairs defied the leadership on tax legislation in 1989. Despite the change, no chair has ever been seriously challenged for reelection to the position.

After Republicans took over the House in 1995, committee chairs exercised greater influence in the selection of subcommittee chairs than had been the case under the Democrats, subject to approval by GOP members of the committee.

Not all full committees employ subcommittees. The House and Senate Budget committees, the ethics committees, and the Senate Rules, Small Business, and Veterans' committees do without subpanels. Some, such as the House ethics committee, employ select subcommittees while others, such as House Armed Services, utilize "panels" for particular nonlegislative tasks. And in the House the Rules and House Administration committees each have only two subcommittees.

Select and Special Committees

Select and special committees are established from time to time in both chambers to study special problems or concerns, such as global warming, population, crime, hunger, or narcotics abuse. On other occasions, they deal with a specific

event or investigation. Major investigations ha ducted by select committees such as the Senat investigated the Watergate scandal in 1973–1 House and Senate panels that jointly investigat contra affair in 1987.

The size and life span of select and special ally are fixed by the resolutions that create th cases, they have remained in existence for only Ordinarily they are not permitted to report although there are exceptions, such as the 1973 Committee on Committees chaired by Rep. Ric D-Mo. But much of Bolling's work was rejecte House reexamined itself again with a new Selec on Committees in 1979–1980, chaired by Rep. son, D-Ca., it withheld legislative authority fro Some of these committees, however, such as the Committee in the Senate, have gone on continu for all intents and purposes, permanent. *(See box ishes Select Committees, p. 166.)* Still others ultim full committees. In June 2002, the House creat Committee on Homeland Security (H.Res. 449 charged with collecting proposals from a variet tee stakeholders regarding the establishment of a ment of Homeland Security. The nine-member by majority leader Dick Armey, R-Texas, acc task in November 2002 and, pursuant to the en tion, promptly disbanded. But as part of the p standing Homeland Security Committee was cr

Unlike most select committees, the Intellig tees in both chambers have legislation referred consider and report legislation to the chamber special case, as the committees are effectively pe ties. Indeed, the House panel is officially the Per Committee on Intelligence. The Intelligence p matter is much narrower than that of most stand tees. In the House the panel is maintained as a s tee and appointed by the Speaker to insulate it mal political competition of the committee assi cess. Speakers have complained of being deluge from members to serve. In 1995 House rules wer make the Speaker himself or herself an ex offici the House panel, replacing the majority leader in new rule replaced an earlier one adopted in 1 given the Speaker the right to attend the commit and to receive access to its information. Both th Senate committees were originally limited tenu term limits for the Senate committee were elimi House committee members, other than the Spea ity leader, may currently serve no more than fo in a period of six successive Congresses.

Joint Committees

Joint committees can be either temporary or They are created by a statute or concurrent re

Both parties are represented on conference committees, with the majority party having a larger number, and a majority of conferees from each house must sign the conference report. In the past, conference committees met on the Senate side of the Capitol, with the most senior senator presiding, but this custom is no longer followed. Conferences now meet anywhere in the House, Senate, or Capitol complexes, with members of either house presiding, though the role is largely honorific. For certain legislation considered on an annual basis, such as appropriations bills and the congressional budget resolution, the chair alternates between the chambers.

Most conference committees met in secret until late 1975 when both chambers amended their rules to require open meetings unless a majority of either chamber's conferees vote in open session to close the meeting for that day. In 1977 the House amended its rules further to require open conference meetings unless the full House voted by recorded vote to close them. That rule was never adopted by the Senate, but in practice Senate conferees have always gone along with the representatives on those occasions—limited to defense and intelligence agency bills—when the House has voted to close a conference committee. Despite the "sunshine" rules, committees have found various ways to avoid negotiating in public, including the use of informal sessions, separate meetings of each delegation with staffers as go-betweens, and meeting rooms too small to accommodate all who wish to attend.

Conferees may be instructed by the House, just before they are appointed and while they are meeting, although the instructions are not binding and are sometimes ignored. When conferees are about to be appointed, the principal manager for the minority is usually recognized to offer a motion to instruct, and sometimes a motion may be offered pro forma to prevent another member from offering a less desirable proposition. The House also has a rule that allows any member, with preference for recognition again going to the minority party, to offer a motion to instruct its conferees or to dismiss them if a conference has not reported after twenty calendar days. This form of motion to instruct may be offered repeatedly by any member until the conferees finally report. This motion has sometimes proved a useful device for the minority to bring attention to a conference's failure to act or to force the House to vote for or against legislative provisions proposed in the Senate. The Senate rarely instructs its conferees, but there have been some indications the practice may be becoming more popular.[2]

After conferees reach agreement, they sign a conference report and submit it and a statement of managers providing a detailed explanation of their actions to each chamber. Unlike a bill reported by a House or Senate legislative committee, conferees who disagree may not include any minority views. Sometimes conferees who sign the report but object to certain provisions include a notation, such as "except section XXX," next to their names, but these caveats have no substantive effect. When conferees are unable to agree, the bill may die in conference if they take no formal action. Sometimes conferees file a report incorporating only matters on which they have agreed, leaving out others on which they disagree to await further negotiation or additional votes on the floor of each house to see if one chamber or the other will compromise. On rare occasions conferees formally report in disagreement and await further amendments by both houses.

Once their report is approved by the first of the two houses to consider it, the conference committee automatically is dissolved and the report goes to the remaining house for a vote. If either chamber rejects the conference report, the legislation remains before it in the form it existed prior to its commitment to conference, to await additional amendments or a new conference. The first chamber to consider the report also has the option to recommit it to conference, usually with instructions, to change an unacceptable provision. This action has the effect of rejecting the initial conference report but does not require the appointment of a new conference. The conferees may simply resume meeting. But it may endanger chances for a new agreement if the other chamber refuses to accede on the issue in question. If an agreement is reached on the issue in dispute, the filing process is repeated. In the Senate, conference reports may be filibustered like other legislation.

1 C. Lawrence Evans and Walter J. Oleszek, "Procedural Features of House Republican Rule." In *New Majority or Old Minority: The Impact of Republicans on Congress,* eds. Nicol C. Rae and Colton C. Campbell. (Lanham, Md.: Rowman & Littlefield, 1999), 127.

2 Bart Jansen, "Capitol Hill's Conferences: Can They Be Revived?" *CQ Weekly,* January 5, 2009, 18.

and Senate cochairs, was tasked with fashioning legislation to achieve at least $1.5 trillion in deficit reductions—the absence of which would trigger across-the-board budget cuts. The novel arrangement would require the committee's bill to be reported against a strict deadline but may then be passed by each chamber on a majority vote with no amendments or dilatory procedures allowed. The act provided a termination date for the committee of less than a year. The committee itself is highly unusual in that it is joint, select, *and* legislative.

Ad Hoc Committees

The Speaker of the House has the authority to create ad hoc committees, if approved by a vote of the House, to consider legislation that might be within the jurisdiction of several committees. Membership of such ad hoc committees would come from committees that would otherwise have exercised legislative jurisdiction. This authority, created in 1977, has been used only twice, most notably in the 95th Congress to handle consideration of major energy legislation proposed by the Carter administration.

In 1995 the new Republican majority extended this idea to oversight, giving the Speaker the power to propose, subject to a House vote, the creation of ad hoc oversight committees to review specific matters within the jurisdiction of two or more standing committees. While aggressive use of oversight to investigate the Clinton administration became

HOUSE ABOLISHES SELECT COMMITTEES

The rise and sudden fall in 1993 of the supposedly temporary House panels known as select committees was a small but significant illustration of the inability of House Democrats to conduct oversight of the committee system. In the 1980s and 1990s it became increasingly difficult for the majority party to get rid of these entities once they had come into existence. They acquired virtually permanent status.

The initial urgency that was often used to justify the creation of a select committee to study an issue and hold hearings was quickly transformed into an argument that the subject matter was important enough to require an ongoing panel. Once established, abolition would have constituted a slap at interest groups, such as the elderly or children's lobbies, which viewed the select committees as friendly forums tailor-made to promote their issues.

In fact, the subject matter may have been a secondary consideration. Select committees were regarded as a prestigious reward for the member chairing the committee, who controlled a staff and budget, and as patronage for the Speaker, who appointed the chair and all other members of such committees. Moreover, members could chair subcommittees of the select committees, even if they already chaired other subcommittees on their permanent committee assignments, because the select subpanels were usually outside the multiple-chairmanship restrictions in Democratic Caucus rules.

Attempts to abolish select committees, or even to conduct oversight of their usefulness, were regarded as challenges to a comfortable status quo. Two of the five select committees present at the end of the 102nd Congress existed as part of the rules of the House. Three others were reestablished by resolutions reported from the Rules Committee at the beginning of each Congress and passed by the House, and their funding was folded into the annual resolution that provided money for most standing committees.

Following the 1992 election, however, the push for reform of Congress was gaining momentum as a result of scandals in the operation of the House. Members of the large new freshman class were looking for potential targets. The Republican minority proposed a raft of changes in the structure and operations of the House, many of them radical, but in the renewed climate of public scrutiny some Democrats also were looking for at least a symbolic way to support reform without causing major disruptions.

Four select committees, each without legislative jurisdiction, proved to be vulnerable.

1. Permanent Select Committee on Aging. Created in 1975, it was made a permanent part of the House rules and was recreated automatically on the opening day of each Congress, along with the Permanent Select Committee on Intelligence, which had legislative jurisdiction. The Aging panel had sixty-eight members, making it larger than any other House committee; a staff of thirty-seven; and a budget of $1,542,240 in 1992.

2. Narcotics Abuse and Control. Created in 1976, it had thirty-five members, a staff of eighteen, and a budget of $729,502 in 1992.

3. Children, Youth, and Families. Created in 1983, it had thirty-six members, a staff of eighteen, and a budget of $764,593 in 1992.

4. Hunger. Created in 1984, it had thirty-three members, a staff of sixteen, and a budget of $654,274 in 1992.

The Democratic Caucus, meeting in December 1992 to organize for the next Congress, eliminated the Select Committee on Aging from House rules as a

one of the new majority's priorities, it was conducted through the standing committees with efforts at coordination by the leadership. Through the end of the 111th Congress (2009–2011), no ad hoc oversight committees had been created by the House.

Task Forces

Task forces operating outside the committee system are not mentioned in the rules of the House and usually have no official status. (Some committees—the House Armed Services Committee in the 112th Congress for example—have created task forces within themselves that perform certain functions of subcommittees.) They are groups of members working collectively for a specific purpose, usually by appointment of party leadership. Both the majority and minority have used task forces, mostly to work within the respective party caucuses. In some cases the task forces produce a useful product that can be further developed, perhaps as a bill referred to a committee. In others, their creation is intended as little more than another title on a member's

stationery. When the Democrats controlled the House there were some complaints from legislative committees that task forces were becoming too visible, but this represented more of an institutional jealousy than reaction to substantive work by task forces.

On rare occasions task forces have played the principal role in creating legislation, most notably in enacting the Ethics Reform Act of 1989 that restricted honoraria and secured enactment of a long-delayed pay raise for members. In the House the bill was written by a bipartisan Leadership Task Force on Ethics and introduced by the Speaker himself. In 1995 Speaker Gingrich created a bipartisan task force on the Corrections Calendar to develop issues that might be considered using that new mechanism. In 1997 a bipartisan task force developed proposals to reform the ethics process in the House after the existing process had created tremendous partisan divisions in reprimanding and fining the Speaker for ethics violations at the beginning of the session. However, its recommendations were substantially changed by the House.

permanent body, effectively abolishing it and requiring it to seek renewal and survive a House floor vote just like the other select committees. The proposal slipped through in part because the chairmanship was vacant, so there was no incumbent to be displaced, and no clearly designated successor. Reps. William J. Hughes, D-N.J., and Marilyn Lloyd, D-Tenn., were competing at the time to get the nod from Speaker Thomas S. Foley, D-Wash., for the position. And few believed the rules change seriously threatened the panel.

Once the 103rd Congress convened in 1993, the Rules Committee reported separate resolutions recreating the four select committees. But the first to be considered by the House, the popular anticrime narcotics panel, went down to a surprising defeat by a vote of 180–237. An unusual coalition of opponents consisted of near-unanimous Republicans, a small number of Democratic reformers, and a group of committee chairs and other senior members. Members of the last group had always regarded the existence of the select committees as an implicit slap at the standing committees, which had legislative jurisdiction, for inattention to these issues, and a source of competition for media coverage and financial resources. They long had waited for an opportunity to be rid of them.

Surprisingly, the large class of freshman Democrats, many of whom had been elected on pledges to reform Congress, strongly supported the narcotics panel chaired by senior Ways and Means Committee member Charles B. Rangel, D-N.Y., a member of the Congressional Black Caucus.

Defeat of the narcotics committee surprised the Democratic leadership. Despite an attempt by the Rules Committee to reverse the result by repackaging all of the select committees in a single resolution to try to maximize support from the combination of special interest constituent groups that wanted them, it quickly became apparent that their time had passed in the House, and no new floor vote was ever held. Rep. Tony Hall, D-Ohio, went on a hunger strike to protest the abolition of the Hunger Committee, which he had chaired.

Only the Permanent Select Committee on Intelligence, created in House rules, which reports the intelligence authorization bill and is a legislative committee but with members appointed by the Speaker instead of elected by the House, survived. Some members had advocated abolishing the panel and creating a joint committee with the Senate to reduce the number of members involved in intelligence issues and the possibility of security leaks. When Republicans assumed control of the House in 1995, they retained the select committee, increased the term of service on the rotating panel, and even added the Speaker as an ex officio member.

In 2002 a new temporary Select Committee on Homeland Security was created in the House to deal with legislation on homeland security that was percolating up from a variety of panels. Pursuant to the enabling resolution, the new select committee was expired upon completing its duties in November 2002 but was then resuscitated in the 108th Congress and became a standing committee in 2005 with both legislative and oversight responsibilities over the new Department of Homeland Security. By this route, the Committee on Homeland Security became the House's newest standing committee.

At the behest of Speaker Nancy Pelosi, House Democrats created the Select Committee on Energy Independence and Global Warming after retaking the House in 2007. The new panel, which was bitterly opposed by Energy and Commerce Chair John Dingell, D-Mich., had no legislative authority but was intended to shine a light on issues about which Dingell was perceived to be less than enthusiastic. The select committee was retained in the 111th Congress but abandoned by Republicans in the 112th amid a fairly major shakeup within the Energy panel.

The House Republican leadership from 1995 to 1998 dramatically increased the use of task forces of Republican members to prepare legislation and for other purposes. The practice had the advantage, from the point of view of the leadership, of maximizing its control over an issue and simplifying the legislative process by reducing controversy surrounding such issues as committee jurisdiction. However, the practice was attacked because much of the work was conducted outside the normal protections of public hearings and written committee reports that allow access by other members, the media, and the public. Task forces in the 104th and 105th Congresses, the two after the Republican Party gained the majority as a result of the 1994 elections, were criticized for meeting in secret, giving too much influence to lobbyists allied with the majority, and weakening the committee system.

Committee Sizes and Ratios

The 1946 reorganization act set not only the jurisdiction of congressional standing committees but also their size. Today, however, the size of committees in both chambers is settled through negotiations between majority and minority party leaders. The House dropped nearly all size specifications from its rules in 1975; in the 112th Congress (2011–2013), only the Permanent Select Committee on Intelligence had one (twenty-one members). Senate standing rules of the 110th Congress still included committee sizes (Senate Rule XXI.2 and .3), necessitating some adjustments at the beginning of a Congress. Each chamber in effect endorses leadership decisions on committee sizes, as well as party ratios, when it adopts resolutions making committee assignments.

One potential disadvantage of the system in the House is that committees consist of the number of members who happen to be assigned to them throughout the Congress, with little consideration given to a committee's optimal size. For some time, the largest committee in either chamber was the popular House Committee on Transportation and Infrastructure with seventy-five members in the 110th Congress. One reason for its recent popularity was the expectation that

Congress would pass well-funded multiyear highway, mass transit, and aviation program reauthorizations. By the 112th Congress, however, Transportation had been sharply cut back, to fifty-nine members. Armed Services thus became the largest House committee with sixty-two members—just one more than the Financial Services Committee. The Senate Appropriations committee was that chamber's largest at twenty-nine members.

Congressional scholars Deering and Smith found that modern House Democratic leaders had expanded committee sizes to meet member demand and maintain party harmony. The authors found less pressure for committee expansion in the Senate, because most senators held two major committee assignments. They also found that senators generally were less concerned with their committee assignments than were their House colleagues.[25] That said, Senate party leaders did agree to add seats to the Foreign Relations Committee to meet increased demand in 2007.

The standing rules of each chamber are silent on the matter of party ratios on committees. The Senate traditionally has more or less followed the practice of filling standing committees according to the strength of each party in the chamber. The House has been less inclined to allocate minority party representation on committees on the basis of the relative strength of the two parties, particularly on the more important panels.

Under Democratic control, that party's caucus rules stipulated that committee ratios be established to create firm working majorities on each committee and instructed the Speaker to provide for a minimum of three Democrats for every two Republicans, although this did not always occur. (The House and Senate committees dealing with ethics matters have equal party representation with the chair from the majority party in the chamber.)

Democrats in the House felt little need to accommodate their political opposition, especially on exclusive House committee assignments such as Appropriations, Rules, and Ways and Means. House Republicans in the 1980s complained bitterly of mistreatment by Democrats and argued that the Democrats had been in the majority for so long that they had become arrogant in the use of power. Fourteen Republicans filed a lawsuit in 1981 after the defeat of their attempts on the floor to change the party ratios on four key committees—Appropriations, Budget, Rules, and Ways and Means—to reflect the gains made by their party in the November 1980 congressional elections. Republicans charged the Democrats with unconstitutionally discriminating against GOP members and their constituents when they set the party ratios. The case was dismissed by the U.S. District Court for the District of Columbia in October 1981, and the U.S. Supreme Court refused to review it in February 1983. In response to the angry Republican protests Democratic leaders in 1985 agreed to give Republicans more seats on most major committees.

When the Republicans took control in 1995, however, these earlier stands were quickly forgotten, given the necessity of controlling the tools of legislative power. The party copied the Democrats' practices of ensuring domination of important committees, even though its majority was far smaller than the ones the Democrats had enjoyed. Even on a housekeeping committee such as House Administration, the leadership took more direct responsibility for sensitive issues involving internal management of the House and expanded its party's ratio of control in the 105th and 106th Congresses to two-to-one (six Republicans and three Democrats, exceeding ratios previously employed by the Democrats.

And so it goes to date. With Democrats in control of the House in 2007, this situation continued to obtain. Likewise, a return to Republican control in 2011 brought little change. House Administration had a 6:3 ratio in favor of the new majority; Appropriations, 29:21; Budget, 22:16; Rules, 9:4; and Ways and Means, 22:15. This suggests that neither party will give up its advantage any time soon.

The Chair's Role

Each committee is headed by a chair, who is a member of the majority party of a chamber. A chair's power once resulted from the rigid operation of the seniority system under which a person rose to a chair through continuous service on a given committee. As long as the chair's party retained control of Congress, he or she normally kept this position. If control passed to the other party, he or she changed places with the ranking member of that party. The seniority system, intermittently observed from the mid-1800s, took firm hold in the Senate after the Civil War and became entrenched in the House within a few decades of the 1910 revolt against Speaker Joseph Cannon, R-Ill.

By the latter part of the twentieth century, because of the Democratic Caucus reforms of the 1970s and the new powers enjoyed by Speaker Gingrich under House Republicans, this was no longer an iron-clad rule in that chamber. In the 104th Congress, the House adopted a new rule limiting committee and subcommittee chairs to a maximum service of three terms. The impact of the provision was felt beginning in 2001, when an unprecedented thirteen new chairs were selected in the House without party turnover. And six of these were not the next most senior member of their respective committee.

The Senate would have been due for its own round of musical chairs at the outset of the 108th Congress (2003), but Vermont Republican James Jeffords's leaving of the party returned Democrats to control of the Senate in June 2001. (Jeffords became an independent but caucused with the Democrats.) As a result, Republicans had to revisit their rule on term limits. The result was a complicated formulation that allowed the former chairs two more years in the top spot once Republicans regained control in 2003. Internal shifts, turnover, and fewer committees meant that the Senate impact was less

Members of the House Committee on Appropriations and the Appropriations Subcommittee on the Legislative Branch meet during the markup of proposed 2008 appropriations for the legislative branch. Subcommittee chair Debbie Wasserman-Schultz, D-Fla., is middle right, full committee chair David R. Obey, D-Wis., is at far left. Rep. Barbara Lee, D-Calif., and ranking member Zack Wamp, R-Tenn., look on.

SOURCE: Scott J. Ferrell, Congressional Quarterly.

dramatic than in the House. Still, four sitting chairs had to relinquish their gavels, although in three of those cases seniority allowed them to chair another committee. Because Senate Democrats have no similar rule, their takeover of the chamber in 2007 meant term limits were gone for the time being.

Even with the many changes, committee chairs remained powerful figures on Capitol Hill, especially in the Senate, although they still had to answer to fellow party members. At the full committee level, the chair calls meetings and establishes agendas, schedules hearings, coordinates work by subcommittees, leads markup sessions, files committee reports, frequently acts as floor manager, recommends conferees, controls the committee budget, supervises the hiring and firing of staff, and serves as spokesperson for the committee and the chair's party in the committee's area of expertise. Committees can establish rules that permit the full committee chairs to issue subpoenas on behalf of the committee in the conduct of an investigation. For example, use of the authority by the chairs of the Government Reform and Oversight and Education and the Workforce committees in the 105th Congress sparked bitter partisan controversies.

The committee's ranking minority member also may be an influential figure, depending to some degree on the person's relationship with the chair. Where the two do not get along, or the committee has a partisan tradition, the minority can be marginalized. The ranking member assists in establishing the committee agenda and in managing legislation on the floor for the minority, nominating minority conferees, and controlling the minority staff. The ranking member serves as spokesperson for the committee's minority members. In the Senate, the ranking minority member benefits, as do all senators, from the powerful rules and traditions that require them to be consulted. Chairs and ranking minority members often sit ex officio on all subcommittees of their committee of which they are not regular members.

COMMITTEE ASSIGNMENTS

House and Senate rules state that the membership of each chamber shall elect its members to standing committees (House Rule X.5 and Senate Rule XXIV). In the House all rules, committees, and assignments from the previous

Congress effectively expire on January 3 of each odd-numbered year, and committees cannot function until they are recreated in the rules on opening day and members are reappointed. That sometimes can create an extended hiatus if the next Congress convenes late in January, during which committees and subcommittees cannot meet because they do not yet exist. Sometimes the committees try to get around this by inviting witnesses for forums that allow the returning committee members to gather and discuss issues or informally question witnesses as guests.

Senate committees remain in existence in that continuing body with members being carried over from the previous Congress while they await a full complement of new members. The committees retain full power to act "until their successors are chosen" (Senate Rule XXV.1)

The committee assignment procedure begins during early organization meetings following an election and formally takes place at the beginning of every Congress and throughout the next two years as vacancies occur. There are numerous changes at the beginning of every Congress, as members switch committee assignments, seeking posts of either greater power or greater personal interest to them. Incumbent members are nearly always permitted to retain their existing assignments—referred to as the property right norm—unless the party ratio changes substantially in the preceding election or partisan control of the chamber shifts. In the House in 1995, 2007, and 2011, dramatic committee ratio changes were involuntary as control shifted between the parties. In each case the new majority assumed control of all committees and reduced the number of minority seats. In 1995, both parties also faced the problem of reassigning members who had served on three committees that were abolished. (In general, they were allowed to "follow the jurisdiction" to the new committee of which it became a part.) The Democrats were forced to remove several members each from the Appropriations, Ways and Means, and Rules committees. The caucus guaranteed these members their old seats back as soon as vacancies developed. By the beginning of the 105th Congress in 1997, all of the dislocated members who wanted to had been returned to their old assignments. This process was repeated again in 2007 and 2011 as Democrats and then Republicans regained control and the minority was forced to give up seats.

Representatives of the two parties negotiate on party ratios in advance and then submit the committee rosters to their party caucuses and finally the full chambers. Key decisions, therefore, are made in each party's Committee on Committees with caucus and floor approval largely pro forma. There are always some adjustments in each new Congress in both chambers to take into account the recent election results, member preferences, and the shifting demands that the ebb and flow of issues place on committee workloads. With some exceptions the method currently in general use was adopted by the Senate in 1846 and by the House in 1911.

In the House nothing in the rules guarantees members any committee assignments. But in practice each member who wants to serve on a committee has at least one assignment. Because House committee assignments originate from political parties (Rule X.5(a)(1)), members who switch parties automatically lose their seats under House rules. (Senate rules are silent on this matter.) The Republicans, who have benefited from most party switches since the 1970s, have made a point of allowing their new recruits to retain their old posts, usually with seniority, or have given them even more desirable assignments to help them win reelection. (This does not always work. Rep. Greg Laughlin, R-Texas, a 1995 party-switcher who was placed on the prestigious Ways and Means Committee, lost the nomination in the subsequent Republican primary.)

Even Rep. Bernard Sanders of Vermont, a self-proclaimed socialist and the House's only independent member for most of his 1991–2007 House career (after which he was elected to the U.S. Senate), received two assignments when there was a Democratic majority in the House. When the Republicans controlled the House in 1995, and thereafter, the committee seats he held came out of the Democrats' minority allotment. Sanders was allowed to become the ranking minority member of House subcommittees in the 105th and 106th Congresses, even though he was not a member of the Democratic Caucus, because no Democratic committee members officially sought to block him.

Until 1995 the number and types of committees and subcommittees on which any member might serve were left almost entirely to the discretion of the Republican Conference and the Democratic Caucus, which presented privileged resolutions to the House for electing committee members. House rules were largely silent and the Rules Committee played no role in this process. As part of its rules changes in the 104th Congress, the Republican majority limited each member to a maximum of two committee and four subcommittee assignments. However, almost immediately exceptions started to be made. The party realized that while rules and formulas for organizing committees sounded good when talking about reform, they were less important than the need to retain effective numerical control of committees and satisfy members' political needs.

The Assignment Process

In the Senate the Democratic committee rosters are drawn up by the Democratic Steering and Coordination Committee (typically about twenty-five members), whose chair and members are appointed by the party leader. The Senate Republican committee rosters are drawn up by the Republican Committee on Committees (typically about eight members), which is appointed by the chair of the Republican Conference. Republican Party leaders are ex officio members.

The committee assignment process in the House, with 435 members, five delegates, and a resident commissioner

LOSS OF COMMITTEE POSITIONS AS PUNISHMENT

Stripping a member of his or her position on a committee as a punishment for political heresy has been resorted to, although somewhat rarely, on Capitol Hill. In 1859 the Senate Democratic Caucus removed Stephen A. Douglas, D-Ill., from his chair on the Committee on Territories because he refused to go along with President James Buchanan and the southern wing of the party on the question of slavery in the territories.

In 1866 three Senate Republican committee chairs were dropped to the bottom of their committees for failing to vote with the Radical Republicans on overriding a presidential veto of a civil rights bill.

In 1923 Sen. Albert B. Cummins, R-Iowa, lost his chair on the Interstate Commerce Committee in a fight with the Progressive wing of his party. But the next-ranking Republican, Sen. Robert M. La Follette, R-Wis., was then passed over because of his unpopularity with the regulars of the party, and the chair was given to the ranking Democrat, Ellison D. Smith, D-S.C.

Members of the Progressive wing of the Republican Party in the House also were denied the fruits of seniority in this period after they put up their own candidate for Speaker in 1925. Two of their leaders were ousted from their committee chairmanships for having campaigned as La Follette Progressives, and nine GOP members from the Wisconsin delegation who voted with the insurgents' candidate for Speaker were either dropped to the bottom rank on their committees or moved to less prestigious committees. La Follette had been the Progressive Party's candidate for president in 1924.

In 1965 and 1969 the House Democratic Caucus dropped three southern Democrats to the bottom of their committees because two of them had campaigned for presidential candidate Sen. Barry Goldwater, R-Ariz., in 1964 and the other for former Alabama governor George C. Wallace (American Independent) in 1968.

Another southern Democrat who had supported Goldwater in 1964, Sen. Strom Thurmond of South Carolina, avoided party discipline by switching to the Republican Party. Republicans rewarded him by allowing him to carry over his seniority rights to the GOP side of his committees.

In 1983 House Democrats stripped conservative Rep. Phil Gramm of Texas of his seat on the Budget Committee because of his two-year collaboration with the White House in supporting President Ronald Reagan's economic initiatives. Gramm's apostasy was especially aggravating to the Democratic leadership because he had been placed on the committee with the strong support of Majority Leader Jim Wright, D-Texas, after Gramm had given assurances that he would be a team player. Gramm resigned from Congress, switched to the Republican Party, and won his seat back in a special election. The Republicans then put him right back on the Budget Committee.

In 1995 some conservative Senate Republicans advocated stripping Sen. Mark O. Hatfield, R-Ore., of his chairmanship of the Appropriations Committee because he had cast the lone Republican—and deciding—vote that defeated a balanced budget amendment to the U.S. Constitution. The amendment was a major element

Republicans removed Christopher H. Smith, R-N.J., from his position as chair of the House Veterans' Affairs Committee after the 108th Congress and awarded it to Steve Buyer, R-Ind. Party leaders upended the seniority system by exercising the option to replace committee chairs with members who had shown more fealty to them and raised more money for the party.

SOURCE: Scott J. Ferrell, Congressional Quarterly.

in the new Republican majority's legislative agenda and had earlier passed the House for the first time. After debate in the Republican Conference, no action was taken against Hatfield. He retained the chairmanship but announced shortly thereafter that he would not seek reelection.

Finally, on January 3, 2001, James A. Traficant Jr., D-Ohio, voted with House Republicans to reelect Speaker J. Dennis Hastert, R-Ill. In response the Democratic Caucus stripped Traficant of his committee assignments from the previous Congress and then ejected him from the caucus itself. For a time, Republicans held open a seat on the Transportation Committee in hopes that Traficant would switch parties. But he refused to do so. Traficant was subsequently indicted and convicted on bribery, racketeering, and other charges and ultimately expelled from the House.

Republicans too have proven willing to depose chairs over substantive disagreements. In January 2005 the Republican Steering Committee refused to renominate Christopher H. Smith of New Jersey as chair of the Veterans' Affairs Committee. Smith had repeatedly opposed his party's position on the funding of veterans' programs and occasionally voted pro-labor. That same month, Republican leaders ousted Joel Hefley of Colorado from the chairmanship of the House ethics committee. During the 108th Congress, Hefley presided over the committee while it admonished Majority Leader Tom DeLay, R-Texas, three times.

---

involved, can be complex in itself and is made more so by mechanisms to ensure that various factions are fairly represented. The Democrats have had basically the same system since 1974. The Republicans have used different methods but

by the mid-1990s had a system that was similar in many respects.

The Democratic committee rosters are drawn up by the party's Steering Committee, a far larger body than its

Republican counterpart—about fifty-five members in 2011, which was up from thirty-five in 1993. The Steering Committee is chaired by the Democratic leader but also has two cochairs who had been appointed by the leader. In a change, however, the two—Rosa DeLauro of Connecticut and George Miller of California—are now elected. In the 112th Congress it consisted of the leader, the whip, the caucus chair, the caucus vice chair, the chair of the Democratic Congressional Campaign Committee, cochairs of the Steering Committee, two vice chairs of the Steering Committee, the assistant leader, the senior chief deputy whip and eight chief deputy whips, a freshman class representative, twelve members appointed from equal regions, thirteen members appointed by the leader, the chair of the Organization, Study, and Review Committee, and the ranking members of the Appropriations, Budget, Energy and Commerce, Rules, Financial Services, and Ways and Means committees. The number of leadership-appointed members has fluctuated. Pelosi reportedly named thirteen for the 112th Congress. Each member has only one vote. (From 1911 until 1974 Democratic committee assignments were made by the Democratic members of the Ways and Means Committee.) An exception applies to the Democratic members of the Rules and House Administration committees. In 1974 the caucus rules gave the Democratic leader the power to nominate all party members of Rules. House Administration was included under this provision in 1994. Nominations to all standing committees are subject to ratification by the caucus.

Republican committee nominations in the House are determined by the party's Steering Committee, which is chaired by the Republican leader. During the 110th Congress it included the floor leader, the whip, the chief deputy whip, the conference chair, the policy committee chair, the policy vice chair, the policy secretary, the National Republican Congressional Committee chair, the chairs of the Appropriations, Budget, Energy and Commerce, Rules, and Ways and Means committees, a California representative, a Texas representative, ten members elected from geographic regions, one small state representative, and one member each from the freshmen classes of the 109th and 110th Congresses. Both the floor leader and the Speaker are members when the Republicans are in the majority. As with the Democratic Steering Committee, the Republican committee has been expanding fairly steadily to include more constituent parts of the party conference. It has, in fact, been so much of a moving target that the Republican leadership has recently declined to make public (even to party members, it appears) its makeup. A motion to codify the committee and make its membership public was rejected prior to the beginning of the 112th Congress.

The two parties' systems diverge as the Republicans allocate additional voting strength to the Speaker and floor leader (when present) and make allowances for the needs of small states. The Rules and the House Administration committees again are exceptions. GOP members of those committees are nominated by the party leader. The Democrats' approach is to allow the party leader to appoint additional members to the committee on the theory that these members will generally be sympathetic to entreaties from the party.

Once the committee rosters are approved by the two parties in each chamber, they are incorporated in resolutions and put to votes before the full chambers. With approval usually automatic, the votes merely formalize recommendations by the two parties and the party ratios previously negotiated by the leadership. Neither party interferes with the individual committee assignments made by the other. To attempt to do so would be a serious violation of comity. However, the minority may not attempt to exceed the allotment of seats on any committee awarded to it by the majority or its assignment resolution would be rejected on the floor. On several occasions House Republicans, when in the minority, forced votes on Democratic committee assignments to protest what they regarded as excessively advantageous majority committee ratios on some committees. In 1995 the Democrats responded in kind by forcing a vote on the assignment of party-switcher Greg Laughlin, R-Texas, to the Ways and Means Committee, which further expanded the majority's ratio there from that set at the beginning of the 104th Congress. In 1997 the Republicans moved to table (kill) a Democratic committee assignment resolution when they believed the minority was attempting to increase its strength on a committee without permission, but after brief discussion the misunderstanding was cleared up and an embarrassing vote avoided.

The Seniority Factor

Both parties in each chamber generally follow seniority in positioning members on committees and in filling vacancies, with new members being ranked at the bottom of their committees. Many factors are involved in the decisions of the party leadership in assigning new members to committees, but once the member has the seat seniority remains the most important single factor in determining his or her advancement on that committee.

Only rarely is a committee seat taken away to punish a member. In 1983 House Democrats attempted to discipline Phil Gramm, D-Texas, for leaking details of their secret caucuses on the Budget Committee in the previous Congress to the Reagan administration. The Steering and Policy Committee did not renominate Gramm to the Budget Committee. He promptly resigned from the House and was reelected as a Republican, and he was then returned to the committee. *(See box, Loss of Committee Positions as Punishment, p. 171.)*

In the 104th Congress, Appropriations chair Bob Livingston, R-La., removed conservative freshman Mark Neumann, R-Wis., from the powerful Defense Appropriations subcommittee because Neumann opposed Republican spending priorities. The outcry from the huge freshman class, however, proved so intense that Speaker Gingrich had to mollify Neumann with an additional committee assignment on the Budget Committee, bumping a senior member off to make room.

Members who stay on the same committee from one Congress to another are given the same seniority ranking they had in the previous Congress unless a death, resignation, or retirement on the committee allows them to move up a notch. But if members, even senior members, transfer from one committee to another they are ranked at the bottom in seniority on their new committees. There are exceptions to these rules in unusual circumstances. The five Democratic House members and the two Democratic senators who switched to the Republican Party in 1995 were given some seniority on their new committee assignments or carried their existing seniority with them on the same committee. This helped newly minted Republican senators Ben Nighthorse Campbell of Colorado and Richard C. Shelby of Alabama to move through the ranks so quickly that they found themselves committee chairs as the 105th Congress began. By contrast, Senator Arlen Specter of Pennsylvania was stripped of seniority in all his committees when he switched from the Republicans to the Democrats in 2009. (He subsequently lost in the primary.)

As a rule members of Congress remain on their major committees throughout their careers, gradually working their way up in seniority. Those who do wish to switch, usually to one of the exclusive committees in the House (Appropriations, Energy and Commerce, Financial Services, Rules, Ways and Means) or the "Super A" committees in the Senate (Armed Services, Appropriations, Finance, Foreign Relations) make the effort early in their careers before they accumulate too much seniority on their original assignments and lose the incentive to leave. If a member continues to be reelected and does not have an equally successful, ambitious, and younger colleague ahead of him or her on the committee roster, that member usually can expect to become a chair or ranking minority member.

Plum Assignments

In both chambers committee assignments are extremely important to members. The Senate, with fewer political selection procedures and proportionately more plum seats than the House, tends to see less maneuvering, lobbying, and horse-trading for desired committee slots. There are fewer members competing for influence and looser floor rules than in the House. Each senator therefore has a greater chance to affect legislation of all stripes.

In the House influence often is closely related to the committee or committees on which a member serves. Moreover, assignment to a powerful committee virtually guarantees large campaign contributions.

Just wanting to be on a committee is not enough. In most cases members have to fight for assignments to the best

Seniority still plays a major role in the power structure of both houses of Congress. In 1998, by virtue of his seniority, Strom Thurmond, R-S.C., was president pro tempore of the Senate and chair of the Armed Services Committee, but in 1999 he chose to give up his committee post.

SOURCE: Scott J. Ferrell, Congressional Quarterly.

committees. In each chamber a few committees are considered most powerful and difficult to get on. But congressional leaders often have to go looking for volunteers to serve on less attractive panels.

Traditionally the premier House committees sought by representatives have been Appropriations, Rules, and Ways and Means, although the attraction of Rules under both Republicans and Democrats was reduced after its members were nominated directly by the two party leaders and lost much of their power to operate and vote independently. In the 1980s members also avidly sought seats on Budget and Energy and Commerce. In the 1990s Public Works and Transportation (now Transportation and Infrastructure), often either desired or reviled by members for its traditional pork barrel programs, regained popularity so quickly that there were jokes that the public seats in the committee room would have to be removed to accommodate all of the new members. Indeed, the committee topped out at seventy-five members during the 111th Congress but was pared back to fifty-nine in the 112th. Finally, by the first decade of the twenty-first century, Financial Affairs also had gained exclusive status—first for Republicans and then for Democrats as well.

In the Senate the most popular committees traditionally have been Appropriations and Finance. Both the Budget Committee and Armed Services also have been in demand. Foreign Relations, once considered highly prestigious, fell steadily in influence and desirability after the defeat of

House, Senate Rules Governing Composition of Committee Membership

The majority party in each chamber chooses all of the committee and subcommittee chairs while the minority party selects the ranking members. House practices are determined by the rules of the Republican Conference and Democratic Caucus, although the rules of the House stipulate certain requirements. The Senate guidelines are governed by the chamber's standing rules, with some party regulations. In general, rules for the selection of committee leaders apply equally to chairs and ranking minority members. The guidelines below cover the principal assignment and leadership selection practices, but not every possible rule, contingency, or exception.

HOUSE REPUBLICANS

The Republicans, through their conference, divide the House committees into three categories: exclusive, nonexclusive, and exempt. Exclusive committees are Appropriations; Energy and Commerce; Financial Services; Rules; and Ways and Means. Nonexclusive committees are almost everything else: Agriculture; Armed Services; Education and Labor; Homeland Security; Foreign Affairs; Judiciary; Transportation and Infrastructure; Budget; Oversight and Government Reform; Natural Resources; Science; Small Business; and Veterans' Affairs. The exempt committees are Standards of Official Conduct, House Administration, and Select Intelligence.

Republicans serving on an exclusive committee generally may not serve on any other standing committee, with the exception of the House Administration, Standards of Official Conduct, and Budget committees. (The Budget Committee is required by House rules to have members from the Appropriations and Ways and Means committees.) GOP membership on the Budget Committee includes three members each from the Appropriations and the Ways and Means committees. (Other GOP Budget members include one member appointed by the Republican leadership.)

Members of the Republican Party may serve on two nonexclusive committees. Membership on exempt committees does not count against the total. This practice technically violates a House rule sponsored by Republicans in the 104th Congress that limited all members to service on no more than two standing committees. To ensure that members serve on these less desirable, internal housekeeping panels, the Republicans got around the House rule by simply having the House vote to approve the additional committee assignments.

Chairs (or ranking minority members) of full committees are recommended by the Steering Committee without regard to seniority and are voted on by secret ballot of the conference. But the Republican leader (Speaker or floor leader) nominates the chair and other Republican members of the Rules, Intelligence, and House Administration Committees, subject to conference approval. If any nominee is rejected by the conference, the Steering Committee, or the Speaker, as the case may be, must make a new nomination until one is approved. Development of procedures for the selection of Republican subcommittee chairs and members is at the discretion of the chair of a committee, unless a majority of the GOP members of the full committee disapprove. Chairs of the Appropriations subcommittees are subject to approval by the Steering Committee.

No Republican may serve as the chair of more than one standing committee or subcommittee of a standing committee, although chairs of the Standards of Official Conduct and House Administration committees are exempt from the restriction. The chair of the Appropriations Committee is not permitted to head a subcommittee of that committee. A subcommittee chair of a standing committee may chair a subcommittee of the Permanent Select Committee on Intelligence. A 1995 House rules change, readopted in 2011, limits committee and subcommittee chairs to three terms in these positions.

HOUSE DEMOCRATS

The rules of the Democratic Caucus also classify committees as exclusive, nonexclusive, and exempt. And the categories contain the same panels. Members assigned to an exclusive committee may be on no other standing committee—although exceptions for Rules now are made routinely. Budget, House Administration, and Standards of Official Conduct are again the exceptions. Two Democrats each from the Appropriations Committee and the Ways and Means Committee serve on the Budget Committee, as well as one leadership member appointed by the minority leader. (When the Democrats control the House, the majority leader always occupies this slot.)

Members of the Permanent Select Committee on Intelligence and joint committees are selected by the Democratic leader and then appointed by the Speaker if the Democrats are in the minority.

No Democrat may serve on more than two nonexclusive committees, with exceptions allowed for House Administration and for Standards of Official Conduct.

Democrats are nominated to serve on most committees by the Steering Committee, subject to Democratic Caucus approval. Members of the Rules and House Administration committees are nominated by the Democratic leader subject to caucus approval.

The rules of the caucus are more restrictive than those of the House regarding service on the Budget Committee. Democratic Budget Committee members may serve for only three terms out of every five consecutive terms, instead of the four-of-six terms permitted in House rules and used by Republicans. Exceptions to this limitation include the Democratic leadership–designated member of the Budget Committee, who may stay indefinitely, as well as the ranking minority member, who may stay on for an additional two years, if required, to serve a second term in that position.

Democrats are limited to one full committee chair (or ranking member position). They may not simultaneously chair another full, select, permanent select, special, ad hoc, or joint committee. Standing committee chairs may not chair any subcommittee, but the chairs of the House Administration and Standards of Official Conduct committees are exempted. The chair of the Appropriations Committee may chair a subcommittee of that committee. No Democrat may chair more than one subcommittee of a committee or select committee with legislative jurisdiction. Ranking minority members of the following nonexclusive committees, which were classified as major committees prior to a 1995 rules change, may not serve on any other committee: Agriculture,

Financial Services, Education and Labor, Judiciary, Armed Services, and Transportation and Infrastructure.

Most nominations for committee leadership positions are made by the Steering Committee and without regard to seniority, though it is extremely rare for Steering to take the initiative to reject an incumbent. (It most recently did so in the 105th Congress, nominating John LaFalce of New York as ranking minority member of the Banking Committee instead of incumbent Henry B. Gonzalez of Texas. Gonzalez then challenged him before the caucus. With a third candidate also in the race, Gonzalez finished first on the initial ballot but lacked a majority. LaFalce then withdrew and Gonzalez was confirmed for another term. The caucus votes on all nominations individually by secret ballot.)

Exceptions to the practice of Steering Committee nominations are the Rules Committee and House Administration Committee chair, who are nominated by the Democratic leader, and the Budget Committee chair, who is selected from among members choosing to run for the position on the floor of the caucus.

Subcommittee chairs of the Appropriations Committee also are voted on by secret ballot in the party caucus. The committee caucus may use subcommittee seniority as the criterion in nominating candidates for subcommittee chairs. Beginning with the 102nd Congress (1991–1993), subcommittee chairs of the Ways and Means Committee also have been ratified by the Democratic Caucus.

On other committees, chairs or ranking subcommittee members are elected by the Democrats on their committee. (Special rules allow such choices to be brought before the full caucus for a vote if they are especially controversial, but this has never been done.) Committee members are entitled to bid for subcommittee leadership slots in the order of their seniority on the full committee, with members choosing which subcommittee they would bid for, and an up-or-down vote is then held on that member's candidacy. If a candidacy is rejected, under a 1995 rules change the next member in order of committee seniority can bid for any open subcommittee ranking post. Before the change, the committee had to fill the post selected by the rejected candidate before moving on.

SENATE REPUBLICANS AND DEMOCRATS

The Senate divides its committees into "A," "B," and "C" committees in its Rule XXV—although those terms are not used in the rule. "A" committees are Agriculture, Nutrition, and Forestry; Appropriations; Armed Services; Banking, Housing, and Urban Affairs; Commerce, Science, and Transportation; Energy and Natural Resources; Environment and Public Works; Finance; Foreign Relations; Governmental Affairs; Homeland Security; Intelligence; Judiciary; and Labor and Human Resources. "B" committees are Budget; Rules and Administration; Veterans' Affairs; Small Business and Entrepreneurship; Aging; and Joint Economic. Committees on Ethics and Indian Affairs and the Joint Committee on Taxation are considered "C" committees but do not count toward the service limits outlined in the paragraph below. And a member of any joint committee on which a senator is required by law to serve also does not count toward the limits.

Senate rules also regulate both service and chairs, but chamber rules may be supplemented or superseded by party rules, sometimes resulting in variations in practice from one Congress to the next. Exceptions from various rules also are granted to individual senators.

Senators may serve on two "A" committees and may serve on one "B" committee. Party practices limit senators to serve on only one of the elite or "Super A" committees—Appropriations, Armed Services, Finance, and Foreign Relations, although there have been exceptions. Senators are limited to membership on three subcommittees of each major committee on which they serve (the Appropriations Committee is exempt from the limit) and on two subcommittees of their minor committee. The chair or ranking minority member of a committee may serve as an ex officio member without a vote on any subcommittee of that committee. There are numerous exceptions to these rules that protect senators who would have been in violation at the time they took effect. By agreement of the majority and minority leaders, the membership of a committee may be temporarily increased above the size limits set by the rules— but by no more than two members—to maintain majority party control. Any senator serving on a committee for this purpose would be allowed to serve on three major committees.

Both parties guarantee their members one seat on a major committee before any member receives a second top assignment.

A senator generally may serve as chair or ranking minority member of only one standing, select, special, or joint committee, though again there may be exceptions, especially with regard to service on joint committees. A Republican Conference rule adopted in 1995 and effective in 1997 (with the 107th Congress exempt) limits GOP senators to no more than three Congresses of service as a committee chair or ranking member.

Under Senate rules, the chair of a major committee may serve as chair of only one subcommittee among all of his or her major committees and one subcommittee of his or her minor committee. The chair of a minor committee may not serve as chair of any subcommittee on that committee. He or she may chair one subcommittee of each of his or her major committees. A senator who does not otherwise chair a committee may chair only one subcommittee of each committee on which he or she serves.

The Senate Republican Conference's Committee on Committees makes committee assignments on major committees and the Rules and Administration Committee. Other assignments are made by their floor leader. Members of each Senate committee elect the chairs or ranking members of their committee by secret ballot subject to the approval of the Republican Conference. Votes in the Committee on Committees and in the conference also are by secret ballot.

Senate Democratic committee assignments and nominations for ranking minority members are made by the Steering and Coordination Committee and circulated to all Senate Democrats. A party rule adopted in 1975 provides for a secret-ballot vote on an individual nominee for chair (or ranking member) if requested by 20 percent of the Senate's Democrats.

Chair J. William Fulbright, D-Ark., in 1974 because of a series of weak chairs and its continuing inability to pass its major bill authorizing foreign aid. After Republicans took control in 1995 activist conservative chair Jesse Helms, R-N.C., brought greater visibility to the panel, but it remained undesirable to most members. The departure of Helms and the onset of the wars in Afghanistan and Iraq somewhat reversed that trend.

While other panels wax and wane, Appropriations, Finance, and Ways and Means have never been wholly eclipsed because they control the flow of money into and out of federal coffers. In the 1980s and 1990s these taxing and spending committees were thrust to the center of action more than ever before by Congress's increasing tendency to pile most of its legislative work onto a handful of fiscal measures.

COMMITTEE PROCEDURES

Committee procedures are regulated by Senate and House rules that incorporate many of the provisions in the Legislative Reorganization Acts of 1946 and 1970 and other measures. In many cases these rules serve to protect minority rights and the rights of witnesses at committee hearings.

One of the basic goals of the 1946 act was to standardize committee procedures in regard to having regular meeting days, keeping committee records and votes, reporting legislation, requiring a majority of committee members to be in attendance as a condition of transacting committee business, and following set procedures during hearings.

The 1946 rules were not uniformly observed by all committees. The continuing dissatisfaction with committee operations led in the 1970 reorganization act to further efforts to reform committee procedures, particularly to make them more democratic and accountable to the membership and the public. The House has more restrictive provisions than the Senate, but the majority still has broad flexibility in running a committee's business. *(See box, Congress Adapts to Demands for Greater Transparency, p. 177.)*

Senate and House committees are required to establish and publish rules of procedure. (In general, see House Rule XI and Senate Rule XXVI.) Each chamber's standing committees also must fix regular meeting days, although chairs are authorized to call additional meetings and set an agenda. In addition, the rules must contain procedures under which a committee majority may call a meeting if the chair fails to do so, even though use of such a procedure would be a serious affront to a chair. House rules also allow a committee majority using this process to place items of its choosing on the agenda.

An attempt to undercut a chair's authority over committee meetings was made in the Senate Foreign Relations Committee in 1997 after Chair Jesse Helms declared his refusal to hold a hearing on President Clinton's nomination of Massachusetts governor William Weld to be ambassador to

Mexico. Helms was adamantly opposed to the moderate Weld, even though he was a fellow Republican, for a variety of philosophical reasons. It appeared likely that a majority of both the committee and the Senate would confirm Weld if allowed to vote. A committee majority was able to force Helms to convene a meeting but was unable to take control of the agenda away from him. With the Senate parliamentarian sitting near him, Helms allowed no debate on the Weld nomination and spent most of the meeting denouncing his opponents. The episode illustrated how little Senate traditions have changed despite reforms of the rules. Senators are still unwilling to push powerful colleagues too far.

Committees were required by the 1970 act to keep transcripts of their meetings and to make public all roll-call votes. In the House the rules require that information about committee votes be made available to the public at the committees' offices and, as of the 112th Congress, also electronically. The committees are directed to provide a description of each amendment, motion, order, or other proposition voted on; the name of each committee member voting for or against the issue; and the names of those present but not voting. The rules also require that the results of all votes to report legislation be published in the committee reports. (See House Rule XI.2(e).)

In 1995 the rules were further amended to require that, on all votes conducted in a committee markup on a reported bill or other matter reported to the House, the report contain the number of votes cast for or against and how individual members voted.

In the Senate the rules are less specific. They require that a committee's report on a bill include the results of roll-call votes on "any measure or any amendment thereto" unless the results have been announced previously by the committee. Senate rules require that in reporting roll-call votes the position of each voting member is to be disclosed (Senate Rule XXVI.7(b)).

The rules stipulate that it is the chair's duty to see to it that legislation approved by his or her committee is reported. And a committee majority has access to procedures to force a bill out of committee if the chair refuses to bring it up for consideration or to report it after the committee has acted favorably (XXVI.10(b)). The rules prohibit a committee from reporting any measure unless a majority of its members are present. Members were allowed time to file supplemental and minority views for inclusion in committee reports, but in the House Republicans restricted the minority's long-standing rights to have three full days following the vote on reporting a bill to submit them. In 1997 the rule was amended to reduce the time by counting the day in which the committee ordered a bill reported as the first day.

House rules require committees and subcommittees to announce hearings at least one week in advance unless the chair and ranking minority member jointly, or the committee

CONGRESS ADAPTS TO DEMANDS FOR GREATER TRANSPARENCY

In the late 1990s Congress continued the process of adapting to demands for greater public access to its proceedings that began with "sunshine" rules in the 1970s requiring open committee and conference committee meetings. The media also gained virtually unfettered access to committee hearings and meetings.

The initial sunshine reforms were part of an effort to improve Congress's image, which had suffered dramatic reversals after a series of widely publicized scandals. They were further accelerated by the public's disgust for excessive government secrecy as revealed by the Watergate scandal in the 1970s that led to the resignation of President Richard M. Nixon. Proponents maintained that open meetings helped protect the public interest and made lawmakers more accountable to the electorate.

During the 1980s there was some retreat from the reforms, including votes by a number of key panels to close their doors during consideration of major legislation. Votes to close committees had to be conducted in open session by a roll call with a quorum present. The House Ways and Means Committee, perhaps the most heavily lobbied committee in the House, chose to close its doors to write such landmark legislation as a historic tax-overhaul bill in 1985 and trade and catastrophic illness insurance bills in 1987. Ways and Means chair Dan Rostenkowski, D-Ill., argued: "It's just difficult to legislate. I'm not ashamed about closed doors. We want to get the product out."[1] Other panels—notably House Appropriations subcommittees—also met privately to draft legislation. Sometimes committees' decisions were made by small groups of members behind the scenes and then ratified in open session. Defenders of closed sessions argued that committee members were more candid, markups more expeditious, and better laws written away from lobbyists' glare.

Efforts to institutionalize a pattern of exceptions to the rules failed, however, in the face of continuing public suspicions about the operations of Congress and the ability of special interest groups to influence the legislative process. In 1995, after Republicans took control of the House, the rules were further amended to prevent committees from closing their sessions merely for the sake of convenience. Committees wishing to close had to determine by roll-call vote that disclosure of testimony or other matters to be considered would endanger national security, compromise sensitive law enforcement information, or tend to defame, degrade, or incriminate any person. The House Committee on Standards of Official Conduct (now Ethics) was exempted from these requirements in 1997. In 2011, an amended House rule (XI 2(e)) further required that reports and votes also be made available electronically.

Despite all these efforts, critics still claim that too much of what is done by committees, and Congress more generally, remains hidden from the public. In the aftermath of the September 11 attacks and attendant to the global war on terror, the proceedings of the Armed Services committees and the Intelligence committees have become more secretive. But even outside of the national security realm, the diminished use of conference committees, long delays in the publication of committee reports, and the expanded role of leadership in legislative drafting continues the long-standing practice of hidden information and hidden decision making. As Ellen Miller, executive director of the Sunlight Foundation, put it: "I don't think Congress has ever been a terribly open institution. It's as if it erected a firewall around its information a long time ago, and there has been a continual cultural resistance to providing information in a timely manner, contemporary fashion."[2]

SUNSHINE RULES

The Legislative Reorganization Act of 1970 took the first steps toward more open committee meetings and hearings and required that all House and Senate committee roll-call votes be made public. The House in 1973 voted to require that all committee sessions be open unless a majority of the committee voted in public to close them. The Senate adopted a similar rule in 1975. Both chambers in 1975 voted to open conference committee sessions, unless a majority of the conferees of either chamber voted in public to close a session. The House amended this rule in 1977 to require a recorded vote by the full House to close a conference committee meeting. Conferences have been closed for legislation dealing with sensitive intelligence and national security matters. With the vast majority of hearings now open this issue has received little attention over the last decade, with the exceptions being the advisability of closed hearings regarding the September 11, 2001, attacks and the Iraq War.

BROADCASTS

While the Senate had a long tradition of broadcasting hearings, the House did not sanction such broadcasts until passage of the 1970 reorganization act. In 1974 it decided to allow broadcasts of markup meetings as well. The Senate left decisions on broadcast coverage to its committees. The House for many years set more stringent standards for broadcast coverage of hearings or bill-drafting sessions, considering it a special privilege to be granted or denied, but the House was eventually forced to stop cherry-picking requests for media access. House rules were amended in 1995 to require that all open committee sessions be opened to press coverage, including radio and television broadcasts, without the need for special permission. Televised broadcasts of floor debate began in the House in 1979 and in the Senate in 1986. *(See box, Televised Floor Debates Here to Stay, p. 82.)*

1 Jacqueline Calmes, "Fading 'Sunshine' Reforms: Few Complaints Are Voiced as Doors Close on Capitol Hill," *CQ Weekly*, May 23, 1987, 1059–1060. library.cqpress.com/cqweekly/WR100401008.
2 Tim Starks, "A Dome under Lock and Key," *CQ Weekly*, December 1, 2008, 3192.

itself by vote, set a shorter period. A Republican proposal to give this power to the chair alone was successfully resisted by the minority in 1995. In most circumstances committees are required to conduct meetings and hearings in open session and to require witnesses to file written statements in advance. The rules allow minority party members to call witnesses during at least one day of hearings on a subject.

JURISDICTIONAL CONFLICTS

Most bill referrals to committees are routine matters handled by the parliamentarians of each chamber. Committee jurisdictions outlined in House Rule X and Senate Rule XXV as well as precedents normally dictate where a bill is sent. But sometimes things are not so clear-cut.

Jurisdictional disputes between and among committees have been evident since the inception of the standing committee system. The Legislative Reorganization Act of 1946 attempted to eliminate the problem by defining each committee's jurisdiction in detail. But it was not able to do so.

As early as 1947 a fight broke out in the Senate over referral of the controversial armed forces unification bill. In the House the measure had been handled by the Committee on Executive Expenditures (now the Oversight and Government Reform Committee), which had jurisdiction over all proposals for government reorganization. But in a Senate floor vote, that chamber's Armed Services Committee successfully challenged the claim of the Expenditures Committee (now the Homeland Security and Governmental Affairs Committee) to jurisdiction over the bill. Such problems have continued to arise because the complexities of modern legislative proposals sometimes make it impossible to define jurisdictional boundaries precisely.

In the House the problem has been aggravated by a failure to restructure the committee system to meet new developments and national concerns. The problem of conflicting and overlapping jurisdictions became obvious in the 1970s as Congress attempted to formulate a coherent energy policy. When President Jimmy Carter in 1977 submitted his comprehensive national energy program, the impending jurisdictional tangle forced Speaker Thomas P. "Tip" O'Neill Jr., D-Mass., to establish an ad hoc energy committee to review the work of five House committees and to guide energy legislation through the House. (An attempt to consolidate energy responsibilities in one committee as the Senate had done in 1977 was soundly defeated in the House in 1980.)

Occasionally, when the opportunity arises, a bill is drafted in such a way that it will be referred to a committee favorable to it. The 1963 civil rights bill, for example, was worded somewhat differently in each chamber so that it would be referred to the Judiciary Committee in the House and the Commerce Committee in the Senate. Both panels were chaired by strong proponents of the legislation, while the chairs of the House Interstate and Foreign Commerce Committee (now the Energy and Commerce Committee) and the Senate Judiciary Committee were opposed to the legislation. Congressional expert Walter Oleszek noted that "careful drafting therefore coupled with favorable referral decisions in the House and Senate prevented the bill from being bogged down in hostile committees."[26]

Most bills, however, are subject to strict jurisdictional interpretation and rarely open to the legerdemain given the 1963 civil rights bill or the special handling the Speaker was able to give the 1977 energy bill. Oleszek observes:

> Committees guard their jurisdictional turfs closely and the parliamentarians know and follow precedents. Only instances of genuine jurisdictional ambiguity provide

opportunities for the legislative draftsman and referral options for the Speaker and the presiding officer of the Senate to bypass one committee in favor of another.[27]

Multiple Referrals

The practice of multiple referrals has been permitted in the Senate by unanimous consent, although it is used less frequently there than in the House, which did not permit the practice until the rules were amended in 1975. In that year the Speaker was permitted to refer a bill to more than one committee.

There were three types of multiple referrals: joint, when several committees considered a bill at the same time; sequential, when a bill was referred first to one committee, then to another, and so on; and split, when parts of a bill were referred to different committees. The most common method was joint referral; split referral was the least used. The Speaker also was given the authority subject to House approval to create an ad hoc committee to consider legislation when there were overlapping jurisdictions.

In 1977 the Speaker was permitted to impose reporting deadlines on the first committee or committees to which a bill was referred. In 1981 Speaker O'Neill announced that in making multiple referrals he would consider not only the content of the original bill but also amendments proposed by the reporting committee. And in 1983 the Speaker announced that he had the authority to designate a primary committee on jointly referred bills and impose time limits on other committees after the primary committee issued its report.

After 1975 the number of multiple referrals grew significantly in the House, as did the importance of multiple-referred bills. "In one form or another multiple referral is now employed on a multitude of significant legislation and exists as a prominent feature of congressional operations," wrote Melissa P. Collie and Joseph Cooper.[28] Collie and Cooper interpreted the arrival of multiple referral in the House "as a signal that committee turf is no longer what it has been cracked up to be." They contended that legislators have surrendered their exclusive autonomy over legislation for access to all legislation to which they have claim.[29]

The growth of multiple referrals in the House affected key aspects of the legislative process, including the Speaker's prerogatives, the work of the Rules Committee, floor proceedings, and relations with the executive branch and interest groups. It encouraged members, committees, and staff aides to negotiate with one another rather than act separately as traditionally done, according to scholars Roger Davidson, Walter Oleszek, and Thomas Kephart. They also said, "More importantly, the procedure at the same time has greatly augmented the powers of the Speaker and the Rules Committee, by strengthening their role in centralizing and coordinating the House's workload. That may well be the most profound effect of the multiple-referral procedure."[30]

These changes came with the price of greater complexity in the legislative process, however, as bills had to be tracked through multiple locations and of battles among committees over jurisdiction and the type of referrals they would receive, creating controversies that the Speaker was often called upon to mediate.

When Republicans assumed control of the House they instituted changes intended to streamline the process and reduce such distractions. Joint referrals were replaced in 1995 in the House by a procedure that required the Speaker in cases in which more than one committee had a jurisdictional claim to designate a committee as the primary committee for consideration. Other committees could be granted secondary or sequential referrals with time limits at the Speaker's discretion. This is sometimes called additional initial referral, perhaps to ease the loss of status by the other committees involved. The change was not radical inasmuch as the Speaker already had the power to designate a committee as the primary panel in cases of multiple referrals even though he or she rarely did so. The change did have the effect of simplifying the referral process and placing greater responsibility in the primary committees. It also reduced the intense competition among committees for referrals that sometimes had produced distracting jurisdictional wars among chairs and staff during the period of Democratic rule, with the Speaker in the middle.

Spending Rivals

The relationships between the Appropriations and authorizing committees traditionally have provided striking illustrations of intercommittee rivalries. Authorizing committees handle bills allowing funding, but usually only the Appropriations committees are permitted to consider the spending allocated for federal agencies and programs. There are exceptions for certain instances of direct spending approved by committees, such as entitlement programs authorized by permanent law.

As a formal matter, the Appropriations committees are barred by the standing rules from inserting legislative provisions in their appropriations bills, but they habitually do so, often out of necessity. While the other committees often grumble about the usurpation of their authority by the appropriators, the committees also often cooperate because they must rely on the appropriations process to include provisions regulating the programs they administer if the normal authorization bills cannot be enacted.

The creation of the House and Senate Budget committees in 1974 added yet another dimension to committee rivalries. The new committees were charged with the task of preparing two congressional budget resolutions (later reduced to only one when the original procedure proved impractical) setting out and enforcing goals for spending and revenues in the next fiscal year and later years. They also were to monitor the revenue and spending actions of the House and Senate.

As the country became increasingly preoccupied with budget deficits in the 1980s, the power relationships among these various committees started to shift. The authorizing committees went from proposing various new programs to a fallback position of defending existing ones. "Squeezed between the budget resolution and appropriations stages there is little time left for debating the recommendations of the authorization committees," Oleszek observes. "As a result these panels have lost influence to the Appropriations and Budget committees."[31]

The Appropriations committees also benefited in the 1980s and the 1990s from Congress's increasing reliance on omnibus continuing appropriations resolutions that were used when legislators routinely failed to pass some or all of the individual appropriations bills. These bills became vehicles for authorizing legislation. As a result, Deering and Smith note:

> [A]ppropriators gained a voice in shaping legislation that they otherwise would not have had, particularly in conference. And the continuing resolutions gave appropriators— as well as other members through appeals to appropriators and through floor amendments—an opportunity to pursue legislative matters without the consent and cooperation of the affected authorizing committee.[32]

Yet the Appropriations committees also lost influence. They had to share power with party and budget leaders in negotiating budget resolutions and then had to operate within the rigid constraints of those resolutions.

Smith and Deering summed up the power shifts.

> As partisan conflict over budget priorities intensified and produced policy stalemates among the House, Senate, and White House, both appropriations and authorizing committees lost autonomy. Party and Budget Committee leaders became central to resolving the conflict. Normal legislative procedures were ignored, set aside temporarily, and in some cases directly altered. All committees learned new legislative tricks to minimize the damage to programs they wanted to protect, but most could not avoid deep encroachments on their traditional autonomy. . . . Thus, in the quite unsettled power structure of Congress, leaders and budget committees fared well, appropriations committees survived but were injured, and authorizing committees took strong blows to their autonomy.[33]

But the Budget committees have had their ups and downs. After being considered power centers with seats carefully balanced, especially in the House, among various other committees and factions, they lost attraction for members as available funds for discretionary government programs were squeezed out in the face of growing deficits. Members preferred the power of awarding funds for programs to other colleagues and to constituents but balked at the pain of searching for cuts year after year. Adoption of a budget resolution each year was often delayed by broad disagreements among the parties or between Congress and the president. Rep. Martin Russo, D-Ill., who rotated off the House Budget Committee in 1991, found service there so painful that he rejoiced, saying that "my sentence is over."

After party control switched in the House in 1995, the Budget Committee regained visibility under the leadership of Rep. John Kasich, R-Ohio, a close ally of Speaker Gingrich. It also benefited from rules changes that expanded the committee's jurisdiction over the structure of the budget process itself. But once again factors beyond the control of Congress were bringing matters full circle. By the end of 1999 a soaring economy was pouring such huge amounts of tax revenue into the federal Treasury that a budget surplus was certain and promised to continue for years. For a time this shifted debate to a subject members of Congress understood better: how to spend or cut taxes.

Flush times did not last long, as the budget slipped back into deficit by 2002. Tax cuts, spending on the wars in Afghanistan and Iraq, and a more sluggish economy all contributed to the return of painful times on the Budget committees. Complicating all this, as the end of the first decade of the twenty-first century approached, House Democrats reinstituted the PAYGO (pay-as-you-go) system in 2007 that had lapsed early in the Bush administration. Under PAYGO, newly enacted tax cuts or spending increases have to be offset by tax increases or spending cuts to survive floor challenges.

Budget Brinksmanship

The frequent emergence of executive-legislative budget battles to work out fiscal issues added yet another twist to the power relationships. Authorizing and appropriations committees—already wary of a budget process that had shifted some of their control over tax and spending issues to the Budget committees—viewed the high-level talks, where budget decisions were further centralized, with even greater suspicion.

A 1989 budget-summit deal collapsed in part because chairs of key committees required to enact the plan were not involved in crucial negotiations. The tax-writing committees were given a revenue-raising target without any agreement on how the figure would be attained. Attempting to avoid a replay, congressional and White House leaders involved key committee chairs in a 1990 budget summit from the start. Although the authorizing committee chairs were still excluded, the congressional negotiating team included the chairs and ranking members of the tax-writing and Appropriations committees in both the House and Senate, along with the Budget committees and other congressional leaders.

After intermittent talks beginning in May 1990, two dozen congressional and White House negotiators in September went into seclusion at Andrews Air Force Base outside Washington, D.C., for what they hoped would be a final round of budget talks. A budget agreement ultimately was reached by eight congressional and administration officials and led to the Budget Enforcement Act of 1990.

But many members of Congress were not pleased with an agreement reached by a handful of leaders in secrecy away from Capitol Hill, a process that seemed to some observers to cast aside the committee system and political accountability. Many committee chairs in the House were up in arms about provisions of the agreement that trod on their turf. More than half of the committee chairs voted against the budget, along with seven of the thirteen Appropriations subcommittee chairs. The summit agreement went down to humiliating defeat in the House, leading to a three-day shutdown of the government.

The budget crisis finally was resolved, and the resulting budget reconciliation package boded further power shifts in the budget process. The new law gave the executive branch closer scrutiny of legislation as it was being crafted. But whatever the near-term outcome, the rivalries among the spending committees were certain to continue. In the following years, budget brinksmanship became the norm as expiring appropriations and soon-to-be-breached debt ceilings triggered interbranch standoffs and down-to-the-wire negotiations that frequently placed committees in little more than a support role. A recent such episode surrounding the near default of the federal government and the debt ceiling led to creation of the Joint Select Committee on Deficit Reduction—a panel with nearly unprecedented powers to change tax and spending laws along with an up-or-down vote on the House and Senate floors that nevertheless failed to reach an agreement.

OVERSIGHT MANDATE

In addition to their lawmaking function, committees bear important responsibilities for overseeing implementation of the laws already on the books. Congress has given the executive branch broad authority over the vast array of agencies and programs it has created. As the range of activities of the federal government has grown, so, too, has the need for Congress to oversee how the executive branch administers the laws it has passed. Oleszek explains:

> A thoughtful, well-drafted law offers no guarantee that the policy intentions of legislators will be carried out. . . . The laws passed by Congress are often general guidelines, and sometimes their wording is deliberately vague. The implementation of legislation involves the drafting of administrative regulations by the executive agencies and day-to-day program management by agency officials. Agency regulations and rules are the subject of "legislative oversight"— the continuing review by Congress of how effectively the executive branch is carrying out congressional mandates.[34]

Members of the Joint Select Committee on Deficit Reduction hold a full committee hearing on considering proposed committee rules on Capitol Hill in Washington, D.C., on September 8, 2011. The bipartisan "super-committee" was tasked to identify at least $1.2 trillion in deficit cuts by November 23, 2011. Its failure to do so triggered automatic spending cuts in defense and nondefense domestic programs, but Congress still had all of 2012 to negotiate an alternate deal.

SOURCE: XINHUA/Landov.

Congress did not officially recognize its responsibility for oversight until enactment of the 1946 Legislative Reorganization Act. That law mandated that the House and Senate standing committees exercise "continuous watchfulness of the execution by the administrative agencies" of any laws under their jurisdiction. The 1946 law divided oversight responsibilities into three areas: the legislative or authorizing committees were to review government programs and agencies, the Appropriations committees were to review government spending, and the committees currently named House Oversight and Government Reform and Senate Governmental Affairs and Homeland Security were to probe for inefficiency, waste, and corruption in the federal government. But, as Oleszek points out, "to some degree all committees perform each type of oversight."[35]

Since enactment of the 1946 law Congress has passed several measures affecting oversight activities. In the 1970 Legislative Reorganization Act, Congress increased staff assistance to all House and Senate committees, recommended that committees ascertain whether programs within their

jurisdiction should be funded annually, and required most committees to issue oversight reports every two years.

Congress acted in 1974 to improve its oversight procedures when it passed the Congressional Budget and Impoundment Control Act. That act strengthened the role of the General Accounting Office (renamed the Government Accountability Office in 2004 and commonly referred to as the GAO) in acquiring fiscal, budgetary, and program-related information from federal agencies, authorized the GAO to establish an office to develop and recommend methods by which Congress could review and evaluate federal programs and activities, and authorized committees to assess the effectiveness of such programs and to require government agencies to carry out their own evaluations.

Congressional committees have a variety of ways of exercising their oversight responsibilities. The traditional and most obvious way is through normal legislative procedures. Congress can examine government activities through committee hearings and investigations—with precedents stretching back to 1792 and the investigation into the disastrous military defeat of General Arthur St. Clair. Today they range from relatively mundane reviews of drug production on public lands (2003) to highly publicized probes such as the 104th Congress's investigations of personnel firings at the White House travel office, access by Clinton administration officials to Federal Bureau of Investigation (FBI) files on former Republican White House staffers, the Whitewater real estate deal involving President and Mrs. Clinton, and the 105th Congress's hearings on alleged campaign finance law violations in the 1996 election and Internal Revenue Service abuses of taxpayers' rights.

It is often difficult to interest members in conducting routine oversight over government agencies unless visible political rewards exist for those participating. Oversight does not involve obtaining funds for projects or trading favors with colleagues. When the House mandated that most committees create subcommittees specifically devoted to oversight, the panels often became the last chosen in the internal subcommittee assignment bidding process and were often chaired by junior members.

Some powerful members vigorously pursued oversight agendas and employed the full range of Congress's investigative powers, in recent years most notably Rep. John D. Dingell, D-Mich., who chaired both the House Energy and Commerce Committee (1981–1995) and its oversight subcommittee. He conducted highly publicized investigations ranging across his committee's vast legislative domain, which he frequently fought to expand. After Democrats lost control of the House in 1995, to make more key subcommittee posts available for other members, Dingell and most other committee ranking minority members were barred from also ranking on any subcommittee. Even though he no longer could control a committee or subcommittee agenda, Dingell vigorously but unsuccessfully fought the change, arguing that it needlessly downgraded the conduct of committee oversight and left it to junior members who either did not care or lacked the expertise to investigate effectively.

Committees can use their subpoena powers broadly to demand information from government agencies and even hold executive officials in contempt for failure to comply, subject to approval by the parent chamber. The House voted several times during the 1980s to hold executive branch officials in contempt, most notably Anne Gorsuch, the administrator of the Environmental Protection Agency during the Reagan administration.

In 1996 the House Government Reform and Oversight Committee voted to hold White House counsel Jack Quinn in contempt for refusing to respond to a committee subpoena for documents, generating controversy over whether a committee had the authority to vote contempt without first giving the person cited a chance to appear and offer some defense. The majority determined that it had the power to proceed. After the vote, White House compliance was obtained and no House vote on contempt was held.

The use of the contempt power may become a first resort, not a last, in highly charged, partisan confrontations between the branches over information. Late in 1997 Attorney General Janet Reno was threatened with contempt by the committee, even before she testified, when it was learned that the Department of Justice would not supply a copy of a memorandum from the director of the FBI to Reno reportedly outlining why he disagreed with her decision not to appoint an independent counsel to investigate allegations of improper fund-raising by the president, vice president, and others during the 1996 election campaign.

Alleged scandals in the Clinton administration provided many opportunities for congressional oversight and substantial media coverage. Republicans seemed to have concluded that by weakening the Democratic president, political prospects might improve for enactment of their legislative agenda.

The GOP leadership, especially in the House, took on a major new role in selecting topics for committees to examine. Leadership intervention extended so far as selecting subcommittee chairs and obtaining additional funds for investigations and expenses in the biennial committee funding resolution passed by the House, and even afterward.

For example, in the 105th Congress Speaker Gingrich recommended that $2.15 million in additional funds be allocated for the Education and the Workforce Committee's Oversight subcommittee to use to investigate organized labor. The money was subsequently provided on a party-line vote of the House Oversight Committee, with no House vote required. New House rules allowed a reserve fund of money in the committee funding resolution that the Speaker could direct to special projects. Democrats called this a slush fund, claiming that it undermined the requirements of fiscal discipline and advance planning that the committee funding resolution was supposed to place on committee activities. They also argued that the investigation was a sham intended as retribution against organized labor for its massive spending to overturn the Republican majority in the 1996 election. The Democrats demanded unsuccessfully that the full House vote on all such reallocations of funds. Republicans countered that flexibility was essential in the conduct of congressional oversight to deal both with new issues and expansions of previously planned investigations and that Congress should not be straight-jacketed by funding priorities made early in a two-year cycle.[36]

Special reports required from agencies, investigations by agencies' inspectors general, audits by the GAO, and studies by congressional support agencies are other oversight tools. The substantial growth in reports required by Congress has triggered some complaints within both the executive branch and Congress that legislative committees are attempting to micromanage administrative details. The 104th Congress passed a Reports Elimination Act in response to these complaints to reduce the number of reports required, but the traditional tension between the legislative and executive branches concerning oversight is unlikely to be relieved simply by paperwork reduction.

The legislative veto had been a popular oversight mechanism since 1932, when Congress began attaching to various statutes provisions giving one or both chambers or individual committees authority to veto government actions, regulations, and orders. The Supreme Court threw out the legislative veto in the 1983 *INS v. Chadha* decision on the grounds that Congress could exercise such power only through the enactment of legislation presented to the president for signature or veto. Some of these provisions continue to exist in statutes, however, and can occasionally still be used under the rules of each chamber to make a political point, even though they no longer have legal effect. For example, in 1998 Rep. Tom Campbell, R-Calif., used a provision of the War Powers Act to force a House vote on a concurrent resolution purporting to force withdrawal of U.S. troops from a peacekeeping mission in Bosnia. (The resolution was reported adversely from committee and defeated on the floor.) In 1999 similar votes occurred relating to the North Atlantic Treaty Organization's military action against Serbia. Since *Chadha*, Congress has either rewritten many of these laws to pass constitutional muster or has found other informal ways to continue to exercise its influence.

Congress also has at its disposal nonstatutory controls, such as informal contacts between executive officials and committee members and staff, and statements made in committee and conference reports as well as statements during hearings and floor debates. Davidson and Oleszek observe: "Although their usage is not measured, nonstatutory controls may be the most common form of congressional oversight."[37]

★

NOTES

1 Woodrow Wilson, *Congressional Government: A Study in American Politics* (Boston: Houghton Mifflin, 1885), 79.

2 Walter J. Oleszek, *Congressional Procedures and the Policy Process*. 4th ed. (Washington, D.C.: CQ Press, 1996), 121.

3 Leroy N. Rieselbach, *Congressional Reform* (Washington, D.C.: CQ Press, 1986), 110.

4 Christopher J. Deering and Steven S. Smith, *Committees in Congress*. 3rd ed. (Washington, D.C.: CQ Press, 1997), 2.

5 Oleszek, *Congressional Procedures and the Policy Process*, 4th ed., 112.

6 George Goodwin Jr., *The Little Legislatures: Committees of Congress* (Amherst: University of Massachusetts Press, 1970).

7 Wilson, *Congressional Government*, 59.

8 George B. Galloway, *Congress at the Crossroads* (New York: Crowell, 1946), 88.

9 Deering and Smith, *Committees in Congress*, 3rd ed., 26.

10 Galloway, *Congress at the Crossroads*, 139–144; and Goodwin, *The Little Legislatures*, 11–12.

11 Steven Smith and Christopher J. Deering, *Committees in Congress*. 2nd ed. (Washington, D.C.: CQ Press, 1990), 33.

12 Ibid., 42.

13 The House Armed Services Committee also had established two temporary "panels."

14 The Senate Budget Committee also had established one "task force."

15 George H. Haynes, *The Senate of the United States*. Vol. 1. (Boston: Houghton Mifflin, 1938), 273–277.

16 Randall B. Ripley, *Power in the Senate* (New York: St. Martin's Press, 1969), 23.

17 Ibid., 47.

18 Wilson, *Congressional Government*, 82.

19 Roger H. Davidson, "Subcommittee Government: New Channels for Policy Making." In Thomas E. Mann and Norman J. Ornstein, eds., *The New Congress* (Washington, D.C.: American Enterprise Institute, 1981), 105–108.

20 Deering and Smith, *Committees in Congress*, 3rd ed., 33.

21 Janet Hook, "Extensive Reform Proposals Cook on the Front Burner," *Congressional Quarterly Weekly Report*, June 6, 1992, 1579.

22 Norman J. Ornstein, Thomas E. Mann, and Michael J. Malbin, *Vital Statistics on Congress: 1997–1998* (Washington, D.C.: Congressional Quarterly, 1998), 123.

23 Senate Temporary Select Committee to Study the Senate Committee System, *First Report, with Recommendations; Structure of the Senate Committee System: Jurisdictions, Numbers and Sizes, and Limitations on Memberships and Chairmanships, Referral Procedures, and Scheduling*, 94th Cong., 2nd sess., 1976, 6.

24 Deering and Smith, *Committees in Congress*, 3rd ed., 141.

25 Ibid., 78–81.

26 Walter J. Oleszek, *Congressional Procedures and the Policy Process*. 3rd ed. (Washington, D.C.: CQ Press, 1989), 87.

27 Ibid., 88.

28 Melissa P. Collie and Joseph Cooper, "Multiple Referral and the 'New' Committee System in the House of Representatives." In Lawrence C. Dodd and Bruce I. Oppenheimer, eds., *Congress Reconsidered*. 4th ed. (Washington, D.C.: CQ Press, 1989), 248.

29 Ibid., 254.

30 Roger H. Davidson, Walter J. Oleszek, and Thomas Kephart, "One Bill, Many Committees: Multiple Referrals in the U.S. House of Representatives," *Legislative Studies Quarterly* 13, no. 1 (February 1988): 4.

31 Oleszek, *Congressional Procedures and the Policy Process*, 3rd ed., 76.

32 Deering and Smith, *Committees in Congress*, 3rd ed., 201.

33 Smith and Deering, *Committees in Congress*, 2nd ed., 211.

34 Oleszek, *Congressional Procedures and the Policy Process*, 4th ed., 300.

35 Ibid., 301.

36 Jeffrey L. Katz, "GOP Preserves Special Fund for Future Probes," *CQ Weekly*, June 27, 1998, 1751.

37 Roger H. Davidson, Walter J. Oleszek, and Frances E. Lee, *Congress and Its Members*. 13th ed. (Washington, D.C.: CQ Press, 2011), 339.

SELECTED BIBLIOGRAPHY

Aberbach, Joel D. *Keeping a Watchful Eye: The Politics of Congressional Oversight.* Washington, D.C.: Brookings Institution, 1990.

Adler, E. Scott. *Why Congressional Reforms Fail: Reelection and the House Committee System.* Chicago: University of Chicago Press, 2002.

Baughman, John. *Common Ground: Committee Politics in the U.S. House of Representatives.* Stanford, Calif.: Stanford University Press, 2006.

Canon, David T., Garrison Nelson, and Charles Stewart, III, comps. *Committees in the U.S. Congress, 1789–1946.* Washington, D.C.: CQ Press, 2002.

Clark, Joseph S. *The Senate Establishment.* New York: Hill and Wang, 1963.

Cooper, Joseph. *Congress and Its Committees: A Historical Approach to the Role of Committees in the Legislative Process.* New York: Garland, 1988.

Cox, Gary W., and Mathew D. McCubbins. *Setting the Agenda: Responsible Party Government in the U.S. House of Representatives.* New York: Cambridge University Press, 2005.

Davidson, Roger H. "Subcommittee Government: New Channels for Policy Making." In Thomas E. Mann and Norman J. Ornstein, eds., *The New Congress.* Washington, D.C.: American Enterprise Institute, 1981.

Davidson, Roger H., Walter J. Oleszek, and Frances E. Lee. *Congress and Its Members.* 13th ed. Washington, D.C.: CQ Press, 2011.

Deering, Christopher J., and Steven S. Smith. *Committees in Congress.* 3rd ed. Washington, D.C.: CQ Press, 1997.

Endersby, James W., and Karen M. McCurdy. "Committee Assignments in the U.S. Senate." *Legislative Studies Quarterly* 21 (May 1996): 219–234.

Evans, C. Lawrence. *Leadership in Committee: A Comparative Analysis of Leadership Behavior in the U.S. Senate.* Ann Arbor: University of Michigan Press, 1991.

Evans, C. Lawrence, and Walter J. Oleszek. *Congress under Fire: Reform Politics and the Republican Majority.* Boston: Houghton Mifflin, 1997.

Fenno, Richard F., Jr. *Congressmen in Committees.* Boston: Little, Brown, 1973.

Finocchiaro, Charles J. *Procedural Efficiency, Leadership Centralization, or Both? Unconventional Patterns of Bill Referral in the Republican Congress.* East Lansing: Michigan State University, 2000.

Frisch, Scott A., and Sean Q. Kelly. *Committee Assignment Politics in the U.S. House of Representatives.* Norman: University of Oklahoma Press, 2006.

Galloway, George B. *Congress at the Crossroads.* New York: Crowell, 1946.

Goodwin, George, Jr. *The Little Legislatures: Committees of Congress.* Amherst: University of Massachusetts Press, 1970.

Groseclose, Tim, and Charles Stewart. "The Value of Committee Seats in the House, 1947–1991." *American Journal of Political Science* 42 (April 1998): 453–474.

Hall, Richard L. *Participation in Congress.* New Haven, Conn.: Yale University Press, 1996.

Hall, Richard L., and C. Lawrence Evans. "The Power of Subcommittees." *Journal of Politics* 52 (May 1990): 335–355.

Haynes, George H. *The Senate of the United States: Its History and Practice.* 2 vols. Boston: Houghton Mifflin, 1938.

Hinckley, Barbara. *The Seniority System in Congress.* Bloomington: Indiana University Press, 1971.

Katz, Jonathan, and Brian Sala. "Careerism, Committee Assignments, and the Electoral Connection." *American Political Science Review* 90 (March 1996): 21–33.

Kiewiet, D. Roderick, and Mathew D. McCubbins. *The Logic of Delegation: Congressional Parties and the Appropriations Process.* Chicago: University of Chicago Press, 1991.

King, David C. *Turf Wars: How Congressional Committees Claim Jurisdiction.* Chicago: University of Chicago Press, 1997.

Krehbiel, Keith. *Information and Legislative Organization.* Ann Arbor: University of Michigan Press, 1991.

Krehbiel, Keith, Kenneth A. Shepsle, and Barry Weingast. "Why Are Committees Powerful?" *American Political Science Review* 81 (September 1987): 929–945.

Longley, Lawrence D., and Walter J. Oleszek. *Bicameral Politics: Conference Committees in Congress.* New Haven, Conn.: Yale University Press, 1989.

Maass, Arthur. *Congress and the Common Good.* New York: Basic Books, 1983.

Maltzman, Forrest. *Competing Principals: Committees, Parties, and the Organization of Congress.* Ann Arbor: University of Michigan Press, 1997.

McConachie, Lauros. *Congressional Committees.* New York: Crowell, 1898.

McCown, Ada C. *The Congressional Conference Committee.* New York: Columbia University Press, 1927.

Miller, Mark C. *The View of the Courts from the Hill: Interactions between Congress and the Federal Judiciary.* Charlottesville: University of Virginia Press, 2009.

Munson, Richard. *The Cardinals of Capitol Hill: The Men and Women Who Control Federal Spending.* New York: Grove Press, 1993.

Nelson, Garrison, and Charles Stewart III. *Committees in the U.S. Congress 1993–2010.* Washington, D.C.: CQ Press, 2011.

Oleszek, Walter J. *Congressional Procedures and the Policy Process.* 8th ed. Washington, D.C.: CQ Press, 2011.

Parker, Glenn R., and Suzanne L. Parker. *Factions in House Committees.* Knoxville: University of Tennessee Press, 1985.

Petersen, R. Eric, and Richard S. Beth. *Senate Committee Activity: Action on Measures Referred, 1973–2000.* New York: Nova Science, 2003.

Reeves, Andree E. *Congressional Committee Chairmen: Three Who Made an Evolution.* Lexington: University of Kentucky Press, 1993.

Robinson, James A. *The House Rules Committee.* Indianapolis: Bobbs-Merrill, 1963.

Rohde, David W. "Committees and Policy Formulation." In Paul J. Quirk and Sarah A. Binder, eds., *The Legislative Branch.* Oxford, U.K.: Oxford University Press, 2005.

Schickler, Eric. *Disjointed Pluralism: Institutional Innovation and the Development of the U.S. Congress.* Princeton, N.J.: Princeton University Press, 2001.

Schickler, Eric, and Frances E. Lee, eds. *The Oxford Handbook of the American Congress.* Oxford, U.K.: Oxford University Press, 2011.

Schneider, Judy, Christopher Davis, and Betsy Palmer. *Reorganization of the House of Representatives: Modern Reform Efforts.* Report no. RL31835. Washington, D.C.: Library of Congress, Congressional Research Service, 2003.

Schneier, Edward V., and Bertram Gross. *Congress Today.* New York: St. Martin's Press, 1993.

Shepsle, Kenneth A. "The Changing Textbook Congress." In John E. Chubb and Paul E. Peterson, eds., *Can the Government Govern?* Washington, D.C.: Brookings Institution, 1989.

———. *The Giant Jigsaw Puzzle: Democratic Committee Assignments in the Modern House.* Chicago: University of Chicago Press, 1978.

Shepsle, Kenneth A., and Barry R. Weingast. "The Institutional Foundations of Committee Power." *American Political Science Review* 81 (June 1987): 85–104.

Smith, Steven S., and Christopher J. Deering. *Committees in Congress.* Washington, D.C.: CQ Press, 1984.

Strahan, Randall W. *New Ways and Means: Reform and Change in a Congressional Committee.* Chapel Hill: University of North Carolina Press, 1990.

Unekis, Joseph K., and Leroy N. Rieselbach. *Congressional Committee Politics: Continuity and Change.* New York: Praeger, 1984.

Van Beek, Stephen D. *Post-Passage Politics: Bicameral Resolution in Congress.* Pittsburgh: University of Pittsburgh Press, 1995.

chapter 4

Congressional Staff

Thousands of people work for Congress, a generally faceless mass of mostly young people who are an integral part of the legislative process. For the public, congressional staff members are represented by the voices at the other end of phone calls to members' offices or the blurred faces behind members at televised congressional committee meetings. Staffers are drawn to Capitol Hill by the exciting prospect of being at the epicenter of important political, social, and economic issues, by the idealistic hope of making a difference in public service, and, often, by raw ambition.

Staff members cannot vote, but their imprint is everywhere: on legislation, in political matters, and on the views of members. The influence of congressional staff members is vast—too vast, say critics who believe they wield excessive power and cost too much tax money. But legislators reply that staffs provide the expertise on complex issues that members could never master alone.

Although thousands of people work for Congress, the term *congressional staff* as it is commonly used applies to men and women who work for committees or for individual members. Capitol Hill staffers may be policy and legal experts—who usually work for congressional committees— or they may be versed in running an efficient office for a member, helping constituents, and doing whatever they can to get their bosses reelected. Members rely heavily on staff during all stages of the legislative process. Some staffers draft legislation, negotiate with lobbyists, and plot strategy for floor action. These "entrepreneurial staffers," a phrase coined by David E. Price, a political scientist and Democratic member of the House from North Carolina, are given considerable responsibility for legislative decision making, with members of Congress backstopping their efforts.[1] Faced with more complex issues, more technical legislation, and more demanding constituents with ever-increasing ways to stay abreast of congressional activity and voice their concerns, members have encouraged the growth of entrepreneurial staff.

Many members of Congress also view staff—especially large staffs—as a symbol of prestige and importance. To some members, the larger the staff, the more powerful a member appears. Similarly, many staffers feel that the more powerful the committee or member they work for, the more powerful they are.

POSTWAR WAVES OF STAFF EXPANSION

Congressional staffs became large and diverse in the half-century following World War II. That worldwide conflict and the Great Depression before it in the 1930s transformed the United States into a global power and an increasingly complex society. With those changes came an unremitting need in Congress for assistance in understanding and legislating on issues of the postwar world.

Huge increases in the size of congressional staff came in two waves: after a landmark congressional reorganization in 1946 and during a period of internal reform in the 1970s that changed many of the traditional ways in which Congress operated. As the size of staff increased, so did the cost of running Congress, which by fiscal year 2010 tallied nearly $4.7 billion before dropping slightly to about $4.5 billion the following fiscal year.[2] By comparison, the cost in 1960 was $118.2 million. Although the 2011 figure includes some congressional support agencies not in existence in 1960, the magnitude of the increase still holds. About one-half of the fiscal year 2010 total was devoted to House and Senate operations, with the largest share going for staff salaries.

Congress has more staff members than any other national legislature. In 2009 about 16,000 aides worked directly for its 541 voting and nonvoting members (including the delegates from American Samoa, the District of Columbia, Guam, the Northern Mariana Islands, and the Virgin Islands, and the resident commissioner from Puerto Rico), for the committees, joint committees, leadership, and chamber officers and officials.[3] Furthermore, 6,300 or so congressional employees are support staff. They work for the Library of Congress, Government Accountability Office, Congressional Budget Office, and other agencies of the legislative branch. This chapter deals primarily with personal and committee staffs.

Although the forces that helped push staff size to record heights remain strong, growth stopped in the late 1980s and 1990s because of budget cuts and reductions of committee staff that emerged in part from changing political control and attitudes on Capitol Hill. Growth began to climb again in the next decade, particularly in the personal offices of members and leadership. Then national economic concerns and a growing political desire among congressional leaders to "set an example" led to a push for tightening in House and Senate expenditures in 2011 that some observers suggested could lead to a reduction in staffing levels or affect staff compensation.

Explaining Staff Growth

Congressional staffs expanded steadily after enactment of the 1946 Legislative Reorganization Act but most dramatically after the 1970 Legislative Reorganization Act and in response to increasing member responsibility. The growth began to level off in the late 1970s but continued to climb, reaching a peak in the early 1990s of about 17,800 before starting a decline in 1995. The level rose again in the early part of the twenty-first century to another peak in 2006, when House and Senate staff totaled more than 15,900 before dropping again.[4]

In 1947 House and Senate committees had 399 aides; in 2009 the number exceeded 2,200, including standing, special, and select committees (but not joint committees), an increase of about 450 percent. (The high point in committee staff occurred in the mid- to late 1980s, when it was around 3,000.)[5]

Staff numbers for the standing committees in the House reached their highest point of 2,201 in 1991 before declining to 1,246, in 1996 and then leveling off. In 2009 there were 1,324 employees. In the Senate, committee staff numbers also shifted but not as dramatically. At its highest point in 1990, the staff numbered 1,090, and in 2009 Senate committee staff numbered 913.[6] (See Table 4.1, p. 193.)

At the start of the twenty-first century, House members' office staff was at about the same level as two decades earlier, even with some declines during the 1990s. In 1977, House member offices had 6,942 employees. That number grew to 7,920 by 1986 before dropping slightly and resting at about 7,200 in the early 2000s. In 2009, member offices employed 6,907. Staff in House leadership offices had dropped from 162 in 1979 to 126 by 1997, then increased dramatically to 179 two years later before leveling off. Leadership offices employed 171 staffers in 2009. Senators' offices also showed a rise in staff hiring, growing from 3,554 in 1977 to 4,294 in 1991, then leveling off and declining in the 2000s. In 2009,

there were 3,884 staffers employed in Senate offices. *(See Table 4.2, p. 195.)* Meanwhile, Senate leadership offices had a dramatic increase in staffing, rising from 91 in 1979 to 214 in 2009.[7]

The initial significant growth in staff after World War II was caused by congressional efforts to be more independent of the executive branch, the growing number of complex legislative issues, competition among committees, and increased constituent mail and services. Further staff growth, especially committee staff, after the 1970 reorganization act was linked to congressional reform efforts at the beginning of that decade. Along with the election of more activist members came the decline of the congressional seniority system, more intense lobbying efforts by special interests, and a growing disdain for how minority party members had traditionally been treated. In 1979, the number of House committee staffers was almost three times the number in 1970, and the number of Senate committee staffers doubled over the same time period.[8] In the House the increase stemmed largely from the creation of many more subcommittees, and the chairs of those panels were given the authority to hire staff, a prerogative previously jealously guarded by the full committee chairs.

In the Senate the passage of S Res 60, allowing senators—often more junior in status—to hire personal staff members to help with committee work, accounted for much of the staffing growth in that chamber.

The relationship between Congress and the executive branch also was a factor in staff growth during the 1970s. Before the mid-1960s Congress still depended to a large extent on the executive branch for information and advice on existing programs and legislative proposals. But growing distrust of the executive branch, partially the result of the Vietnam War and, in the 1970s, the Watergate scandal that drove President Richard M. Nixon from office, prompted Congress to hire more and better-qualified committee staff to monitor and evaluate executive branch performance as well as to provide independent analysis of issues and proposals. In addition, the larger staff increased Congress's capacity to initiate more legislation rather than depend heavily on executive branch agencies.

Also during the 1970s vast expansion occurred in White House and executive office staff. As the executive branch grew, Congress felt greater urgency to create its own bureaucracy as a counterbalance. Former Sen. Daniel Patrick Moynihan, D-N.Y., termed this process the "Iron Law of Emulation": "Whenever any branch of government acquires a new technique which enhances its power in relation to the other branches, that technique will soon be adopted by those other branches as well."[9]

Similarly, the growth of special interest groups in Washington, D.C., contributed to an increase in Capitol Hill staff as members sought better assistance in evaluating the claims and proposals of the proliferating groups representing

Maryland senator John Marshall Butler and his entire staff pose in the 1950s. Congressional staff sizes ballooned in the 1960s and 1970s.

SOURCE: U.S. Senate Historical Office.

business, labor, environment, and citizens. All of these factors added up, in the minds of members, to more work, longer days, more difficult issues, and larger controversies. Although some indicators of the congressional workload—the number of bills introduced, reported, and passed; the number of votes taken; and the number of subcommittee and committee meetings—decreased in the 1990s, the workload remained heavy. The decrease in the number of bills reflected Congress's penchant, developed in the 1980s and into the 1990s, for using omnibus bills, one big package containing many separate bills. In addition, the budget deficit restrained members from considering any legislation that cost considerable amounts of money.

The number of committee and subcommittee meetings may have decreased, but contentious confirmation hearings in the Senate, rooted in the increased partisanship characterizing Washington politics from the 1970s on, became especially time-consuming as members and interest groups used the process as a vehicle to debate social and political issues such as abortion and race relations. By November 2010, nearly 20 percent of President Barack Obama's key policy-making positions remained vacant. The following June, the

Senate sought to reduce the workload associated with confirmations by passing a bill removing 169 low-level agency positions from the list of more than 1,200 requiring Senate confirmation. But then it languished in the Republican-controlled House. Also in June, the Senate passed a resolution requiring nominations for about 200 mostly part-time positions with federal advisory boards and councils directly to the floor, allowing them to bypass committee review.[10] (Later, frustrated with Republicans blocking his nominations, and bearing criticism for some recess appointments, Obama in his 2012 State of the Union address proposed reforms rules on nominations to require a Senate vote within ninety days of a nomination.) Congressional and executive ethics investigations also increasingly added to the committee workload.

After the September 11, 2001, terrorist attacks, national security became a priority in both the executive and legislative branches, adding once again to the committee workload. The House responded by creating a Select Committee on Homeland Security with both legislative and oversight functions. The committee was to have oversight of the new Department of Homeland Security, which merged all or part of twenty-two federal agencies. The new committee, which became a permanent standing committee at the start of the 109th Congress (2005–2007), was given parts of the jurisdictions of the Transportation, Judiciary, Intelligence, and Science committees, among others. The committee also established five subcommittees, and in 2007 added a sixth subcommittee focused on cybersecurity and infrastructure protection. The Senate opted to place homeland security oversight under the Governmental Affairs Committee, which was renamed Homeland Security and Governmental Affairs at the start of the 109th Congress. In the 112th Congress, it too had six subcommittees. Each chamber also established a new Appropriations subcommittee on homeland security during the 108th Congress (2003–2005).

In 2007, with an increasing interest among Democrats in tackling legislation to address climate change, House Speaker Nancy Pelosi, D-Calif., created a new Select Committee on Energy Independence and Global Warming. The committee was disbanded when Republicans took over the House in 2011.

At the end of the twentieth century and into the twenty-first, Congress was closely divided between Republicans and Democrats, and partisan stalemates worsened, matching a growing dissatisfaction among the public and leading to changes in majority control. The GOP held a razor-thin voting margin in both the House and Senate until the 2006 elections, when Democrats regained control of both chambers. But the GOP won back the House in the 2010 elections and further narrowed the Democrats' rule in the Senate. The flip-flop caused high staff turnover, as is typical with majority changeover,[11] and a national financial crisis in the late 2000s led to changes in legislative priorities and a tightening of government budgets, with some increasing scrutiny of staff expenditures.

Employment Practices

Until the latter years of the twentieth century, congressional aides—for all the power and prestige they possessed—were treated differently from the vast majority of American workers. For the most part, federal labor, safety, and health laws did not cover staffers. After Congress was criticized for being unable to live under the laws it passed for others, lawmakers in 1995 enacted a workplace compliance bill, known as the Congressional Accountability Act, which applied eleven federal labor and antidiscrimination laws to most congressional employees. *(See box, Congress and Workplace Compliance, p. 210.)*

Still, even with these new protections, and for all the glamour of working for Congress, aides often face long hours, cramped quarters, and the sometimes capricious demands of the politicians at whose pleasure they serve. In October 2012, the Congressional Management Foundation and the Society for Human Resource Management released the first of three studies on work-life experiences in Congress. It showed D.C.

staffers on average working 53 hours per week while Congress is in session, often not getting everything done and desiring more flexibility but also highly valuing meaningful work. The next two studies cover legislators' experiences and staffers' overall job satisfaction.

Earlier studies showed that women and African Americans were at a particular disadvantage. A 1998 study of House personal staffs concluded that, even though women made up 57 percent of employees, they often held lower-paying jobs. The same study also found that black House staff members received 87 percent of the pay of their white counterparts and made up 5.9 percent of the total staff, while Latino staffers earned 70 percent of the salaries of white staffers. These differences in average salary largely stemmed from the positions held by minority staff compared with those held by white staff.[12]

A 2000 study of congressional personal staff found that women on House personal staffs held 38 percent of the executive positions and 41 percent of the policy positions. In the Senate in 1999, women held 37 percent of the executive positions and 53 percent of the policy jobs.[13] In 2011, *National Journal* profiled 319 staffers it called "top aids" who worked for congressional leaders and House and Senate committees. Of those, 32 percent were female and 93 percent were white.[14]

EVOLUTION OF THE CONGRESSIONAL STAFF

During the early years of Congress, senators and representatives were reluctant to admit they required staff assistance, either in the committees or in their own offices. According to William L. Morrow, in his book *Congressional Committees*, "Legislators were considered more erudite than most citizens and they believed any suggestion for staff assistance might be interpreted as a lack of confidence in their ability to master their jobs."[15]

Congressional staffing began as clerical assistance. Harrison W. Fox Jr. and Susan Webb Hammond noted in their 1977 book, *Congressional Staffs*, that the term *clerk-hire* was applied in the early days to the account used to pay personal staffers.[16] The term remained common in the decades that followed even though both chambers moved to consolidate accounts and give members more flexibility in hiring staff.

Until the 1820s standing committees were few and far between. Even though more were created, members handled business without paid assistance. Congress rejected requests to employ permanent committee clerks until about 1840 when, after pleas by committee chairs, some clerical help was permitted in emergencies on a per diem or hourly basis. Funds for these part-time assistants were made available through special appropriations.

In 1856 the House Ways and Means and Senate Finance committees became the first to obtain regular appropriations for full-time clerks. Appropriations for other committees followed, but their staffing generally was limited to persons hired for housekeeping duties, such as stenographers and receptionists. Members or their personal aides (who were still paid out of members' own pockets) usually handled substantive committee work and bill drafting. The number of committee employees continued to increase gradually, however. By 1891 committee staff numbered forty-one in the Senate and sixty-two in the House.

George B. Galloway, a specialist on Congress with the Library of Congress for many years, observed that the turn of the twentieth century found Congress adding line items to appropriations acts specifying funds for the standing committees of the House and Senate. The first comprehensive pay bill authorizing appropriations for all legislative employees, including committee clerks, was enacted in 1924. That act appropriated $270,100 for 141 Senate committee clerks and $200,490 for 120 House committee employees.

Senators were first authorized to hire personal aides in 1885, at a pay rate of six dollars a day. The House passed similar provisions in 1893. Before this time, members who were not committee chairs either worked without personal assistance or paid aides with personal funds.[17]

In the late nineteenth century, an ill-defined line, in practice and by statute, separated committee and personal staffs. Clerks appointed by committee chairs to assist on committee business often worked on the chairs' district business as well. Some superfluous committees were kept in business to provide chairs with clerk services and to provide the offices that accompanied a committee bureaucracy.

Distinctions between the duties of committee employees and members' personal staff remained blurred well into the twentieth century. Under provisions of the Legislative Pay Act of 1929, for example, when a senator assumed leadership of a committee, the three senior clerks of his office staff became ex officio clerk and assistant clerks of that committee. Furthermore, the act stipulated that the clerical staff of a Senate committee would serve as secretarial workers for its chair.

Personal staffs did not increase much in size between the turn of the century and World War II. In 1946 representatives were authorized to employ five aides, and the average Senate office had six staffers. Committee staffs also did not expand greatly. In 1943 Senate committees employed 190 aides; House committees, 114.[18]

Birth of the Modern Congress: The 1946 Reorganization Act

The organization of the modern Congress—its procedures, organization, structure, staffing—dates, by most accounts, from the Legislative Reorganization Act of 1946.

As early as 1941, senators and representatives realized that congressional operations—including staffing procedures and the committee structure—required modernization to

deal with the challenges faced by the national government in the wake of the Great Depression and in the face of the looming world war. Members pointed out that the growing congressional workload placed too heavy a burden on them and their staffs. In addition, improved communications and transportation permitted voters to ask more of elected officials, thereby increasing constituency casework. And from the depression-inspired New Deal days of the 1930s onward, issues and legislation became more complicated as the federal government expanded.

Faced with more complex legislation, Congress realized it lacked staff with technical knowledge and skills. It had to rely instead on the executive branch and private groups for specialized assistance and help with drafting bills. Members, then, began to fear that their excessive dependence on the executive branch would make Congress a secondary, instead of a coequal, institution in the national government. This apprehension was underscored by a warning issued in 1942 by President Franklin D. Roosevelt, who was frustrated with delays in enacting key administration proposals: "In the event that Congress fails to act, and act adequately, I shall accept the responsibility, and I shall act."[19]

Congress, however, did not have money to expand its staff; the United States was entering World War II:

[In 1941] of every seven dollars it authorized the federal government to spend, Congress spent only one cent on itself. Its thirty-two-hundred-member staff was predominantly clerical and custodial, with not more than two hundred persons who could be considered legislative professionals. [Members] were often required to use their office clerks as the principal staff of any committee they chaired, thus ignoring professional competence as the foundation for committee staffing.[20]

The lack of professional staff, however, was to an extent self-inflicted. Members were reluctant to increase their own funding lest the public view them as unable "to carry traditional legislative burdens."[21] In 1941, for example, senators balked when Sen. A.B. "Happy" Chandler, D-Ky., suggested allowing each senator one "research expert." Senior members who chaired committees objected to adding specialists to the clerical ranks, fearing it might establish a cadre of political assistants who could eventually compete for their bosses' jobs.[22]

Nevertheless, as frustrations rose with the workload and institutional ineffectiveness, Congress passed legislation in 1944 creating the Joint Committee on the Organization of Congress to study the organization, operation, and staffing of the House and Senate; House, Senate, and committee interaction; and congressional-executive relations. Two years later Congress incorporated most of the committee's recommendations into the Legislative Reorganization Act of 1946.

Laws and Rules Governing the Hiring of Staff

Since 1946 Congress has approved major laws and regulations that affect the hiring and placement of congressional staff, among which are the following:

LEGISLATIVE REORGANIZATION ACT OF 1946

This act established a permanent complement of professional staff for all standing committees and directed that staff be appointed on the basis of merit and not political affiliation. The latter directive is not always observed because committees prefer to hire their own Democratic or Republican experts. Under the act, committees were allowed to hire four professional staff aides and six clerical aides. Although a provision recommending that each member hire an administrative assistant on his or her personal staff was dropped from the act, the Senate instituted the reform later that year.

POSTAL RATE–FEDERAL PAY LAW OF 1967

This 1967 postal rate–federal pay law contained a ban on nepotism. It prohibited public officials, including members of Congress, from hiring, appointing, promoting, or advancing relatives in the agency in which the officials serve. The ban did not include relatives already employed, and it did not prevent an official in one agency or chamber of Congress from seeking to obtain employment for a relative in another agency or chamber.

LEGISLATIVE REORGANIZATION ACT OF 1970

This act increased from four to six the number of professional aides that could be employed by most standing committees of the House and Senate. The minority party was authorized to hire two of them and one of the six clerical aides. Committees were permitted to provide training for staff and to hire consultants. The act also required that one-third of House investigative staff funds be allocated to the minority (this provision was deleted in 1971 by the House Democratic Caucus).

HOUSE COMMITTEE AMENDMENTS OF 1974

Changes adopted in 1974 (H Res 988) tripled the staffs of most House standing committees. The number of professional aides went from six to eighteen and of clerical employees from six to twelve, with the minority party allowed to appoint one-third of each category. (The latter provision was killed in 1975.)

HOUSE DEMOCRATIC CAUCUS ACTION OF 1975

In 1975 the House Democratic Caucus overturned the 1974 House committee reorganization plan that had given Republicans one-third of investigative staff. Instead, it increased the number of statutory staff working on subcommittees by allowing subcommittee chairs and ranking minority members to hire one staff person each to work on their subcommittees. The increase of up to twelve aides (because standing committees are permitted a total of six subcommittees) was considered to be an overall increase in committee staff to forty-two statutory aides. The number of committee aides permitted by statute remained at thirty, however.

HOUSE RESOLUTION 359

In 1979 the House approved a rules change that permitted representatives to hire up to four additional employees if their jobs fit into one of the following five categories: a part-time employee; a shared employee; an intern; a temporary employee hired for three months or less; or a person who replaced an employee on leave without pay. This brought the total number of House personal staffers in a member's office to eighteen full time and four part time. (There are no limits on the number of Senate personal staff.)

SENATE RESOLUTION 60

The Senate in 1975 adopted S Res 60 authorizing senators to hire up to three staffers, called associate staff, to help them with their committee work. The resolution

---

The central elements of the 1946 act reduced the number of standing committees in the Senate from thirty-three to fifteen and in the House from forty-eight to nineteen and authorized the hiring of professional committee staff. Senators were assigned two committees instead of as many as nine. Representatives served on one committee instead of five. Each committee's jurisdiction was more strictly defined.

Congress also tried in the reorganization to separate the roles of committee and personal staffs by specifying that the former could only work on "committee business" and nothing else.

The House and Senate Appropriations committees and the Joint Committee on Taxation had begun building nonpartisan professional staffs in the 1920s. According to political scientist Michael J. Malbin, the success of those staffs led Congress in 1946 to institutionalize the practice by allowing each standing committee to hire a total of ten staff members—four professional and six clerical—selected

"solely on the basis of fitness to perform the duties of office."[23] The professional staff provided expert knowledge on a subject while the clerical staff supplied nonpolicy administrative and secretarial support. Although the terminology has changed some, and other names—such as investigative, associate, or temporary—have come into use, this broad distinction continues.

In 1946 the Appropriations committees were permitted to determine their staff needs by majority vote. Thus the total number of committee aides allowed under the 1946 act was 340, plus the additional staffers hired by the Appropriations committees.

The Joint Committee on the Organization of Congress also recommended that each member be allowed to hire an administrative assistant for his or her personal staff. Although this recommendation was dropped from the final act because of House resistance, it was instituted separately by the Senate shortly after the act's passage.[24]

permitted each senator to hire up to three committee assistants. S Res 60 later was changed from a Senate rule to a statute that forms the basis for the legislative assistance allowance now provided to all senators regardless of their committee leadership posts.

SENATE COMMITTEE AMENDMENTS OF 1977

Legislation (S Res 4) enacted in 1977 to reorganize Senate committees required committee staffs to be in proportion to the number of majority and minority members on each standing committee. The measure introduced a standing rule that a "majority of the minority members of any committee may, by resolution, request that at least one-third of all funds of the committee for personnel ... be allocated to the minority members of such committee."[1]

SENATE RESOLUTION 281

Approved in 1980, S Res 281 directed each Senate committee, except the Select Committee on Ethics, to submit a single budget for all expenses anticipated for the fiscal year. (Money requested by the ethics committee comes from the Senate contingent fund.) The resolution eliminated the distinction between statutory and investigative committee staffs, which previously had separate budgets, and the change itself made it much easier to get a true picture of Senate committee expenditures.

CONGRESSIONAL ACCOUNTABILITY ACT OF 1995

In 1995 Congress passed legislation that ended exemptions from workplace laws that both chambers long enjoyed. The law established an Office of Compliance for employees to file grievances regarding an alleged violation but also allowed eventual recourse to the courts. *(See box, Congress and Workplace Compliance, p. 210.)*

COMMITTEE CUTS

At the beginning of the 104th Congress in 1995, Republicans revised House rules (H Res 6) to change some of the ways the House conducted business. One change was the restructuring of committees, with a directive that committee staff be reduced by one-third. Moreover, no committee was permitted more than five subcommittees, except the Appropriations Committee, the Government Reform and Oversight Committee, and the Transportation and Infrastructure Committee. The rules also gave control of staff hiring for subcommittees to the full committee chair. Subcommittee chairs and ranking members no longer had the authority to hire one staffer each.

LEGISLATIVE BRANCH APPROPRIATIONS ACT, FISCAL 1999

A provision of this act gave the Senate Appropriations Committee the authority to determine its own staffing needs and budget. The committee had been exempt from the annual funding process from 1946 to 1981, when the Senate's overall biennial funding process was applied to it like other panels. The House Appropriations Committee has continuously had such funding independence since 1946.

SENATE COMMITTEE AUTHORIZATIONS, FISCAL 2012

When discussing committee authorizations for fiscal 2012, Majority Leader Harry Reid, D-Nev., and Minority Leader Mitch McConnell, R-Ky., urged a departure from the biannual negotiations on the majority-minority divisions of committee funding that had become common practice over the previous decade. Such negotiations focused closely on party divisions in the chamber. But in a committee report accompanying the fiscal 2012 authorizations, the pair wrote that regardless of the party division, they encouraged a new practice ensuring that the minority share never be less than 40 percent and the majority share never exceed 60 percent.

1 U.S. Senate Committee on Rules and Administration, *Standing Rules of the Senate, Rule XVII.* rules.senate.gov/public/index.cfm?p=RuleXXVII.

Under the 1946 act, majority party members were responsible for hiring and firing committee staff, although in practice committees usually delegated that power to the chair, who often consulted with the senior minority party member. Normally, chairs obtained most staff funding from the House Administration and the Senate Rules and Administration committees. But the first professional committee staffs were nonpartisan, assigned to work with either party no matter which controlled the chamber. "The same staff member might write the committee report for a bill and a statement in opposition," said Senate historian Donald A. Ritchie.[25]

In two other important reforms, the 1946 act expanded the Legislative Reference Service (now the Congressional Research Service) and created senior specialist positions in subject areas roughly equivalent to those of the standing committees. The specialists received salaries comparable to those of their counterparts in the executive branch. In addition, the act expanded the bill-drafting service available through the Office of the Legislative Counsel.

Although members thought the 1946 act improved staffing procedures, concern about staff quality remained. By 1948 ninety-three senators had appointed administrative assistants, but some senators complained that unqualified personal secretaries had been promoted. Some members also felt that committees were not always using the staffing authority or hiring well-trained experts.[26] And by the 1970s, minority members were complaining that committee staff more reflected the ideology and interests of the chairs.[27]

Reform Era: Reorganization Act of 1970

By 1965 a new joint committee was looking into the concerns about the quality and availability of staff that had arisen since the landmark 1946 reorganization law. The committee focused on increasing the number of personal and committee staff, expanding staff with scientific and technical expertise,

HOUSE AND SENATE SUPPORT OFFICES

In its day-to-day operations Congress is supported by the offices and staffs of the clerk of the House, the secretary of the Senate, the House chief administrative officer (CAO), the House and Senate sergeants at arms, and parliamentarians, among others.

The functions of the clerk of the House and the secretary of the Senate are administrative as well as quasi-judicial. The full chamber elects each official, who usually is the nominee of the majority party. These officials are elected every two years at the beginning of each new Congress, but normally remain in their posts until that party loses control of the chamber (although each house retains the power to remove its officials).

The clerk and secretary perform a wide range of tasks. They process all legislation; prepare the "Daily Digest" and periodic reports for the *Congressional Record;* provide for the recording and printing of bills and reports; compile lobby registration information; prepare and deliver messages to the Senate and receive messages from the Senate and president; and supervise, respectively, the House and Senate libraries and the document rooms.

In the House, other administrative functions that used to rest with the clerk are now the responsibility of the House CAO, a position dating from 1992. The CAO oversees cyber-security functions; furnishes stationery supplies, electrical and mechanical equipment, and office furniture; manages the payroll and employee benefits; and supervises repair services.

Initially the position was promoted as nonpartisan and titled the director of nonlegislative and financial services, but House Republicans charged it was a Democratic cover-up for various House scandals that had erupted around that time. When the GOP took control of the House in 1995, it instead created the position of CAO as part of a package of rules changes. The CAO is nominated by the Speaker, reports directly to the Speaker, and oversees the six hundred technical and administrative staff. The Senate secretary, responsible for these same functions, oversees twenty-six departments.

The House and Senate sergeants at arms do not wear uniforms, but they are the police officers of their respective chambers. They attend all House and Senate floor sessions and are responsible for enforcing rules and maintaining decorum, ensuring the security of buildings and visitors, and supervising the Capitol police. In addition, the House sergeant at arms is in charge of the Mace, a traditional symbol of legislative power and authority.

The House and Senate sergeants at arms also introduce the bearers of all messages, official guests, and members attending joint sessions; supervise doormen and supervise the pages (although the House page program was disbanded in 2011); issue gallery passes; and perform a variety of custodial services. On the House side the doorkeeper performed these duties until 1995, when the position was abolished.

The House and Senate chaplains are officers of their respective chambers. The chaplains open each day's session with a prayer and provide other religious services to members, their families, and congressional staff.

The parliamentarians of the House and Senate sit in on all sessions to advise the presiding officers on parliamentary procedures. They help refer legislation to committees, and they maintain compilations of the precedents of each chamber.

The Office of the Senate Legal Counsel advises and represents senators, committees, officers, and staffers on legal matters related to official Senate work and civil proceedings.

The House Office of the Law Revision Counsel develops and updates an official classification of U.S. laws. The office periodically prepares and publishes a new edition of the United States Code, including annual cumulative supplements of newly enacted laws.

Other officials include the inspector general, the historian, and—in the House—the legislative counsel.

---

increasing pay to attract more qualified candidates, and providing more staff for the minority.

Five years later Congress passed the Legislative Reorganization Act of 1970. That law

- Increased from four to six the number of permanent professional staff employees authorized for each standing committee. Two of the six professional staffers, in addition to one of six permanent clerical staffers provided under previous law, were to be reserved for the exclusive use of the committee's minority party members. That provision did not apply to the House and Senate Appropriations committees or to the House Committee on Standards of Official Conduct. Equally important, the 1970 changes established a procedure by which a committee could seek annual funding for additional staff, which later led to substantial growth in staff that came to be called investigative or temporary. In the

decades that followed, the bulk of committee staff fell under these, not statutory, categories.

- Authorized standing committees, with the approval of the Senate Rules and Administration Committee or House Administration Committee, to provide staff members with specialized training.

- Authorized salary levels for Senate committee staff personnel comparable to those of House committee staff personnel.

- Redesignated the Legislative Reference Service in the Library of Congress as the Congressional Research Service; redefined its duties to better assist congressional committees by providing research and analytical services, records, documents, and other information and data, including memorandums on proposed legislation; and expanded its staff resources.

- Allowed the minority party one-third of a House committee's investigative funds. (The House voted in

1971 to disregard this provision. It was revived in 1974, killed in 1975, and taken up again in 1989.) By 1999 most House committee and subcommittee staffs were considered investigative, although funds for them were provided through biennial resolutions. (See "Committee Staffs," p. 196; "Partisanship and Minority Staffing," p. 200.)

Changes in 1974–1979

The expansion of committee and personal staffs continued into the 1970s, pushing Congress toward what would become, in the late 1980s and early 1990s, the high-water mark in support staff numbers.

House Committee Staffing

Another change in House committee staffing levels occurred in 1974 when the number of permanent professional staff employees was increased to eighteen and the number of clerical aides to twelve. This brought the total number of permanent committee aides to thirty, where it remained in the 112th Congress (although the Appropriations Committee is allowed to hire as many staff members as it deems necessary).[28] At the request of the minority party, up to ten of these thirty professionals within each committee can be assigned to the minority. Committee staff increasingly took on responsibility for drafting legislation, conducting negotiations, and preparing questions for witnesses testifying at hearings.[29]

In addition to permanent statutory staff, House—as well as Senate—committees continued to rely heavily on temporary or investigative aides. At first these employees were funded annually, but currently they are provided under biennial resolutions covering a full Congress, increasing their resemblance to regular statutory employees. Even though temporary employees, they often remain with a committee year after year.

House Subcommittee Expansion

A principal goal of reformers in the 1970s was to break the iron grip of seniority and the power held by a handful of the most senior members—usually full committee chairs. Reformers sought to diffuse this power by creating new enclaves, subcommittees, where that power could be exercised and to give protection in the rules to those entities.

In 1973 the House Democratic Caucus adopted a "subcommittee bill of rights" empowering each committee's majority caucus to determine subcommittee chairs, jurisdictions, and budgets. In 1974 the House required all committees with more than fifteen members to establish at least four subcommittees, a threshold changed to twenty members by the caucus in 1975. The changes during these years also gave subcommittee leaders the right to staff support paid from committee funds. These significant moves institutionalized House subcommittees to an unprecedented

TABLE 4.1   **Congressional Committee Staffs**

From 1935 to 2009 the committee staffs in Congress expanded, then shrank, and then began to show some growth again. The table below lists the number of statutory and investigative staff members of standing committees (special and select committees are not included). Staff growth in both chambers began after the Legislative Reorganization Act of 1946 but accelerated in the 1970s. The highest number of staff positions in the House was recorded in 1991 (2,201), and in the Senate in 1975 (1,277). The House numbers began to decline in the early 1990s and dropped dramatically in 1995 when the Republicans took control after winning a majority in the 1994 elections. In the Senate the numbers began to decline in the late 1970s, stabilizing at around 1,000–1,100 through the 1980s, with a further drop in the 1990s. A slight increase in numbers was seen in the 2000s before concerns about a national economic crisis caused Congress to begin to scrutinize its own budget.

The personal staff of members also increased during these years but, unlike committee staffs, stabilized in the 1990s, before dropping in the next decade. (See Table 4.2, p. 195.)

Year	House	Senate
1935	122	172
1947	167	232
1960	440	470
1965	571	509
1970	702	635
1975	1,460	1,277
1979	1,909	1,269
1980	1,917	1,191
1985	2,009	1,080
1990	1,993	1,090
1995	1,246	732
1999	1,238	805
2000	1,176	762
2001	1,177	805
2002	1,222	869
2003	1,193	857
2004	1,249	838
2005	1,272	887
2006	1,225	929
2007	1,014	874
2008	1,297	919
2009	1,324	913

SOURCE: Norman J. Ornstein, Thomas E. Mann, and Michael J. Malbin, *Vital Statistics on Congress, 2012* (Washington, D.C.: Brookings Institution Press, forthcoming), Table 5-5.

degree. Then, as the power of subcommittees grew, so did their staffs. By the late 1970s the number of staffers working for subcommittees equaled the number assigned to full committees in the 1960s.

A further change in House practices adopted in 1975 affected the growth of subcommittee staff. The new rule allowed subcommittee chairs and the ranking minority member on each panel to hire one staff person each to work directly for them on their subcommittee business.

The 1970 changes were dramatic, increasing staff by about 650 percent. Congressional scholars Christopher J. Deering and Steven S. Smith noted that in 1970 twelve House committees had no separate subcommittee staff. Of the seven that did, only Appropriations and Government Operations functioned under clearly decentralized systems in which a subcommittee staff worked almost, if not entirely, exclusively for the subcommittee chair. By the end of the decade, in 1979, only three House committees with subcommittees had not created separate staffs.[30]

The movement to separate and distribute staffs to subcommittees continued in the new decade where it peaked between 1985 and 1988. After that, the percentage of committee staff assigned to subcommittees in the House started to drift downward, reaching a point in 1995, after the Republican takeover, not seen since the late 1970s.

Senate Committee Staffing

Whereas House subcommittee staff grew nearly 650 percent in the 1970s, Senate subcommittee staff grew less than 50 percent. In 1979 just two committees, Judiciary and Governmental Affairs, employed nearly three-fourths of the Senate's subcommittee staff.

Senate subcommittee staff did not grow as quickly because the Senate retained far more centralized staffing arrangements than the House. By the 110th Congress, a few specialized Senate committees, including Budget, Permanent Select Committee on Intelligence, Small Business and Entrepreneurship, and Veterans' Affairs, had no subcommittees.

Nevertheless, the Senate—like the House—moved to provide better staffing for members. A key event occurred in 1975 when the Senate authorized an increase in committee staff in response to the complaints of junior senators. They wanted, according to Sen. Bob Packwood, R-Ore., "the same access that the senior senators do to professional staff assistance."[31] Senators were allowed to hire up to three staffers, called associate staff, depending on the type and number of committees assigned each senator.

That change (S Res 60) was intended to prevent a senator who already had staff on a committee from getting more staff for that committee. Thus it benefited primarily junior senators who had been excluded from separate staff on their committees because of their low-seniority status. The plan cut into the traditional power base that senior members enjoyed through their control of committee staff and was opposed by many of them for that reason. Over time S Res 60 increased staff for all senators.

The 1975 change also required senators to certify that their new aides worked only on committee business. The funds to pay for the additional committee aides were merged with senators' general clerk-hire funds, allowing members to use the money as they wished but thereby undermining the original premise for personal committee staff. In addition, today most of these staffers work out of senators' personal offices and often are difficult to distinguish from the legislative assistants on senators' personal staffs.

Senate Subcommittees

Senate committees, unconstrained by rules requiring separate subcommittee staff, varied widely in their staffing. Committees such as Governmental Affairs, Judiciary, and Health, Education, and Labor resembled House committees in allowing subcommittee leaders to appoint staff. Others, such as Armed Services and Banking, Housing, and Urban Affairs, did not appoint separate staffs but assigned certain subcommittee responsibilities to full committee staff members, giving the staff assistant two masters—the full committee chair and the subcommittee chair. In some committees, such as Agriculture, Nutrition, and Forestry, there was little meaningful differentiation among committee staff and usually little separate subcommittee activity, particularly with respect to drafting legislation.[32]

Growth of Personal Staffs

Like committee staff, the number of personal assistants to senators and representatives continued to grow throughout the 1970s and 1980s until the numbers stabilized in the Senate and gradually declined in the House during the 1990s, with fluctuations in the next decade. In 2009 more than 6,900 personal staffers were working for members of the House and nearly 3,900 for senators.[33]

Each House member can hire up to eighteen full-time and four part-time aides in his or her Washington and district offices. The average House member's full-time staff numbers about fifteen. There is no Senate limit other than that imposed by the funds available to a senator. Senators' personal staffs range in size from thirteen to seventy-one. The average is about thirty to thirty-five full-time employees.[34]

Before 1979 a representative could hire a maximum of eighteen personal aides, with no exceptions. In July of that year the House approved a rules change permitting members to add up to four more staffers to their payrolls—without counting them toward the ceiling of eighteen—if their jobs fit into one of five categories.

1. A part-time employee, defined as one who does not work more than fifteen full working days a month or who is paid $1,270 a month or less.

2. A shared employee—an employee, such as a computer expert, who is on the payroll of two or more members simultaneously.

3. An intern in the member's Washington office, defined as an employee hired for up to 120 days and paid $1,160 a month or less.

4. A temporary employee, defined as a staff member hired for three months or less and assigned a specific task or function.

5. A person who temporarily replaces an employee on leave without pay.

TABLE 4.2   **Personal Staffs in Congress**

Similar to the growth of committee staffs, personal staffs began to increase in the late 1960s, reaching their height in the 1980s. But unlike committee staffs, which declined under budget and political pressures, personal staffs stabilized in the late 1980s and 1990s before dropping in the 2000s. In 2007, the House personal staff numbers had dropped below the 1977 level and the Senate numbers had nearly matched the 1980 level. *(See Table 4.1, p. 193.)*

Year	House	Senate
1935	870	424
1947	1,440	590
1957	2,441	1,115
1967	4,055	1,749
1972	5,280	2,426
1977	6,942	3,554
1980	7,371	3,746
1982	7,511	4,041
1984	7,385	3,949
1986	7,920[a]	3,774[a]
1988	7,564	3,977
1990	7,496	4,162
1992	7,597	4,249
1994	7,390	4,200
1996	7,288	4,151
1999	7,216	4,272
2000	7,226	4,087
2001	7,209	3,994
2002	7,263	4,024
2003	7,048	3,998
2004	6,742	3,687
2005	6,804	3,934
2006	7,117	3,944
2007	6,735	3,753
2008	6,903	3,908
2009	6,907	3,884

NOTE: a. Senate figures reflect the period immediately after congressionally mandated staffing cuts in legislation known as the Gramm-Rudman Bill. House figures are for the entire fiscal year, thus averaging post–Gramm-Rudman staffing levels with previous, higher ones.

SOURCE: Norman J. Ornstein, Thomas E. Mann, and Michael J. Malbin, *Vital Statistics on Congress, 2012* (Washington, D.C.: Brookings Institution Press, forthcoming), Table 5-1.

A senator's personal staff was enhanced primarily through the adoption in 1975 of S Res 60, which allowed hiring a personal staffer to do work connected with the senator's committee assignments.

Staff Contraction in the 1980s and 1990s

Even with these changes, the staff began to contract during the 1980s and on through the next decade. One factor in the slowdown of staff expansion was the effort begun by Republican president Ronald Reagan in 1981 to shrink the size of the federal government. The total executive staff, including the White House and related support groups such as the National Security Council, had peaked at 5,639 in 1972; by 1988, Reagan's last full year in office, the staff had dropped to

1,645. The executive staff grew slightly during the succeeding term of President George H. W. Bush, reaching 1,855 in 1992. Democratic president Bill Clinton moved into the White House with the promise of cutting staff. By 1997, the first year of his second term, White House staff had declined to 1,565.[35]

Lawmakers in Congress—especially Republicans, who had taken over the Senate—echoed Reagan, calling for a reduction of the congressional bureaucracy. Thus both the House and Senate cut committee budgets 10 percent in 1981. The Republican-controlled Senate led the way, cutting its committee staffs by 14 percent. More than half the cuts, however, came from a single committee, Judiciary.[36] The Democratic House felt pressure to follow suit.

In 1981 political considerations forced the House Democratic leadership to combine investigative funds for all committees in a single package. Until then, the House had taken up each committee's budget one at a time on the House floor. Given the Republican move to trim congressional budgets, Democrats feared that funds for some committees might suffer further cuts if each committee's request was considered individually.

House Democrats cut committee staffs by around 10 percent at the start of the 103rd Congress in 1993, primarily by abolishing four temporary select committees. But major reductions came only after Republicans took control of Congress in 1995. As part of their Contract with America, the GOP's political platform in the 1994 elections, House Republicans cut committee staff by more than a third. (In part this also was the result of the House GOP's effort to rein in the committee system.[37]) Senate Republicans, who controlled that chamber, also reduced committee staff, although not as much.

Personal staffs for individual members of Congress are evenly distributed regardless of party. Cuts in committee aides allowed GOP leaders in 1995 to claim credit for a significant overall staff reduction while minimizing damage to individual lawmakers, the majority of whom were now Republican. (However, Republicans did make some changes to member staffing allowances, including cutting back on an extra staff allowance allotted to junior members of the Appropriations Committee.[38]) Most of the committee staff cuts forced by the GOP that year affected the now-minority Democrats, largely through dismissal of former Democratic majority staff. Republicans then limited the number of staffers hired to replace those previously serving Democrats.[39] They also gave committee chairs control over hiring subcommittee staff.[40]

Some critics complained that staff reductions were too severe. The Republicans "went too far in downsizing committee staffs, hurting their ability to advance their own agenda," wrote a former GOP staff aide in 1996.[41] And in the opinion of Sen. Robert C. Byrd, D-W.Va., staff reductions had affected "the ability of members to adequately address issues of national importance which arise in Congress every day."[42]

But overall staff levels showed their sharpest decrease only right after the GOP takeover, as they rose briefly again in

1997, followed by fluctuations over the next decade and some increases since 2007. The Congressional Research Service (CRS), which tracked a more consistent increase in the 2000s, most notably in personal staffing, attributed the change to a greater need among members for professionalism in the legislative process as well as of the use of more sophisticated communication and business technologies. CRS analysts also suggested that the increasing personal staff sizes might indicate a shift of focus on traditional committee activities, such as legislative and investigative work, to "more individualized activities" in members' offices, including constituent service and political activity.[43] Nevertheless, with a continued focus on government spending amid a troubled economy, and repeated cutbacks to appropriations bills, staff numbers—or at least expenditures on staff—were only expected to decrease in subsequent years.

COMMITTEE AND PERSONAL STAFF: WHAT THEY DO

As legislative activities and work have expanded, paralleling growth in the executive branch, Congress has changed as an institution. The legislative staff has changed as well, becoming larger and less collegial, more expert-oriented, and often more activist. These changes reflect the demands made on staff as Congress has faced more complex issues and, increasingly in the past few decades, more sharply partisan divisions on both domestic and international problems. David Price, a political scientist and Democratic House member from North Carolina, said while working as a staff member in the Senate in the 1960s that he saw an increased focus on "the importance of entrepreneurship in congressional staffs—a continual search for policy gaps and opportunities, a job orientation that stressed the generation and promotion of policy initiatives designed to heighten the public visibility of the senator and his or her leadership role in the chamber."[44]

One matter remained as true at the start of the twenty-first century as in 1946 when Congress adopted its major post–World War II reorganization: Members of the Senate and House need the support and advice of staff, both on committees and in their own offices, to carry out their jobs. The late Sen. Edward Kennedy, D-Mass., who served forty-seven years in the Senate, said toward the end of his tenure that "95 percent of the nitty-gritty work" of drafting and negotiating legislation was performed by staff.[45]

Staff is roughly divided into two types: those who work for a committee, usually serving either the majority or minority party on the panel, and those who work in a member's office serving that person's requirements. Staffers in a member's office may be assigned to work on the issues that are before the committee on which the member serves. But even without this close link, all members have someone on staff to handle legislative issues.

Committee Staffs

While congressional committees vary in their organization, most at one time had dual staffs—one professional and one clerical. By the end of the 1990s, however, this distinction had all but disappeared in Congress.

Yet the work to be done has not fundamentally changed. Certain staff members are responsible for the day-to-day running of the committee and assisting the members and other staff colleagues who concentrate on substantive issues. Some of the routine tasks include keeping the committee calendar up to date, processing committee publications, referring pending bills to appropriate executive branch offices for comment, preparing the bill dockets, maintaining files, announcing hearings and contacting witnesses, opening and sorting mail, and—increasingly—preparing or updating electronic data, including committee websites. Other staff members handle committee policy and legislative matters, including legal and other types of research, public relations, statistical and other technical work, and drafting and redrafting legislative language and amendments.

All of these staffers are a committee's statutory, or permanent, staff. Their positions are established by rules of the House or Senate or by law and are funded annually in the legislative branch appropriations bill. Committees also hire additional personnel for special work. These so-called investigative employees are considered temporary, but they often remain with the committees for extended periods.

Although permanent staff funding and investigative staff funding were once handled separately, by 2000 both chambers had eliminated the distinction to gain better financial control over staff costs. Senate committees now submit all funding requests in one budget document to the Rules and Administration Committee for review.

Permanent House committees are entitled to thirty staffers paid out of statutory funds. Most of the committees put their highest-paid staff in this category and not under the investigative budget, which is reviewed by the House Administration Committee. Over the years, investigative employees have accounted for much of the increase in committee staff costs, as the budgets for these aides are flexible. In addition to staff salaries, House investigative budgets include money for office equipment, consultants, publications, and travel within the United States.

House investigative budgets do not include funds for hiring statutory staff or for printing expenses, stenographic costs, foreign travel, stationery, and some communications expenses. The investigative total also does not include funding for the House Appropriations or Budget committees, both of which are included directly in the annual legislative appropriations bill and are not limited to thirty statutory staffers. The House Appropriations Committee in 2009 had 303 staff members. Its counterpart in the Senate had 100.[46]

Democratic Staff Director for the House Budget Committee Tom Kahn meets with representatives during a break in the House Budget markup of the fiscal 2005 concurrent budget resolution.

SOURCE: Scott J. Ferrell, Congressional Quarterly.

Committees seeking additional investigative help may use the services of legislative or executive branch agencies under rules employed by the housekeeping committees in both chambers. The congressional Government Accountability Office (formerly the General Accounting Office), the Treasury Department, and the FBI, among others, frequently are called on for assistance.

Functions

Colton C. Campbell and Paul S. Herrnson note in their book *War Stories from Capitol Hill*: "In the high-pressure, overworked environment of the contemporary Congress, committee staffers turn the wheels of the committee system."[47] While committee responsibilities vary, most staff perform these basic functions:

Planning Agendas. Staffers help chairs set committee agendas, select issues to consider, schedule hearings and bill markups, and plan floor action.

Organizing Hearings. Staffers set up hearings on legislation and issues under the committee's jurisdiction. Aides select witnesses, prepare questions, inform the press, brief committee members, and occasionally substitute for members who

cannot attend hearings, often asking questions prepared by the absent legislator. Even when the chair is present, senior aides with special knowledge sometimes question witnesses on technical subjects.

Oversight and Investigations. Staff members conduct original research on issues, which often takes the form of critiques of existing legislation, court decisions, and current practices. Aides on the Armed Services and foreign policy committees, for example, often travel to areas or countries to research matters the committee is considering. Sometimes staffers organize regional hearings for members held outside Washington, D.C.

Bill Markup and Amendment Drafting. Staff aides assist in marking up (amending) bills by explaining technical provisions, outlining policy questions, analyzing proposed changes following committee decisions, and incorporating decisions in successive revisions of the bill. They also often serve as liaisons among the Office of the Legislative Counsel in each chamber, committee members, government agencies, and special interest groups during the drafting of legislation.

Preparing Reports. Committee reports that accompany bills sent to the full chamber are almost entirely written by staff and generally include a background of the bill, a section-by-section analysis, and a comparison of the bill with existing law. Often the reports are the only information available to noncommittee members when the House or Senate considers a bill. Staff aides consult with the chair or the majority party members about information and emphasis in the report. Minority party members and opponents of a bill often file views, usually drafted by the committee's minority staff members. *(See Chapter 2, The Legislative Process.)*

Preparing for Floor Action. Top aides most familiar with the legislation often accompany the committee chair or another sponsor of the bill when the legislation is debated by the full Senate or House. They advise the bill's supporters and sometimes help prepare amendments. They also may draft a script for the bill's managers to follow during the floor debate, including opening and closing remarks.

Conference Committee Work. The staffs of corresponding committees in each chamber work together on the preparation of conference reports and in resolving differences in legislation initially considered by those committees and subsequently passed by the House and Senate.

Liaison with Executive Branch, Special Interests. Staff aides communicate frequently with executive branch officials, special interest groups, and lobbyists on legislative proposals before the committee. Some members regard this activity as the most consequential of all staff work.

Press Relations. Committee staffers also perform press-related tasks. They alert reporters to upcoming hearings, markup sessions, and floor action on committee-reported measures. Aides answer questions from the press and public, provide background information on legislation before the committee and on recent committee decisions on legislation, and write press releases. In addition, they make committee members accessible to the media and generally work to obtain favorable publicity for the committee.

Recruitment and Tenure

The chair or the top-ranking minority party member of a committee selects most committee employees, as a perquisite of office, subject only to nominal approval by the full committee.

From surveys and interviews with committee staff, certain generalizations about committee professionals emerge. They are relatively young, although not as young as personal office staffers, and most are male. The majority of aides have advanced degrees, particularly law, and many have previous experience in the executive branch. Although congressional scholars have, since the 1970s, observed a trend toward career development in committee staff positions, staff experience does decline sharply in periods of shifting party control, such as in 1995 when Republicans took control of the House for the first time in nearly four decades. The same phenomenon occurs when committee leadership posts change frequently, which may occur when a senior member retires or is defeated.

Also when majority control shifts from one party to the other, the turnover in committee jobs creates a much larger displacement. When the Democrats won the majority in 2006 and retained the majority's two-to-one staffing advantage, about 600 to 800 Republican aides, mostly attorneys, staff investigators, and legislative specialists, were expected to lose their jobs. An even larger layoff occurred when Republicans took back the House in 2011; an estimated 1,800 Democratic congressional staffers—about 500 of them committee aides—lost their jobs with the change in leadership.[48]

Congressional aides accept positions knowing there is no job security. Employees' tenure is subject to the whims of the hiring chair or member, and aides can be fired with or without cause. As one Capitol Hill observer pointed out, "Staff members all have friends whose chair retired, switched committees, or was beaten, leaving them with a new chair wanting to 'clean house.' They all know competent people who were fired without warning because the boss sensed a slight, or just felt it was time for a change."[49]

Power of Committee Staff

Congress's reliance on staff assistance prompts some observers to call these individuals unelected representatives. As senators and representatives spend more time on policy issues, constituency service, and campaign fund-raising, they delegate additional responsibilities to staff professionals, many of whom have advanced degrees and considerable experience and come to Capitol Hill hoping to make substantive policy decisions. The extent of that influence is often debated.

Staff members usually do the initial work that gives lawmakers the information needed to make informed judgments on policy matters. For example, *National Journal* reported that a "team totaling 20 [Senate Governmental Affairs] aides, including detailees from the [Federal Bureau of Investigation] and [Central Intelligence Agency]" drafted the 2004 bill that reorganized the nation's intelligence community.[50] California Democratic Rep. Henry Waxman, who formerly served as a subcommittee chair and later as chair of the House Energy and Commerce Committee, wrote in 2009 that one benefit of being a chair is having additional staff who can help monitor issues throughout government. Waxman, who counts the Ryan White CARE Act among his successes in the House, said that "staffers are invaluable in this regard, because by circulating through the agencies they can vastly expand a congressman's range of knowledge. This is how I first learned about AIDS."[51]

Sometimes they travel to foreign countries to conduct investigations. A study released in 2006 by the Center for Public Integrity, Medill News Service of Northwestern University, and American Public Media found that congressional

Signs in the Rayburn House Office Building in November 2006 advertise a resume drop-off for congressional staff and briefing for departing members. With Democrats regaining a majority in the House and Senate for the 110th Congress, staff turnover was high. In the 111th Congress, where Republicans made great gains in the House and Senate, turnover was elevated yet again.

SOURCE: Scott J. Ferrell, Congressional Quarterly.

staff members were more likely to travel than the members of Congress for whom they worked. The study reported that congressional aides took $30 million in trips paid for by private groups from 2000 through mid-2005, surpassing the privately sponsored travel of their bosses by nearly $10 million over the same time. Together, aides and members of the House and Senate filed twenty-three thousand public disclosure forms on their individual trips, the survey found, for an estimated price tag of about $50 million.[52]

The Center for Public Integrity reported in 2007 a drop in congressional travel, finding staffers took an estimated twenty-seven hundred trips in a one-year period ending June 30, 2006, compared to forty-seven hundred trips in the previous year. The drop was noted to have occurred just as Congress prepared to vote on new travel and gift rules. But the Center continued to find that staffers took most of the trips, accounting for 70 percent of the total. In 2010, Tim Johnson, R-Ill., called on CRS to review international congressional travel since 1994, then followed up with legislation calling for a more detailed GAO report.

During hearings, aides recruit witnesses on their own or at the direction of the chair and plan when and in what order they should appear. In addition, committee staff aides accompany committee members to the floor to give advice, draft amendments, and negotiate compromises.[53]

In his 1988 book, *The Power Game,* journalist Hedrick Smith quoted members who said they were highly dependent on their aides. House majority whip Tony Coelho, D-Calif., said: "When I leave a meeting, I don't have time to do the follow up. . . . The staff controls that meeting, that issue. I don't have time to make phone calls, to listen to the lobbyists. What is power? Information. Follow-through. Drafting an op-ed article."[54]

Daniel Lipinski, D-Ill., a former political scientist, describes in *Congress Reconsidered* how leadership often relies on its own staff to meet with committee staff in order to apply pressure for certain legislative outcomes. Such staff relationships can work in the other direction for members and committees, as well. "Staff can play a significant role in policy making and it is important not to underestimate which relationships can help a member make an impact," he states.[55]

Some senators bemoan the trend toward communication through aides. William S. Cohen, then a Republican senator from Maine and later President Clinton's secretary of defense, said to Smith: "More and more you are dependent on your staff. There is so much competition among staffs, fighting over issues, that sometimes you'll call a senator and ask, 'Why are you opposing me on this?' and he'll say, 'I didn't know I was.' And you'll say, 'Well, check with your staff and see.'"[56] It so happened that Cohen was succeeded in the Senate by Susan Collins, one of his staff aides.

A former long-term staffer for the House Appropriations Committee, Scott Lilly, is quoted in a 2008 book by Thomas Mann and Norman Ornstein, *The Broken Branch*, about how an erroneous provision that provided staff access to individual tax returns slipped into a three-thousand-page appropriations bill during an all-night staff negotiation in December 2004:

> Why do we conduct the people's businesses this way? Some say it's that Members of Congress have become too lazy to do their own work.... But my experience indicates that the vast majority of Members of both parties would love to revert to the old system in which the people elected to make these decisions actually do. I also know that nearly all of the staff who have been called on to participate in these exercises are deeply troubled by the process that has evolved.[57]

Partisanship and Minority Staffing

Partisanship of committee employees has long been controversial. The 1946 Legislative Reorganization Act did not apportion the professional committee staff between the chair and the ranking minority member. The act simply stated that "staff members shall be assigned to the chair and ranking minority member of such committee as the committee may deem advisable." Committees interpreted that provision in different ways, but generally the chair's preferences dictated the number—if any—of aides made available to minority party members. The result was that for the most part the minority had little or no staff support to assist in developing proposals to counter the program of the majority. Because Democrats were the majority most of the years after 1946, this meant that Republicans were at a disadvantage in advancing their own ideas.

In the 1960s Republicans began to press for formally recognized and permanently authorized minority staffing. Newspaper columnist Roscoe Drummond succinctly gave the GOP argument in 1961.

> If the Republican members of Congress are ever to be in a position to clarify, expound, and defend their stand on the major issues . . . and to advance constructive alternatives of their own, they must get a steady flow of adequate, reliable, competent research and information from an adequate,

reliable, and competent professional staff. This staff must be in the service of the minority, selected by the minority, and working for it.[58]

Historically, another problem facing minority staff was inequitable treatment. Sometimes minority staffers were paid less than their counterparts working for the majority. In addition, minority senators and representatives often waited longer than majority members to appoint staff. In the 1970s several changes were made in minority staffing. The 1970 Legislative Reorganization Act provided that at least three full-time minority staff aides were to be assigned to most committees of the House and Senate. Since then, however, the two chambers have traveled somewhat different paths in their approaches to minority staffing.

House. In January 1971 the House voted to delete the provisions of the 1970 Legislative Reorganization Act allocating one-third of committee investigative funds—those used to hire part-time professionals and otherwise to assist members—to the minority side. The Democratic Caucus had voted to bind all House Democrats to vote for the deletion, a move that infuriated Republicans and emphasized the importance members attach to congressional staffing. Although the GOP did eventually win additional staffing, the highly partisan Democratic actions fed Republican discontent. That discontent led in the 1980s and early 1990s to Republican vilification of the majority for its arrogant and unrestrained use of its power, which contributed to the GOP takeover of the House in the 1994 elections.

The minority staffing issue resurfaced in late 1974, as representatives debated a proposal to reorganize House committees. That plan called for giving Republicans ten of thirty staff members assigned to committees by statute and one-third of the investigative staff allotted to subcommittees by the House Administration Committee. But when the Democratic Caucus met in January 1975, a resolution was introduced to nullify the one-third minority investigative staff guarantee. The caucus agreed to a compromise that allowed subcommittee chairs and top-ranking minority members to hire one staff person each to work on their subcommittees—up to a maximum of six subcommittees—but dropped the one-third minority investigative staff guarantee. House rules permitted standing committees a total of six subcommittees. Although the staff increase applied specifically to subcommittees, the revision was widely billed as an increase of twelve in the number of statutory committee employees. The number of committee employees permitted by statute remained at thirty.

The minority staffing compromise produced one of the most significant changes of the many revisions made in House rules during the 1970s. Incorporated into the rules on January 14, 1975, the compromise was seen as crucial to strengthening the subcommittees and giving House minority members a meaningful opportunity to influence legislation.

Dispersing power among committee members and reducing the authority of House committee chairs also meant dispersing control over committee staffs and budgets.

The idea of allocating one-third of investigative staff to the minority came up again in 1989. This time, House Democrats agreed to let the minority have at least 20 percent of committee investigative staff positions, with an eventual goal of one-third. By 2001, in the wake of party control shifts and changes in House committee staffing procedures, more than half of the committees in that chamber allotted at least 30 percent of their staff positions to the minority, which by then was the Democrats.

Senate. As part of the Senate's 1975 change in committee staffing (S Res 60), all minority members were authorized to hire up to three personal committee aides, except for those who already had staff appointment authority on a particular committee. In 1977 a Senate committee reform resolution (S Res 4) directed that committee staffs be allocated in proportion to the number of the majority and minority members on a standing committee. The measure further specified that a "majority of the minority members of any committee may, by resolution, request that at least one-third of the funds of the committee for statutory, investigative, and clerical personnel . . . be allocated to the minority members." The reform resolution set a four-year timetable for Senate committees to provide one-third staffing to the minority.

Since the mid-1990s, the Senate has been more likely than the House to adjust the division of funding to reflect the partisan makeup of the chamber in each Congress. In early 2011, while discussing budget allocations for fiscal 2012, Senate leaders Harry S. Reid, D-Nev., and Mitch McConnell, R-Ky., urged that for all future Congresses, the minority share shall never be less than 40 percent and the majority's not exceed 60 percent.[59]

Majority-Minority Staff Cooperation. The degree of cooperation between the majority and minority staffs varies among committees. It is difficult to be nonpartisan on Capitol Hill, and most staffers have party or philosophical preferences. Even more important, most staffers work for a single member or the majority or minority committee leadership and must act in accordance with their wishes. A few committees—Appropriations, Ethics, and Joint Taxation, among others—have traditions of professional nonpartisan staffing. But that tradition has faltered somewhat in recent years.

From the late 1940s to the late 1970s the Senate Foreign Relations Committee had a bipartisan staff that served all committee members. In 1979, however, a group of Republican senators led by Jesse Helms of North Carolina, S. I. Hayakawa of California, and Richard G. Lugar of Indiana requested and received separate minority staff. In 1981, when Republicans took control of the Senate, the partisan staffing arrangement continued.

Political scientist Michael Malbin, who studied the Joint Taxation Committee in the late 1970s, found there are benefits to nonpartisan staffing. These aides served as the principal staff on tax legislation for both the House Ways and Means and Senate Finance committees. On all major issues likely to be considered by the two committees on tax-related measures, the joint committee aides outlined the political interests of both major parties. This information was published before the committees met to allow all members of the House and Senate, the press, and the public to understand the issues and political implications of committee deliberations.[60]

Washington journalists Jeffrey H. Birnbaum and Alan S. Murray, who followed the passage of the 1986 Tax Reform Act in their book, *Showdown at Gucci Gulch,* painted a similar picture.

[The staffers of the joint committee] were not beholden to any single member. Their job was not political, and their bosses were many. . . . [They] served as a reservoir of in-house expertise for the entire Congress, especially the two tax-writing committees. Joint Tax aides shaped and analyzed every change in tax law proposed by their bosses and often came up with suggestions themselves. Their revenue estimates on the changes were gospel. In tax reform, an exercise driven by revenue estimates and income-distribution charts, Joint Tax pronouncements were crucial.[61]

In the 1990s, however, growing partisanship—particularly in the House—altered this respect for comity on certain committees as some members argued that the Joint Taxation Committee, as well as other panels that have had traditions of nonpartisan staffing, had moved toward partisanship. For example, during a 1997 House Appropriations Committee debate, Rep. Vic Fazio, D-Calif., attempted to eliminate the extra funding that would have allowed the Joint Taxation Committee to increase its staff by twelve. Fazio claimed the panel had swerved from its nonpartisan roots to become an advocacy arm for the Republican majority in charge of the House Ways and Means Committee.[62]

The tradition of nonpartisanship also broke down in the House Committee on Standards of Official Conduct (commonly known as the House ethics committee) during the panel's investigation of House Speaker Newt Gingrich, R-Ga., in the 104th Congress. The panel always had depended on members to put their politics aside for the sake of maintaining the honor of the House's self-policing system, but the poisonous political atmosphere that prevailed in the House during the 1990s, in part stemming from Gingrich's attacks on Democrats for many years, caused Democrats to respond in kind. Gingrich became the first Speaker in U.S. history to be reprimanded by the House after the ethics committee found that he had used tax-exempt money for political purposes and had submitted false information to the ethics subcommittee investigating him. Democrats had pushed for the

Senate Appropriations chair Ted Stevens, R-Alaska, consults with aides as House and Senate conferees gather to consider legislation that would make supplemental fiscal 2004 appropriations for the wars in Iraq and Afghanistan.

SOURCE: Scott J. Ferrell, Congressional Quarterly.

reprimand as Gingrich in 1988 had filed the ethics complaints that led to the resignation of Speaker Jim Wright, a Democrat from Texas.

Nonpartisanship broke down again in 2005, when House Republican leaders opened the 109th Congress by pushing through a package of rule changes that included how the ethics committee conducted business. The committee had angered the leadership in 2004 by admonishing Majority Leader Tom DeLay of Texas for three instances of inappropriate conduct. The rules changes specified that any complaint against a House member would be allowed to die after forty-five days if the committee did not proceed with an investigation. Democrats, who make up half of the ten-member panel, said the changes undermined the ethics process and were meant to protect DeLay. The rules changes were adopted along party lines on January 4 and led to a virtual shutdown of the committee. The five Democrats blocked approval of the panel's rules, making it impossible for the panel to function. Finally, on April 27, the House voted overwhelmingly to adopt a resolution that had the effect of reversing the January changes.[63]

The panel's credibility continued to be questioned, particularly as an investigation of Rep. Maxine Waters, D-Calif.,

that began in early 2010, lingered into 2011 after the GOP took control of the House. Waters had come under scrutiny from government watchdog groups who alleged her family had made more than $1 million doing business with various companies and political candidates that she had helped. She stood firm against the charges, particularly after Politico in 2011 reported that internal documents "showed the committee and its professional, nonpartisan staff were riven with infighting and conflicting agendas as the committee" in 2010 took on the case of Waters as well as that of Rep. Charles Rangel, D-N.Y., who had been forced to give up his chairmanship of Ways and Means following ethics violations charges. The committee was forced to turn to outside counsel to complete the Waters investigation.[64]

Personal Staff

Members of the House are entitled to withdraw funds from the chamber's members' representational allowance (MRA, formerly called the clerk-hire allowance) to run and staff their offices. The funds are divided equally among representatives. For senators, the money is divided according to their state's population.

TABLE 4.3   **Congressional Staffs in House District and Senate State Offices**

A sizable portion of the personal staff of a senator or representative is assigned to work in district or state offices instead of in Washington, D.C. For the House the percentage of staff in district offices grew steadily until 2005 (followed by slight decreases), reflecting in part the importance of direct contact with constituents. In the Senate the percentage has grown as well.

	House employees	Percentage of personal staff in district offices	Senate employees	Percentage of personal staff in state offices
1972	1,189	22.5	303	12.5
1978	2,317	33.4	816	25
1980	2,534	34.4	953	25.4
1985	2,871	38.1	1,180	28.8
1990	3,027	40.4	1,293	31.1
1995	3,459	48.1	1,278	30.1
1997	3,209	44.1	1,366	31
1999	3,192	44.2	1,414	33.2
2000	3,216	44.5	1,405	34.4
2001	3,004	41.7	1,228	30.7
2002	3,302	45.5	1,456	36.2
2003	3,241	45.9	1,440	36
2004	3,392	50.3	1,468	39.8
2005	3,450	50.7	1,534	39
2006	3,506	49.3	1,562	39.6
2007	3,314	49.2	1,495	39.8
2008	3,418	49.5	1,590	40.7
2009	3,377	48.9	1,589	40.9

SOURCE: Norman J. Ornstein, Thomas E. Mann, and Michael J. Malbin, *Vital Statistics on Congress, 2012* (Washington, D.C.: Brookings Institution Press, forthcoming), Tables 5-3 and 5-4.

The characteristics of personal staff vary greatly from those of committee staff. A former House legislative assistant (LA), Mark Bisnow, has painted a vivid picture of personal aides.

> House LA's tend to be young, commonly in their twenties; theirs can be an entry-level professional position requiring no previous Hill experience. . . . (Committee staffers, in contrast, tend to be more specialized, and therefore older and of greater experience.) Their workaday world is informal and often frenetic. . . . Fifty-to-sixty hour work weeks are not unusual. Under constant time pressure and a multitude of urgent assignments, LA's typically switch among projects and topics by the half hour; they learn to write quickly, think politically, and argue combatively. In crowded offices, their desks nudged up against each other in ways that would affront a fire marshal, they do their own typing, photocopying, and phone-calling. They then suspend any calm reflections until things settle down again at six or seven or eight o'clock at night.[65]

Political scientist Nicol Rae, who served as a congressional fellow in the office of Sen. Thad Cochran, R-Miss., noted that "Senate aides are older and more seasoned than their House counterparts," and he observed a stronger sense of professionalism in Senate offices.[66]

Personal staffs are set up differently in each congressional office, although clear patterns exist. Whether a representative or senator chooses to emphasize constituent service or legislation probably makes the biggest difference in how the office is organized. A member's personality is another factor.

Most congressional offices have an administrative assistant (AA), a legislative director, legislative assistants, caseworkers, and at least one press secretary. Many also have an office manager, appointments secretary, legislative correspondent, and systems or computer manager.

The administrative assistant, sometimes called the chief of staff, often serves as the member's alter ego and chief political adviser, keeping him or her abreast of district and Capitol Hill politics. Ted Kaufman worked for twenty years as chief of staff to Sen. Joe Biden, D-Del., before he was appointed to fill the remainder of his boss's term when Biden was elected vice president under President Barack Obama in 2008. Kaufman told *Time* magazine in 2010: "It's like volleyball. . . . There are setters and spikers. The chief of staff is a setter, putting the ball in the air so the Senator can spike it."[67] The AA also usually directs and supervises the staff or shares these supervisory responsibilities with others who manage the legislative staff in Washington, the clerical staff, and staff in the state or district offices.

Functions

In the modern Congress no senators or representatives try to manage their activities entirely unassisted. Members generally depend on staff to handle the routine work of a congressional office. Reliance on staff is underscored by this picture of a member's typical day.

> On a normal day, a senator or [representative] has two and sometimes three simultaneous committee hearings, floor votes, issues caucuses, meetings with other congressmen from his state or region, plus lobbyists, constituents, and press to handle. He will dart into one hearing, get a quick fill-in from his staffer, inject his ten minutes' worth and rush on to the next event, often told by an aide how to vote as he rushes onto the floor. Only the staff specialist has any continuity with substance. The member is constantly hop scotching.[68]

Constituent Service. A congressional office today more closely resembles the customer service department of a large company than the typical legislative office of an earlier period. Until World War I a single clerk handled a member's entire correspondence. In those days congressional mail usually involved awarding rural mail routes, arranging for Spanish-American War pensions, sending out free seeds, and, occasionally, explaining legislation.[69]

Today a major responsibility of personal staffs, especially in the House, is responding to the myriad constituent requests from a member's state or district. For example, staffers untangle bureaucratic snarls in collecting Social Security or veterans' benefits; answer questions about student loans and similar programs; help home state or district organizations obtain federal grants; respond to constituent questions and comments on legislative and national issues by mail and e-mail; and produce newsletters, other mailings, and electronic news updates to keep constituents informed of their boss's activities.

Such services are important not only for the benefits they provide to constituents but also for the benefits they bring to the relationship between a member of Congress and a voter. According to former congressional staffer Bisnow,

> [Constituent service] is often considered one of the more beneficial things congressmen do, but the motivation goes beyond mere charity; personal touches typically matter to voters as much as larger issues of ideology, voting record, or even public reputation. As a result, constituents occupy almost deified status in the eyes of Hill offices, a flotilla of paid aides poised to handle their problems. Too bad for a challenger who can do nothing more than walk the district at his own expense.[70]

Junior members of Congress tend to pay more attention to constituent services than more senior members, and House members spend more time on casework than senators. In both chambers, however, senior legislators are likely to receive proportionately more casework requests than junior members, in part because they are better known to the public and, being senior, presumably are more powerful and thereby

better equipped to resolve constituents' problems. Senators often receive casework requests from outside their home states, particularly if they are prominent national figures; representatives rarely do.

With the recent explosion of Internet resources, congressional staff are able to communicate more easily through websites, e-mail, Facebook, Twitter, and YouTube with an increasing number of politically active constituents.

A 2005 study by the Congressional Management Foundation (CMF) concluded that the initial introduction of electronic communication—via e-mail—dramatically expanded the workload of personal staff. Congress received four times more communications in 2004 than in 1995, and most of the increase was from Internet-based communications. In 2004 the House and Senate, combined, received more than 200,000,000 postal and e-mail messages. The House received 10,400,000 communications by post and 99,053,399 via the Internet; the Senate received 7,935,594 by post and 83,000,000 via the Internet, the study reported.

CMF also found that congressional offices were devoting more resources to managing the growing volume of constituent communications. And it found that a large percentage of the communications to Congress was in mass form messages—multiple copies of the same text sent under different constituents' names. In addition, some of the staff members surveyed believed these mass form messages were sent without the constituents' knowledge and approval.[71]

In 2010, CMF conducted another study on communication between Congress and citizens, reporting that senior staff managers indicated their offices had more fully integrated social media into their operations. The report concluded that "Congressional staffers have new and instant means for assessing public opinion on emerging policies and issues."[72] Almost two-thirds of staffers said they used Facebook to study constituent views, 42 percent said Twitter was useful, and 34 percent said they trusted YouTube. More offices used the same tools to distribute information and member views to citizens: 74 percent said Facebook was important for such activity, 51 percent said Twitter was an important communication tool, and 72 percent said YouTube was a useful tool. Furthermore, 59 percent of those surveyed said they felt social media was worth the time spent on it, and 55 percent said it offers more benefits than risks. More than one-third of the staffers surveyed said their offices spent too little time on online town hall meetings, posting videos, and updating their website, Twitter, or Facebook page.

Those results coincide with an earlier CMF survey that found that 57 percent believe the Internet has made members of Congress more accountable, and the majority of staff indicated they believe constituents have more influence on lawmakers than lobbyists do.[73]

The emphasis on constituent services is reflected in the increase in personal staff working in member offices in both chambers, particularly in district and state offices. In 2009 senators deployed 40.9 percent of their staff to their state offices—up from 12.5 percent in 1972. Representatives sent 48.9 percent of their aides to their districts in 2009, as opposed to 22.5 percent in 1972. The growth in home office staffing levels suggests a trend of members and senators spending more time at home focused not only on constituent service, but also on fund-raising and reelection, according to CRS.[74] *(See Table 4.3, p. 203.)*

This change in staff dynamics can be illustrated by the growth of New York Democratic senator Charles E. Schumer's staff levels between 2001 and 2007. Schumer had forty-nine staff members working for him in 2001, twenty-five of whom worked outside of Washington in offices in the state or in New York City. His non-Washington staff included six regional representatives throughout the state and four caseworkers. Schumer also had two counsels, a policy director, two other policy assistants, a legislative director, five legislative assistants, and two legislative correspondents. His personal allowance to pay for staff salaries and benefits was $2,114,796.[75] In 2007, he had sixty-two staff members, twenty-seven of whom worked in eight regional offices. He also had increased his legal counsels from two to four. His staff allowance at that time was $3,125,171.[76]

Legislation. Lawmaking is the primary task of members of Congress. In undertaking this task, members rely on their legislative assistants for substantive and political guidance as they weave their way through the daily thicket of complex, interdependent issues. More committee meetings are held than a member can prepare for or attend. Other members, federal officials, special interest groups, and sometimes even White House staff must be consulted before decisions are made, and often floor debates last well into the evening.

Specifically, legislative assistants work with members to draft bills and amendments and recommend policy initiatives and alternatives. LAs also monitor committee sessions that members cannot attend and may prepare lawmakers' speeches and position papers. In many offices, LAs are supervised by a legislative director, normally the senior legislative assistant.

In Senate offices, which have more staffers, a team of LAs often will specialize in different issues. Members of the House may rely simply on one or two LAs to handle legislation. In some cases the member delegates legislative correspondence and personally takes care of monitoring pending legislation.

Other Duties. Casework and legislation are only some of the chores handled by personal staffers. The press secretary serves as the member's chief spokesperson to the news media. Press aides compose news releases about legislative issues and newsworthy casework or federal grants, write newsletters, and organize press conferences. Because they deal almost exclusively with hometown media outlets, some House press aides are based in the district offices instead of in Washington. Where there is no press secretary, press relations are handled by the administrative assistant or a legislative assistant, or sometimes by a chief of staff—particularly for a larger media outlet. Senators, who receive more national publicity and represent larger areas than members of the House, often have several deputy press secretaries or assistant press staff.

The office manager, who often is the second-level manager in a congressional office, is in charge of handling clerical functions.

The appointments secretary, called the executive secretary or scheduler in some offices, normally handles personal appointments and travel arrangements for the member. An executive secretary who has been in a member's office for some time often exercises direct or indirect control over other staff members.

The legislative correspondent drafts responses to letters about pending legislation. In some offices, the LA may draft letters in a particular subject area; in others, the legislative correspondent drafts letters for the LAs regardless of the subject.

The systems manager coordinates the member's computerized correspondence operations and often the e-mail and Internet homepage setup and maintenance. Given the enormous amount of mail members of Congress receive each year, correspondence operations have become an important function.

Relations with Committee Staff

Besides the help they get from personal aides, senior senators and representatives are assisted on legislative matters by staffs of the committees and subcommittees on which they serve. In addition, all senators since 1975 have been authorized up to three aides to help with their committee business. The chair of a standing committee has two staffs. It is not unusual for an aide to do both committee work and personal casework for a member, no matter which payroll he or she is on.

Recruitment

Representatives and senators hire their own personal aides. Although House and Senate employment offices are available, most hiring is based on informal contacts, but word of mouth and just plain luck are important as well. Potential staffers may seek out members who are involved in particular issue areas, who are known to pay well, who are from a certain area of the country, or who have a particular ideological bent. Conversely, members may hire staffers for some of the same reasons.[77] In recent years members with private business backgrounds have used the congressional employment offices and even newspaper ads to solicit job applications.

In seeking knowledge and experience, members must decide whether to hire from the state or district or from Washington circles. This is an especially delicate problem for first-term members who may have limited Washington contacts and who feel indebted to their campaign staff and stress cultivating state and district contacts. A staffer who came to Washington with Sen. Pete V. Domenici, R-N.M., said he soon realized how important it is to strike a balance when hiring staff.

> We had a lot of people we felt we had to hire from the campaign. We brought a lot of them with us.... The big mistake we made was that we did not hire anyone who knew the Senate.... I had to check ten offices every time I wanted to find out how you did something. It was insane.[78]

Rep. David Price described setting up his staff after his first election in 1986: "I was well aware of the need to hire relatively senior people with Washington experience for the top positions. For most other staff positions I hired younger people hoping to gain in experience and exposure what I couldn't pay them in dollars." Price, a long-term member of the Committee on Appropriations, served four terms before losing reelection in 1994, but was back in 1997. He said he had the same number of staffers but that they were "more experienced, better compensated, and far more focused on appropriations issues."[79] Amy Black, a political science professor who worked as a congressional fellow in the office of former Rep. Melissa Hart, R-Pa., described the congresswoman taking a different tactic: she tried to hire "loyal and dedicated workers who would assimilate to her office's culture and stay."[80]

A staffing study conducted by the Congressional Management Foundation urged new House members to balance applicants' knowledge of constituencies and Washington politics in choosing their Hill staff. According to the study:

Most members find it essential that at least one senior staffer be from the district to advise on the local political ramifications of positions and actions. Hiring all, or virtually all, of your Washington staff from the district, however, may cause your office to go through a long learning curve. Many freshman offices advise hiring an experienced office manager and an experienced legislative staffer. An experienced manager will save months of muddling through in the crucial phase of establishing your office. Similarly, an experienced legislative staffer can guide your inexperienced legislative staff.[81]

Party loyalty of staff, while important, may be a secondary consideration to many representatives and senators when making hiring decisions. "It may be [that members] consider their aides already self-screened: If someone wants to work for them, their politics must be compatible."[82] But loyalty does count and on occasion turns up in startling ways. In 1999 Republican Michael P. Forbes, who represented the First District of New York, switched to the Democratic Party, saying that the GOP "has become an angry, narrow-minded, intolerant and uncaring majority, incapable of governing at all, much less from the center, and tone-deaf to the concerns of a vast majority of Americans."[83] His staff, as loyal Republicans, declined to go with him, resigning en masse two days after his announcement and forcing the Democrats to quickly put together a temporary replacement group of aides.

Increasingly, diversity of congressional aides has become a concern. A University of Texas at San Antonio professor analyzed staff employment in the House in 2010 and reported that Latinos made up only 7 percent of staff and noted that Republicans particularly lagged in hiring Latinos.[84] An ICF International study of House compensation in 2010 indicated that 24 percent of the 133 House offices questioned said they reached out to groups like Congressional Tri-Caucus (Hispanic, Black, or Asian Pacific Caucus) or black or Latino educational institutions—down from nearly 33 percent in 2009.[85] And the *National Journal* 2011 study of top Hill aides indicated that 93 percent of the respondents were white.

Qualifications and Tenure of Hill Staffers

Staffers working for the modern Congress are more qualified than ever before and come increasingly from professional instead of political backgrounds, giving members better information for making decisions. Yet some

CONGRESSIONAL INTERNS

For years, members of Congress have been assisted by temporary employees known generally as congressional interns. The origins of the practice are obscure, but it probably began when members hired students of American government or the sons and daughters of constituents to work in their offices during the summer. This diverse and informal method of employment expanded greatly during the 1960s.

Congressional interns vary widely in their experience and their office responsibilities. Younger ones may undertake clerical tasks, help to answer mail, or guide visitors around the Capitol. Those with more experience may be assigned to constituent casework, draft speeches and reports, or help committee staff.

Interns may be paid from a member's annual staff allowance or other funds available to the office, but many are not paid at all. Those under private internships are paid by their sponsors. The Congressional Fellowship program of the American Political Science Association, for example, brings each year a few dozen experienced journalists, teachers, and government officials to Congress. Employees of federal agencies may be assigned to Congress for a time if necessary. Many student interns receive academic credit for their work from their colleges and universities.

No central clearinghouse exists for internships. Every congressional office, committee, caucus, and supporting organization manages its own internship program. Interns can do better by targeting their own representative or senators for a position. Lawmakers often prefer interns from their own district or state. Some interns volunteer to work first in the state or district office of the lawmaker.

SOURCES: Harrison W. Fox Jr. and Susan Webb Hammond, *Congressional Staffs: The Invisible Force in American Lawmaking* (New York: Free Press, 1977), 137–138; and Roger H. Davidson and Walter J. Oleszek, *Congress and Its Members*, 13th ed. (Washington, D.C.: CQ Press, 2012), A4–A5.

FROM LOBBYIST TO STAFFER

Political observers for decades have analyzed the flow of members and staff into the lobbying community, calling the phenomenon the "revolving door." More recently, analysts also have focused on the reverse phenomenon—lobbyists moving into staffing positions on Capitol Hill as members have increasingly sought to employ staff with special expertise or knowledge of Washington gained outside the doors of Congress. The apparently seamless transition between the lobbying industry and legislative employment for many decades has raised questions about the influence of lobbyists in the congressional lawmaking and appropriations process that is difficult to document. Studies tend to focus on the level of staff turnover and the level of staff experience.

A 2011 survey by an online disclosure site called LegiStorm revealed that 5,400 current and former congressional staffers had gone through the revolving door in the past decade—meaning they had both been registered as lobbyists and been paid as staffers at some point during that time period. LegiStorm's research found that 605 former registered lobbyists had taken jobs working for lawmakers in the past decade. "For every person the American people have elected to sponsor legislation of public benefit, special interests have more than one former legislative advocate now working on the inside in Congress," Jock Friedly, founder and president of LegiStorm, told the *Washington Post*. "That represents a large network of people to influence decisions and to provide valuable intelligence."[1]

A 2010 study by the London School of Economics, based in part on 2000–2008 salary data provided by LegiStorm, found 1,113 lobbyists who had previously worked in members' offices on Capitol Hill. LegiStorm said that study's lower finding was likely due to a different methodology.

Just after Democrats regained control of the House and Senate in the 2006 elections, 207 lobbyists took jobs on the Hill, most of them Democrats, according to LegiStorm. And it reported that by the time of the release of its study in September 2011, 155 lobbyists had been hired as congressional staffers just that year. Meanwhile, about 388 congressional aides had left Capitol Hill for registered lobbying jobs for the first time in 2011, LegiStorm reported. "On average, every business day this year at least two Hill staffers have decided to cash in their experience and connections to become registered lobbyists," Friedly said.

The Center for Responsive Politics (CRP) released a report in July 2011 showing at the start of the 112th Congress—when Republicans regained control of the House and narrowed the majority in the Senate after a wave of election successes among young conservatives—a doubling of the number of lobbyists employed in powerful staff positions from the previous Congress. During the 111th Congress, 60 former lobbyists were employed in "critically important staff positions" in Congress—33 by Democrats and 27 by Republicans. During the 112th Congress, 128 former lobbyists held such positions, 79 of them working for Republicans, 48 for Democrats, and 1 for an independent. The study points to a disproportionate number of lobbyists hired by Republicans as chiefs of staff and legislative directors.

CRP also points to a large number of lobbyists hired by freshman Republicans in the House—a common tendency among any freshmen seeking to compensate for their lack of experience in Congress. Of the thirty-eight freshmen in 2011 who hired lobbyists, all but two were Republican. Sen. Marco Rubio, R-Fla., hired lobbyists as his chief of staff and legislative director. Chief of staff Cesar Conda represented dozens of clients while working for the lobbying firm Navigators Global LLC (formerly DC Navigators LLC) for eight years. Legislative director Sally Canfield had represented Sanofi-Aventis, a global pharmaceutical company, the year before Rubio hired her.

Several lobbyists for major companies or firms also are sometimes hired to work for the congressional committees they had previously lobbied. CRS reported that the number of lobbyists working directly for congressional committees increased from seven in the 111th Congress to twenty-four in the 112th Congress. But many committees have a dozen or more lobbyists working for members of that committee. The House Energy and Commerce and House Financial Services committees have the highest number of lobbyists employed by their members.

Rep. Fred Upton, R-Mich., chair of the House Energy and Commerce Committee, hired Howard Cohen, formerly president of the health care lobbying firm HC Associates, as chief health counsel for the committee. He had previously served as counsel for the committee from 1995 to 1998. Gary Andres, former vice chair at Dutko Worldwide, also was hired by the committee as staff director. He had represented one hundred clients before taking the committee job, according to CRS. Overall, the LegiStorm study found at least eleven former lobbyists working on the GOP staff of both the Energy and Commerce and Ways and Means committees, while reporting that Democratic members of those committees together employ five former lobbyists.

The practice of hiring lobbyists is not new, and even more senior and long-term members have done so. In December 2008, Senate Democratic leader Harry Reid of Nevada hired David B. Krone, who had worked as a telecom lobbyist and worked on several bills in Reid's jurisdiction, including a 2001 broadband access measure that Reid cosponsored. He has also been a major contributor to Reid's campaigns and in 2011 became the senator's chief of staff.

Jason Cole, who was hired as chief of staff to newly elected Rep. Jim Hines, D-Conn., in 2009, previously was a registered lobbyist for UBS Americas Inc., the U.S. subsidiary of Swiss financial services giant UBS AG. Cole had lobbied on five bills in 2008. Hines sat on the Committee on Financial Services.

Telecommunications lobbyists as well as defense lobbyists also have found jobs in Congress. Sen. Al Franken, D-Minn., hired Drew Littman as his chief of staff in 2009. Littman had previously represented both SBC Communications (which merged with AT&T in 2005) and Nextel Communications in the early 2000s. He also had lobbied on behalf of the United States Telecommunications Association, the Children's Defense Fund, and Electrum USA. In the 112th Congress Franken sat on the Judiciary; Health, Education, Labor and Pensions; and Energy and Natural Resources committees.

1 T. W. Farnam, "Revolving Door of Employment between Congress, Lobbying Firms, Study Shows," *The Washington Post*, September 13, 2011. www .washingtonpost.com/politics/study-shows-revolving-door-of-employment-between-congress-lobbying-firms/2011/09/12/gIQAxPYROK_story.html.

SOURCES: firststreet.cqpress.com; Sarah McKinnon Bryner, *From Hired Guns to Hired Hands: "Reverse Revolvers" in the 111th and 112th Congresses: A Center for Responsive Politics Report* (Washington, D.C.: Center for Responsive Politics, 2011); "Former Lobbyists Working for Congress Outnumber Elected Lawmakers," September 13, 2011, www.legistorm.com; *The Hill People 2011*, National Journal Special Edition, June 18, 2011; Darren Samuelsohn, "Fred Upton Hires Ex-Health-Care Lobbyist," Politico.com, December 24, 2010, www.politico .com/news/stories/1210/46785.html; Jordi Blanes i Vidal, Mirko Draca, and Christina Fons-Rosen, "Revolving Door Lobbyists" (London: London School of Economics, 2010).

Capitol Hill employees, especially those with long service, believe many staffers see their jobs as way stations on the road to other opportunities—that is, employment on the Hill helps prepare them through training, experience, and contacts for other careers, often in the private sector at much larger salaries.

Despite the presence of many highly qualified staffers on the Hill, congressional staff experience has declined. A 2010 study by ICF International for the House's Chief Administrative Office found that tenure of personal staff ranged from 1.8 years for a staff assistant in the D.C. office to 6.7 years for a chief of staff.[86] Former CMF executive director Rick Shapiro attributed the House decline to the fast turnover of lawmakers: "As member experience declines, the experience they bring with them is going to decline."[87]

An earlier CMF study found that, in 1998, personal staff members on the House side had an average of 2.7 years of experience in their current jobs, a 27 percent decline from 1992 but higher than the 2010 estimate by ICF International. Personal staff on the Senate side in 1997 had 2.8 years of experience in their current position. In 1993 it was 3.5 years.[88] But in 2011, the average tenure for a Senate aide was about 5.3 years.[89]

Many political scientists in recent decades have noted the trend of staffers moving to jobs in the lobbying sector, but more recently observers have noted an increasing trend of professionals leaving other careers to work on the Hill. The Center for Responsive Politics in 2011 released a study concluding that the number of lobbyists working in staff positions in Congress had increased more than twofold between the 111th Congress and 112th Congress.[90]

THE COST AND PAY OF CONGRESSIONAL STAFF

The steady expansion of congressional staffs stemming from the 1946 and 1970 reorganization acts contributed significantly to the higher cost of running Congress. The expansion of House and Senate committees from 399 aides in 1947 to 2,237 in 2009 and personal staffs from 2,030 to about 10,791 drove up costs. For example, in fiscal 1960 approximately $12.3 million was appropriated for permanent committee and investigative staffs in both the House and Senate. In fiscal 2011 the amount was about $182 million.[91]

The expansion of personal staffs also produced a substantial increase in the funding needed to run a member's office. In 1970 each representative was entitled to an annual clerk-hire allowance of $149,292 for a staff not to exceed fifteen employees for a district under 500,000 persons, or $157,092 for a staff not to exceed sixteen employees for a member representing a larger district. In 1979 the annual clerk-hire allowance for a staff of up to twenty-two employees was $288,156.

House Allowance

Since November 1995 representatives have paid for staff salaries, office expenses, and official mail out of the members' representational allowance, which included three former expense allowances—clerk-hire, official expenses, and official mail. Although the members' representational allowance is calculated on the basis of those three components, members may spend the MRA as they see fit. In 2010 this allowance averaged $1,522,114, with $944,671 permitted for personnel; the House in January 2011 reduced the MRA for 2011 and 2012 by 5 percent, setting it at an average of $1,446,009. Under the MRA, members can hire up to eighteen full-time and four nonpermanent aides in their Washington and district offices.[92] The representational allowance also includes travel funds for each member calculated by the distance between the District of Columbia and the farthest point in a member's district, as well as funds for rental of district office space. Funding for official mail is based on the number of nonbusiness addresses per district.

When Republicans took over the House in 2011, with fiscal 2011 appropriations incomplete and an outcry among new conservatives for belt tightening amid a national economic crisis, legislative branch appropriations were trimmed and soon after further cuts were recommended for fiscal 2012. In the House, funding for committee employees dropped from $171.2 million in fiscal 2010 to $163 million the next year, while authorized expenditures for MRAs dropped from $660 million to $613 million. In 2011, the House Appropriations Committee sought further reductions, sending to the full House a bill that it said "reflects an acknowledgment that the Legislative Branch must set itself as an example for fiscal restraint while continuing to serve the Nation." Among the recommended reductions was a cut in the authorization for MRAs by 6.4 percent to $573.9 million and a reduction for committees to $152.6 million. The Appropriations Committee also approved a 6.4 percent reduction in salaries and expenses for House leadership office staff.[93]

Senate Allowance

Three allowances make up senators' official personnel and office expense account: the administrative and clerical assistance allowance; the legislative assistance allowance; and the office expense allowance.

The administrative and clerical assistance allowance varies with the size of the senator's state. For fiscal year 2011, the Senate originally allocated an annual allowance ranging from $2,512,574 for states with fewer than five million residents to $3,993,206 for states with more than twenty-eight million. A measure adopted later reduced that amount by 5 percent.[94] Overall, the fiscal 2010 appropriation of $422 million for senators' official personnel and office expenses was cut to $410 million.

Senators may hire as many aides as they wish within their allowance. In practice, the range of employees is from thirteen to seventy-one, depending on the size of the state and the salary level. Senators employ an average of thirty to thirty-five full-time staffers.[95]

In 1975 senators were provided a separate allowance to hire personal staffers for specialized work on a senator's committees, up to a maximum of three committee assignments. Although initially limited to senators without other staff support on committees, the fiscal 1978 appropriations bill for the legislative branch gave this additional legislative assistance allowance to all senators along with the administrative and clerical allowance, thereby making the Senate clerk-hire allowance two separate allowances. In fiscal 2011 each senator was authorized $508,377 to appoint up to three legislative assistants. That allowance was later cut by 5 percent.[96]

The original intent of the 1975 change was to give junior senators assistance in meeting their committee responsibilities. But because there no longer is any limit on the number of staff that can be employed, senators can use their legislative aides for either committee or personal staff work and appoint as many staff as funds from the two accounts will permit.

The office expense allowance, like the clerk-hire allowance, is governed by a formula, in this instance based primarily on the distance between Washington, D.C., and the senator's home state, and the population of the senator's state. The initial fiscal 2011 authorization for senators ranged from $128,585 to $465,922, although those figures were later cut by 5 percent.[97]

Changes in Staff Salaries

The salaries of committee employees increased dramatically in the decades after World War II. In 1945, House employees were listed under clerk-hire categories with an annual base pay of $2,500. The 1970 Legislative Reorganization Act converted the base pay system of the House into a monthly salary system and raised the compensation levels of committee employees. In 2009, committee and leadership aides could earn a maximum of $172,500, and forty-three staffers reached that maximum. A Politico study based on data from LegiStorm showed that the number of staffers who were earning within the upper 3 percent of House salaries had increased by nearly 39 percent in the previous four years. And in members' personal offices, a total of fifty-three were making the maximum $168,411—a level set by a House-issued pay order, which remained the same in 2010. The lowest-paid staffers made under $30,000 a year. While there are maximum levels set for House and Senate salaries, Congress also is regulated by the minimum wage requirement, which as of July 2009 was $7.25 an hour.[98]

Both the House and the Senate are required by law to report the salaries, allowances, and expenses paid to members and members' personal and committee staffs. The "Statement of Disbursements of the House" (known before 1993 as the "Report of the Clerk of the House") is issued quarterly; the "Report of the Secretary of the Senate," every six months. (Both reports are available to the public through the House and Senate Document rooms and online at www.legistorm.com). The House began providing its reports for the public online in 2009, and the Senate followed suit in late 2011.

Outside the maximum and minimum level requirements, salaries as well as benefits for personal staff are left to the discretion of each member of Congress. Staff receive the same cost-of-living increases and insurance and retirement benefits as do other Capitol Hill employees, but formal policies on working hours, vacation time, sick leave, and maternity leave also vary from office to office. In 1995 Congress included the Fair Labor Standards Act in its workplace compliance bill, which applied to the legislative branch eleven federal labor and antidiscrimination laws. However, the Office of Compliance, created with the workplace compliance bill to carry out the statutes, decided to exempt from overtime pay requirements many of the legislative employees who often work longer hours. The Office of Compliance maintained that the overtime policy reflected standards found elsewhere in the government and in many private businesses.

Most House and Senate employees, like all federal employees, qualify for annual salary increases, or cost-of-living adjustments. But the additional earnings are not automatically included in congressional staffers' paychecks. Instead, they are added to the members' committee and personal payroll funds, to be paid out to staff members only at the discretion of the Hill employer. Members, committee chairs, or administrative officers can choose among giving their employees the increase, using the money to hire more staffers, or returning the money to the Treasury at the end of the year.

The salaries of some congressional staff—such as the clerk of the House, secretary of the Senate, parliamentarians, House counsel, and legislative counsel—are set by statute. Thus their salaries (and raises) are funded by legislative appropriations and, like those of senators and representatives, are normally ensured. But if the pay of officers gets too close to that of members, they will not get an annual adjustment unless members also accept adjustment for their pay.

CONGRESSIONAL STAFF: ETHICS AND LEGALITIES

The highly charged political atmosphere on Capitol Hill leads inevitably to close public scrutiny of the personal conduct of members and staff. The result more often than not is controversy and conflict and, at times, changes in rules and procedures.

Four of the most prominent ethics and legality issues emerging in the last several decades have been congressional compliance with laws governing other public as well as private

CONGRESS AND WORKPLACE COMPLIANCE

The first bill enacted by the Republican-led 104th Congress (1995–1997) was S 2, which amended eleven federal labor and antidiscrimination laws to apply specifically to Congress and its related offices. Among other things, the Congressional Accountability Act allowed congressional employees to take claims to federal court after an initial mediation and counseling stage. The amended laws were:

1. Civil Rights Act of 1964—prohibited discrimination in employment on the basis of race, color, religion, sex, or nationality.

2. Occupational Safety and Health Act of 1970—set safety regulations for workplaces.

3. Age Discrimination in Employment Act of 1967—prohibited workplace discrimination against people age forty and older.

4. Rehabilitation Act of 1973—provided federal aid for a variety of programs for disabled workers and for the training of personnel to work with the disabled.

5. Americans with Disabilities Act of 1990—prohibited workplace discrimination against people with disabilities.

6. Family and Medical Leave Act of 1993—set criteria for unpaid parental and medical leave for employees seeking to spend time with children or ailing family members.

7. Fair Labor Standards Act of 1938—dealt with minimum wage and mandatory overtime or compensation for employees who worked more than forty hours per week, as updated in 1989. (The minimum wage was increased again in 1996 and 2007.)

8. Employee Polygraph Protection Act of 1988—restricted the use of polygraph tests of employees by employers. The use of legal lie detector tests by the Capitol police was not affected by application of this law.

9. Worker Adjustment and Retraining Notification Act of 1988—required a sixty-day advance notice of a plant closing or large layoffs of permanent workers.

10. Veterans Re-employment Act of 1994—required employers to rehire for the same or similar position returning veterans who left their jobs after being called into military service.

11. Labor-Management Dispute Procedures—a part of the United States Code (Chapter 71 of Title V) that established procedures for resolving federal labor-management disputes.

OFFICES COVERED

Congressional offices and officers covered by the 1995 Congressional Accountability Act were:

- Each office of the House and Senate, including each office of a member and each committee
- Each joint committee
- Capitol police
- Congressional Budget Office
- Office of the Architect of the Capitol
- Senate and House restaurants and gift shops
- Botanic Garden
- Office of the attending physician
- Capitol Guide Service
- Office of Compliance

---

workers, use of staff at public expense for political—particularly election—purposes, relations with outside interest groups and lobbyists, and nepotism. Workplace compliance, as it was usually called, was addressed forthrightly in 1995, but only after years of struggle by reformers. Political use of staffers remains a sensitive issue as members and their aides walk a blurred line between appropriate committee or personal staff work and efforts to help get the boss reelected. A lack of a disclosure of gifts and travel paid for by lobbyists caused Congress to revisit ethics rules in 2006 and 2007. Finally, the nepotism issue has faded almost from sight after a few high-profile scandals.

Workplace Compliance

Until nearly the end of the twentieth century, members of Congress exempted themselves from most of the civil rights laws and other worker protection standards that they, by law, imposed on other employers. This policy earned Congress the unwelcome epithet as "The Last Plantation."

Members argued that their employment practices should not be regulated like those of a private business because Congress's work was political. Defenders of no regulation believed elected officials must be free to choose staffers who would be loyal to them. Many members also believed the principle of separation of powers would be violated if the executive branch had the power to enforce employment laws in the legislature. But the exemptions from laws governing most other employers eventually became a target of reformers inside and outside Congress, who attacked the practice as a failure of Congress to live under the very laws it passed.

When legislation to subject Congress to the labor laws governing private sector employment stalled in 1994, the House at first changed its rules to impose the compliance requirements on members. But in 1995 the newly Republican-controlled Congress moved farther, passing as its first bill the Congressional Accountability Act. This legislation, which applied eleven federal labor laws to all congressional employees, replaced a haphazard mix of voluntary rules and internal protections for congressional staff. It also allowed congressional employees to take claims to federal court after an initial mediation and counseling stage. Many members remained skeptical of allowing employees to haul them into court, particularly during an election campaign, but supporters said this enforcement mechanism was essential to allow meaningful redress under the law. Nevertheless, members could still fire, or refuse to hire or promote, anyone for "political incompatibility."

The statutes to which Congress made itself subject included the Civil Rights Act of 1964, which prohibited discrimination in employment on the basis of race, color, religion, sex, or nationality, and the Occupational Safety and Health Act of 1970, which set safety rules for workplaces. Other statutes included the Americans with Disabilities Act of 1990, which prohibited workplace discrimination against people with disabilities, and the Family and Medical Leave Act of 1993, which allowed unpaid leave to care for sick family members. *(See box, Congress and Workplace Compliance, p. 210.)*

Even before the 1995 legislation, the House did attempt to create procedures allowing employees to file complaints alleging mistreatment by supervisors, including members of Congress. An Office of Fair Employment Practices was set up in-house, under supervision of the clerk of the House, to handle complaints. Critics, however, said internal policing was inherently flawed. In fact, the complaint procedures were rarely used, which critics attributed to employees' fear of retribution, including firing, if they spoke out.

The 1995 Congressional Accountability Act addressed this issue squarely by setting up complaint procedures. Under this act, both House and Senate employees with grievances must go through a formal complaint, mediation, and hearing process conducted by the newly created Office of Compliance. Employees must request private counseling by the office within 180 days of the alleged violation. No later than fifteen days after the counseling phase, which is normally thirty days, the aggrieved employee who wants to proceed must file a request for mediation with the office. Mediation typically involves communication among all the parties involved in the case. If unsatisfied, the employee can file a formal complaint with the office to request a hearing and a decision by a hearing officer, or he or she may abandon the internal review process and file a civil lawsuit in U.S. District Court or in the District of Columbia District Court. Appeals are permitted if the parties are not satisfied with the hearing officer's decision. An aggrieved party not satisfied with the final court decision can appeal it to the U.S. Court of Appeals for the Federal Circuit. A final appeal can be made to the U.S. Supreme Court.[99] Employees may go to the courts first only if the claim is based on the U.S. Constitution, not the statutes of the 1995 law. Before 1995, court action was another main avenue for settling congressional employment grievances.

One important event that increased pressure for an employee rights law was a precedent-setting congressional job discrimination suit based on the Constitution that was settled out of court in 1979 for an undisclosed sum of money. The suit was filed in 1974 against former representative Otto E. Passman, D-La., by one-time aide Shirley Davis.

The case established the constitutional right of a congressional employee who claims sex discrimination to sue a member of Congress for damages. The out-of-court settlement, however, left undecided the question of whether the Constitution's speech or debate clause (Article I, Section 6) provides a member of Congress with immunity from job discrimination suits in at least some circumstances. This clause protects members from court suits for actions taken in Congress as part of their official duties.

The suit filed by Davis against Passman initially was thrown out of court by a federal district judge, who ruled that no existing law provided Davis with protection from job discrimination by a member of Congress. On appeal, however, the Supreme Court ruled that the Constitution itself gives individuals the right to sue members of Congress, regardless of the provisions of any particular statute, for alleged constitutional violations.[100]

In its decision, the Court dealt only with Davis's right to sue Passman, not the merits of her complaint. The case was then sent back to the lower federal courts to be decided on the merits, but the out-of-court settlement was announced before the courts acted. Nevertheless, the specter of future court actions by employees, under the precedent of Passman's case, helped to buoy the case of reformers seeking a statutory employment protection law.

Legislative Work versus Politics

The issue of employing congressional staff for political gain invariably comes up at election time when incumbents are accused of using staffers to help in their reelection campaigns.

When members return home to campaign they take with them the customary entourage of staff aides, who must juggle their political work with their status as government employees paid with federal tax dollars. No specific federal law forbids congressional staff to perform political duties, but the practice is somewhat limited by rules in the House and, to a lesser extent, in the Senate.

Personal staff members may play an important role in the reelection campaigns of their members of Congress. House rules allow a House employee to work on a campaign—compiling mailing lists and organizing fundraisers, for example—if assigned congressional duties also are being fulfilled. The Senate has no formal procedures to govern the practice. Congressional staff aides are not allowed to engage in campaign duties. They may take leave and transfer to the campaign organization for the duration of the campaign season.[101]

ETHICS RULES FOR CONGRESSIONAL STAFF

Like members of Congress, House and Senate employees must abide by certain ethics rules. These restrictions deal with honoraria, outside income, gifts, meals, travel, financial disclosure, and postemployment lobbying. Most of the rules were amended in 1989 when Congress passed the Government Ethics Reform Act and in 1995 when Congress adopted new gift rules.

The rules were amended again in 2007 at the start of the 110th Congress after charges of influence peddling by lobbyists were revealed in 2006. The House initially passed new rules that applied just to members of that chamber. Then both chambers passed, and President George W. Bush signed, the Honest Leadership and Open Government Act (P.L. 110-81), which amended the Lobbying Disclosure Act of 1995 and the Federal Election Campaign Act of 1971. The new law set detailed restrictions for members and staff on accepting gifts, meals, and travel expenses, eliminating the previous exemption of gifts under $50 and further restricting "officially connected" travel of members and aides paid for or arranged by lobbyists. The law also restricts aides' contact with their boss's spouse if that spouse is a lobbyist and bars staff members from lobbying their former bosses or offices in Congress for one year.

Under the 2007 law, lobbyists must file quarterly, rather than semiannual, electronic reports identifying state or local government clients and revealing their expenditures. Semiannual reporting is required of all political committees that lobbyists establish or control, fund-raising activities, and political contributions, and lobbyists must certify that rules regarding gifts and travel had been abided. The law also expanded the information lobbyists must provide. The law increased the civil penalties for violating the disclosure rules, from $50,000 to $200,000.

HONORARIA

As of January 1, 1991, members and staff of the House were prohibited from accepting honoraria. House employees could request, however, that charitable contributions be made in their name in lieu of honoraria for speeches and appearances. Charitable contributions, which were limited to $2,000 per speech, appearance, or article, could not be made to any organization that benefited the person who spoke or any of his or her relatives, and the House employee could not seek tax advantages from the contribution. In mid-1991 the Senate, in return for a pay raise, also eliminated honoraria for members and staff, although charitable contributions could be made.

OTHER OUTSIDE INCOME

Senior staff in the House—employees compensated at or above the GS-16 salary level—were barred from keeping more than 15 percent of the Executive Level II salary, $136,700 in 1999, in outside earned income; from being paid for working or affiliating with a law or other professional firm (they were allowed to teach for pay if the House Committee on Standards of Official Conduct approved); and from serving on boards of directors. Outside earned income included "wages, salary, fees, and other amounts paid for personal services, as opposed to items such as interest, rents, dividends, and capital gains, which represent a return on investments."

Also as of 1991, senior staff in the Senate were subject to a cap on outside income that was equal to or more than 15 percent of their Executive Level II salary.

House rules restrict the amount of outside earned income allowed for House members and certain "senior" staff. According to a rule set in 1977 and amended in 1981 and 1989, the amount is limited each year to 15 percent of the rate of pay for Level II of the Executive Schedule in effect on January 1 of the year. In 2009, the outside earned income limit was $26,550.[1]

GIFTS

Rules approved in 1989 limited House members and staff to $200 in gifts. Senators and their staff were prohibited from receiving gifts totaling more than $100 a year from anyone with a direct interest in legislation or gifts totaling more than $300 a year from anyone else but relatives. In both chambers, nominal gifts worth less than $75 were exempted.

Under rules approved in 1991, senators, representatives, and their employees could accept up to $250 in gifts annually. Members and staff did not have to count gifts worth $100 or less. The rules, which eased those passed less than two years earlier under the Ethics Reform Act of 1989, eliminated almost all requirements to disclose the receipt of gifts.

In 1995 the Senate placed a $50 limit on gifts that senators and employees could receive. The rules placed a $100 annual limit on gifts from any one source. Senators and staff could accept unlimited gifts from family members and close friends but had to get approval from the ethics committee for gifts valued at more than $250. House members could no longer accept any gifts, unless the items were of nominal value. Members could still accept unlimited gifts from family and friends, but gifts valued at more than $250 required ethics committee approval. At the beginning of the 106th Congress in 1999, the House voted to permit its members to accept gifts valued at up to $50 as well.

The 2007 law bans all gifts from registered lobbyists, foreign agents, or private entities employing either, including gifts under $50.

The Senate rule changes as provided under legislation passed only by the Senate in January 2007 (known as the Legislative Transparency and Accountability Act) prohibited members and their staff from accepting any gifts from registered

A former congressional aide commented in 1990 on the fine line between legislative work and politics.

> [Congress] by its nature is so intensely political that it becomes a practical impossibility to say in many instances where the discharge of official duties leaves off and aspirations to higher office (or reelection) begin. A congressman and his staff, for example, are not supposed to use office typewriters, photocopy machines, and phone lines to solicit financial contributions for election campaigns, but who is to judge their ulterior motives in taking positions, proposing bills and amendments, writing speeches, or issuing press releases that happen to be of value in both legislative and campaign contexts?[102]

To avoid being criticized for using government-paid staff to work on their campaigns, incumbents seek legitimacy, or the appearance of legitimacy, through several different

lobbyists or the companies or organizations that hire them. The rules also required that tickets to entertainment and sporting events be valued at the market rate.

The Senate also approved a new rule that would bar senators from attending any event in their honor during a national party convention if the event is paid for by a lobbyist or an entity that retains or employs lobbyists.

Under both the House and Senate rules, lobbyists or the groups they represent may continue to pick up the tab for a meal if it fits under one of the exceptions that existed before and are still in the rules. The one that is most likely to be used day to day is known informally as the "reception exception" or the "toothpick rule." That rule allows lawmakers to sample food at receptions sponsored by private groups.

TRAVEL

One of the exceptions to rules restricting gifts has been the payment of expenses for travel in connection with official duties, provided it is not paid for by a lobbyist. For both House and Senate members and staff, the 2007 law further bars such expenses paid by clients of lobbyists or foreign agents, or if the trip was planned or arranged by a lobbyist or a lobbyist accompanies the member or staff for any duration. In the Senate, travel expenses can be paid for by a "charitable organization," even if it employs lobbyists, but for only a one-day event. The House allows travel to be compensated by an "institution of higher education," even if it employs lobbyists. Otherwise, permissible "officially connected" travel is limited to three days for domestic travel and seven days for foreign travel for Senate employees and senators, and four days for domestic travel and seven days for foreign travel for House employees and members. The rules also require that senators and Senate staff pay the higher charter rate for private planes, while the House bans members and staff from accepting flights on private aircraft.

FINANCIAL DISCLOSURE

The Government Ethics Act of 1989 for the first time brought all three branches of government under the same financial disclosure law, although each branch continued to be responsible for administering requirements for its own employees. The new rules on financial disclosure became effective with the reports due in 1991. Income of more than $200 from any source had to be reported. Gifts worth less than $75 did not have to be reported.

Employees who had charitable contributions made on their behalf in lieu of honoraria had to disclose the source and amount of the contributions. The charities receiving such contributions had to be disclosed in confidential reports to the House Committee on Standards of Official Conduct. In addition, the source and amount of any honoraria received by the spouse of a reporting individual had to be disclosed. Travel reimbursements, including an itinerary and dates of travel, also had to be reported. Finally, within thirty days after leaving office staffers were required to file a termination report containing complete financial disclosure information for the previous year up to the date of departure.

The 2007 law requires members and staff to report all gifts and to make disclosures of travel expenses received within thirty days after the trip, including a description of the meetings or events attended.

POSTEMPLOYMENT LOBBYING

Effective January 1, 1991, former House and Senate staff members (those at the GS-17 salary level or above) were barred for one year after leaving employment from lobbying the member, office, or committee for which they had worked. In 1999 an attempt to extend the postemployment ban to two years failed to win approval in a House-Senate conference committee. Leadership staff members were barred from lobbying the members and employees of the leadership for the chamber in which they served. The 2007 law extended the postemployment lobbying ban, or "cooling-off period," to two years for members of the Senate. The 2007 law also restricts "senior" Senate staff—those compensated for sixty days at a rate of at least 75 percent of a member's salary—from making lobbying contact with any senator, officer, or employee in the Senate. All Senate staffers are barred from lobbying the member or committee for whom they worked. (The rules had already provided an exception for those representing Indian tribes, but that exception under the 2007 law only applies for those who act as an employee or an elected or appointed official of the tribal organization.)

The House in 2007 added postemployment restrictions that affected lawmakers, House officers, and "very senior staff"—those staff members paid at an annual rate of $123,900 or more for at least sixty days. For one year after leaving office, they may not "communicate with or appear before a member, officer, or employee of either house of Congress or any Legislative Branch office with intent to influence official action on behalf of anyone else."

1 "The Outside Earned Income Limitation Applicable to Members and Senior Staff," House Ethics Committee. ethics.house.gov/outside-employment-income/outside-earned-income-limitation-applicable-members-and-senior-staff.

SOURCES: House Committee on Standards of Official Conduct and the Senate Rules and Administration Committee; Jack Maskell, "Lobbying Law and Ethics Rules Changes in the 110th Congress" (Washington, D.C.: Congressional Research Service, 2007).

approaches. "Because of what has gone under the bridge in the past, people are more aware and more careful," said one legislative aide who took a 50 percent pay cut in 1978 to help his boss, Sen. Robert P. Griffin, R-Mich., in his unsuccessful effort to win a third term. "My sense is that everybody is overly sensitive and overly paranoid about it."[103]

In some cases House and Senate staffers go on vacation or temporarily take themselves off the government payroll. Others try to mix their congressional job with election campaign duties and agree to a cut in pay to reflect the reduction in their congressional work. Others remain on the payroll to avoid losing benefits but claim to put in a full day of constituent service at the member's district office before going to campaign headquarters to help their boss in the reelection bid. Nonetheless, staffers "simply doing their ordinary job is a large contribution in itself."[104]

Supreme Court Case

In March 1981 the Supreme Court let stand an appeals court ruling that said it was up to Congress to determine whether and under what restraints congressional aides may double as campaign workers. The Court's decision appeared to clear the way for a senator or representative to keep staff aides on the government payroll even when they were working almost exclusively on the member's reelection campaign.

The 1981 appeals court ruling was issued in a 1977 suit brought by former Federal Election Commission attorney Joel D. Joseph against Sen. Howard W. Cannon, D-Nev., and Chester B. Sobsey, Cannon's $40,000-a-year administrative assistant. Joseph charged that Sobsey had remained on the Senate payroll from March 1975 through November 1976 while working for Cannon's reelection.

The suit also claimed that Cannon's approval of Sobsey's salary payments under those circumstances constituted a fraudulent claim against the government. But the appeals court held that to judge the legality of Cannon's actions would violate the Constitution's separation of powers doctrine. Only the House and Senate can judge such "political questions," the appeals court ruled.

The appeals court based much of its ruling on the conclusion that Congress itself had set no hard-and-fast standard that would have enabled Cannon to determine where to draw the line between Sobsey's official duties and his political chores. Existing rules governing staff campaign work were lenient and subject to differing interpretations. In the past both chambers had been extremely reluctant to police their members' use of staff in political campaigns. Congress had never allowed its own staffers to be restricted by the 1939 Hatch Act, which prohibits civil service employees from participating in partisan political activities.

Today, under House regulations staff members, while not permitted to contribute cash to a campaign, may assist a member's reelection effort so long as their assigned congressional duties also are being fulfilled. Those duties are set by each member, as is the amount of vacation time granted.

Senate restrictions are even more lax. The guiding document on the subject was a Senate Rules and Administration Committee report of October 17, 1977, which states that "other than actual handling of campaign funds, the Senate has not imposed any restrictions on the participation of a member of a senator's staff in that senator's reelection campaign." Several weeks after the 1981 appeals court decision in the Cannon case, the Senate Select Committee on Ethics proposed incorporating into the Senate ethics code a 1977 ruling by the committee declaring that senators should remove from their congressional payrolls staffers who undertake political work to the detriment of their official Senate duties. But the full Senate never acted on the proposal.

Flexibility of Staff Use

Unlike the House, which does not allow personal staff to solicit and receive campaign contributions, the Senate provides that three members of each senator's staff may be designated for that purpose. In Cannon's Supreme Court case, the senator argued that he had designated Sobsey as one of the staffers allowed to solicit and receive campaign funds.

The use of congressional staff on a campaign offers an enormous advantage to members over their challengers, who must use their own campaign funds to finance staff support. But it is difficult to differentiate political activities from legislative work that is also usable in an election campaign. Some activities, such as managing a campaign, raising money, and dealing with poll results, are clearly political. But casework, speech writing, and preparation of responses on particular issues falls into a gray area.

Most of those engaged in campaign efforts at high levels are the administrative assistants. An AA is usually a member's top congressional aide and the one having the most political as well as legislative experience.

In close races it is not unusual to find a massive shift of personnel from congressional work to the campaign. Because this shift offers an obvious target for an opponent, staff members in these contests almost always leave the government payroll.

In 1985 the Senate ethics committee issued an interpretive ruling (No. 402) stating that an unnamed senator's personal secretary could receive pay from the campaign committee for off-hours work she did for the senator's reelection. The secretary had been designated to receive campaign contributions for the senator.

In 1986 the House ethics committee investigated complaints that Rep. Mac Sweeney, R-Texas, was threatening to fire staff members who refused to perform campaign activities. The committee said it found no evidence of impropriety and took no further action.

House Minority Whip Newt Gingrich, R-Ga., later Speaker, was investigated by the House ethics committee in 1989–1990 for suggestions that he improperly used his congressional payroll for political purposes. The *Atlanta Business Chronicle* reported in its July 24, 1989, issue that Gingrich had given large, but temporary, year-end pay raises to staff members when they returned to his congressional office after taking leave without government pay to work on his campaign in the 1986 and 1988 elections. Gingrich denied any wrongdoing and said he was being chastised for a legitimate practice that is widespread on Capitol Hill—members giving their staff year-end bonuses. The investigation of Gingrich, which included other charges, was dropped in March 1990.

In 2004 the House ethics committee began an informal investigation of John Conyers Jr., D-Mich., after a Detroit newspaper published a story suggesting that his congressional office staff conducted campaign work and did personal chores for him during office hours. Former Conyers staff members also complained to the ethics committee about the alleged misuse of personnel. In December 2006 the committee wrapped up work on Conyers's case after the Detroit representative agreed to meet certain conditions. Conyers, who became chair of the Judiciary Committee in 2007, was prohibited from using his congressional staff for any campaign-related work during the 110th Congress unless the aides took unpaid leave and shifted to paid service for his campaign. Even then, they had to receive advance approval from the ethics committee.

Conyers had initially denied the charges, but later "acknowledged what he characterized as a 'lack of clarity' in his communications with staff members regarding their official duties and responsibilities." He also agreed to improve and increase the education and training of his staff to ensure that they do not improperly engage in campaign-related work.[105]

Staff Relations with Lobbyists

The influence of lobbyists on members of Congress and their staffs became a major concern in the 109th Congress as revelations became public about lobbyist Jack Abramoff, who had charged more than $80 million to various Indian tribes for his lobbying services, and his connections to House members. Both GOP majority leader Tom DeLay of Texas and House Administration Committee chair Bob Ney of Ohio were implicated in the Abramoff influence-peddling scandal. Former DeLay press secretary Michael Scanlon, an associate of Abramoff's, pleaded guilty in November 2005 to conspiracy to bribe members of Congress and their staffs. John Albaugh, former chief of staff to Ernest Istook, R-Okla., pleaded guilty in 2008 to conspiracy to defraud the House and working in conspiracy with an Abramoff associate, and agreed to cooperate with prosecutors. Abramoff pleaded guilty in March 2006 to federal conspiracy and fraud charges.

Ney had tried to insert into elections reform legislation language that would have benefited an Indian gambling casino operated by one of Abramoff's clients. Ney and DeLay both received golf trips to Scotland that were paid for by Abramoff, although the payments for the trip were reported as made by a charity operated by Abramoff. DeLay, a close associate of Abramoff's, was fighting separate criminal charges in Texas from alleged election violations. So although both DeLay and Ney were found to have had contacts with Abramoff, only Ney was convicted of two felonies and sent to jail. DeLay resigned his House seat on June 9, 2006. Ney resigned from his on November 3, 2006. Scanlon in February 2011 was sentenced to twenty months in federal prison; he reportedly had earned about $7 million a year working with Abramoff between 2001 and 2003. Albaugh in April 2011 was sentenced to five years of probation and four months in a halfway house; U.S. District Judge Ellen Segal Huvelle said

GOP Majority Leader Tom DeLay of Texas looks on as his attorney answers questions as they arrive for his trial in October 2010. DeLay was convicted the following month of money laundering for illegally channeling $190,000 in corporate contributions into Texas legislative races in 2002 through a money swap. Unlike several members of his staff, he was not brought to trial for his ties to disgraced lobbyist Jack Abramoff.

SOURCE: AP Photo/Jack Plunkett/file.

Albaugh was not given a prison sentence because she believed members of Congress were to blame for the incident.

Abramoff had developed ties to staff and members in part by showering them with gifts, travel, and meals. Neil Voltz, a former aide to Ney, testified in federal court in May 2006 about being given tickets to sporting events and concerts and free food, for example. "In return, I gave preferential treatment to my lobbying buddies," he said.[106] Such reports of lobbyists providing trips, dinners, and gifts to lawmakers and their staff forced the Republican leadership in both the House and Senate to put together legislation in 2006 overhauling the way politicians and their staff can interact with corporate lobbyists. The bills addressed such issues as limiting congressional junkets funded by private interests, setting new bans on gifts from lobbyists, and strengthening disclosure and conflict-of-interest laws. These changes to the 1995 lobbying disclosure law also would have affected senior staff members who are governed by many of the same travel and post-employment rules that govern lawmakers.

The House bill ran into trouble, however, when Republican rank-and-file members loudly voiced their opposition. Many called the tighter gift limits insulting and complained that a travel ban would eliminate useful trips with educational value.

Meanwhile, the Democrats introduced their own bill in February 2006 that also made sweeping changes to House rules governing ethics and lobbying practices, including banning privately funded travel and providing more rigorous requirements for disclosure and enforcement of ethics and lobbying laws and regulations. The Republicans brought a scaled-back measure to the floor, and it passed in May, although many Democrats said it did not go far enough. The Senate lobbying bill was broader and banned all gifts and meals from lobbyists, while increasing to two years the cooling-off period that keeps senators from taking lucrative private sector lobbying jobs after they leave the Senate. The Senate bill passed in March 2006, but the two bills were never reconciled in conference.[107]

110th Congress: Lobbying and Ethics Changes

One of the first actions taken by the Democrats after winning back control in the 110th Congress was to draft new ethics and lobbying disclosure rules. The House initially drafted changes to its own rules, prohibiting members and aides from accepting most meals and gifts from lobbyists, banning most privately funded travel, and making it virtually impossible for House members to travel on private jets—rules that had been in effect in January 2007. The Senate also approved a package of new gift and travel rules for the chamber that month, but many of the changes were included in a separate bill to amend the Lobbying Disclosure Act of 1995 and Federal Election Campaign Act of 1971. A final bill, titled the Honest Leadership and Open Government Act, was cleared later that year and signed into law by President George W. Bush.

The new rules required, among other things, more detailed lobbying disclosures by paid lobbyists; set more detailed restrictions for members and their staff on accepting gifts and travel expenses; imposed additional restrictions on lobbying activities of former members and staff; and restricted members and staff from seeking earmarks in appropriations measures.

Previous House and Senate rules had permitted members and staff to accept gifts valued under $50, but the new rules expressly bar such gifts from lobbyists, foreign agents, or their clients. That includes meals or tickets to events, except for "food or drink of nominal value," such as hors d'oeuvres and drinks at receptions. Also, members and aides must get advance approval to accept travel expenses related to their official duties, and they must certify that it is not paid for by a lobbyist or his or her clients and is not for recreational purposes and that a lobbyist will not be traveling with them for any duration of the trip. The Senate permits "official travel" to be paid for by a "charitable organization," even if it employs lobbyists, but only for a one-day event. The House permits travel to be compensated by a higher education institution, even if it employs lobbyists. Also, senators and their staff must reimburse for the use of a noncommercial aircraft at a higher charter rate, while in the House it is virtually impossible for members to travel on private jet.[108]

Campaign fund-raisers for members of Congress are exempt from the lobbying rules. Those are covered by Federal Election Commission rules, which limit contributions from lobbyists and others and require that money raised and spent be disclosed publicly and on a regular schedule.

The "Cooling-Off" Period

The 2007 rules also include language that bars lawmakers, House and Senate officers, and senior staff of the House and Senate from lobbying contacts in Congress for one year after leaving office. In the Senate, senior staff (those who made at least 75 percent of their boss's salary for sixty days) cannot communicate "with intent to influence" any senator or officer or employee of the Senate for one year if that staff member becomes a registered lobbyist. All other Senate staff who become registered lobbyists are barred from such communication with the senator or committee for whom they worked. In the House, staff from a member's personal office are barred from lobbying only that member, and staff of a committee are barred from lobbying any members of that committee for one year.

A 2005 study of members and top staff of Appropriations Committees revealed thirty instances in which a relative lobbied members or staff for money in an appropriations bill. Twenty-two such cases were successful, resulting in $750 million in projects.[109]

The rules also prohibit staff from having any lobbying contact with their boss's spouse or, in the Senate, any member of the senator's immediate family who may be registered lobbyists.

The ethics rules go a step farther to set restrictions on lawmakers and staffers looking for new employment, such as after losing a reelection campaign. Senior aides in the House or Senate must notify the ethics committee within three business days that they are negotiating an agreement for future employment, and they must recuse themselves from any matter in the chamber that would potentially present a conflict of interest.

Questionable Hiring Practices

Nepotism has been a recurring problem in Congress. Some members have used their staff allowances to hire relatives and, in effect, supplement their own incomes.

On May 20, 1932, the House adopted a resolution providing that: "The Clerk of the House of Representatives is hereby authorized and directed to keep open for public inspection the payroll records of the disbursing officer of the House." The resolution was adopted without debate. Few members on the floor understood its import. The next day, however, newspapers published stories based on examinations of the disbursing officer's records. They disclosed that ninety-seven members of the House devoted their clerk-hire allowance, in whole or in part, to paying persons having the

Speaker Tom Foley's staff, pictured here in 1989, included his wife, seated beside him; under the nepotism rule, she served without pay as his chief of staff.

SOURCE: R. Michael Jenkins, Congressional Quarterly.

same names as their own. Presumably these persons were relatives. The names were published, and nepotism in Congress became the subject of wide public discussion. At that time, however, nepotism was not illegal or even a violation of the standing rules.

Senate payroll information did not become available for public inspection until twenty-seven years later. On June 26, 1959, the Senate by voice vote adopted a resolution requiring the secretary of the Senate to make public the name, title, salary, and employer of all Senate employees. The resolution was the outgrowth of critical newspaper stories on the withholding of payroll information, coupled with additional disclosures of congressional nepotism.

A few years later nepotism became a problem for Rep. Adam Clayton Powell Jr., D-N.Y., in a case that was one of a series of events leading to a landmark Supreme Court decision on qualifications of members of Congress. Soon after marrying in December 1960, Powell employed his Puerto Rican wife, Yvette Marjorie Flores, as a paid member of his congressional office staff. Mrs. Powell remained in Puerto

Rico after the birth of a son in 1962 but continued to draw a $20,578 annual salary as a clerk whose job was to answer mail from Spanish-speaking constituents.

In 1964 the House adopted a resolution aimed specifically at the Powell situation: It forbade members to hire employees who did not work either in the member's home district or in the member's Washington, D.C., office. (That provision was made permanent in 1976.) Mrs. Powell, however, continued to live in Puerto Rico. Following a select committee investigation of that and other charges against Powell, the House on March 1, 1967, voted to exclude him from the 90th Congress. The Supreme Court ruled later, however, that the House action was unconstitutional, and Powell returned to Congress in 1969.

In 1967 Congress approved a measure to curb nepotism in federal employment. The measure, added to a postal rate–federal pay bill, prohibited public officials, including members of Congress, from appointing or trying to promote the appointment of relatives in the agency in which the officials served. The ban covered all officials, including the president,

Rep. Bob Filner, D-Calif., worked for three lawmakers—Sen. Hubert H. Humphrey, and Reps. Donald Fraser and Jim Bates—before he became a member of Congress.

SOURCE: Scott J. Ferrell, Congressional Quarterly.

but it did not cover relatives already employed. And it did not prevent an official in one agency or chamber of Congress from seeking to obtain employment for a relative in another agency or chamber.

The *U.S. Senate Handbook and the House Members' Congressional Handbook,* prepared for all new members and updated periodically by the Senate Rules and Administration Committee and the House Administration Committee, lists twenty-seven classifications of relatives whose employment by representatives and senators is prohibited by law. Certification that an employee is related to a member of Congress must be made on payroll authorizations by the employing member or by the committee or subcommittee chair.

In 1995 and 1996 the conservative Landmark Legal Foundation requested that the ethics committee investigate whether House Democratic whip David E. Bonior of Michigan violated nepotism rules by employing his wife. The ethics committee eventually found no substance to the nepotism charge. Bonior said his wife worked in his office four years before they were married in 1991 and thus was exempt from the ban.[110]

Moving Beyond a Staff Job

One of the benefits of working for a member of Congress is that the knowledge gained on the job often leads to an elected office. In the 110th Congress, seventy-four members and one delegate—Eni F. H. Faleomavaega of America Samoa—had previously worked on the personal staff of a member of Congress or a House or Senate committee.[111]

California Democratic representative Bob Filner has the distinction of having worked for three lawmakers before becoming a member of Congress himself. In the 1970s, he worked for Sen. Hubert H. Humphrey of Minnesota and then Minnesota Democratic representative Donald Fraser. In the 1980s, he worked for California Democrat Jim Bates. Filner then won the newly drawn Fiftieth District seat in 1992.

Former Democratic representative Jane Harman, also of California, worked for Democratic senator John Tunney of California for two years and the Senate Judiciary Committee for another two years and also served in the administration of President Jimmy Carter.

Rep. Paul Ryan, R-Wis., was first elected in 1998 at age twenty-eight and worked his way up to become chair of the House Committee on Budget in 2011. Ryan had at one time served as an aide to Wisconsin GOP senator Bob Kasten and to Kansas Republican Sam Brownback in the House and Senate. In between those stints, he worked as a speechwriter for former New York representative Jack Kemp, then worked for the think tank Empower America founded by Kemp and conservative pundit William Bennett. Michigan Democrat John Conyers Jr., chair of the House Judiciary Committee in the 110th Congress, served for three years as a district staff member to Michigan Democratic representative John D. Dingell. And Missouri Democratic representative William Lacy Clay put himself through college at the University of Maryland by working as a doorman for the House for six years.

In the Senate, Robert F. Bennett of Utah made his first run for the Senate at the age of fifty-nine, but he was no stranger to Washington. His father, Wallace F. Bennett, was a four-term U.S. senator from 1951 to 1974. Bennett worked as an aide for his father for two years, after having worked for Utah Republican representative Sherman P. Lloyd.

Iowa Democratic senator Tom Harkin was elected to the House after working in 1969 for Rep. Neal Smith, D-Iowa, as an aide on the House select committee investigating the U.S. military's progress in Vietnam. He made a name for himself with his discovery of South Vietnam's "tiger cages," in which hundreds of men, women, and children were crammed into underground cells. Harkin's photographs and story in *Life* magazine energized the antiwar movement and forced South Vietnam to shutter the tiger cages. The move cost the thirty-year-old Harkin his job on Capitol Hill. But he came back to the House in 1975 as the representative from western Iowa.

NOTES

1 Michael J. Malbin, *Unelected Representatives: Congressional Staff and the Future of Representative Government* (New York: Basic Books, 1980), 28.

2 Ida A. Brudnick, *Legislative Branch: FY2011 Appropriations.* (Washington, D.C.: Library of Congress, Congressional Research Service, 2011), Table 4; Ida A. Brudnick, *Legislative Branch: FY2012 Appropriations* (Washington, D.C.: Library of Congress, Congressional Research Service, 2011), Table 4.

3 Norman J. Ornstein, Thomas E. Mann, and Michael J. Malbin, *Vital Statistics on Congress, 2012* (Washington, D.C.: American Enterprise Institute, forthcoming), Table 5-1.

4 Ibid.; Norman J. Ornstein, Thomas E. Mann, and Michael J. Malbin, *Vital Statistics on Congress, 2008* (Washington, D.C.: Brookings Institution, 2008), Table 5-1.

5 Ibid., Table 5-1.

6 Ornstein et al., *Vital Statistics in Congress 2012*, Tables 5-1, 5-6, 5-7.

7 Ibid., Table 5-1.

8 Ibid., Table 5-5.

9 Hedrick Smith, *The Power Game: How Washington Works* (New York: Random House, 1988), 282.

10 William A. Galston, *Increased Efficiency for Senate Confirmation of Presidential Appointments* (Washington, D.C.: Brookings Institution, 2011); Dan Friedman, "Senate Approves Cut in Jobs Requiring Conformation," NationalJournal.com, June 29, 2011.

11 R. Eric Petersen, Jennifer E. Manning, and Ida A. Brudnick, *Administrative Issues Related to a Change in Majority in the House of Representatives* (Washington, D.C.: Library of Congress, Congressional Research Service, 2010).

12 Bradley S. Keare, *1998 House Staff Employment Study* (Washington, D.C.: Congressional Management Foundation, 1998), 3, 93–94.

13 Susan Webb Hammond, "Life and Work on the Hill: Careers, Norms, Staff and Informal Caucuses," in *Congress Responds to the Twentieth Century,* eds. Sunil Ahuja and Robert Dewhirst (Columbus: Ohio State University, 2003).

14 "The Hill People, 2011," *National Journal,* June 18, 2011, 16.

15 William L. Morrow, *Congressional Committees* (New York: Scribner, 1969), 52.

16 Harrison W. Fox Jr. and Susan Webb Hammond, *Congressional Staffs: The Invisible Force in American Lawmaking* (New York: Free Press, 1977), 15.

17 Ibid.

18 Ibid., 20.

19 Richard A. Baker, *The Senate of the United States: A Bicentennial History* (Malabar, Fla.: Krieger, 1988), 89–90.

20 Lindsay Rogers, "The Staffing of Congress," *Political Science Quarterly* 56, March 1991, 1–2.

21 Robert C. Byrd, *The Senate, 1789–1989: Addresses on the History of the United States Senate* (Washington, D.C.: Government Printing Office, 1988), 538.

22 Baker, *Senate of the United States,* 89–90.

23 Michael J. Malbin, "Delegation, Deliberation, and the New Role of Congressional Staff," in *The New Congress,* eds. Thomas E. Mann and Norman J. Ornstein (Washington, D.C.: American Enterprise Institute, 1981), 138.

24 Byrd, *The Senate, 1789–1989,* 550.

25 Donald A. Ritchie, *The U.S. Congress: A Very Short Introduction* (Washington, D.C.: Library of Congress, 2010), 49.

26 Fox and Hammond, *Congressional Staffs,* 22.

27 Ritchie, *The U.S. Congress,* 49.

28 Rules of the House of Representatives: One Hundred Twelfth Congress, Rule X 9(a) and 9(d).

29 Ritchie, *The U.S. Congress,* 49.

30 Christopher J. Deering and Steven S. Smith, *Committees in Congress.* 3rd ed. (Washington, D.C.: CQ Press, 1997), 166.

31 Remarks of Senator Packwood, 121 *Congressional Record* (daily edition, 10 June 1975), S. 10281.

32 Deering and Smith, *Committees in Congress,* 166.

33 Ornstein et. al., *Vital Statistics on Congress, 2012,* Table 5.1.

34 Roger H. Davidson, Walter J. Oleszek, and Frances E. Lee, *Congress and Its Members.* 13th ed. (Washington, D.C.: CQ Press, 2011), 132.

35 Lyn Ragsdale, *Vital Statistics on the Presidency: Washington to Clinton* (Washington, D.C.: CQ Press, 1998), 266–268.

36 Ornstein et al., *Vital Statistics on Congress, 2008,* 114.

37 Lawrence C. Dodd and Bruce I. Oppenheimer, *Congress Reconsidered.* 9th ed. (Washington, D.C.: CQ Press, 2009), 381.

38 David E. Price, *The Congressional Experience.* 3rd ed. (Cambridge, Mass.: Westview Press, 2004), 68.

39 Lawrence C. Dodd and Bruce I. Oppenheimer, *Congress Reconsidered.* 6th ed. (Washington, D.C.: CQ Press, 1997), 379.

40 Colton C. Campbell and Paul S. Herrnson, *War Stories from Capitol Hill* (Upper Saddle River, NJ: Pearson Education, 2004), 11.

41 Bruce Bartlett, "Downsizing Staff with Painful Results," *Washington Times,* November 22, 1996, A18, cited in Roger H. Davidson and Walter J. Oleszek, *Congress and Its Members.* 7th ed. (Washington, D.C.: CQ Press, 2000), 219.

42 U.S. Congress, *Congressional Record,* daily ed., 105th Cong., 1st sess., July 30, 1996, S9117, cited in Davidson and Oleszek, *Congress and Its Members,* 220.

43 Eric Petersen, Parker H. Reynolds, and Amber Hope Wilhelm, *House of Representatives and Senate Staff Levels in Member, Committee, Leadership and Other Offices, 1977–2010* (Washington, D.C.: Library of Congress, Congressional Research Service, 2010).

44 Price, *The Congressional Experience,* 95.

45 Ritchie, *The U.S. Congress,* 123.

46 Ornstein et al., *Vital Statistics on Congress, 2012,* Tables 5-6, 5-7.

47 Campbell and Herrnson, *War Stories from Capitol Hill,* 7.

48 Martin Kady II, "Thousands of Hill Jobs at Stake on Election Day," *CQ Today,* October 27, 2006; Erika Lovely, "On the Agenda: Packing and Shredding," Politico.com, November 15, 2010.

49 Malbin, "Delegation, Deliberation, and the New Role of Congressional Staff," 151.

50 Siobhan Gorman and Richard Cohen, "Hurtling toward an Intelligence Overhaul," *National Journal,* September 18, 2004, 2808, as cited in Davidson et al., *Congress and Its Members,* 204.

51 Henry A. Waxman, *The Waxman Report: How Congress Really Works* (New York: Hachette Book Group, 2009), 35.

52 "Power Trips: How Private Travel Sponsors Gain Special Access to Congress," Center for Public Integrity, 2006, www.public integrity.org/powertrips; Kate Phillips, "Trip Study Finds More Was Spent on Aides Than Lawmakers," *New York Times,* June 6, 2006.

53 Davidson et al., *Congress and Its Members,* 205.

54 Smith, *The Power Game,* 284.

55 Lawrence C. Dodd and Bruce I. Oppenheimer, *Congress Reconsidered.* 9th ed. (Washington, D.C.: CQ Press, 2009), 343.

56 Smith, *The Power Game,* 289–290.

57 Thomas E. Mann and Norman J. Ornstein, *The Broken Branch: How Congress Is Failing America and How to Get It Back on Track* (New York: Oxford University Press, 2008), 174.

58 Quoted in Kenneth Kofmehl, *Professional Staffs of Congress* (West Lafayette, Ind.: Purdue Research Foundation, 1962), 212.

59 Senate Committee on Rules and Administration, Report 112-009, Authorizing Expenditures by Committees of the Senate, March 31, 2011.

60 Malbin, *Unelected Representatives,* 170–187.

61 Jeffrey H. Birnbaum and Alan S. Murray, *Showdown at Gucci Gulch: Lawmakers, Lobbyists, and the Unlikely Triumph of Tax Reform* (New York: Vintage Books, 1987), 217, 214.

62 *Congressional Quarterly Almanac, 1997,* vol. 53 (Washington, D.C.: Congressional Quarterly, 1998), 9–59.

63 Amol Sharma, "Focusing on a Fresh Start," *CQ Weekly,* January 2, 2006, 31.

64 John Bresnahan, "Maxine Waters Ethics Case Outsourced," Politico.com, July 20, 2011.

65 Mark Bisnow, *In the Shadow of the Dome: Chronicles of a Capitol Hill Aide* (New York: Morrow, 1990), 91.

66 Nicol C. Rae, "The Race for Senate Majority Leader," in *War Stories from Capitol Hill* (Upper Saddle River, NJ: Pearson Education, 2004), 40.

67 Joe Klein, "Ted Kaufman, the Temporary Senator," *Time* magazine, October 21, 2010.

68 Smith, *The Power Game,* 282.

69 Stephen Isaacs, "The Capitol Game," *Washington Post,* February 16–20, 22–24, 1975.

70 Bisnow, *In the Shadow of the Dome,* 76.

71 Congressional Management Foundation, *Communicating with Congress: How Capitol Hill Is Coping with the Surge in Citizen Advocacy* (Washington, D.C.: Congressional Management Foundation, 2005).

72 Congressional Management Foundation, *Social Congress: Perceptions and Use of Social Media on Capitol Hill* (Washington, D.C.: Congressional Management Foundation, 2011).

73 Congressional Management Foundation, *Communicating with Congress: Perceptions of Citizen Advocacy on Capitol Hill* (Washington, D.C.: Congressional Management Foundation, 2011).

74 Ornstein et. al., *Vital Statistics on Congress, 2012,* Tables 5-3 and 5-4; Eric Petersen, Parker H. Reynolds, and Amber Hope Wilhelm, *House of Representatives and Senate Staff Levels in Member, Committee, Leadership and other Offices, 1977–2010* (Washington, D.C.: Library of Congress, Congressional Research Service, 2010).

75 Norman J. Ornstein, Thomas E. Mann, and Michael J. Malbin, *Vital Statistics on Congress, 2001–2002* (Washington, D.C.: American Enterprise Institute Press, 2002), 21.

76 Ornstein et al., *Vital Statistics on Congress, 2008,* 18.

77 Fox and Hammond, *Congressional Staffs,* 49.

78 Richard F. Fenno Jr., *The Emergence of a Senate Leader: Pete Domenici and the Reagan Budget* (Washington, D.C.: CQ Press, 1991), 4–5.

79 Price, *The Congressional Experience,* 67–68.

80 Amy E. Black, *From Inspiration to Legislation: How an Idea Becomes a Bill* (Upper Saddle River, NJ: Pearson Education, 2007), 7.

81 David Twenhafel, ed., *Setting Course: A Congressional Management Guide.* 4th ed. (Washington, D.C.: Congressional Management Foundation, 1992), 30.

82 Bisnow, *In the Shadow of the Dome,* 131.

83 Gebe Martinez, "Forbes' Independent Streak Persists during His Debut as a Democrat," *CQ Weekly,* July 24, 1999, 1777.

84 Erika Lovley, "GOP Hires Fewer Hispanics," Politico.com, November 30, 2010.

85 ICF International, *2010 House Compensation Study: Guide for the 112th Congress* (Fairfax, Va.: ICF International), 68.

86 Ibid.

87 Guy Gugliotta, "House Aides' Experience Drops, 'Pay Gap' Grows," *Washington Post,* November 12, 1998, A19.

88 Keare, *1998 House Staff Employment Study,* 3; Thomas J. Klouda, *1997 Senate Staff Employment: Salary, Tenure, Demographics,* *and Benefits* (Washington, D.C.: Congressional Management Foundation, 1997), 3.

89 Davidson et al., *Congress and Its Members,* 204.

90 Sarah McKinnon Bryner, *From Hired Guns to Hired Hands: 'Reverse Revolvers' in the 111th and 112th Congresses* (Washington, D.C.: Center for Responsive Politics, 2011).

91 Paul E. Dwyer, *Legislative Branch Appropriations for Committee and Personal Staff and Agency Contributions: FY 1960–FY 1984* (Washington, D.C.: Library of Congress, Congressional Research Service, 1984); Paul E. Dwyer, *Appropriations for FY 1999: Legislative Branch* (Washington, D.C.: Library of Congress, Congressional Research Service, 1998); Ida A. Brudnick, *Legislative Branch: FY 2012 Appropriations* (Washington, D.C.: Library of Congress, Congressional Research Service, 2011); Senate Report 111-294, Legislative Branch Appropriations, 2011.

92 Ida A. Brudnick, *Congressional Salaries and Allowances* (Washington, D.C.: Library of Congress, Congressional Research Service, 2011); Ida A. Brudnick, *Members' Representational Allowance: Usage and History* (Washington, D.C.: Library of Congress, Congressional Research Service, 2011); Ida A. Brudnick, *Congressional Salaries and Allowances* (Washington, D.C.: Library of Congress, Congressional Research Service, 2012).

93 House Report 112-148, Legislative Branch Appropriations Bill, 2012; Brudnick, *Legislative Branch: FY2012 Appropriations;* Brudnick, *Legislative Branch: FY 2011 Appropriations.*

94 Brudnick, *Congressional Salaries and Allowances.*

95 Davidson et al., *Congress and Its Members,* 132.

96 Brudnick, *Congressional Salaries and Allowances.*

97 Ibid.

98 Ibid.; Erika Lovley, "2,000 House Staffers Make Six Figures," Politico.com, March 26, 2010; www.dol.gov/dol/topic/wages/mini mumwage.htm.

99 *Congress and the Nation Vol. IX, 1993–1996* (Washington, D.C.: Congressional Quarterly, 1998), 892–893.

100 Davis v. Passman, 442 U.S. 228 (1979).

101 Davidson et al., *Congress and Its Members,* 133.

102 Bisnow, *In the Shadow of the Dome,* 192.

103 Christopher Buchanan, "Campaigning by Staff Aides Is Still a Common Practice," *Congressional Quarterly Weekly Report,* October 28, 1978, 3116.

104 Bisnow, *In the Shadow of the Dome,* 192.

105 Susan Ferrechio, "House Ethics Committee Wraps up Work on Conyers, Weldon, Feeney Investigations," *CQ Weekly,* January 8, 2007, 129.

106 Danielle Knight, "House of Horrors," *U.S. News and World Report,* September 3, 2006.

107 David Nather, "A Session Squandered," *CQ Weekly,* December 18, 2006, 3341.

108 Jack Maskell, *Lobbying Law and Ethics Rules Changes in the 110th Congress* (Washington, D.C.: Library of Congress, Congressional Research Service, 2007); Jack Maskell, *Acceptance of Gifts by Members and Employees of the House of Representatives under New Ethics Rules of the 110th Congress* (Washington, D.C.: Library of Congress, Congressional Research Service, 2008); Senate Select Committee on Ethics' Regulations and Guidelines for Privately-Sponsored Travel.

109 Steven S. Smith, Jason M. Roberts, and Ryan J. Vander Wielen, *The American Congress* (New York: Cambridge University Press, 2009), 340.

110 *Congress and the Nation Vol. IX,* 902.

111 Chuck McCutcheon and Christina L. Lyons, eds., *CQ's Politics in America 2010* (Washington, D.C.: Congressional Quarterly, 2009) 1142–1143.

SELECTED BIBLIOGRAPHY

The Almanac of the Unelected: Staff of the U.S. Congress. Washington, D.C.: Almanac of the Unelected, 1988.

Baker, Richard A. *The Senate of the United States: A Bicentennial History.* Malabar, Fla.: Krieger, 1988.

Baughman, John. *Common Ground: Committee Politics in the U.S. House of Representatives.* Stanford, Calif.: Stanford University Press, 2006.

Birnbaum, Jeffrey H., and Alan S. Murray. *Showdown at Gucci Gulch: Lawmakers, Lobbyists, and the Unlikely Triumph of Tax Reform.* New York: Vintage, 1987.

Bisnow, Mark. *In the Shadow of the Dome: Chronicles of a Capitol Hill Aide.* New York: Morrow, 1990.

Byrd, Robert C. *The Senate, 1789–1989: Addresses on the History of the United States Senate.* 2 vols. Washington, D.C.: Government Printing Office, 1988.

Congressional Management Foundation. *Working in Congress: The Staff Perspective.* Washington, D.C.: Congressional Management Foundation, 1995.

Cooper, Joseph, and G. Calvin Mackenzie. *The House at Work.* Austin: University of Texas Press, 1981.

Cummings, Frank. *Capitol Hill Manual.* 2nd ed. Washington, D.C.: Bureau of National Affairs, 1984.

Davidson, Roger H., Walter J. Oleszek, and Frances E. Lee. *Congress and Its Members.* 13th ed. Washington, D.C.: CQ Press, 2011.

Deering, Christopher J., and Steven S. Smith. *Committees in Congress.* 3rd ed. Washington, D.C.: CQ Press, 1997.

Dodd, Lawrence C., and Bruce I. Oppenheimer. *Congress Reconsidered.* Washington, D.C.: CQ Press, 2009.

Fenno, Richard F., Jr. *The Emergence of a Senate Leader: Pete Domenici and the Reagan Budget.* Washington, D.C.: CQ Press, 1991.

———. *The Making of a Senator: Dan Quayle.* Washington, D.C.: CQ Press, 1989.

———. *The Presidential Odyssey of John Glenn.* Washington, D.C.: CQ Press, 1990.

Fox, Harrison W., Jr., and Susan W. Hammond. *Congressional Staffs: The Invisible Force in American Lawmaking.* New York: Free Press, 1977.

Jones, Rochelle, and Peter Woll. *The Private World of Congress.* New York: Free Press, 1979.

Kofmehl, Kenneth. *Professional Staffs of Congress.* 3rd ed. West Lafayette, Ind.: Purdue University Press, 1977.

Leal, David L., and Frederick M. Hess. "Who Chooses Experience? Examining the Use of Veteran Staff by House Freshmen." *Polity* 36, no. 4 (July 2004): 651–664.

Malbin, Michael J. "Delegation, Deliberation, and the New Role of Congressional Staff." In Thomas E. Mann and Norman J. Ornstein, eds., *The New Congress.* Washington, D.C.: American Enterprise Institute, 1981.

———. *Unelected Representatives: Congressional Staff and the Future of Representative Government.* New York: Basic Books, 1980.

Mann, Thomas E., and Norman J. Ornstein. *The Broken Branch: How Congress Is Failing America and How to Get It Back on Track.* New York: Oxford University Press, 2008.

Miller, James A. *Running in Place: Inside the Senate.* New York: Simon and Schuster, 1986.

Morrow, William L. *Congressional Committees.* New York: Scribner, 1969.

Nelson, Garrison, and Charles Haines Stewart. *Committees in the U.S. Congress 1993–2010.* Washington, D.C.: CQ Press, 2011.

Ornstein, Norman J., Thomas E. Mann, and Michael J. Malbin. *Vital Statistics on Congress 2008.* Washington, D.C.: Brookings Institution, 2008.

———. *Vital Statistics on Congress 2012.* Washington, D.C.: Brookings Institution, forthcoming.

Price, David E. *The Congressional Experience.* 3rd ed. Boulder, Colo.: Westview Press, 2004.

Redman, Eric. *The Dance of Legislation.* Seattle: University of Washington Press, 2001.

Reid, T. R. *Congressional Odyssey: The Saga of a Senate Bill.* New York: Freeman, 1980.

Ritchie, Donald A. *The U.S. Congress: A Very Short Introduction.* New York: Oxford University Press, 2010.

Setting Course: A Congressional Management Guide. 7th ed. Washington, D.C.: Congressional Management Foundation, 2000.

Smith, Steven S., Jason M. Roberts, and Ryan J. Vander Wielen. *The American Congress.* New York: Cambridge University Press, 2009.

Waxman, Henry. *The Waxman Report: How Congress Really Works.* New York: Hachette Book Group, 2009.

★ REFERENCE MATERIALS

HOW A BILL BECOMES A LAW

This graphic shows the most typical way in which proposed legislation is enacted into law. There are more complicated, as well as simpler, routes, and most bills never become law. The process is illustrated with two hypothetical bills, House bill No. 1 (HR 1) and Senate bill No. 2 (S 2). Bills must be passed by both houses in identical form before they can be sent to the president. The path of HR 1 is traced by a gray line, that of S 2 by a black line. In practice, most bills begin as similar proposals in both Houses.

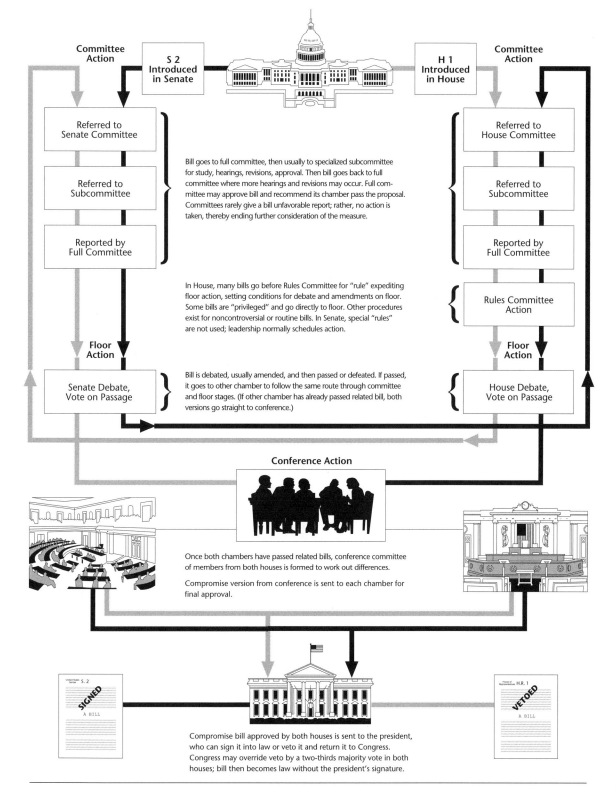

Committee Action

S 2 Introduced in Senate

Referred to Senate Committee

Referred to Subcommittee

Reported by Full Committee

Bill goes to full committee, then usually to specialized subcommittee for study, hearings, revisions, approval. Then bill goes back to full committee where more hearings and revisions may occur. Full committee may approve bill and recommend its chamber pass the proposal. Committees rarely give a bill unfavorable report; rather, no action is taken, thereby ending further consideration of the measure.

In House, many bills go before Rules Committee for "rule" expediting floor action, setting conditions for debate and amendments on floor. Some bills are "privileged" and go directly to floor. Other procedures exist for noncontroversial or routine bills. In Senate, special "rules" are not used; leadership normally schedules action.

Floor Action

Senate Debate, Vote on Passage

Bill is debated, usually amended, and then passed or defeated. If passed, it goes to other chamber to follow the same route through committee and floor stages. (If other chamber has already passed related bill, both versions go straight to conference.)

Committee Action

H 1 Introduced in House

Referred to House Committee

Referred to Subcommittee

Reported by Full Committee

Rules Committee Action

Floor Action

House Debate, Vote on Passage

Conference Action

Once both chambers have passed related bills, conference committee of members from both houses is formed to work out differences.

Compromise version from conference is sent to each chamber for final approval.

United States Senate S. 2 — SIGNED — A BILL

House of Representatives H.R. 1 — VETOED — A BILL

Compromise bill approved by both houses is sent to the president, who can sign it into law or veto it and return it to Congress. Congress may override veto by a two-thirds majority vote in both houses; bill then becomes law without the president's signature.

POLITICAL PARTY AFFILIATIONS IN CONGRESS AND THE PRESIDENCY, 1789–2011

(Affiliations are as of the beginning of the Congress.)

Year	Congress	House Majority party	House Principal minority party	Senate Majority party	Senate Principal minority party	President
1789–1791	1st	AD-38	Op-26	AD-17	Op-9	F (Washington)
1791–1793	2nd	F-37	DR-33	F-16	DR-13	F (Washington)
1793–1795	3rd	DR-57	F-48	F-17	DR-13	F (Washington)
1795–1797	4th	F-54	DR-52	F-19	DR-13	F (Washington)
1797–1799	5th	F-58	DR-48	F-20	DR-12	F (J. Adams)
1799–1801	6th	F-64	DR-42	F-19	DR-13	F (J. Adams)
1801–1803	7th	DR-69	F-36	DR-18	F-13	DR (Jefferson)
1803–1805	8th	DR-102	F-39	DR-25	F-9	DR (Jefferson)
1805–1807	9th	DR-116	F-25	DR-27	F-7	DR (Jefferson)
1807–1809	10th	DR-118	F-24	DR-28	F-6	DR (Jefferson)
1809–1811	11th	DR-94	F-48	DR-28	F-6	DR (Madison)
1811–1813	12th	DR-108	F-36	DR-30	F-6	DR (Madison)
1813–1815	13th	DR-112	F-68	DR-27	F-9	DR (Madison)
1815–1817	14th	DR-117	F-65	DR-25	F-11	DR (Madison)
1817–1819	15th	DR-141	F-42	DR-34	F-10	DR (Monroe)
1819–1821	16th	DR-156	F-27	DR-35	F-7	DR (Monroe)
1821–1823	17th	DR-158	F-25	DR-44	F-4	DR (Monroe)
1823–1825	18th	DR-187	F-26	DR-44	F-4	DR (Monroe)
1825–1827	19th	AD-105	J-97	AD-26	J-20	DR (J. Q. Adams)
1827–1829	20th	J-119	AD-94	J-28	AD-20	DR (J. Q. Adams)
1829–1831	21st	D-139	NR-74	D-26	NR-22	DR (Jackson)
1831–1833	22nd	D-141	NR-58	D-25	NR-21	D (Jackson)
1833–1835	23rd	D-147	AM-53	D-20	NR-20	D (Jackson)
1835–1837	24th	D-145	W-98	D-27	W-25	D (Jackson)
1837–1839	25th	D-108	W-107	D-30	W-18	D (Van Buren)
1839–1841	26th	D-124	W-118	D-28	W-22	D (Van Buren)
1841–1843	27th	W-133	D-102	W-28	D-22	W (W. H. Harrison); W (Tyler)
1843–1845	28th	D-142	W-79	W-28	D-25	W (Tyler)
1845–1847	29th	D-143	W-77	D-31	W-25	D (Polk)
1847–1849	30th	W-115	D-108	D-36	W-21	D (Polk)
1849–1851	31st	D-112	W-109	D-35	W-25	W (Taylor); W (Fillmore)
1851–1853	32nd	D-140	W-88	D-35	W-24	W (Fillmore)
1853–1855	33rd	D-159	W-71	D-38	W-22	D (Pierce)
1855–1857	34th	R-108	D-83	D-40	R-15	D (Pierce)
1857–1859	35th	D-118	R-92	D-36	R-20	D (Buchanan)
1859–1861	36th	R-114	D-92	D-36	R-26	D (Buchanan)
1861–1863	37th	R-105	D-43	R-31	D-10	R (Lincoln)
1863–1865	38th	R-102	D-75	R-36	D-9	R (Lincoln)
1865–1867	39th	U-149	D-42	U-42	D-10	R (Lincoln); R (A. Johnson)
1867–1869	40th	R-143	D-49	R-42	D-11	R (A. Johnson)
1869–1871	41st	R-149	D-63	R-56	D-11	R (Grant)
1871–1873	42nd	R-134	D-104	R-52	D-17	R (Grant)
1873–1875	43rd	R-194	D-92	R-49	D-19	R (Grant)
1875–1877	44th	D-169	R-109	R-45	D-29	R (Grant)
1877–1879	45th	D-153	R-140	R-39	D-36	R (Hayes)
1879–1881	46th	D-149	R-130	D-42	R-33	R (Hayes)
1881–1883	47th	R-147	D-135	R-37	D-37	R (Garfield); R (Arthur)
1883–1885	48th	D-197	R-118	R-38	D-36	R (Arthur)
1885–1887	49th	D-183	R-140	R-43	D-34	D (Cleveland)

		House		Senate		
Year	Congress	Majority party	Principal minority party	Majority party	Principal minority party	President
1887–1889	50th	D-169	R-152	R-39	D-37	D (Cleveland)
1889–1891	51st	R-166	D-159	R-39	D-37	R (B. Harrison)
1891–1893	52nd	D-235	R-88	R-47	D-39	R (B. Harrison)
1893–1895	53rd	D-218	R-127	D-44	R-38	D (Cleveland)
1895–1897	54th	R-244	D-105	R-43	D-39	D (Cleveland)
1897–1899	55th	R-204	D-113	R-47	D-34	R (McKinley)
1899–1901	56th	R-185	D-163	R-53	D-26	R (McKinley)
1901–1903	57th	R-197	D-151	R-55	D-31	R (McKinley); R (T. Roosevelt)
1903–1905	58th	R-208	D-178	R-57	D-33	R (T. Roosevelt)
1905–1907	59th	R-250	D-136	R-57	D-33	R (T. Roosevelt)
1907–1909	60th	R-222	D-164	R-61	D-31	R (T. Roosevelt)
1909–1911	61st	R-219	D-172	R-61	D-32	R (Taft)
1911–1913	62nd	D-228	R-161	R-51	D-41	R (Taft)
1913–1915	63rd	D-291	R-127	D-51	R-44	D (Wilson)
1915–1917	64th	D-230	R-196	D-56	R-40	D (Wilson)
1917–1919	65th	D-216	R-210	D-53	R-42	D (Wilson)
1919–1921	66th	R-240	D-190	R-49	D-47	D (Wilson)
1921–1923	67th	R-301	D-131	R-59	D-37	R (Harding)
1923–1925	68th	R-225	D-205	R-51	D-43	R (Coolidge)
1925–1927	69th	R-247	D-183	R-56	D-39	R (Coolidge)
1927–1929	70th	R-237	D-195	R-49	D-46	R (Coolidge)
1929–1931	71st	R-267	D-167	R-56	D-39	R (Hoover)
1931–1933	72nd	D-220	R-214	R-48	D-47	R (Hoover)
1933–1935	73rd	D-310	R-117	D-60	R-35	D (F. D. Roosevelt)
1935–1937	74th	D-319	R-103	D-69	R-25	D (F. D. Roosevelt)
1937–1939	75th	D-331	R-89	D-76	R-16	D (F. D. Roosevelt)
1939–1941	76th	D-261	R-164	D-69	R-23	D (F. D. Roosevelt)
1941–1943	77th	D-268	R-162	D-66	R-28	D (F. D. Roosevelt)
1943–1945	78th	D-218	R-208	D-58	R-37	D (F. D. Roosevelt)
1945–1947	79th	D-242	R-190	D-56	R-38	D (F. D. Roosevelt); D (Truman)
1947–1949	80th	R-245	D-188	R-51	D-45	D (Truman)
1949–1951	81st	D-263	R-171	D-54	R-42	D (Truman)
1951–1953	82nd	D-234	R-199	D-49	R-47	D (Truman)
1953–1955	83rd	R-221	D-211	R-48	D-47	R (Eisenhower)
1955–1957	84th	D-232	R-203	D-48	R-47	R (Eisenhower)
1957–1959	85th	D-233	R-200	D-49	R-47	R (Eisenhower)
1959–1961	86th	D-283	R-153	D-64	R-34	R (Eisenhower)
1961–1963	87th	D-263	R-174	D-65	R-35	D (Kennedy)
1963–1965	88th	D-258	R-177	D-67	R-33	D (Kennedy); D (L. B. Johnson)
1965–1967	89th	D-295	R-140	D-68	R-32	D (L. B. Johnson)
1967–1969	90th	D-247	R-187	D-64	R-36	D (L. B. Johnson)
1969–1971	91st	D-243	R-192	D-57	R-43	R (Nixon)
1971–1973	92nd	D-254	R-180	D-54	R-44	R (Nixon)
1973–1975	93rd	D-239	R-192	D-56	R-42	R (Nixon); R (Ford)
1975–1977	94th	D-291	R-144	D-60	R-37	R (Ford)
1977–1979	95th	D-292	R-143	D-61	R-38	D (Carter)
1979–1981	96th	D-276	R-157	D-58	R-41	D (Carter)
1981–1983	97th	D-243	R-192	R-53	D-46	R (Reagan)
1983–1985	98th	D-269	R-165	R-54	D-46	R (Reagan)
1985–1987	99th	D-252	R-182	R-53	D-47	R (Reagan)
1987–1989	100th	D-258	R-177	D-55	R-45	R (Reagan)
1989–1991	101st	D-259	R-174	D-55	R-45	R (G. H. W. Bush)
1991–1993	102nd	D-267	R-167	D-56	R-44	R (G. H. W. Bush)
1993–1995	103rd	D-258	R-176	D-57	R-43	D (Clinton)
1995–1997	104th	R-230	D-204	R-53	D-47	D (Clinton)
1997–1999	105th	R-227	D-207	R-55	D-45	D (Clinton)

Year	Congress	House		Senate		President
		Majority party	*Principal minority party*	*Majority party*	*Principal minority party*	
1999–2001	106th	R-222	D-211	R-55	D-45	D (Clinton)
2001–2003	107th	R-221	D-212	R-50	D-50	R (G. W. Bush)
2003–2005	108th	R-229	D-205	R-51	D-48	R (G. W. Bush)
2005–2007	109th	R-232	D-202	R-55	D-44	R (G. W. Bush)
2007–2009	110th	D-233	R-202	D-49	R-49	R (G. W. Bush)
2009–2011	111th	D-257	R-178	D-55	R-41	D (Obama)
2011–2013	112th	R-242	D-193	D-51	R-47	D (Obama)

NOTE: Figures are for the beginning of the first session of each Congress. Key to abbreviations: AD—Administration; AM—AntiMasonic; D—Democratic; DR—Democratic-Republican; F—Federalist; J—Jacksonian; NR—National Republican; Op—Opposition; R—Republican; U—Unionist; W—Whig.

SOURCES: U.S. Bureau of the Census, *Historical Statistics of the United States: Colonial Times to 1970* (Washington, D.C.: Government Printing Office, 1975); U.S. Congress, Joint Committee on Printing, *Official Congressional Directory* (Washington, D.C.: Government Printing Office, 1967–); and *CQ Weekly*, selected issues.

★ SPEAKERS OF THE HOUSE OF REPRESENTATIVES, 1789–2011

Congress		Speaker	Congress		Speaker
1st	(1789–1791)	Frederick A. C. Muhlenberg, Pa.	54th	(1895–1897)	Reed
2nd	(1791–1793)	Jonathan Trumbull, F-Conn.	55th	(1897–1899)	Reed
3rd	(1793–1795)	Muhlenberg	56th	(1899–1901)	David B. Henderson, R-Iowa
4th	(1795–1797)	Jonathan Dayton, F-N.J.	57th	(1901–1903)	Henderson
5th	(1797–1799)	Dayton	58th	(1903–1905)	Joseph G. Cannon, R-Ill.
6th	(1799–1801)	Theodore Sedgwick, F-Mass.	59th	(1905–1907)	Cannon
7th	(1801–1803)	Nathaniel Macon, D-N.C.	60th	(1907–1909)	Cannon
8th	(1803–1805)	Macon	61st	(1909–1911)	Cannon
9th	(1805–1807)	Macon	62nd	(1911–1913)	James B. "Champ" Clark, D-Mo.
10th	(1807–1809)	Joseph B. Varnum, Mass.	63rd	(1913–1915)	Clark
11th	(1809–1811)	Varnum	64th	(1915–1917)	Clark
12th	(1811–1813)	Henry Clay, R-Ky.	65th	(1917–1919)	Clark
13th	(1813–1814)	Clay	66th	(1919–1921)	Frederick H. Gillett, R-Mass.
	(1814–1815)	Langdon Cheves, D-S.C.	67th	(1921–1923)	Gillett
14th	(1815–1817)	Clay	68th	(1923–1925)	Gillett
15th	(1817–1819)	Clay	69th	(1925–1927)	Nicholas Longworth, R-Ohio
16th	(1819–1820)	Clay	70th	(1927–1929)	Longworth
	(1820–1821)	John W. Taylor, D-N.Y.	71st	(1929–1931)	Longworth
17th	(1821–1823)	Philip P. Barbour, D-Va.	72nd	(1931–1933)	John Nance Garner, D-Texas
18th	(1823–1825)	Clay	73rd	(1933–1934)	Henry T. Rainey, D-Ill.[a]
19th	(1825–1827)	Taylor	74th	(1935–1936)	Joseph W. Byrns, D-Tenn.
20th	(1827–1829)	Andrew Stevenson, D-Va.		(1936–1937)	William B. Bankhead, D-Ala.
21st	(1829–1831)	Stevenson	75th	(1937–1939)	Bankhead
22nd	(1831–1833)	Stevenson	76th	(1939–1940)	Bankhead
23rd	(1833–1834)	Stevenson		(1940–1941)	Sam Rayburn, D-Texas
	(1834–1835)	John Bell, W-Tenn.	77th	(1941–1943)	Rayburn
24th	(1835–1837)	James K. Polk, D-Tenn.	78th	(1943–1945)	Rayburn
25th	(1837–1839)	Polk	79th	(1945–1947)	Rayburn
26th	(1839–1841)	Robert M. T. Hunter, D-Va.	80th	(1947–1949)	Joseph W. Martin Jr., R-Mass.
27th	(1841–1843)	John White, W-Ky.	81st	(1949–1951)	Rayburn
28th	(1843–1845)	John W. Jones, D-Va.	82nd	(1951–1953)	Rayburn
29th	(1845–1847)	John W. Davis, D-Ind.	83rd	(1953–1955)	Martin
30th	(1847–1849)	Robert C. Winthrop, W-Mass.	84th	(1955–1957)	Rayburn
31st	(1849–1851)	Howell Cobb, D-Ga.	85th	(1957–1959)	Rayburn
32nd	(1851–1853)	Linn Boyd, D-Ky.	86th	(1959–1961)	Rayburn
33rd	(1853–1855)	Boyd	87th	(1961)	Rayburn
34th	(1855–1857)	Nathaniel P. Banks, R-Mass.		(1962–1963)	John W. McCormack, D-Mass.
35th	(1857–1859)	James L. Orr, D-S.C.	88th	(1963–1965)	McCormack
36th	(1859–1861)	William Pennington, R-N.J.	89th	(1965–1967)	McCormack
37th	(1861–1863)	Galusha A. Grow, R-Pa.	90th	(1967–1969)	McCormack
38th	(1863–1865)	Schuyler Colfax, R-Ind.	91st	(1969–1971)	McCormack
39th	(1865–1867)	Colfax	92nd	(1971–1973)	Carl Albert, D-Okla.
40th	(1867–1869)	Colfax	93rd	(1973–1975)	Albert
	(1869)	Theodore M. Pomeroy, R-N.Y.	94th	(1975–1977)	Albert
41st	(1869–1871)	James G. Blaine, R-Maine	95th	(1977–1979)	Thomas P. O'Neill Jr., D-Mass.
42nd	(1871–1873)	Blaine	96th	(1979–1981)	O'Neill
43rd	(1873–1875)	Blaine	97th	(1981–1983)	O'Neill
44th	(1875–1876)	Michael C. Kerr, D-Ind.	98th	(1983–1985)	O'Neill
	(1876–1877)	Samuel J. Randall, D-Pa.	99th	(1985–1987)	O'Neill
45th	(1877–1879)	Randall	100th	(1987–1989)	Jim Wright, D-Texas
46th	(1879–1881)	Randall	101st	(1989)	Wright;[b]
47th	(1881–1883)	Joseph Warren Keifer, R-Ohio		(1989–1991)	Thomas S. Foley, D-Wash.
48th	(1883–1885)	John G. Carlisle, D-Ky.	102nd	(1991–1993)	Foley
49th	(1885–1887)	Carlisle	103rd	(1993–1995)	Foley
50th	(1887–1889)	Carlisle	104th	(1995–1997)	Newt Gingrich, R-Ga.
51st	(1889–1891)	Thomas Brackett Reed, R-Maine	105th	(1997–1999)	Gingrich
52nd	(1891–1893)	Charles F. Crisp, D-Ga.	106th	(1999–2001)	J. Dennis Hastert, R-Ill.
53rd	(1893–1895)	Crisp			

Congress		Speaker	Congress		Speaker
107th	(2001–2003)	Hastert	110th	(2007–2009)	Nancy Pelosi, D-Calif.
108th	(2003–2005)	Hastert	111th	(2009–2011)	Pelosi
109th	(2005–2007)	Hastert	112th	(2011–)	John A. Boehner, R-Ohio

NOTES: Key to abbreviations: D—Democrat; F—Federalist; R—Republican; W—Whig.
  a. Rainey died in 1934 but was not replaced until the next Congress.
  b. Wright resigned and was succeeded by Foley on June 6, 1989.

SOURCES: *CQ Weekly,* selected issues.

★

HOUSE FLOOR LEADERS, 1899–2011

Congress		Majority	Minority
56th	(1899–1901)	Sereno E. Payne, R-N.Y.	James D. Richardson, D-Tenn.
57th	(1901–1903)	Payne	Richardson
58th	(1903–1905)	Payne	John Sharp Williams, D-Miss.
59th	(1905–1907)	Payne	Williams
60th	(1907–1909)	Payne	Williams; Champ Clark, D-Mo.[a]
61st	(1909–1911)	Payne	Clark
62nd	(1911–1913)	Oscar W. Underwood, D-Ala.	James R. Mann, R-Ill.
63rd	(1913–1915)	Underwood	Mann
64th	(1915–1917)	Claude Kitchin, D-N.C.	Mann
65th	(1917–1919)	Kitchin	Mann
66th	(1919–1921)	Franklin W. Mondell, R-Wyo.	Clark
67th	(1921–1923)	Mondell	Claude Kitchin, D-N.C.
68th	(1923–1925)	Nicholas Longworth, R-Ohio	Finis J. Garrett, D-Tenn.
69th	(1925–1927)	John Q. Tilson, R-Conn.	Garrett
70th	(1927–1929)	Tilson	Garrett
71st	(1929–1931)	Tilson	John N. Garner, D-Texas
72nd	(1931–1933)	Henry T. Rainey, D-Ill.	Bertrand H. Snell, R-N.Y.
73rd	(1933–1935)	Joseph W. Byrns, D-Tenn.	Snell
74th	(1935–1937)	William B. Bankhead, D-Ala.[b]	Snell
75th	(1937–1939)	Sam Rayburn, D-Texas	Snell
76th	(1939–1941)	Rayburn; John W. McCormack, D-Mass.[c]	Joseph W. Martin Jr., R-Mass.
77th	(1941–1943)	McCormack	Martin
78th	(1943–1945)	McCormack	Martin
79th	(1945–1947)	McCormack	Martin
80th	(1947–1949)	Charles A. Halleck, R-Ind.	Sam Rayburn, D-Texas
81st	(1949–1951)	McCormack	Martin
82nd	(1951–1953)	McCormack	Martin
83rd	(1953–1955)	Halleck	Rayburn
84th	(1955–1957)	McCormack	Martin
85th	(1957–1959)	McCormack	Martin
86th	(1959–1961)	McCormack	Charles A. Halleck, R-Ind.
87th	(1961–1963)	McCormack; Carl Albert, D-Okla.[d]	Halleck
88th	(1963–1965)	Albert	Halleck
89th	(1965–1967)	Albert	Gerald R. Ford, R-Mich.
90th	(1967–1969)	Albert	Ford
91st	(1969–1971)	Albert	Ford
92nd	(1971–1973)	Hale Boggs, D-La.	Ford
93rd	(1973–1975)	Thomas P. O'Neill Jr., D-Mass.	Ford; John J. Rhodes, R-Ariz.[e]
94th	(1975–1977)	O'Neill	Rhodes
95th	(1977–1979)	Jim Wright, D-Texas	Rhodes
96th	(1979–1981)	Wright	Rhodes
97th	(1981–1983)	Wright	Robert H. Michel, R Ill.
98th	(1983–1985)	Wright	Michel
99th	(1985–1987)	Wright	Michel
100th	(1987–1989)	Thomas S. Foley, D-Wash.	Michel
101st	(1989–1991)	Foley/Richard A. Gephardt, D-Mo.[f]	Michel
102nd	(1991–1993)	Gephardt	Michel
103rd	(1993–1995)	Gephardt	Michel
104th	(1995–1997)	Dick Armey, R-Texas	Richard A. Gephardt, D-Mo.
105th	(1997–1999)	Armey	Gephardt

Congress		Majority	Minority
106th	(1999–2001)	Armey	Gephardt
107th	(2001–2003)	Armey	Gephardt
108th	(2003–2005)	Tom DeLay, R-Texas	Nancy Pelosi, D-Calif.
109th	(2005–2007)	DeLay; Roy Blunt, R-Mo;[g] John A. Boehner, R-Ohio[h]	Pelosi
110th	(2007–2009)	Steny H. Hoyer, D-Md.	John A. Boehner, R-Ohio
111th	(2009–2011)	Hoyer	Boehner
112th	(2011–)	Eric Cantor, R-Va.	Pelosi

NOTES:

a. Clark became minority leader in 1908.

b. Bankhead became Speaker of the House on June 4, 1936. The post of majority leader remained vacant until the next Congress.

c. McCormack became majority leader on Sept. 26, 1940, filling the vacancy caused by the elevation of Rayburn to the post of Speaker of the House on September 16, 1940.

d. Albert became majority leader on January 10, 1962, filling the vacancy caused by the elevation of McCormack to the post of Speaker of the House on January 10, 1962.

e. Rhodes became minority leader on December 7, 1973, filling the vacancy caused by the resignation of Ford on December 6, 1973, to become vice president.

f. Gephardt became majority leader on June 14, 1989, filling the vacancy created when Foley succeeded Wright as Speaker of the House on June 6, 1989.

g. Blunt became interim majority leader on September 29, 2005, filling the vacancy created by the resignation of DeLay following his indictment in Texas.

h. Boehner became majority leader on February 2, 2006.

SOURCES: Randall B. Ripley, *Party Leaders in the House of Representatives* (Washington, D.C.: Brookings Institution, 1967); *Biographical Directory of the American Congress, 1774–1996* (Alexandria, Va.: CQ Staff Directories, 1997); and *CQ Weekly,* selected issues.

★

SENATE FLOOR LEADERS, 1911–2011

Congress		Majority	Minority
62nd	(1911–1913)	Shelby M. Cullom, R-Ill.	Thomas S. Martin, D-Va.
63rd	(1913–1915)	John W. Kern, D-Ind.	Jacob H. Gallinger, R-N.H.
64th	(1915–1917)	Kern	Gallinger
65th	(1917–1919)	Thomas S. Martin, D-Va.	Gallinger; Henry Cabot Lodge, R-Mass.[a]
66th	(1919–1921)	Henry Cabot Lodge, R-Mass.	Martin; Oscar W. Underwood, D-Ala.[b]
67th	(1921–1923)	Lodge	Underwood
68th	(1923–1925)	Lodge; Charles Curtis, R-Kan.[c]	Joseph T. Robinson, D-Ark.
69th	(1925–1927)	Curtis	Robinson
70th	(1927–1929)	Curtis	Robinson
71st	(1929–1931)	James E. Watson, R-Ind.	Robinson
72nd	(1931–1933)	Watson	Robinson
73rd	(1933–1935)	Joseph T. Robinson, D-Ark.	Charles L. McNary, R-Ore.
74th	(1935–1937)	Robinson	McNary
75th	(1937–1939)	Robinson; Alben W. Barkley, D-Ky.[d]	McNary
76th	(1939–1941)	Barkley	McNary
77th	(1941–1943)	Barkley	McNary
78th	(1943–1945)	Barkley	McNary
79th	(1945–1947)	Barkley	Wallace H. White Jr., R-Maine
80th	(1947–1949)	Wallace H. White Jr., R-Maine	Alben W. Barkley, D-Ky.
81st	(1949–1951)	Scott W. Lucas, D-Ill.	Kenneth S. Wherry, R-Neb.
82nd	(1951–1953)	Ernest W. McFarland, D-Ariz.	Wherry; Styles Bridges, R-N.H.[e]
83rd	(1953–1955)	Robert A. Taft, R-Ohio; William F. Knowland, R-Calif.[f]	Lyndon B. Johnson, D-Texas
84th	(1955–1957)	Lyndon B. Johnson, D-Texas	William F. Knowland, R-Calif.
85th	(1957–1959)	Johnson	Knowland
86th	(1959–1961)	Johnson	Everett McKinley Dirksen, R-Ill.
87th	(1961–1963)	Mike Mansfield, D-Mont.	Dirksen
88th	(1963–1965)	Mansfield	Dirksen
89th	(1965–1967)	Mansfield	Dirksen
90th	(1967–1969)	Mansfield	Dirksen
91st	(1969–1971)	Mansfield	Dirksen; Hugh Scott, R-Pa.[g]
92nd	(1971–1973)	Mansfield	Scott
93rd	(1973–1975)	Mansfield	Scott
94th	(1975–1977)	Mansfield	Scott
95th	(1977–1979)	Robert C. Byrd, D-W.Va.	Howard H. Baker Jr., R-Tenn.
96th	(1979–1981)	Byrd	Baker
97th	(1981–1983)	Howard H. Baker Jr., R-Tenn.	Robert C. Byrd, D-W.Va.
98th	(1983–1985)	Baker	Byrd
99th	(1985–1987)	Bob Dole, R-Kan.	Byrd
100th	(1987–1989)	Byrd	Bob Dole, R-Kan.
101st	(1989–1991)	George J. Mitchell, D-Maine	Dole
102nd	(1991–1993)	Mitchell	Dole
103rd	(1993–1995)	Mitchell	Dole
104th	(1995–1997)	Bob Dole, R-Kan.; Trent Lott, R-Miss.[h]	Tom Daschle, D-S.D.
105th	(1997–1999)	Lott	Daschle
106th	(1999–2001)	Lott	Daschle
107th	(2001–2003)	Tom Daschle, D-S.D.; Trent Lott, R-Miss.; Tom Daschle, D-S.D.	Trent Lott, R-Miss.;[i] Tom Daschle, D-S.D.;[j] Trent Lott, R-Miss.[k]
108th	(2003–2005)	Bill Frist, R-Tenn.	Tom Daschle, D-S.D.
109th	(2005–2007)	Frist	Harry Reid, D-Nev.

Congress		Majority	Minority
110th	(2007– 2009)	Harry Reid, D-Nev.	Mitch McConnell, R-Ky.
111th	(2009–2011)	Reid	McConnell
112th	(2011–)	Reid	McConnell

NOTES:

a. Lodge became minority leader on August 24, 1918, filling the vacancy caused by the death of Gallinger on August 17, 1918.

b. Underwood became minority leader on April 27, 1920, filling the vacancy caused by the death of Martin on November 12, 1919. Gilbert M. Hitchcock, D-Neb., served as acting minority leader in the interim.

c. Curtis became majority leader on November 28, 1924, filling the vacancy caused by the death of Lodge on November 9, 1924.

d. Barkley became majority leader on July 22, 1937, filling the vacancy caused by the death of Robinson on July 14, 1937.

e. Bridges became minority leader on January 8, 1952, filling the vacancy caused by the death of Wherry on November 29, 1951.

f. Knowland became majority leader on August 4, 1953, filling the vacancy caused by the death of Taft on July 31, 1953. Taft's vacant seat was filled by Democrat Thomas Burke on November 10, 1953. The division of the Senate changed to 48 Democrats, 47 Republicans, and 1 Independent, thus giving control of the Senate to the Democrats. However, Knowland remained as majority leader until the end of the 83rd Congress.

g. Scott became minority leader on September 24, 1969, filling the vacancy caused by the death of Dirksen on September 7, 1969.

h. Lott became majority leader on June 12, 1996, following the resignation of Dole on June 11, 1996.

i. The Senate began the 107th Congress evenly split, 50–50. As vice president, Democrat Al Gore held the constitutional authority to break ties in the Senate, giving Democrats the majority. Daschle became majority leader on January 3, 2001.

j. On January 20, 2001, Republicans George W. Bush and Dick Cheney were inaugurated as president and vice president, respectively. This gave Republicans the majority in the Senate because of Cheney's tie-breaking power. Lott became majority leader.

k. Daschle became majority leader on June 6, 2001, after Republican Sen. James M. Jeffords of Vermont declared himself an Independent. The division of the Senate changed to 50 Democrats, 49 Republicans, and 1 Independent, thus giving control of the Senate to the Democrats.

SOURCES: *Biographical Directory of the American Congress, 1774–1996* (Alexandria, Va.: CQ Staff Directories, 1997); *Majority and Minority Leaders of the Senate,* comp. Floyd M. Riddick, 94th Cong., 1st sess., 1975, S. Doc. 66; and *CQ Weekly,* selected issues.

RECORDED VOTES IN THE HOUSE AND SENATE, 1947–2011

Year	House	Senate	Year	House	Senate
1947	84	138	1980	604	546
1948	75	110	1981	353	497
1949	121	226	1982	459	469
1950	154	229	1983	498	381
1951	109	202	1984	408	292
1952	72	129	1985	439	381
1953	71	89	1986	451	359
1954	76	181	1987	488	420
1955	73	88	1988	451	379
1956	74	136	1989	368	312
1957	100	111	1990	511	326
1958	93	202	1991	428	280
1959	87	215	1992	473	270
1960	93	207	1993	597	395
1961	116	207	1994	497	329
1962	124	227	1995	867	613
1963	119	229	1996	454	306
1964	113	312	1997	633	298
1965	201	259	1998	533	314
1966	193	238	1999	609	374
1967	245	315	2000	600	298
1968	233	280[a]	2001	507	380
1969	177	245	2002	483	253
1970	266	422	2003	675	459
1971	320	423	2004	543	216
1972	329	532	2005	671	366
1973	541	594	2006	543	279
1974	537	544	2007	1186	436
1975	612	611	2008	690	210
1976	661	700	2009	991	397
1977	706	636	2010	664	299
1978	834	520	2011	916	227
1979	672	509			

NOTES: Totals do not include quorum calls. a. This figure does not include one yea-or-nay vote that was ruled invalid for lack of a quorum.

SOURCES: *CQ Almanac,* selected volumes (Washington, D.C.: Congressional Quarterly, selected years); Congressional Record's *Résumés of Congressional Activity*; Norman J. Ornstein, Thomas E. Mann, and Michael J. Malbin, *Vital Statistics on Congress, 1997–1998* (Washington, D.C.: Congressional Quarterly, 1998), 166; and Library of Congress, THOMAS (http://thomas.loc.gov/home/rollcallvotes.html).

ATTEMPTED AND SUCCESSFUL CLOTURE VOTES, 1919–2011

The filibuster, recognized by the public primarily as nonstop speech, has been an enshrined Senate tradition throughout the chamber's history but became a focus of increasing criticism in the twentieth century as a device to thwart majority decisions. It was not until 1917 that the Senate adopted a rule, known as cloture, that allowed a majority—albeit a supermajority—to end a filibuster and bring a measure to a vote. The number of votes required to invoke cloture has varied over the years, standing at sixty in 2011 if there are no Senate vacancies. (The rules require a three-fifths majority of members to invoke cloture. The Senate has one hundred members.)

Congress		First session		Second session		Total	
		Attempted	Successful	Attempted	Successful	Attempted	Successful
66th	(1919–1921)	1	1	0	0	1	1
67th	(1921–1923)	1	0	1	0	2	0
68th	(1923–1925)	0	0	0	0	0	0
69th	(1925–1927)	0	0	2	1	2	1
70th	(1927–1929)	5	2	0	0	5	2
71st	(1929–1931)	0	0	0	0	0	0
72nd	(1931–1933)	0	0	0	0	0	0
73rd	(1933–1935)	1	0	0	0	1	0
74th	(1935–1937)	0	0	0	0	0	0
75th	(1937–1939)	0	0	2	0	2	0
76th	(1939–1941)	0	0	0	0	0	0
77th	(1941–1943)	0	0	1	0	1	0
78th	(1943–1945)	0	0	1	0	1	0
79th	(1945–1947)	0	0	4	0	4	0
80th	(1947–1949)	0	0	0	0	0	0
81st	(1949–1951)	0	0	2	0	2	0
82nd	(1951–1953)	0	0	0	0	0	0
83rd	(1953–1955)	0	0	1	0	1	0
84th	(1955–1957)	0	0	0	0	0	0
85th	(1957–1959)	0	0	0	0	0	0
86th	(1959–1961)	0	0	1	0	1	0
87th	(1961–1963)	1	0	3	1	4	1
88th	(1963–1965)	1	0	2	1	3	1
89th	(1965–1967)	2	1	5	0	7	1
90th	(1967–1969)	1	0	5	1	6	1
91st	(1969–1971)	2	0	4	0	6	0
92nd	(1971–1973)	10	2	10	2	20	4
93rd	(1973–1975)	10	2	21	7	31	9
94th	(1975–1977)	23	13	4	4	27	17
95th	(1977–1979)	5	1	8	2	13	3
96th	(1979–1981)	4	1	17	9	21	10
97th	(1981–1983)	7	2	20	7	27	9
98th	(1983–1985)	7	2	12	9	19	11
99th	(1985–1987)	9	1	14	9	23	10
100th	(1987–1989)	24	6	20	6	44	12
101st	(1989–1991)	9	6	15	5	24	11
102nd	(1991–1993)	20	9	28	14	48	23
103rd	(1993–1995)	20	4	22	10	42	14
104th	(1995–1997)	21	4	29	5	50	9
105th	(1997–1999)	24	7	29	11	53	18
106th	(1999–2001)	36	11	22	17	58	28
107th	(2001–2003)	22	11	39	22	61	33
108th	(2003–2005)	22	1	26	11	48	12
109th	(2005–2007)	21	14	33	20	54	34
110th	(2007–2009)	78	30	34	31	112	61
111th	(2009–2011)	45	35	46	28	91	63
112th	(2011–)	34	19	N/A	N/A	N/A	N/A

NOTE: The number of votes required to invoke cloture was changed March 7, 1975, from two-thirds of those present and voting to three-fifths of the total Senate membership, as Rule XXII of the standing rules of the Senate was amended.

SOURCES: United States Senate Virtual Reference Desk (www.senate.gov/reference/reference_index_subjects/Cloture_vrd.htm); *Congress and the Nation*, selected volumes (Washington, D.C.: CQ Press, selected years); *CQ Almanac*, selected volumes (Washington, D.C.: Congressional Quarterly, selected years); and Richard S. Beth, Library of Congress, Congressional Research Service.

CONGRESSIONAL INFORMATION ON THE INTERNET

A huge array of congressional information is available for free at Internet sites operated by the federal government, colleges and universities, and commercial firms (including the free version of pay services). The sites offer the full text of bills introduced in the House and Senate, voting records, campaign finance information, transcripts of selected congressional hearings, investigative reports, and much more.

THOMAS AND THE BIOGRAPHICAL DIRECTORY

The most important site for congressional information is **THOMAS** *(http://thomas.loc.gov)*, which is named for Thomas Jefferson and operated by the Library of Congress. THOMAS's highlight is its databases containing the full text of all bills introduced in Congress since 1989 (101st Congress), the full text of the *Congressional Record* since 1989, and the status and summary information for all bills introduced since 1973 (93rd Congress).

THOMAS also offers special links to bills that have received or are expected to receive floor action during the current week and newsworthy bills that are pending or that have recently been approved. House floor actions are updated every fifteen minutes. THOMAS has full text of most committee reports since 1995, an index of treaties since the 94th Congress, answers to frequently asked questions about accessing congressional information, publications titled *How Our Laws Are Made* and *Enactment of a Law*, and links to many other congressional websites *(http://thomas. loc.gov/links)*. Finally, THOMAS allows one to track the status of appropriations bills or find bill numbers and public law (PL) numbers, which can be hard to find for appropriations bills as they move through Congress before getting an actual number.

Another very useful site hosted by the Library of Congress at Congress.gov is the **Biographical Directory of the United States Congress, 1774–Present** *(http://bioguide.congress.gov)*. This page allows one to search for information about every member of Congress, both current and historical, by last name, first name, party (including a host of third parties), state, position, and year. Every member has a short biographical summary, and on the left of an individual biography one can access research collections that feature this individual as well as a bibliography of related sources, if there are such.

HOUSE OF REPRESENTATIVES

The **U.S. House of Representatives site** *(www.house.gov)* offers the schedule of bills, resolutions, and other legislative issues the House is to consider in the current week. It also has updates about current proceedings on the House floor and a list of the next day's meeting of House committees. Other highlights include a database that helps users identify their representative, a directory of House members and committees, the House ethics manual, a calendar of congressional primary dates and candidate-filing deadlines for ballot access, the full text of all amendments to the U.S. Constitution that have been ratified and those that have been proposed but not ratified, and information about Washington, D.C., for visitors. House.gov hosts the websites maintained by House members, where one can find a range of information including individual biographies, district maps, copies of press releases, Dear Colleague letters, details of draft legislation, and editorials written. It also hosts committee websites, which often feature press releases and reports, hearings schedules, copies of witness testimony, and in some cases video of committee proceedings. The House also hosts the **Black Americans in Congress** *(http://baic.house.gov)* and **Women in Congress** *(http://womenincongress.house.gov)* websites.

Another key House site is the **Office of the Clerk On-line Information Center** *(http://clerk.house.gov)*, which has records of all roll-call votes taken since 1990 (101st Congress). The votes are recorded by bill. The site also has lists of committee assignments, a telephone directory for members and committees, mailing label templates for members and committees, rules of the current Congress, election statistics from 1920 to the present, biographies of Speakers of the House, biographies of women who have served since 1917, information on public disclosure, and a virtual tour of the House chamber.

The site operated by the **House Committee on Rules** *(www. rules.house.gov)* has posted dozens of Congressional Research Service reports about the legislative process. Some of the available titles include *Legislative Research in Congressional Offices: A Primer; Hearings in the House of Representatives: A Guide for Preparation and Conduct; How Measures Are Brought to the House Floor: A Brief Introduction; House and Senate Rules of Procedure: A Comparison;* and *Presidential Vetoes 1789–1996: A Summary Overview.*

The office of the **Law Revision Counsel** operates a site *(http://uscode.house.gov)* that has a searchable version of the U.S. Code, which contains the text of public laws enacted by Congress, and a tutorial for searching the Code.

SENATE

The Senate is not as active in the Internet world as the House. The main **Senate website** *(www.senate.gov)* has records of all roll-call votes taken since 1989 (101st Congress, arranged by bill), brief descriptions of all bills and joint resolutions introduced in the Senate during the past week, and a calendar of upcoming committee hearings. The site also provides the standing rules of the Senate, a directory of senators and their committee assignments, lists of nominations that the president has submitted to the Senate for approval, and a virtual tour of the Senate. As with the House website, Senate.gov hosts websites operated by both senators and committees. Senate.gov has a particularly rich historical section, accessible at *www.senate.gov/ history* (the page will redirect to a landing page) with a wealth of essays, pictures, and statistics.

GENERAL REFERENCE

Information about the membership, jurisdiction, and rules of each congressional committee is available at the new U.S. Government Printing Office site, **Federal Digital System** *(www.gpo. gov/fdsys)*. It has transcripts of selected congressional hearings, the full text of selected House and Senate reports, and the House and Senate rules manuals.

The **U.S. Government Accountability Office** (GAO, which changed its name in 2004 from General Accounting Office), the investigative arm of Congress, operates a site *(www.gao.gov)* that provides the full text of its reports from October 1995 to the present as well as summaries of legal decisions. The reports cover a wide range of topics: animal welfare, aviation safety, combating terrorism, counternarcotics efforts in Mexico, defense contracting, electronic warfare, the Federal Reserve system, food assistance programs, hurricane preparedness, health insurance, illegal immigrants, information technology, long-term care, mass transit, Medicare, military readiness, money laundering, national parks, nuclear waste, organ donation, student loan defaults, and prescription drugs, among others.

GAO e-mail updates are excellent current awareness tools. Electronic mailing lists distribute daily and monthly lists of reports and testimony released by the GAO. Subscriptions are available by filling out a form and identifying topic interests at *www.gao.gov/subscribe/index.php.*

Current budget and economic projections are provided at the **Congressional Budget Office** (CBO) website *(www.cbo.gov)*. The site also has reports about the economic and budget outlook for the next decade, the president's budget proposals, federal civilian employment, Social Security privatization, cost analyses of war operations, tax reform, water use conflicts in the west, marriage and the federal income tax, and the role of foreign aid in development, among other topics. Additional highlights include monthly budget updates, historical budget data, cost estimates for bills reported by congressional committees, and transcripts of congressional testimony by CBO officials. The information is highlighted by what the CBO terms "infographics."

The congressional **Office of Technology Assessment** (OTA) was eliminated in 1995, but every report it ever issued is available at The OTA Legacy *(www.princeton.edu/~ota)*, a site operated by the Woodrow Wilson School of Public and International Affairs at Princeton University. The site has more than 100,000 pages of detailed reports about aging, agricultural technology, arms control, biological research, cancer, computer security, defense technology, economic development, education, environmental protection, health and health technology, information technology, space, transportation, and many other subjects. The reports are organized in alphabetical, chronological, and topical lists.

The primary nonpartisan source of research into Congress is the **Congressional Research Service** (CRS), which is organized under the Library of Congress. While not all CRS reports are public, they are collected independently at *http://opencrs.com*. A further list of sites hosting some CRS reports is available at *http://archive-it.org/collections/1078*. Others are available for sale at *www.pennyhill.com*. Many reports will show up in an Internet search on the topic.

FINANCIAL TRANSPARENCY

Several Internet sites provide detailed campaign finance data for congressional elections. The official site is operated by the **Federal Election Commission** (FEC, *www.fec.gov)*, which regulates campaign [or election] spending. The site's highlight is its database of campaign reports filed from May 1996 to the present by House and presidential candidates, political action committees, and political party committees. Senate reports are considered "unofficial" because they are officially filed with the secretary of

the Senate. The older reports in the FEC's database are scanned images of paper reports filed with the commission, while reports that were filed electronically can be viewed on the website or downloaded in comma-delimited format.

The FEC site also has summary financial data for House and Senate candidates in the current election cycle, abstracts of court decisions pertaining to federal election law from 1976 to the present, and a directory of national and state agencies that are responsible for releasing information about campaign financing, candidates on the ballot, election results, lobbying, and other issues. Another useful feature is a collection of brochures about federal election law, public funding of presidential elections, the ban on contributions by foreign nationals, independent expenditures supporting or opposing a candidate for federal office, contribution limits, filing a complaint, researching public records at the FEC, and other topics. Finally, the site provides the FEC's legislative recommendations, its annual report, a report about its first thirty years in existence, the FEC's monthly newsletter, several reports about voter registration, election results for the most recent presidential and congressional elections, and campaign guides for corporations and labor organizations, congressional candidates and committees, political party committees, and nonconnected committees.

Another online source for campaign finance data is **CQ Money Line** *(http://moneyline.cq.com*, formerly PoliticalMoneyLine.com and FECinfo.com) from CQ Roll Call. Its searchable databases provide extensive itemized information about receipts and expenditures by federal candidates and political action committees from 1980 to the present. The detailed data are obtained from the FEC. For example, candidates' contributions can be searched by ZIP code. The site also has data on soft-money contributions, lists of the top political action committees in various categories, lists of the top contributors from each state, and much more. Most information is free, although some sections of the site are limited to subscribers.

More campaign finance data are available from the **Center for Responsive Politics** *(www.opensecrets.org)*, a public interest organization. The center provides a list of all soft-money donations to political parties of $100,000 or more in the current election cycle and data about leadership political action committees associated with individual politicians. Other databases at the site provide information about travel expenses that House members received from private sources for attending meetings and other events, activities of registered federal lobbyists, and activities of foreign agents who are registered in the United States.

The **Sunlight Foundation** is another nonprofit organization following funds passing to and from the federal government. Its site *(http://sunlightfoundation.com)* has a blog and newsfeed following the financial data generated by government activity. Its data site, called **Transparency Data** *(http://transparencydata.com)*, tracks not only campaign contributions but also federal grants and earmarks. It also publicly discloses lobbying fees and settlements with government contractors. A robust search function is combined with the capacity for "bulk" downloads of these data.

LegiStorm *(www.legistorm.com)* is particularly noted for making congressional staff salaries and expenses (including foreign travel) readily available. The subscription section of its site (LegiStorm PRO) also has a congressional directory and looks at the "revolving door" between lobbying and Congress.

First Street by CQ Press combines the publicly available lobbying disclosures with a deep history of congressional and federal directories, making it possible to easily track who has worked with whom within Congress and who has lobbied whom on what bills. While these data are only available through library or organizational subscription, the free site *(http://firststreet research.cqpress.com)* offers periodic journalistic reports generated from the FirstStreet database, including an annual ranking of the top ten earning lobbyists in three categories: former members of Congress, former congressional staffers, and lobbyists from outside Congress.

The Center for Public Integrity, *(www.publicintegrity.org/ news/Watch-News)* is a more purely journalistic and aggressive investigator of public finances and other corruption. It is not specifically focused on Congress, but its policy areas—money and politics, government waste/fraud/abuse, the environment, health care reform, the financial system, national security, and state government transparency—often involve the federal legislative branch.

ELECTIONS AND POLITICS

Thousands of Internet sites provide information about elections and politics. They are operated by candidates, political parties, interest groups, think tanks, trade associations, labor unions, businesses, government agencies, news organizations, polling firms, universities, and individuals. These sites can have very short lives. Many spring up just before a particular election and then disappear once the ballots are counted. The sites listed below, however, had proven themselves to be stable sources of ongoing election information as of mid-2011.

Several websites focus on election reform. One such site is **Ballot Access News** *(www.ballot-access.org)*, run by Richard Winger. The newsletter (archived on the site back to 1994) publishes news about efforts around the country to overturn laws that restrict ballot access by candidates, and it contains extensive information on minor parties nationwide. **The Century Foundation Election Reform** website *(www.tcf.org/elections)* is the home of the National Commission on Federal Election Reform, organized in the wake of the 2000 presidential election by the Miller Center of Public Affairs at the University of Virginia and the Century Foundation.

Other sites simply focus on making available accurate and in-depth voter and elections data. The **Census: Voting and Registration Data** site *(www.census.gov/hhes/www/socdemo/voting/index .html.)*, operated by the U.S. Census Bureau, has data about registration and voting by various demographic and socioeconomic groups from 1964 to the present. **Electionline.org** *(www.election line.org)* is produced by the Pew Center on the States' Election Initiatives. A nonpartisan, nonadvocacy site, Electionline.org provides current news and analysis on election reform. Another Pew site is **The Pew Research Center for the People & the Press**

(www.people-press.org). This site presents the results of polls regarding the press, politics, and public policy issues conducted from 1995 to the present. The polls measure public attitudes about topics such as China policy, Congress, the economy, elections, and the Internet's impact on elections. The **League of Women Voters' Voter Information** site *(www.smartvoter.org)* has links to information about state and local candidates around the country, details about how to register to vote, voter registration contact numbers for every state, and links to other election sites.

Finally, the **U.S. Election Atlas** site *(www.uselectionatlas.org)* site features maps detailing the results of recent presidential, senatorial, and gubernatorial elections by state. It also includes polling information and predictions for upcoming elections. Note to users: The site reverses the use of blue and red colors often employed by news organizations to designate Republicans and Democrats.

Still other sites provide information to voters about the way the system works or has been working. The **Electoral College Home Page** *(www.archives.gov/federal-register/electoral-college)* provides background information about how the Electoral College operates. It also has results for popular votes and Electoral College votes in presidential elections from 1789 to the present and provisions of the U.S. Constitution and federal law pertaining to presidential elections. The **Project Vote Smart** site *(www .votesmart.org)* provides biographies of thousands of candidates and elected officials in offices ranging from state legislator to president, voting records for members of Congress, detailed campaign finance data for members of Congress, the texts of ballot initiatives from states around the country, links to thousands of other political websites, and lots more.

Some of the many major websites that cover Capitol Hill are **CQ Roll Call** *(http://rollcall.com/politics)*, the publisher of *CQ Weekly; The Hill* *(www.thehill.com)*, a newspaper focused on Congress that publishes daily when Congress is in session; the *National Journal* *(www.nationaljournal.com)*; the *New York Times:* Politics *(www.nytimes.com/pages/politics/index.html)*; **Politico** *(http://politico.com)*, **PoliticsOnline** *(www.politicson line.com)*, which features a large collection of links to news stories about how the Internet is being used in elections and politics around the world; and the *Washington Post:* Politics *(www .washingtonpost.com/politics)*, which includes a U.S. Congress Votes database.

For more political websites, visit **Politics1** *(www.politics1. com)*, which provides a huge set of annotated links to websites operated by candidates, political parties, election offices, and election news sources in states across the country. Politics1 also has links to sites for presidential candidates, the two major parties, third parties, and political news sources. Another source is **Political Resources on the Net** *(www.politicalresources.net)*, with links to more than 24,000 election- and politics-related websites around the world.

★ INDEX

Page numbers in italics denote a figure, a table, an image, or an illustration.

A

Abourezk, James G., 117, 120
Abramoff, Jack, 215
ad hoc committees, 165–166
   See also committees
Adams, John Quincy, 45, 132
Akaka, Daniel K., 40
Albert, Carl, 149
Aldrich, Nelson W., 10, 45–46
Alexander, Bill, 122
Alexander, Lamar, 58
Alito, Samuel A., Jr., 120
Allen, James B., 109, 117
Allison, William B., 10, 45–46
amendments
   amending process, 101–105, 114–116
   debate on, 104
   degrees of, 104–105
   offering, 71
Anderson, Glenn M., 156
Andres, Gary, 207
Annals of Congress (Gales & Seaton), 122
Annunzio, Frank, 156
appropriations bills, 93
Arends, Les, 153
Armey, Dick, 15, 34
Army-McCarthy hearings, 80
Aspin, Les, 156

B

Bach, Stanley, 95
Baker, Howard H., Jr., 53–54, 82
Baker, Robert G. "Bobby," 48
Bankhead, William B., 19
Banks, Nathaniel P., 14
Barbour, Philip P., 14
Barkley, Alben W., 10, 46
Base Realignment and Closing laws, 73
Bates, Jim, 218
Baucus, Max, 123
Bayh, Evan, 68
Becerra, Xavier, 42
Bell, Chris, 37–39
Bennett, Robert F., 218
Bennett, William, 218

Biden, Joe, 203
bills
   action on, 5, 105–107
   adoption of the rule, 99–100
   appropriations bills, 93
   clean bills, 81
   holds on, 108–111
   markup, 80–81, 197
   numbering of, 74–76
   prefixes of, 76
   presidential action on, 129–133
   private bills, 102–103
   reading of, 77
   referral to committee, 77–78
   scheduling, 70–74
   text of, *105*
   See also legislative process
bipartisanship, success through, 11
Birnbaum, Jeffrey H., *Showdown at Gucci Gulch* (1987), 201
Bisnow, Mark, 203
Black, Amy, 206
Black, Barry C., *111*
Blaine, James G., 12–13, 21
blanket waivers, 94
Blunt, Roy, 15, *29*, 30, 35
Boehner, John A., *33*
   as conference chair, 43
   fundraising efforts, 6
   as House minority leader, 39–40
   as House Speaker, 32–33
   intentional inaction of, 7–8
   as majority leader, 15, 34
   profile in the media, 6
   on self-executing rules, 99
   See also campaign financing
Boggs, Hale, 20
Bolling, Richard, 15, 23, 150
Bonior, David E., 218
Bork, Robert H., 80
Boyd, Linn, 12
Brademas, John, 15
Breaux, John, 123
The Broken Branch (Mann & Norman 2008), 31, 119, 200
Brown, George Rothwell, 12
budget deficit, and the legislative process, 68